M. J. Flynn J. N. Gray A. K. Jones K. Lagally
H. Opderbeck G. J. Popek B. Randell
J. H. Saltzer H. R. Wiehle

Operating Systems

An Advanced Course

Edited by
R. Bayer, R. M. Graham, and G. Seegmüller

Springer-Verlag
Berlin Heidelberg New York 1979

Editors
Prof. Dr. R. Bayer
Institut für Informatik
der TU München
Arcisstraße 21
D-8000 München 2

Prof. Dr. R. M. Graham
Computer and Information Science
Graduate Research Center
University of Massachusetts
Amherst, Mass. 01002/USA

Prof. Dr. G. Seegmüller
Institut für Informatik der
Universität und Leibnitz-Rechenzentrum
der Bayrischen Akademie der Wissenschaften
Barerstraße 21
D-8000 München 2

Originally published in the series
Lecture Notes in Computer Science, Vol. 60
Springer-Verlag Berlin Heidelberg 1978

AMS Subject Classifications (1970): 68-02

ISBN 3-540-09812-7 Springer-Verlag Berlin Heidelberg New York
ISBN 0-387-09812-7 Springer-Verlag New York Heidelberg Berlin

This work is subject to copyright. All rights are reserved, whether the whole or part of the material is concerned, specifically those of translation, reprinting, re-use of illustrations, broadcasting, reproduction by photocopying machine or similar means, and storage in data banks. Under § 54 of the German Copyright Law where copies are made for other than private use, a fee is payable to the publisher, the amount of the fee to be determined by agreement with the publisher.

© Springer-Verlag Berlin Heidelberg 1979
Printed in Germany

Printing and binding: Beltz Offsetdruck, Hemsbach/Bergstr.
2145/3140-54321

PREFACE

The Advanced Course on Operating Systems was held at the Technical University in Munich from July 28 to August 5, 1977, and was repeated from March 29 to April 6, 1978. The course was organized by the Institute for Informatics of the Technical University Munich and the Leibniz Computing Center of the Bavarian Academy of Sciences, in co-operation with the European Communities, sponsored by the Ministry for Research and Technology of the Federal Republic of Germany.

Contents

CHAPTER 1.: INTRODUCTION

R. Bayer
R. M. Graham
J. H. Saltzer
G. Seegmüller

INTRODUCTION 1

CHAPTER 2.: MODELS

A. K. Jones

THE OBJECT MODEL: A CONCEPTUAL TOOL
FOR STRUCTURING SOFTWARE 7

1. *The Object Model* 8
2. *The Object Model Applied to Operating Systems* 11
3. *Mechanics of Supporting Type Modules* 15
4. *Observation* 16
5. *References* 16

M. J. Flynn

COMPUTER ORGANIZATION AND ARCHITECTURE 17

1. *Machine Mapping and Well Mapped Machines* 19
2. *Name Space - Memory Space* 37
3. *Traditional Machine Language Problems and Some Fundamental Concepts* 52
4. *Towards Ideal Program Representations* 56
5. *Parallel Processor Forms of Computing Systems* 81
   References 97

CHAPTER 3.: ISSUES AND RESULTS IN THE DESIGN OF OPERATING SYSTEMS

J. H. Saltzer

NAMING AND BINDING OF OBJECTS 99

A. *Introduction* 102
1. *Names in Computer Systems* 102
2. *A Model for the Use of Names* 104
3. *Problems in the Use of Names* 110
4. *Some Examples of Existing Naming Systems* 114
5. *The Need for Names with Different Properties* 120
6. *Plan of Study* 123
B. *An Architecture for Addressing Shared Objects* 124
1. *User-Dependent Bindings and Multiple Naming Contexts* 129
2. *Larger Contexts and Context Switching* 136

	3. *Binding on Demand, and Binding from Higher-Level Contexts*	145
	C. *Higher-Level Naming Contexts, or File Systems*	151
	1. *Direct-Access and Copy Organizations*	151
	2. *Multiple Catalogs and Naming Networks*	157
	3. *The Dynamics of Naming Networks*	165
	4. *Binding Reference Names to Path Names*	168
	5. *Context Initialization*	175
	D. *Implementation Considerations*	178
	1. *Lost Objects*	178
	2. *Catalogs as Repositories*	182
	3. *Indirect Catalog Entries*	183
	4. *Search Rules*	185
	E. *Research Directions*	186
	References	190
	Appendix A: *Case Study of Naming in Multics*	193
	1. *The Addressing Architecture of Multics*	193
	2. *The Multics File System*	200
	3. *Context Initialization in Multics*	202
	4. *Bibliography on Naming in Multics*	208
G. J. Popek C. S. Kline	ISSUES IN KERNEL DESIGN	209
	1. *Introduction*	210
	2. *Effects of Design Constraints on Kernel Architecture*	211
	2.1. *Security Policy*	212
	2.2. *System Functions*	212
	2.3. *Hardware Effects*	213
	2.4. *Performance*	215
	3. *Principles of Kernel Design*	216
	3.1. *Overall System Architecture*	216
	3.2. *Resource Pools*	216
	3.2.1. *Type Integrity*	217
	3.2.2. *Resource Management*	218
	3.2.3. *Naming*	218
	4. *More on Overall System Architecture*	219
	4.1. *Trusted Processes*	219
	4.2. *Levels of Kernels*	220
	5. *Internal Kernel Architecture*	221
	5.1. *Hardware Selection*	222
	5.2. *Parallelism*	222
	5.3. *Abstract Type Structures*	222
	6. *Confinement*	223
	6.1. *Importance*	223
	6.2. *Storage and Timing Channels*	224
	6.3. *Timing Independent Scheduling Channels*	225
	7. *Conclusion*	226
	Bibliography	226
A. K. Jones	PROTECTION MECHANISMS AND THE ENFORCEMENT OF SECURITY POLICIES	228
	1. *Introduction*	229
	2. *Security Policies*	230
	3. *Protection Mechanisms*	233
	4. *Enforcing a Policy of Isolation*	233
	5. *Enforcing Access Control Policies*	236
	5.1. *Implementation of Access Control Protection Mechanisms*	240

	5.2.	Authority Lists	241
	5.3.	Capability Based Implementation	242
	5.3.1.	Extended Object Types	244
	5.3.2.	Status	248
	6.	Enforcing Information Control Policies	248
	7.	References	250

K. Lagally   SYNCHRONIZATION IN A LAYERED SYSTEM   252

1.	Introduction	253
2.	General Concepts	253
2.1.	Synchronization	253
2.2.	Processes and Messages	255
2.3.	Process Hierarchy	257
3.	Implementation Tools	258
3.1.	Semaphores	258
3.2.	Conditional Critical Regions	259
3.3.	Monitors	260
3.4.	Path Expressions	261
3.5.	Object Managers	262
4.	Examples	263
4.1.	Readers and Writers	263
4.1.1.	Semaphores	264
4.1.2.	Conditional Critical Regions	268
4.1.3.	Monitors	269
4.1.4.	Path Expressions	270
4.1.5.	Object Managers	271
4.2.	The Five Dining Philosophers	275
5.	Conclusion	277
6.	References	278

B. Randell   RELIABLE COMPUTING SYSTEMS   282

1.	Introduction	283
2.	Basic Concepts	286
2.1.	Systems and Their Failures	286
2.2.	Errors and Faults	287
3.	Reliability Issues	290
3.1.	Requirements	290
3.2.	Types of Fault	291
3.3.	Fault Intolerance and Fault Tolerance	293
3.4.	Design Fault Tolerance	294
4.	System Structure	296
4.1.	Static Structure	296
4.2.	Dynamic Structure	298
4.3.	Atomic Actions	299
4.4.	Forms of Atomic Action	302
4.5.	Levels of Abstraction	303
4.6.	Faults and Structuring	306
5.	Fault Tolerance Techniques	308
5.1.	Protective Redundancy	308
5.1.1.	Triple Modular Redundancy	309
5.2.	Error Detection	311
5.2.1.	Types of Check	312
5.2.2.	Interface Checking	313
5.3.	Fault Treatment	314
5.4.	Damage Assessment	317
5.5.	Error Recovery	318
5.5.1.	Backward Error Recovery	318

5.5.2.	Forward Error Recovery	325
5.5.3.	Multi-Level Error Recovery	328
6.	Summary and Conclusions	332
7.	Acknowledgements	334
8.	References	335
	Appendix 1: Bell Laboratories ESS No. 1A Processor	340
A1.1	System Description	340
A1.2	Reliability Strategies	342
A1.3	Reliability Evaluation	348
	Appendix 2: HIVE	350
A2.1	System Description	350
A2.2	Reliability Strategies	352
	Appendix 3: The JPL-STAR Computer	355
A3.1	System Description	355
A3.2	Reliability Strategies	356
A3.3	Reliability Evaluation	359
	Appendix 4: The Newcastle Reliability Project	362
A4.1	The EML System	362
A4.2	System Description	364
A4.3	Reliability Strategies	364
A4.4	Reliability Evaluation	366
A4.5	The Recoverable Filing System	366
A4.6	Resource Contention System	367
	Appendix 5: The Plessey System 250 Computer	368
A5.1	System Description	368
A5.2	Reliability Strategies	369
A5.3	Reliability Evaluation	371
	Appendix 6: Pluribus	374
A6.1	System Description	374
A6.2	Reliability Strategies	376
A6.3	Reliability Evaluation	378
	Appendix 7: PRIME	381
A7.1	System Description	381
A7.2	Reliability Strategies	383
A7.3	Reliability Evaluation	385
	Appendix 8: The SIFT Computer	387
A8.1	System Description	387
A8.2	Reliability Strategies	388

J. N. Gray   NOTES ON DATA BASE OPERATING SYSTEMS   393

	Acknowledgements	394
1.	Introduction	395
1.1.	A Sample System	395
1.2.	Relationship to Operating System	396
1.3.	General Structure of Data Management Systems	397
1.4.	Bibliography	398
2.	Dictionary	400
2.1.	What it is	400
2.2.	Bibliography	401
3.	Data Management	402
3.1.	Records and Fields	402
3.2.	Sets	402
3.3.	Cursors	404
3.3.2.	Operations on Cursors	404
3.3.3.	Cursor Positioning	405
3.4.	Various Data Models	406
3.4.1.	Relational Data Model	406
3.4.2.	Hierarchical Data Model	407
3.4.3.	Network Data Model	408
3.4.4.	Comparison of Data Models	409

3.5.	*Views*	409
3.5.1.	*Views and Update*	411
3.6.	*Structure of Data Manager*	411
3.7.	*A Sample Data Base Design*	412
3.8.	*Comparison to File Access Method*	414
3.9.	*Bibliography*	414
4.	*Data Communications*	415
4.1.	*Messages, Sessions, and Relationship to Network Manager*	415
4.2.	*Session Management*	417
4.3.	*Queues*	417
4.4.	*Message Recovery*	418
4.5.	*Response Mode Processing*	418
4.5.	*Conversations*	419
4.6.	*Message Mapping*	419
4.7.	*Topics not Covered*	420
4.8.	*Bibliography*	420
5.	*Transaction Management*	421
5.1.	*Transaction Scheduling*	424
5.2.	*Distributed Transaction Management*	425
5.3.	*The Data Management System as a Subsystem*	427
5.4.	*Exception Handling*	428
5.5.	*Other Components Within Transaction Management*	429
5.6.	*Bibliography*	429
5.7.	*Lock Management*	430
5.7.1.	*Pros and Cons of Concurrency*	430
5.7.2.	*Concurrency Problems*	431
5.7.3.	*Model of Consistency and Lock Protocols*	431
5.7.4.	*Locking, Transaction Backup and System Recovery*	437
5.7.5.	*Lower Degrees of Consistency*	438
5.7.6.	*Lock Granularity*	438
5.7.7.	*Lock Management Pragmatics*	446
5.7.8.	*Bibliography*	458
5.8.	*Recovery Management*	459
5.8.1.	*Model of Errors*	459
5.8.2.	*Overview of Recovery Management*	460
5.8.3.	*Recovery Protocols*	462
5.8.4.	*Structure of Recovery Manager*	472
5.8.5.	*Log Management*	478
5.8.6.	*Examples of a Recovery Routine*	480
5.8.7.	*Historical Note on Recovery Management*	480
5.8.8.	*Bibliography*	481

H. Opderbeck — COMMON CARRIER PROVIDED NETWORK INTERFACES — 482

1.	*Introduction*	483
2.	*Protocoll Characteristics*	485
2.1.	*Connection Establishment and Clearing*	485
2.2.	*Error Control*	485
2.3.	*Flow Control*	486
2.4.	*Multiplexing*	487
2.5.	*Synchronization*	488
2.6.	*Transparancy*	489
3.	*Terminal Emulation Interface*	490
4.	*Character Concentration Interface*	493
5.	*X.25 Interface*	495
5.1.	*Introduction*	495
5.2.	*Link Access Procedure*	496
5.3.	*Packet Level Interface*	498

	6. Terminal Handling Through Public Networks	502
	6.1. Introduction	502
	6.2. PAD Parameters	502
	6.3. PAD-User Interaction	504
	6.4. PAD-Host Interaction	505
	6.5. Network Virtual Terminal	506
	References	507

G. J. Popek
C. S. Kline

DESIGN ISSUES FOR SECURE COMPUTER NETWORKS — 517

1.	Introduction	518
1.1.	The Environment and its Threats	519
1.2.	Operational Assumptions	520
2.	Relevant Issues in Encryption	520
2.1.	Public Key Encryption	522
2.2.	Algorithms Based on NP Completeness	522
2.3.	Error Detection	523
2.4.	Block vs Chain Ciphers	524
2.5.	Applications of Encryption	524
2.6.	Limitations of Encryption	526
3.	Key Distribution	529
3.1.	Public Key Based Distribution Algorithms	531
4.	Levels of Integration	533
5.	Encryption Protocols	534
5.1.	Confinement	535
5.2.	Authentication	536
6.	Network Encryption Protocol Case Study: Process-Process Encryption	538
6.1.	The Encryption Connection Protocol	539
6.2.	Discussion	542
6.3.	ARPANET Application	543
6.4.	Efficiency Considerations	543
6.5.	System Initialization Procedures	544
6.6.	Symmetry	545
7.	Conclusion	545
8.	Bibliography	546

CHAPTER 4: FUTURE OUTLOOK AND RESEARCH PROBLEMS

H. R. Wiehle

ON SYSTEM SPECIFICATION — 547

A.	Introduction	548
B.	Definitions and Examples	556
C.	Sequentializing Units	564
D.	Specification of Units and Decomposable Systems	573
E.	Some Remarks on Relations between Systems	579
	References	582

J. H. Saltzer

RESEARCH PROBLEMS OF DECENTRALIZED SYSTEMS WITH LARGELY AUTONOMOUS NODES — 583

Coherence and the Object Model	586
Other Problems in the Semantics of Coherence	589
Heterogeneous and Homogeneous Systems	590
Conclusion	591
References	591

CHAPTER 1: INTRODUCTION

R. Bayer
Technical University Munich
Munich, Germany

R. M. Graham
University of Massachusetts
Amherst, Mass., USA

J. H. Saltzer
Massachusetts Institute of Technology
Cambridge, Mass., USA

G. Seegmüller
Leibniz Computing Center
of the Bavarian Academy of Sciences
Munich, Germany

CHAPTER I

INTRODUCTION

R. Bayer, R.M. Graham, J.H. Saltzer, G. Seegmüller

This book contains the lecture notes of an Advanced Course on Operating Systems held at the Technical University Munich in 1977 and 1978. The material of the course was discussed and organized during a preparatory seminar attended by all lecturers in early 1977.

An attempt was made to agree upon a uniform approach to the field of Operating Systems. The course differs from the usual approaches in its emphasis and selection of topics. We presume that the reader has had the experience of a more traditional operating systems course and that he has worked with some real operating systems also. The set of topics of this course is not the traditional set. It is strongly influenced by two considerations. The first observation is the beginning of a dramatic change in trade-offs in view of decreasing hardware costs. The second one has to do with recently emerging new results in computer science which reflect a better understanding of several areas closely related to operating systems. So we are not going to present much on programs, processes, scheduling, resource control blocks, building of file systems and performance modelling. Rather an attempt will be made at a more intensive treatment of areas like protection, correctness, reliability, networks and decentralization.

What is an operating system? Although there are many terms used for the versions of existing operating systems, and no universally accepted definition, there is certainly agreement that operating systems are essential parts of at least the following three conceptual kinds of computing systems.

Programming systems consisting of

>editors, compilers, debuggers, ...
>the operating system,
>the hardware.

Data base systems consisting of

>data base managers,
>the operating system,
>the hardware.

Application systems consisting of

>application programs,
>the operating system,
>the hardware.

There is also agreement on those aspects that are at the heart of operating systems. In fact, the terms nucleus or kernel are often used for the most essential functions of an operating system. Much of the research and development in operating systems has focused on resource management and the user's interface to this management. Our view of operating systems and the focus of this course is resource management in a very wide sense and the attendant user interface. We shall concentrate on the semantics of this interface, on internal system structure and, to some extent, on hardware architecture.

It is interesting and instructive to look briefly at the history of modern computer systems. In the beginning, computers were small, simple, and free standing. Each individual could use the machine on a one-to-one basis. Generally, there has been an evolution from this state to the current large, complex, multiprogramming, multiprocessor, central systems with virtual memory and many ancillary devices and subsystems. The major trends have been: from one user to many users of the same system; from isolated users to cooperating users; from sequential batch to multiprogramming, to time sharing; and, in both hardware and software, an increase in the degree of concurrency. Most importantly, we see a trend toward increased concern with the management of non-physical resources.

The first computer users always had the entire computer all to themselves for some interval of time. A user always had all the resources. Any resource management facilities provided by an operating (or programming) system were entirely for the user's convenience. As the user community grew it was necessary to insure efficient, equitable distribution of the system's physical resources among all the contenders. It has become clear that any kind of sharing, even sharing between the operating system and a single user, requires resource management for the shared resources.

Even in a sequential batch system, a user had to be prevented from monopolizing the computer. Thus, system management of the central processor was required, at least to the extent of limiting the execution time of user programs. Memory was another resource that was managed quite early. The operating system itself required some primary memory. The programs and data of other users in the batch had to be protected from destruction by the user program currently executing. This was especially true as soon as direct access secondary memory was available in sufficient quantity to make permanent data storage feasible. Hence, system management of I/O devices and secondary memory were required.

As the hardware became more complex, the management of these physical resources became more comprehensive and complex. Multiprogramming and time sharing had a substantial impact on resource management. Management of the processor evolved from simply enforcing the maximum execution time for a user's program to multiplexing the central processor(s) among a number of different user programs. Primary memory management evolved from a simple division between the system and a single user to virtual memories, which facilitate simultaneous sharing of primary memory among many users and the treatment of secondary memory as a direct extension of primary memory.

It is a principle of science that as complexity increases, the need for abstractions to deal with this complexity also increases. The evolution of operating systems is no exception. Early abstractions were files and processes. In each instance the abstraction takes the form of some non-physical resource and benefits both the user and the system. The abstraction of a file gives the user a unit of information that is extremely useful in organizing his data. Complex movement and manipulation of large amounts of data can be expressed very simply by the user in a device/location independent way. At the same time, because of the abstract nature of files, system management of these resources translates easily into the management of physical secondary storage and I/O devices. In addition, since the user does not specify details, the system has much greater latitude in physical memory management and more potential for efficient utilization of it.

In like manner, the abstraction of a process permits more efficient systems management of the central processor(s) as well as indirectly contributing to the ease of management of all other resources. The user also benefits from the process abstraction. With it he can establish sets of cooperating concurrent processes which not only take maximum advantage of the system's parallelism, but often result in clearer formulation of the problem to be solved. The notion of an <u>abstract machine</u> which is available to each user encompasses the essence of this direction of abstraction.

What is the current state of affairs? In a recent workshop the lecturers of this course concluded that the classic problems of physical resource management and concurrency management are well understood, at least to the extent that their implementation is routine and minor enough that operating systems that are satisfactory to the market place are being built. We have chosen to omit from this course any consideration of these problems. Acceptable solutions are widely known. In fact, all of the recent textbooks on operating systems contain extensive discussions of these problems and their solutions. Rather we tried to focus on problems that were less well understood in the past - that are on or near the frontier of the field and that showed significant progress within the last few years. For example, none of the textbooks has an adequate discussion of protection, yet this is one of the most important problems in the design of new operating systems.

Abstractions are based on <u>models</u>. We recognize that models are not only needed to cope with complexity, but ultimately they are needed to verify or validate the correctness and other desired properties of a specific system design. <u>Models for the underlying hardware</u> are the foundation upon which more abstract, general models are built, since they give us insight into the fundamental mechanisms for the final interpretation of a program that is required to produce actual results. In addition, through them we can glimpse a future kind of architecture with many parallel activities, highly distributed.

The <u>object model</u> is the basis for the abstract resource, an object. This very general model is applicable to both software and hardware. It has benefitted from more recent developments in the study of programming languages. This benefit is not incidental. There, the need for careful specification of interfaces with total protection of their implementation has led to the introduction of abstract data types. Objects in operating systems correspond to data types as they appear in some more recent programming languages. The object model seems, in some sense, to capture fundamental properties that pervade all aspects of modern operating systems: protection, naming, binding, data, procedures, and physical devices. A model of this nature seems to be necessary in order to realistically consider the validation of important properties of an operating system, such as correctness and reliability.

There are a substantial number of major problems that affect the entire fiber of the more advanced operating systems. Most of these problems appear in the newer system organizations, such as, data base operating systems, distributed systems, and networks of computers. In these new settings the problems tend to be an order of magnitude more difficult. Naming and binding are fundamental. Resources cannot be managed without the use of names. The value of symbolic names was recognized long ago. Symbolic names need to be bound to specific objects. The complexity of this problem, when conjoined with protection and multiple computers networked together, is staggering. Protection, difficult enough in multiuser, timesharing systems, is far more complex when the access controls must extend throughout a network with a distributed data base. An important property of networks and distributed systems is that distinct components are often under different administrative controls, thereby adding new problems of coordination, protection, naming, and reliability.

The importance and need for correctness and reliability of operating systems has always been recognized. However, sensitive applications are currently being implemented within unreliable systems. Correctness and reliability issues are not unique to operating systems, but they are much more significant in this context. An undiscovered, minor bug in the system or a breach of the protection mechanism can result in great financial loss or even the loss of human lives.

What about the future? New hardware developments always influence the organization and function of new operating systems. Advances in communications technology have made networks of computers possible. New production and miniaturization techniques make it possible to mass produce cheap processors. Distributed systems and highly parallel machines are inevitable. What are the advantages and disadvantages of such systems? What is the appropriate user interface? Current models are inadequate to deal with questions of correctness and reliability - nor are they of much help in guiding the designer to a simple and efficient implementation. Many of the readers will be deeply involved in these problems. In the lectures that follow, we hope that we will be able to help the reader prepare to cope with these problems.

CHAPTER 2.A.

Anita K. Jones
Carnegie-Mellon University
Pittsburgh, Pa., USA

The Object Model:
A Conceptual Tool for Structuring Software

THE OBJECT MODEL:
A CONCEPTUAL TOOL FOR STRUCTURING SOFTWARE

Anita K. Jones
Department of Computer Science
Carnegie-Mellon University
Pittsburgh, PA 15213 USA

Computers are programmed to simulate complex physical and abstract systems. To design, construct, and communicate these programmed systems to others, human beings need appropriate conceptual tools. The object model is both a concept and a tool. It provides guidelines for characterizing the abstract entities in terms of which we think. In particular, use of the object model can lead to clear and explicit expression of the dependency relations between these entities in a way that is conducive to rendering them as programs. An example benefit is that different programmers can be assigned different parts of a design to program, and their products can be integrated with a minimum of inconsistencies. The object model provides a framework in terms of which to think about and communicate designs for programmed systems; it is implicitly and explicitly used in other papers in this volume. Thus, it is appropriate to explore the model itself.

The notion of the object model has evolved over the past decade or so. It has roots at least as far back as the Simula language design [Dahl68]. Researchers in the area of programming methodology are investigating the object model and the kinds of abstractions it enables [Liskov76]. Some recently designed programming languages incorporate constructs to assist the programmer thinking in the framework of the object model [Wulf77, Liskov77]. In this paper I will not develop the arguments for and against use of the object model, nor will I explore its many nuances. I will explain the model generally, and consider some of its ramifications with respect to operating systems.

1. The Object Model

In the object model emphasis is placed on crisply characterizing the components of the physical or abstract system to be modeled by a programmed system. The components, that are thought of as being "passive', are called objects. Objects have a certain "integrity" which should not--in fact, cannot--be violated. An object can only change state, behave, be manipulated, or stand in relation to other objects in ways appropriate to that object. Stated differently, there exist invariant properties that characterize an object and its behavior. An elevator, for example, is characterized by invariant properties including: it only travels up and down inside its shaft; it cannot be moving and stopped at the same time; it can stop at only one floor at a time; it's maximum capacity, measured in volume and weight, cannot be exceeded. Any elevator simulation must incorporate these invariants, for they are integral to the notion of an elevator.

The object model dictates that these invariant properties are preserved by a set of <u>operations</u> that are the only means by which an object can be directly manipulated. To alter or even to determine the state of the object, an appropriate operation must be invoked. Thus, the set of operations for an object collectively define its behavior. In practice, the number of operations required for an object is relatively small (say, from three to twelve).

The behavior of any elevator object could be defined using three operations. The first one would be used only once to 'install' the elevator, initializing its state. For example, the Install operation would fix the relevant parameters of the building, such as the number of floors, in which the elevator exists. Once an elevator is Installed, the other two operations, Up and Down, can be invoked by passengers who wish to change floors. In a programmed simulation of the elevator, only the procedures implementing the three operations would be able to alter the state of the elevator. For example, synchronization of actions necessary to preserve elevator invariants are found in the code bodies of the procedures implementing the Up and Down operations.

Because many objects essentially have the same behavioral characteristics, it is convenient to define a single set of operations, perhaps parameterized, that are equally applicable to many objects. Two objects are said to be of the same <u>type</u> if they share the same set of operations. The literature on programming methodology contains numerous articles explicating the notion of type. For our purposes it is not necessary to delve into the theology that surrounds the issue of precisely what constitutes a type definition. I will rely on the reader's intuitions.

In a programmed implementation of a type, the programmed operations are collected together in what is called a <u>type module</u>. Some recently designed languages provide syntactic constructs designed to permit and encourage a programmer to build his program as a set of independent type modules. Alphard [Wulf77] includes the <u>form</u> construct; Clu [Liskov77] includes the <u>cluster</u>. Within a type module definition appears a description of the representation, if any, that is created when an object is instantiated, as well as the procedures that implement the operations of the type. Scope rules are defined so that only the code that is part of the type module can directly manipulate the representation of an object of that type. As a result, only the code in the type module implementation must be considered to determine the invariant properties that hold for objects of the type. Every type has a specification that expresses all that is known or can be assumed by programs outside the type module. Details of implementation, both of an object's representation and the exact algorithm followed in the implementation of an operation, are hidden behind the type module boundary. The intent is that from the type specifications a user can understand enough about the type to use it, but cannot make use of type module implementation details.

To express a new abstraction, a designer specifies a new type. New types are defined using existing types. First, one assumes the existence of some primitive types provided by a language or a machine. Objects may be--in fact, usually are--represented in terms of other component objects. Operations for the new type are implemented assuming the existence of the specified operations for manipulating component objects. To implement an entire system a programmer constructs a set of type module definitions related by dependence; a second type module depends upon a first, if operations in the first are assumed for the implementation of the second.

The object model is merely a structuring tool; it does not imply a particular design technique. It is amenable to use with both the "top down" and "bottom up" design techniques. Using the "top down" technique, a programmer designs the main program in terms of whatever, as yet, nonexistent, types seem convenient, then implements the types found necessary for designing the main program. This process is repeated until all types are defined, either by the programmer or as primitives. Alternatively, a designer using the "bottom up" design technique constructs types that express low level abstractions that are deemed to be useful building blocks. He successively builds up to the higher level abstractions, and eventually to the entire system. In either case, at each step in the design process a programmer implementing a type can ignore unnecessary detail. He focuses only on the specifications and the implementation of the new type he is currently defining and on the specifications of the types he is using to construct the new type.

To illustrate the object model and the corollary notion of type modules, consider an example of a customer of a telephone service as seen by those who provide the service. Relevant operations that need to be performed for the customer include:

Lookup -- given a customer's name, determine customer's primary telephone number

ChangeService -- alter the current service provided to a customer, e.g., remove the phone, or install a new extension

Credit -- credit the customer's account by a certain amount

Debit -- debit the customer's account by a specified amount

WriteBill -- output a formatted copy of a customer's bill suitable for sending to him for payment

Each customer can be represented in the computer by an object called a telephone-service-customer. Each customer is characterized by a name and address, the kind of telephone service presently provided, as well as billing and credit information. There are various groups of people that cooperate to provide telephone service; each group has a need to reference telephone-service-customer objects. A telephone operator needs to Lookup telephone numbers upon request. Likewise, the service representatives of the company should be able to assign new numbers or otherwise alter (ChangeService) the current service that is provided to a customer. Business office employees need to be able to print bills, inspect billing and service data, and to credit and debit a user's account (WriteBill, Debit, Credit). Each of the above sees the customer from a different perspective and has available operations which support that perspective.

As part of the type definition, a customer might be represented by a record containing at least the following component objects (of types not specified here):

```
name
address
current service (an array, one entry for each installed phone number)
    assigned phone number
    location of phone
    number of extensions
    color/type of phone
billing data (an array, one entry for each installed phone number)
    rate schedule
    local call charges
    itemized long distance charges
    credit or debit carried from previous month
    billing address
```

As stated earlier, the representation of the telephone-service-customer object is not available for manipulation except by code that implements the telephone-service-customer type module, in particular the operations sketched above. Thus, details of implementation, such as record formats, are not available outside the type module.

2. The Object Model Applied to Operating Systems

An operating system provides a variety of services--address space management, i/o support, and process management including synchronization and interprocess communication. Following the object model, an operating system can be described as a set of types, each of which can be thought of as a kind of resource. Some resources have a direct physical realization, such as i/o devices. Others are further removed from the hardware, such as processes, semaphores, mailboxes (for communication of messages between processes), and files. Each resource is an object. As an example, intuitively described operations for two types, processes and mailboxes, are listed below:

process operations:

> Create -- create a new process capable of executing code
>
> Destroy -- destroy an existing process
>
> Fork -- create a new process to execute in parallel with the invoker of the Fork operation
>
> Join -- two processes are joined together so that one is destroyed and the other continues execution
>
> Schedule -- cause a process to compete for CPU resources
>
> Unschedule -- remove a process from competition for CPU resources

mailbox operations:

> Create -- create empty mailbox
>
> Destroy -- destroy an existing mailbox
>
> Send -- place a particular message into a specified mailbox
>
> Receive -- take a message from a specific mailbox, waiting until a message appears, if necessary
>
> ConditionalReceive -- take a message from a specific mailbox, but do not wait if the mailbox is empty

Any dependency between operating system types may or may not be of interest to the user. For example, implementation of the mailbox type relies on the existence of a message type. A user must be able to create and initialize a message, otherwise mailboxes will not be very useful. In addition the mailbox type module relies upon some synchronization module. Note that the user need not be concerned with whether or not code implementing a particular type executes in privileged mode. The object model paradigm is a basis for designing an operating system in which different facilities are provided in different domains of privilege. In particular, the code of each type module has the privilege to manipulate the components of an object of the type; no other code executes with that privilege. Note also that when both operating systems and application programs can be designed using the object model, the boundary between two modules is the same; no artificial boundary separates the operating system and the application.

Next I consider three operating system features--naming, protection, and synchronization--from the perspective of the object model. My objective is to discuss how these features common to operating systems manifest themselves as viewed in the object model framework. First, consider <u>naming</u>. When thinking or programming in the terms of the object model, it is appropriate to be able to name <u>objects</u>. In contrast, most extant systems provide to users a space of names for one or more memory segments. From the perspective of the object model such systems provide for naming of only a single type of object--segments. Let us consider the ramifications of segment naming.

In systems that restrict the space of names to segments only, other types of objects are usually named in one of the two following ways. In one case, the name of an object is the address of the segment used for representing the object. For example, in many systems a process context block is maintained by the operating system to represent a process object. The address of the first word in that block is used as the name for the process. This necessitates either validating an address each time it is used (e.g., presented to the operating system as a parameter), or, if possible, restricting its use to trusted programs. It is very sad to read code in which a check of whether an address is on a double word boundary is made, as a futile attempt to determine whether a parameter is a process name or not. Such a naming scheme is inadequate.

The second technique for naming an object is to introduce a new name interpreter for each new type of object. For example, process objects may be named, say using integers that are interpreted as indices into a table of process representations. Only code in the process type module can access this table, so the interpreter of process names is part of the process type module. But this means only that the process type module maps integers to processes, not that it can determine from a submitted parameter whether that integer name designates a legitimate process, or that the caller should be able to access it in any way. This second naming scheme is also inadequate.

It would seem that a facility to name objects--not just segments--is desirable. Such a facility would make programming more convenient, and would free the programmer from the burden of mentally translating from the object to the details of that object's representation. It is unclear how such a facility should be implemented. Such naming of objects can be supported dynamically by the operating system or, applications programmers can be constrained to write programs only in languages that provide object naming syntax and a compiler to map objects to their representations.

Closely related to naming is protection, a facility provided by an operating system to constrain the way information is used and changed. Because logically separate pieces of information are encoded in different objects, it is appropriate to provide protection for each object individually. Manipulation of an object is requested by specifying an operation to be performed on that object. A straightforward technique for constraining arbitrary manipulation of an object is to constrain the ability to perform operations on that object. Rights to perform certain operations defined for an object are distributed only to those who should be able to manipulate the object. A protection mechanism permits an operation to be successfully invoked only if the invoker possesses the right to do so. Controlling the use of an object based on the operations defined for it is desirable. Certainly, it is more meaningful to users than protecting on the basis of read/write access to the memory cells used for representing objects. Such protection mechanisms enable fine distinctions between the manipulations allowed to various users. In the telephone-service-customer example the operator can be granted only the right to Lookup telephone numbers, while the telephone service office can be granted the right to perform both the Lookup and ChangeService operations, yet not be permitted to perform the billing operations. Thus, the service office can cause the customer object to be altered, but only in constrained ways related to the responsibilities of the service office.

Our conclusion is that both naming and protection can profitably be provided on the basis of objects. In an operating system in which both naming and protection are provided for all objects--not just segments, there exist implementations in which protection and naming are integrated. For now, an implementation will be sketched. It will be investigated in more detail in the paper on protection. Let the set of objects that are accessible during the execution of a program, in particular, an operation, be called the domain. A domain can be expressed as a set of descriptors, sometimes called capabilities [Dennis66]. Each descriptor is an unforgeable token that identifies a particular object. The name of an object is a local name, say an integer offset into a list of descriptors. The system name interpreter locates the unique object specified by information in the descriptor. Using this naming mechanism, code is restricted to use of only those objects in its domain. For the naming mechanism and the protection mechanism to be well defined, the alteration of domains, i.e., the acquisition and dispersion of descriptors via execution in a domain must be controlled in a disciplined manner.

This naming mechanism can be extended to support protection if a domain is redefined to be not just a set of objects, but a set of rights to objects. We extend the descriptor to encode rights to an object in addition to the information needed to find a unique object. An operation can be successfully performed in a domain only if the right to do so is in that domain.

There are a number of extant systems which support the naming of objects of types besides memory segments [Burroughs61, Lampson76, Wulf74, Needham77]. It remains a research issue to determine how to provide object naming and protection cost-effectively. If the operating system supports generalized object naming, an interesting issue is what hardware support, if any, should be provided. Indeed, how inexpensive can object naming be made? Another alternative is to provide a language system as the "front end" to the operating system and have the language system support object naming. As exemplified by the Burroughs 5000 system, the compiler, and a minimal run time system would support the mapping between an object and the (virtual) memory used to represent it. The supporting operating system need only provide more modest naming and protection mechanisms. A disadvantage of this is the lack of support for individual naming and protection of objects for debugging and for runtime reliability checks.

Synchronization is yet another facility which is affected by adoption of the object model paradigm. According to the object model, each different manipulation of an object is performed by a different operation. It is frequently the case that synchronization is naturally expressed at the level of operations, i.e., that only certain sequences of operations are allowed. For example, one invariant property of a mailbox is that the number of messages removed cannot exceed the number of messages sent to that mailbox. This can be expressed by saying that the Receive operation cannot be performed more times than the Send operation. Habermann [77] has developed a notation called path expressions to express permissible operation sequences. One advantage of expressing synchronization restrictions as relations among operations is that synchronization constraints can be meaningfully stated as part of the specification of the type module. Thus, synchronization constraints are expressed to the user in natural terms--i.e., in terms of permissible operation sequences on object. One can view a path expression as a declarative statement of what synchronization constraints are to be observed. The code actually realizing that synchronization may not even be written by the author of the type module, but may be provided statically by the language system or dynamically by the operating system.

In this section I have tried to argue that three of the features that every operating system provides all have a natural expression, given the object model paradigm. In particular, each one can be phrased in terms of the objects and operations that are meaningful to the user. It is my opinion that some model, and perhaps the object model is the correct one, is needed to raise operating system designers and implementors above the level of that common denominator, the memory word, and all the extraneous, debilitating detail it forces us to think about.

3. Mechanics of Supporting Type Modules

Consider the invocation of operations defined as part of a type. The operations are implemented as procedures in hardware, firmware, and more often, in software. Provisions must be made to invoke these procedures in a well defined manner, and to provide a domain containing the objects that are to be accessible for the duration of the procedure's execution. To support the notion of a type module there must exist an invocation mechanism that, at a minimum, locates the procedure that implements the desired operation, acquires or constructs a domain to make available to the procedure those objects required for its correct execution, and causes execution of the procedure to begin at the procedure entry point.

Because objects are specified as parameters to operation invocations, a question arises: does the ability to perform operations on an object change as a result of its being passed as a parameter? If one program passes an object as a parameter to a slave program that is to perform a task that the caller could conceivably perform, the second program should not have any rights to manipulate the parameter object that the caller program does not have. In fact, the second program may have less.

In contrast, if an object is passed as a parameter to an operation defined as part of the object's type, the code implementing that operation will require the ability to manipulate the object's representation. Thus, some means for __amplification__, i.e., for obtaining additional rights to manipulate an object is required [Jones75]. Most extant hardware provides only an extremely primitive amplification mechanism. When a user program invokes an operation that happens to be provided by a module of the operating system, the hardware state changes so that when the operating system code is entered, it has access to __all__ of main memory. In particular, it has all necessary access to the representation of the parameter object, but it also has __much, much__ more.

Such a mechanism does not support the object model very well. It places an undue burden on the implementor of the operating system, because that programmer has no means to restrict the objects, or memory, that are accessible to his code, making debugging more difficult. Such mechanisms inadequately support the concept of software reliability. More selective amplification mechanisms can be designed. The Multics hardware permits domains of execution to be ordered so that segments, the nameable objects in the Multics system, that are available to one domain are available both to it and to domains lower in the ordering [Organick72]. The Multics hardware can be augmented so that each domain can be treated independently eliminating the ordering constraint [Schroeder72]. Other systems, such as Hydra, that lack hardware to perform amplification provide such support in software [Wulf74]. Programming languages that support the concept of abstract data types provide such amplification mechanisms [Jones76].

So, to support the object model requires support for the notion of a domain. Ideally, domains are small; only the rights and objects necessary to perform the task at hand are available. Domain support must include a facility for suspending execution in one domain in order to enter another, and subsequently to return to the first. Some provision for amplification is required. Domain management needs to be efficient for domain entry and exit occur often. Current operating system research and some programming language research is addressing these issues.

4. Observation

The fidelity with which a particular system adheres to the object model varies widely. Some operating systems, such as Multics, define a single type of object, the segment, and permit users to create segments at will. Other systems, such as Hydra, permit users to dynamically create new object types, as well as new objects. Hydra, in particular, provides naming and protection of objects of user defined types, as well as operating system types, as was sketched above. However, even in cases where the operating system design does not closely adhere to the object model, the model often provides a convenient vehicle for describing system components. Consequently, in the other papers in this volume authors have used the notion with greater or less fidelity, as suited their needs and their taste.

5. References

Burroughs Corporation, The Descriptor--A definition of the B5000 Information Processing System. Detroit, MI (February 1961).

Dahl, O.-J., B. Myhrhaung and K. Nygaard, The Simula 67 Common Base Language, Norwegian Computing Center, Oslo, Norway (1968).

Dennis, J. B. and Van Horn, E. C., Programming Semantics for Multiprogrammed Computations, CACM 9, 3 (March 1966) 143-155.

Habermann, A. N., On the Concurrency of Parallel Processes, Perspectives in Computer Science, A. Jones, editor, Academic Press (1977).

Jones, A. K. and W. A. Wulf, Towards the Design of Secure Systems. Software--Practice and Experience, 5, 4 (October-December 1975) 321-336.

Jones, A. K. and B. H. Liskov, A Language Extension for Controlling Access to Shared Data. IEEE Transactions on Software Engineering SE-2, 4 (December 1976) 277-284.

Lampson, B. W. and H. Sturgis, Reflections on an Operating System Design. CACM 19, 5 (May 76), 251-266.

Liskov, B. H. and S. Zilles, Specification Techniques for Data Abstractions. Proceedings of the International Conference on Reliable Software, SIGPLAN Notices 12,3 (1977).

Liskov, B. H., A. Snyder, R. Atkinson, and C. Schaffert, Abstraction Mechanisms in CLU. Proceedings of the ACM Conference on Language Design for Reliable Software, SIGPLAN Notices 10,6 (1975), 534-545.

Needham, R. and R. D. H. Walker, The Cambridge CAP Computer and its Protection System. Proceedings of the 6th ACM Symposium on Operating System Principles (November 77) 1-10.

Organick, E. I., The Multics System: iAn Examination of its Structure. MIT Press (1972).

Schroeder, M. D. and J. H. Saltzer, A Hardware Architecture for Implementing Protection Rings. CACM 15, 3 (March 1972) 157-170.

Wulf, W. A., et al, Hydra: the Kernel of a Multiprocessor Operating System. CACM 17, 6 (June 1974) 337-345.

Wulf, W. A., R. L. London and M. Shaw, Abstraction and Verification in Alphard. IEEE Transactions on Software Engineering (April 1976).

CHAPTER 2.B.

M. J. Flynn
Stanford University
Stanford, Ca., USA

Computer Organization and Architecture

COMPUTER ORGANIZATION AND ARCHITECTURE[*]

M. J. Flynn
Department of Electrical Engineering
Digital Systems Laboratory
Stanford University
Stanford, CA 94305

ABSTRACT

The instruction set is a defining influence on the machine organization that interprets it. A well mapped machine is one whose organization directly supports a single instruction set and whose state transition matches those called for by the instruction.

An important determinant in the architecture is the mechanism for naming and locating an object in the storage hierarchy. Three classes of issues are involved in name specification; the process name space which deals with issues unique to a single program, the processor name space which is concerned with interprocess communication issues and finally a memory space which is concerned with the physical parameters of access time and bandwidth.

A Canonic Interpretive Form (CIF) of higher level languages programs is proposed to measure the "minimum" space to represent and time to interpret a given program. This "ideal" is a basis for a comparison with traditional machine languages which require ten times more program space than the CIF.

Synthesis of program forms (called Directly Executed Languages--DELs) which approach CIF measures is proposed as well as results of a recently completed FORTRAN DEL (DELTRAN).

Within the context of traditional machine architectures, concurrency or parallel arrangement of processors is possible to improve performance. Two classes of organizations are discussed: the single instruction multiple data stream type and the multiple instruction multiple data stream. These organizations, together with a performance analysis based on certain program behavior characteristics, is reviewed.

---

[*] This research was partly supported by the Department of Energy under contract number EY-76-S-03-0326-PA 39 and the ARO-Durham under contract number DAAG-26-76-G-0001.

I. MACHINE MAPPING AND WELL MAPPED MACHINES

Introduction

A machine is largely known by its instruction set. Of course, other issues such as space, power, algorithms used, may be important in certain applications but the user basically sees the instruction set of the machine. The instruction set, thus, is the interface between programs and resources. The program is a sequence of instructions that accomplish a desired user end. The instructions are interpreted by a control unit which activates the system's resources (data paths) to cause proper transformations to occur (Figure 1).

The instruction set is sometimes called the architecture of the processor. It is, of course, actually a language. Its usefulness is best measured by the space it requires to represent a program and time required to interpret these representations. Recent developments in technology allow a great deal more flexibility in control unit structure while a variety of current research efforts have brought additional understanding in the nature of the instruction set. It is the purpose of these notes to explore these developments. In this first section we shall be more concerned with a review of fundamental notions related to computer architecture. This will allow us to discuss issues and concepts in traditional machine architectures.

Instruction Action

The instruction consists of a pair of rules, an action rule and a sequencing rule. The action rule specifies a function which takes n domain arguments--where n is the order of the function--maps it into a (usually) single range element. Both domain arguments and range element are finite, in fact, the bound is established a priori. Thus, the action rule has the following form:

$$f_i(x_1, x_2, x_3, \ldots, x_n) = y_i$$
$$f_{i+1}(x_1, x_2, x_3, \ldots, x_n) = y_{i+1}$$

The number of different types of functions, f, is the number of elements in the vocabulary of the instruction set. For general purpose computers, the order of f rarely exceeds 2 and the order of the range is usually 0 or 1.

Since a program is a sequence of instructions, the instruction must contain a sequencing mechanism. That is, a method of specifying the successor to itself, f_{i+1}. The successor in all familiar computer organizations is a unary rule; each single instruction specifies a single successor. However, a particular instruction may require inspection of several arguments before determining which of several possible successors is the correct one. This is a variation of the familiar condi-

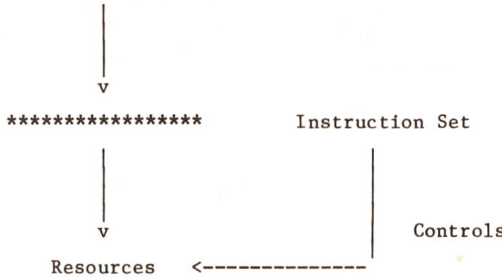

Figure 1: The Instruction Set

tional branch instruction.

Specification

From the above there are five objects to be specified: the operation element, f_i; two source arguments (assuming a binary order instruction); a single result argument; and finally a successor instruction. Now, specification may be accomplished by one of the four methods: (Figure 2)

    (i)   by fragment identification
    (ii)   by coordinate address
    (iii) by implication
    (iv)   immediately

(i) Specification by <u>fragment identification</u> is also called specification by association or content. In specification by <u>record fragment</u>, as the name implies, we must be in possession of a piece of the object or record to be retrieved. This piece is usually called the tag. The entire storage is searched and records whose tags match the inquiring tag are retrieved. Since multiple matches may develop, retrieval must be done with care.

(ii) <u>Coordinate address</u>-- specification by coordinate address is the familiar direct addressing scheme. Every element, object, that can be retrieved has an associated index, or address. A number of objects can be retrieved from storage is called the range and the size of an individual object that is retrieved from storage is called the resolution. When binary addresses are used, then clearly the size of the address, or object specification, must contain $\log_2$ of the range.

(iii) Specification by <u>implication</u> is a useful method of more efficient coding of

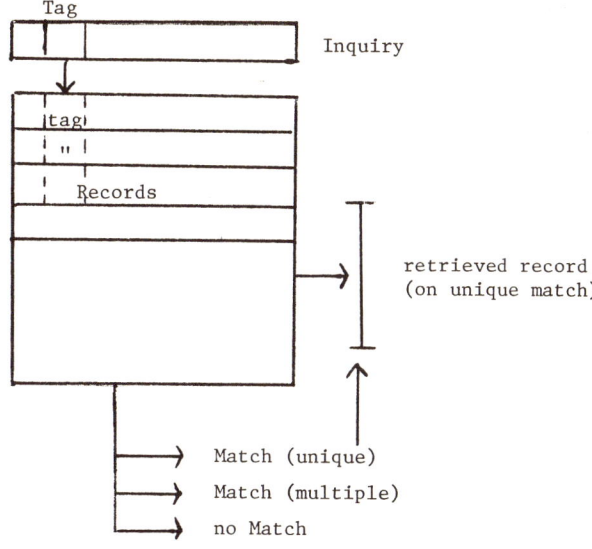

(i) Specification by Fragment Identification (tag association)

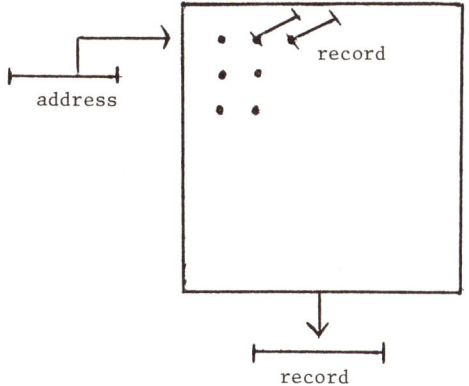

(ii) Specification by Coordinate Address

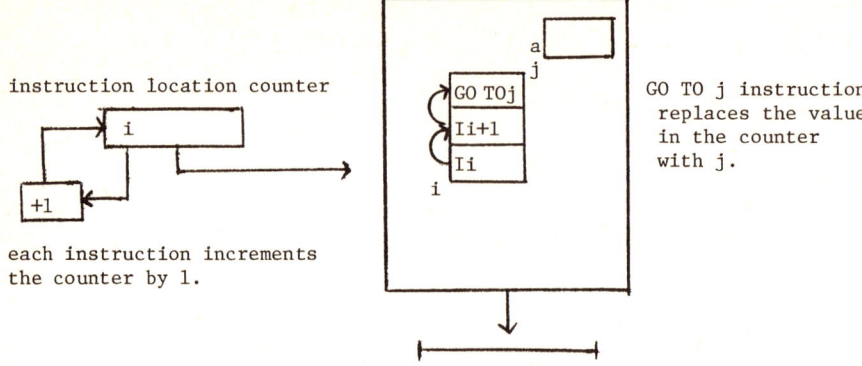

(iii) Specification by Implication (for in-line instruction convention)

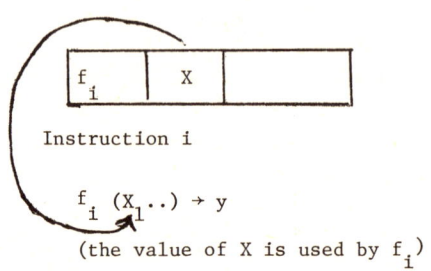

Instruction i

$f_i(X_1..) \to y$

(the value of X is used by f_i)

(iv) Immediate Specification

Figure 2: Object Specification

instructions. Effectively, both the programmer and the control unit agree on an interpretation. Thus, for example, instructions could be assumed to lie in line, i.e. one following another. This would avoid the need for an explicit specification of the successor function. Of course, when the programmer did not wish the next instruction to be located at the present location plus one, he must insert a special instruction which will tell the interpreter to jump or go to the correct location

(iv) The <u>immediate reference</u> corresponds to placement of the desired operand, or object, directly in the instruction itself. Clearly, this has its limitations. The program is no more general than its ability to operate on a variety of variable objects. Once an object is placed directly in the instruction, the variability of that object is largely lost. However, for certain specific functions and instruction artifacts immediate specification is useful.

Most general specification schemes, as used in instruction set design, concentrate on the coordinate address/implication specification approaches. Addressing by fragment is limited in efficiency since, if one uses too short a tag the problem of multiple matches becomes acute. This in turn forces the interpreter to examine each of the multiple matches until it finds the desired one. It corresponds to, for example, a telephone book inquiry where the retriever is given only the first two or three letters of the last name in searching for a particular record. Even though other information may be known about the record so as to resolve the retrieval to one record, too many objects must be examined to find the correct one, thus lowering the overall space-time efficiency. Thus, we find that specification by record fragment is usually restricted in use to particular applications where the multiple match problem is not significant. Also, as mentioned earlier, immediate specification has some notable drawbacks. It may tend to increase program size and certainly limits the generality of the result in program representation. Thus, combinations of coordinate addressing and implication really form the basis of instruction set design. In fact, they provide the basis for probably the most popular categorization of instruction sets--by the number of addresses that the instruction set contains. See Table 1 for a list of the five classes of instruction sets.

The Interpretation of an Instruction (see [1, 2])

In order to get a better understanding of the execution unit and the control mechanism, consider the functional units that make up the processor: control unit, execution unit, and storage. As shown in Figure 3, the execution unit may further be broken down into two basic pieces--addressing and operation. The storage module is a conventional memory with data retrieval by address. All system elements are activated by the control unit acting on registers in the processor. The registers can be thought of as separate from storage and the execution unit. By separating the registers in this way we remove the facility to store or hold exit data information from storage and the execution unit. Thus, the operation involves transfer of information from one or two registers through the execution unit and the return of a result to another register (perhaps one of the source registers).

After an instruction has been transmitted to the instruction register from storage, the operation part of the instruction drives the control unit through a sequence of control steps. For example, the first control steps calculate a source address and fetch the source datum into the storage register. Following that, a sequence of steps is performed with two registers as sources and another register as a result. These control signals are determined, in part, by the operation itself. Certain test signals are examined continuously by the control unit to determine the next control command. the instruction is executed in four basic phases as shown in Figure 4. The operation in the execution phase might be an ADD, for example. In order to accomplish this, however, a number of suboperations are necessary as shown in Figure 5.

First, the sign of each of the source data has to be inspected. If a complement of the operand is required, it may involve the injection of an additional 1 into the least significant data position (as in two's complement arithmetic). Finally, after the ADD there is a potential recomplementation (again, depending upon the representation) and an inspection for overflow.

Before discussing techniques of control we must review what is being controlled. Information is processed within a functional unit by a specific configuration of logic gates (combinatorial logic) in a single time unit or by a sequence of steps through such logic configurations (sequential logic). The communicated data may be transmitted and transformed in one time unit by the data paths of the system. A sequence of transmissions from register to register requires multiple time units. These units are called the internal cycles of the system. This section investigates the general requirements for controlling both the data paths of the system as well as various kinds of internal cycles which the designer may use.

Data Paths and Control Points

A machine, exclusive of control, consists largely of registers and combinatorial execution logic (adders, shifters, and so on). Each register position in the system can be gated to one of a number of other registers during one cycle. The inter-register connections together with the registers and resources are referred to as the data paths of the system. The output of each register activates AND gates which are directed to each of the destinations reachable from the source register in one cycle. (Figure 6).

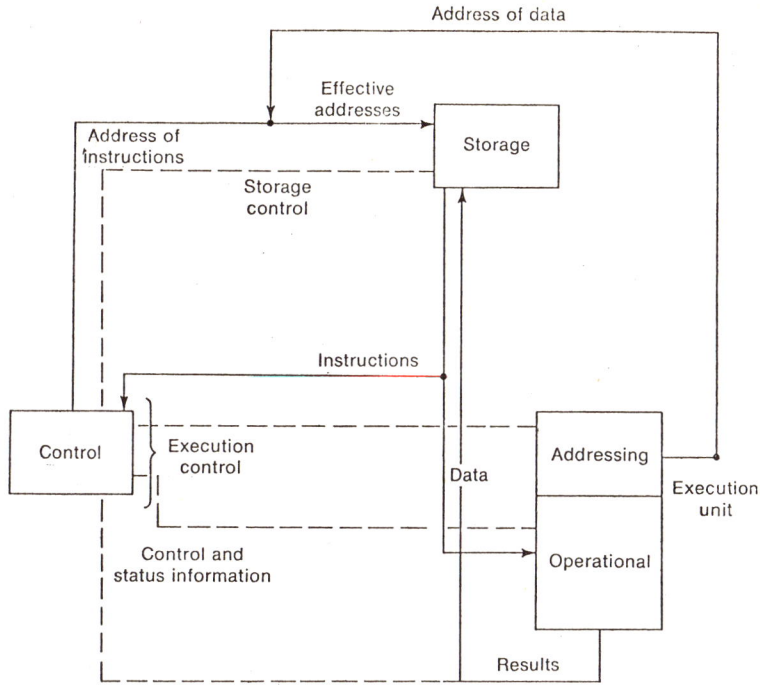

Figure 3: Control in a Computer

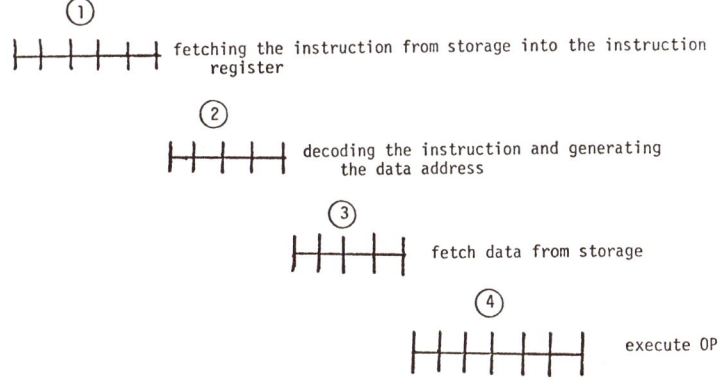

Figure 4: Instruction Timing

TABLE 1: Instruction Formats

NOTATION
    OP: Operation to be performed
    SR1:   Address of the first soruce data item
    SR2:   Address of the second source data item
    RL: Address of the location where the result is to be placed
    NI: Address of the next instruction in the sequence
    c(A):   The contents of the location whose address is A
    (A):   Value contained in A
    *:   Address of the instruction currently being interpreted
    ACC: An accumulator register; the implied location of a source or
            result operand for certain formats

FOUR ADDRESS

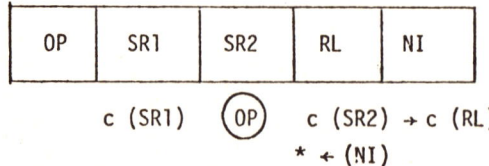

TWO ADDRESS

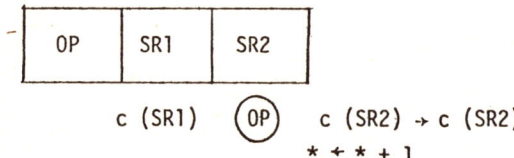

ONE ADDRESS

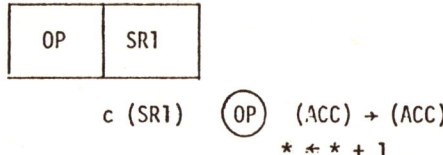

ZERO ADDRESS

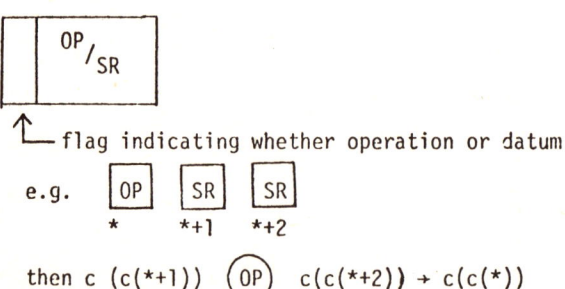

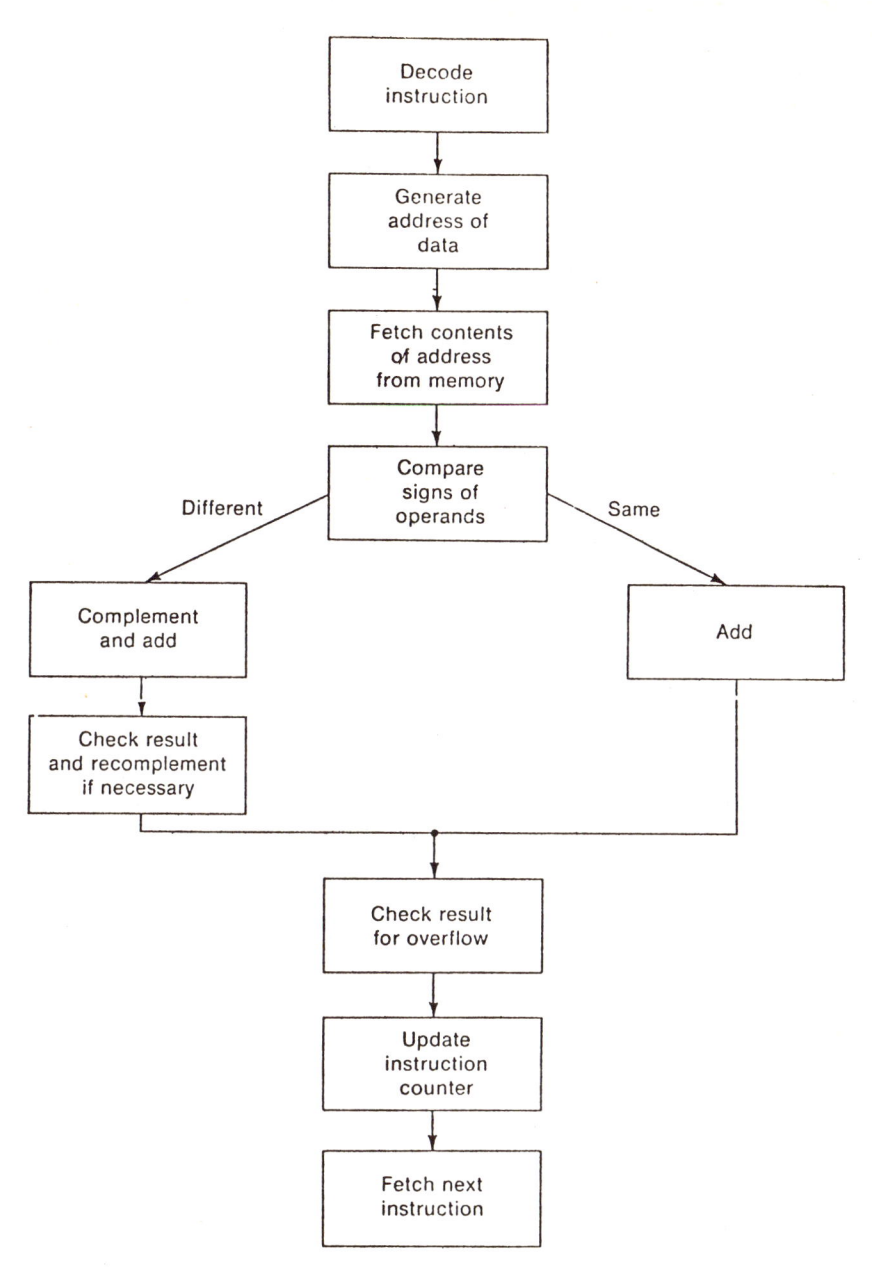

Note: The primitive operations (*)
correspond to the ADD microinstruction.

Figure 5: Instruction Interpretation

There are two types of data paths:
(1) Those paths that connect the source register to a destination register (perhaps itself) without any intervening transformational logic.
(2) Those paths connected from a source register into an execution unit and then directed to a destination register.

Figure 7 shows the ith bit of a storage register, an adder, and an accumulator. In this example, the accumulator register is added to a word from memory which has been placed in the storage register; the sum is returned to the accumulator. This occurs during the execute phase shown in Figure 4. A simple ADD instruction may have a three-cycle execute. One cycle is used for inspection of the signs of each of the operands before the addition, the second cycle is used for the addition, and the third cycle is used for sign and overflow inspection. During the second cycle the information in bit i of the storage register is gated to bit i of the adder, activated by an appropriate control single, label SR-to-adder. This allows the information from bit i of the accumulator and bit i of the storage register to activate the two inputs to the ith position of the adder. This together with the carry from bit i-1 position determines the sum, which is gated through an OR into the accumulator. The accumulator does not actually change its value upon receiving this signal, but at the end of the cycle a sample pulse is used to set this new information into the accumulator. At the same time, new information can be entered into the storage register. If the instruction, instead of being an ADD instruction, were a SHIFT instruction, we would use a path from the accumlator to its neighbor. Notice that operations involving the adder require a substantial number of logic decisions before the value can be determine and set into the accumulator, while the SHIFT operation involves only two decisions.

In general, if the execution unit (for example, the adder in the preceding example) has internal storage, it may be treated as a multiple-cycle operation. If it does not, then the tioe required to direct information from a register through the execution unit and back to a register defines the cycle time. Combinatorial logic has no memory by itself; all information is lost at the end of one cycle, unless it is stored in a register.

Control points are the hardware locations at which the output of the processor instruction decoder activates specific registers and operation units. Control points basically govern intercycle register-to- register communications. For each register in the processor there is a fixed number of other registers to which data may be transmitted in one cycle. For each such possibility, a separate AND circuit is placed on the output of each bit of the source register with the entry into the destination register being collected from all possible resources by an OR circuit.

For example, consider a 32-bit computer with eight registers. Assume that each

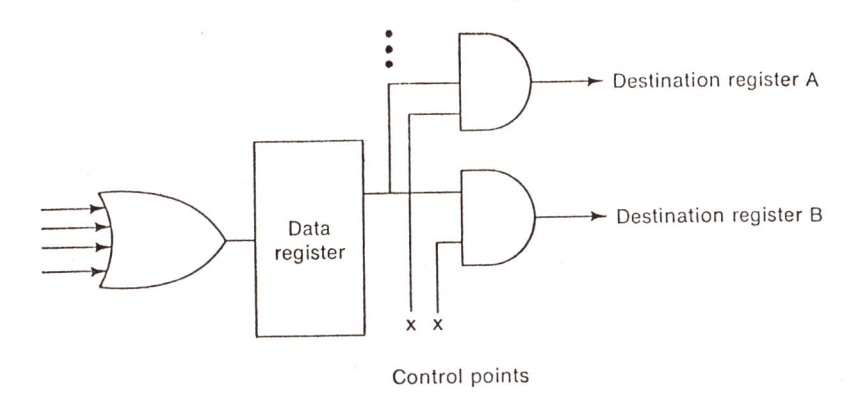

Figure 6: Control Points

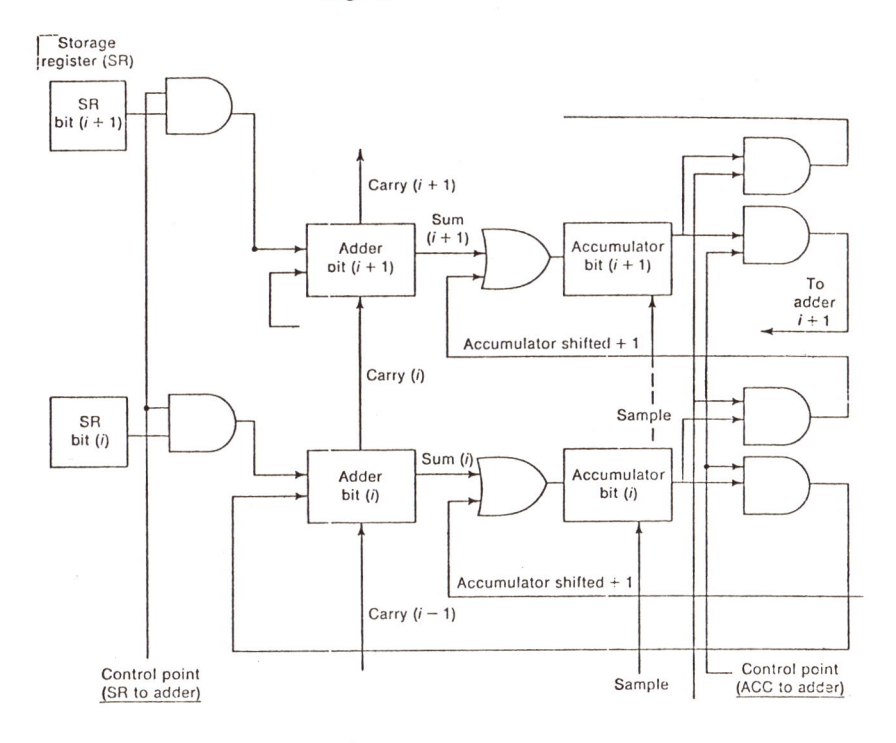

Figure 7: Control Distribution

register can communicate with three other register in one cycle. The number of control points required for register communication is therefore 3 X 8 X 32 or 768. In addition, assume the machine has three execution units, each of whose 32-bit outputs can be gated to one of four registers. This accounts for an additional 3 X 4 X 32 or 364 control points. There are additional control points for the selection of a particular function within a designated module. This might account for 100 more control points. Thus, there are a total of somewhat over 1200 control points that must be established each cycle by the output of the instruction decoder. Fortunately, in most computer design situations many of these control points are not independent. For example, bit 7 of a certain register is not gated to another register, but rather the entire contents of the register is gated to its destination register. Since only one line is required to control these multiple control points, the total number of outputs required can be significantly reduced. These outputs are then referred to as <u>independent control points</u>. For the hypothetical system described, there might be anywhere from 50 to 200 independent control points depending upon the variety of instructions.

The operation code specifies the operation to be performed; by itself it is insufficient to specify multiple control steps for the execution of an instruction; some additional counting mechanism is also required. If the control implementation is to be done with hardware implementation--using a combinatorial network--then a counter is used to sequence through the control steps to transmit signals to control points. This counter identifies the particular step of the instruction that is executed at any moment. The combination of the sequence count and the operation is the input to the network which then describes the exact state of each control point at each cycle of every instruction. (Figure 8)

<u>Cycle Time</u>

The cycle time of a computer is the time required to change the information in a set of registers. This is also sometimes referred to as a state transition time. The internal cycle time may be of constant value; there are basically three different ways of clocking a processor.

1. <u>Synchronous Fixed</u> -- In this scheme all operations are composed of one or more clock cycles with the fundamental time quantum being fixed by the design. Such systems are also referred to as clocked, since usually a master oscillator (or clock) is used to distribute and define these cycles.

2. <u>Synchronous Variable</u> -- This is a slight variation of the former scheme in which certain long operations are allowed to take multiple cycles without causing a register state transition. In such systems there may be several

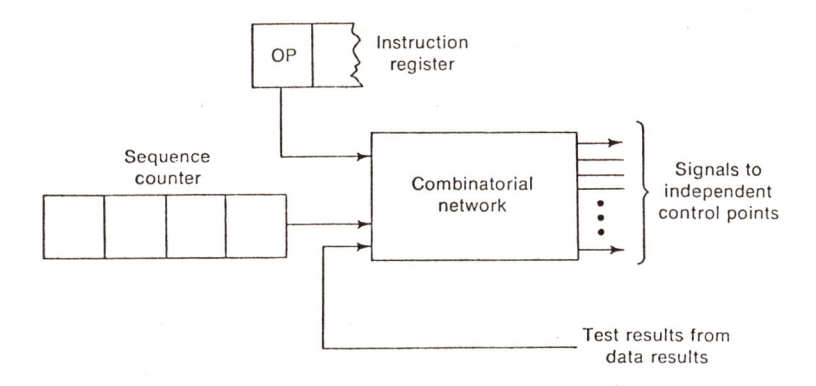

Figure 8: Instruction Decoder

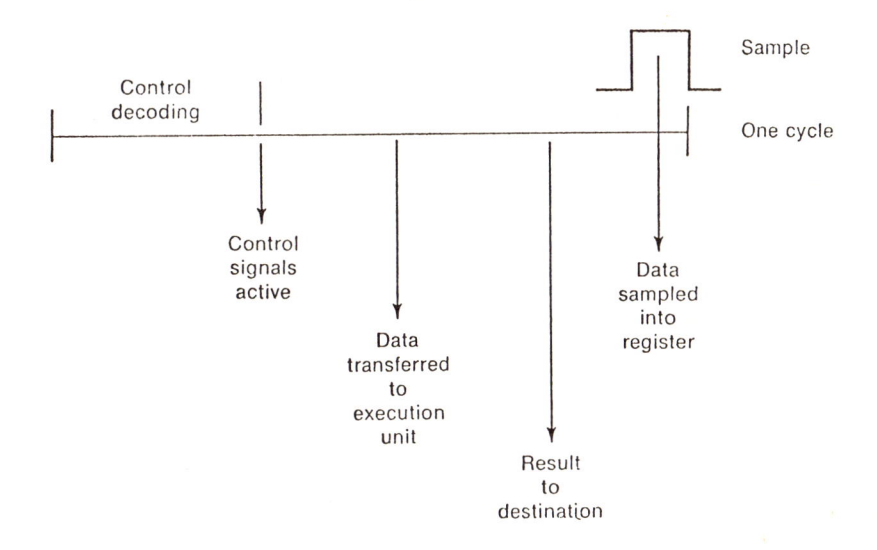

Figure 9: Internal Cycle

different cycle lengths. For example, a register-to-register transfer of information might repesent one basic cycle while a transfer from a register to an adder with return to a register required perhaps two or three basic cycles. The fundamental difference between these two schemes is that the fixed synchronous scheme stores information into registers at the end of every cycle time, while the variable synchronous scheme sets information into registers after a number of cycles depending upon the type of operation being performed.

3. <u>Asynchronous Operation</u> -- In a completely asynchronous machine there is no clock or external mechanism that determines a state transition. Rather the logic of the system is arranged in stages. When the output value of one stage has been stablized, the input at the stage can admit a new pair of operands.

Asynchronous operation is advantageous when the variation in cycle time is significant since a synchronous scheme must always wait for the worst possible delay in the definition of the time quantum required. On the other hand, when logic delays are predictable, synchronous techniques have an advantage since several additional stages of logic are required in the asynchronous scheme to signal completion of an operation. In actual practice, most systems are basically synchronous (either fixed or variable) with some asynchronous operations used for particular functions of the machine, such as in accessing main memory.

The cycle itself is composed of two components: (1) the time necessary to decode the control information and set up the control points, and (2) the time necessary to transmit and transform the data (the data state transition). In simple machines the cycle is the sum of the control decoding time and the data state transition time. In second generation computers with hard-wired control logic, control time was approximately 35 percent of the entire cycle and the data state transition was the remaining 65 percent of the cycle. With the use of microprogram store for the implementation of the control function in third generation computers, the control time increased and overlapping of the two became more prevalent. (Figure 9)

Machine Mapping

How should one arrange the data paths and resources in response to a given instruction set? On the surface this sounds like a relatively straightforward challenge. However, as we shall shortly see, things are not quite as simple as would seem.

When a user examines an instruction set, he visualizes certain sequences of actions and certain data paths implied by these actions. In fact, the instruction set definition, together with the cycle time specifications, both internal and memory, largely determine the data paths and instruction timings for most instructions in machines. The machine for which the data paths and instruction timings are thus predicted are called <u>well mapped machines</u>. A <u>well mapped machine</u> has internal and memory state transitions corresponding to those specified in the instruction set. Thus, its timing is by definition predictable from the instruction set.

Two other machine classes are possible. We call these <u>partially mapped</u> and <u>overlapped</u>. A <u>partially mapped machine</u> has significantly more internal state transitions and memory state transitions than that called for by the instruction set. Partial mapping usually comes about for one of two reasons, (1) the designer, in an effort at economy, retrieves, for example, only half or quarter of a record specified by the instruction at a time and operates on the record in piecemeal fashion; (2) the universal host machine represents a configuration which is designed to interpret not one but several different machines. Universal host structures will require additional state transitions to interpret the various fields of the instruction as well as reconfigure data paths.

The <u>overlapped machine</u>, on the otherhand, will execute an instruction in fewer effective state transitions than that specified in the instruction set. The key here is the effective number of state transitions since all state transitions must properly occur, but by having a number of instructions in various phases of execution—concurrently executing—the effect is to reduce the number of apparent state transitions required for the interpretation of a particular instruction.

Example 1: The Well Mapped 7094

(a) The Basic Instruction:

```
   12      1   3     15
┌────────┬───┬───┬────────┐
│   OP   │ I │▓X │  ADDR  │
└────────┴───┴───┴────────┘
```

ACC OP C(ADDR - C(Reg X)) → ACC

Parameters:
    Referend size: 36^b = 1 word
    Internal cycle: 333 nsec fixed synchronous
    Memory cycle: 2 μsec (6 internal cycles)
          1 μsec read - 1 μsec write/regenerate
    Memory range: $2^{15b} \approx 32^K$
          resolution 36^b word

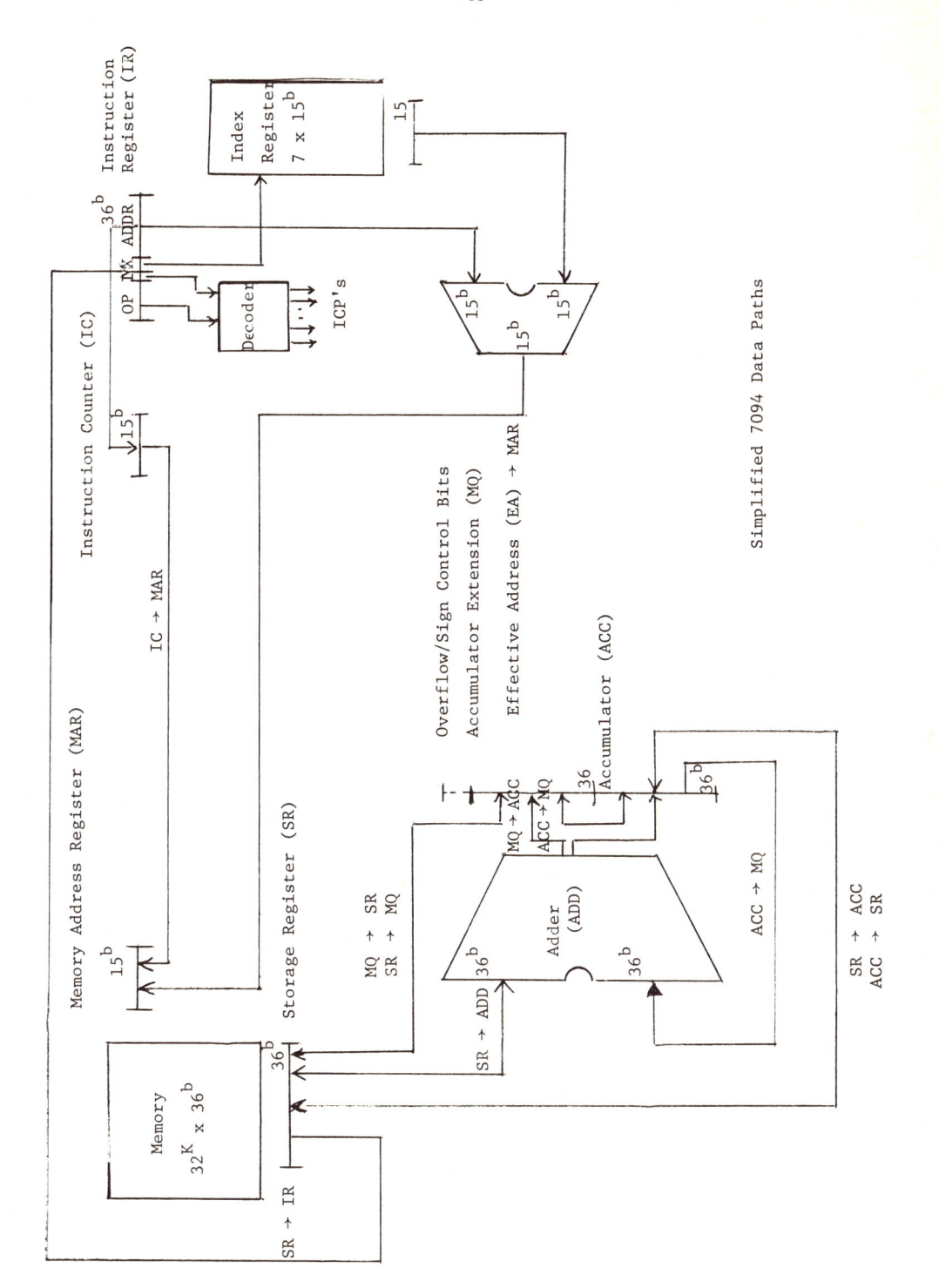

Simplified 7094 Data Paths

A Well Mapped Instruction Timing for Simplified 7094

ADD Instruction (without indirection)

Instruction Fetch |—|—|—|
  C(MAR) → SR

  SR → IR |—|

  Decode |—|

  Address−C(RegX) → MAR |—|

Data Fetch
  C(MAR) → SR |—|—|—|—|—|

  SR /ACC sign instruction |—|

  SR ADD ACC → ACC |—|

  overflow check/sign control |—|

Next Instruction Preparation
  IC + 1 → IC |—|

  IC → MAR |—|

II. NAME SPACE - MEMORY SPACE

The primary issue we wish to study in this section is the relationship between names or unique identifiers and objects that contain the desired information.

It has long been recognized that the management of memory requires multiple mappings (Denning [3]):
1. the compiler performs a naming function by translating symbolic addresses into unique identifiers,
2. typically a loader performs a naming function by translating these unique identifiers into memory locations,
3. the contents function then retrieves the data contained in the identified locations.

Simply speaking, it would seem that a set of unique identifiers defines the name space for a program while the set of memory locations defines a memory space. Unfortunately, as we shall see, things are not this simple for either terms since many issues related to the way programs reference one another complicate the name space definition on the one hand, while complex algorithms for buffering memory disguise the real picture of physical memory on the other.

A program consists of a set of action rules defined over a space of object names. A set of all object names that can be acted on directly by the program defines the name space of the program. The key word here is directly. When a program accesses a file it cannot act directly on the data in that file. Rather, it must first move it into the name space available to the program. While perhaps somewhat moot, the key issue is that the program uses an object in the same space as an action argument. Note here how cloudy the issue can be if one defines an architecture which is completely register oriented; that is, operands must be first brought into registers before any transformation can be performed on them. By strict interpretation then, the name space would be the register set, thus, the program itself would lie outside its own name space--a very undesirable situation. Thus, we must be a little less formal and somewhat more intuitive about the name space notion. Name space consists of all locations visible to the action rules (or instruction set) of the program clearly including the program locations themselves, the register sets and all possible data areas, but excluding the I/O space (if one exists).

One program's name space is another program's I/O space, one might say; since with respect to I/O one could surely conceive of channel or disc controller action rules which operate directly on the space of named objects which contain blocks of information which are sought by the central processor. The main purpose of these notes is to review the structure of a program's and a processor's name space. Our attention is primarily directed at the main memory and process actions which can be defined upon it as distinct from focusing on peripheral units.

What is a process? A _process_ is a program together with its state vector. A _state vector_ consists of an initial program state together with an assignment of values for all objects initially referred to by the program. Thus, a program differs notably from a process in the sense that a program is a pure piece of code, whereas a process is a program in execution. Execution here is used in a logical not necessarily a physical, sense. By identifying a mapping between objects and values we _bind_ them. Because of the multiple levels of interpretation active in the overall processor, a single process may be actively executed at one level, suspended at a lower level, and not even be a process at still a lower level, since values are not bound to a space at that level. Thus, it is again very important to stress that our view is of one level: a process resident in a space called memory being interpreted by a processor and memory system. Thus, a process is created with respect to this level when it is assigned and enters the name space of the processor. The name space of the processor and the process need not necessarily be the same. The process, in general, will have a proper subset of the name space of the processor.

Some Definition on Naming
(1) A _process name space_ is the set of objects that can be used by a process.
(2) A _processor name space_ is the set of objects that can be used by all processes.
(3) The _memory space_ is the set of locations used to interpret a processor name space.
(4) _Virtual memory_ space is an informal term indicating a multiple level interpretive process associating a physical location to a process or processor name space object.
(5) _Binding_ is an association between objects or between objects and locations or between locations and values (the contents map). For binding to be nontrivial the association, or mapping, is restrictive. The binding function actually restricts the domain of possible objects, locations or contents.

Name Spaces and Memory Space

It is instructive to separately consider the issues posed by the process name space, the processor name space and the memory space. While considering these issues separately, one should realize that any intelligent design will provide consistent and congruent handling of objects across each of these boundaries so as to minimize interpretation time and overall cost.

Process Name Space--Issues

A name used by a process is a surrogate for a value. This value, or name space object, is also called the referand. The assignment of meaning to referand template is the data representation problem where the template is merely a partitioning of bits, or symbols, within the referand. Our discussion here is limited only to the name and not the value or even to the referand template. Values are assigned to names by an operation called "content map" so that the contents of the name produces the correct value. For purposes of this discussion we assume that the content map is established externally (by the loader).

Some naming issues that are unique to the name space (Figure 10) of a process include:
1. range and resolution of objects,
2. range extension--I/O handling and files,
3. homogeneity of the space,
4. reference coding.

1. <u>Range and resolution</u> -- the range and resolution refer to the maximum number of objects that can be specified in a process space and the minimum size of an object in that name space respectively. Traditionally, instructions provide resolution usually no smaller than an 8 bit byte, and frequently a 16 bit or larger word, and range defined as large as one can comfortably accomodate within the bounds of a reasonable instruction size and hence program size. Thus, ranges from 2^{16} for minicomputers to 2^{24} for System 360 include most common arrangements.

2. <u>Range extension</u> -- I/O and file handling--since the process range is bounded, it is essential that an extension mechanism be provided. The need for range extension stems from the bounded nature of the process name space range. After all, if the range were unlimited then as soon as objects were entered anywhere in the system, that place of entry could be regarded as part of the process name space. An associated problem is that of attaching records to an established process name space. Usually this attachment must be done by a physical movement of the data from its present location to an area within the bounds of the present process name space before it can be operated on. The programmer must manage data movement from the I/O space into the process name space through I/O commands. This binding or attachment is the responsibility of the programmer and must be performed at the correct sequential interval so as to insure the integrity of the data and yet not exceed the range requirements of the name space objects--overflow buffers, for example. This ability to communicate between an unbounded I/O media and a bounded processor name space allows the programmer to simulate for himself an open ended name space. However, it is a requirement placed on the programmer and it is frequently a cumbersome and inefficient operation. Of course, the larger the range, the more precise and vari-

able the resolution, the more easily managed objects in a process name space. Having flexibility at this level allows conciseness of code representation.

From the above, the desirability of an unbounded name space with flexible attachment possibilities is clear.

3. <u>Homogeneity of the space</u> -- the name space may be partitioned in different ways but the type of partitioning referred to here is that distinguished by the action rule within a process. Action rules or instructions generally cannot treat all objects in the same way. Certain classes of objects are established such as registers, accumulators, and memory objects. Action rules are applied in a non-symetric way: one of the arguments for an action rule must be a register whereas the other may be a register or a memory object. The premise of this partitioning is performance, i.e. the assumption that access to registers is faster than access to memory. Thus, many familiar machines have their name space partitioned into a register space and memory space: 360, PDP-11, etc. As the partitioning of the name space increases, its <u>homogeneity</u> decreases.

4. <u>Reference coding</u> -- the actual identification of the object, i.e., its name or address, is a subtle series of design issues--a constant series of tradeoffs between intepretation time and program size or representation size. We outline below traditional issues in the design of the address reference facilities.

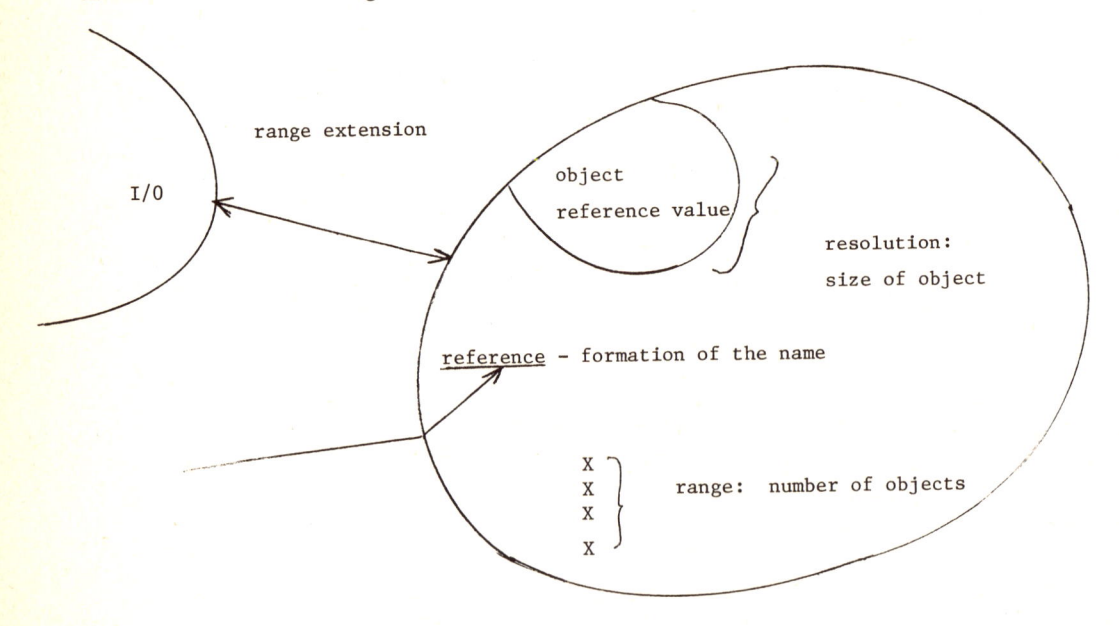

Figure 10: Process Name Space

Reference

    Generation of address

        direct
        indexed
        computed

        Types

            multiple indexed
            combination index, look-up, etc.
            sub-program computation

    Use of address

        immediate
        direct
        indirect
            depth

    Format

        full address
        short

        Types

            reference
            relative address
            base: zero, implied, register

    implied

        Multiplicity

            multiple choice in operation code

The Processor or System Name Space

The processor or system name space is actually the space of all process name spaces. Thus, many of the same issues that existed between objects in a process name space now exist between the processes and the processor name space. Processes must be located relative to one another, they cannot occupy the same space at the same time. The processor name space then may be considerably larger than the process name space, although the resolutions need not be the same. The processor name space (Figure 11) for example may deal with much larger objects if the proper conventions are followed at all levels. Listed below are some of the more notable processor name space issues:

1. range, resolution and range extension
2. dimensionality
3. process reference coding:

1. <u>Range, resolution and range extension</u> -- the issues here are the same as they were in the process name space: unbounded versus bounded range, and given that the range is bounded how can the range be extended--what are the I/O and file conven-

tions for introducing new tasks data sets.

2. <u>Dimensionality</u> -- one method of dealing with range extension is to use a multidimensional processor name space; where one dimension identifies a process or process data set name, the other dimension identifies an index within that process name space. If neither the process names nor the indicies are bounded, we have a two dimensional unbounded range processor name space.

In general, processor name spaces may have single linear dimension or be two dimensional with ordered or unordered prefix. Two dimensional name spaces are frequently called segmented [4]. This type of name space is composed of a set of separate linear name spaces. Each linear name space is part of a process name space within which objects have been ordered to form a segment. A segmented name space is a two dimensional space since it is necessary to specify two names (name of the segment and name of the index within the segment) in order to access an item or an object. The disadvantage of segmented processor name spaces over linear name space is the added complexity of the addressing mechanism required for address interpretation. Notice that segmented name spaces may be homogeneous, i.e. no partition of the space by action rules is required. Rather, the space is partitioned by process requirements themselves and the partitioning is dynamic. As pointed out by Randall [5], two types of segmented name spaces are of particular interest, the linear segmented name space and the symbolic or unordered segmented name space. The basic difference between these two is that in the latter the segments are in no sense ordered. The segment name is arbitrary and operations on segments names do not produce another name. This lack of ordering means that there is no name contiguity to cause problems of task allocation and reallocation of addresses. Whereas the advantage of the linear segmented name space is that they permit indexing across segment names. This can be of benefit where the segment had a bounded range.

3. <u>Process or segment reference coding</u> -- [6]

```
Process (Segment) Relocation
       Map type        - Contiguous - Base and Bound
                       - Non-contiguous - fixed block size
                           . associative
                           . direct
                           . set associative
Process (Segment) Relocation
                       - Contiguous - Base and Bound
                       - Non-contiguous - Keyed Direct
                                        - Ordered Priority
Process (Segment) Communications
                       - accessing rights
                           . read
                           . write
                           . read/write
                       - acquiring rights
                       - modifying rights
```

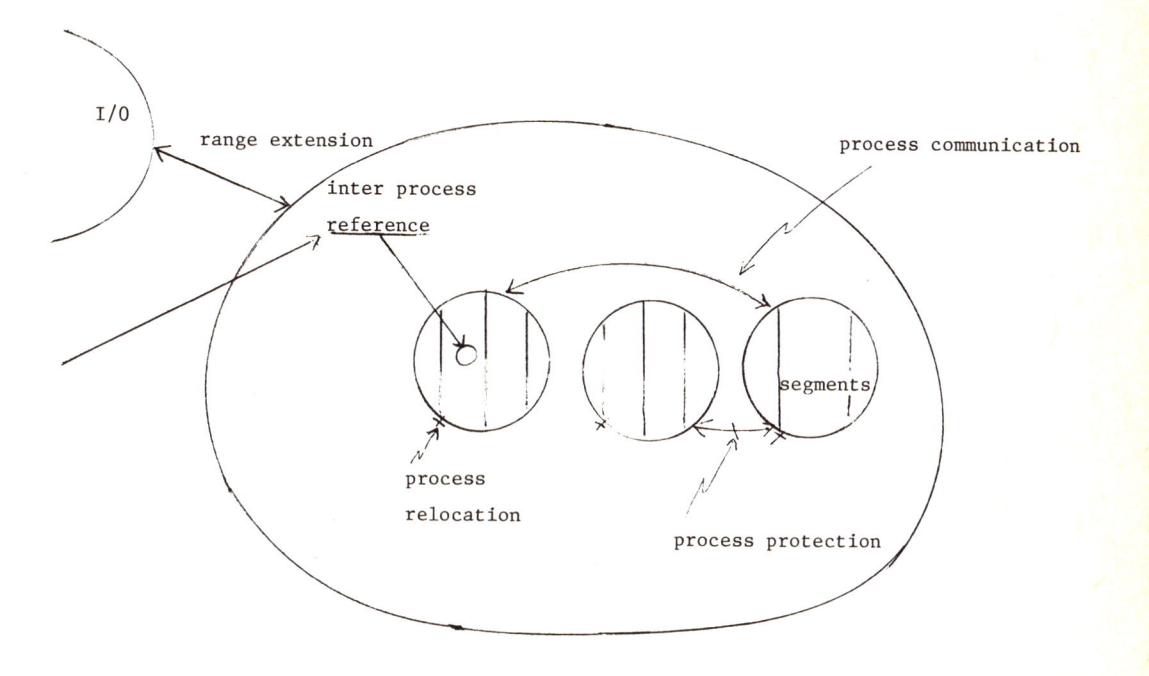

Figure 11 : Processor Name Space

Memory Space

Memory space issues are focused on the physical arrangement of elements in the memory hierarchy. There are basically only two parameters that the system observes: the memory space latency and memory space bandwidth.

Latency is the time for a particular request to be completed. Bandwidth refers to the number of requests supplied per unit time. In order to provide large memory spaces with desirable access time (latency) and bandwidths, modern memory systems employ multiple levels of storage (Figure 12). Smaller, faster levels have greater cost per bit than larger, slower levels. If there are n levels in the storage hierarchy, then the levels may be ordered by their size and access time from S_o, T_o the smallest, closest level to S_n, T_n for the largest level. The goal of a good memory system design is to provide the processor with an effective memory space of S_n with an access time close to T_o. How well this goal will be achieved depends on a number of factors--the physical characteristics of the device used in each level as well as the behavioral properties of the programs or processes being executed.

Program Behavior [7,8]

Three important principles of program behavior assist in design of a virtual memory system. The three principles are:

(1) The principle of reference locality or spacial locality: Assume that U is probability of any address at random being accessed then given that reference S_i has just occured then the probability of another reference ocurring in this region is much greater than U. That is, given S_i then the

$$\text{Prob.} \{S_j \mid S_j \in (S_i \pm \Delta)\} \gg U$$

within t references following S_i. The principle of spacial locality allows us to determine the size of a block to be transferred among the levels. Block size need not be uniform--although designs would certainly be simplified if they were.

(2) The principle of temporal locality: Given a reference pattern R during which a sequence of N addresses has been made to the storage hierarchy then the probability that within t references following R there are elements of the reference string R that will be accessed with much greater probability than U. That is given $R = S_i$, $S_{i+1}, \ldots, S_j, \ldots, S_{i+N}$ the

$$\text{Prob.} \{S_j \mid S_j \in R\} \gg U$$

within t references following R. The principle of temporal locality helps identify the number of blocks to be contained at each level.

(3) The principal of sequentiality: Given that reference S_i has just occurred, then

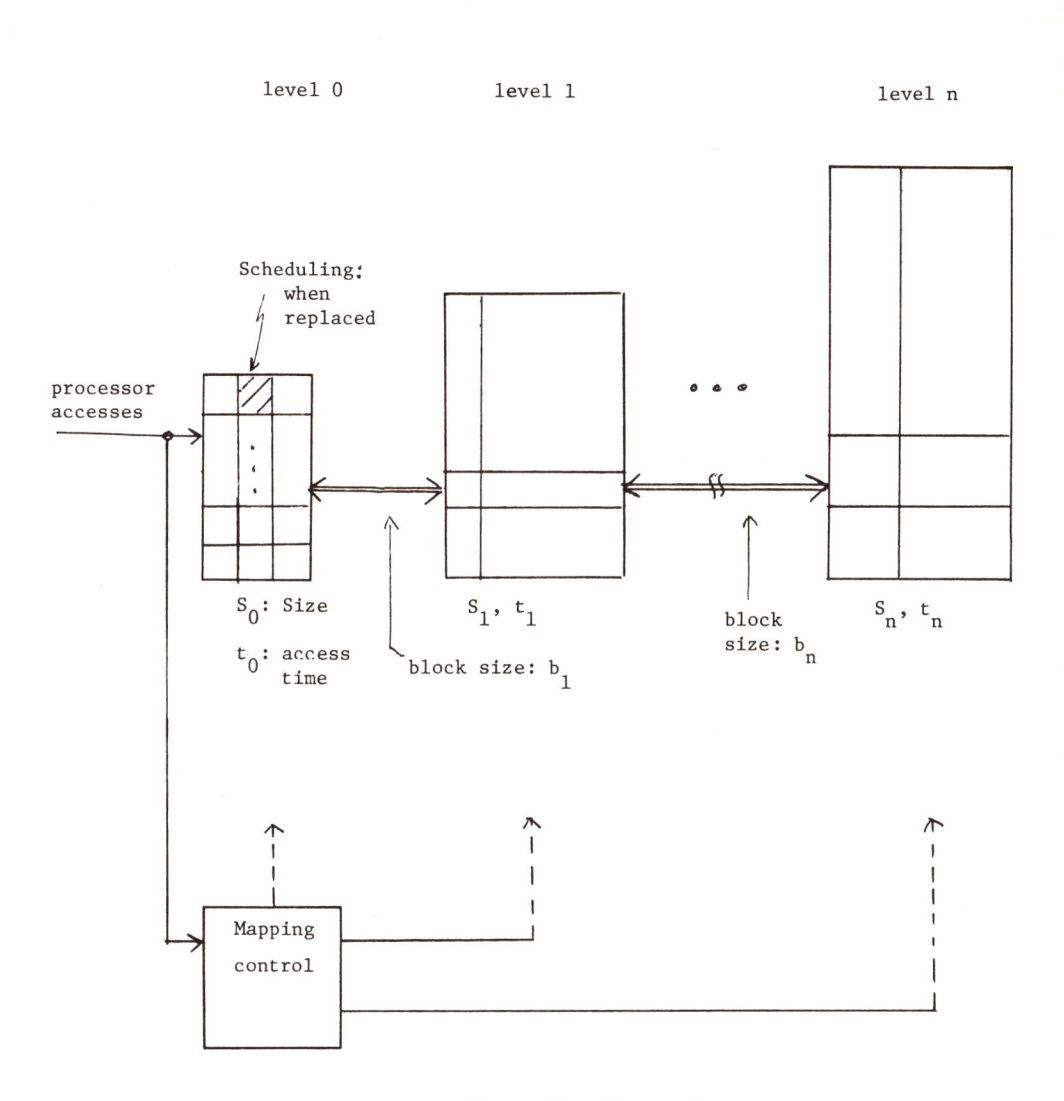

Figure 12: Memory Space

it is likely within the next several references that the successor to S_i will be accessed. That is, given that S_i has occurred:

$$\text{Prob. } \{S_i+1\} \gg U$$

within t references of S_i, with t usually less than 4. The principle of sequentiality allows address distribution to concurrently operating devices for certain levels of hierarchy.

Individual programs have individual characteristics with respect to each of the aforementioned principles--each program behaves slightly differently.

The more the designer understands the program environment for which his design is expected to operate the better the design. Fundamental to any design is an understanding of the miss rate as a function of program size. The miss curve is illustrated in Figure 13. A typical miss curve has distinct regions of locality.

Assuming a reasonable fixed choice of block size (determined in part by the physical characteristics of the storage media), then figure 13 illustrates 3 regions of locality. The W_0 region includes the active, data and instruction pages, which are being processed at a particular moment. Usually at least four pages--1 for program and perhaps 3 for data sets is required to capture this most intimate region. As additional pages are added to a particular storage level, the miss rate remains constant until a larger environment is captured. Perhaps now several pages encompassing a significant program function together with its data sets are contained in the W_1 region. Finally, as additional pages are added for the same program, the entire program will eventually be captured and the fault or miss rate diminishes to a constant level. This sets a lower bound for demand page systems and is determined by the first incidence of a particular page and explicit I/O movement.

The Physical Memory System

The physical memory system is illustrated on Figure 12. Of course the smallest level must be big enough to contain a significant number of elements from the W_0 and significant elements from the W_1 region. Even when the program behavior is well known (which is almost never) design of a multi-level memory hierarchy system is complex, involving a significant number of design issues and tradeoffs.

Design issues include:

(1) The number of levels in the hierarchy--clearly a two level hierarchy is limited especially if the ratio of T_0 to T_1 is significant--several orders of magnitude. A small number of levels force the designer to use large sizes at low levels resulting in expensive designs.

(2) Device characteristics--at each level the bandwidth and access time form

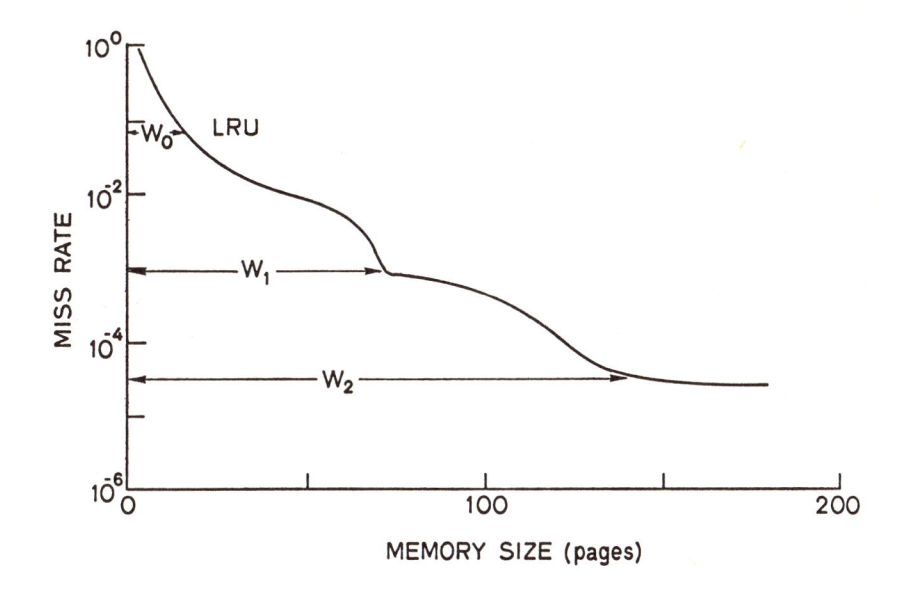

Figure 13

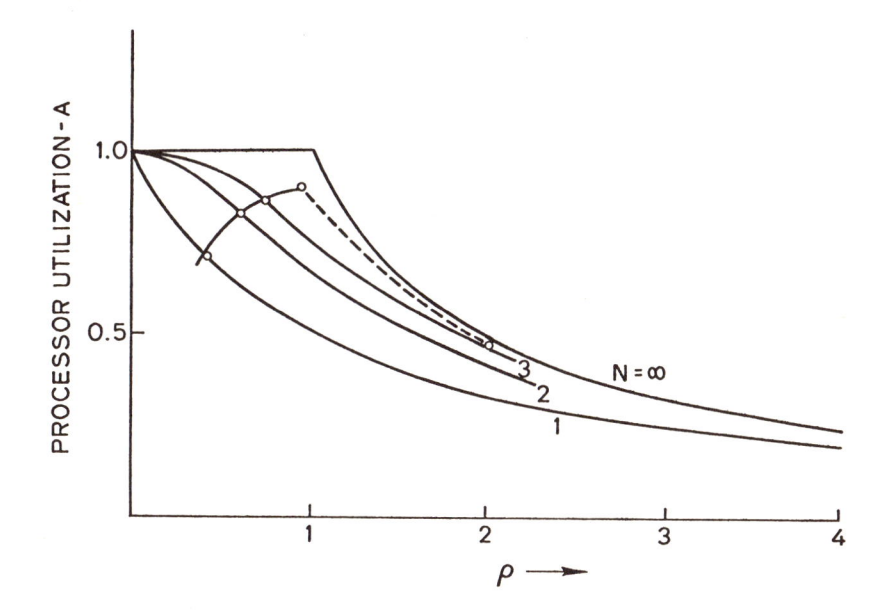

Figure 14

important parameters and are significant in determining such issues as the number of levels and the block size. Also many physical devices such as drum or disc have natural size increments which determine the total number of blocks available at a particular level.

(3) Block size--as mentioned earlier block size need not be uniform across the levels of the hierarchy. While program locality considerations alone argue for somewhat smaller block sizes of the order of perhaps 64 or 256 bytes, access time versus bandwidth considerations of rotational devices force designers to use larger blocks--1K to 4K bytes--when dealing with these devices.

(4) Number of blocks--clearly, at the highest level, S_n, the number of blocks and the block size determine the total number of entries that can be stored in this physical memory space. At intermediate levels there is a cost performance tradeoff.

(5) Replacement algorithm--since lower levels of the hierarchy can only contain a small fraction of the memory space only the most active regions can be stored in it. The problem is identifying the "most active" regions without needlessly complicating the overall design. Simple algorithms such as LRU (Least Recently Used) or FIFO (First In First Out) are widely used.

(6) Write strategy--there are two basic strategies for stores into the system. The "store through" philosophy and the "swap" philosophy. Under the store through regime, when a store type reference is made to a locality currently in level S_0 that entry is updated in S_0 as well as in each higher level of the hierarchy. Under the swapping regime, the write reference is updated only at the lowest level where it is contained in the memory hierarchy. Then when this page is to be replaced it must be swapped back to its higher level. In store through, swapping is not necessary since each level of the hierarchy always has an updated picture of the memory system. In actual practice, combinations of store through and swapping are used in most modern memory systems. Store through is used for the S_0S_1 (cache-main memory) transaction while swapping is used at higher levels.

Sharing

Two types of sharing are quite significant to the memory systems designer-- process and processor sharing. Under process sharing, or multiprogramming, a single processor contains multiple processes. When a miss occurs in process P_i, rather than waiting for the required block to be swapped in, the processor moves on to another process in the system. This requires that multiple processes be available at reasonably low levels in the memory hierarchy. The number of such active processes is called the degree of multiprogramming allowed in the system. Since higher degrees of multiprogramming result in a particular hierarchy level of the memory hierarchy being allocated in smaller and smaller pieces to various processes, its exercise can rapidly be self-defeating because of potentially higher miss rates per process. The degeneration of performance due to inadequate availability of low levels of storage is called <u>trashing</u>.

Processor sharing for multiprocessing involves several processors sharing the same space. The principle design problems for multiprocessing systems involves the updating problem--several processes simultaneously require the same data set or storage block. The memory system design must take care that the multiple copies are appropriately updated.

<u>Performance Models of Processor Memory Interactions</u>

Review of Stochastic Models [9,10]

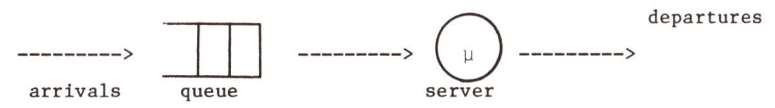

```
                                                            departures
-------->   [queue]   -------->   ( μ )   -------->
arrivals                         server
```

Arrival Process: Requests made on a system. The interarrival times are random variables with arrival time probability distribution.

Server: Service by the system, service times are random variables with service time probability distribution.

<u>Markovian Distributions</u> (M)

Poisson Arrival: Probability of n arrivals at time t (λ is average arrival rate):

$$P_n(t) = \frac{(\lambda t)^n}{n!} e^{-\lambda t}$$

Exponential Service-Time Distributions: Probability that service is completed by time t (μ is average service rate)

$$F(t) = 1 - e^{-\mu t}$$

Other distributions: $C = \frac{\sigma^2}{\mu^2}$ coef. of variation

    M: $C = 1$
    G: General C = anything
    D: Constant $C = 0$
    Er: Erlangian $C < 1$
    H: Hyperexponential $C > 1$

Queue Models are categorized by

Arrival Dist/Service Dist/Number of Servers

thus, M/M/1 is a singler server queue with Markovian arrival and server distributions.

Queue Properties: if Q is average queue length (including request being serviced) and T_w is average waiting time for completion of service:

$$Q = \lambda T_w$$
$$\rho = \frac{\mu}{\lambda}$$

and M/G/1

$$T_w = \frac{1}{\lambda} \{ \rho + \frac{\rho^2(1+C^2)}{2(1-\rho)} \}$$

for M/M/1 C = 1

$$T_w = \frac{1}{\lambda} \{ \rho + \frac{\rho^2}{1-\rho} \}$$

Closed Queueing Systems

Consider simple CPU - Drum Model:

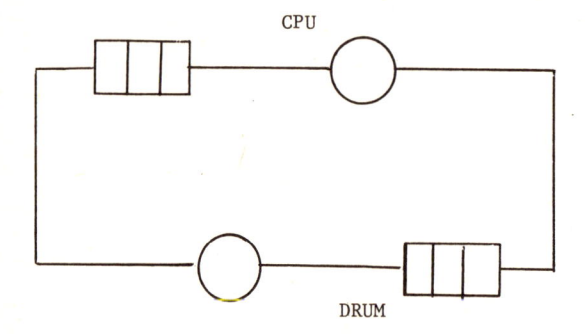

[Diagram: CPU and DRUM in closed loop with queues]

queue length cannot grow beyond CPU limits.

Let drum act as server of memory system faults: (τ, rotation period)

$$\mu = \frac{1}{\tau}$$

Requests depend memory size, miss rate, and processing ability of CPU. In particular:

request/sec = miss rate (faults/memory references)
        x(references/instruction)
        x instructions/sec

In a multiprogramming system if a fault occurs, control is transferred to another process. This transfer procedure continues until either the fault has been handled or there are not other available processes.

Let n be the degree of multiprogramming and the fraction of processor activity. Then

$$A = \frac{\rho^n - 1}{\rho^{n+1} - 1},$$

this is plotted in Figure 14. Note that the optimum degree of multiprogramming can be computed if the program fault behavior is known. This is illustrated in the Figure 14 by the computed points. Note that extending the degree of multiprogramming leads to an activity falloff since the average memory size allocated to a process has decreased to a point that higher fault rates dominate.

III. TRADITIONAL MACHINE LANGUAGE PROBLEMS AND SOME FUNDAMENTAL CONCEPTS [11]

Traditional instruction sets have been designed within the following constraints:

(a) The instruction repertoire is static and cannot be dynamically modified. The introduction of new instructions is a difficult procedure at best.

(b) Instruction execution time is dominated by the time required to fetch an instruction and its operands from memory. As many as ten or twenty internal operations (cycles) comprise the interpretation of an instruction.

(c) Since most of the time is spent accessing memory, the instruction set is chosen to minimize the number of memory references at the expense of new and more complex instruction sets of second and third generation architectures.

These constraints, while understandable in the context of slow memory technology, give rise to significant inefficiencies in program representation. Moreover, substantial improvements in memory technology have yet to be reflected in improvements in these representations. Some more notable inefficiencies include:
1. fixed name space representations
2. rigid operational environments
3. limited format types.

We review each of these areas as well as a preliminary evaluation of efficiency in the remainder of this section.

Name Space

As discussed in the preceding section, some characteristics of the process name space include:
1. range and resolution
2. homogeneity
3. flexibility in interpreting object structures

(1) <u>Range and Resolution</u> -- The traditional instruction set arrangement has resolution to an 8 bit byte and range defind as large as possible within the bounds of a reasonable instruction size. The information content of such an arrangement is very low, Hammerstrom [12] estimates less than 5% information content in the address field. The principal of locality in programs defines regions of current activity which can be captured in a small fast working storage. Since each region is of small size, it is clear that the actual entropy in the address information is far less than the total range of the program address.

(2) <u>The Homogeneity of the Name Space</u> -- Many machines have their name space parti-

tioned into a register space and memory space: System 360, PDP-11, etc. As we shall see, available data does not support such partitions for performance improvement. In order to improve performance, the incidence of load and store instructions into registers from the memory space must be small enough to justify the partition. For example consider the following accumulator oriented sequence:

   Load accumulator, A
   Add accumulator, B
   Store accumulator, C

compared to a three address instruction. The reason for the accumulator in the designers eye was to avoid unnecessary data references to memory. The premise is that programs could be partitioned into relatively long sequences of arithmetic operations with a minimum of register initialization. When the average incidence of load and store instructions approach twice the incidence of functional operations, this premise has vanished.

(3) <u>Interpretation Flexibility</u> -- Flexibility of interpetation of the object structure refers to the number, variety and richness of the data structures available to the operation vocabulary. Inflexible object structures result in considerable program representation manipulation being required to cause proper functional transformations.

Operational Environments

Higher level language representation of programs presents a serious mismatch between the functional operations in the language and the actual operation vocabulary of the processor. Thus, inconsistencies between arithmetic types as well as procedural facilities in the instruction set representation and the higher level language representation create additional instructions, requiring additional interpretation time to fully execute the higher level language statement.

Familiar examples include the IF statement--a three way branch in FORTRAN which may require three machine language instructions; the DO statement involves at least the same number of machine instructions. Even a simple assignment often requires both a load and a store instruction as a result of the previously mentioned splitting of the name space.

Format Limitations

Most familiar machines used for large computation are of the fixed format type. The size of the instruction may vary but not the interpretation or the transformation of the operands. Thus, A op B := A is the familiar System 360 transformation, where A, B may be either a register name or memory space name. It is generally impossible to do A op B := B if op is non-commutative. It is also not possible to implicitly specify a stack or accumulator.

This rigidity in type of transformation and incompleteness of classes of transformation represents another source of inefficiency in machine instruction program representation that will be discussed next.

Measuring the Efficiency of Machine Instruction Program Representation [13]

In this section we review some well known data describing instruction usage in the IBM 7090 computer series, System 360 and PDP-10. This code usage data is examined as to the relationship between a computer architecture to its user environment. Different architectures exist because they presume to provide more efficient program representations and executions. That is, the static program size (amount of storage required to represent a program) as well as the dynamic program size (number of instructions required for program execution) have in some sense been minimized.

One measure of this "optimization" is to compare program statistics for a particular architectue against an ultimately simple, fully explicit architecture. In a simple architecture nothing is implied--no registers or counters are invisible to the problem state programmer. Each instruction contains an operation, the full generalized address specification (allowing, if necessary, multiple levels of indirectin through tables, etc.) for both source operands, a result operand, and a test of the result which selects an address for the next instruction. Of course, familiar architectures achieve their compact instruction representation at the expense of additional "over- head" instructions to load and store registers, and alter the inline sequence of code (branch), etc.

> We define three types of instructions[1]
> M-instructions are memory partition movement instructions; such as the LOAD and STORE instruction which move data items within a storage hierarchy.
> P-instructions are procedural instructions which perform functions associated with instruction sequencing, i.e., TEST, BRANCH, COMPARE, etc., but perform no transformation on data.
> F-instructions perform computational functions in that they operate on data. They include arithmetic operations of all types, as well as logical and shifting operations.

Instructions which merely rearrange data across partitions of a memory name space or which alter ordinary sequencing are "overhead" instructions. The ratio of

---

[1] The categorization of M, P and F type instructions is for the technical code presented only. Obviously for a SORT program a MOVE might be a F-type instruction: pointing up the more general problem of separating an architectural artifact from a true program function.

these overhead instructions to functional instructions is indicative of the use of an architecture. An overhead instruction exists in the representation of a program so as to match the original program requirements to the requirements of the machine languages. The most common overhead instructions concern the range, resolution and homogeneity of the name space: e.g. load and store of registers, push and pop the stack, etc. Overhead instructions are clearly undesirable because they require additional space for the program as well as additional interpretation time of the execution of the program.

To quantify "overhead" we define three ratios:
1. M-ratio: ratio of M-instructions to F-instructions
2. P-ratio: ratio of P-instructions to F-instructions
3. NF-ratio: ratio of the sum of M and P instructions to F instructions

These ratios are tabulated in Table 2 for IBM 7090, System 360 and PDP-10 [14].

TABLE 2

Processor	"Ideal"	7090	360	PDP-10
M-ratio	0.0	2.0	2.9	1.5
P-ratio	0.0	0.8	2.5	1.1
NF-ratio	0.0	2.8	5.5	2.6

Note that the "ideal" machine would have a zero entry for all ratios. Also note that for these machines between 2.6 and 5.5 non-functional instructions are required for each functional instruction implying that the size of programs could be reduced by this factor.

IV. TOWARDS IDEAL PROGRAM REPRESENTATIONS [11]

By what criteria should program representations be judged? Clearly, an efficiency measure should lie in some sort of space-time product involving both the space needed to represent an executable program and the time needed to interpret it; although other factors--such as the space and time needed to create executable representations, or the space needed to hold the interpreter--may also be important. This report considers only the space and time needed to represent and execute a program.

Canonic Interpretive Forms

Characterizing "ideal" program representations is either trivial or extremely complicated, depending on one's point of view. Neither extreme offers significant insight into the problems at hand, however. It is therefore imperative to develop constructive space-time measures that can be used to explore practical alternatives. Although these measures need not be achievable, they should be satisfied only by clearly superior representations, easy to define, easy to use, and in clear agreement with both a programmer's intuition and pragmatic observations. We propose the following Canonic Interpretive Form, or CIF, as a measure of statement representation in a high level programming language.

1:1 Property

Instructions -- one CIF instruction is permitted for each non-assignment type operation in a HLL statement.

Name Space -- One CIF name is permitted for each unique[1] HLL name in a HLL statement.

Log$_2$ Property

Instructions -- each CIF instruction consists of:
A single operation identifier of size $[\log_2(F)]$[2]; and one or more operand identifiers, each of size $[\log_2(V)]$[3].

Referencing Property

Instructions -- each HLL procedural (program control) statement causes one canonic reference.

---

[1] I.e., distinct name in the HLL statement; "A = A+1" contains two unique names--the variable "A" and the constant "1".

[2] F is the number of distinct HLL operators in the scope of definition for the given HLL statement.

[3] V is the number of distinct HLL program objects--variables, labels, constants, etc.--in the relevant scope of definition.

Name Space -- one reference is allowed for each unique variable or constant in the HLL statement.

Space is measured by the number of bits needed to represent the static definition of a program; time by the number of instructions and name space references needed to interpret the program. Source programs to which these measures are applied should themselves be efficient expressions of an optimal abstract algorithm -- so as to eliminate the possible effects of algorithm optimization during translation -- such as changing "X = X/X" to "X = 1."

Generating canonic program representations should be straight forward because of the 1:1 property. Traditional three address architectures[4] also satisfy the first part of this criteria, but do not have the unique naming property.

For example, the statement "X = X + X" contains only one unique variable, and hence can be represented by a single CIF instruction consisting of only one operation identifier and one operand identifier. The three address representation of this statement also requires only a single instruction, but it would consist of four identifiers rather than the two required by the CIF.

There may be some confusion as to what is meant by an "operation". Functional operators (+, -, *, /, SQRT, etc.) are clear enough; however, allowance must also be made for selection operators that manipulate structured data. For instance, we view the array specification "A(I,J)" as a source level expression involving one operator (two dimensional qualification) and at least three operands (the array A, and its subscripts I and J). Therefore, unlike the previous case, the canonic equivalent of "A(I,J) = A(I,J) + A(I,J)" requires two instructions -- the first to select the proper array element, and the second to compute the sum. Thus:

Example 1:   X = X + X

| + | X |

Example 2:   A(I,J) = A(I,J) + A(I,J)

| @ | A | I | J | A_{IJ} |
| + | A_{IJ} |

The operator "@" computes the address of the doubly indexed element "A(I,J)", and dynamically completes the definition of the local identifier "A_{IJ}". This identifier is then used in the same manner as the identifier "X" is used in the first example.

We count each source level procedural operator, such as IF or DO, as a single operator. The predicate expression of an IF must, of course, be evaluated independently if it is not a simple variable reference. Distinct labels are treated as

---

[4] I.e., instruction sets of the form OP X Y Z -- where OP is an identifier for a (binary) operation; X the left argument; Y the right argument; and Z the result.

distinct operands , so that:

Example 3:   IF (X-Y) 10,20,30

-	X	Y	
IF	10	20	30

Two accesses to the process name space (references) are required to execute the first example: one to fetch the value of X as an argument, and one to update its value as a result of executing the statement. In example two, four references are required: one each to fetch the values of I and J for the subscripting operation; one to fetch the value of A_{IJ} as an argument; and one to update the value of this array element after execution. Note that no references are required to access the array A, even though it appears as an operand of the @ function -- in general, no single identifier in a CIF instruction can cause more than one reference unless it is bound to both an argument and a result, and then it will initiate only two references. No references are needed for either example just to maintain the instruction stream, since the order of execution is entirely linear[5]. The 1:1 property measures both space and time, while the $\log_2$ property measures space alone, and the referencing property measures time alone. These measures may be applied either statically or dynamically -- although static reference counts are strictly comparative, and hence of limited value.

The 1:1 property defines, in part, a notion of <u>transformational completeness</u> -- a term which we use to describe any intermediate language satisfying the first canonic measure. Translation of source programs into a transformationally complete language should require neither the introduction of synthetic variables, nor the insertion of non-functional memory oriented instructions[6]. However, since the canonic measures described above make no allowance for distinguishing between different associations of identifiers to arguments and results, it is unlikely that any practical language will be able to fully satisfy the CIF space requirements.

<u>Comparison of CIF to Traditional Machine Architectures</u>

Consider the following three line excerpt from a FORTRAN subroutine:

    1   I = I + 1
    2   J = (J-1)*I
    3   K = (J-1)*(K-I)

Assume that I, J, and K are fullword (32 bit) integers whose initial values are

---

[5] The assumption here is that such reference activity can be fully overlapped since it is so predictable.

[6] E.g., to hold the results of intermediate computations, or move data about within the storage hierarchy merely to make it accessible to functional operators.

stored in memory prior to entering the excerpt, and whose final values must be stored in memory for later use before leaving the excerpt. The canonic measures for this example are:

CANNONIC MEASURE OF THE FORTRAN FRAGMENT

Instructions

    Statement 1 -- 1 instruction   (1 operator)
    Statement 2 -- 2 instructions   (2 operators)
    Statement 3 -- 3 instructions   (3 operators)

    Total   6 instructions   (6 operators)

Instruction Size

  Identifier Size

    Operation identifier size = $\lceil \log_2 4 \rceil$ = 2 bits
         (operations are: +, -, *, =)

    Operand identifier size = $\lceil \log_2 4 \rceil$ = 2 bits
         (operands are: 1, I, J, K)

  Number of Identifiers

    Statement 1 -- 3 identifiers   (2 operand, 1 operator)
    Statement 2 -- 5 identifiers   (3 operand, 2 operator)
    Statement 3 -- 7 identifiers   (4 operand, 3 operator)

    Total   15 identifiers   (9 operand, 6 operator)

Program Size

    6 operator identifiers x 2 bits = 12 bits
    9 operand identifiers x 2 bits = 18 bits

    Total   30 bits

References

    Instruction Stream -- 1 reference   (nominal)
    Operand Loads   -- 9 references
    Operand Stores   -- 3 references

    Total   13 references

The following listing was produced on an IBM System 370 using an optimizing compiler[7]:

```
    1   L     10,112(0,13)
        L     11,80(0,13)
        LR    3,11
        A     3,0(0,10)
        ST    3,0(10)

    2   L     7,4(0,10)
        SR    7,11
        MR    6,3
        ST    7,4(0,10)
```

---

[7]FORTRAN IV level H, OPT = 2, run in a 500K partition on a Model 168, June 1977.

```
3   LR    4,7
    SR    4,3
    LCR   3,3
    A     3,8(0,10)
    MR    2,4
    ST    3,8(0,10)
```

A total of 368 bits are required to contain this program body (we have excluded some 2000 bits of prologue/epilogue code required by the 370 Operating System and FORTRAN linkage conventions) -- over 12 times the space indicated by the canonic measure. Computing reference activity in the same way as before, we find 48 accesses to the process name space are required to evaluate the 370 representation of the FORTRAN excerpt. If allowance is made for the fact that register accesses consume almost no time in comparison to accesses to the execution store, this count drops to 20 references -- allowing one access for each 32 bit word in the instruction stream.

The increase in program size, number of instructions, and number of memory references is a direct result of the partitioned name space, indirect operand identification, and restricted instruction formats of the 370 architecture. In order to facilitate the discussion at this point, it is useful to define [13] three general classes of instructions:

M-instructions, which simply move data items within the storage hierarchy (e.g., the familiar LOAD and STORE operators);

P-instructions, which modify the default sequencing between instructions during execution (e.g., JUMP, BRANCH and LINK operators); and

F-instructions, which actually perform functional computations by assigning new values to result operands after transforming the current values of argument operands (e.g., all arithmetic, logical, and shifting operators).

Instructions that merely rearrange data accross partitions of a memory name space, or that alter the normal order of instruction sequencing, are "overhead" in the sense that they do not directly contribute to a computation. The ratio of these overhead instructions (i.e., M- and P- type instructions in our terminology) to functional instructions (F-instructions) is indicative of the use of an architecture. Overhead instructions must be inserted into the desired sequence of F-instructions to match the computational requirements of the original program to the capabilities of the machine architecture. Statically, M-instructions are by far the most common overhead instructions -- indeed, they are the most common type of instruction in almost all existing machines. Dynamically, however, P-instructions become equally significant.

The table below illustrates the use of ratios for the foregoing example.

Synthesis of Canonic Program Representations

Before treating the synthesis problem the introduction of some additional concepts will be useful.

COMPARISON FOR THE EXAMPLE

	370 FORTRAN-IV (level H extended) optimized	non optimized	CIF
No. of Instructions	15	19	6
M-type Instructions	9	13	0
F-type Instructions	6	6	6
M-ratio	1.5	2.7	0
Program Size	368 bits	604 bits	30 bits
Memory References	20	36	13

Target Machine: The semantics of a program representation at any hierarchical level J defines the target machine for that representation. Traditional machine languages are usually thought of as target machines for emulation while newer concepts in environmentally oriented program representations are referred to as directly executed languages (DELs).

Directly Executed Languages (DEL): We define the DEL as the target machine which corresponds to a simple one step mapping of a higher level language program representation. The DEL, being a target machine, consists of:
1. a name space
2. operation vocabulary
3. sequence rules.

Host Machine and DEL Interpreter: A host machine, together with a particular DEL interpreter, is the agent that responds to DEL rules and causes correct transitions in the DEL name space. The host machine is actually a target machine at level J-1. In turn, it may be interpreted by a J-1 interpreter together with a J-2 host machine. While not important in our context, the level 0 machine is the final physical realization of the required state transformations.

The interpreter then is that program written for the host machine which takes a particular DEL and causes, corresponding to the DEL transformation rules, appropriate state transformations in the DEL name space. In order to accomplish this, the interpreter must have its own name space and cause its own host machine state transitions. The name space of the interpreter and the DEL should be separate, the interpreter for example residing in "control store" which is otherwise unaddressable by any other entity.

Synthesis of Simple Host Machines

Simple Host Machine Structures

Since the host machine will undergo a number of state transitions before it completes the interpretation of a single DEL instruction unit, and since presumably the host machine will not be designed uniquely for the interpretation of a single DEL, the need for speed in interpretation is obvious. The program for the interpretation of the DEL must be stored in high speed read write storage. Since this storage will by and large determine host machine state transition time, it will therefore also determine the interpretation speed of the host machine. Since the traditional machine instructions premise of slow memory access is no longer true, at least for small memory sizes, a new arrangement of host machine instructions seem to be in order. This would stress:

(1) multiple simultaneous access to the resources of the system
(2) overlapped access to fast interpretive store which contains interpretive parameters.

Additionally, a number of specific host machine attributes have been identified [16] which are significant in producing interpretive performance. We mention several of these below:

(1) Flexible field extraction and manipulation for generalized decoding.
(2) Residual control for dynamically reconfiguring both internal and external environment.
(3) Capability for constructing complex address mapping functions.
(4) A large amount of writeable interpretive storage with simple mechanisms for reading or writing any portion.
(5) Flexible host instruction sequencing with comprehensive facility for bit setting and testing which can be used for sequencing.
(6) Parallelism within a host instruction and host environment arranged to aid in eliminating host overhead instructions.

A Sample Host Architecture

Consider the organization outlined in Figure 16. The general purpose registers contain the instruction register and instruction counter. Assume that the instruction width is the same as the data word width (perhaps 32 bits). A typical host instruction is partitioned into three fragments, each of which is essentially a primitive instruction with simultaneous action of typically host instruction fragments shown below:

I.   (F) $C(R_1)$ OP $C(R_2) := C(R_1)$

II. (M) $C(R_3)$ $\begin{array}{c}\text{LOAD}\\\leftarrow\\:=\\\rightarrow\\\text{STORE}\end{array}$ C(MICROSTORAGE ADDRESS)

III.   (P)   IF   (TEST = 1)
             THEN   * ← * + Δ
             ELSE   * ← * + 1

(a) A register-to-register operation of the F-type. OP uses the contents of R_1 and the contents of R_2 as arguments, placing the result in R_1.

(b) A load or store from microstorage into the general purpose registers. Immediate values can be contained in the address field in this structure fragment.

(c) The branch instruction or P-type. This includes specification of a test mask and an offset value (Δ) relative to the location counter (*).

The net effect is to simultaneously control the operation of three finite state machines; an F machine, an M machine, and a P machine. Actually it will not always be possible to exploit concurrent operations. Inconsistent use of the registers by two of the fragments could cause a confict. Also it may not be possible in many instances to write code which uses all three fields.

The concurrency gives us to an interesting type of overlapped operation: while the F fragment transforms current data values, the P fragment tests the results of the preceding instruction and the M fragment fetches ahead new data for the following F instruction fragment. Notice that while a split name space is still used, no additional time is required to manage the partition; since every F fragment carries an M fragment with it. (We make no pretense here that a split name space is always required in an efficient host or that the above is the only way to handle it.) In any event, the foregoing instruction resembles a familiar microinstruction. This instruction executes in essentially one machine cycle--perhaps 200 nanoseconds--using ordinary circuitry. Depending upon the arrangement of microstorage, conflicts between the load/store fragment and next-instruction-fetch mechanism could double the instruction execution time.

For transfer of input data to and from main memory, an alternate instruction format is used. This instruction format is block-oriented and asynchronously moves blocks of data between microstorage and main storage. Thus, main memory is in many ways treated as an I/O device. Notice that this treatment, except for its explicit nature, is very similar to cache-based memory systems already in use.

The example is actually an abstraction of a machine in use at Stanford called EMMY [17,18]. EMMY word size, timing and parallel host instruction philosophy are similar to this example. Other host machine structures designed for similar interpretive purposes should also be mentioned [16], especially Burroughs B1700 [19].

DEL Synthesis[8]

---

[8] The material presented in this section is a much simplified version of [20].

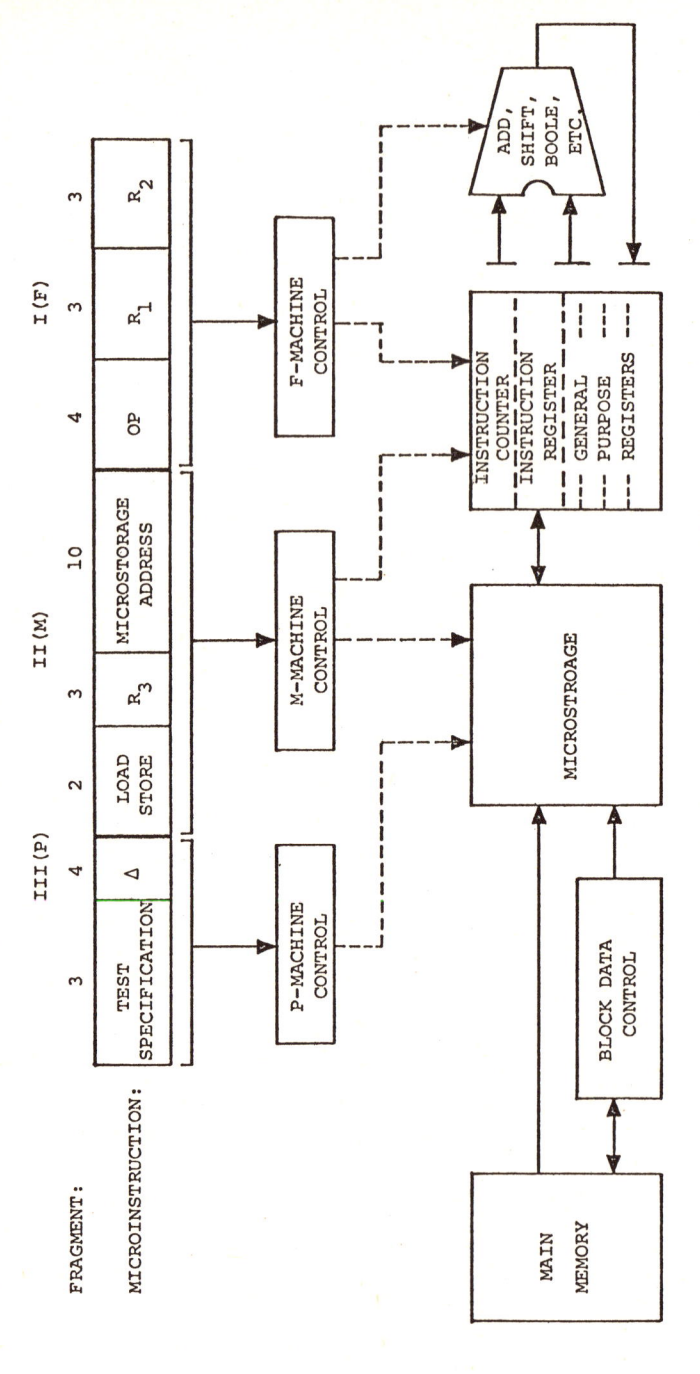

Fig. 16: Sample Host Machine

Terms and Assumptions

In order to synthesize simple "quasi-ideal" DELs, let us make some fairly obvious straight forward assignments and assumptions:
  (1) The DEL program representation lies in the main storage of the host machine.
  (2) The interpreter for the DEL lies in a somewhat faster, smaller interpretive storage. The interpreter includes the actual interpretive subroutines as well as certain parameters associated with interpretation.
  (3) A small number of registers exist in the host machine which contain local and environmental information associated with the interpretation of the current DEL instruction. Further assume that communicatins between interpretive storage and this register set can be overlapped with transformations on the register set (Figure 17).

Before proceeding, an elaboration on some notions concerning DEL instruction structure will be useful. A _template_ is a binary string partitioned into _containers_ by action of the interpretive program. A _container_ is an element of the vector bit string. It is an identifier for either a format, operand field, or operation field. In general, the containers specify the following information:
  (1) format and (implicitly) the number of operands
  (2) the operands
  (3) operations to be performed (of a most binary order) on the identified operands
  (4) sequencing information, if required.

A _format_ is a transformation rule identifying:
  (1) template partition (i.e. number and meaning of containers)
  (2) the order of the operation: i.e. whether the operation is nullary, unary or binary
  (3) ordering precedence among operands.

The container size is the maximum size that a field may take on. Container size is determind by the number of elements required in a locality, thus, the structure of the DEL instruction unit might consist of a template outlined below.

(a) Storage Assignments

DEL INSTRUCTION ENVIRONMENT	DEL INTERPRETER / CURRENT DEL SCOPE	DEL PROGRAM REPRESENTATION
HOST REGISTERS	INTERPRETIVE STORAGE	MAIN MEMORY
DEL INSTRUCTION ENVIRONMENT	DEL SUBROUTINE ENVIRONMENT	DEL TARGET PROGRAM

(b) DEL Instruction Unit

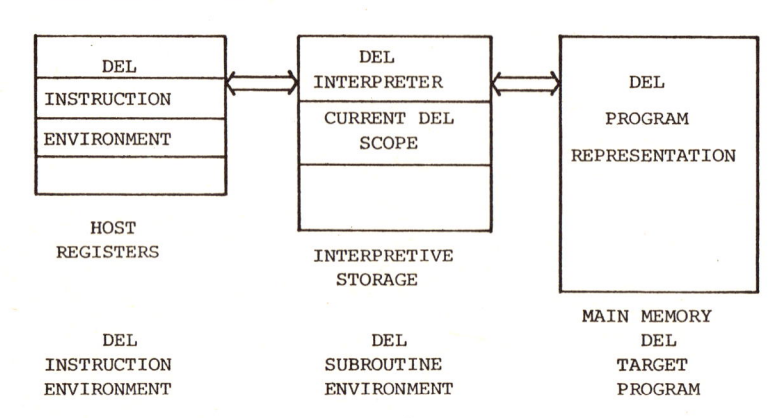

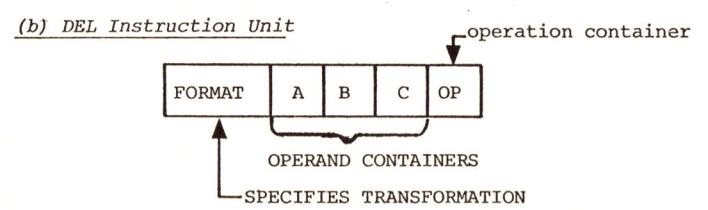

| FORMAT | A | B | C | OP |

- OP → operation container
- A, B, C → OPERAND CONTAINERS
- FORMAT → SPECIFIES TRANSFORMATION

Figure 17: DEL Model

DELs Which Approach Canonic Form

There four notions useful in defining a DEL which approaches canonical form: environment, contour, operation and format.

Environment

The notion of environment is fundamental not only to DELs but also to traditional machine languages as evidenced by widespread adoption of cache and virtual memory concepts. What is proposed here is akin in some respects to the cache concept and yet quite distinct from it. We recognize locality as an important property of a program name space and handle it explicitly under interpreter control. Thus, locality is transparent to the DEL name space but recognized and managed by the interpreter. Properties of the environment are:

(1) The DEL name space is homogeneous and uniform with an a priori unbounded range and variable resolution.

(2) Operations, involving for example the composition of addresses which use registers, should not be present in the DEL code but should be part of the interpreter code only. Thus, the register name space and the interpreter name space are largely not part of the DEL name space. It is the function of the interpreter to optimize register allocation.

(3) The environmental locality will be defined by the higher level language for which this representation is created. In FORTRAN, for example, it would correspond to function or subroutine scope.

(4) Unique to every environment is a scope which includes:
    (i) a label contour,
    (ii) an operand contour,
    (iii) an operation table.

Contours

Following the model of J. Johnson [21], contour is a vector (a table) of object descriptors. When an environment is invoked, a contour of label and variable addresses must be placed (or be already present) in the interpretive storage. For a simple static language like FORTRAN this creation can be done at load time. For languages that allow recursion, etc., the creation of the contour wowld be done before entering a new environment. An entry in the contour consists of the (main memory) address of the variable to be used; this is the full and complete DEL name space address. Type information and other descriptive details may also be included as part of the entry.

The environment must provide a pointer into the current contour. Environment further mwst provide an index of width of the container for labels and variables.

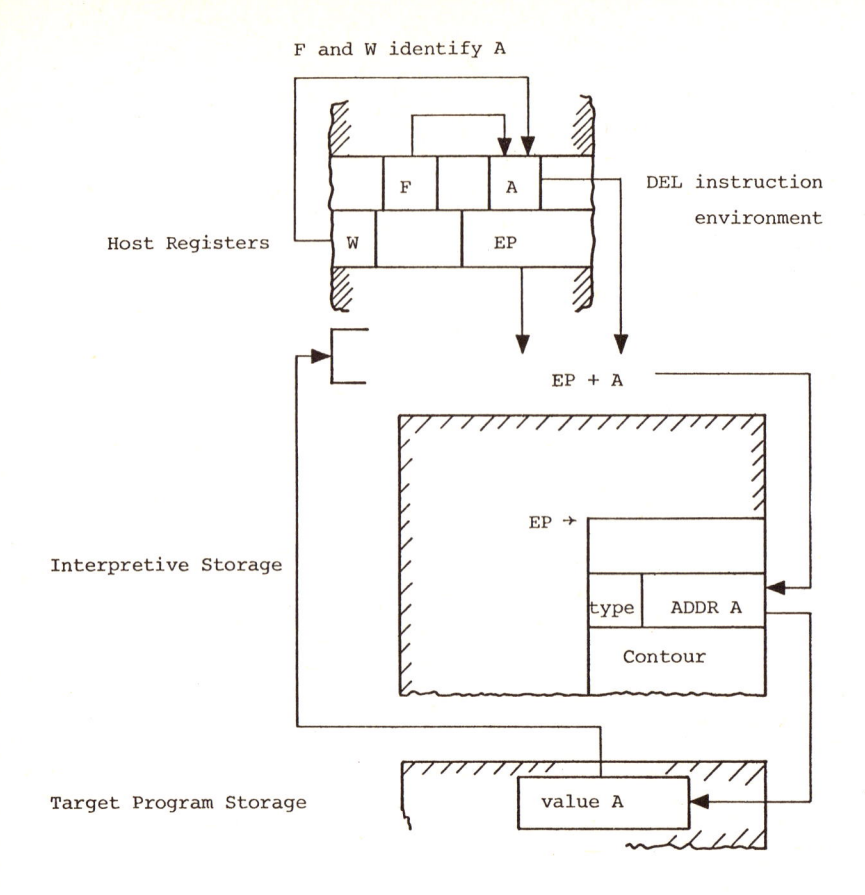

Fig. 18a: Variable Accessing in DEL

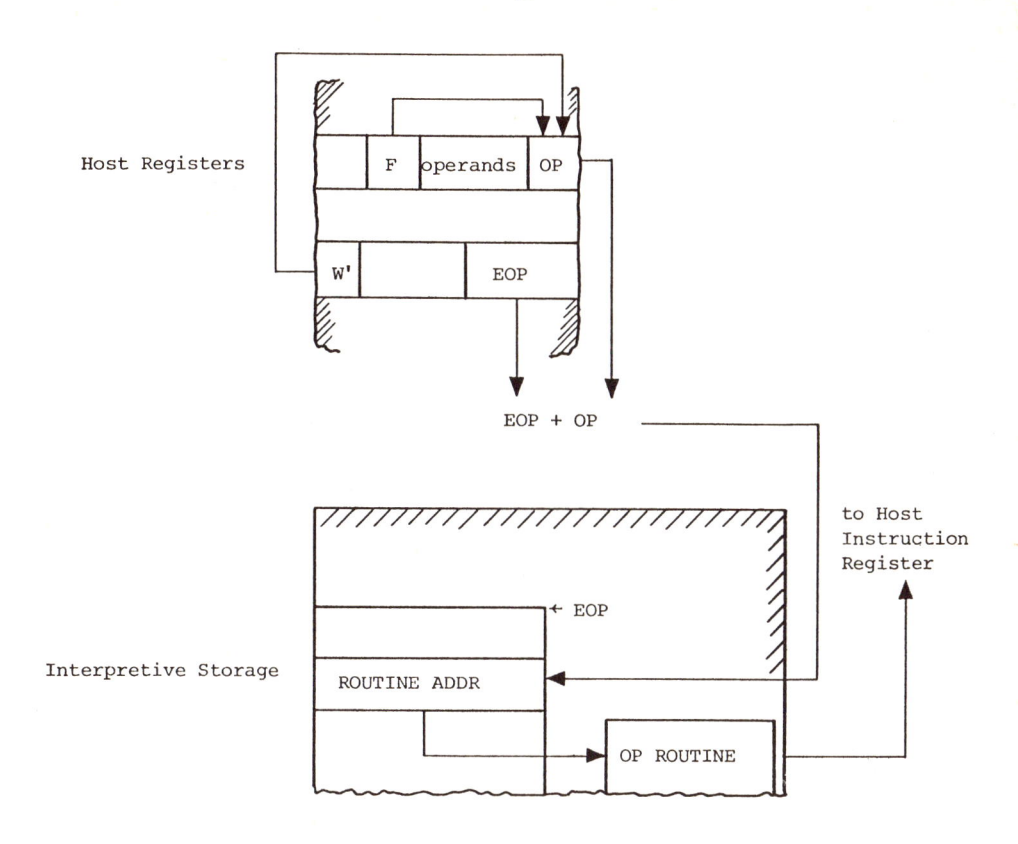

Fig. 18b: Operation Access in DEL

Typically, the environoent pointer and width index would be maintained in the registers of the host machine. If W is the index of width of the environment and EP is the environmental pointer into the current contour contained in interpretive storage, then Figure 18a illustrates the accessing process. Both labels and variables may be indexed off the same environmental pointer. The DEL source instruction unit has containers which define indices in the current contour that identify a target name space address.

Operations

Each verb or operation in the higher level language identifies a corresponding interpretive operator in the DEL program representation (exclude for the moment control actions which will be discussed shortly). The routines for interpreting all familiar operations are expected to lie in the interpretive storage. Certain unusual operations, such as the trigonomentric functions may not always be contained in the interpretive storage. A pointer to an operator translation table must be part of the environment; the actual operations used are indicated by a small index container off this pointer (Figure 18b). The table is also present in the interpretive storage. For simple languages, this latter step is probably unnecessary since the total number of operations may be easily contained in, for example, a six bit field and the saving in DEL program representation may not justify the added interpretive step.

Formats for Transformational Completeness

In order to achieve a form of the transformational completeness property mentioned earlier, three distinct kinds of transformation must be considered based on the order of the operation--the nullary operation which assumes no operand, the unary operation which assumes one source and produces one result, and the binary operation which takes two source operands and produces a single result. In order to achieve completeness, a stack should also be available. However, the DEL formats should contain no overhead instructions: for handling the stack. That is, the stack will always be "pushed" when used as a sink and always be "popped" when used as a source.

Then for tranformational completeness we have the following formats.

nullary case, one format

$F_{0,1}$	OP

unary case, five formats (T is top of stack)

| $F_{1,1}$ | A | B | OP | OP A → B
| $F_{1,2}$ | A | OP | | OP A → T
| $F_{1,3}$ | A | OP | | OP T → A
| $F_{1,4}$ | A | OP | | OP A → A
| $F_{1,5}$ | OP | | | OP T → T

binary case, formats (T,U are top and under the top elements of the stack, respectively)

| $F_{2,1}$ | A | B | C | OP | A OP B → C
| $F_{2,2}$ | A | B | OP | | A OP B → B
| $F_{2,3}$ | A | B | OP | | A OP B → A
| $F_{2,4}$ | A | B | OP | | A OP A → B
| $F_{2,5}$ | A | OP | | | A OP A → A
| $F_{2,6}$ | A | B | OP | | A OP B → T
| $F_{2,7}$ | A | B | OP | | A OP T → B
| $F_{2,8}$ | A | B | OP | | T OP A → B
| $F_{2,9}$ | A | OP | | | T OP A → A
| $F_{2,10}$ | A | OP | | | A OP T → A
| $F_{2,11}$ | A | OP | | | A OP A → T
| $F_{2,12}$ | A | OP | | | A OP T → T
| $F_{2,13}$ | A | OP | | | T OP A → T
| $F_{2,14}$ | A | OP | | | T OP T → A
| $F_{2,15}$ | A | OP | | | T OP U → A
| $F_{2,16}$ | OP | | | | T OP U → T

The binary formats vary from all explicit ABC type formats to all stack oriented formats, TUT format. Note that A, B and C are explicit variables, T infers the top of the stack, U the element underneath the top of the stack. While there are a total of over three hundred format transformations possible, it is easy to show more formally that the above 21 accomplish all possible valid transformations without overhead. Note that transformatins such as U OP B :=A, U OP T := T do not follow a uniform stack discipline while transformations such as C OP B := A are merely identifier permutations and unnecessary.

Furthermore, the size of a transformationally complete (to a binary order) set can be minimized by observing that the trailing OP container can specify the order of the operation. This allows F_0 and F_1 formats to be subsumed into the binary. Also the four "identical" source formats (such as A OP A := B) require the compiler to identify argument equivalence. Given such a compiler, it would more likely optimize the source to eliminate the redundancy rather than require such formats for representation.

Thus, practical <u>binary transformational completeness</u> is achievable with twelve formats. So far we have ignored the control problem; statements such as IF, DO or GOTO actually represent a transformation on the sequencing structure and are more appropriately recognized as distinct formats rather than functional operations. A format for each of the aforementioned procedures would add three to the twelve previously discussed totaling fifteen formats as a useful complete set of formats.

AN EXAMPLE AND SOME RESULTS   [11]

Again consider the previous example:

```
1    I = I+1
2    J = (J-1)*I
3    K = (J-1)*(K-I)
```

This might be implemented as:

Statement	Implementation				Semantics
	4	2	2	2	
1	ABA	I	1	+	I := I+1
2	ABT	J	1	–	T := J-1
	TAB	I	J	*	J := T*I
3	ABT	J	1	–	T := J-1
	ABT	K	I	–	T := K-I
	TUA	K	*		K := T*U

where T and U are the top and next-to-top (under top) stack elements, respectively. The size, in bits, of each identifier field in the first instruction appears directly above the corresponding mnemonic. Note that the stack is "pushed" automatically by the 5th instruction and the 6th instruction "pops" the stack for further use.

Our CIF rules apply directly to container size--two bits are allowed to identify the four variables and two bits are used for the four operations. The canonic number of instructions are achieved, as are the variable and operation container sizes; however, 4 additional bits per instruction are needed in this implementation to identify the correct format (out of the fifteen instruction formats discussed in the preceding section).

There is a difference between the transformational completeness required by the canonic rules, and the achieved transformational completeness. The two agree only for statements containing at most one functional operator--so that the implementation contains an additional J-identifier in instruciton 3 and an additional K-identifier in instruction 6. These do not, however, necessitate additional memory references since separate domain and range references are also required in the CIF if a single variable is used both as a source and sink within a given statement. The comparison with the CIF measures are shown below.

ACHIEVED vs. THEORETICAL EFFICIENCY

Number of	Achieved	CIF
Instruction Units	6	6
Operand Identifiers	11	9
Operator Identifiers	6	6
Memory References	2 (i.u.) 12 (data)	1 (i.u.) 12 (data)
Totals	14 total	13 total
Size of	Achieved	CIF
Each Identifier	2 bits	2 bits
Total Program	58 bits	30 bits

We assume that 32 bits are fetched per memory reference during the instruction fetch portion of the interpretation process. While the program size has grown with respect to CIF measure, it is still substantially less than System 370 representation; other measures are comparable to CIF.

The example discussed in the preceding section may be criticized as being non-typical in its DEL comparisons:

i. The containers are quite small, thus reducing size
   size measures for the DEL code.
ii. Program control is not included.
iii. The program reduction in space may come at the
   expense of host machine interpretation time.

With respect to the first criticism, note that the size of a program representation grows as a log function of the number of variables and operations used in an environment. If sixteen variables were used, for example, program size would increase by 50% (to 90 bits). It is even more interesting, however, to observe what happens to the same three statements when they are interspersed in a larger context with perhaps 16 variables and 20 statements and compiled into System 370 code. The size of the object code produced by the compiler for either optmized or unoptimized versions increases by almost exactly the same 50%--primarily because the compiler is unable to optimize variable and register usage.

The absence of program control also has no significant statistical affect. A typical FORTRAN DO or IF is compiled into between 3 and 9 System 370 instructions (assuming a simple IF predicate) depending upon the size of the context in which the statement occurs. Thus, the inclusion of program control will not significantly alter the statistics and may even make the DEL argument more favorable.

The third criticism is more difficult to respond to. We submit that host interpretation time *should* not be noticeably increased over a traditional machine instruction if the same premises are made, since

i. 16 DEL formats must be contrasted against perhaps 6 or 8 System 370 formats (using the same definition of format)--not a significant implementation difference.
ii. Some features are required by a 370 instruction even if not required by the instruction--e.g., indexing. Name completion through base registers is a similar situation since the base values remain the same over several instructions.
iii. Approximately the same number of state transitions are required for either a DEL instruction or a traditional machine instruction if each is referred to its own "well mapped" host interpreter. In fact, for an unbiased host designed for interpretation the interpretation time is approximately the same for either a DEL instruction or a System 370 instruction.

The language DELtran, upon which the aforementioned example was based, has been developed as a FORTRAN DEL. The performance and vital statistics of DELtran on the host EMMY [24] is interesting, especially when compared to the 370 performance on the same system. The table below is constructed using a version of the well-known Whetstone benchmark and widely accepted and used for FORTRAN machine evaluation. The EMMY host system referred to in the table is a very small system--the processor consists of one board with 305 circuit modules and 4096 32 bit words of interpretive storage. It is clear that the DELtran performance is significantly superior to the

370 in every measure.

DELtran vs. System 370 Comparison for the Whetstone Benchmark

Whetstone Source -- 80 statements (static)
                 -- 15,233 statements (dynamic)
                 -- 8,624 bits (excluding comments)

	System 370 FORTRAN-IV opt 2	DELtran	ratio 370/DELtran
Program Size (static)	12,944 bits	2,428 bits	5.3:1
Instructions Executed	101,016 i.u.	21,843 i.u.	4.6:1
Instructions/Statement	6.6	1.4	4.6:1
Memory References	220,561 ref.	46,939 ref.	4.7:1
EMMY Execution Time (370 emulation approximates 360 Model 50)	0.70 sec.	0.14 sec.	5:1
Interpreter Size (excludes I/O)	2,100 words	800 words	2.6:1

Before concluding, a further comparison is in order, Wilner [31] compares the S-language for FORTRAN on the B-1700 as offering a 2:1 space improvement over System 360 code. The FORTRAN S-language instruction consists of a 3 or 9 bit OP code container followed by operand containers of (usually) 24 bits--split as descriptor, segment and displacement (not unlike our interpretive storage entry). The format set used in this work is of limited size, and does not possess transformational completeness. However, even this early effort offers noticable improvement of static program representation.

Language Directed Operating Systems

Thus far in this paper we have examined the implication of fast interpretive host machines on program representation largely in the absence of an operating system or operating system functions. In this section we outline some of the implications of language oriented machines on operating systems.

To repeat an ideal discussed earlier: representation is the issue--and interpretation is an implementation technique which provides efficient realizations and executions of this representation. If the representation is poor with respect to the initial problem there is nothing that the operating system designer or the machine designer can do to recover efficiency. Thus, both the machine designer and the operating systems designer are forced to closely examine the initial representations in which they find the programs--the higher level language. If one of the messages of the preceding section was that machine designers have blinded themselves by looking too closely at machines and not nearly closely enough at the languages which were initially used to perform the program representations; so too the same can be said about operating systems designers. Just as we have seen that t'e universal instruction set is inefficient when compared to environmentally oriented (or language oriented) instructions sets so too the concept of a universal operating system catering to all environments is probably just as inefficient. The concept of a single layered operating system is not able to efficiently represent the multilingual interpretively oriented machine design situation. The thesis of this note is that the inner layer of the traditional operating system must be tailored to each language environment and that further, a new model of the operating system is required in which levels are associated with interpretive functional parameters.

What we are actually attempting to define is a language directed operating system based on interpretation. A discussion of this involves two distinct aspects:

(A) the identification of OS entities, and
(B) the image language switching problem.

(A) The Interpretive Operating System:

In order to identify the operating system which is appropriate to varying environments let us examine some general concepts.

A primary concept[9] in developing such operating systems is that of an atomic function. An atomic function is a noninterruptable process usually in one:one correspondence with a language primitive. Clearly one would like to make an atomic function as large as possible and thus minimize the relative significance of entry and exit overhead during interpretation. This prescribes a certain viewpoint in specification of semantics of the image machines. However, physical and device requirements mandate that interrupts be serviced at regular intervals. For example an atomic function cannot mask interrupts indefinitely.

A sequence of atomic functions may now be defined, each performing a significant computation. Of course, each computation is interruptable on atomic boundries. Notice that this is define with respect to physical time. Naturally one can cascade higher level abstractions in which interrupts are masked at one level and yet visible at another. Such hierarchies of interrupt structures are beyond the scope of this short outline but are obvious extensions.

With the above concepts in mind we now examine the layers of interpreted language oriented operating system. As in the earlier discussion of machines, the operating system is now considered an enviromental object. Significant aspects are variable and associated with a particular higher level language; other aspects

---

[9] I am indebted to Professor Freeman for pointing out the utility of the atomic function concept in this context [15,40,41].

remain stable over many environments. The most variable aspects of an OS are those most closely associated with linguistic operations and semantics. We propose a typical four layer hierarchy consisting of (Figure 15):

(1) Absorbed functions
(2) Constituent atoms
(3) Constructed OS functions
(4) Meta lingual functions.

(1) <u>Absorbed functions</u> -- These are functions that lie completely within the linguistic operation, such as name interpretation. While name interpretation may be common to several linguistic subroutines it is a sub-atomic function that lies completely within a semantic operation--which is itself an OS atom. Here we find all processor name space issues, as discussed in the preceding section; including relocation, protection, checking, communication, etc. as well as the memory management. Handling memory faults, however, probably cannot be considered an absorbed function since it adds a considerable amount of time to the interpretation of a linguistic operation. Normally fault handling occupies its own atom.

Absorbed OS functions are really the most intimate types of linguistic mappings. These functions make the image machine match the linguistic environment in so far as names, operations, context, etc. are concerned [15,40,41].

(2) <u>Constituent Atoms</u> -- There are many routines in an operating system which are outside the specified language primitive yet essential for ordinary operation. Such extra lingual constituent atoms arise from one of two sources.

(a) an exceptional condition arises in the course of the interpretation of a linguistic atom and absorbed OS function. The exceptional condition handler then is an atom of its own. Examples include, the memory fault handler memory protect exception, arithmetic exception (overflow), access rights violation, etc.

(b) The second class of constituent atoms arise from the fact that certain language primatives cannot (due to real time constraints) be represented as OS atoms but must be expressed in terms of lower level atomic functions not found in the language. Thus primitive I/O atoms each corresponding to specific device control commands must be available in the system.

(3) <u>Constructed OS Functions</u> -- Higher level language primatives such as PRINT and READ are operations which must be composed of constituent OS atoms. Thus, the PRINT command is actually a subroutine of constituent atoms which performs the PRINT

(i) Traditional View   (ii) Language Oriented View

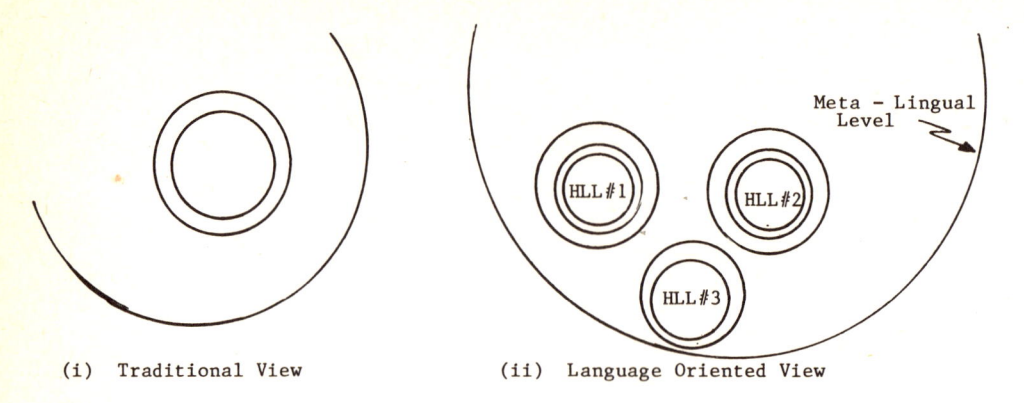

Figure 15(a):   Layers of Interpretation in an Operating System

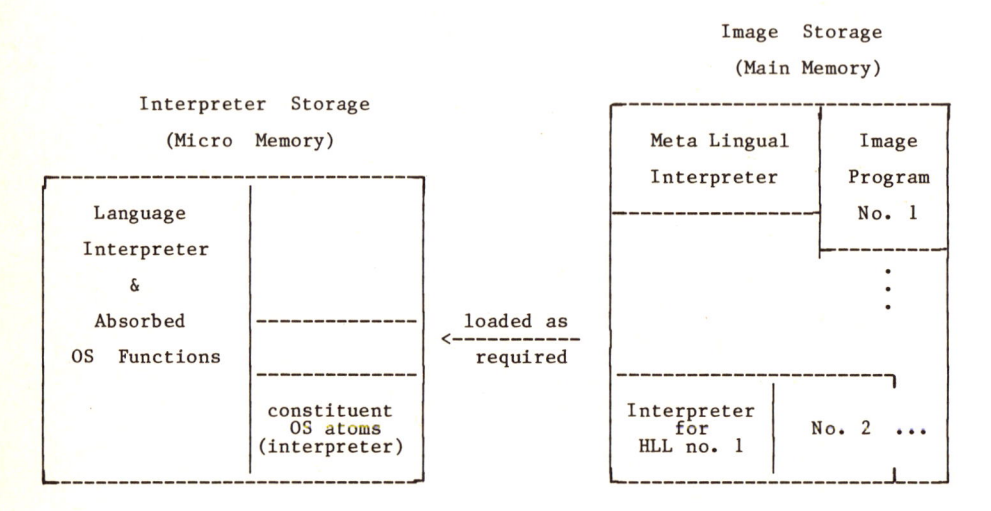

Figure 15(b):   Storage Assignments

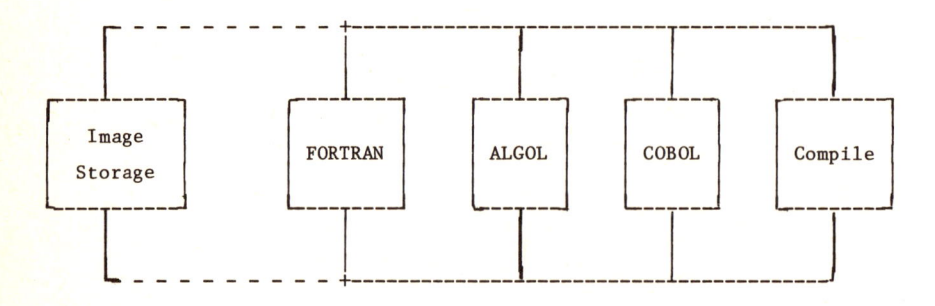

Figure 15(c): Switching Processors vs. Switching Interpretive Memory

semantics. Usually these contructs are restricted to the I/O comoands, although extensive library operations also fall into this class--they might include the trignametric and logarithmic functions not interpretable in the time required for atomic interrupt handling. These utility functions would then become constructed functions which are designed about a minimum number of constituent atoms.

(4) <u>Meta Lingual Functions</u> -- these include actions, labels and names which surround the user program, such as instructions to the loader, definition of resources required by a process, overall security checking, etc.

It is in the meta lingual function definition that the OS designer becomes a language designer. Many an operating system fails because the designer forgets that representation is the issue. Conciseness, straightforwardness and usefullness of representation are the hallmarks of successful meta lingual command design. Even at this level, however, flexibility is possible so that the meta lingual artifacts may have aterable definition depending upon the environment. The interpretation of meta lingual functions is a dual level interpretation of constituent atoms and subsequent host instructions.

Figure 15(b) shows the levels of OS function assignment in an interpretive processor. The absorbed functions naturally lie within the language interpreter itself. The routines for commonly used constituent atoms also reside in the interpretive storage, while constructed OS functions written in constituent atoms and requiring a dual level of interpretation may lie in either the interpretive storage or in the image storage. Meta lingual functions, which will surely consist of special constituent atoms as well as constructed functions, reside outside program storage until required.

(B) <u>Language Directed OS Machines</u>

The basic issue here is one of separate machines versus image machine switching. Figure 15(c) illustrates an arrangement of multiple language oriented machines sharing a coomon storage. Here absorbed functions are dedicated to each of the language machines as are both common constituent atoms and constructed functions. The underlying issue is one of performance versus cost. The interpreter for an image language consists of at least 2 to 4 thousand words of interpretive storage. This would require, within the current state of the art, from 200 micro seconds--to 1 millisecond for an image switching time. With continuing decrease in the cost of hardware it may be more reasonable to dedicate specific machines to a language function rather than paying the speed penalty for image switching among machines as various environments are encountered. The sharing of multiple interpreters within a single host system requires very careful systems analysis to insure that the most commonly used and important parts are captured in the interpretive store at the critical moments of the program execution. The success of such shared interpreters depends largely on the stability of the environment and the care with which the original allocation and analysis was formed. Since the interpretive storage, in order to be fast, will invariably be of limited size and hence unable to capture complete environments the issue of critical section analysis and routine placement is a critical one in environmentally oriented systems.

V. PARALLEL PROCESSOR FORMS OF COMPUTING SYSTEMS [24]

Gross Structures

In order to discribe a machine structure from a macroscopic point of view, on the one hand, and yet avoid the pitfalls of relating some descriptions to a particular problem, the stream concept will be used [25]. Stream in this context simply means a sequence of items (instructions or data) as operated on by a processor. The notion of "instruction" or "datum" is defined with respect to a reference machine. To avoid trivial cases of parallelism, the reader should consider a reference instruction or datum as similar to those used by familiar machines (e.g., IBM 7094). In this description, organizations are categorized by the magnitude (either in space or time multiplex) of interaction of their instruction and data streams. This immediately gives rise to four broad classifications of machine organizations.

(1) The single-instruction-stream single-data stream organization (SISD), which represents most conventional computing equipment.

(2) The single-instruction-stream multiple-data stream (SIMD), which includes most array processes, including Solomon [26] and Illiac IV.

(3) Mutiple-instruction-stream single-data stream type organizations (MISD), which include specialized streaming organizations using multiple-instruction streams on a single sequence of data and the derivatives thereof. The plug board machines of a bygone era are a degenerate form of MISD wherein the instruction streams are single instructions, and a derived datum (SD) is passed from program step i to program step i + 1 (MI).

(4) Multiple-instruction stream-multiple-data stream (MIMD), which include organizations referred to as "multiprocessor." Univac [27], among other corporations, was an early proposer of MIMD structures.

These are qualitative notations. They could be quantified somewhat by specifying the number of streams of each type in the organization or the number of instruction streams per data stream, or vice versa.

SIMD and Its Effectiveness

There are three basic types of SIMD processors, that is, processors characterized by a master instruction applied over a vector of related operands. These include (Figure 19) the following types.

(1) The Array Processor: One control unit and m directly connected processing elements. Each processing element is independent, i.e., has its own registers and storage, but only operates on command from the control unit.

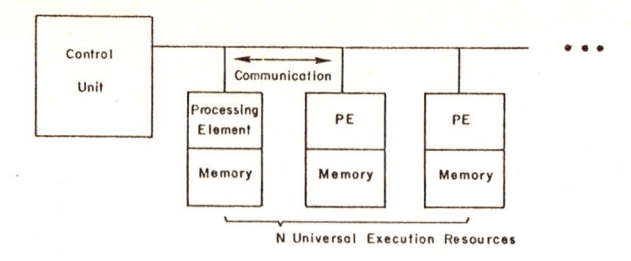

Fig. 19a: Array Processor

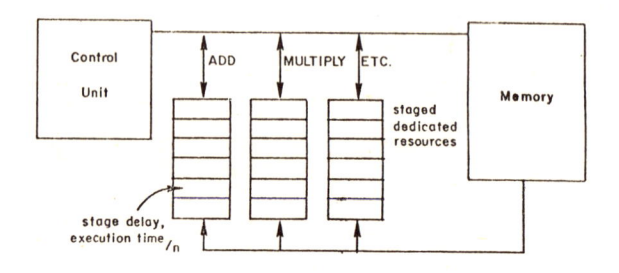

Fig. 19b: Pipeline Processor

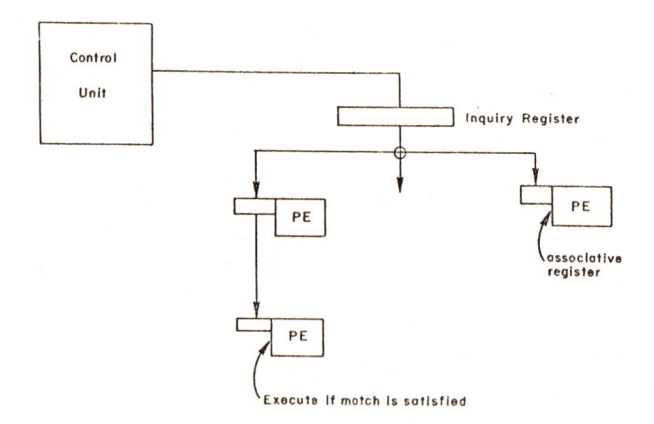

Fig. 19c: Associative Processor

(2) The Pipelined Processor: A time-multiplexed version of the array processor, that is, a number of functional execution units, each tailored to a particular function. The units are arranged in a production line fashion, staged to accept a pair of operands every Δt time units. The control unit issues a vector operation to memory. Memory is arranged so that it is suitable to a high-speed data transfer and produces the source operands which are entered a pair every Δt time units into the designated function. The result stream returns to memory.

(3) The Associative Processor: This is a variation of the array processor. Processing elements are not directly addressed. The processing elements of the associative processor are activated when a generalized match relation is satisfied between an input register and characteristic data contained in each of the processing elements. For those designated elements the control unit instruction is carried out. The other units remain idle.

A number of difficulties can be anticipated for the SIMD organization. These would include the following problems:
(1) Communications between processing elements.
(2) Vector Fitting: This is the matching of size between the logical vector to be performed and the size of the physical array which will process the vector.
(3) Sequential Code (Nonvector): This includes housekeeping and bookkeeping operations associated with the preparation of a vector instruction. This corresponds to the Amdahl [28] effect. Degradation due to this effect can be masked out by overlapping the sequential instructions with the execution of vector type instructions.
(4) Degradation Due to Branching: When a branch point occurs, several of the executing elements will be in one state, and the remainder will be in another. The master controller can essentially control only one of the two states; thus the other goes idle.
(5) Empirically, Minsky and Papert [29] have observed that the SIMD organization has performance portional to the $\log_2 m$ (m, the number of data streams per instruction stream) rather than linear. If this is generally true, it is undoubtedly due to all of the preceding effects (and perhaps others). We will demonstrate an interpretation of it based upon branching degradation.

Communication in SIMD organizations has been widely studied [30]-[32]. Results to date, however, indicate that it is not as significant a problem as was earlier anticipated. Neuhauser [33], in an analysis of several classical SIMD programs, noted that communications time for an array-type organization rarely exceeded 40 percent of total job time and for the matrix inversion case was about 15 percent.

The fitting problem is illustrated in Figure 20. Given a source vector of size m, performance is effected in an array processor when the M physical processing elements do not divide m [34]. However, so long as m is substantially larger than M, this effect will not contribute significant performance degradation. The pipeline processor exhibits similar behavior, as will be discussed later.

The Amdahl effect is caused by a lack of "parallelism" in the source program; this can be troublesome in any multistream organization. Several SIMD organizations use overlapping of "sequential type" control unit instructions with "vector operations" to avoid this effect, with some apparent success.

Multiple-execution organizations such as SIMD have potential difficulty in the use of the execution resources. The reason for this is that all units must process the same instruction at a particular unit of time. When nested decisions are considered (Figure 21), difficulty arises because the execution units are not available to work on any other task.

Consider an SIMD system with p data streams. Now a single instruction will act uniformly on p pairs of operands. With respect to our reference instruction I (which operates on only a pair of operands) the SIMD instruction, designated I*, has p times the effect.

To achieve close to the 1/p bound, the problem must be partitionable in p identical code segments. When a conditional branch is encountered, if at least one of the p data differs in its condition, the alternate path instuctions must be fully executed. We now make a simplifying assumption: the number of source instructions are the same for the primary branch path and the alternate. Since the number of data items required to be processed by a branch stream is p, only the fraction available will be executed initially and the task will be reexecuted for the remainder. Thus, a branch identifying two separate tasks, each of length N, will take twice the amount of time as their unconditional expectation.

Assume that the overhead for reassigning execution elements to alternate paths tasks is prohibitive. This is usually true when the task size is small or when the swapping overhead is large (an array processor, each of whose data streams has a private data storage). Based on empirical evaluation of program performance in a general scientific environment (i.e., not the well- known "parallel type" programs such as matrix inversion, etc.) it has been suggested [29] that the actual performance of the SIMD processor is proportional to the $\log_2$ of the number of slave processing elements rather than the hoped for linear relation. This has been called Minsky's conjecture:

$$\text{perf.}_{\text{SIMD}} \approx \log_2 M.$$

While this degradation is undoubtedly due to many causes, it is interesting to interpret it as a branching degradation: Now define q_i: probability that program will require nested branches to level i $\sum_i q_i = 1$. Assume that the probability of

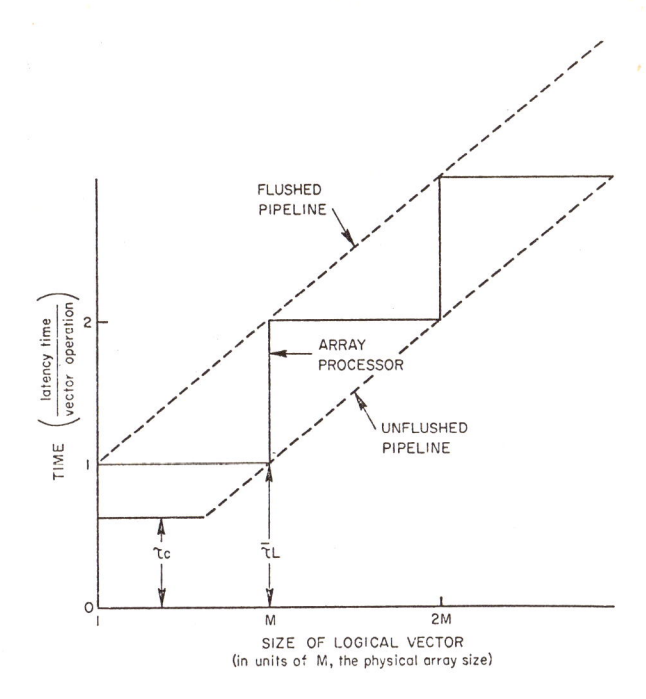

Figure 20: Vector Fitting

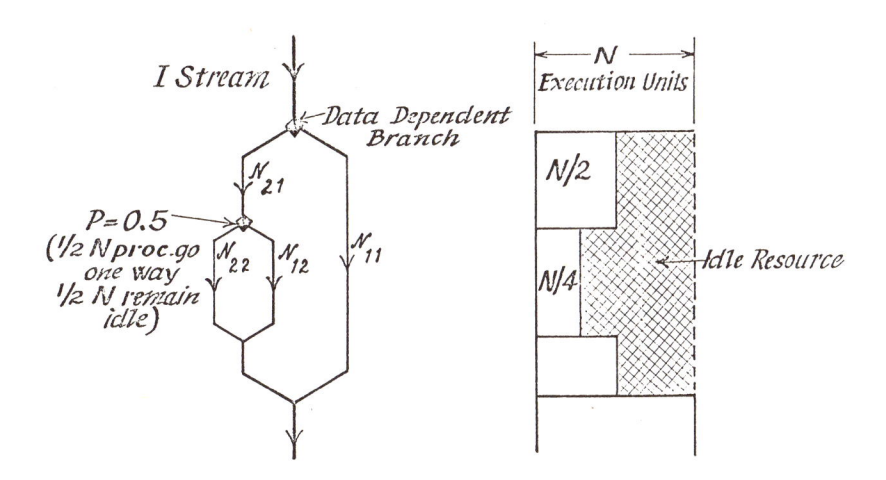

Figure 21: SIMD Branching

being at one of the lower levels of nesting is uniform. That is, it is equally likely to be at level 1, 2, ..., $[\log_2 M]$ and $q_{[\log M]+i} = 0$ for $i = 1$ to ∞.

Now also define:
T_1: the time required to do the whole computation by a SISD (uniprocessor)
T_2: the time required to do same computation by an SIpD processor ($M = p$).

Let S_p be the computation speedup:

$$S_p = \frac{T_1}{T_p} = \frac{\text{execution time SISD}}{\text{execution time SIpD}}$$

Now T_p can be computed under the assumed uniform distribution of q.

$$T_p = q_0 \frac{T_1}{p} + q_1 \frac{T_1}{p/2} + q_2 \frac{T_1}{p/4}$$

$$+ \quad q_i \cdot \frac{T_1}{\frac{p}{2^i}} + q_{[\log_2 p]} \cdot \frac{T_1}{\frac{p}{p}}$$

Since $q_0 = q_1 = q_2 \cdots q_{[\log_2 p]}$

$$T_p = \frac{q_0 T_1}{p} [1 + 2 + 4 + \ldots + 2^{\log_2 p}]$$

assuming intergal values of $\log_2 p$:

$$T_p = \frac{q_0 T_1}{p} [p - 1]$$

let $q_0 = \frac{1}{\log_2 p}$ and compute S_p

$$S_p = \frac{p \log_2 p}{p - 1} \quad \text{or} \quad \log_2 p \text{ for p large.}$$

Thus we have a plausible performance relation based on a particular nesting assumption. Of course this degradation is not due to idle resources alone; in fact, programs can be restructured to keep processing elements busy. The important open question is whether these restructued programs truly enhance the performance of the program as distinct from just keeping the ressources busy. Empirical evidence suggests that the most efficient single-stream program organization for this larger class of problems is presently substantially more efficient than an equivalent program organization suited to the SIMD processors. Undoubtedly this degradation is a combination of effects; however, branching seems to be an important contributor--or rather the ability to efficiently branch in a simple SISD organization substantially enhances its performance.

Certain SIMD configurations, e.g. pipelined processors, which use a common data storage may appear to suffer less from the nested branch degradation, but actually the pipelined processor should exhibit an equivalent behavior. Let C be an n element result vector and A and B be n element source vectors. Several members of C will satisfy a certain criterion for a type of future processing and other will not. Elements failing this criterion are tagged and not processed further, but the vector C is usually left unaltered. If one rearranges C, filters the dissenting elements, and compresses the vector, then an overhead akin to task swapping in the array processor is introduced. Notice that the automatic hardware generation of the compressed vector is not practical at the high data rates required by the pipeline.

If the pipelined processor is logically equivalent to other forms of SIMD, how does one interpret the number of data streams? This question is related to the vector fitting problem. Figure 20 illustrates the equivalence of an array processor to the two main categories of pipeline processors.

1) <u>Flushed</u>: The control unit does not issue the next vector instruction until the last elements of the present vector operation have completed their functional processing (gone through the last stage of the functional pipeline).

2) <u>Unflushed</u>: The next vector instruction is issued as soon as the last elements of the present vector operation have been initiated (entered the first state of the pipeline).

Assuming that the minimum time for the control unit to prepare a vector instruction, τ_c, is less than the average functional unit latency, τ_{cL}, for the flushed case the equivalent number of data streams per instruction stream m is

$$m = \frac{\overline{\tau_L}}{\Delta t} \quad \text{flushed pipeline}$$

where t is the average stage time in the pipeline.

With the unflushed case, again assuming the $\overline{\tau}_L > \tau_c$, the equivalent m is

$$m = \frac{\tau_c}{\Delta t} \quad \text{unflushed pipeline.}$$

Notice that when $\tau_c = \Delta t$, m = 1, and we no longer have SIMD. In fact, we have returned to the overlapped SISD.

<u>MIMD and Its Effectiveness</u>

The multiple-instruction stream organizations (the "multiprocessors") include at least two types.

1) **True Multiprocessors**: Configurations in which several physically complete and independent SI processors share storage at some level for the cooperative execution of a multitask program.

2) **Shared Resource Multiprocessor**: As the name implies, skeleton processors are arranged to share the system resources. These arrangments will be discussed later.

Traditional MIMD organizational problems include: 1) available program parallelism; 2) communicatins overhead; 3) cost increases linearly with additional processors, while performance increases at a lesser rate (due to interference); and 4) providing a method for dynamic reconfiguration of resources to match changing program environment, (critical tasks)--this is related to 1).

Kuck [35] and others have studied the question of available parallelism in programs for MIMD organizations. Again we define terms:

T_1: uniprocessor (SISD) cooputation time
p: number of independent processors: pIpD
T_p: time for computation as pIpD
S_p: $\frac{T_1}{T_p}$
q_i: probability of i processors being active simultaneously

$$\sum_{i=1}^{P} q_i = 1$$

Kuck has emperically observed

$$S_p \doteq \frac{p}{10 \log_{10} 10}$$

R. Lee [36] presents an interesting argument for Kuck's empirical result based on a generalized Amdahl argument:

Since for every program some time must be spend without benefit of parallelism (or low parallelism)--if only to issue FORK and JOIN type operations--q_1 is not equal to zero. In fact some activity will certainly occur at low i, q_i.

Then we know that

$$S_p \leq \frac{1}{\sum_{i=1}^{P} \frac{q_i}{i}} \leq \frac{1}{q_1}$$

now recall that $H_p = \sum_{i=1}^{P} \frac{1}{i}$ is the pth harmonic number and

$$H_p = \ln p + \gamma + \frac{1}{2p} - \frac{1}{12p^2} + \frac{1}{120p^4} - \varepsilon$$

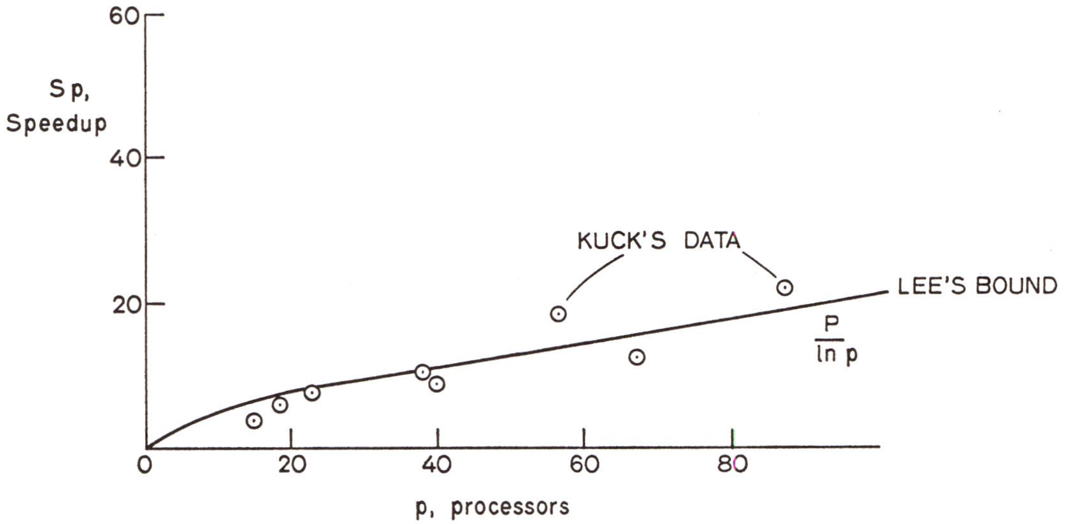

Figure 22: S_p vs processors (MIMD)

where $\gamma = 0.57721..$ (Euler's constant)

and $\epsilon < \dfrac{1}{252p^6}$

thus $H_p > \ln p$

Now if $q_1 = q_2 = \ldots q_p = \dfrac{1}{p}$

$$S_p \leq \dfrac{p}{H_p} \leq \dfrac{p}{\ln p}$$

since $S_p \leq \dfrac{1}{\sum_i q_i} = \dfrac{1}{\frac{1}{p}\sum_i \frac{1}{i}}$

In fact, Lee shows that the same result holds under the weaker condition

$$\sum_{i=1}^{p} \dfrac{q_i - \frac{1}{p}}{i} \geq 0$$

Lee's Bound and Kuck's data are plotted in Figure 22.

Communications is a primary source of degradation in MI systems. When several instruction steams are processing their respective data streams on a common problem set, passing of data points is inevitable. Even if there is naturally a favorable precedence relationship among parallel instruction streams insofar as use of the data is concerned, delays may ensue, especially if the task exeuction time is variable. The time one instruction stream spends waiting for data to be passed to it from another is a macroscopic form of the strictly sequential problem of one instruction waiting for a condition to be established by its immediate predecessor.

The "lockout" problem associated with multiple-instruction streams sharing common data may cause serious degradation. Note that multiple-instruction stream programs without data sharing are certainly as sterile as a single-instruction stream program without branches.

Madnick [37] provides an interesting model of software lockout in the MIMD environment. Assume that an individual processor (instruction stream control unit) has expected task execution time (without conflicts) of E time units. Suppose a processor is "locked out" from accessing needed data for L time units. This locking out may be due to interstream communications (or accessing) problems (especially if the shared storage is an I/O device). Then the lockout time for the jth processor (or instruction stream) is

$$L_j = \sum_i P_{ij} T_{ij}$$

where T_{ij} is the communications time discussed earlier and P_{ij} is the probability of task j accessing data from data stream i. Note that the lockout may be due to the broader communications problem of the jth processor requesting a logical data stream i. This includes the physical data stream accessing problem as well as additional sources of lockout due to control, allocation, etc.

In any event, Madnick [37] used a Markov model to derive the following relationship:

$$\mathcal{E}(\text{idle}) = \sum_{i=2}^{n} \frac{(i-1)}{\left(\frac{E}{L}\right)^i (n-i)!} \bigg/ \sum_{i=0}^{n} \frac{1}{\left(\frac{E}{L}\right)^i (n-i)!}$$

where $\mathcal{E}(\text{idle})$ is the expected number of lock-out processors and n is the total number of processors. If a single processor unit performance, then for n processors

$$\text{perf.} = n - \mathcal{E}(\text{idle})$$

and normalized performance (max = 1) is given by

$$\text{perf.}_N = \frac{n - \mathcal{E}(\text{idle})}{n}$$

Figure 23 is an evaluation of the normalized performance as the number of processors (instruction stream-data pairs) are increased for various interaction activity ratios L/E.

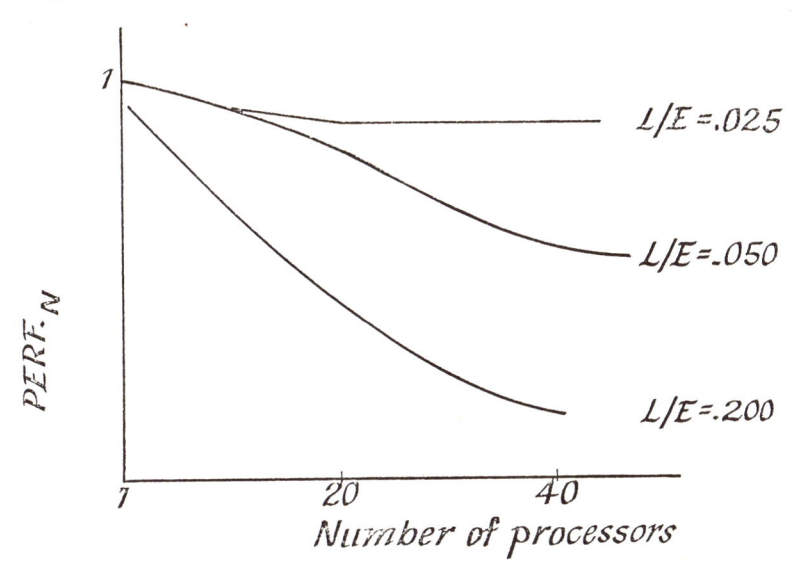

Figure 23: MIMD Lockout

Shared Resource Multiprocessors

Whether an interpreted language is fixed (conventional machine code) or variable, processor faults still occur during execution. The faults are especially severe in high performance, pipelined systems. Faults may arise for a number of reasons:

(a) A _memory fault_ in the storage hierarchy occurs when an operand is not available because of its location in physical memory. This causes a delay in moving an operand to a machine-accessible part of memory.

(b) A _procedural fault_ occurs when a conditional branch or similar artifact is encountered and the condition is not yet available or known. Here again, the system must wait for the resolution of the condition.

(c) An _operand fault_ occurs when there is a data dependency. That is, the source data for one operation has not yet been provided by a preceding operation.

(d) A _resource fault_ is also possible. That is, because of the physical implementation of the system, two otherwise independent operations are in conflict because they both require a single physical facility.

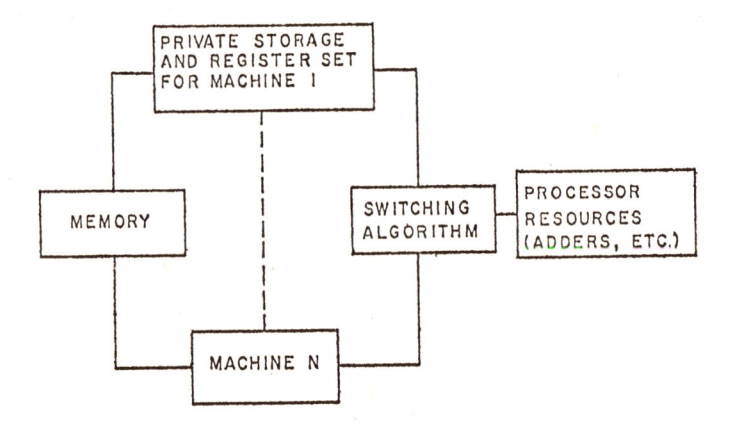

Figure 24: Shared Resource Multiprocessors

The degenerative effects of these conflicts are especially notable in high performance systems which try to execute multiple sequential instructions simultaneously. Effects such as nonresolvable branches, stores into the instruction stream, etc.--with subsequent fault penalty--confirm the difficulty. In order to avoid these problems, multiple skeleton machines have been proposed [38,39] which share the internal resources of a processor--adder, shifter, etc.--but separaely manage their own progam states through physically independent sets of registers (Figure 24).

There are two approaches to switching control among these skeleton machines:
(a) The <u>switch on fault</u> philosophy is the most obvious. As soon as a fault of significant duration is detected, control is switched to an alternate skeleton machine. The principal advantage of this approach is that it is potentially very effective in its use of resources. That is, given enough skeleton machines, one can have arbitrarily high resource usage ratios. A major difficulty is the complexity of the switching algorithm. It may be expensive to implement, and it surely represents a critical additional time overhead which mitgates some of the advantages of the shared resource concept. Another complication is that the switching algorithm should guarantee that each machine achieves a minimum processing rate. This insures timely handling of interrupts and avoids a situation where code in one machine seizes control by simply "never faulting".
(b) <u>Synchronous switching</u> implies time multiplexing of the resources among skeleton machines. Time multiplexing "gears" the machine down so that <u>within each machine</u> there is only one instruction being exeucted at a time, and the effect of faulting is largely reduced on a per machine basis. The ensemble, on the other hand, processes instructions at a very high rate. In other words, we are overlapping machines rather than instructions in a single program. For critical code segments and tasks, subcommutation can be arranged which allows a limited amownt of instruction overlapping in certain critical skeleton machines. The advantage of synchronous switching is that the switching algorithm is simple and predictable, and hence may be implemented with less overhead. It is not as flexible, however, as the switch on fault scheme, and it may not be as effective in its use of resources.

A possible optimal arrangement is a combination of space-time switching (Figure 26). The time factor is the nuober of skeleton processors multiplexed on a time-phase ring, while the space factor is the number of multiplexed processor "rings", K, which simultaneously request resources. Note that K processors will contend for the resources and, up to $K - 1$, may be denied service at that moment. Thus, a rotating priority among the rings is suggested to guarantee a minimum performance. The partitioning of the resources should be determined by the expected request statistics.

When the amount of "parallelism" (or number of identifiable tasks) is less than the available processors, we are faced with the problem of accelerating these tasks. This can be accomplished by designing certain of the processors in each ring with additional staging and interlock [39] (the ability to issue multiple instructions simultaneously) facilities. The processor could issue multiple-instruction execution requests in a single-ring revolution. For example, in a ring $N = 16$, 8 processors could issue 2 requests per revolution, or 4 processors could issue 4 requests per revolution; or 2 processors could issue 8 requests per revolution; or 1 processor could issue 16 requests per revolution. This partition is illustrated in Figure 26. Of course mixed strategies are possible. For a more detailed discussion the reader is referred to [38], [39] and [24].

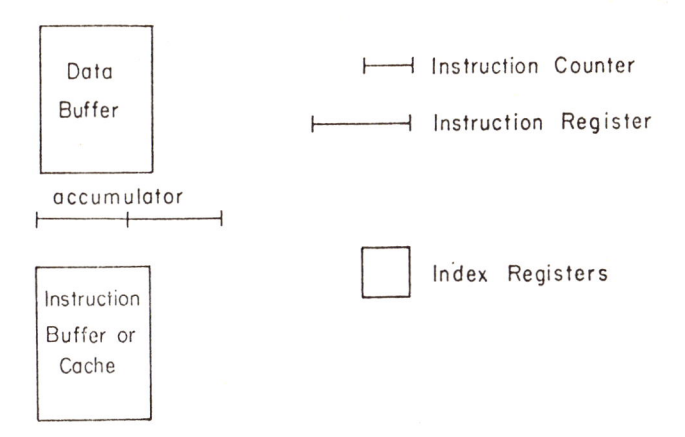

Figure 25a: Skeleton Processor

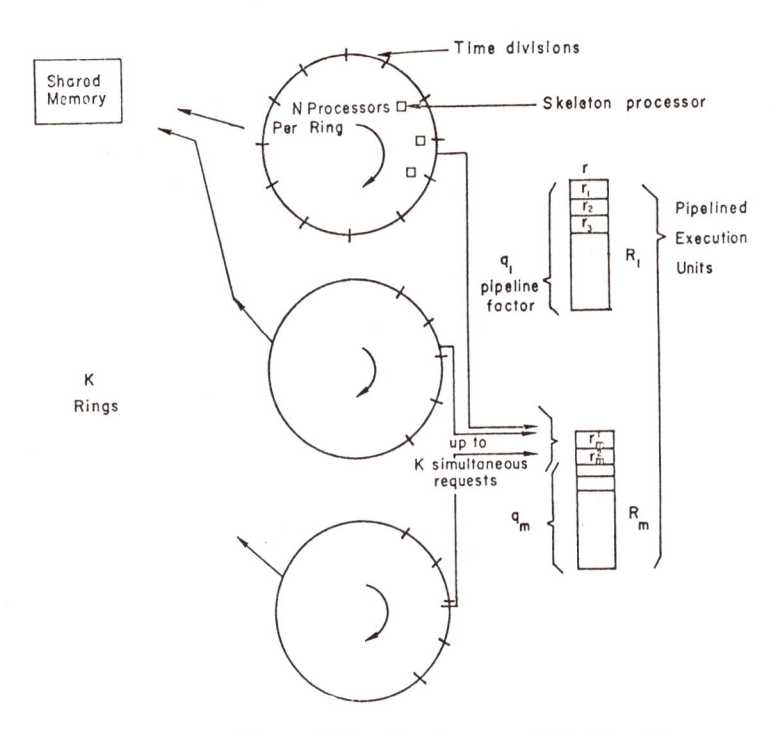

Figure 25b: Synchronous Switching MP

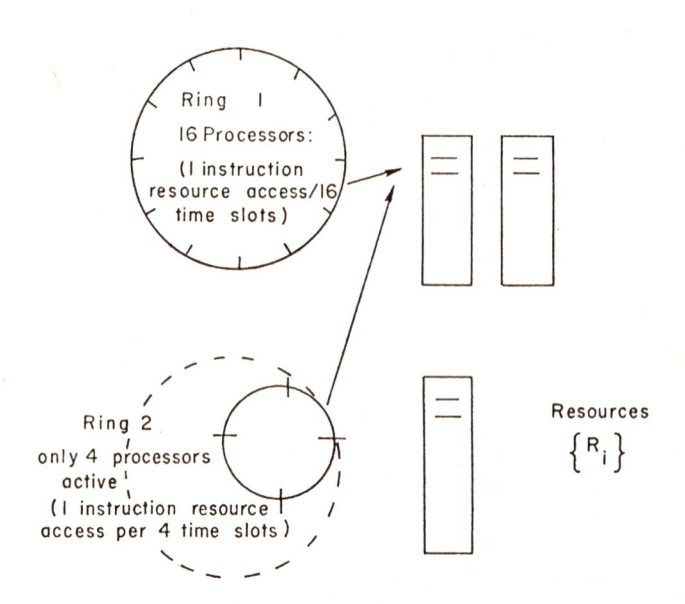

Figure 26: Sub Commutation

References

[1] Flynn, M. J., "Microprogramming: Another Look at Internal Computer Control", *Proc. of IEEE*, Vol. 63, No. 11, November 1975.

[2] Flynn, M. J., "Microprogramming and the Control of a Computer", Chapter 10, *Introduction to Computer Architecture*, H. Stone (Ed.) Science Research Assoc. (Pub.), 1975, pp. 432-473.

[3] Coffman, E. G. and Denning, P. J., *Operating Systems Theory*, Prentice Hall, 1973.

[4] Dennis, J., "Segmentation and the Design of Multiprogrammed Computer Systems", *JACM*, Vol. 12, No. 4, October 1965.

[5] Randall, B., and Kuehner, C. J., "Dynamic Storage Allocation Systems", CACM, Vol. 11, No. 5, pp. 297-305, May 1968.

[6] Habermann, A. N., *Introduction to Operating Systems Design*, SRA (Pub.) 1976.

[7] Denning, P., "The Working Set Model for Program Behavior", CACM, Vol. 11, No. 5, pp. 323-333, May 1968.

[8] Denning, P. and Graham, G. S., "Multiprogrammed Memory Management", *Proc. of the IEEE*, Vol. 63, No. 6, pp 924-939, June 1975.

[9] Fuller, S., "Performance Evaluation" Chapter 11 in *Introduction to Computer Architecture*, H. Stone (Ed.), SRA (Pub.), 1975.

[10] Kleinrock, L., *Queueing Systems*, 2 Volumes, Wiley-Interscience Publ., 1975.

[11] Flynn, M. J., "The Interpretive Interface: Resources and Program Representation in Computer Organization", *Proc. of the Symposium on High Speed Computers and Algorithms*, April 1977, University of Illinois, Academic Press (Pub.).

[12] Hammerstrom, D. W. and Davidson, E. S., "Information Content of CPU Memory Referencing Behavior", *Proc. of Fourth Symposium on Computer Architecture*, March 1977.

[13] Flynn, M. J., "Trends and Problems in Computer Organizations", *IFIP Proceedings 74*, North-Holland Pub., pp. 3-10.

[14] Lunde, A., "More Data on the O/W Ratios", Computer Architecture News, Vol. 4, No. 1, pp. 9-13, March 1975, Pub. ACM.

[15] Freeman, Martin, et al, "PERSEUS: An Operating System Machine," unpublished manuscript, December 1977.

[16] Rossman, G., Flynn, M., McClure, R., and Wheeler, N. D., "The Technical Significance of User Microprogrammable Systems", Technical Report, Palyn Associates, San Jose, CA., for U. S. National Bureau of Standards Contract, No. 4-36045, November 1974.

[17] Flynn, M. J., Neuhauser, C. J. and McClure, R. M., "EMMY--An Emulation System for User Microprogramming", AFIPS, Vol. 44, NCC, 1975, pp. 85-89.

[18] Flynn, M. J., Hoevel, L. W., and Neuhauser, C. J., "The Stanford Emulation Laboratory", Digital Systems Lab., Technical Report No. 118, Stanford University, June 1976.

[19] Burroughs Corp., "B-1700 Systems Reference Manual", Burroughs Corp., Detroit, Mich., 1972.

[20] Hoevel, L. W. and Flynn, M. J., "The Structure of Directly Executed Languages: A New Theory of Interpretive System Support", Digital Systems Lab., Technical Report No. 130, Stanford University, March 1977.

[21] Johnson, J. B., "The Contour Model of Block Structured Processes", *SIGPLAN Notices*, Vol. 6, pp. 52-82, February 1971.

[22] Hoevel, L. W., "DELtran Principles of Operation", Digital Systems Lab., Technical Note No. 108, Stanford University, March 1977.

[23] Wilner, W., "Burroughs B-1700 Memory Utilization", AFIPS Proceedings, Vol. 41-I, FJCC, 1972, pp. 579-586.

[24] Flynn, M. J., "Some Computer Organizations and Their Effectiveness", *IEEE Transactions on Computers*, Vol. C-21, No. 9, pp. 948-960, September 1972.

[25] Flynn, M. J., "Very High-Speed Computing Systems", *Proc. IEEE*, Vol. 54, pp. 1901-1909, December 1966.

[26] Slotnick, D. L., Borch, W. C. and McReynolds, R. C., "The Soloman Computer--A Preliminary Report", in *Proc. 1962 Workshop on Computer Organization*, Washington, D.C.: Spartan, 1963, p. 66.

[27] Lewis, D. R. and Mellen, G. E., "Stretching LARC´s, Capability by 100--A New Multiprocessor System", presented at the 1964 Symp. Microelectronics and Large Systems, Washington, D.C.

[28] Amdahl, G. M., "Validity of the Single Processor Approach to Achieving Large Scale Computing Capabilities", in *1967 Spring Joint Computer Conf. AFIPS Conf. Proc.*, Vol. 30. Washington, D.C.: Thompson, 1967, p. 483.

[29] Minsky, M. and Papert, S., "On Some Associative, Parallel, and Analog Computations", in *Associative Information Techniques*, E. J. Jacks, Ed., New York: Elsevier, 1971.

[30] Stone, H. S., "The Organization of High-Speed Memory for Parallel Block Transfer of Data", *IEEE Trans. Comput.*, Vol. C-19, pp. 47-53, January 1970.

[31] Pease, M. C., "An Adaptation of the Fast Fourier Transform for Parallel Processing", *J. Ass. Comput. Mach.*, Vol. 15, pp. 252-264, April 1968.

[32] Pease, M. C., "Matrix Inversion Using Parallel Processing", *J. Ass. Comput. Mach.*, Vol. 14, pp. 69-74, 1971.

[33] Neuhauser, C., "Communications in Parallel Processors", The Johns Hopkins University, Baltimore, MD, Comput. Res. Rep. 18, December 1971.

[34] Chen, T. C., "Parallelism, Pipelining and Computer Efficiency" *Comput. Des.*, Vol. 10, pp. 69-74, 1971.

[35] Kuck, D., Muraoka, Y., and Chen, S. C., "On the Number of Operations Simultaneously Executable in Fortran-like Programs and Their Resulting Speedup", IEEE TC, 1972.

[36] Lee, R. B., "Performance Bounds for Parallel Processors", Digital Systems Lab., Technical Report No. 125, Stanford University, November 1976.

[37] Mednick, S. E., "Multiprocessor Software Lockout", in *Proc. 1968 Ass. Comput. Mach. Nat. Conf.*, pp. 19-24.

[38] Flynn, M. J., Podvin, A. and Shimizu, K., "A Multiple Instruction Stream Processor With Shared Resources", in *Parallel Processor Streams*, C. Hobbs, Ed., Washington, D.C.: Spartan, 1970.

[39] Flynn, M. J., "Shared Internal Resources in a Multiprocessor" in *1971 IFIPS Congr. Proc.*

[40] Freeman, Martin, et al, "A Model for the Construction of Operating Systems," unpublished manuscript, in preparation 1977.

[41] Jacobs, W. W., "Control Systems in Robots," *Proceedings of the ACM 25th Anniversary Conference*, vol. 1, 1972, pp. 110-117.

CHAPTER 3.A.

J. H. Saltzer
Massachusetts Institute of Technology
Cambridge, Mass., USA

Naming and Binding of Objects

Overview

A property of a computer system that determines its ease of use and its range of applicability is the way it creates and manages the objects of computation. An important aspect of object management is the scheme by which a system names objects. Names for objects are required so that programs can refer to the objects, so that objects can be shared, and so that objects can be located at some future time. This chapter introduces several rather general concepts surrounding names, and then explores in depth their applicability to two naming structures commonly encountered inside computer systems: addressing architectures and file systems. It examines naming functions that are usually implemented (or desired) in these two areas, and some of the design tradeoffs encountered in a variety of contemporary computer systems. It ends with a brief discussion of some current research topics in the area of naming.

Glossary

bind — to choose a specific lower-level implementation for a particular higher-level semantic construct. In the case of names, binding is choosing a mapping from a name to a particular object, usually identified by a lower-level name.

catalog — an object consisting of a table of bindings between symbolic names and objects. A catalog is an example of a context (q.v.).

closure — abstractly, the mechanism that connects an object that refers to other objects by name with the context in which those names are bound.

component — an object that is contained by another object.

context — a particular set of bindings of names to objects: a name is always interpreted relative to some context.

© 1978 by J. H. Saltzer. All rights reserved.

indirect entry	- in a naming network, an entry in a catalog that binds a name, instead of to an object, to the path name of some catalog entry elsewhere in the naming network.
library	- a shared catalog (or set of catalogs) that contains objects such as programs and data to which several users refer. A computer system usually has a __system library__, which contains commonly used programs.
limited context	- a context in which only a few names can be expressed, and therefore names must be reused.
modular sharing	- sharing of an object without the need to know of the implementation of the shared object. From the point of view of naming, modular sharing is sharing without need to know of the names used by the shared object.
name	- in practice, a character- or bit-string identifier that is used to refer to an object on which computation is performed. Abstractly, an element of a context.
naming hierarchy	- a naming network (q.v.) that is constrained to a tree-structured form.
naming network	- a catalog system in which a catalog may contain the name of any object, including another catalog. An object is located by a multi-component path name (q.v.) relative to some working catalog (q.v.).
object	- a software (or hardware) structure that is considered to be worthy of a distinct name.
path name	- a multiple component name of an object in a naming network. Successive components of the path name are used to select entries in successive catalogs. The entry selected is taken as the catalog for use with the next component of the path name. For a given starting catalog, a given path name selects at most one object from the hierarchy.
reference name	- the name used by one object (e.g., a program) to refer to another object.
resolve	- to locate an object in a particular context, given its name.
root	- the starting catalog of a naming hierarchy.
search	- abstractly, to examine several contexts looking for one that can successfully resolve a name. In practice, the systematic examination of several catalogs of a naming network, looking for an entry that matches a reference name presented by some program. The catalogs examined might typically include a working catalog, a few other explicitly named catalogs, and a system library catalog.

shared object — 1) a single object that is a component of more than one other object. 2) an object that may be used by two or more different, parallel activities at the same time.

synonym — one of the multiple names for a single object permitted by some catalog implementations.

tree name — a multiple component name of an object in a naming hierarchy. The first component name is used to select an entry from a root catalog, which selected entry is used as the next catalog. Successive components of the tree name are used for selection in successively selected catalogs. A given tree name selects at most one object from the hierarchy.

unique identifier — a name, associated with an object at its creation, that differs from the corresponding name of every other object that has ever been created by this system.

unlimited context — a context in which names never have to be reused.

user-dependent binding — binding of names in a shared object to different components depending on the identity of the user of the shared object.

working catalog — in a naming network, a catalog relative to which a particular path name is expressed.

A. Introduction

1. Names in computer systems

Names are used in computer systems in many different ways. One of these ways is naming of the individual variables of a program, together with rules of scope and lifetime that apply to names used within a collection of programs that are constructed as a single unit. Another way names are used is in database management systems, which provide retrieval of answers to sophisticated queries for information permanently filed by name and by other attributes. These two areas are sufficiently specialized that they have labels of their own: the first is generally studied under the label "semantics of programming languages" and the second is studied under the label "database management".

Yet another use of names, somewhat less systematically studied, is the collection together of independently constructed programs and data structures to form subsystems, inclusion of one subsystem as a component of another, and use of individual programs, data structures, and other subsystems from public and semi-public libraries. Such activity is an important aspect of any programming project that builds on previous work or requires more than one programmer. In this activity, a systematic method of naming objects so that they may contain references to one another is essential. Programs must be able to call on other programs and utilize data objects by name, and data objects may need to contain cross references to other data objects or programs. If true modularity is to be achieved it is essential that it be possible to refer to another object knowing only its interface characteristics (for example, in the case of a procedure object, its name and the types of the arguments it expects) and without needing to know details of its internal implementation, such as to which other objects it refers. In particular, use of an object should not mean that the user of that object is thereafter constrained in the choice of names for other, unrelated objects. Although this goal seems obvious, it is surprisingly difficult to attain, and requires a systematic approach to naming.

Unfortunately, the need for systematic approaches to object naming has only recently been appreciated, since the arrival on the scene of systems with extensive user-contributed libraries and the potential ability easily to "plug together" programs and data structures of distinct origin.* As a result,

---

* Examples include the Compatible Time-Sharing System (CTSS) constructed at M.I.T. for the IBM 7090 computer, the Cambridge University System, the Honeywell Information Systems Inc. Multics, IBM's TSS/360, the TENEX system developed at Bolt, Beranek and Newman for the Digital Equipment PDP-10 computer, the M.I.T. Lincoln Laboratory's APEX system for the TX-2 computer, the University of California (at Berkeley) CAL system for the Control Data 6400, and the Carnegie-Mellon HYDRA system for a multiprocessor Digital Equipment Company PDP-11, among others.

the mechanisms available for study are fairly ad hoc "first cuts" at providing the necessary function, and a systematic semantics has not yet been developed.* In this chapter we identify those concepts and principles that appear useful in organizing a naming strategy, and illustrate with case studies of contemporary system naming schemes.

2. A _model_ _for_ _the_ _use_ _of_ _names_

We shall approach names and binding from an object-oriented point of view: the computer system is seen as the manager of a variety of objects on which computation occurs. An active entity that we shall call a _program interpreter_** performs the computation on these objects. Objects may be simply arrays of bits, commonly known as segments, or they may be more highly structured, for example containing other objects as components. There are two ways to arrange for one object to contain another as a component: a copy of the component object can be created and included in the containing object (containment by _value_) or a name for the component object may be included in the containing object (containment by _name_).

In containment by value, an object would be required to physically enclose copies of every object that it contains. This scheme is inadequate because it does not permit two objects to share a component object whose value changes. Consider, for example, an object that is a procedure that

---

* Early workers in this area included A. Holt, who was among the first to articulate the need for imposing structure on memory systems [Holt, 1961] and J. Iliffe, who proposed using indirect addressing (through "codewords") as a way of precisely controlling bindings [Iliffe and Jodeit, 1962]. J. Dennis identified the interactions among modularity, sharing, and naming in his arguments for segmented memory systems [Dennis, 1965]. A. Fraser explored the relation between naming in languages and naming in systems [Fraser, 1971].

** In various systems, the terms "execution point", "processor", "process", "virtual processor", "task", and "activity", have been used for this active entity. For the present discussion we shall adopt the single term "program interpreter" for its mnemonic value, and assume that there are potentially many active sites of computation (and thus many active program interpreters) at the same time, as in typical time-sharing and multiprocessing systems.

calculates the current Dow-Jones stock price average. Assume that this procedure uses as a component some data base of current stock prices. Assume also that there is another procedure object that makes changes to this data base to keep it current. Both procedure objects must contain the data base object. With containment by value, each procedure object must include a copy of the data base. Then, however, changes made by one procedure to its copy will not affect the other copy, and the second procedure can never see the changes.

A fundamental purpose for a name, then, is to accomplish sharing, and the second scheme is to include a name for a component object in a containing object. When names are used, some way is then needed to associate the names with particular objects. As we shall see, it is common for several names to be associated with the same object, and for one name to be associated with different objects for different purposes. In examining these various possibilities, we shall discover that they all fit into one abstract pattern. This abstract pattern for containment by naming is as follows: a context is a partial mapping from some names into some objects of the system.* To employ a component object, a name is chosen for the object, a context that maps that name into that component object is identified or created, the name is included in the containing object, and the context is associated with the containing object. At some later time, when the containing object is the target of some computation, the program interpreter performing the

---

* In the study of programming language semantics, the terms universe of discourse, context, and environment are used for a concept closely related to the one we label context. Usually, the programming language concept is a mapping with the possibility of duplicate names, a stack or tree structure, and a set of rules for searching for the correct mapping within the environment. Our concept of context is simpler, being restricted to an unstructured mapping without duplicates. The names we deal with in this chapter correspond to free variables of programming language semantics, and we shall examine a variety of techniques for binding those free variables. Curiously, we use a simpler concept because in systems we shall encounter a less systematic world of naming then in programming languages.

computation may need to refer to the component object. It accomplishes this reference by looking up the name in the associated context. Arranging that a context shall map a name into an object is called _binding_ that name to that object in that context. Using a context to locate an object from a name is called _resolving_ that name in that context. Figure 1 illustrates this pattern.

In examining figure 1, two further issues are apparent: 1) the context must include, either by value or by name, the contained object; 2) the containing object must be associated with a context. Figure 2 illustrates the handling of both these issues in the familiar example of a location-addressed memory system in a simple computer that has no sophisticated addressing machinery at all. Electrical wiring in effect places a copy of the contained object in its context and also places a copy of the context in the containing object. (In both cases, the "copy" is the only copy, the original.)

The alternative approach for handling the connection between the context and the contained object is for the context to refer to the contained object with another name, a lower-level one. This lower level name must then be resolved in yet another context. Figure 3 provides an example in which an interpreter's internal symbol table is the first, higher-level context, and the location-addressed memory of figure 2 provides the lower-level context. A more elaborate example could be constructed, with several levels of names and contexts, but the number of contexts must be finite: there must always be some context that contains its objects by value (as did the location-addressed hardware memory) rather than naming them in still another context. Further, since a goal of introducing names was sharing, and thus avoiding multiple copies of objects, each object ultimately must be contained by value in one and only one context.

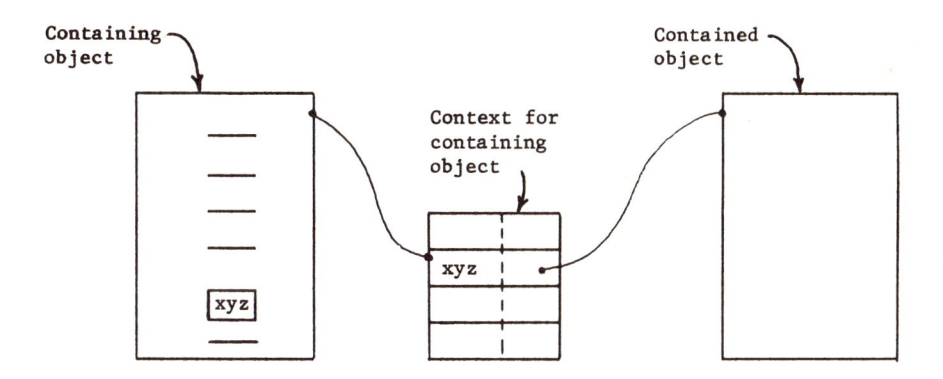

Figure 1 -- Pattern for use of names. The containing object includes a use of the name "xyz". The containing object is somehow associated with a context. The context contains a mapping between the name "xyz" and enough information to get to the contained object. Because the contained object has not been copied into the containing object, it is possible for some third object also to contain this object; thus sharing can occur.

```
                 Memory addressing
                    hardware               Memory
                 ┌────┬────┬────┐    ┌──────────────┐
Processor        │    │    │    │    │              │
                 │    │    │    │    │              │
   ┌─────┬────┐  │    │    │    │    │              │
   │     │9742│──┤    │    │    │    │              │
   │     └────┘  │    │    │    │    │              │
   │  ↑          │    │    │    │    │              │
   │program      │ 9742    │    │    │              │
   │counter      │         │    │    │next instruction│
   └─────────┘   │    │    │    │    │              │
                 └────┴────┴────┘    └──────────────┘
                         ⎵_____⎵
                        location addressed memory system
```

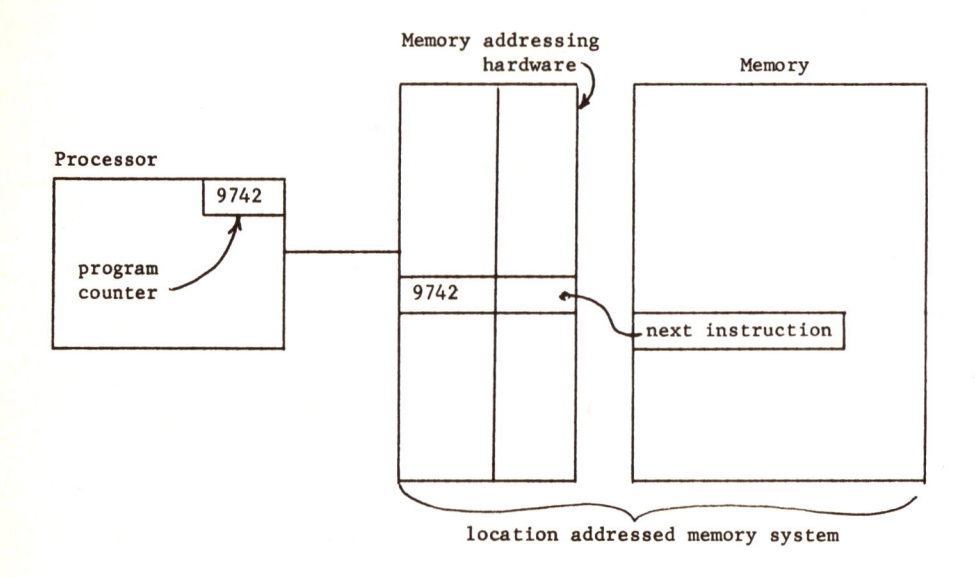

Figure 2 -- Instruction retrieval as an example of naming. In this
          simple computer the processor program counter names the
          next instruction to be interpreted. The processor is
          associated with a context, the memory addressing hardware,
          by means of an electrical cable. The context maps the name
          "9742" into the physical location in memory of some particu-
          lar word of information, again using electrical cable to
          form the association. (Note that, except in the simplest
          microprocessors, one does not usually encounter a processor
          that actually uses such a primitive scheme.)

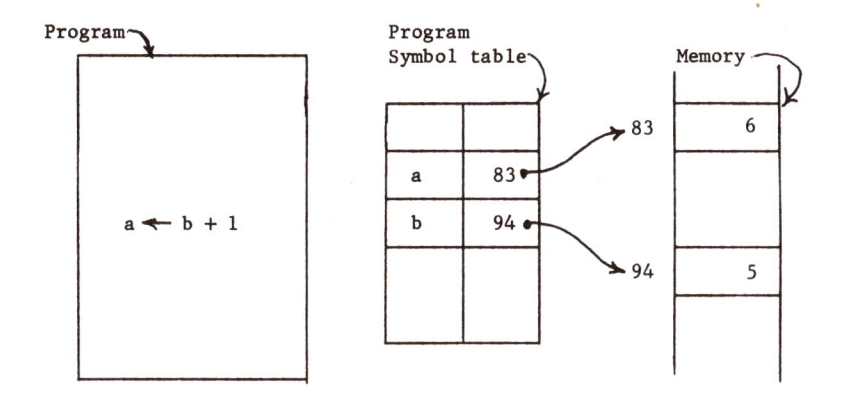

Figure 3 -- A two-level naming example. An interpreter executes
a program containing the names "a" and "b". The
interpreter resolves these names using the context
represented by a symbol table that maps the names
"a" and "b" into lower level names, which are
addresses in the memory. These lower level names
might be resolved as in figure 2.

Returning to figure 1, it is also necessary for a containing object to be associated with its context. If the context happens to be implemented as an object in its own right (a common strategy) this association may be provided by creating a new object that contains (using either lower-level names or copies, as appropriate) both the original containing object and the appropriate context as components. A mechanism that exists for the purpose of associating some name-containing with its context is known as closure, and an object that performs this function is a closure object. In many cases, the closure is implicitly supplied by the program interpreter rather than being implemented as an explicit object. For example, in figure 3, the interpreter automatically uses the program's symbol table (which might be a data object contained in the interpreter itself) as a context. For another example, in many systems the user's catalog is an automatically provided context for file names. Yet another example is the context associated with each virtual processor in a system for resolving the addresses of words in memory; this context is called the virtual processor's address space, and in a paged system is represented by a page map. The concept of a closure is fundamental to naming, but explicit closure objects will not appear to be of much interest until we consider the problem of changing contexts when calling from one procedure to another.

3. Problems in the use of names

This simple model for the use of names seems straightforward in that it allows objects to be shared. However, there are several more objectives usually wanted in a naming system: modularity of sharing, multiple contexts, and user-dependent bindings. Failure to meet one or more of these objectives shows up as an awkward problem. These troubles may arise from deliberate design compromises or from unintentional design omissions.

One common problem arises if the wrong implicit context is supplied by the program interpreter. This problem can occur if the interpreter is dealing with several objects and does not fully implement closures. Such an interpreter may not keep distinct the several contexts, or may choose among available contexts on some basis other than the object that contained the name. For example, file names in many systems are resolved relative to a "current working catalog"; yet often the working catalog is a static concept, unrelated to the identity of the object making the reference.

Names permit sharing, but not always in the most desirable way. If use of a shared object requires that the user know about the names of the objects that the shared object uses (for example, by avoiding use of those names) we have not accomplished the goal of modularity. We shall use the term modular sharing to describe the (desirable) situation in which a shared object can be used without any knowledge whatsoever of the names of the objects it uses.

Lack of modular sharing can show up as a problem of name conflict, in which for some reason it seems necessary to bind the same name to two or more objects in one context. This situation often occurs when putting together two independently conceived sets of programs in a system that does not provide modular sharing. Name conflict is a serious problem since it requires changing some of the uses of the conflicting names. Making such changes can be awkward or difficult, since the authors of the original programs are not necessarily available to locate, understand, and change the uses of the conflicting names.

Sharing should also be controllable, in the following apparently curious way: different users of an object (that is, users with distinct, simultaneously active program interpreters) should be able to provide private <u>user-dependent</u> <u>bindings</u> for some of its components. However, one user's private bindings should not affect other users of the shared object. The most common example of a user-dependent binding is the association between arguments to a function and its formal parameters, but in modular systems other examples abound also. When a single subprogram is used in different applications, it may be appropriate for that subprogram to have a different context for each application. The different contexts would be used to resolve the same set of names, but some of those names might resolve to different objects. There are three common situations in which the users of an object might need different contexts for different applications:

1. When the object is a procedure, and its operation requires memory private to its user. The storage place for the private memory can be conveniently handled by creating a private context for this combination of user and program and arranging that this private context be used whenever the program serves this user. In the private context, the program's name for the memory area is bound to a storage object that is private to the user. A concrete example might be the storage area used as a buffer by a shared interactive text editor in a word processing system.

2. When a programmer makes a change to one part of a large subsystem, and wants to run it together with the unchanged parts of the subsystem. For example, suppose a statistics subsystem is available that uses as a component a library math routine. One user of the statistics subsystem has a trouble, which he traces to inaccuracy

in the math routine. He develops a specialized version of the math routine that is sufficiently accurate for his use, and wants to have it used whenever he invokes the statistics subsystem. Copying the entire subsystem is one way to proceed, but that approach does not take advantage of sharing, and in cases where writable data is involved may produce the wrong result. An alternative is to identify those contexts that refer to the modified part, and create special versions that refer to the new part instead of the original.

3. Two multimodule subsystems (for example a theatre ticket and an airline reservation system) might differ in only one or two modules (for example the overbooking policy algorithm). Yet it may be desirable to maintain only one copy of the common modules. To handle those cases where a common module refers to a non-common module by name, user-dependent bindings are required.

In each of these situations some provision must be made for a name-using object to be associated with different contexts at different times, depending on the identity of the user. This provision is usually made by allowing the establishment of several closures, each of which associates the name-using object with a different context, and providing some scheme to make sure that the name interpreter knows which closure to use for each different user.

Yet another problem in using names is _unstable bindings_; that is, bindings that change unpredictably between definition and use. For example, file system catalogs often serve as contexts, and usually those catalogs permit names to be deleted or changed. Employing one object in another by using a name and a changeable context can make it impossible to ensure that when the time comes to use that name and context the desired object will be obtained.

Sometimes, these naming troubles arise because a system uses a single compromise mechanism to accomplish naming and also some other objective such as economy, resource management, or protection. A common example is a limitation on the number of names that can be resolved by a single context. Thus, the limited size of the "address space" of a location-addressed memory system often restricts which subprograms can be employed together in forming a program, producing non-modular sharing, name conflicts, or sometimes both. For example, some operating systems allow several users to share a text editor or compiler by assigning those programs fixed locations, the same in every user's address space. In such a system if a single user wants to construct a subsystem that uses both the editor and the compiler as components, they must have been assigned different fixed locations. If more than a handful of shared programs are required, name conflict will occur, and restrictions must be placed on which sets of programs any one user can invoke as part of a single subsystem. What is going wrong is simply that with a limited number of names available, one cannot make the universally usable name assignment needed to accomplish modular sharing.

4. Some examples of existing naming systems

Most existing systems exhibit one or more of the problems of the previous section. Two types of naming systems are commonly encountered: systems growing out of a programming language, and operating systems with their own, language-independent naming systems.

FORTRAN language systems are typical of the first type [IBM, 1961]. For purpose of discussion here, separately translated subprograms play the part of objects*. Each subprogram is given a name by its programmer, and may contain the names of other subprograms that it calls. When a set of

---

* The names of individual FORTRAN variables and arrays are handled by the compiler using another, distinct naming system.

subprograms is put together (an activity known as "loading"), a single, universal context is created associating each subprogram with its name. Uses of names by the subprograms of the set, for example where one subprogram calls another by name, are then resolved in this universal context. The creator of the set must be careful that all of the objects named in an included object are also included in the set. The set of loaded subprograms, linked together, is called a "program".

Because a universal context is used for all subprograms loaded together, two subprograms having the same name are incompatible. The common manifestation of this incompatibility is name conflicts discovered when two collections of subprograms, independently conceived and created, are brought together to be part of a single program.

Loading subprograms involves making copies of them. As discussed in the previous section, this copying precludes sharing of modifiable data among distinct programs. Some systems provide for successive programs to utilize data from previous programs by leaving the data in some fixed part of memory. Such successive programs then need to agree on the names for (positions of) the common data.

Loading a set of subprograms does not create another subprogram. Instead, the resulting program is of a different form, not acceptable input to a further loading operation, and not nameable. This change of form during loading constrains the use of modularity, since a previously loaded program cannot be named, and thus cannot be contained in another program being created by the loader.

In contrast with FORTRAN, APL language systems give each programmer a single context for resolving both APL function names and also all the individual variable names used in all the APL functions [Falkoff and Iverson, 1968]. This single context is called the programmer's "workspace".

APL functions are loaded into the workspace when they are created, or when they are copied from the workspace of another programmer.

Problems similar to those of FORTRAN arise in APL: name conflicts lead to incompatibility, and in the case of APL, name conflicts extend to the level of individual variables. The programmer must explicitly supply all contained objects. Copying objects from other workspaces precludes employing shared writable objects.

In an attempt to reduce the frequency of name conflicts, APL provides some relief from the single context constraint by allowing functions to declare private variables and placing these variables in a name-binding stack, thus creating a structured naming environment. Stacking has the effect that the names in a workspace may be dynamically re-bound, leading to unreliable name resolutions. When a function is entered, the names of any variables or other functions defined in that function are temporarily (for the life of that function invocation) added to the workspace stack, and if they conflict with names already defined they temporarily override all earlier mappings of those names. If the function then invokes a second function that uses one of the remapped names, the second function will use the first function's local data. The exact behavior of a function may therefore depend upon what local data has been created by the invoking function, or its invoker, and so forth. This strategy, named "call-chain name resolution," is a good example of sharing (any one function may be used, by name, by many other functions) but without modularity in the use of names.

Consider the problem faced by a team of three programmers creating a set of three APL functions. One programmer develops function A, which invokes both B and C. The second programmer independently writes function B, which itself invokes C. The third programmer writes function C. The second programmer finds that a safe choice of names for private temporary variables of B is impossible without knowing what variable names the other two programmers are using for communication. If the programmer of B names a variable "X" and declares it local to B, that use of the name "X" may disrupt communication between procedures A and C in the following scenario: suppose the other programmers happened to use the name "X" for communication. B's variable "X" lies along the call chain to C on some--but not all--invocations of C. Each programmer must know the list of all names used for intermodule communication by the others, in violation of the definition of modular sharing.

LISP systems have extremely flexible naming facilities, but the way they are conventionally used is very similar to APL systems [Moses, 1970]. Each user has a single context for use by all LISP functions. Functions of other users must be copied into the context of an employing function. Call-chain name resolution is used.

LISP is usually implemented with an internal cell-naming mechanism that eliminates naming problems within the scope of a single user's set of functions. The atoms, functions, and data of a single user are all represented as objects with unique cell names. When an object is created, it is bound to this cell name in a single context private to the user. (The implementation of this mechanism varies among LISP systems. It usually is built on operating system main-memory addressing mechanisms and a garbage collector or compactor.) These cell names usually cannot be re-bound, although they are a scarce resource and may be reallocated if they become unbound. Cell names are used by LISP objects to achieve reliable references to other LISP objects.

LISP permits modular sharing, through explicit creation of closure objects, comprising a function and the current call-chain context. When such a function is invoked, the LISP interpreter resolves names appearing in the function by using its associated context. The objects and data with bindings in the context contained in the closure are named with internal names. Internal names are also used by the closure to name the function and the context.

In many LISP systems the size of the name space of internal names is small enough that it can be exhausted relatively quickly by even the objects of a single application program. Thus potential sets of closures can be incompatible because they would together exhaust the internal name space.

As far as name conflicts are concerned, however, two closures are always compatible. Closures avoid dynamic call-chain name resolution. So within the confines of a single user's functions and data, LISP permits modular sharing through exclusive, careful use of closures*.

Most language systems, including those just discussed, have been designed to aid the single programmer in creating programs in isolation. It is only secondarily that they have been concerned with interactions among programmers in the creation of programs. A common form of response to this latter concern is to create a "library system". For example, the FORTRAN Monitor System for the IBM 709 provided an implicit universal context in the form of a library, which was a collection of subprograms with published names [IBM,1961]. If, after loading a set of programs, the loader discovered that one or more names was unresolvable in the context so far developed, it searched the library for subprograms with the missing names, and added them to the set being loaded. These library subprograms might themselves refer to other library subprograms by name, inducing a further library search. This system exhibited two kinds of problems. First, if a user forgot to include a subprogram, the automatic library search might discover a library subprogram that accidentally had the same name and include it, typically with

---

* This particular discipline is not a common one among LISP programmers, however. Closures are typically used only in cases where a function is to be passed or returned as an argument, and call-chain name resolution would likely lead to a mistake when that function is later used.

disastrous results. Second, if a FORTRAN subprogram intentionally called a library subprogram, it was in principle necessary to review the lists of all subprograms that that library subprogram called, all the subprograms they called, and so on, to be sure that conflicts with names of the user's other subprograms did not occur. (Both of these problems were usually kept under control by publishing the list of names of all subprograms in the libraries, and warning users not to choose names in that list for their own subprograms.)

A more elaborate form of response to the need for interaction among programmers is to develop a "file system" that can be used to create catalogs of permanent name-object bindings. Names used in objects are resolved automatically using as a context one of the catalogs of the file system. The names used to indicate files are consequently called "file names".

However, because all programmers use the same file system, conflict over the use of file names can occur. Therefore it is common to partition the space of file-names, giving part to each programmer. This partition is sometimes accomplished by assigning unique names to programmers and requiring that the first part of each file name be the name of the programmer choosing that file name.

On the other hand, so that programs can be of use to more than one programmer, file names appearing within a program and indicating objects that are closely related may be allowed to omit the programmer's name. This omission requires an additional sophistication of the name resolution mechanisms of the file system, which in turn must be used with care. For example, if an abbreviated name is passed as a parameter to a program created by another programmer, the name resolution mechanisms of the file system may incorrectly extend it when generating the full name of the desired object. Mistakes in extending abbreviated names are a common source of troubles in achieving reliable naming schemes.

As a programmer uses names in his partition of the file names, he may eventually find that he has already used all the mnemonically satisfying names. This leads to a desire for further subdivision and structuring of the space of file names, supported by additional conventions to name the partitions*. Permitting more sophisticated abbreviations then leads to more sophisticated mechanisms for extending those abbreviations into full file names. This in turn leads to even more difficulty in guaranteeing reliable naming.

Many systems permit re-binding of a name in the file system. However, one result of employing the objects of others is that the creator of an object may have no idea of whether or not that object is still named by other objects in the system. Systems that do not police re-binding are common; in such systems, relying on file names can lead to errors.

The preceding review makes it sound as though systems of the kinds mentioned have severe problems. In actual fact, there exist such systems that serve sizable communities and receive extensive daily use. One reason is that communities tend to adopt protocols and conventions for system usage that help programmers to avoid trouble. A second reason is that much of the use of file systems is interactive use by humans, in which case ambiguity can often be quickly resolved by asking a question.

In the remainder of this chapter, we shall examine the issues surrounding naming in more detail, and look at some strategies that provide some hope of supporting modular sharing, at least so far as name-binding is concerned.

5. <u>The need for names with different properties</u>

A single object may have many kinds of names, appearing in different contexts, and more than one of some kinds. This multiple naming effect arises from two sets of functional requirements:

---

* For example, Multics provided a tree-structured file naming system [Bensoussan, 1972].

1) Human versus computational use:

   a) Names intended for use by human beings (such as file names) should be (within limits) arbitrary-length character strings. They must be mnenomically useful, and therefore they are usually chosen by a human, rather than by the computer system. Ambiguity in resolving human-oriented names is often acceptable, since in interactive systems, the person using the name can be queried to resolve ambiguities.

   b) Names intended for computational use (such as the internal representation of pointer variables) need not have mnemonic value, but must be unambiguously resolvable. They are usually chosen by the system according to some algorithm that helps avoid ambiguity. In addition, when speed and space are considered, design optimization leads to a need for names that are fixed length, fairly short, strings of bits (for example, memory addresses).

2) Local versus universal names:

   a) In a system with multiple users, every object must have a distinct, unique identity. To go with this unique identity, there is often some form of universal name, resolvable in some universal context.

   b) Any individual user or program needs to be able to refer to objects of current interest with names that may have been chosen in advance without knowledge of the universal names. Modifying (and recompiling) the program to use the universal name for the object is sometimes an acceptable alternative, but it may also be awkward or impossible. In addition, for convenience, it is frequently useful to be able to assign temporary, shorthand names to objects whose universal names are unwieldy. Local names must, of course, be resolved in an appropriate local context.

Considering both of these sets of requirements at once leads to four combinations, most of which are useful. Further, since an object may be referred to by many other objects, it may have several different local names. As one might expect, most systems do not provide for four styles of names for every object. Instead, compromise forms are pressed into service for several functions. These compromises are often the root cause of the naming troubles mentioned in the previous section.

A further complication, especially in names intended for human consumption, is that one may need to have synonyms. A synonym is defined as two names in a single context that are bound to the same object or lower-level name*. For example, two universal names of a new PL/I compiler might be "library.languages.pℓ1" and "library.languages.new-pℓ1", with the intent being that if a call to either of those names occurs, the same program is to be used. Synonyms are often useful when two previously distinct contexts are combined for some reason.

Finally, a distinction must be made between two kinds of naming contexts: <u>unlimited</u>, and <u>limited</u>. In an unlimited naming context, every name assigned can be different from every other name that has ever been or ever will be assigned in that context. Character string names are usually from unlimited naming contexts, as are unique identifiers, by definition. In a limited context the names themselves are a scarce resource that must be allocated and, most importantly, must be reused. Addresses in a location-addressed physical memory system, processor register numbers, and indexes of entries in a fixed size table are examples of names from a limited context.

---

* Note that when a higher-level name is bound, through a context, to a lower-level name, the higher and lower level names are <u>not</u> considered synonyms.

One usually speaks of _creating_ or _destroying_ an object that is named in an unlimited context, while speaking of _allocating_ or _deallocating_ an object that is named in a limited context.* Names for a limited context are usually chosen from a compact set of integers, and this compactness property can be exploited to provide a rapid, hardware-assisted implementation of name resolution, using the names as indexes into an array.

Because of the simplicity of implementation of limited contexts, the innermost layers of most systems use them in preference to unlimited contexts. Those inner layers can then be designed to implement sufficient function, such as a very large virtual memory, that some intermediate layer can implement an unlimited context for use of outer layers and user applications.

6. _Plan of study_

Up to this point, we have seen a general pattern for the use of names, a series of examples of systems with various kinds of troubles in their naming strategies, and a variety of other considerations surrounding the use of names in computer systems. In the remainder of this chapter, we shall develop step-by-step two related, comprehensive naming systems, one for use by programs in referring to the objects they compute with (an _addressing architecture_,) and one for use by humans interactively directing the course of the programs they operate (a _file system_). We shall explore the way in which these two model naming systems interact, and some implementation considerations that typically affect naming systems in practice. Finally, we shall briefly describe some research problems regarding naming in distributed computer systems.

---

* Both the name for the object and resources for its representation may be allocated (or deallocated) at the same time, but these two allocation (or deallocation) operations should be kept conceptually distinct.

B. **An architecture for addressing shared objects**

An addressing architecture is an example of a naming system using computation-interpretable names, in which the program interpreter is usually a hardware processor. Although we shall see points of contact between these machine-oriented names and the corresponding human-oriented character string names, those contacts are incidental to the primary purpose of the addressing architecture, which is to allow flexible name resolution at high speed. Typically, the interpretation of a single machine instruction will require one name resolution to identify which instruction should be performed and one or more name resolutions to identify the operands of the instruction, so the addressing architecture must resolve names as rapidly as the hardware processor interprets instructions in order not to become a severe bottleneck.

Figure 2 illustrated an ordinary location-addressed memory system. Sharing is superficially straightforward in a location-addressed memory system: an object is named by its location, and that name can be embedded in any number of other objects. However, using physical locations as names guarantees that the context is limited. If there exist more objects than will fit in memory at once, names must be reused, and reuse of names can lead to name conflict. Further, since selective substitution requires multiple contexts, the single context of a location-addressed memory system appears inherently inadequate. To solve these problems, we must develop a more hospitable (and unfortunately more elaborate) addressing architecture.

The first step in this development is to interpose an object map between the processor and the location-addressed memory system, as in figure 4 , producing a structured memory system. Physical addresses of the location-addressed memory system appear only in the object map, and the processor must use logical names--object numbers--to refer to stored objects. The object map acts as an automatically supplied context for

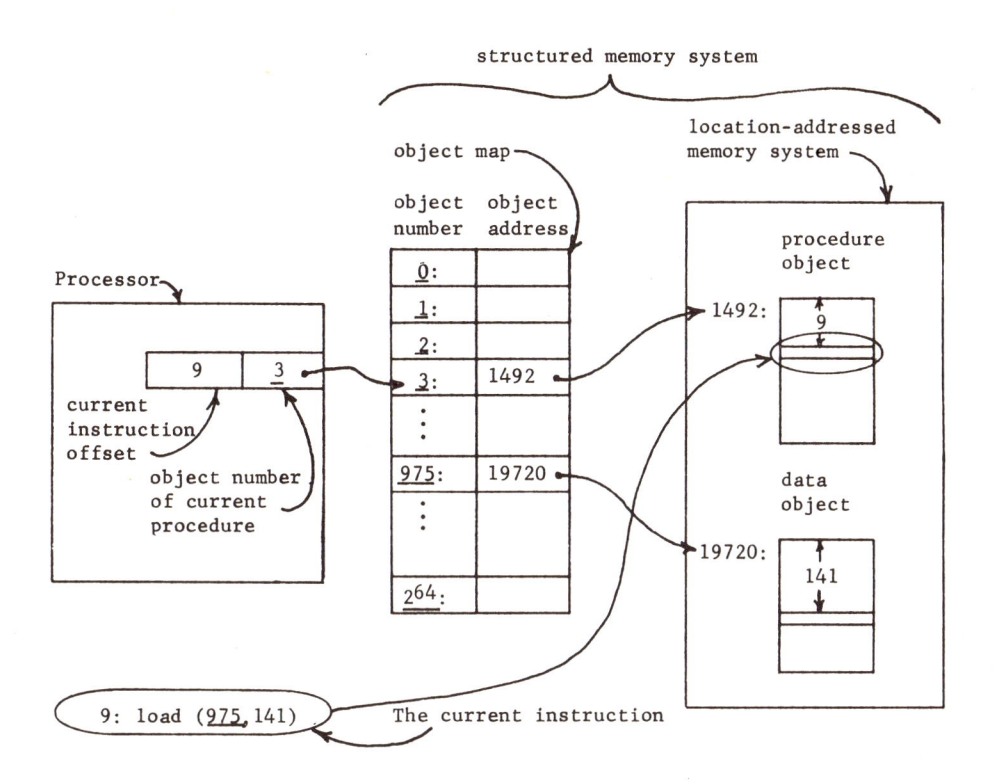

Figure 4 -- The structured memory system. The processor is executing
instruction 9 of procedure object 3, located at address
1501 in the memory. That instruction refers to location
141 of data object 975, located at address 19861 in the
memory. The columns of the object map relate the object
number to the physical address. In a practical implementation, one might add more columns to the object map to
hold further information about the object. For example,
for a segment object, one might store the length of the
segment, and include checking hardware to insure that all
data offsets are of values within the length of the segment.

resolving object numbers provided by the processor; it resolves these object numbers into addresses in the location-addressed memory to which it is directly attached. We assume that this one object map provides a universal context for all programs, all users, and all real or virtual processors of the system, and that the range of values is large enough to provide an unlimited context; the object numbers are thus unique identifiers. To simplify future figures, we redraw figure 4 as in figure 5, with the unique identifiers directly labeling the objects to which they are bound. We can now notice that the procedure has embedded within itself the name of its data object; the context in which this name is interpreted is the same universal context in which the processor's instruction address is interpreted, namely the object map of the structured memory system. We shall occasionally describe this name embedded in the procedure as an outward reference, to distinguish it from references by the procedure to itself.

Since the structured memory system provides an unlimited context, the procedure can contain the name of the data object without knowing in advance anything about the names of objects contained in the data. Further, if the location-addressed memory system is small, one set of programs and data can be placed in it at one time, and another set later, with some objects in common but without worry about name conflict. We have provided for modular sharing, though with a minor constraint. The procedure cannot choose its own name for the data object, it must instead use the unique identifier for the data object previously assigned by the system. Table I will be used as a way of recording our progress toward a more flexible addressing architecture. Its first two columns

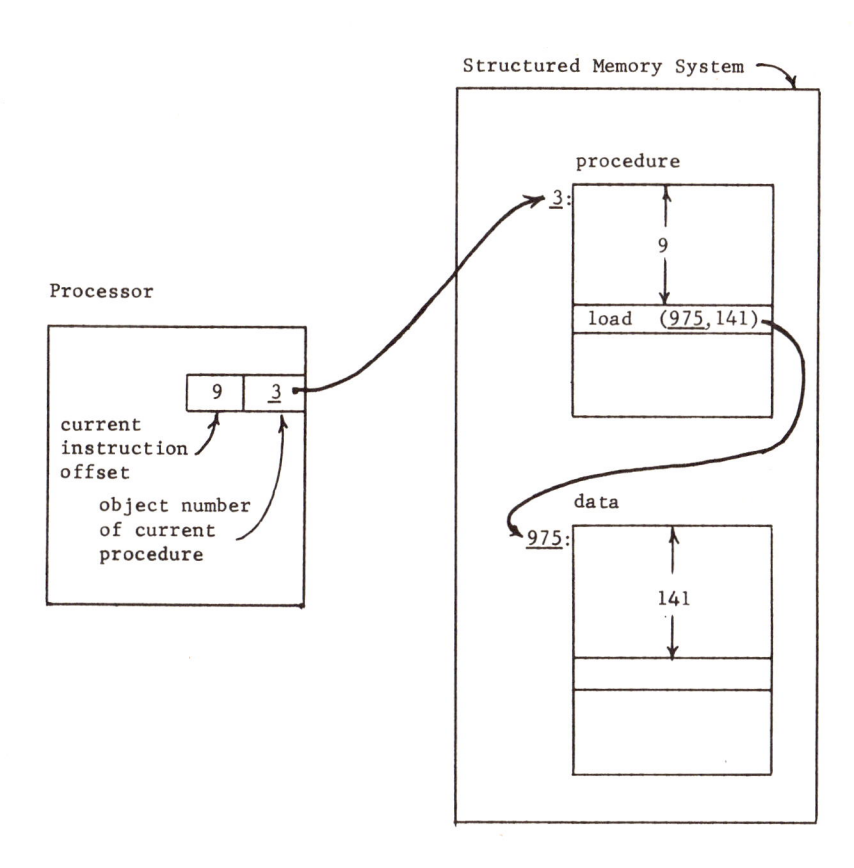

Figure 5 -- The structured memory system of figure 4 with the object map assumed and therefore not shown. Note that the procedure object contains the name of the data object, _975_. To emphasize the existence of the context that the now-hidden object map implements, all object numbers in this and the following figures are italicized (underlined).

Table I -- Naming objectives and the addressing architecture

Naming Objective	architectural feature					
	Location Addressed Memory System	Structured Memory System	SMS with pointer register context	SMS with context objects	SMS with closure table	SMS with closures and name source register
sharing of components	yes	yes	yes	yes	yes	yes
sharing of component objects without knowing subcomponents	no	yes	yes	yes	yes	yes
sharing procedure components with user-dependent binding of subcomponent names	no	no	yes	yes	yes	yes
ability to easily change contexts on procedure calls	no	no	no	yes	yes	yes
automatic change of context on procedure calls	no	no	no	no	yes	yes
sharing data objects with user-dependent binding of subcomponent names	no	no	no	no	no	yes

indicate the effect of adding an object map that allows unique identifiers as object names.* Its later columns and lower rows are the subjects of the next few sections.

1. **User-dependent bindings and multiple naming contexts**

As our system stands, every object that uses names is required to use this single universal context. Although this shared context would appear superficially to be an ideal support for sharing of objects, it goes too far; it is difficult to avoid sharing. For example, suppose that the data object of figure 5 should be private to the user of the program, and there are two users of the same program. One approach would be to make a copy of the procedure, which copy would then have a different object number, and modify the place in the copy where it refers to the data object, putting there the object number of a second data object. From the point of view of modularity, this last step seems particularly disturbing since it requires modifying a program in order to use it. What is needed is a user-dependent binding between the name used by the program and the private object.

Improvement on this scheme requires that we somehow provide a naming context for the procedure that can be different for different users. An obvious approach is to give each user a separate processor, and then to make the context depend on which processor is in use.** This approach leads to figure 6, in which two processors are shown, and to provide

---

* Although unique-identifier object maps have been proposed [Radin and Schneider, 1976; Redell, 1974] there seem to be formidable problems in implementing unlimited contexts in hardware (a very large map may be needed, thereby producing interactions with multilevel memory management) and most real object addressing systems provide limited contexts that are just large enough to allow short-lived computations to act as though the context were unlimited. Multics [Bensoussan et al., 1972] was a typical example.

** In the usual case that there are not enough real hardware processors to go around, one would implement virtual processors in their place. This discussion will continue to use the term "processor" for the program interpreter, since from the point of view of naming, it is of no concern whether a processor is virtual or real.

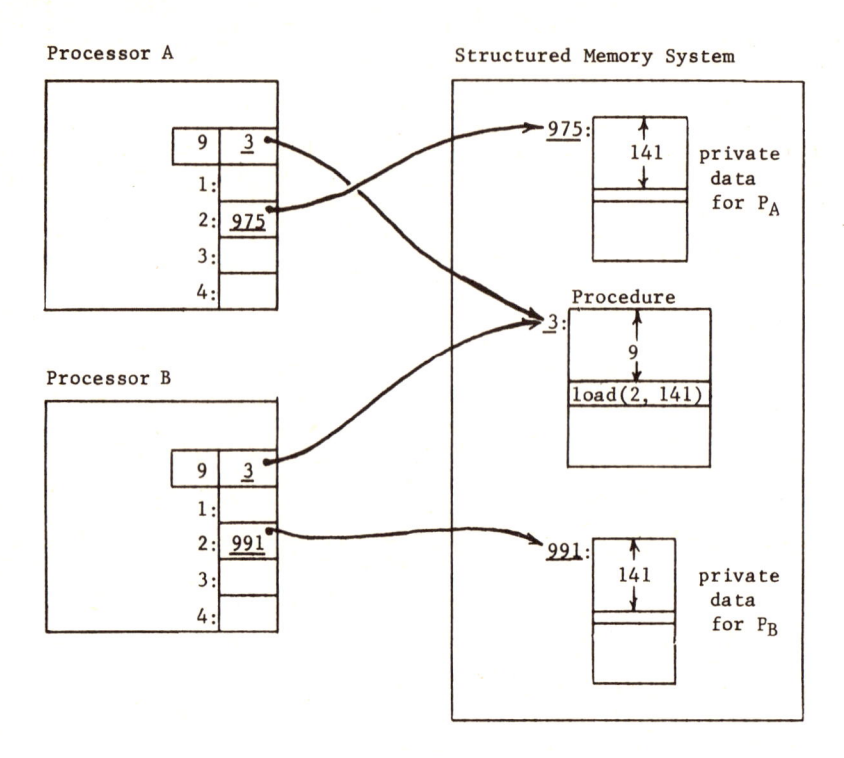

Figure 6 -- Addition of pointer registers to the processor, to permit a single procedure to have a processor-dependent naming context.

a per-user context each processor has been outfitted with an array of pointer registers, each of which can hold one object number. The name-interpreting mechanics of the processor must be more elaborate now, since interpretation of a name will involve going through two layers of contexts.

This more elaborate name interpretation goes as follows: the pointer registers are numbered, and the processor interprets an operand reference, which used to be an object number, as a register number instead. The register number names a register, whose contents are taken by the processor to be an object number in the context of the structured memory system.

Thus, in figure 6, the current instruction now reads "load (2,141)" with the intent that the name "2" be resolved in the context of the processor registers. If processor A resolves "2", it finds object number 975, which is the name of the desired object in the context of the structured memory system. Thus when processor A interprets the operand reference of the instruction (3,9) it will obtain the 141st item of object 975. Similarly, when processor B interprets the same operand reference, it will obtain the 141st item of object 991.

We have thus arranged that a procedure can be shared without the onerous requirement that everything to which the procedure refers must also be shared-- we are permitting selective user-dependent bindings for objects contained by procedure objects.

The binding of object numbers to particular objects was provided by the structured memory system, which chose an object number for each newly created object and returned that object number to the requester as an output value. We have not yet described any systematic way of binding register numbers to object numbers. Put more bluntly, how did register two get loaded with the appropriate object number, different in the two processors? Suppose the procedure were created by a compiler. The choice that register name "2" should be used would have been made by the compiler, so in accordance with the standard pattern for using names, the compiler should also provide for binding of that name to the correct object. In this case, it might do so as in figure 7 , by producing as output not only the procedure object containing the "load" instruction, but also the necessary context binding information. If the procedure uses several pointer registers, the context binding information should describe how to set up each of the needed registers. As shown, the context binding information is a high level language description of the context needed by the procedure; this high level description must be reduced to a machine understandable version of the context for the program to run. The combination of the program and its context binding information is properly viewed as a prototype of a closure.*

The same technique can be used by the compiler to arrange for the procedure to access a shared data object, too. Suppose, for example, the compiler determines from declarations of the program that variable b is to be private (that is, per-processor) while variable a is to be shared by all users of this procedure. In that case it might create, at compilation time, an object to hold variable a (say in location 5 of that object) and include its object number with the context binding information as in figure 8 . The result would be the pattern of reference shown in figure 9 .

Translation from the high level context description of figure 8 to the register context of figure 9 is accomplished by a program known

---

* In the terms of programming language semantics, the compiler is a function that produces as its output value another function: this output function contains free variables planted in it by the compiler and that should be bound in a way specified by the compiler. Thus the compiler should return not a function, but a closure that provides for binding of the free variables of the enclosed function.

input to compiler:

```
.
.
a ← b
.
.
```

Compiler

output from compiler:

① text

```
.
.
.
load (2, 141)
.
.
.
```

② Context binding information

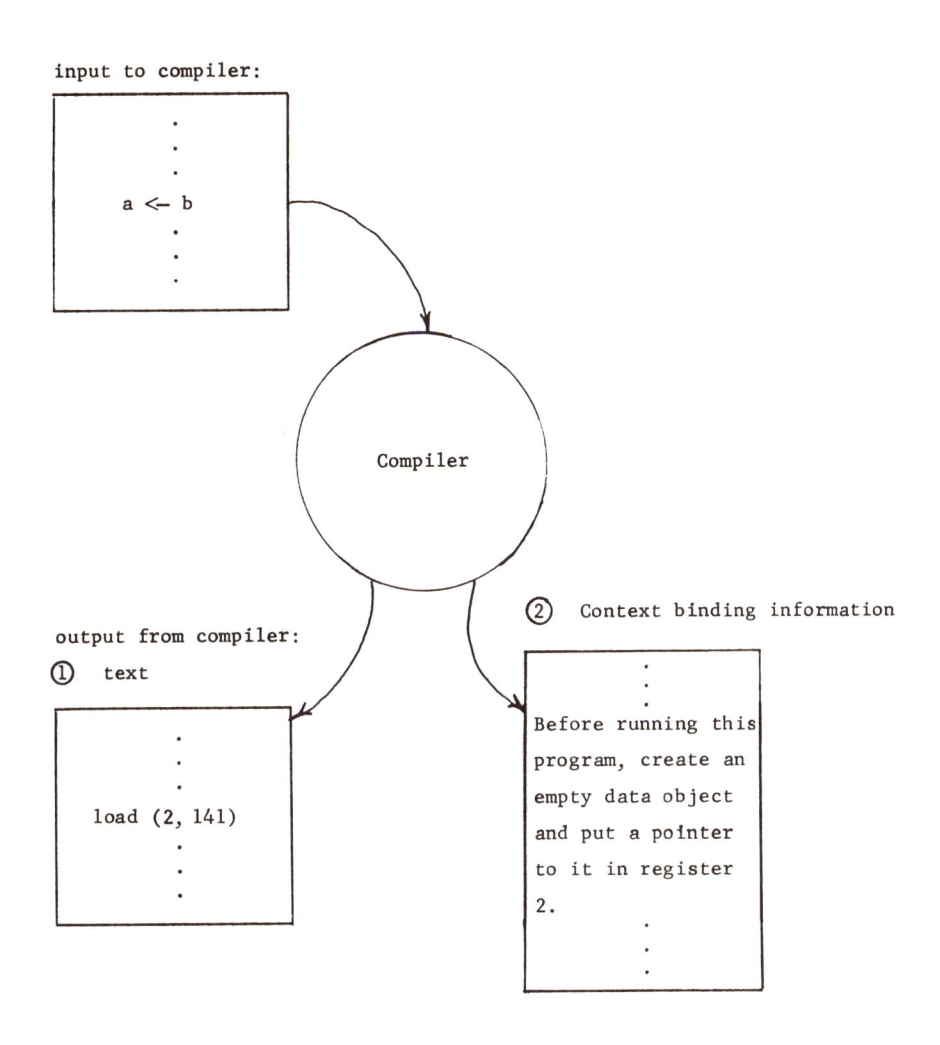

```
.
.
.
Before running this
program, create an
empty data object
and put a pointer
to it in register
2.
.
.
.
```

Figure 7 -- When a per-processor addressing context is used, one of the outputs of the compiler is information about the bindings needed to create that context. In this example, the empty data object should have had some values placed in it (by earlier instructions in this program) before the load instruction is encountered.

input:

```
      .
      .
      .
   a ← b
      .
      .
      .
```

Compiler

output text:
```
      .
      .
      .
  load  (2, 141)
  store (3, 5)
      .
      .
```

output context:

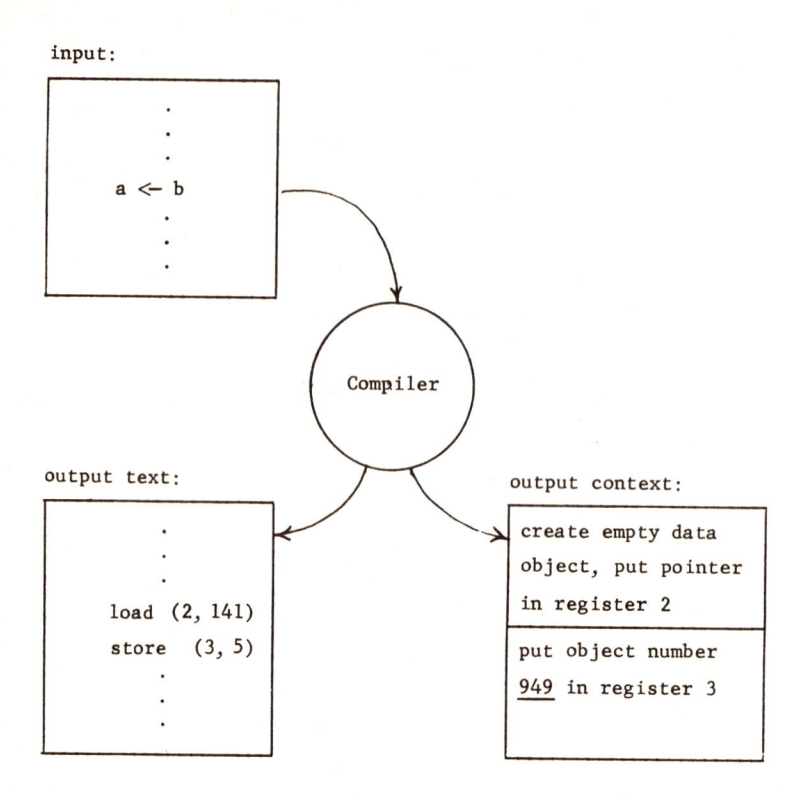

| create empty data object, put pointer in register 2 |
| put object number 949 in register 3 |

Figure 8 -- Shared data objects can be handled by appropriate entries in the context part of the compiler's output. This output context produces the reference pattern of figure 9.

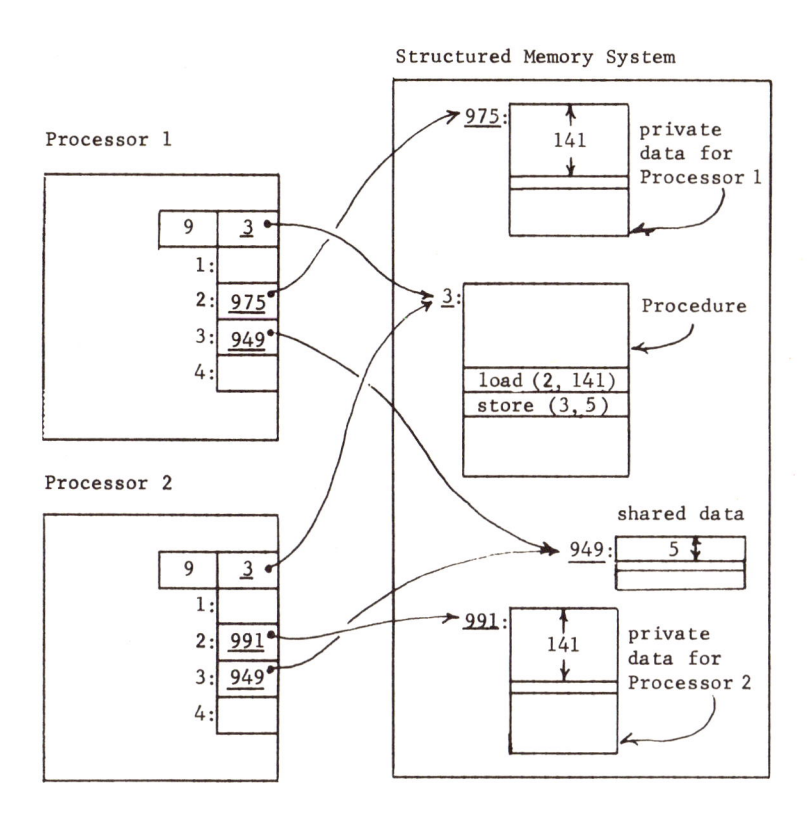

Figure 9 -- A shared procedure, using both per-processor private data and shared data, with a context in the processor registers and bindings supplied by the compiler of figure 8 .

here as a context initializer* and most such programs permit a wider variety of object interlinking possibilities than illustrated in figure 8. Before getting into that subject, we should first consider three elaborations on the naming conventions already described.

2. Larger contexts and context switching

In order to achieve user-dependent bindings, we have arranged that each procedure has its own private context, so the first of these elaborations is to arrange for switching from one context to another when calling from one procedure to another. We encounter an interesting implementation dilemma: how many pointer registers should be provided? If there are only a few, some procedure will undoubtedly need to refer to more objects than there are available pointer registers. (Recall that a limited context is a common naming problem.) On the other hand, if there are a large number, context switching will require reloading all of them, which could be time-comsuming. This dilemma can be resolved by moving the processor context into memory, in a data object, and leaving behind a single processor register, the current context pointer, that points to this context object. Now, a single register swap will suffice to change contexts, at the cost of making the name interpreter more complex and, maybe, slower. Figure 10 illustrates this architecture, figure 11 shows the corresponding changes needed in the context-establishing information that the compiler must supply, and Table I continues to chart our progress**. With this addition to the addressing architecture, in preparation for context switching, we should note that we have quietly introduced explicit closures. The processor now contains a pair of pointers, to a procedure and to a context for the procedure: this pair of

---
* Various other names for this program are loader, linker, link-editor, or binder.

** For an example of this form of architecture, in Multics the linkage section played the role of the context object, a linker initialized it, and compilers routinely produced prototype linkage sections as part of their output. One of the processor base registers, known as the linkage pointer, played the part of the current context pointer. [Daley and Dennis, 1968].

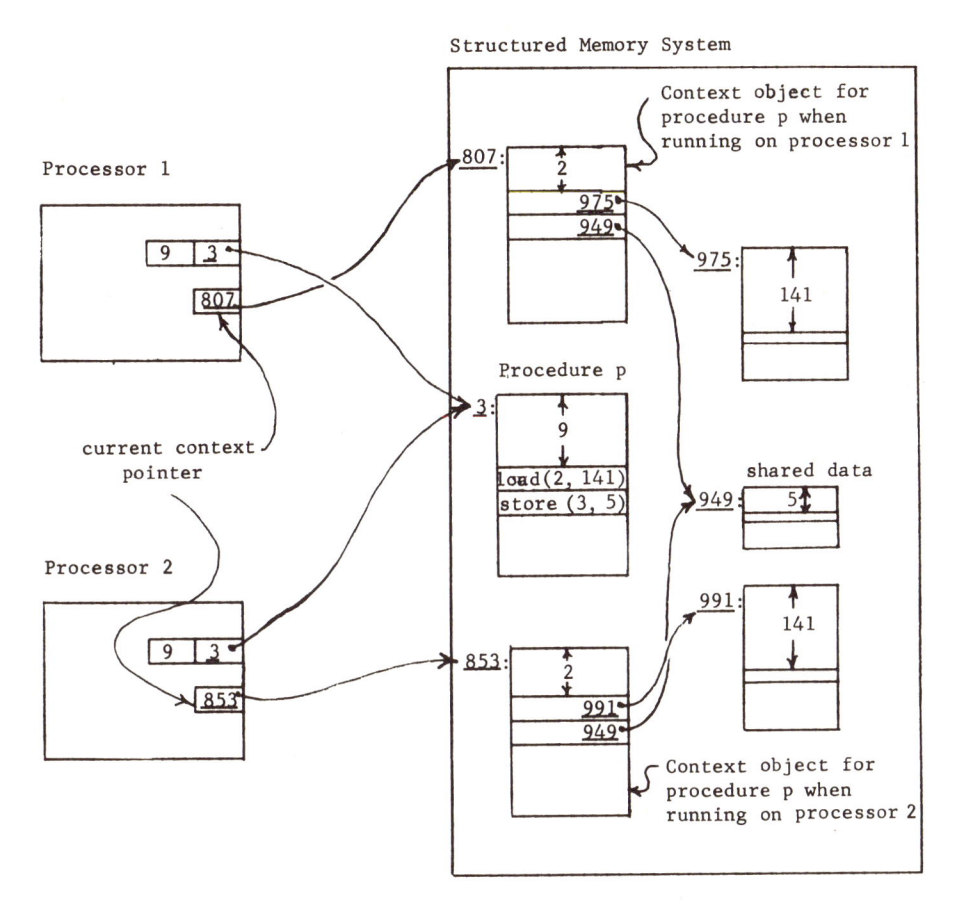

Figure 10 -- By placing the per-processor context in a data object in memory, and adding a current context pointer register to the processor, the context is not limited to the number of processor registers. Instead, all addresses are assumed to be interpreted indirectly relative to the segment named by the current context pointer. For example, the instruction at location (3,9) in procedure p contains the address (2,141). The name "2" is resolved by referring to the second location of the object named by the current context pointer. All of the context objects for a given procedure have the same layout, as determined by the compiler, but the bindings to other objects can differ. Note that the combination of the current context pointer and the current instruction pointer in any one processor represents an object, the current closure.

input:

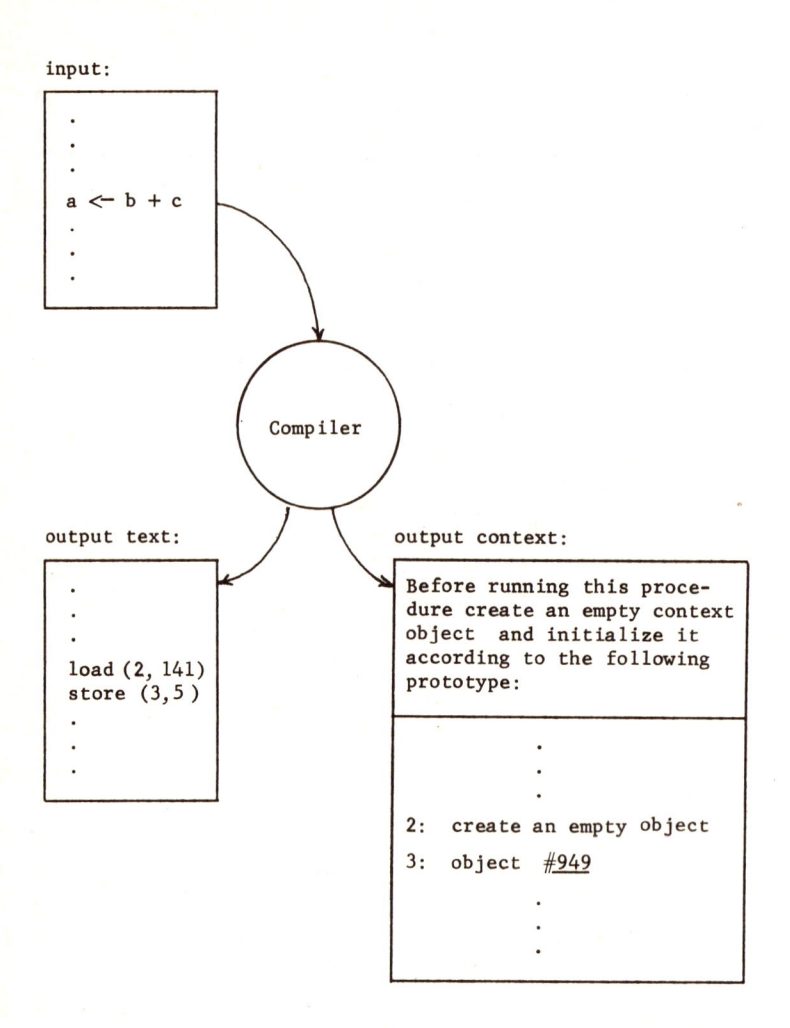

```
.
.
.
a ← b + c
.
.
.
```

Compiler

output text:
```
.
.
.
load (2, 141)
store (3, 5)
.
.
```

output context:

Before running this procedure create an empty context object and initialize it according to the following prototype:

```
     .
     .
     .
2:   create an empty object
3:   object  #949
     .
     .
     .
```

Figure 11 -- Compiler output needed to initialize the context objects of figure 10. In addition to the instructions provided by the compiler, one further step is needed: just before calling procedure "p", the object number of its context object for this processor must be loaded into the current context pointer register.

pointers can be considered to be an object in its own right, a closure. (In a moment we shall take the final step of placing these explicit closures in memory.)

The establishment of the context for resolving names of the procesure spans **three different times**:

1) compile time, when names within the context object are assigned, and the compiler creates the context-establishing information with the aid of declarations of the source program,
2) just before the program is first run, when the context initializer creates and fills in the context object and creates any private data objects,
3) just before each execution of the program, when part of the calling sequence loads the current context pointer register with a pointer to the context object.

We have distinguished between the second and the third times in this sequence on the chance that the program will be used more than once, without need for reinitialization, by the same processor. In that case, on second and later uses of the program, only the third step may be required.

The second elaboration of our per-procedure context scheme is to provide for automatically changing the context when control of the processor passes from one procedure to another. Suppose, for example, the procedure "p" calls procedure "q". In that case, as control passes from "p" to "q" the current context pointer of this processor should change from the processor's context object for "p" to the processor's context object for "q"; upon return of control, the context pointer should change back. In terms of the naming model, the meaning of a call is that the processor should switch its attention from one closure to another.

Mechanically, we may accomplish these changes by adding one more per-processor object: a <u>closure table</u>, which contains a mapping from procedure object number to the private context object number for every procedure used by this processor. At the same time, we replace the current context pointer with a processor register that contains the object number of the closure table. The name interpreting part of the processor must once again be made more complex. To interpret a name, found as the operand part of an instruction, the processor first uses the closure table pointer and the object number of the next instruction register to look up in this processor's closure table the object number of this procedure's context. It can then proceed as before to interpret the name in that context. Figure 12 illustrates this new <u>closure table pointer register</u>, and a typical object layout just before a call. The call instruction, after resolving the name "4" in the current context to be object number <u>98</u>, inserts that number in the object number part of the instruction location counter. From then on, the processor will automatically use the context object for procedure "q" in resolving names. When procedure "q" returns to "p", the context automatically is restored to that of "p" when the object number part of the instruction location counter is reset to the object number of "p".* Table I again identifies the additional function gained.

---

* We have not specified the way in which procedure "p" tells procedure "q" where its arguments are located or where to return, because it would lead to a distracting discussion of calling mechanisms. Both the return point and the arguments should be viewed as temporary bindings to names already in some naming context of "q", and some machinery is needed both to effect those temporary bindings and to reverse them when "q" returns. For example, the argument addresses and the return point might be pushed onto a stack by "p" and popped off the stack by "q" when it returns. The top frame of the stack is then properly viewed as a distinct naming context for "q". Automatic hardware to perform all the functions of a procedure call is becoming commonplace, as in Multics [Schroeder and Saltzer, 1974] and the Cambridge Capability System [Needham, 1972]. Both of these systems had versions of the closure table in some form.

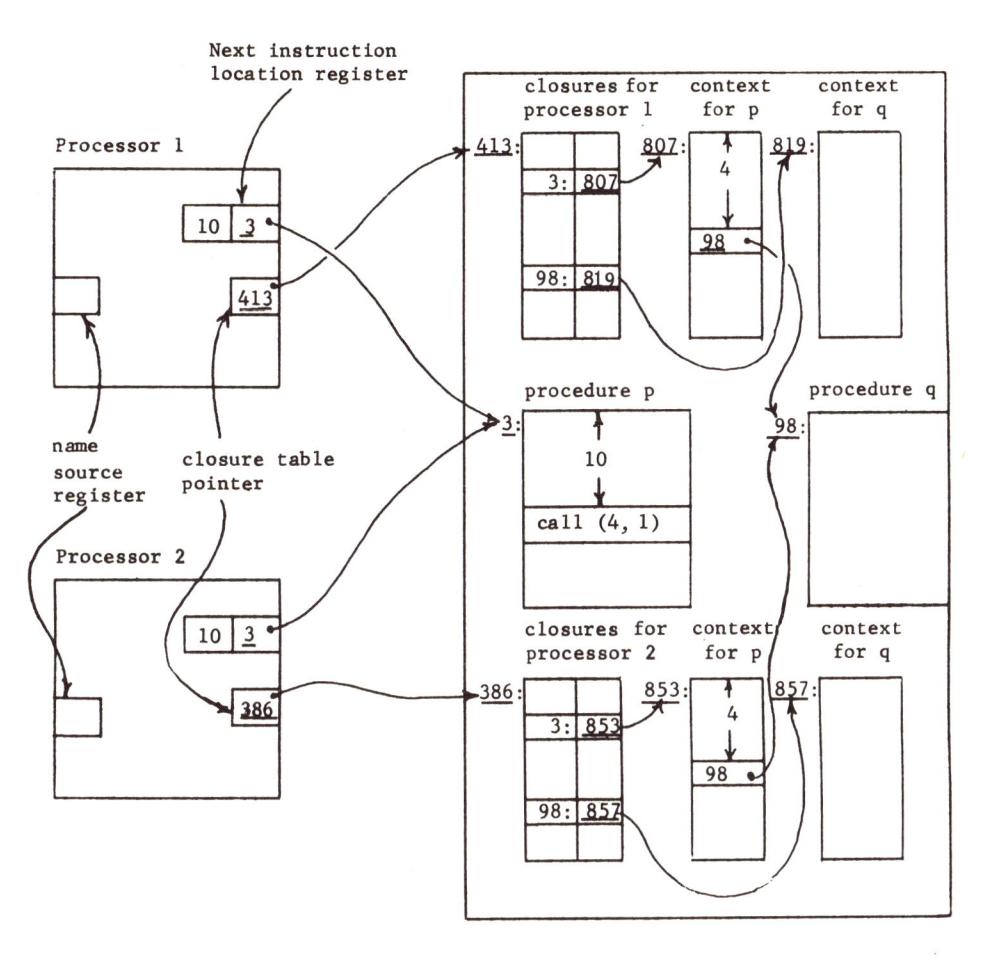

Figure 12 -- Context switching. Procedure "p" is just about to call
procedure "q", in both processors. The current context
for resolving names is located in two steps, starting
with the closure table pointer and the object number
of the current procedure. This pair (for processor 1,
the pair is (413,3)) leads to a location containing the
context for "p" (for processor 1, p's context is object
807). Note that the call instruction in procedure "p"
refers to its target using a name in the context for "p"
exactly as was the case for data references. The name
source register enters the picture when data objects refer
to other data objects, as described in the text.

The final elaboration, which is actually omitted in most real systems, is to provide for the possibility that a shared data object should have a user-dependent context. This possibility would be required if it is desired to share some data object without sharing all of its component objects. Such user-dependent binding of course requires that the data object have a per-processor context, just like a procedure object, and one's initial reaction is that figure 12 seems to apply if we are careful to create a context for each such data object and place a pointer to it in the appropriate closure table. A problem arises, though, if we follow a reference by a procedure to a data object and thence to a component named in that object, an operation that may be called an _indirect_ reference. Consider first the direct data reference that occurs if the instruction

$$\text{get} \quad (19,7)$$

is executed. The number "19" is a name in the current procedure's context object, which selects a pointer to the data object, and the number "7" is an offset within that object; the result would be to retrieve the 7th word and perhaps put it in an arithmetic register. Now suppose the instruction

$$\text{get } (19,7)*$$

is executed, with the asterisk meaning to follow an indirect reference. Presumably, location 7 of the data object contains, instead of an arithmetic item, an outward reference (say (4,18)) that should be interpreted relative to the per-processor context object associated with this data object by the closure table. If we are not careful, the processor may get the wrong context, for example, the context of the current procedure. To be careful, we can explicitly put in the processor a _name source register_ that the processor always automatically loads with the object number of the object from which it obtained the name it is currently resolving. To obtain the correct context, the processor always uses the current value of the name source register as the index into the closure table. Since it obtains most names from instructions of the current procedure, the name source register will usually contain the object number of the current procedure. However, whenever an indirect reference chain is being followed, the name source register follows along, assuring that for each indirect reference evaluated, the correct context object will be used*.

Another interesting problem arises when a program stores a name into an object. The program must also ensure that the name is correctly bound in the context where that object's names are resolved. Such an operation would occur if dynamic rearrangement of the internal organization of a partially shared structured object were required. Again, since most programming languages do not permit partially shared structures, they also do not provide semantics for rearranging such structures.

We should also note that when a procedure or data object refers to an object by name, we have constructed a fairly elaborate mechanism to resolve the name, to wit:

1) The closure table pointer and the name source register are read to form an address in the closure table.

2) The closure table is read to retrieve the current context object number.

---

* As mentioned, the elaboration of a pointer source register is rarely required, because per-processor data contexts are rarely implemented in practice. (One example of a pointer source register appeared in the Honeywell 68/80 protection ring hardware [Schroeder and Saltzer, 1974].) Most programming languages have no provision at all for describing data objects that have per-user private contexts. The TENEX copy-on-write feature can be interpreted as an example of per-user data contexts [Murphy, 1972].

3) The current context object number and the originally presented name of the object are used to form an address within the current context object.

4) The current context object is read to obtain the object number of the desired object.

5) The object number of the object is combined with the offset to form an address for the data reference.

6) The data is read or written.

Thus for each data access, three accesses to the structured memory subsystem (steps 2, 4, and 6) are required. And we might expect that inside the structured memory subsystem, a single access may require three accesses to the location-addressed memory system, if both an object table and also block allocation (paging) are used. Thus it appears that we could be requiring a nine to one expansion of the rate of memory accesses over that required for a single data reference. One solution to this problem lies in speed-up tricks of various kinds, the simplest being addition to the front of the structured memory system of a small but very fast buffer memory for frequently used data items. Since the processor's name interpreter refers to the current context object once for every instruction that has an operand reference, its object number would almost certainly remain in even the smallest buffer memory. A similar observation applies to frequently resolved names within the context. Thus, although there are many memory references, most of them can be made to a very fast memory.

A second approach is to reduce the number of object-to-object cross references. Depending on the level of dynamics that a set of programs actually uses, it may be feasible to prebind many references, and thereby avoid exercising much of the addressing architecture. For example, in figure 12 , a "prebinder" may be able to take procedure p and procedure q, and construct from them a single procedure object with a single, combined context, and with the call from p to q replaced by an internal reference. In effect, the prebinder replaces containment by name with containment by copy. This kind of prebinding would be appropriate if p and q are always used together, and there are no name conflicts in their outward references. Doing prebinding irrevocably commits the connection between p and q; a user of the combined procedure cannot substitute a different version of q. If an application is sufficiently static in nature, and does not share writeable objects with other applications, one could in principle prebind all of the objects of that application into a single big object containing only self-references, and thereby completely avoid use of any special hardware architecture support at all. Such a strategy might be valuable in converting a system from development to production. The development system might over use a software interpreted version of the addressing architecture. The extreme slowness of such software interpretation would be less important during development, and prebinding would eliminate the interpretation when the production system is generated.

3. Binding on demand, and binding from higher-level contexts

Figure 12 illustrates a static arrangement of contexts surrounding procedures, but does not offer much insight into how such an arrangement might come into existence. Since there are two levels of contexts, there are now two levels of context initialization. The creation of a new virtual processor must include the creation of a new, empty closure table and the placement of the object number of that table in the closure table pointer of the new virtual processor. The filling in of the closure table,

and the creation and filling in of individual contexts, may be done at the
same time, by the creator of the virtual processor. Alternatively the creator
may supply only one entry in the closure table, and one minimally completed
context for the context initializer procedure itself, and expect that procedure to fill in the remainder of its own context and add more context
objects to the closure table as those entries are needed.

This latter procedure we shall term <u>binding on demand</u>*, and it is
usually implemented by adding to the processor the ability to recognize
empty entries in a context or the closure table. When it detects an empty
entry, the processor temporarily suspends its normal sequence, saves its
current state, and switches control to an entry point of the context initializer
program. (The processor may have a special register that was previously set to
contain a pointer to the context initializer. Alternatively, it may just
transfer to a standard address, in some standard context, with the assumption that that address has been previously set to contain an instruction
that transfers to the context initializer.) The context initializer examines
the saved processor state, to interpret the current address reference so as to
determine which entry in which context is missing, and proceeds to initialize
that entry.

Binding on demand is a useful feature in an on-line programming
system, in which a person at a terminal is interactively guiding the course
of the computation. In such a situation it is frequently the case that a
single path through a procedure, out of many possible paths, will be followed,
and that therefore many of the potential outward references of the procedure
will not actually be used. For example, programs designed for interactive
use often contain checks for typing errors or other human blunders, and

---

* The term <u>dynamic linking</u> was used in Multics, one of the few systems that actually implemented this idea (Daley and Dennis, 1968].

when an error is detected, invoke successively more elaborate recovery
strategies, depending on the error and the result of trying to repair it.
On the other hand, if the human user makes no error, the error recovery
machinery will not be invoked, and there is no need for its contexts to
have been initialized. For another example, consider the construction
of a large program as a collection of subprograms. It can be important
for one programmer to begin trying out one or a few of the subprograms
before the other programmers have finished writing their parts. Again,
if the programmer can, by adjusting input values, guide the computation
through the program in such a way as to avoid paths that contain calls to
unwritten subprograms, it may be possible to check out much of the logic
of the program. Such partial checkout requires the ability to initialize
partially a context (leaving out entries for non-existent subprograms).*

A second idea related to context initialization stems from the
suggestion, made earlier, that a context initializer can perform more
elaborate operations than simply creating empty data objects or copying
object numbers determined at compile time. Returning to figure 11, the
compiler creates a prototype context object for use by the context
initializer. If the context initializer were prepared for it, this prototype could also contain an entry of the form "look for an object named
'cosine' and put its object number in this entry of the context". This
idea requires that the name "cosine" be a name in some naming context
usable by the context initializer, and it is really asking the context

---

* Binding on demand is an idea closely related to a programming language
technique named <u>lazy evaluation,</u> in which either binding or calculation
or both are systematically postponed until it is apparent that the result
is actually needed. [Henderson and Morris, 1976].

initializer to perform the final binding, by looking up that name at run
time, discovering the object number, and binding it in the context being
initialized. There are several situations in which it might be advantageous
to do such binding from a higher-level context at context initialization
time rather than at compile time:

1) The program is intended to run on several different computer
   systems and those different systems may use different object
   numbers for their copies of the contained objects.

2) At the time the program is compiled, the contained object does
   not yet exist, and no object number is available. However,
   a symbolic name for it can be chosen. (This situation
   arises in the large-system programming environment mentioned
   before. It also arises when programs call one another
   recursively.)

3) There may be several versions of the contained object, and the
   programmer wants control at execution time of which version
   will be used on a particular run of the program.

Bindings provided at compile time are created with the aid of declaration
statements appearing inside the program being compiled. As we shall see,
bindings created at run time must be created with the aid of declarations
external to, but associated with, the program. It is exactly because the
declarations are external to the program that we obtain the flexibility
desired in the three situations described above.

Most computer operating systems provide some form of highly structured,
higher-level, symbolic naming system for objects that allows the human programmer or user of the system to group, list, and arrange the object with
which he works: source programs, compiled procedures, data files, messages,

and so on. This higher-level context, the file system, is designed primarily for the convenience of people, rather than programs. Among typical features of a file system designed for interactive use by humans are synonymous names, abbreviations, the ability to rename objects, to rearrange them, and to reorganize structures.

A program, in referring to computational objects, usually does so in an addressing architecture like that developed up to this point, using names that are intelligible to hardware, and explicitly attempting to avoid potential troubles such as uncertain name resolutions, name conflict, and incorrect expansion of abbreviations. Thus the machine-oriented program addressing architecture is usually made as distinct and independent as possible from the human-oriented file system. The program context initializer, however, acts as a bridge between these two worlds, prepared to take symbolic names found in the program execution environment, interpret them in the context of the file system, and return to the program execution environment an object binding that is to match the programmer's intent.

Development of the higher-level file system and that part of the program context initializer that uses it is our next topic. First, however, it may be helpful to review, in Table II , all of the examples of naming and name binding that occur in our addressing architecture alone. This table emphasizes two points. First, in even a simple naming system there are many examples of naming and name binding. Second, in the course of implementation of appropriate name-binding facilities for modular programming, there are many places in which naming is itself used as an internal

Table II -- Examples of naming and binding in the model of addressing architecture.

	object that contains the name	form of the name	closure implementation	context
1.	location-addressed memory system	none	none	none (objects are directly included)
2.	object map	absolute address of object	name interpreter has only one choice	location-addressed memory system
3.	virtual processor retrieving instructions	procedure object number	name interpreter has only one choice	object map
		instruction location counter	procedure object number register	procedure object
4.	procedure context object	object number	only one choice	object map
5.	procedure object	offset within context object	closure table	procedure context object
6.	closure table	object number of context object	only one choice	object map
7.	processor retrieving operand, step 1 of name interpretation	procedure object number	closure pointer	closure table
8.	processor retrieving operand, step 2 of name interpretation	offset within context	dynamically constructed in step 1	procedure context
9.	symbolic name in prototype context	symbolic object name	supplied by context initializer	file system
10.	symbolic name in source program	name resolvable to compile time	supplied by compiler	file system
		name not resolvable at compile time	containment in procedure text	prototype context

implementation technique. This internal use of naming and binding is conceptually distinct from the external facility being implemented, but real implementations often blur the distinction, as an implementation shortcut or out of confusion. These two points should be pondered carefully, because in developing a higher-level naming concept in the next sections, we will utilize the naming contexts of the addressing architecture, create intermediate levels of contexts, and have several opportunities to confuse the problem being solved (building up a naming context) with the method of solution (using naming concepts).

C. <u>Higher-Level Naming Contexts, or File Systems</u>

1. <u>Direct-Access and Copy Organizations</u>

Higher-level naming contexts, or <u>file systems</u>. are provided in computer systems primarily for the convenience of the human users of the systems. In on-line systems, a file system may assume a quite sophisticated form, providing many features that are perceived to be useful to an interactive user.*

The foremost property of a file system is that it accepts names that are chosen and interpreted by human beings--ideally arbitrarily chosen, arbitrary length strings of characters. The context used to resolve these user-chosen names is called a <u>catalog</u>**, which in its simplest form is an object containing pairs: a character string name and a unique identifier of the object to which that character-string name is bound***. The unique

---

* A similar, but typically less-sophisticated file system is often used for batch processing job control languages.

** In many systems, the term <u>directory</u> is used.

*** In many systems, catalogs are also used as repositories for other things of interest about an object, such as details of its physical representation, measures of its activity, and information about who is authorized to use the object. Such use of a catalog as a repository as well as a naming context tends to confuse naming issues with other problems, so we shall assume for our present discussion that the underlying storage system provides for the repository function and that catalogs are exclusively naming contexts. In a later discussion of implementation considerations, some of the effects of mixing these ideas will be examined.

identifier names the object in the context of the underlying storage system. Normally, the name-resolution mechanism of the file system is sufficiently cumbersome that it is not economically feasible for a running program to use it for access to single words. Therefore, some mechanism must be provided for making sure that most references are to a high-speed addressing architecture. There are two commonly-found ways of organizing a file system's relation to this addressing architecture: the <u>copy</u> file system, and the <u>direct</u>-<u>access</u> file system.

In a <u>copy</u> file system, the catalog manager operates quite independently of the addressing architecture. A program may call upon the catalog manager to create an object with a given file system name. When the program wishes to read or write data from or to the object, it again calls the catalog manager, at a read or write entry point, giving the character-string name of the object, and the address of a data buffer in the addressing architecture. The catalog manager looks up the character-string name, finds the object identifier, and then performs the read or write operation by copying the data from its permanent storage area to the addressing architecture or back. Thus, in a copy file system, use of an object by name is coupled with the kind of data movement usually associated with multilevel memory management; usually the file system uses secondary storage devices that have their own addressing structure, but this addressing structure is hidden from the user of the file system. Figure 13 illustrates a copy file system.

In a <u>direct</u>-<u>access</u> file system, the catalog manager also creates a higher-level naming context, but it uses the addressing architecture itself as the mechanism for data access. Instead of performing copying read and write operations for its caller, it provides an entry that we may name "get

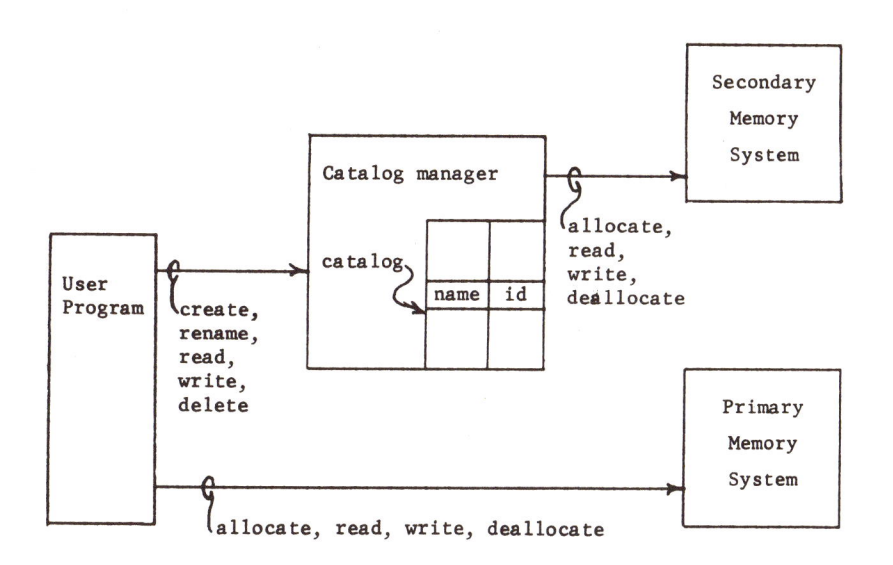

Figure 13 -- Organization of a simple copy file system. The
user calls on the catalog manager to create objects and
record character-string names for them. The identifiers (labelled id) stored by the catalog manager
are names in the context of a secondary memory system,
not directly accessible to the user program. The user
program, to manipulate an object, must first copy part
or all of it into the primary memory system by giving
a read request to the catalog manager, and specifying
the character-string name of an object and the name
of a suitable area in the primary memory system.

identifier", which returns to its caller an object identifier, for a given character-string name, suitable for use directly with the lower level addressing architecture. Figure 14 shows a direct access file system.

Which of these two kinds of designs is preferred depends on the arrangement of the available addressing architecture. If a structured memory system that provides multilevel management of all primary and secondary memory is available, then names of the structured memory system may be embedded in program contexts, and a direct-access file system seems preferable. If, on the other hand, permanent storage of large volumes of data on secondary memory is managed separately from the primary memory system used by programs, then the object names stored in a catalog would refer to a context not available to a program, and the copy form of file system design is appropriate*.

The distinction between these two kinds of file systems is an important one, since programs must be written differently in the two kinds of design. The direct-access file system is sometimes called a <u>one-level store</u> [Kilburn, 1961], because a program can consider all other programs and data to be nameable in a single context, rather than in two contexts with the necessity for explicitly copying objects from one context (the permanent storage system) to another (the program execution environment) in order to manipulate them.* Note that a direct-access file system can be used to simulate a copy file system, by copying objects from one part of it to another. The

---

* Most copy file systems obscure our precise distinction by providing a temporary context consisting of currently active files. Upon some program's declaring an interest in a certain file, the file system allocates a name for the file in the temporary context, and hands that name back to the program for use in future read/write calls. Despite the similarity in structure to the "get identifier" call, such systems are not direct-access because it is still necessary to explicitly copy things from the context of the file system to the context of the addressing architecture in order to manipulate them.

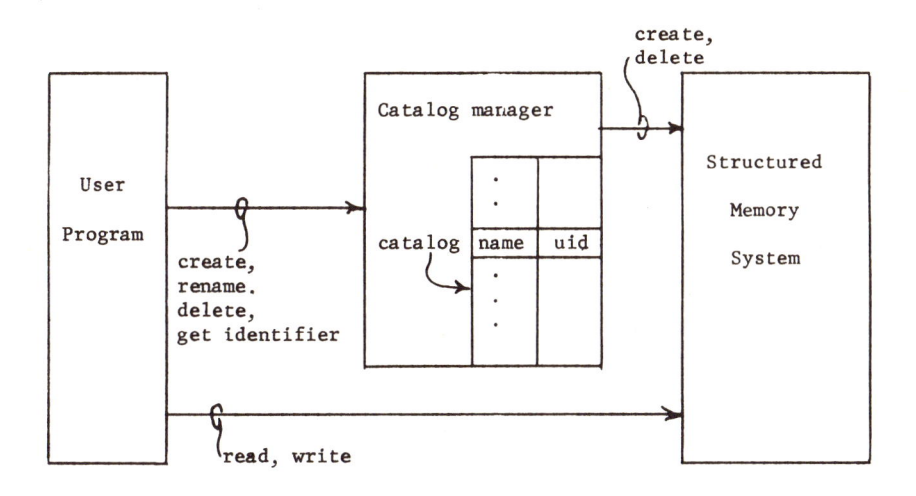

Figure 14 -- Organization of a simple direct-access file system.
The user calls on the catalog manager, as before, to
create objects and to record character-string names.
However, the entry "get identifier" returns the object
number, or unique identifier (labelled <u>uid</u>) by which
an object is known in the structured memory system.
The objects themselves are created and stored by the
structured memory system, in response to direct
requests from the catalog manager. The catalog
manager may itself use the structured memory system
to store the catalog, but that use is both unimportant
and invisible to the user of the catalog so long as
there is only one catalog, since the user does not
need to know the name by which the catalog manager
refers to the catalog. As shown, there is nothing to
prevent a user program from additionally making direct
create and delete calls on the Structured Memory Subsystem, thus creating uncatalogued objects, or destroy-
ing catalogued objects without the knowledge of the
catalog manager.

reverse is quite a bit harder to do, since a one-level store requires that the base level system implement a single, universal naming context.

In either a direct-access or a copy file system that implements a single catalog, the operation of a context initializer program (the program, described in part B, that connects the higher level file system context to lower level program execution contexts) is relatively straightforward. Consider the direct-access case first. The context initializer starts with a character-string name found in a prototype context. The context initializer calls the "get identifier" entry of the direct-access file system, takes the returned identifier as an object number, and inserts it in the program context being initialized. In the case of a copy file system, the context initializer goes through an extra step, known as <u>loading</u> the object. That is, it allocates a space for the object in primary memory, and then it asks the copy file system to read a copy of the referenced object into primary memory. Finally, it places the primary memory address of the newly-copied object in the context being initialized. To avoid copying a shared object (that is, one named by two or more other objects) into primary memory twice, the context initializer must also maintain a table of names of objects already loaded, a <u>reference name table</u>. Before calling on the file system, the context initializer must first look in the reference name table to see if the name refers to an object already loaded. Because the higher-level file system requires copying of objects in order to use them, the context initializer for the addressing architecture is forced

---

* Another name sometimes used for the direct access file system is the "Virtual Access Method".

to develop in the reference name table an image of those parts of the higher-level file system that are currently in use*.

In examining the operation of the context initializer in the environments of copy and direct-access file systems, we have identified the most important operational distinctions between the two designs. For simplicity in the succeeding discussion, we shall assume that a direct-access file system is under discussion, and that the adaptation of the remarks to the copy environment is self-evident.

2. <u>Multiple catalogs and naming networks</u>

The single-catalog system of figure 13 and 14 is useful primarily for exposing the first layer of issues involved in developing a file system, although such systems have been implemented for use in batch-processing, one-user-at-a-time operating systems**. As soon as the goal of multiple use is introduced, a more elaborate file system is needed. Since names for objects are chosen by their human creators, to avoid conflict it is necessary, at a minimum, to provide several catalogs, perhaps one per user***.

---

* In practice, dealing with shared objects also involves several other complicated issues, such as measuring activity for multilevel memory management or accounting, and maintaining multiple copies for reliability; such issues lead a good distance away from the study of name binding and will not be pursued here.

** The FORTRAN Monitor System (FMS) for the IBM 709 computer is a typical example of a batch processing system that had a single catalog, for a library of public subroutines.

*** Most of the first generation of time-sharing systems, such as CTSS, APEX, the SDS-940, TYMSHARE, DTSS, VM/370-CMS, and GCOS III TSS provided one catalog per user. OS/360 provided a single system-wide catalog with multicomponent names that could be used to provide the same effect.

If there are several catalogs available, any of which could provide the context for resolving names presented to the file system, some scheme is needed for the file system name interpreter to choose the correct catalog. Technically, some mechanism is needed to provide a closure. A scheme used in many systems that provide one catalog per user is as follows: the state of a user's virtual processor usually includes a register (unchangeable by the user) that contains the user's name, for purposes of resource usage accounting and access control*. The file system name interpreter simply adds another use to this name: as a closure identifier. The name interpreter resolves all object names presented to it by first obtaining the current user name from the virtual processor name register, and looking that up in some catalog of catalogs, called a master user catalog. The user's name is therein bound to that user's personal catalog, which the interpreter then uses as the context for resolving the originally presented object name. This scheme is simple, and easy to understand, but it has an important defect: it does not permit the possibility of sharing contexts between users. Even if one user knows another user's name, and has permission to use the second user's file, the first user cannot get his program to contain the correct file system name for the file in the other user's catalog: the user's own catalog is automatically provided as the implicit context for all names found in his programs. Reusing the account or principal identifier as a closure identifier, while simple, is inflexible.

To understand the reason why shared contexts are of interest, we must recall that the file system is a higher-level naming context provided for the convenience of the human user rather than a facility of direct interest to the user's programs. The commands typed by the user at the terminal to

---

* In discussions of information protection, this name is usually called a principal identifier.

guide the computation specify the names of programs and data that he wishes the computation to deal with, and he expects these names to be resolved in the context of the file system. The user would like to be able to express conveniently a name for any object that is of interest to him. If he makes frequent use of objects belonging to other users, then to minimize confusion he should be able to use the same names for objects that their owners use. These considerations suggest a need for a scheme that allows contexts to be shared.

A simple scheme that supplies the minimum of function is to add a second, user-settable register to the user's virtual processor, dedicated exclusively to the function of closure identification. We shall name this new register the <u>working catalog</u> register; and have the file system resolve names starting from that register rather than some register intended for a purpose only accidentally connected with naming. The working catalog register would normally contain a name that is bound, for example in a master user catalog, to the user's personal catalog.* When the user wishes to use a name found in some other catalog, he first arranges that the working catalog register be reloaded with the name of the other catalog. This scheme has been widely used, and is of considerable interest because it exposes several issues brought about by the desire to share information:

1) In some systems, protection of information from unauthorized use is achieved primarily by preventing the user from naming things not belonging to him. For example, before the working catalog register was added, the file system name interpreter resolved all names relative to the protected principal identifier register, thereby preventing a user from naming objects belonging to

---

* For implementation speed, the working catalog might actually be represented by its object number rather than by a character-string name requiring resolution every time a name is used.

others. With the addition of the working catalog register, the user can suddenly name every object in the file system. Protection must be re-supplied either by restricting the range of names of catalogs that the user can place in the working catalog register (for example, permitting the user to name either his catalog or a public library catalog, but nothing else) or else by developing a protection system that is more independent of the naming system--an access control list for each object, for example*.

2) The change of context involved when the working catalog is changed is complete--<u>all</u> names encountered in the program being executed, or the context initializer program, will be resolved relative to the name of the current working catalog. If program A contains a reference to object B, and the context initializer is expected to dynamically resolve the name "B" at the time it is first used, that resolution will depend on the working catalog in force at the instant of the first reference to B. Here we have a potential conflict between the intention of the programmer in embedding the name "B" in the program and the intention of the current user of the program, who may want to adjust the working catalog to assure correct resolution of some other name to be typed at the terminal as input to program A. Since there are two effectively independent sources of names, perhaps there should be two working catalogs, and an automatic way of choosing the correct working catalog depending on the source of the name. Unfortunately, inside the computer both kinds of names are presented to the file system by similar-appearing

---

* The lack of ability to name other users' objects was the primary file system protection scheme of M.I.T.'s Compatible Time-Sharing System. The equivalent of the working catalog register in that system was restricted to the users' catalog, the library, or a catalog held in common among a designated group of users [Crisman, 1965].

sources--some program calls, giving the name as an argument. (We are here encountering a problem described earlier, that the wrong implicit context may be supplied by the name interpreter.)

3) Having once changed the context in which names are resolved, the human user (or the program writer) must constantly remember that a new context is in force, or risk making mistakes. As an example of a complication that can arise, many systems provide an **attention** feature that allows a user, upon pressing some special key at his terminal, to interrupt the current program and force control to some standard starting place. If the working catalog register was changed by the current program (perhaps in response to a user request to that program) then the "standard" starting place may start with a "non-standard" naming context in force.

These last two issues suggest that an alternative, less drastic approach to shared contexts is needed: some scheme that switches contexts for the duration of only one name resolution.

One such scheme is to provide that each name that is not to be resolved in the working catalog carry with it the name of the context in which it should be resolved. This approach forces back onto the user the responsibility to state explicitly, as part of each name, the name of the appropriate context. We assume, as before, that catalogs are to have human-readable character-string names, and therefore there must be some context in which catalog names can be resolved. Figure 15 shows one such arrangement, called a **naming network**, an arrangement characterized by catalogs appearing as named objects in other catalogs. We have chosen the convention that to express the name of an object that is not in the working catalog, one concatenates the name of the containing catalog with

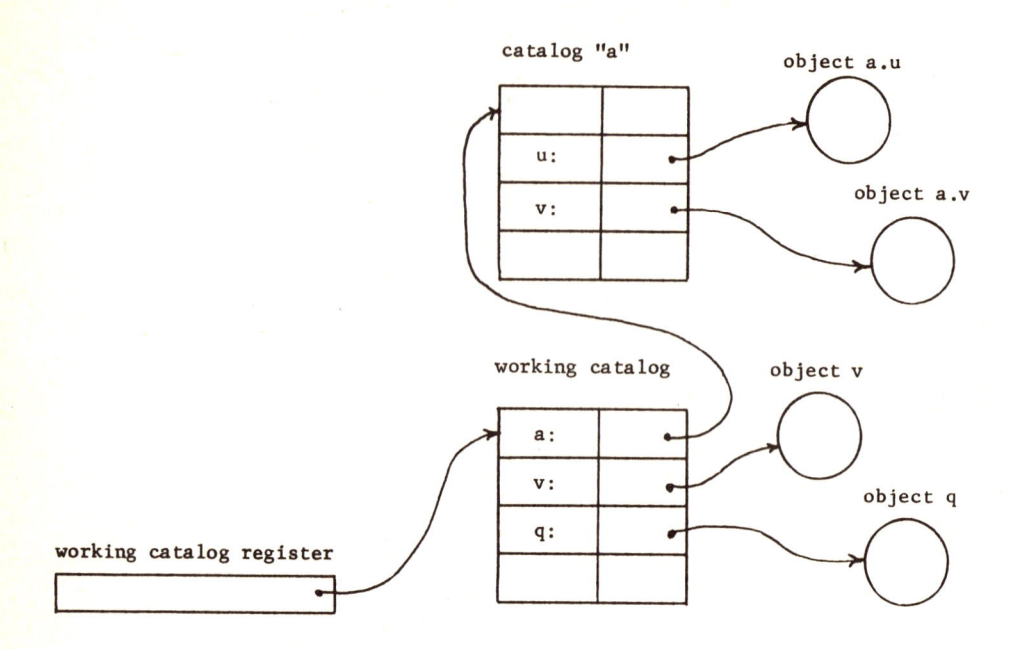

Figure 15 -- A simple naming network. All single-component names given to the file system are resolved in the context named by the working catalog register. All two-component names are resolved by resolving the first component in the working catalog, which leads to another catalog in which the second component may be resolved. As in earlier figures, the arrows represent object addressing; the (italicised) object numbers have been omitted to simplify the figures. (The working catalog register refers to the working catalog by object number in this example, although it could also be implemented as a multicomponent path name relative to some standard starting catalog known to the file system).

the name of the object, inserting a period between the two names. The
absence of a period in a name can then be taken to mean that the name is
to be resolved in the working catalog. One would expect names containing
periods to come to programs as input arguments, originating perhaps from
the keyboard; they represent a way for the user to express intent precisely
in terms of the current naming structure, which can change from day to day.
On the other hand, one would permanently embed in a program only single-component names, to avoid the need to revise programs every time objects are
rearranged in the catalog structure. We shall return to the topic of binding
names of the program to names of the catalog structure after first exploring
naming networks in some depth.

A naming network generalizes in the obvious way if we admit names
consisting of any number of components--these names are called path names.
Thus, in figure 15, it might be that the object named "a.v" is yet
another catalog, and that it contains an object named "cosine"; the user
could refer to that object by providing the path name "a.v.cosine".* Note
also that the path names "v" and "a.v" refer to distinct objects--either
may be referred to despite the apparent name conflict.

A naming network admits any arbitrary arrangement of catalogs,
including what is sometimes called a recursive structure: in figure 16,
catalog "a.v" contains a name "c", bound to the identifier of the original
working catalog. The utility of a recursive catalog structure is not
evident from our simple example--it merely seems to provide curious

---

* If it should turn out that object "a.v" is not a catalog, the user
has made a mistake; in a well-designed system the file-name interpreter should have some provision for detecting this mistake. For
example, in an object-oriented system, each object contains as part
of its representation the identification of its type, and the underlying system would report an error to the file system if it attempted
to perform a catalog lookup on an object not of the catalog type.
If an object-oriented system is not used, perhaps the higher level
catalog would contain for each entry a flag that indicates whether
or not that entry describes another catalog.

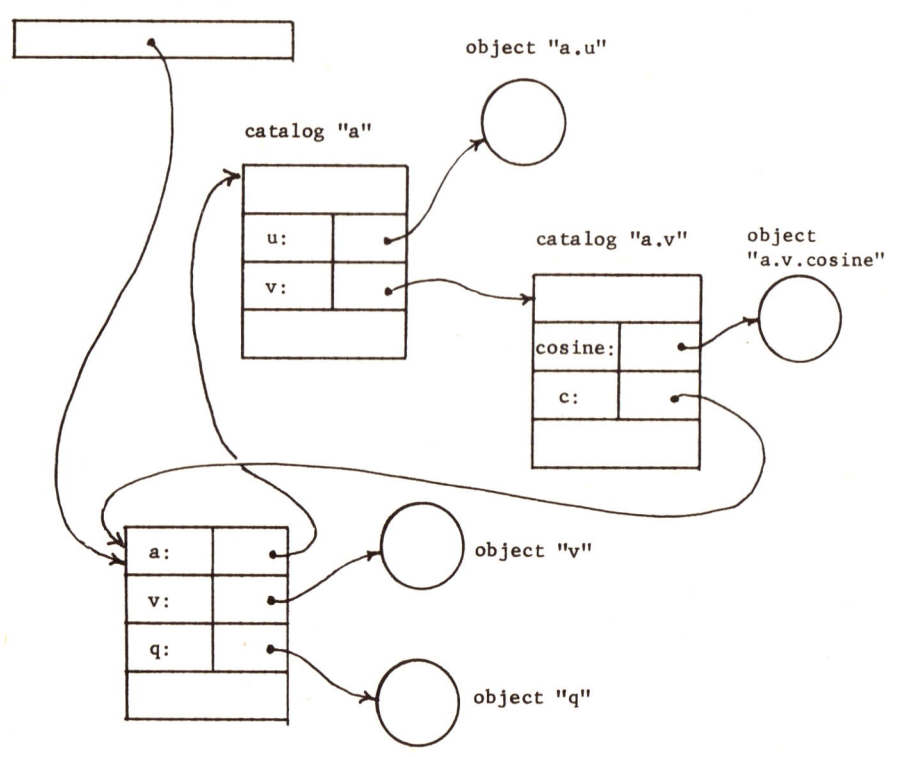

Figure 16 -- A naming network with recursive structure. Object "v" is also known by the name "a.v.c.v".

features such as allowing the object named "q" to be referred to also as "a.v.c.q" or "a.v.c.a.v.c.q". But suppose that some other processor has its working catalog register set to the catalog we have named "a.v". Then from the point of view of that processor, objects in catalog "a.v" can be referred to with single component names, while the object that the first processor knew as "q" could be obtained by the name "c.q". By admitting a recursive catalog structure, every user can have a working catalog that contains named bindings to any other user's catalog. Thus the original goal, of providing shared contexts, has been met.*

3. **The dynamics of naming networks**

If we were to implement the file systems of figures 13 or 14, with the intent of having a naming network, we would probably discover an important defect: although we could easily implement entries to "read", "write", or "get identifier" that understood path names in an existing naming network, and we could also implement an entry to create a new object or catalog, we could not write a program that called those entries to <u>create</u> a naming network with recursive structure--we would be limited to creating a simple tree structure. Unless our applications were sufficiently static that we could insert in advance all recursive cross-references among catalogs that might ever be needed, we should make provision for programs dynamically to add recursive cross-references by calling the file system. These provisions must include:

1) some way to add to a catalog an entry that represents a binding to a previously existing object.

---

* Naming networks are not often encountered in operating systems. The CAL time-sharing system [Lampson and Sturgis, 1976] and the CAP system [Needham and Birrell, 1977] are two examples. In data base management systems, the CODASYL standard data base system defined by their Data Base Task Group (DBTG) called for a recursive naming network [CODASYL, 1971].

2) some way of naming previously existing objects, so that
provision one can be accomplished.

The first provision seems straightforward enough, but the second one implies a fundamental limitation of some kind in the conception of naming networks, at least so far as dynamically constructing them is concerned: **one can dynamically extend a naming network only by**

1) creating new objects, or
2) adding "short-cut" bindings to objects that were already nameable by some other name.

Thus, in figure 17, one could imagine a request to the file system like "Add to my working catalog a cross-reference, named 'm', to the catalog currently nameable as 'b.x.m'," or "Add to catalog 'b.x.m' a cross-reference, named 'r', to catalog 'b'." These two requests would add the bindings indicated in the figure with dashed lines, but neither request increases the range of objects that can be named. Meanwhile, there is no way available to express the concept "add a cross-reference named 'z' to catalog 'b', that allows access to the catalog labelled 'unnameable' in figure 17." Note that this catalog is unnameable only from the point of view of the working catalog register; some other user might have a name for it. If <u>no</u> one had a binding for it, it would be a "lost object", about which more will be said later.

In practice, the problem of inaccessibility is not so serious as it might initially seem: a modest discipline on creation of catalogs can control the situation. A typical strategy for a time-sharing system might be as follows:*

1) When the time-sharing system is first brought into existence, create a "root" catalog, and place in it two more newly created catalogs, one for the library (named "library") and another for individual users' home catalogs (named "users".)

---

* This is a version of the strategy used in the CAL time-sharing system.

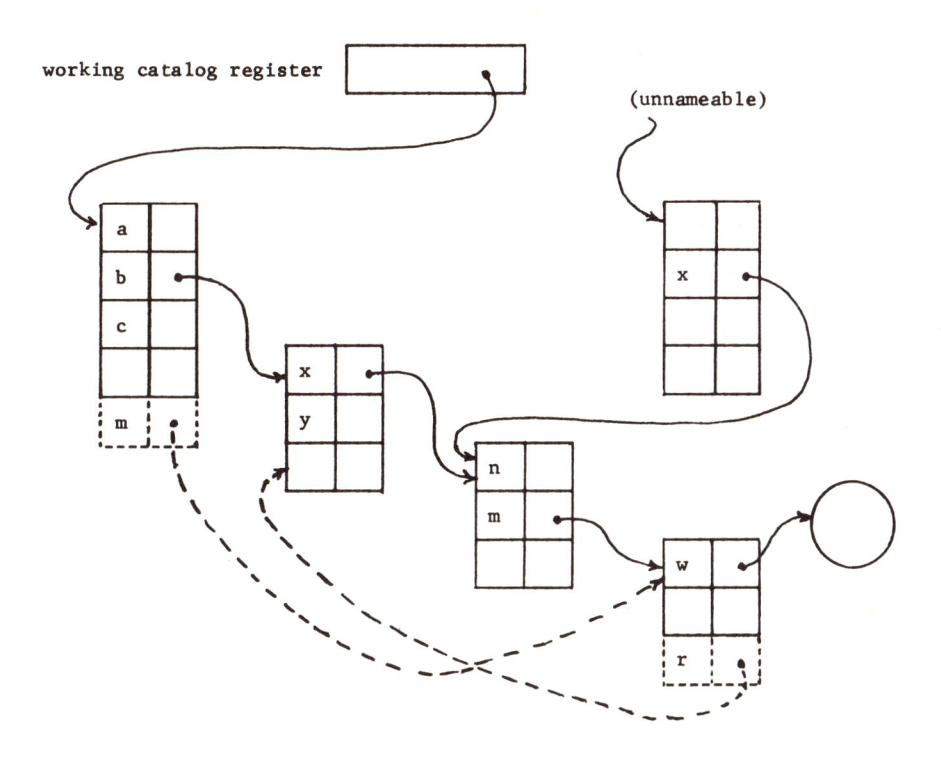

Figure 17 -- A naming network containing an unnameable catalog.

2) For each user of the time-sharing system, create a home catalog, arrange that whenever that user logs in, the working catalog register be loaded by the login procedure to contain the path name (relative to the "root" catalog) of that user's home catalog, and place in the user's home catalog a (recursive) entry binding the name "root" to the unique identifier of the root catalog.

Now, each user will find that he can refer to his own files by simply giving their names, he can refer to library programs by preceding their names with "root.library.", and he can refer to a file in the catalog of his friend "Lenox" by preceding its name with "root.users.Lenox.". If he finds that he makes frequent use of files belonging to Lenox, he can place in his own catalog a new entry directly binding some appropriate name (say "Lenox") to the identifier of Lenox's catalog. The only obvious effect of this extra binding is that shorter names can now be used to refer to objects in Lenox's catalog.

Notice that if a user accidentally destroys the cross-reference to the catalog named "root", that user would find that he could name nothing but things in his own catalog. The root catalog therefore plays an important part in making a naming network useful in practice.

4. <u>Binding reference names to path names</u>

It remains for us to pick up several loose ends and glue them together to complete the picture of name binding operations that appear in a computer system. However, before inventing any further mechanisms, let us first stop and review the collection of machinery we have developed already, so as to understand just what functions have been provided and what is missing.

We began by assuming as an underlying base a universal naming context in which all objects have unique, system-wide identifiers. We then developed on this base a systematic way of using hardware-oriented reference names and contexts in which those names resolved to underlying universal names--an addressing architecture. The purpose of these reference names was to allow programs to be constructed of distinct data and procedure objects that refer to one another using hardware-interpretable names that are unambiguously resolved in closely associated contexts. We also observed that these contexts must be initialized, either as part of the construction of the program or else dynamically as the program executes (in order to avoid modifying the program when it is used in a different application). We briefly outlined the place of the context initializer program as a bridge between the machine-oriented naming world of the addressing architecture and a higher-level, human-oriented file system naming world. The purpose of the context initializer is to take symbolic names found in the prototype context segment of a program, interpret those names in the higher-level context of the naming network, and place in a context object accessible to the addressing architecture an appropriate binding to a specific object.

Next, we developed the outline of a human-engineered file system--a naming network--to be used as the context for people guiding computations. During this development we observed that the dynamic initialization of the lower-level reference name context, say of a procedure, sometimes can involve resolution of symbolic names in the higher-level file system. A problem we noticed, but never quite solved, was that these symbolic names are of two origins: some are supplied by the _writer_ of the procedure, and are intended to be resolved according to that writer's goals, and some are supplied by the <u>user</u> of the procedure, in the course of supplying instructions to the program at execution time. These latter names are presumably intended by the user to be resolved in the file system relative to the user's current working catalog.

Thus, for example, a user may have a working catalog containing a memorandum needing revision, which the user has named "draft". The user invokes an editing procedure, and asks that editor to modify the object he knows by the name "draft" in the working catalog. But it is possible (even likely) that the author of the editor program organized the editor to make a copy of the object being edited (so as not to harm the original if the user changes his mind); perhaps that author chose the name "draft" for the object meant to contain the copy. We have, in effect, two categories of outward symbolic references from the program, the first category to be resolved relative to the working catalog, and the second relative to some, as yet unidentified, place in the naming network. The name interpreter used for the translation from file system names to unique identifiers is being called upon to supply one of two different implicit contexts; we have so far provided only one, the working catalog.

To inform the name interpreter which context to use is straightforward: the semantics of use are different and apparent to the translator or interpreter of the program. A name supplied by the author of the program appears as a character string in the source program in some position where reference to an object is appropriate, while a name supplied by the user appears as a data character string in a position where the programmer has indicated that it should be converted into a reference to an object*. Thus if we simply arrange that explicitly programmed conversions from character string to reference be done with the working directory as a context, while all other names found in the source program be interpreted in some other (as yet unspecified) context, we can distinguish the intents of the author and the user of the program.

This approach leaves one final question: what is the appropriate other context in which to resolve outward symbolic references provided by the author of an object? We are here dealing with a situation similar to that posed by some programming languages, in which a procedure is defined, and then passed (or returned) as an argument to be invoked at a time when some context is in effect that is different from the one in which the procesure was defined**. The standard way to deal with the problem of resolving free variables found in functional arguments is to create and pass not a procedure, but a closure, consisting of the procedure and the context in which its names are to be interpreted. In the case at hand, a name-containing object is being interpreted, and we are trying to discover the closure that defines its symbolic naming context.

A simple (though not quite adequate, as we shall see approach to providing a closure is to require that each catalog that contains the object also contain entries for every symbolic name used in that object. Then, we design the context initializer so that whenever any object is discovered to require a symbolic name to be resolved, the context initializer should resolve that name by looking in the file system catalog in which it originally

---

* It should be noted that few languages provide direct semantics for conversion of character-string data into external object references. To fill this gap in language semantics, many operating systems provide subroutines to perform the conversion. Such a subroutine typically takes a character string argument representing the name of some object, and returns a reference (sometimes called a pointer or an address) to that object.

** Accomplishing correct name resolution when a function containing references to free variables is passed or returned as an argument is known, in the programming language community, as the "FUNARG problem". In our case, a compiler or assembler has returned as its output value a procedure that contains free variables--unresolved outward symbolic references. Thus, we should expect that solutions to the FUNARG program might provide a clue how to proceed.

found that object. The author (or user) of an object that uses symbolic names is instructed that in order for the object to operate correctly, someone must prepare its containing catalog by installing entries for every name used by the object. These entries are the externally-provided declarations that replace the internal-to-the-object declarations whose absence caused context initialization to be needed in the first place.

Using the containing catalog as a context for resolving symbolic names handles part of the problem, but it fails to provide modular sharing. Consider the catalog of figure 5-18 named "root.users.Smith". Smith has in mind declaring that the name "b" should be bound to a program written by Lenox, which Smith can refer to as "root.users.Lenox.b". Unbeknownst to Smith, Lenox organized "b" in several pieces, one of which is named "a". If Smith binds the name "b" directly to Lenox's procedure, and the containing catalog is used as a context, Lenox's procedure will get the wrong "a" whenever it is invoked by Smith. What is really needed is an explicit closure, rather than an implicit one, so we conclude that we should arrange things as in figure 19, with each named procedure replaced by a closure object containing a pointer to the procedure, and a pointer to the appropriate context. Now, there is no problem about how to bind the name "b" in Smith's catalog: it can be bound to the closure for procedure b, as shown. With this arrangement, when Smith's procedure "a" calls on procedure "b" the name "b" will be resolved in Smith's catalog, and it will cause initialization of a new (addressing architecture) context for b that is based on the file system context of Lenox's catalog. When procedure "b" calls for "a" it will get the "a" bound in Lenox's catalog, as intended. Although we have described the problem in terms of procedures, the same problem arises for any name using object, and the same solution, binding to the object through a closure rather than directly,

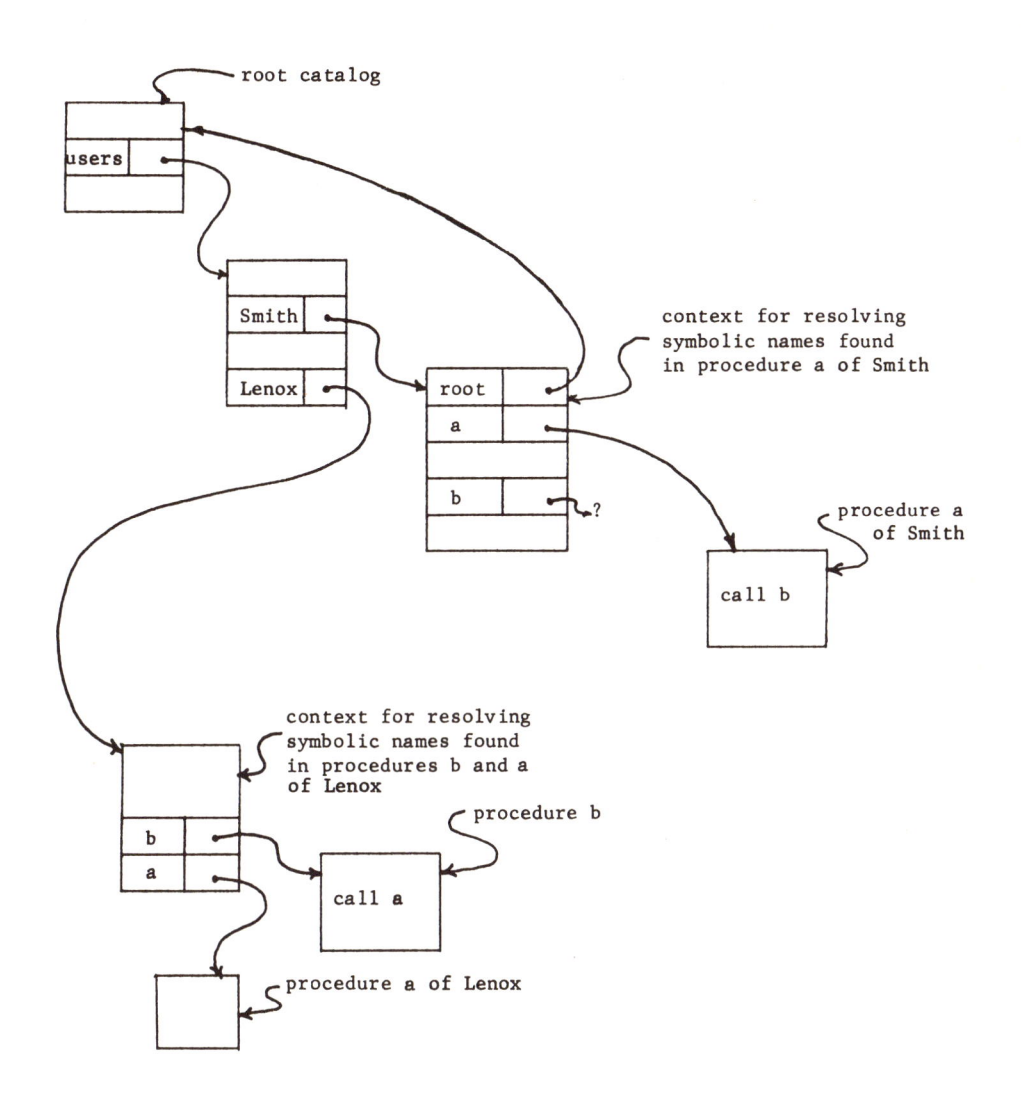

Figure 18 -- Sharing of a procedure in the naming network. If
the name "b" in Smith's catalog is bound to procedure
"b" in Lenox's catalog, the context initializer will
make a mistake when resolving procedure b's reference
to "a".

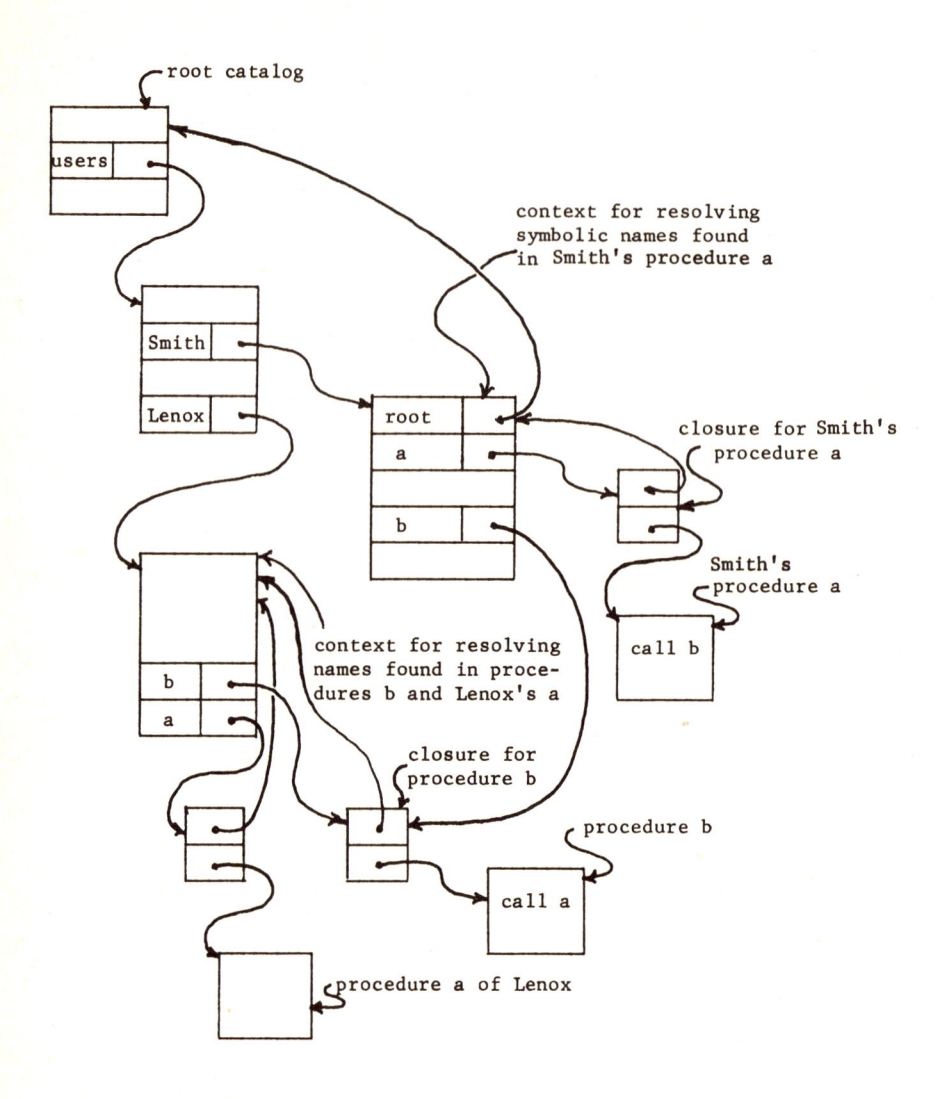

Figure 19 -- Addition of closures to allow sharing of procedures to work correctly.

should be applied. The goal of modular sharing, namely that correct use of an object should not require knowing its internal naming structure, is then achieved.

5. Context initialization

The careful reader will note that we have not quite tied everything together yet: we have not shown how the context initializer of the addressing architecture makes systematic use of the file system closure mechanism. As a final step we should look into how this bridge between the addressing architecture and the file system might be organized. We approach this integration by considering one possible implementation of the context initialization programs involved.

First, let us suppose there is a catalog management function named "resolve", of two arguments, that looks up the symbolic name provided as its first argument in the catalog that has the object number supplied as the second argument. Thus to look up the name "xyz" in the catalog with object number 415, one would write

$$xyznum = resolve\ ("xyz",\ 415);$$

and upon return from "resolve", xyznum would contain the object number of "xyz". Actually, we must be a little careful here: xyznum would actually contain the object number of the file system closure of object "xyz".

The next step is to recognize explicitly the operation of making an object addressable by a running processor. This operation involves three steps:

1) creating and initializing an addressing architecture context for this processor to use when interpreting names found in the object. Let us suppose that the prototype context information is tucked away somewhere inside the object itself, in a standard, easy-to-find place.

2) inserting in this processor's closure table the addressing closure for this object; that is, the association between the object's object number and the object's just-created addressing context.

3) obtaining from the file system closure for the object the actual object number, for use by the processor in addressing the object.

Thus, we might imagine a context initialization program named "install" that would take as an argument the object number of a file system closure, and would go into the closure, find the object itself and perform those three steps. Step one, creating and initializing an addressing architecture context, may require resolving symbolic names (assuming some names are to be bound in advance of execution rather than on demand) so "install" will need to call on "resolve", giving as the second argument the catalog found in the file system closure for the object being installed. For each name so resolved, "install" will also have to call itself recursively, so as to make that object addressable, too. If binding on demand is involved, install should leave in the addressing context a copy of the object number of the file system closure, so that later demand binding faults can be correctly resolved. Figure 20 illustrates a simplified sketch of the function "install".

We might expect that the initial call to "install" comes, say, from an interactive program that has just read a line from the user's terminal, and discovered that the line contains the name of some object on which computation should be performed. The program might call "resolve" to convert the symbolic name to a closure object number, specifying as a context for this symbolic name resolution the current working catalog. Then it would call "install", possibly triggering a wave of recursive calls to "install", and it could then manipulate the object as required. It is instructive to follow through this sequence in detail for the file system catalog arrangement of figure 19, assuming that the working catalog is "root.users.Smith", and that Smith has typed a command

```
install (closure-num):   begin;
                         proc-num := closure-num.second part;
                         file-context-num := closure-num.first-part;
                         addr-context-num := create-new-object;

                         "examine the procedure proc-num to find
                         the prototype of its addressing context";
                         "initialize addr-context from that prototype";
                         "place a copy of file-context-num in addr-context";
                         "identify the symbolic names in the prototype";

                         for each such name do;
                             if name is to be bound now then do;
                                 cl-num := resolve (name, file-context-num);
                                 p-num := install (cl-num);
                                 "insert p-num in addr-context";
                             od;
                             else
                                 "insert bind-on-demand flag in addr-context";
                         od;

                         "insert proc-num and addr-context-num in
                         closure table";

                         return proc-num;

                         end;
```

Figure 20 -- Outline of the "install" function of the context initializer.

that calls for execution of a program named "a". In following the sequence,
note that we have provided, in a single mechanism, independent contexts for
resolutions of symbolic names typed at the terminal and for symbolic names
provided by the programmer; and that even when different programmers happen
to use the same symbolic name for different objects, use of both their programs as components of the same subsystem is still possible.

This completes our conceptual analysis of higher-level naming systems.
Table III summarizes the objectives that we have identified and also the
file system facilities that implement those objectives. It remains for us to
look at a variety of implementation strategies actually used in practice,
most of which consist of shortcuts that abridge one or more of the objectives
of the naming systems of figures 12 and 19.

D. Implementation considerations

Up to this point we have developed two models of name binding that
relentlessly pursue every implication and admit no compromise. The results
are naming structures more sophisticated than any encountered in practice,
although every portion of the structures described has appeared in some form
in some system. In this section we explore some pressures that lead to compromise, and also investigate the effects of compromise to see which simpler
structures might be acceptable for certain situations.

1. Lost objects

One potential trouble with naming networks is called the "lost object"
problem. When a user deletes a binding in a catalog, the question arises
of whether or not the file system should destroy the formerly referenced
object and release the resources being used for its representation. If
there are other catalogs containing bindings to the same object, then
it should not be destroyed, but there is no easy way to discover whether

Table III -- The objectives of a file system, and the facilities used to accomplish them.

Objectives	file system facilities					
	single catalog system	multiple catalog system	working catalog register	naming network	catalogs used as closures	distinct closure objects
human-oriented names	yes	yes	yes	yes	yes	yes
multiple users	no	yes	yes	yes	yes	yes
shared contexts	no	no	yes	yes	yes	yes
selectively shared contexts	no	no	no	yes	yes	yes
distinguish intent of programmer and user	no	no	no	no	yes	yes
modular sharing	no	no	no	no	no	yes

or not other bindings exist. One approach is not to destroy the object, on the chance that there are other bindings, and occasionally leave an orphan that has no catalog bindings. If the system has a modest amount of storage it is then feasible to scan periodically all catalogs to mark the still accessible objects, and then sweep through storage looking for unmarked orphans, a technique known as "garbage collection". A substantial literature exists on techniques for garbage collection [Knuth, 1968], but these techniques tend not to be applicable to the larger volume of storage usually encountered in a file system.

An alternative approach is the following: when an object is created, the first binding of that object in some catalog receives a special mark indicating that this catalog entry is the "distinguished" entry for that object. If the user ever asks to delete the distinguished entry, the file system will also destroy the object.* This alternative approach burdens the naming system with the responsibility of remembering, in addition to a name-to-object binding, whether or not the entry is distinguished. This burden is significant: the mechanisms of naming and those of storage allocation are being tangled; the catalog has become the repository for an attribute of the object that has nothing to do with its name. Even when "garbage collection" is used there is a subtle entanglement of naming with storage allocation: that strategy calls for destruction of objects whenever they become nameless. Entanglement of mechanisms with different goals is not necessarily bad, but it should always be recognized. As we shall see in the next section, it can easily get out of hand.

Finally, a more drastic approach to avoiding lost objects is to eliminate the multiple bindings completely: require that each object appear in one and only one catalog. Then, when the binding is deleted, the object can be destroyed without question. But this constraint has

---

* This approach was used, for example, in the CAL time-sharing system [Lampson and Sturgis, 1976].

far-reaching consequences for the naming goals. The naming network is restricted to a rooted tree, called a naming hierarchy. Although any object in such a hierarchy can refer symbolically to any other object, it can do so only by expressing a path name starting either from its own tree position or from the root, and thereby embedding the structure of the naming hierarchy in its cross references. User-dependent bindings become impossible.

Also, the constraint is more drastic than necessary. One can allow non-catalog objects to appear in as many catalogs as desired, and maintain with the representation of each object a counter (the <u>reference count</u>) of the number of catalogs that contain bindings to the object. As bindings are created or deleted, the counter can be updated, and if its value ever reaches zero, it is time to destroy the object.* (This scheme would fail if applied to the more general naming network. Consider what would happen in figure 16 if the only binding to the structure shown were the pointer in the working catalog register, and that binding were destroyed. Since all of the objects in the figure have at least one binding from other objects in the figure, the reference count would not go to zero, and the entire recursive structure would become a lost object.**)

---

* This strategy of reference counts to allow a file to appear in many catalogs was used in the file system for the UNIX time-sharing system [Ritchie and Thompson, 1974].

** The CAP system actually used this approach, on the basis that abandoned recursive structures will occur infrequently, and that occasional reload of the entire contents of the file system from backup copies will have the effect of reclaiming the last storage. A mixed scheme has been suggested by R. Needham, but never implemented. The idea would be to use both distinguished entries and reference counts, and to refuse to delete a distinguished entry if non-distinguished entries still existed, as indicated by a reference count greater than one [Needham and Birrell, 1977].

2. Catalogs as repositories

In many real systems, to minimize the number of parallel mechanisms and to allow symbolic names to be used for control and in error messages, the catalog is used as a repository for all kinds of other attributes of an object besides control of its destruction.* These other attributes are typically related to physical storage management, reliability, or security. Some examples of attributes for which some repository is needed are:

a)   the amount of storage currently utilized by the object,

b)   the nature of the object's current physical representation,

c)   the date and time the object was last used or changed,

d)   the location of redundant copies of the object, for reliability,

e)   a list of users allowed to use the object, and what modes of use they are permitted.

f)   the responsible owner's name, to notify in case of trouble.

The most significant effect of this merging of considerations of naming with considerations of physical storage management, reliability, and security is this: to provide control there should be only one repository for the attributes of any one object. Therefore, systems with this approach usually begin with the rule that there can be no more than one catalog entry for any one object. Thus the form of the naming network is restricted to that of a rooted tree, or naming hierarchy, with the ills for naming mentioned in the previous section. The use of the catalog as a general repository indeed distorts the structure of the naming system. However, there are two refinements that have been devised to restore some of the lost properties, indirect catalog entries and search rules.

---

* In fact, the UNIX time-sharing system appears to be the only widely-used system that completely avoided the repository functions [Ritchie and Thompson, 1974].

3. **Indirect catalog entries**

Some systems provide an ingenious approximation to a naming network within the constraint that there be a single repository for each object. They begin with a naming hierarchy, as described above, but they permit two kinds of catalog entries. A *direct entry* provides a binding of a name to an object and its attributes, as usual. Exactly one direct entry appears for each object. An *indirect entry* provides a binding of a name to a path or tree name of some object elsewhere in the catalog hierarchy. The meaning of such an indirect entry is that if the user attempts to refer to an object with that name, the references should be redirected to the object whose path name or tree name appears in the indirect entry. There can be any number of indirect entries that ultimately lead to the same object.* Indirect entries provide most of the effect of a naming network: a single object may appear in any of several contexts. Yet the systematic use of indirect entries can confine the embedding of path names or tree names to catalogs. Further, a convention can be made that all symbolic references made by an object are to be resolved in the context consisting of the catalog in which that object's direct entry appears. In effect, this convention provides an automatic rule for associating a procedure with its symbolic naming context, and eliminates the need for an explicit closure to make the association.** Figure 21 illustrates the situation of figure 19, except that a naming network allowing indirect entries is used.***

---

* Most such systems permit the possibility that the target of the redirected reference can redirect the reference to yet another catalog entry. In such cases, protection must be provided to prevent the name interpreter from going into a loop when a careless user leaves two indirect entries referring to each other.

** It also means that any one procedure can be associated with one and only one context, whereas with explicit closures, several closures could be provided for a single procedure, each naming different contexts.

*** The CTSS system was probably the first to provide indirect catalog entries, doing so under the name "links". IBM's TSS/360 and Honeywell's Multics also were organized this way. The CAL time-sharing system allowed both indirect entries ("soft links") and any number of direct entries ("hard links").

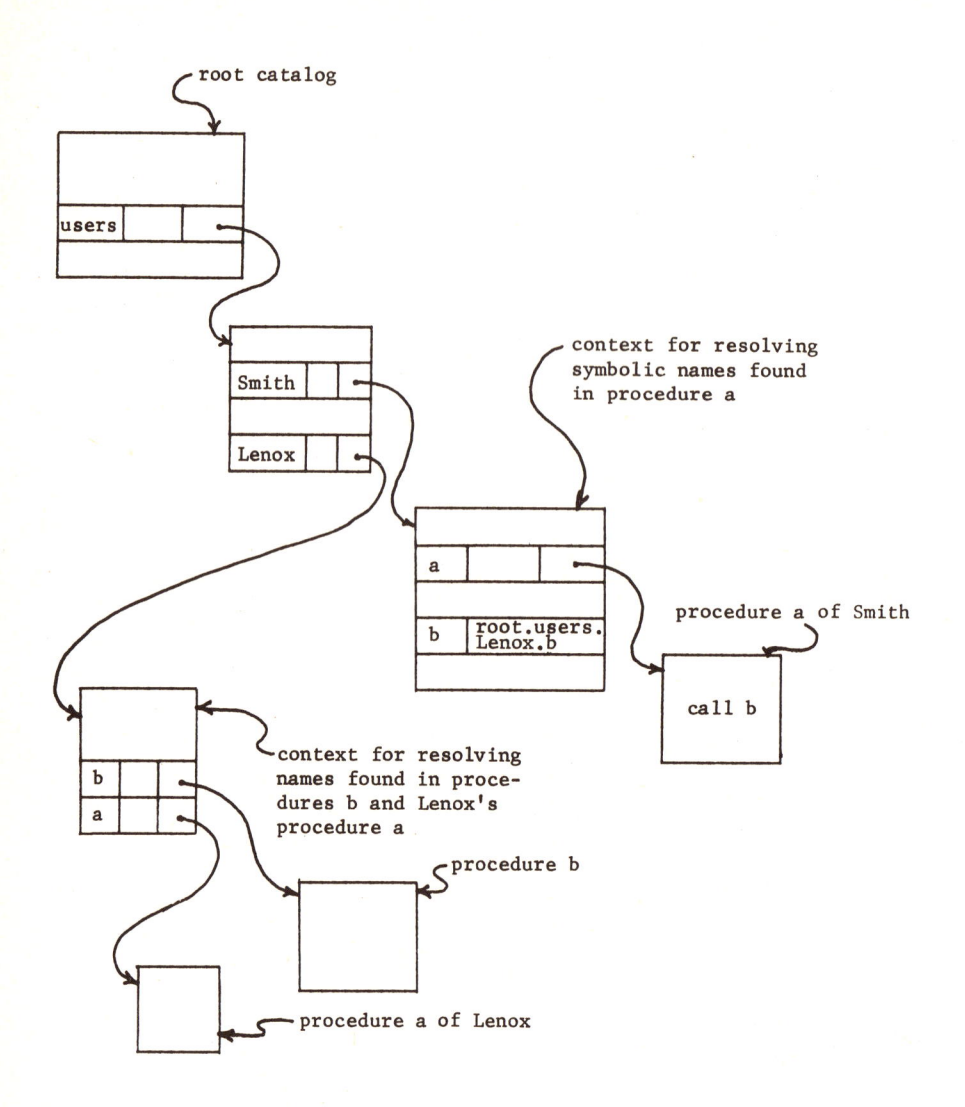

Figure 21 -- Sharing of procedures in a naming hierarchy with indirect catalog entries. The name "b" in Smith's catalog is bound to the tree name of Lenox's procedure, rather than its unique identifier. Since in a naming hierarchy the root catalog is distinguished, Smith no longer needs a binding for it; the name interpreter is assumed to know its unique identifier.

4. <u>Search</u> <u>rules</u>

Yet another approach to operation within the constraint of one catalog entry per object and a hierarchical naming tree is to condition the name interpreter to look in several different catalogs when resolving a name. Thus, for example, many systems arrange that names are looked up first in the user's working catalog, and failing there, in some standard library catalog. Such a simple system correctly handles a large percentage of the outward name references of traditional programs, since many programs call on other programs written by the same programmer or else universally available library programs.

The search rule scheme becomes more elaborate if other patterns of sharing are desired. One approach allows the user to specify that the search should proceed through any sequence of catalogs, including the working catalog, the catalog containing the referencing object, and arbitrary catalogs specified by path name. Further, a program may dynamically change the set of search rules that are in effect. This set of functions is intended to provide complete control over the bindings of outbound programs and data references, and allow sharing of subsystems in arbitrary ways, but the control tends to be clumsy. Unintended bindings are common, since a catalog belonging to another subsystem may contain unexpected names in addition to the ones for which the catalog was originally placed in the search path, yet every name of the catalog is subjected to this search. Substitution of one object for another can also be clumsy, since it typically requires that the search rules be somehow adjusted immediately before the reference occurs, and returned to their "normal" state before any other name reference occurs. To make this substitution more reliable, an artificial reference is sometimes used, with no purpose other than to force the search at a convenient time, locate the substituted object, and get its bindings installed for later actual use.*

Table IV summarizes the effect of using catalogs as repositories, indirect entries, and search rules on the various objectives that one might require of a file system and the reference name resolution ability of the context initializer for the addressing architecture.

E. Research directions

Name binding in computer systems, as should by now be apparent, is relatively ad hoc and disorganized. Conceptual models capture only some parts of what real system designers face. The simple model of names, contexts, and closures can be used to describe and better understand many observed properties and misbehaviors of practical systems, but one's intuition suggests that there should be more of an organized approach to the subject. Since the little bit of systemization so far accomplished grows out of studying equivalent, but smaller scale, problems of the semantics of naming within programming languages, one might hope that as that study progresses, further insight on system naming problems will result.

Apart from developing high-level conceptual models of name binding in file systems and addressing architectures, there are several relatively interesting naming topics about which almost nothing systematic is known, and the few case studies in existence are more intriguing for their irregularity, inconsistency, and misbehavior than for guidance on naming structure. These topics arise whenever distributed systems are encountered.

---

* The search rule strategy described here is essentially that used in Multics [Organick, 1972].

Table IV -- Effect on objectives of various implementation strategies.

Objective	model file system	distinguished catalog entries	general repositories, naming hierarchy	indirect entries	search rules
no lost objects	no	yes	yes	yes	no effect
independence of naming and storage allocation	yes	no	no	no	no
control of object attributes	no	no	yes	no effect	no effect
cross references without knowledge of tree structure	yes	yes	no	yes	yes
multiple contexts for an object	yes	yes	no	no	yes, but clumsy
Resolving reference names: easy to predict result	yes	yes	yes	yes	no
easy to specify	no	no	no	no	yes
correct operation under local rearrangement	yes	sometimes	no	no	no
old object still available to old users if reference name is rebound	yes	sometimes	no	no	no
precise substitution	yes	yes	no	yes	no

A system is distributed from the point of view of naming whenever two or more parallel and independently operating naming systems are asked to cooperate coherently with each other. For example, two or more separate computers, each with its own addressing architecture and file system, are linked by a communication network that allows messages to flow from any system to any other. The unsolved questions that arise surround preparing the addressing architectures and file systems so that:

1) Within each system the goals of sharing named objects are met essentially as in the models of this chapter.

2) Object sharing can occur between systems, so that an object in one system can have as constituents objects physically stored in other systems. Sharing between systems seems to involve maintaining contexts that work with multiple, independent name generators.

3) Objects can, if desired, be permanently moved from one system to another without the need to modify cross references to and from that object, especially cross references arising on systems not participating in the move.

4) Operations can proceed smoothly and gracefully even if some systems are temporarily disabled or are operating in isolation. This goal leads to consideration of keeping multiple copies of objects on different systems, and produces some real questions about how to name these multiple copies. It also means that name generation within any one system must be carried out independently of name generators on other systems, and it leads to problems of keeping name generators coordinated.

These descriptions of goals barely scratch the surface of the issues that must be explored, and until there are more examples of distributed systems that attempt coherent approaches to naming, it will not be clear what the next layer of questions is.

There are several activities underway that could shed some light on these questions. At the University of California at Irvine, a system named D.C.S. (for Distributed Computing System) has been designed and is the subject of current experimentation [Farber, et al., 1973]. At Bolt, Beranek, and Newman, a program named RSEXEC was developed that attempts to make all the file systems of a network of TENEX computers look to the user as a single, coherent file system [Thomas, 1973]. The Advanced Research Projects Agency of the U. S. Department of Defense has developed a "virtual file system" that operates on a variety of networked computers as part of a research program known as the National Software Works [Carlson and Crocker, 1974].

The current direction of hardware technology, leading to much lower costs for dedicated computers and networks to interconnect them, is making feasible a decentralization that has always been desired for administrative convenience, and one should expect that the problems of inventing ways of providing coherence across distinct computers that run independent naming systems will rapidly increase in importance.

Acknowledgements

The initial view of organization of this chapter grew out of conversations with M.D. Schroeder. Extensive and helpful technical comments on early drafts were made by D. Clark, L. Svobodova, G. Popek, and A. Jones, and observations about pedagogical problems were provided by J.C.R. Licklider and M. Hammer. Suggestions on style were made by K. Sollins. For several years, undergraduate students in the M.I.T. subject "Information Systems" suffered through early, somewhat muddled attempts to explain these ideas.

Sections A.2, A.3, and A.4 of the introduction follow closely the development by A. Henderson in his Ph.D. thesis [Henderson, 1975, pp. 17-26], with his permission.

Suggestions for further reading

1) The mechanics of naming [Henderson, 1975; Fabry, 1974; Dennis, 1965; Redell, 1975; Clingen, 1969].

2) Case studies of addressing architectures [Organick, 1972; Bell and Newell, 1971; Organick, 1973; Radin and Schneider, 1976; Needham, 1972; Watson, 1974, Chapter 2].

3) Case studies of file system naming schemes [Murphy, 1972; Bensoussan et al., 1972; Lampson and Sturgis, 1976; Needham and Birrell, 1977; Ritchie and Thompson, 1974; Organick, 1972; Watson, 1974, Chapter 6].

4) Object-oriented systems [Wulf et al., 1974; Janson, 1976; Redell, 1974].

5) Historical sources [Holt, 1961; Iliffe and Jodeit, 1962; Dennis, 1965; Daley and Dennis, 1968].

6) Semantics of naming in systems [Fraser, 1971].

References

Bell, C.G., and Newell, A., *Computer Structures*, McGraw-Hill, New York (1971). (SR)

Bensoussan, A., Clingen, C.T., and Daley, R.C., "The Multics virtual memory: concepts and design," *CACM* 15, 4 (May, 1972), pp. 308-318. (A.4, B, SR, App)

Bratt, R.G., "Minimizing the Naming Facilities Requiring Protection in a Computing Utility," S.M. Thesis, M.I.T. Dep't of Elec. Eng. and Comp. Sci. (Sept., 1976). (Also available as M.I.T. Lab. for Comp. Sci. Technical Report TR-156.) (App)

Carlson, W.E., and Crocker, S.D., "The impact of networks on the software marketplace," *Proc. IEEE Electronics and Aerospace Convention* (EASCON 1974), pp. 304-308. (E)

Clingen, C.T., "Program naming problems in a shared tree-structured hierarchy," *NATO Science Committee Conference on Techniques in Software Engineering 1*, Rome (October 27, 1969). (SR)

CODASYL (Anonymous), *Data Base Task Group Report*, Association for Computing Machinery, New York (1971). (C.2)

Crisman, P., Ed., *The Compatible Time-Sharing System: A Programmer's Guide*, 2nd ed., M.I.T. Press, Cambridge (1965). (C.2)

Daley, R.C., and Dennis, J.B., "Virtual memory, processes, and sharing in Multics," CACM 11, 5 (May, 1968), pp. 306-312. (B.2,B.3, SR,App)

Dennis, J.B., "Segmentation and the design of multiprogrammed computer systems," JACM 12, 4 (October, 1965), pp. 589-602. (A.1, SR, SR)

Fabry, R.S., "Capability-based addressing," CACM 17, 7 (July, 1974), pp. 403-412. (SR)

Falkoff, A.D., and Iverson, K.E., APL\360: User's Manual, IBM Corporation, White Plains, New York (1968). (A.4)

Farber, D.J., et al., "The distributed computing system," Proc. 7th IEEE Computer Society Conf. (COMPCON 73), pp. 31-34. (E)

Fraser, A.G., "On the meaning of names in programming systems," CACM 14, 6 (June, 1971), pp. 409-416. (A.1, SR)

Henderson, D.A., Jr., "The binding model: A semantic base for modular programming systems," Ph.D. thesis, M.I.T. Dep't of Elec. Eng. and Comp. Sci. (February, 1975). (Also available as M.I.T. Project MAC Technical Report TR-145.) (SR)

Henderson, P., and Morris, J.H., "A Lazy Evaluator," Proc. 3rd ACM Symposium on Principles of Programming Languages, (January, 1976), pp. 95-103. (B.3)

Holt, A., "Program organization and record keeping for dynamic storage allocation," CACM 4, 10 (Oct., 1961), pp. 422-431. (A.1,SR)

IBM (Anonymous) Reference Manual: 709/7090 FORTRAN Operations, IBM Corporation, White Plains, New York (1961). C28-6066 (A.4,A.4)

Iliffe, J., and Jodeit, "A dynamic storage allocation scheme," Computer Journal 5, (Oct., 1962), pp. 200-209. (A.1,SR)

Janson, P.A., "Removing the Dynamic Linker from the Security Kernel of a Computing Utility," S.M. Thesis, M.I.T. Dep't of Elec. Eng. and Comp. Sci. (June, 1974). (Also available as M.I.T. Project MAC Technical Report TR-132.) (App)

Janson, P.A., "Using type extension to organize virtual memory mechanisms," Ph.D. Thesis, M.I.T. Dep't of Elec. Eng. and Comp. Sci. (Sept., 1976). (Also available as M.I.T. Lab. for Comp. Sci. Technical Report TR-167.) (SR)

Kilburn, et al., "One-Level Storage System," IRE Trans. on Elec. Computers EC-11, 2 (April, 1962), pp. 223-235. (C.1)

Knuth, D., The Art of Computer Programming, Volume 1/Fundamental Algorithms, Addison Wesley, Reading, Mass. (1968), Chapter 2. (D.1)

Lampson. B.W., and Sturgis, H.E., "Reflections on an operating system design," CACM 19, 5 (May, 1976), pp. 251-265. (C.2,D.1, SR)

Moses, J., "The function of FUNCTION in LISP," SIGSAM Bulletin (July, 1970), pp. 13-27. (A.4)

Murphy, D.L., "Storage organization and management in TENEX," AFIPS Conf. Proc. 41 I (FJCC, 1972), pp. 23-32. (B.2,SR)

Needham, R., "Protection systems and protection implementation," AFIPS Conf. Proc. 41 I (FJCC, 1972), pp. 571-578. (B.2,SR)

Needham, R.M., and Birrell, A.D., "The CAP filing system," Proc. 6th ACM Symposium on Operating Systems Principles (November, 1977), pp. 11-16. (C.2,D.1, SR)

Organick, E.I., The Multics System: an Examination of its Structure, M.I.T. Press, Cambridge (1972). (D.4,SR, SR,App)

Organick, E.I., Computer System Organization, The B5700/B6700 Series, Academic Press, New York (1973). (SR)

Radin, G., and Schneider, P.R., "An architecture for an extended machine with protected addressing," IBM Poughkeepsie Lab Technical Report TR 00.2757 (May, 1976). (B,SR)

Redell, D.D., "Naming and protection in extendible operating systems," Ph.D. Thesis, Univ. of Cal. at Berkeley, (Sept., 1974). (Also available as M.I.T. Project MAC Technical Report TR-140.) (B,SR, SR)

Ritchie, D.M., and Thompson, K., "The UNIX time-sharing system," CACM 17, 7 (July, 1974), pp. 365-375. (D.1,D.2, SR)

Schroeder, M.D., and Saltzer, J.H., "A hardware architecture for implementing protection rings," CACM 15, 3 (Mar., 1972), pp. 157-170. (B.2,B.2)

Thomas, R.H., "A resource sharing executive for the ARPANET," AFIPS Conf. Proc. 42 (1973 NCC), pp. 159-163. (E)

Watson, R.W., Timesharing System Design Concepts, McGraw-Hill New York (1974). (SR,SR, App)

Wulf, W., et al., "HYDRA: The kernel of a multiprocessor operating system," CACM 17, 6 (June, 1974), pp. 337-345. (SR)

Appendix A: Case Study of Naming in Multics

The Multics system implements a shared-object addressing architecture and a variation of a direct-access file system. In doing so, this system illustrates an interesting set of design choices and compromises. To a close approximation, the designers of Multics had in mind achieving all of the naming objectives discussed in this chapter, but they had to work within the framework of modest extensions to an existing, fairly simple addressing architecture, that of the General Electric 635 computer. In addition, Multics was one of the first designs to be ventured in this area, and some of its design decisions would undoubtedly be handled differently today. For clarity in this case study, we shall examine only the user-visible naming facilities of Multics. We shall ignore the closely-related, but user-invisible multilevel memory management (paging) machinery, and also the closely-related information protection facilities. The reader should, however, realize that these three functions are actually implemented with integrated, overlapping mechanisms.

1. The addressing architecture of Multics

Multics implements a single, simple kind of object known as a segment. A segment is an array of 36-bit words, containing any desired number of words between zero and 262,144. An individual word within a segment is named by specifying its displacement, or distance from word zero of the segment, as in figure 22.[1] Although segments have unique identities, the addressing architecture does not use unique identifiers to name segments.* Thus there is no universal, underlying context for naming segments. Instead, Multics implements a large number of small segment-naming contexts, known as address spaces. Typically, one address space is provided for each distinct

---

* The Multics file system, described below, maintains a unique identifier for each file, but that unique identifier cannot be used by the addressing architecture.

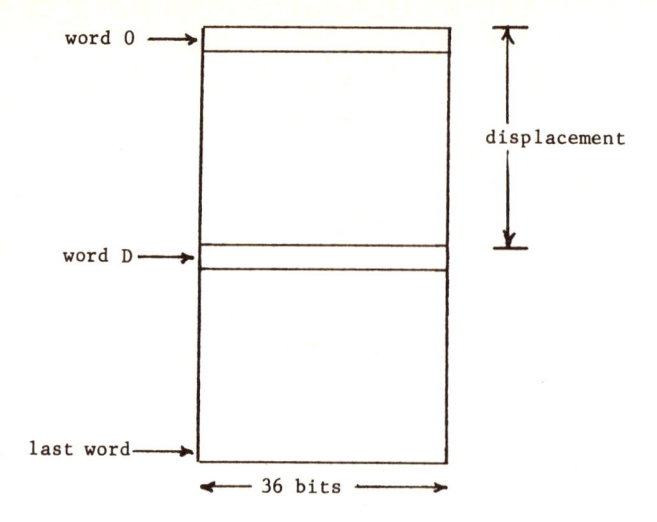

Figure 22 -- A Multics segment.

---

active user of Multics, and an address space has the lifetime of a user terminal session.

The reason for such a choice is that each individual address space need be no larger than the number of segments actually used in the lifetime of a terminal session, and the names resolved by the address space can therefore be a small, compact set of integers, known as __segment numbers__. Only a few address bits are then needed to hold a segment number, and the context itself can be implemented as a small array of entries using the segment number as an array index: the context is called a __descriptor segment__, and a segment number is simply a displacement within some descriptor segment. (See figure 23.) Although the hardware architecture allows

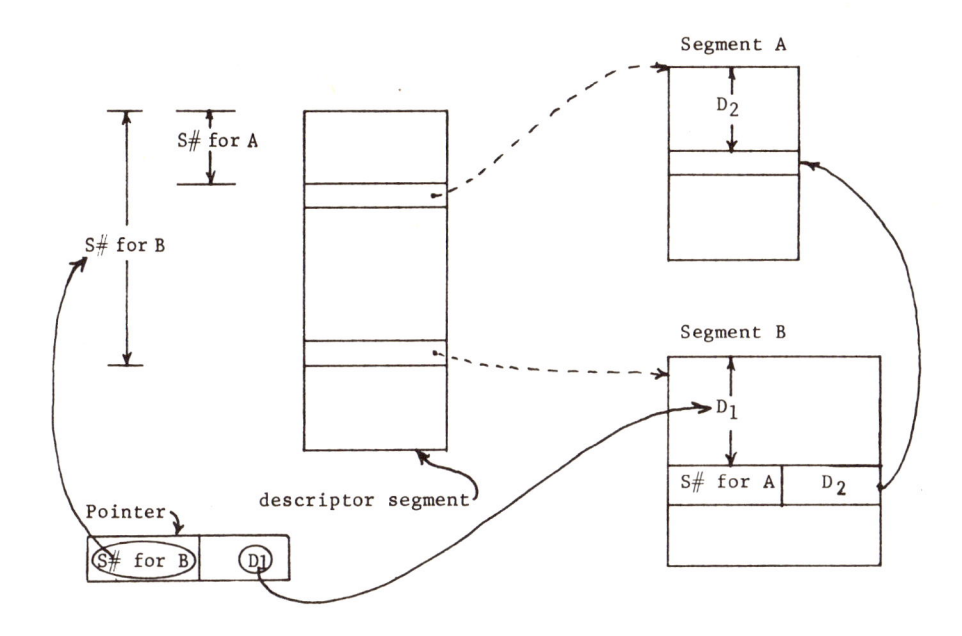

Figure 23 -- Pointer addressing in Multics. A pointer contains a
segment number (S#), which is a displacement in the
descriptor segment that identifies the lower-level
(physical) address of the segment. The pointer also
contains a displacement that identifies a word within
the ultimately addressed segment. The pointer on the
left refers to a word in the segment labelled B, and
that word happens to contain a pointer to a word in
the segment labelled A.

segment numbers up to 18 bits in length, typical address spaces have only a few hundred segments, and the software tables required to keep track of what those segment numbers mean have size limits of only a few thousand entries.

The compromise involved is that segment numbers are meaningful only in the context in which they were defined: if one user passes a segment number to another user, there is no reason to expect that number to have the same meaning in the other user's address space. Thus, segment numbers cannot be used to implement complex, linked structures that are shared between different users. On the other hand, sharing is still quite feasible since, as we saw in section B.2, when user-dependent bindings are a goal, one takes care not to embed object numbers in shared objects anyway. A second aspect of the compromise is that there is no a priori relationship between segment identities and segment numbers; when a job begins a new address space must be created and the segments of interest must be mapped (Multics literature uses the word _initiated_) into the new address space. Initiation represents a run-time cost, and requires supporting tables to keep track of which segments have been initiated.

One segment may contain a reference to another in two ways in Multics. The simplest way, but usable only in segments not shared with other address spaces and having a lifetime no greater than the current address space, is by means of a _pointer_, which is just a segment number and displacement address stored in a standard format. (See figure 23.) Because segment numbers have different bindings in different address spaces, a more complex form of inter-segment reference is required if the containing segment is to be shared. For example, procedure segments need to refer to data segments and other procedure segments, but procedures are commonly shared. This second form of reference is by way of a per-procedure context, known in Multics as a <u>linkage section</u>. A pointer register in the processor, known as the <u>linkage pointer</u>, points to the beginning of the linkage section, as shown in figure 24 . An instruction that refers to an object outside the procedure uses for its operand address an indirect address, specifying some displacement relative to the linkage pointer. The linkage section contains at that displacement an ordinary pointer to the desired object.

If a second user shares the procedure segment, a second linkage section is involved, as in figure 25 . Note that there are two address spaces involved in this figure, but that no pointers in either address space lead to the other. The only segments shared between the two address spaces contain no embedded pointers. In addition, all references to the shared segments are by way of pointers in either the processor or linkage section private to an address space, so a shared segment can have different segment numbers in the two address spaces.

Finally, for speed, each processor contains eight pointer registers (actually, the linkage pointer is one of them) that a program may load with any desired pointer. Once such a register is loaded, that register can then be used as an operand address, thus avoiding the use of the slower indirect reference through memory.

When calling from one procedure to another, the value of the linkage pointer must be changed to point to the linkage section of the new procedure. This change is not accomplished by automatic hardware in Multics, but rather by a conventional sequence of instructions in the called program. A per address space table of closures, known as the <u>linkage offset table</u>, contains pointers to every linkage section, one for each procedure in the address space. One of the processor pointer registers conventionally

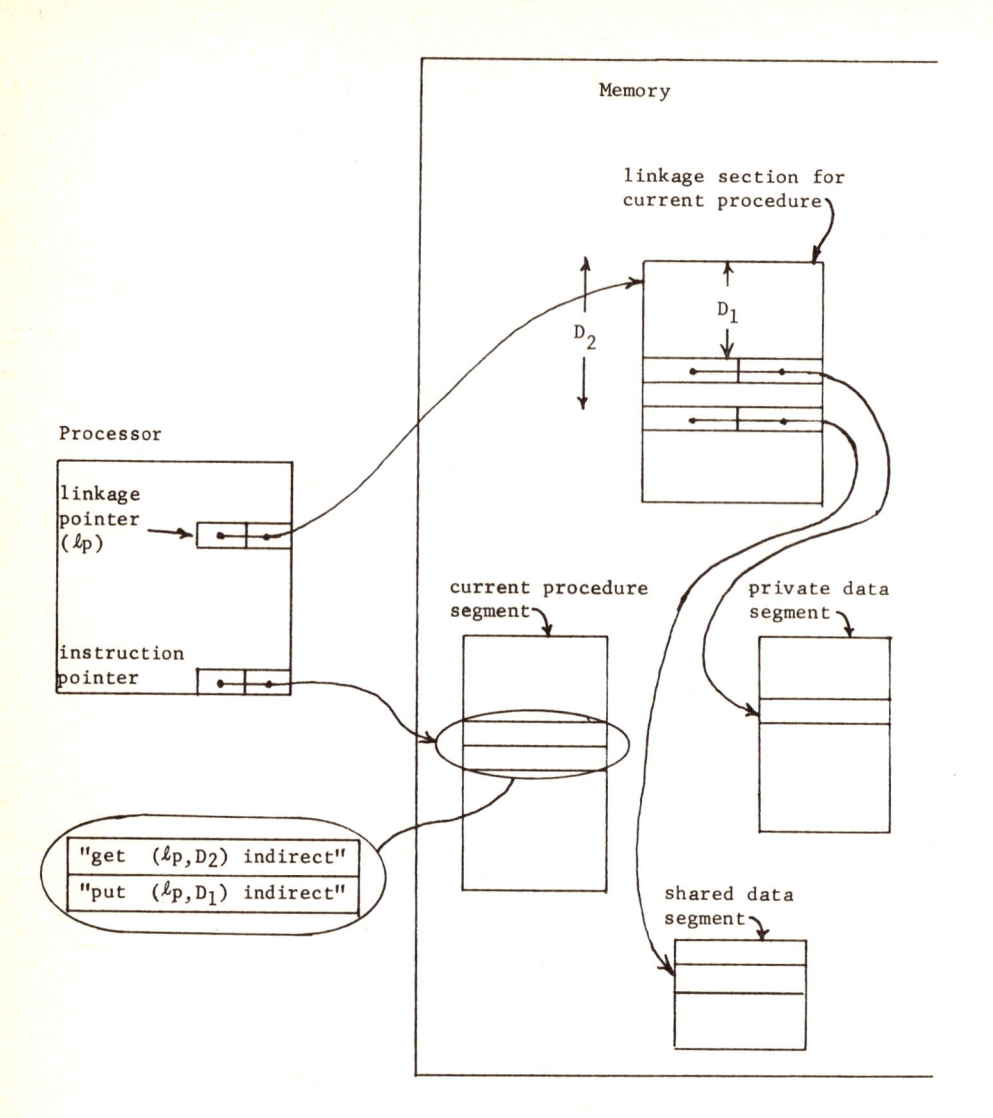

Figure 24 -- Intersegment references in Multics by procedure. The operand address specifies indirect addressing via the Dth word of the segment that is the current target of the linkage pointer register. The linkage section is thus a context for the current procedure. For simplicity, the descriptor segment is not shown, but all four of the pointer references of the figure, it should be remembered, are interpreted using the descriptor segment as the context.

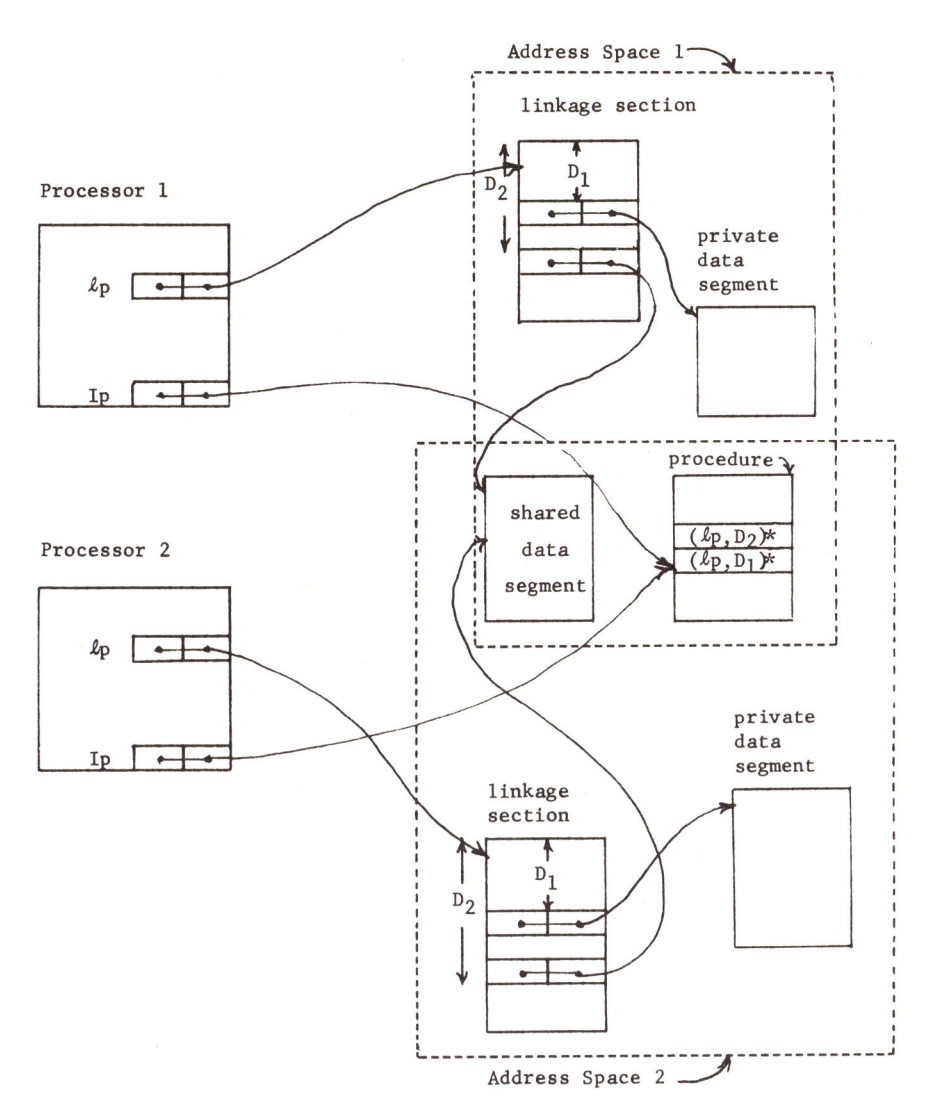

Figure 25 -- Shared address spaces in Multics. Hidden in each processor (and not shown in this figure) is a register (the <u>descriptor segment base register</u>) that contains the physical address of a descriptor segment (also not shown). The two processors above are using different descriptor segments, and thus different address spaces. However, these address spaces overlap in that a procedure segment and a shared data segment appear in both. Note that the shared segments can have different segment numbers in the two address spaces, yet all intersegment references work correctly. The notation $(\ell p, D_2)*$ means that the pointer addressed by the pair $(\ell p, D_2)$ should be used as an indirect address. This figure should be compared with figure 10, which illustrates a similar configuration.

contains a pointer that leads (after indirection through a stack segment, not of concern to us here) to the base of the linkage offset table. The conventional sequence upon entry to a procedure is then the following: sometime before the first intersegment reference of the procedure is encountered, use this procedure's segment number as a displacement in the linkage offset table to load the linkage pointer register with a pointer to the linkage section of this procedure. This operation is so similar to the corresponding operation of the addressing architecture developed earlier that figure 12 can be used directly to illustrate it, with a slightly different caption.

2. The Multics file system

For its file system, Multics implements a direct-access hierarchy of named catalogs and files. The catalogs are known as directories, and for each catalogued object contain not only any number of synonymous names, but also are the repository for a physical storage map, a unique identifier, an access control list, reliability control, and resource accounting information. A root directory is "known to the system" and when a user program presents a tree name the file system resolves it by starting in that root directory. Every directory and file except the root is represented by exactly one direct entry, known as a branch, in some directory, so a strict hierarchy results. This strict hierarchy was chosen on the basis of simplicity--the lost object problem need not be considered--and expediency--using the directory as a repository seemed the quickest design to implement.

For flexibility, then, indirect directory entries are also provided, called <u>links</u>. Any number of indirect entries can lead to the same directory or file. A link is a directory entry that binds a directory entry name to an associated tree name that leads from the root directory to the desired object.* If the entry named by the link is another link, then that second link is followed; a link depth counter limits such successive links to ten, so as to catch links accidentally arranged in an infinite loop.

The file system maintains for each user a cell containing the absolute path name of some directory, called the user's <u>working</u> directory. One can then more briefly express the name of some objects by a <u>relative</u> path name that starts from the working directory. Names typed at the terminal are usually interpreted relative to the working directory, although the user can also type in an absolute path name by using a distinctive syntax.

The pattern of use of the file system is as follows: suppose the user is in interactive communication with an application program, such as an editor, and he types to the editor the instruction to look at something in a file named "a". The editor takes the relative path name "a", and first passes it to a utility program that combines it with the name of the current working directory and returns an absolute path name, suitable for presentation to the file system. The editor then calls the <u>initiate</u> entry of the file system, presenting the absolute path name. The file system resolves this name through its directory hierarchy, following any links encountered along the way. Assuming it finds a file by that name, this user has permission to use it, and it has not previously been initiated, the file system then selects an unused segment number in the current address space,

---

* A link may actually contain an <u>absolute</u> <u>path</u> <u>name</u>; that is, a name that begins at the root and proceeds, possibly via other links, to lead to some named object in the directory hierarchy. (The difference between an absolute path name and a tree name is that a tree name may not involve links.) Allowing links to contain absolute pathnames makes links to directories useful; however the procedure that resolves tree names may become resursive.

fabricates a descriptor segment entry, and returns the segment number to the editor. The file system also makes an entry in a table for this address space, the _Known Segment Table_, relating the unique identifier of the file, the chosen segment number and the directory in which the file was found. If the file in question had previously been initiated in this address space, its unique identifier would already be in the known segment table, and the segment number found there would be returned, rather than a new one. In either case, the editor program uses the returned segment number and an appropriate displacement to fabricate a pointer, and it then reads the contents of the file by direct reference to memory.

The file of the file system has been mapped into a segment of the addressing architecture, and neither the file system nor the addressing architecture make any interpretation of the contents--they are simply an array of up to 262,144 36-bit words.* A file may be larger than 262,144 words, in which case the addressing architecture provides a window into some portion of the file, up to 262,144 words in size. The window can be moved by a call to the address space manager.**

3. _Context initialization in Multics_

The previous example of mapping of a file of the file system into a segment of the addressing architecture started with an interactively supplied file name. Initialization of procedure naming contexts also may involve a step of mapping a file system file into a segment of the addressing architecture.

---

*   Interpretations such as "indexed sequential" files are provided by application level library programs that use the file system and addressing architecture as tools.

** Files larger than 262,144 words and movable windows have not yet been implemented as of Spring, 1978.

Consider a procedure named "a", which contains within it a call to another procedure named "b"*. The compiler of "a" produces an object program consisting of the instructions to carry out procedure "a" and a prototype of the linkage section that will serve as that procedure's context during execution. Contained in that prototype linkage section is a dummy pointer, corresponding to the outbound reference to "b", and consisting of a flag (which will cause the hardware addressing architecture to signal a fault) and the character string "b".** Suppose that the segment containing procedure "a" and its linkage section have been previously mapped into the addressing architecture, and procedure "a" attempts to call "b" for the first time. Upon trying to interpret the dummy pointer, the addressing architecture will signal the fault, passing control to the context initializer program, known in Multics as the dynamic linker.*** The dynamic linking program retrieves from the dummy pointer the character string name "b", resolves it into a segment number, replaces the dummy pointer with a real one containing the segment number and displacement of the entry point, and restarts the interrupted procedure "a". Since the dummy pointer has been replaced with a real one, the procedure call will now work correctly. Further, if procedure "a" ever calls procedure "b" again, that later call will be resolved at the speed of the addressing architecture, rather than the speed of the dynamic linker. The outbound reference from "a" to "b" has been bound, at the addressing architecture level, for the lifetime of the address space.

---

*   Multics includes an entry-point naming scheme that allows one program to call on a named entry point, say "c", of a named procedure, say "b". The following discussion ignores that feature; strictly it describes what happens if program "a" calls entry point "b" of procedure "b", which is the most common case, and the default if only one name is supplied by the calling program.

**   Note that, because segment numbers for a given procedure are different in different address spaces, the compiler cannot place an operational pointer in the prototype linkage segment.

***   As may be apparent by now, the word <u>link</u> is used in Multics for at least two unrelated but similar concepts: indirect catalog entries and the pointers of procedure contexts. Sentences containing the word "link" do not always come supplied with closures, so confusion is common.

The interesting aspect of the dynamic linking sequence is, of course, how the dynamic linker resolves the name "b" into a segment number. As we noted in the general discussion of context initialization, the goal is to resolve the name "b" according to the intent of the subsystem writer who chose to use "a", rather than the current interactive user, so the name resolution takes this goal into account, though imperfectly. The first step is to look in a table for this address space, called the reference name table, which the dynamic linker maintains for this purpose. Each time it maps a procedure or data object into the address space, the dynamic linker places the name of that procedure and its segment number in the reference name table. Thus, the name "a" is certain to be in the reference table, and if it has been previously called from within the address space, so will the name "b". The primary purpose of the reference name table is to avoid the expense of following a path name through the file system directory hierarchy more than once per procedure; often, procedures of a subsystem are used by more than one other procedure of that subsystem. A related effect of the reference name table is to capture a single, address-space-wide binding for a name, so as to guarantee that all callers for that name consistently get the same result, independent of what we shall see is a potentially variable strategy used by the dynamic linker for name binding. The difficulty with the reference name table is that when two independently conceived subsystems are invoked in the same address space, they share the single reference name table, and name conflict can occur.

So much for the reference name table. What if the name "b" is not
found there, indicating that procedure "b" has never been mapped into
this address space? Actually, the check of the reference name table is
properly viewed as the first search rule of a multistep search for the
procedure named "b". If that rule fails, the search is carried on to the
file system, using the assumption that the procedure "b" is to be found
in some file named "b" in the directory hierarchy. As an approximation
to the idea that the directory containing a procedure can be used as a
closure for that procedure's outbound references, the next step of the
search is to look for the name "b" in the directory that the calling procedure, "a", came from. (Remember that the known segment table contains
for each segment, among other things, the directory that the segment was
found in. One reason was to allow this search rule to be implemented easily.)
The dynamic linker thus attempts to initiate a segment named "b" from that
same directory. If that attempt succeeds, it creates an empty linkage section
for "b" to use as its context, places a pointer to that linkage section in the
linkage offset table for this address space, installs "b" in the reference
name table, and then proceeds as if "b" had always been in the reference name
table. If it fails, it continues with the search. The next step is to try
the current working directory, and then to begin going down a list of tree
names of other directories, attempting to initiate the file "b" in each of
those directories in turn. These directories are usually system and project
libraries, though a user may place the tree name of any directory in his
search list. The user may also rearrange the search rules in any order, for
example by placing the search of the reference name table last, or even
deleting it from the list. (Note that even if the reference name table is
not part of the search, it is used to prevent duplicate context initialization.)

Probably the chief virtue of the search rule strategy of Multics is that its imprecision in binding can be exploited to accomplish things for which specific semantics would otherwise need to be provided. For example, the proprietors of the system library can move a library program from, say, the normal library to a library containing obsolete procedures. Users of that program will discover the move through a failure report from the dynamic linker, but they can recover simply by adding the obsolete library directory to their search rules, without changing any programs or links. For a different example, a procedure can be moved from a project library directory to the system library directory; users of that procedure will continue to find it in the normal course of a search without any change to their programs or operation at all.

On the other hand, as was suggested earlier, in the general discussion of adjustable search rules, they are a fairly clumsy and error-prone way to accomplish user-dependent bindings. Probably the primary reason that search rules have persisted in the Multics design, rather than being superceded or augmented by addition of catalogued closure objects, is that most other operating systems, both previous to and contemporary with Multics, have used some form of search at least for system libraries, so this pattern of operation is familiar to both system designers and users.

An interesting complication arises from the combination of design compromises in the addressing architecture and file system of Multics. The addressing architecture provides a very large address space, in which it is feasible to map simultaneously several closely communicating but independently conceived subsystems. On the other hand, the address space survives only for the time of a user's terminal session (or batch job) and therefore inter-procedure linkages cannot be bound in advance; they must be initialized dynamically. But dynamic initialization involves a search, which can be relatively expensive. As a result, two strategies have evolved for minimizing the number of times the dynamic linker is actually invoked.

First, a utility routine, known as the binder, will take as input several procedures, and combine them and their linkage sections into a single procedure and linkage section, with all cross-references among the set resolved into internal displacements rather than pointer references. This new single procedure is written out into a single file, and when used is mapped into a single segment of the addressing architecture. Using the binder eliminates a large percentage of dynamic linking operations, but if one library procedure is used in two different subsystems, to avoid dynamic linking the shared procedure must be copied into both of them.

Second, the conventional way of using the Multics system is to leave all procedure contexts, once initialized, in place for the duration of the terminal session or batch job, so that if the procedure should be used again as part of another command interaction or job step, it will not be necessary to repeat initialization of its context. Thus the interprocedure links are persistent.

Although at first glance this persistence seems to be exactly right, actually it is desirable to be able to reverse or adjust these bindings occasionally. For example, when a programmer is testing out a newly-written set of procedures, and discovers an error, the usual approach is to correct the symbolic version of the procedure, and then recompile it. Conventionally, the compiler overwrites the old procedure with the new one, so the procedure's segment number does not change, but occasionally the entry point of the procedure moves to a new displacement, as a result of fixing the error.

When that happens, any old pointers to this procedure found in linkage sections of other procedures become obsolete, and should be readjusted. Multics does not attempt to maintain the tables and backpointers that would be required to automatically readjust interprocedure linkage pointers, so when the displacement of an entry point changes the usual result is an attempt to enter the procedure at the wrong displacement, followed by some rather baffling failure of the application. The user can request a fresh address space at any time, and that fixes the problem by initializing a fresh set of contexts, all consistent with one another. Unfortunately, completely initializing a fresh address space is a relatively expensive operation. In addition, a beginning programmer typically encounters the first example of an incorrect, persistent interprocedure link long before he is prepared to understand the complex underpinnings that cause it; many programmers consider the need to occasionally request a fresh address space to be a mystery as well as a nuisance.

4. Bibliography on naming in Multics

Primary sources (original research papers) [Daley and Dennis, 1968; Bensoussan, Clingen, and Daley, 1972; Bratt, 1975; Janson, 1974]. Secondary sources (tutorials and texts) [Organick, 1972; Watson, 1974].

CHAPTER 3.B.

G. J. Popek and C. S. Kline
University of California at Los Angeles
Los Angeles, Ca., USA

Issues in Kernel Design

Issues in Kernel Design*

by

Gerald J. Popek and Charles S. Kline

University of California at Los Angeles

Abstract

Considerable activity recently has been devoted to the design and development of operating system kernels, as part of efforts to provide much more reliably secure systems than heretofore available. The resulting kernel architectures differ substantially from more traditional systems of similar function and, in particular, appear superior with respect to reliability, simplicity, and security.

Understanding of the intrinsic characteristics of kernel architectures, including design principles, costs and values, is just now being developed. This paper considers these issues in general, as well as in the context of specific systems.

1. Introduction

As operating systems became larger and more complex, interest increased in segmenting that software in a rational fashion. With respect to operating systems, a number of efforts were made to develop a low level base that would provide basic system functions in a highly reliable way. On top of this skeletal software base, extensive operating system functions and user supports would be built. Early efforts in this direction, although significantly different in scale and goals, include IBM's virtual machine system CP-67 [IBM 72], Brinch-Hansen's RC-4000 nucleus [Bri 73], and CAL-TSS [Lam 76].

However, the greatest impetus to this activity grew recently out of the desire for secure operating systems -- those that could assure that the access to data stored within was controlled and protected in an uncircumventable way. Efforts have been made by a number of groups to design and develop operating system bases that, in addition to providing necessary primitive functions, were wholly responsible for the security of the operating system, including whatever was built on top of that nucleus. Part of the goal of these efforts typically was to minimize the size and complexity of the resulting nucleus, in the well founded belief that to do so would greatly increase the likelihood that the resulting software would be correctly imple-

----
*This research was supported by the Advanced Research Projects Agency of the Department of Defense under Contract DAHC-73-C-0368.

mented. Desires to apply program verification methods to this software have heightened the importance of these minimization goals, since current verification methods are applicable only to modest sized, simply structured programs. Such a minimum size, security oriented operating system nucleus is typically called a "security kernel" [Sch 74].

It should be noted that these efforts have taken place in an environment where reliable security has become of increasing concern. No general purpose operating system of a more traditional design has successfully provided a satisfactory degree of assurance for those who are seriously concerned about control over their data. Known flaws are so numerous that it is generally recognized a highly systematic approach is required. Since it appears that kernel based architectures will make considerable strides in improving that situation, an understanding of their characteristics is useful.

There are several considerations that make a kernel based operating system architecture significantly different from a more traditional architecture developed without security as a major design criterion. Reliable security demands that the software upon which security depends be as small and simple as practical. As a result, functions included in operating system bases to enhance performance or increase the convenience of writing software above that base are not needed for security purposes and consequently not included in a kernel. Kernel designs would typically exclude that software despite potentially increased performance overhead or greater non-kernel software complexity. Naturally, the architecture is structured to avoid these costs as much as possible, and it appears that such penalties can generally be minimized.

Conversely however, the kernel must contain all security related software if correct enforcement is not to depend on non-kernel software. Therefore, as a countering influence, functions are forced into the kernel that may have been omitted from an operating system base and implementable at an outer level. The body of this paper characterizes the architectural principles that lead to these changes. Examples of the relocation of system functions in an architecture are also given.

2. Effects of Design Constraints on Kernel Architectures

While kernel architectures in general exhibit many common characteristics and differ substantially from traditional operating system architectures, they also differ significantly among themselves. The technical constraints concerning security policy, function, hardware and performance must be specified before it will be possible to develop appropriate kernel specifications. Each of these considerations is discussed in turn below.

2.1 Security Policy

The amount of mechanism that must be included in a security kernel is greatly affected by the particular security policy (control discipline [Pop 74] or level of function [Sal 75]) that it is desired to enforce. For example, the support required for isolation is considerably less than what is needed for general support of intimate controlled sharing with domain switches within an individual process.

Kernel architectures have been directed primarily at the goal of reliable "data security": assuring that it is possible for users only to access data to which they are specifically entitled. Issues such as confinement or denial of service have generally not been directly addressed, although care usually has been taken to minimize such problems. Clearly, the more sophisticated the security policy that it is desired to enforce, the more kernel mechanism will likely be needed.

Data security policies themselves may be subdivided on a number of criteria. What are the objects that are protected? An operating system kernel might support any one of the subsets of an extensive list of potential objects: processes, pages, segments, files, file subtrees, messages and/or message channels, records, fields, mini-disks, entire devices (tape drives, disk packs, terminals) or partitions of devices (blocks on a tape, windows on a crt terminal).

Next, what is the _object grain_: the size of the objects protected. Are processes the active objects, or can a procedure call within a process coincide with a domain change, as in Hydra. [Wul 75] Perhaps, in a system that supports a family tree of processes for a given user, the entire family is the active object, with no distinction made among processes. That is, all processes in the tree might be required to have the same access rights. This design was used in the TENEX operating system.

What are the rules governing the alteration of system data that records the security policy? That is, what is the _policy grain_. Is control over objects and groups of objects hierarchically distributed as in Multics[Sal 74], or is it strictly centralized, as in the IBM operating systems. What is the precision with which one can specify access control decisions? Can a file be marked with the exact list of users to be given access, or can one only set the access mode as either public or private, to illustrate two extremes.

2.2 System Functions

Apart from the question of the security policy supported by a kernel, a serious impact on the actual kernel design and implementation results from the functions and services to be supported by that kernel. Is it possible, for instance, to create and destroy objects of all types supported by the kernel, or do certain cases, such as mini-disks, have their allocation fixed at the time the kernel is assembled. To what degree is the number of objects of each type supported and protected by the kernel fully variable. How rich are the set of operators provided to access the kernel protected objects. Are sophisticated message synchronization primitives built, or is a simpler, less efficient facility provided, out of which user software must simulate the desired features.

Type extensibility is another aspect of system function. Is it possible for user programs to create new objects of new types and have these new objects protected in a fashion similar to previously existing objects. This type extensibility first appeared in programming languages, and subsequently in the CAL-TSS system.[Lam 76]

Another aspect of system functionality that invariably affects a security kernel concerns device support. For reasons discussed later, most hardware designs require, for security to be reliably enforced, that there be additional kernel software for each device type. Therefore, the more general hardware base to support, the larger and potentially more complex a kernel can result.

Another significant consideration affecting a security kernel is the convenience with which operating system software can be constructed on top of the primitives which are provided. If certain facilities are entirely absent, selected functions may be impossible to provide. The existing Unix kernel does not permit asynchronous I/O within a user process.[Rit 74] Other functions may be possible to build, but only in a relatively inconvenient way. The UCLA kernel does not support the process hierarchies required by UNIX, although they can be built outside the kernel using inter-process communication facilities.

In general, one wishes as little functionality in the kernel as is sufficient. In applying this philosophy, one should examine the necessary functions and determine whether a different, smaller and simpler set would suffice. A large collection of real time functions and synchronization primitives might be replaced by a few I/O calls (probably needed anyway), a simple signaling method and a way to mark a user process uninterruptible for a short period. The rest may be constructable on that simpler base.

2.3 Hardware Effects

The hardware base on which a kernel is built can significantly impact the resulting kernel, including its size, complexity, overall architecture, and details of implementation. The richness of the hardware base that must be supported will have considerable effect. A multiple processor system, in which more than one cpu executes kernel functions, may require support for processor coordination within the kernel that single processor systems do not. Certain types of I/O channels may need detailed cpu software support.

Typically, the accesses made by central processors are constrained by memory management units, protection keys, or other hardware support. That support has the characteristic that privileged cpu software can set the controls and then permit untrusted software to run with assurance that it is not possible for software to exceed those access rights recorded in the hardware controls. The hardware implemented control features associated with channel accesses to main memory and to secondary storage are typically much less convenient, or even non-existent. Channels on most machines use absolute addresses to access main memory, instead of having a virtual reference modified and controlled by relocation hardware. Therefore, unless some other form of hardware enforced protection, such as IBM's storage keys, limit the channel's access, additional kernel software is required to check and perhaps modify the addresses used by the channel in performing I/O. This task can be quite complex and error prone, even on IBM hardware, as reported by Belady and Weissman [Bel 74].

While in some existing machines, channels' main memory access is controlled by programmable hardware assists, it is even rarer also to find hardware support for control of access to the secondary storage connected to the channel. Therefore it is generally necessary for kernel software to check or modify the secondary storage addresses and relevant commands that compose channel programs. Certain machines such as the IBM 360/370 series have some limited hardware supported control over secondary storage access. There, changes in cylinder or track can be blocked for the duration of a channel program's execution. However, such facilities are generally insufficient for direct use by the kernel to protect pages, segments or file systems.

I/O is clearly one area where hardware characteristics considerably affect the security kernel, but it is not the only one. A simple example, the time of day clock on many machines is located in a way so that only privileged software can read it, despite the fact that the time of day is not relevant to most definitions of data security. On the PDP-11, both the word size and cpu arithmtic are organized on a 16 bit basis. Absolute addresses are larger however. I/O device registers (each 16 bits) have the additional bits located in additional registers, with little commonality among devices where those bits are to be found. Sometimes carry from the 16-th to 17-th bit is implemented, sometimes not. As a result, special software for each device is typically needed to check address bounds. As a result, additional kernel code is required that could have been eliminated with judicious hardware planning.

There are often a number of such hardware characteristics that considerably complicate the task of building a secure kernel, and that would not require significant changes to greatly diminish those difficulties. The previous examples were largely of this class. More dramatic changes to the hardware base could of course greatly contribute to reliable system security. Capability based architectures have considerable promise in that respect. Kernel designs such as those being pursued at UCLA particularly lend themselves to implementation in firmware. The attractive feature about many of these points is that their adoption should not necessarily imply significantly increased fabrication costs, and both the simplicity and reliability of software would be enhanced.

2.4 Performance

The last significant issues which affect the size and complexity of the kernel are performance constraints. Stringent performance requirements as expected make it difficult to develop a straightforward design and implementation. For example, while it may be possible for scheduling decisions to be made through a separate user process which is only interrogated by the kernel, the additional process switch overhead to invoke the scheduler for each expected user process switch may impose unacceptable delays. Expensive domain changing usually exerts pressures that lead to larger, more complex kernels, since one is tempted to integrate such functions as scheduling into kernel code.

The costly effects of this phenomenon are well illustrated by the Multics experience.[Sal 76] On its original GE 645 hardware base, ring crossings (domain changes) were quite expensive, since the existence of rings were simulated in software by a complete switch of segment tables and status at each ring crossing. As a result, performance pressures led the highly privileged ring zero to be composed of approximately 80,000 lines of PL/1 code, and a number of security errors. Subsequent research has shown that a majority of that code can be removed.[Sch 75]

Even if performance requirements do not alter the functional specifications of a kernel, complexity may be increased by the need to code certain functions in a highly efficient manner. It may be necessary to replace a simple sequential search by a more complex hashing algorithm that uses chaining in a overflow area for collision resolution, as just one example.

These issues of security policy, system function, hardware impact, and performance requirements all affect the size and complexity of a security kernel which can be built. Within any given set of such constraints, however, certain designs are far superior to others. The next section of this paper discusses kernel design principles that generally seem to apply to most of the likely sets of constraints.

3. Principles of Kernel Design

A number of design principles have been developed as guides to the design of secure systems, notably "least privilege" and "least common mechanism". See Saltzer [Sal 75] or Popek [Pop 74]. However, they are little help without explanation of their architectural effect, examples of their application, or discussions of their effect on such operating system problems as resource management or performance.

Here we first make several general observations regarding kernel designs and illustrate specific tradeoffs with examples from existing systems. Most of these observations and illustrations are concerned with the tasks of developing as small and simple a kernel as is practical, under the design constraints discussed earlier.

3.1 Overall System Architecture

One of the first questions concerns the relationship of the kernel to the rest of the operating system. There are a number of possibilities. In both the Multics system and a Unix prototype under development at the Mitre Corporation, the kernel is essentially part of the user process, even sharing the process address space in the Multics case. Kernel code and data is protected from user process software by a variety of mechanisms. Kernel tables are shared among all processes. Interrupts may occur at nearly any time, even while running kernel code. Typically, at that point the current process can be suspended and a process switch performed. Therefore kernel data and tables must be designed for parallel access and modification.

An alternate approach, examined at UCLA, more completely separates the kernel from all other software. As in the RC 4000 kernel, the UCLA security kernel is not part of any process. It is run in its own address space, and is better thought of as a hardware extension. That is, each software implemented primitive instruction provides some security relevant function, and runs from invocation to completion without interruption. Functionally it acts as one hardware instruction. Therefore, a process state that indicates running in a powerful mode is never saved or restored, and parallelism complexities are considerably reduced or eliminated. While such an approach may reduce kernel complexity, it requires care in the overall architecture if adequate functionality is to be obtained. The values of each of these approaches are discussed in more detail elsewhere [Pop 75].

3.2 Resource Pools

One of the most effective ways to reduce the size and complexity of an operating system kernel is to remove, as much as possible, all of the resource management functions for a particular type of resource and relegate those functions to untrusted code. The degree to which this goal can be attained, of course, will vary from system to system, and from one object type to another within a given system.

There are three significant aspects to resource handling in operating systems that are subject to removal from an operating system kernel and supportable by user software. They are type integrity, management policy, and naming. Each is discussed in turn below.

3.2.1 Type Integrity

The most extreme action possible is to remove the entire resource as well as all of its supporting software from the base level of the system. As a result, The kernel does not provide protection of these resources as such. Any structure which is needed to insure the type integrity of the resource is the responsibility of the user software. The only protection enforced by the kernel is that provided for the kernel recognized object in which the user implemented resources are placed: segments, pages, disk blocks and the like.

What this strategy generally means is that a single common pool of resources, usually maintained for all processes by the operating system, has now been broken up into a number of smaller subpools, each managed independently. This approach is illustrated by the I/O buffer management in OS/360. Buffer integrity is not assured, since whatever pointer the user supplies in certain SVCs is used by the operating system so long as the indicated transfer involves that user's core.

The tradeoffs involved in pursuing this design are straightforward. By moving all of the resource handling out of a kernel, including the maintenance of the structure or type of the resource, the kernel is further simplified, sometimes considerably. The performance cost is clear from elementary queuing theory. Separate subpools are in general more poorly utilized than the same number of resources in a single common pool, because some subpools may contain idle resources while others are exhausted and unable to fulfil requests directed at them. Alternately, additional resources will be required to maintain the same level of service. A designer must decide what the cost of additional memory or other resources is, or how much delay in response can be tolerated in return for what is likely to be a more secure system.

There are many resources that an operating system typically manages that are not so obvious as I/O buffers. Name spaces are a good example. There are a number of cases where unique names are needed for convenience in communication, like socket numbers in the ARPA net, which are usually assigned and reclaimed by the operating system. However, they could be preallocated to various domains, with each domain expected to do its own management. A kernel, using lower level names (see 3.2.3), can assure that messages are properly delivered to the appropriate domains in the ARPA net example, but need not be concerned with management of sockets [Gai 76].

3.2.2 Resource Management

In those cases where it is not possible to completely exclude support of a resource type from the kernel, it may be possible to remove the management of the resource, but leave that portion of the software responsible for the integrity of the resource objects. That is, the mechanisms which actually operate on the resource are part of the kernel, but the policy software which decides which operations should be performed, and under what circumstances, is untrusted, and part of user processes. This approach, which leaves type integrity as a kernel responsibility but resource management relegated to user code, is essentially the distinction made by Wulf between mechanism and policy.[Wul 75]

A good example of the application of this approach occurs in the UCLA kernel architecture. [Pop 74a] There, process scheduling as well as the management of main memory is the sole responsibility of one particular user level process, containing untrusted code. It issues kernel calls to switch processes, initiate page swaps, and so forth. While this scheduling process therefore can move around the objects that it has the responsibility to manage, it cannot examine any of their contents. This method supports usual functionality requirements and permits sophisticated scheduling, while it considerably simplifies the kernel. However, certain confinement problems are not solved, as discussed later.

3.2.3 Naming

As pointed out by Janson [Jan 74], a considerable amount of code in an operating system is devoted to managing the names of resources, in addition to the management of the resources themselves. A resource may in fact be known by several names, at differing levels of abstraction. In addition to enforcing conventions such as uniqueness of names, the mapping of one name to another must also be done. An example of this mapping can be seen in the handling of segments in Multics. Character string names for segments are used by the file system software (and by users) to specify a segment (analagous to a file). Segment numbers are used by running programs to refer to active segments. The Known Segment Table of that user contains the physical address of the page table for the corresponding segment. Thus there are three different name spaces used to refer to segment resources, and mappings among these spaces must be maintained correctly.

The more of this name management that can be removed from the kernel, the simpler the resulting kernel software. There are several ways to do so. One can consider supporting in the kernel only the lowest level naming. The rest, including mapping software, could be built as part of user domains. This approach generally amounts to partitioning the higher level name spaces, with separate partitions managed by separate processes. However, such a design requires care if controlled sharing is supported by the architecture. User software needs to know the names maintained by other user software in order to coordinate references to shared objects. The coordination can be accomplished if each name maintenance package follows the same conventions, and messages are used to exchange relevant information.

Of course, it is true that in any system some conventions must be externally agreed upon, and some information externally exchanged between people, in order to get coordination started, even if it is only where (in what directory perhaps) to look to find relevant information. Here it is being suggested that much of this coordination and convention handling need not be part of the security enforcement of an operating system. The one potential limitation in this viewpoint, concerning so called trojan horses, is discussed in a later section.

One should note that it is possible to move only a portion of the name support out of the kernel, too. One might partition the name space, allocating each partition to a different user process, and then have the kernel merely enforce that partition. Each user would do his own name management within a given partition. This view is similar to that of type integrity, discussed earlier, with the resource being the names, and the operations implemented in the kernel which operate on names being very limited.

4. More on Overall System Architecture

Up until this point we have maintained the fiction that the appropriate system architecture for highly reliable security placed all security relevant code in the core of the operating system, the kernel, running on the bare hardware. The rest of the system software is encapsulated within user processes, running under the control of the kernel, and making calls to it.

4.1 Trusted Processes

However, this structure is not the best, as recognized by work at M.I.T., [Sal 76] UCLA, [Pop 75] SRI, [Rob 75] as well as in specifications for the military network SATIN-IV. Rather, there are a number of security relevant functions that can profitably be moved out of the kernel and placed in so called "trusted processes".

These processes architecturally are the same as user processes, except that the information they pass to the kernel is used by the kernel to take security relevant actions.

A good example of such a trusted process appears both in the Multics system at M.I.T. as well as in the UCLA Secure Unix development. One process has responsibility for handling free terminals, logging and authenticating users, and starting up the appropriate software for them. The Multics logger and the UCLA initiator both run as standard processes, except that the Multics ring zero software and the UCLA kernel both accept the authentication decision made by that process, and make security relevant decisions using that information.

4.2 Levels of Kernels

One sometimes finds that the software composing these trusted processes can be segregated into security relevant and non-security relevant parts. That is, the trusted processes can often themselves be structured so as to be composed of a kernel and other, untrusted software.

The degree to which this segregation is successful can be increased if a few redundant checks are made. For example one might build a sophisticated hashing algorithm with clever collision resolving for password checks, but after the appropriate entry in the hashing table has supposedly been found by untrusted code, the table index can be given to a trusted subroutine to make the actual check and pass information to the operating system kernel. In VM/370, channel program translation is followed by a security check of the resulting code.

The net result of this segregation is a system composed of levels of kernels. Each kernel depends, for its correct operation, only on the correctness of its own implementation, together with that of the lower level kernels that provide security relevant functions. In this way, the necessity that there be security relevant, trusted code at various levels in a large system is met, while at the same time the total amount of code upon which the overall system's security depends has been minimized. Note that this viewpoint differs markedly from that taken at SRI, in which it is argued that the entire operating system design and implementation should be certified or verified.[Rob 75]

A more powerful example of the utility of a second level kernel concerns name mapping and file systems. There, conditions occur under which the user needs to refer to system supported objects by names that are from a different name space than that supported by the kernel. For example, as already mentioned, the kernel may maintain segment numbers, while the user will invariably wish to refer to those segments by character string names, especially when setting access control information, but perhaps also when stating which segment to read or modify. Because of these usage patterns, mapping between name spaces may be highly security relevant. File systems provide an important case of this problem. In the UCLA Unix system, file management is done by a user level process. [Kam 76] The kernel of that file manager is responsible for elementary directory management, and other untrusted software in the process can take care of positioning pointers within files, scheduling I/O operations and maintaining resource allocation limits. The directory management consists largely of mapping string names to disk block names supported by the kernel, handling allocation matters, and checking and maintaining protection data.

This multiple level kernel architecture can yield significant advantages in the design and implementation of the base level kernel. If applied in conjunction with other design principles discussed above, the base level kernel can become little more than an implementor of abstract types. It makes segments, processes, messages, and so forth out of hardware memory, status registers, and the like. For some systems, this simplification of the base level kernel may permit further improvement. It may be possible to implement each kernel call (including the interrupt handler, which is just a hardware forced call) as uninterruptible code, without losing any relevant performance characteristics. This design virtually eliminates any concern for parallelism in the security relevant code, and therefore enhances its reliability. If the kernel is simple enough, it is a candidate for implementation in microcode. A packet switch communications processor that hosts no user programming is an example of an application that might only require a kernel simple enough for such an implementation.

A final note on levels of kernels concerns the updating of the protection data used by trusted software to make access control decisions. If a user at a terminal is to have confidence in the security enforced by a system, he must be able to view and change the system's protection data in a highly reliable way. He needs a secure channel between his terminal and kernel code. One easy method to implement that channel is to provide a simple facility by which the user can switch his terminal to a trusted process and back. In this way he need not be concerned with any software running in his own process(es). While this solution, unless extended, suffers from the inability to permit program generated changes in protection data, such actions do not seem to occur often in practice anyway, except as a way of compensating for some other lack in functionality or flexibility of the protection controls.

5. Internal Kernel Architecture

Much of the discussion up to this point has concerned the architectural place of a kernel in the larger system architecture, and the effect of kernel goals on that structure. Naturally, the internal structure of a kernel is also important. In general, the task of constructing a reliable kernel is little different from that of developing other highly reliable software. However, there are considerations peculiar to this application which deserve mention, including hardware selection, parallelism, and the effect of finite resource limits on attempts to use abstract type methods for organizing kernel code.

5.1 Hardware Selection

Since hardware is the zero-th level in a structured, layered software architecture, unnecessary complexity in that interface is as undesirable as complexities in the specification of any other layer in the software, for the usual, good reasons. Therefore, hardware selection requires care, as illustrated earlier. It is worth noting that since the kernel software has already been minimized, the hardware impact on what remains can be substantial. In the UCLA kernel for example, approximately 40% of the code is device drivers, much of which could be eliminated if address relocation applied to device transfers.

5.2 Parallelism

While there may be some argument over whether algorithms that are expressed as parallel computations or strictly sequential code are inherently easier to understand (to some degree it certainly depends on the algorithm), it seems rather clear that certification or verification of sequential code is presently less difficult. That is the reason for specifying physical or logical uninterruptibility in the software architecture. This goal is, of course, one that has been followed at higher levels in systems since the early days of multiprogramming.

5.3 Abstract Type Structures

The concept of using extended types (such as illustrated by Simula classes [Dah 66], CLU clusters [Lis 76], Alphard forms [Wul 75], or Euclid modules [Pop 76]) to organize software is quite valuable. However, Janson [Jan 76] points out that most efforts to employ strict type extension methods in programming are done with the underlying assumption of unlimited quantities of resources available. In the internal structure of an operating system or its kernel, this assumption is invalid, of course. One of the most obvious cases where finite resource limits interact with system structure occurs in virtual memory systems, potentially resulting in a structural circularity. Main memory is finite, so system software is constructed to give the illusion of a larger address space by sensing page faults and performing necessary I/Os in a manner invisable to the process involved. However, one may well wish to run this virtual memory software as a process like other processes. Further, the process management software can benefit from being written with the assumption that a large, virtual address space is available. With the obvious circular dependency in mind, it is not clear whether process types or virtual memory types should be the lower level, with the other built on top. Reed [Ree 76] outlines a method of defining multiple levels of types to break the cycle. Lower levels implement a small fixed number or amount of the resource, using small amounts of resources in so doing. Higher levels reimplement the resource in large numbers or amounts, by multiplexing the lower level ones. In medium sized systems such as UCLA Unix, such a multiple tiered structure is not necessary.

6. Confinement

The problem of constructing a system so that an arbitrary program can be run in a fashion that assures the program cannot leak any of the information that it contains, is in practice unsolved. While clearly solvable in principle, [Fen 74] [Lam 75] [Mil 75] no actual solutions have been designed or implemented for real systems.

6.1 Importance

Some have argued instead that confinement is not a serious issue in practical applications. While this viewpoint is clearly reasonable when taken in the context of the current absense of reliable data security, several experiments with the Multics system have illustrated how real the problem may be. It was found possible in principle to drive a user terminal through inter-process communication performed by modulation of paging behavior in one process and the sensing of that modulation by the other. In a separate experiment, a similar bandwidth was discovered through use of the directory system. One process repeatedly made and deleted entries in a directory. This action changed the size of that directory, a value recorded in its parent directory. A second process read the size of that parent directory. In this particular test, the first process was not supposed to be able to communicate to the second.[Sal 76]

These two examples are instructive, for they illustrate a timing dependent and timing independent channel, respectively, both involving resource management. The bandwidth is enough to be of concern both to the military (one job might be a "trojan horse" running with top secret classification, and the other running unclassified) as well as to industry (consider disgruntled programmers).

From a practical point of view, virtually all the channels mentioned by Lampson [Lam 75] or illustrated above are related to the allocation or management of resources, and the changes in system data that occurs as a result of resource allocation decisions.

6.2 Storage and Timing Channels

Millen et al. [Mil 75] partition these channels into storage channels and timing channels. Storage channels are those which permit the passing of information through direct modification and reading of cells in the computer memory. Timing channels are those which permit one user to vary the real time rate at which another receives service, to a degree that the second user can sense. As the examples earlier show, the bandwidth of both types of channels can be significant.

It appears, however, that all resource storage channels can be changed into timing channels, and, on a large system, the bandwidth of the timing channels can be severely limited. Further, it appears that these actions can be taken without losing the values of multiprogramming, which is the primary cause of the problem. Resource storage channels can in general be changed to timing dependent channels in the following way. First, it appears that all direct reads and writes of system storage, such as that illustrated by the Multics file system problem, can be blocked by proper definitions of domains and the association of status data in the appropriate domains. What remains are resource allocation requests and status notifications. The use of resource availability as a channel can then be prevented merely by blocking the process requesting the resource until it is available. To be practical, this replacement of resource status replies by delays should be accompanied by the use of some form of a deadlock detection or prevention algorithm to insure that the system operates efficiently. That code need not necessarily be implemented in a security relevant way, as shown by the discussion of scheduling below.

Some believe that the bandwidth of timing channels can be limited by the scheduling characteristics that can be introduced in a large system. However, the existence of a timing channel is in principle more difficult to identify than a storage channel, since in the latter case there are explicit cells which are being accessed, even if interpretively through system code. While one might argue that if a process has only virtual time available to it, the timing channels are blocked, this viewpoint is probably not practical, given how many real time devices (therefore, clocks) actually exist on real systems. Nevertheless, once the bandwidth is limited to an amount comparable to that expected external to the computer system, the problem has in effect been solved.

6.3 Timing Independent Scheduling Channels

While the preceding paragraphs may suggest a general approach to confinement, considerable care in the system architecture and implementation is required, as illustrated below. Earlier it was pointed out that functions such as the scheduling policy for resource allocation could be done outside a kernel. With respect to confinement, however, this approach creates difficulties. A reasonable scheduler must receive considerable information if it is to perform effective optimization. Since it can transmit information by ordering the completion of user requests, there is a clear potential for covert communication whether or not the scheduler had been written to cooperate.

Storage channels can in large degree be blocked however if the scheduler is designed as an information sink. This action can be taken if each user is permitted to submit only one request at a time, and wait for its completion before submitting another. Device completion status can be returned via the kernel. Studies have shown that, for a reasonable number of jobs on a multiprogramming system, these restrictions are generally not ones with significant impacts on performance. [Bel 74]

However, such restrictions do not prevent collusion among user processes from providing timing independent channels. That is, a group of cooperating, legally communicating processes may be able to communicate with another such group, with which they are not permitted, even in the face of a scheduler designed to be an information sink. Whether or not this is possible depends on scheduler characteristics. Whenever it is possible for one process, by its own resource utilization actions, to affect the _relative order_ in which members of other groups of processes are served, communication is possible.

That is, let processes A and B be one group, X and Y the other. Inter-group communication is not to be permitted. (They may be Ford and G.M. programs). Suppose that A (or B) increases its cpu to I/O ratio so much that the system's adaptive scheduler stops favoring cpu bound processes and begins favoring I/O bound jobs. X is cpu bound, Y is I/O bound. The order in which X and Y are run was changed by A or B. X and Y can easily determine the relative order in which they are run since they can legally communicate. Thus the A,B group has sent one bit to the X,Y group. Clearly this mechanism serves as a basis for extended bidirectional communication.

Many of the interesting scheduling algorithms that are used in practice have the characteristic outlined above, and in fact those that don't seem to ignore precisely that kind of information concerning user behavior upon which meaningful optimization is based. However, not all useful algorithms permit collusion. Round robin does not. The simple, limited algorithm implemented in the new Mitre Unix kernel, in which each process can only set its own priority, and the kernel merely runs that user process with the highest priority, also blocks collusion.

If confinement is felt to be important, considerable auditing of resource management mechanisms and policy will be necessary to block or satisfactorily limit the bandwidth of these kinds of channels.

7. Conclusion

We have attempted to distill the knowledge gained from various security kernel research efforts into a form that will be useful in guiding others who wish to develop highly secure, reliable system bases. It is also hoped that these perspectives are applicable to other environments than operating systems, especially such higher level software projects as message systems and data management, where privacy considerations are especially sensitive.

Acknowledgements

This paper would not have been written had it not been for Clark Weissman, who often asked one of the authors how one designed a kernel. We also wish to thank Evelyn Walton, who largely built the UCLA kernel, and all the members of the UCLA Security Group who participated in discussions that helped form and refine these ideas.

Bibliography

Belady, L. and C. Weissman "Experiments with Secure Resource Sharing for Virtual Machines", Proceedings of IRIA International Workshop on Protection in Operating Systems, Rocquencourt, France, August 13-14,1974, pp 27-34.

Brinch Hansen, P. Operating System Principles, Prentice Hall 1973, 366 pp.

Gaines, R. S. and C. Sunshine, "A Secure NCP for Kernel Based Systems", RAND Internal memo, 1976.

Janson, P. A.,"Removing the Dynamic Linker from the Security Kernel of a Computing Utility", MIT, Masters Thesis, June 1974, MAC TR-132, 128 pp.

Kampe, M., C. Kline, G. Popek, E. Walton, "The UCLA Data Secure Unix Operating System", UCLA Technical Report, 9/76.

Lampson, B., "A Note on the Confinement Problem", Communications of the ACM, Vol. 16, No. 10, October 1973, pp 613-615.

Lampson, B. W. and H. Sturgis, "Reflections on an Operating System Design", Communications of the ACM, 1976.

Millen, J. K., "Security Kernel Validation in Practice", Communications of the ACM, 1976.

Popek, G. and C. Kline, "Verifiable Secure Operating System Architectures", Proceedings of 1974 NCC, pp 145-151.

Popek, G., "Protection Structures", IEEE Computer, June 1974, pp 22-33.

Popek, G. and C. Kline "A Verifiable Protection System", Proceedings of the International Conference on Reliable Software, May 1975, Los Angeles, California.

Popek G., and C. Kline, "The UCLA Secure Unix Design" , Internal memo, unpublished.

Ritchie, D. and K. Thompson, "The Unix Timesharing System" Communications of the ACM, Vol. 17, No. 7, July 1974, pp 365-375.

Robinson, et.al., "On Attaining Reliable Software for a Secure Operating System", 1975 International Conference on Reliable Software, April 21-23, 1975, Los Angeles, California.

Saltzer, J. H. and M. Schroeder, "The Protection of Information in Computer Systems", Proceedings of the IEEE, Vol. 63, No. 9, September 1975, pp 1278-1306.

Saltzer, G. Private communication, 1976.

Schell, R., private communication, 1974.

Wulf, W., et.al., "HYDRA: The Kernel of a Multiprocessor Operating System", Communications of the ACM, Vol. 17, No. 6, June 1974, pp 337-345.

CHAPTER 3.C.

Anita K. Jones
Carnegie-Mellon University
Pittsburgh, Pa., USA

Protection   Mechanisms   and
the Enforcement of Security Policies

PROTECTION MECHANISMS AND
THE ENFORCEMENT OF SECURITY POLICIES

Anita K. Jones
Department of Computer Science
Carnegie-Mellon University
Pittsburgh, PA 15213 USA

1. Introduction

Information is a valuable commodity--whether encoded within a computer system or without. Society, and individuals as well, have always had policies governing the use and dispersal of information. For example, doctors may disclose health information about an individual to other doctors for the purpose of consultation, but may not make public an individual's health history without the individual's consent. Increased use of automated systems to gather and maintain such information in an accessible form have recently caused the public's attention to focus on policies governing information usage. In some cases, policies are entirely lacking; and, in others, they are not enforced.

This public concern is legitimate; automated systems have substantially expanded that ability to gather, maintain, and process information. There are several reasons for this. First, the volume of information that can be maintained has increased; automated storage media require orders of magnitude less space than paper-based systems. Second, the cost to access an item of information, even in a massive data bank, is low. Third, automation has increased the ability to transmit information from one site to another. Data, i.e. encoded information, is routinely shipped rapidly across thousands of miles via telephone lines or satellites; computer readable media, such as magnetic tapes and disks, are also physically transportable by hand or by mail. Last, automation gives us the ability to quickly and cost-effectively transform one encoding of information to a different form. All of these attributes of automated information-keeping have qualitatively altered the environment in which we live. Information previously unavailable can now be obtained. For example, it is now possible to select a multitude of individual items of information and process them to derive a statistical summary at very low cost.

One example policy for information control is the policy of "individual privacy". Using paper-based technology the cost of gathering, recording, and processing information is high. This helps ensure an individual's privacy. Computer-based technology expands our options so that information about an individual can be obtained from many sources, and in such a way that the individual involved is not even aware of the transmission of information about him. The reality of our recently acquired computer technology has given rise to considerable concern about defining new privacy policies to regulate information flow.

It is society that is responsible for formulating the necessary policies dictating how information is to be used or even accumulated. The technical term **security policy** will be used to refer to a policy governing who may obtain or modify information stored in a computer, and in some cases how they may use the information. In contrast, it is the computer science community that is responsible for the invention and implementation of **protection mechanisms** with which to reliably enforce the security policies deemed by society to be required. Without such technical tools, society's choices are limited; developing unenforceable policies is merely an exercise in the abstract.

Interest in policies for controlling information usage also arises from yet another source--the desire for well-behaved programs. Constraining information flow and interactions between software units simplifies and makes more manageable the development and maintenance of software. The "principle of least privilege" [Saltzer75] applied to software dictates that a program have the least set of privileges required to perform its function. This minimizes the possible interactions between the program and other pieces of software, and hopefully simplifies the task of developing and maintaining that software. Ideally, the protection mechanisms used to enforce security policies can be used to good purpose for software management.

2. Security Policies

All security policies are based on the **sharing** of information. In some cases information must be shared between multiple users or the collection of information cannot provide the function for which it was designed. Thus, information sharing is an intrinsic property of information collections, whether they be recorded in paper-based or automated systems. In addition, sharing is sometimes introduced for efficiency reasons, even though it is not strictly necessary. For example, sharing executable code among many users where possible, reduces the cost of maintaining a computer utility. But, this is feasible only if the system enforces the policy that users cannot alter shared code.

Thus, enforcing policies that govern controlled sharing is a facility that operating systems must include for two reasons: because, by their very nature, the applications to which people apply computers require controlled sharing; and, because such enforcement mechanisms can be usefully employed to help with the difficult task of software management.

Another aspect of security policies that needs to be clearly defined is the notion that Saltzer and Schroeder [75] have termed a **principal**. The principal is the authority, usually a person, accountable for the use or misuse of some encoded information. Policies, then, relate principals to information, or encodings of information. When policies are interpreted inside a computer system, executed programs act on behalf of principals. Sometimes it is useful to regard an executing program itself as a principal because some programs are relied on to act within given constraints, regardless of the requests made by their human users. This trend will increase as program verification techniques become more powerful and their use becomes widespread.

In order to consider their enforcement, I will identify two classes of security policies: <u>information control</u> policies and <u>access control</u> policies. The access control policies are a subset of the information control policies, and are of particular interest because they are the policies for which operating systems generally provide protection mechanisms. The two classes of policies contrast with one another as follows: Information control policies state restrictions on the flow of information; access control policies state restrictions on the way encoding of information are used, i.e. accessed. To appreciate the distinction, consider a tax data base containing a financial description of each taxpaying citizen. Imagine, for the moment, that all the income tax forms for this year are stored in individual folders. An access control policy will be defined in terms of <u>containers</u>, the folder holding an individual's tax record. A sample <u>access</u> control policy may grant to an individual the ability to read all the data in his own folder, i.e. all the data about himself. In addition, he may be allowed to add documents to the folder, but not to alter existing data in the folder. The access control policy is stated in terms of access to the folder, not in terms of the information encoded within it.

Information control policies are more subtle than access control policies because they constrain a principal from learning information. They are expressed in terms of information, whether explicitly or implicitly encoded, and wherever it is encoded. We could define an information control policy that permits legislators considering a tax law change to be accorded statistical summaries derived from a subset of the individual tax records. The policy might specify that no legislator is to be able to determine the tax status of an individual, even though that individual's tax record is used to derive statistics available to legislators. Implementing such a policy can be difficult, if not impossible, because the agent responsible for enforcement may not have control over all sources of information, or even the transmittal of that information. Continuing with this tax example, assume that the manager of the tax data base determines what statistical summaries a particular legislator will receive. Unknown to the data base manager, that legislator knows certain information that, taken together with the summaries, will permit him to deduce information about an individual. The data base manager will find it difficult, if not impossible, to enforce the information control policy that constrains legislators from determining an individual's tax situation using statistical summaries.

To make the enforcement of information control policies even more difficult. There are even cases in which the absence of activity or information is sufficient to deduce some fact. This is called <u>negative inference</u> and is a tool that the sleuths of fact and fiction use to great effect. Enforcing any policy in the presence of negative inference is often extremely difficult, unless one cuts off all information flow.

Perhaps the simplest policy to discuss is that of isolation of principals, an information control policy. Isolation can be enforced manually by allocating the computer system to one user at a time and returning the computer to a fixed known state before each allocation. Early systems attempted to implement a policy of isolating principals through the agency of the operating system. By properly initializing the storage protection mechanism, the system ensured that no user could <u>directly</u> read or change the code or data of another user. However, isolation was not complete, because the operating system itself provided numerous indirect communication channels. For example, one user could detect patterns of resource usage of a second user, whether or not the second user intended to communicate to the first. Such channels will be illustrated later.

The policy of isolation dictates that each separate protected entity "belongs to", and is accessible to, only one principal. This is unacceptable in an environment where sharing is intrinsic to the application at hand. Indeed, isolation of users is neither necessary, nor cost-effective, in most situations. As the number of integrated data collections increases, the need for controlled sharing increases.

Defining more sophisticated securities policy can be difficult; one may not forsee all the situations in which a policy will be applied. It may even be the case that a security policy specification clashes with the functional specification of an operating system, so that there does not exist an implementation that satisfies both. One way to define a policy is in mechanistic terms--i.e., by specifying a protection mechanism that enforces the desired policy, rather than stating the policy directly. Such a policy allows any action of a principal that is permitted by the mechanism. For example, if principals are isolated except for a message mechanism which they can use to communicate, the principals can share information by sending copies of the encoded information that they wish to share with one another; but they may not share a single copy of encoded information. Note that a policy relying on a system implemented mechanism does not state what information can be used by what principal; instead, each principal determines what information encodings it shares with others and takes action to cause the sharing to happen or not. Note also that it may be difficult to determine the possible ramifications of a principal's action.

In contrast to policies of isolation, which only address who can access what information, controlled sharing policies also address how the different principals can use the information they can access. It is often found to be desirable to grant to the different principals different permissions to use and to modify shared data. For example, it may be appropriate for one user to be able only to read some data, while a second user may be able to alter it. Such policies are more sophisticated than the policy of isolation or the policy permitting message communication; and, as we will see, require more mechanism to enforce.

3. Protection Mechanisms

Before considering protection mechanisms for particular policies, I should note that the design and implementation of many types of protection mechanisms is still a state-of-the-art activity. There exists no major software system that has withstood penetration efforts. Flaws of realization range from implementation errors involving only a few instructions to system design errors. Hoffman [77] gives a listing of some typical classes of flaws. One typical flaw is that the supervisor does not validate user-supplied parameters sufficiently. A second class of flaws arises from the interaction of asynchronously executing processes. Assume that a user process supplies parameters in user space to be checked by the supervisor. Between the time of the check and subsequent use of the parameter values by the supervisor, they are altered by an asynchronously executing parallel process. This process may not be a traditional process, but an I/O program "executing" on a channel or device.

The Multics designers [Saltzer75] reported the following system design flaw. Card input is performed by a separate process. Data read in from cards is placed in a file object. The card I/O process is given permission to place an entry for the file in the directory of the user requesting input. The card I/O process could place any entry in a user's directory; in particular, it could enter a file that performed an arbitrary, malicious action. If that file has a common command name, the user would unintentionally invoke it; the malicious program could act with the privileges of the unsuspecting user, and cause havoc.

In the following sections I discuss protection mechanisms for enforcement of the two classes of policies defined above: access control policies and information control policies. The relevant mechanisms will be described as though they are entirely dynamic--i.e., protection data is available at run-time and protection enforcement is implemented dynamically. The possibility of alternative, more efficient implementations, such as compile-time enforcement is not precluded. I will not often discuss optimizations that make a mechanism more efficient when such optimization complicates presentation of the mechanism itself.

4. Enforcing a Policy of Isolation

I will begin with the policy of isolation because it is a member of both classes of policies: access control and information control. There are several approaches that can be used to enforce the policy of isolation. One approach relies on physical separation, where principals have dedicated computer system resources. A second approach relies on time separation, where computer resources are sequentially made available to the different principals. This management technique is sometimes referred to as _periods processing_. One disadvantage of periods processing is that the computer resources are totally unavailable between periods when the machine is being "scrubbed" to prepare for processing by a different principal or group of principals. Scrubbing can take 45 minutes to an hour [Gold77].

Another approach is to provide a programmed computer system which separates principals or groups of principals ensuring that, though they share physical resources, groups cannot communicate with one another in any way. One way to do this is to provide each principal, i.e., a group of users who are considered a single principal for security purposes, with their own simulated machine. We have systems called virtual machine monitors [Buzen73] to do this. The virtual machine monitor effects the charade of replicating the underlying machine once for each different principal. Each principal is unaware of the existence of the others. Effectively, the virtual machine monitor multiprograms virtual machines; each virtual machine runs a different principal at his own security level or classification. In practice, we find virtual machines executing operating systems. If an application requires several different security levels, then several copies of the operating system are executed, one on each virtual machine.

An advantage of the virtual machine approach is that processing resources are simultaneously available to people who work at different security levels. Thus, people can have processing resources available during their entire work day, not just in "shifts". There is no time lost to scrubbing the processor between security level changes in order to purge it of information which might be erroneously communicated from one level to another across a change in principals. During the interval that one virtual processor is idle, perhaps awaiting input from one of its users, another virtual processor can make progress.

Virtual machine monitors are an expedient, designed to provide multiple copies of a machine, each of which executes without functionally interacting with the others. To enforce a policy of isolation the virtual machine monitor must, in addition, ensure that a user at some security level can in no way determine any information about other security levels that are running concurrently. It is relatively simple to ensure that no bit in the image of one operating system, running on a virtual machine, can have a value that can be directly altered by the action of any other operating system, i.e., one running at some different security level. Thus, a virtual machine monitor can act as an access control mechanism because it partitions the machine resources into security levels, permitting no direct access between two levels.

More difficult to deal with are the information <u>leakage channels</u> that arise as a byproduct of interaction of different virtual machines with the virtual machine monitor itself. The simulated machines are entire computer systems, not only processors, but also I/O devices including some secondary storage media. It is the virtual machine monitor that is responsible for simulating the existence of that secondary storage. An I/O operation executed by a virtual machine is effectively a request to the virtual machine monitor, which must translate it so that the appropriate I/O appears to take place in the virtual machine making the request. The virtual machine monitor itself has a state and all responses to requests are going to be a function of that state. Thus, the monitor itself is potentially a means for leaking information from one virtual machine to another. To enforce a strict isolation policy, such information flow has to be stopped.

I will discriminate two kinds of leakage channels: storage channels and modulation channels. Though the definitions are given in terms of virtual machines to be more concrete, analogous leakage channels exist in most programmed systems. An illegal <u>storage channel</u> exists if one virtual machine can cause a bit in the virtual machine monitor state to be set, so that bit can be later read by another virtual machine. Generically, storage channels exist if one party can induce a second to set its state to a value that can be detected by yet a third. Communication between the first party and the third is achieved. A team at the System Development Corporation investigated leakage channels in IBM's VM/370 in an effort to see if it could be extended to enforce a policy of isolation [Gold77]. One detected storage channel involved disk cylinder addresses. Principals were permitted to know physical addresses allocated to them. To communicate a single bit of information, a principal could allocate a large number of cylinder and free cylinders with either even, or odd, addresses. The receiver would detect that bit by noting a high percentage of evenly, or oddly, addressed cylinders among those he subsequently allocated.

<u>Modulation channels</u>, or timing channels, exist if one party can detect the pattern of use or non-use of resources (across time) by another. In the SDC study one modulation channel involved the disk manager. Co-resident, but separate storage areas, called "minidisks", are maintained on the same physical disk for the various virtual machines by the monitor. I/O requests for the same physical disk are placed in the same queue. One principal can communicate to another by making little or heavy use of its minidisks. Communication occurs if the second principal can detect or not detect slowdown in the response to minidisk requests.

Such modulation channels can be blocked, but at the cost of substantially reduced system performance. For example, the modulation channel just described can be eliminated by giving each virtual machine a certain amount of I/O service every time quantum, idling the physical processor when no I/O is requested by the virtual machine for which the I/O service time is reserved. Whenever physical resources are shared among multiple principals who have access to a clock, modulation channels can only be blocked by providing each principal a constant service, i.e. a service that cannot be altered by the action of other principals.

Most leakage channels can be blocked, but at a great loss in efficiency. In applications where it is not considered important to block such leakage paths, the virtual machine approach may be expedient. In the worst case, the virtual machine system will run as at the same rate as dedicated resources. That is, if n principals share a single computer, each sees a computer that is 1/n-th of the original computer. In such a situation a security officer would probably feel safer dedicating physical computers to each principal, thus avoiding the problem of verifying the absence of leakage channels in the virtual machine monitor.

5. Enforcing Access Control Policies

Recall that access control policies are expressed not in terms of the control of information, but in terms of the containers of encoded information. No one policy of controlled sharing of such containers would suit all situations, especially in a general purpose operating system. Consequently, the most often used approach is to define the notion of a protected container, along with an access control protection mechanism to constrain the use of these protected containers and their contents. Every protected container is accessible to some principals who, depending on their privilege, may be able to invoke the protection mechanism in order to grant the right to access a container to others. Any policy which can be translated into such a framework can then be enforced.

The formulation of access control mechanisms relies on the object model discussed elsewhere in this volume. The protected containers are objects, presumably with non-overlapping representations. For each object there exists a set of algorithms for extracting information or altering its content. Each algorithm is called an access. In a simple case where it is only appropriate to distinguish manipulations of an object that do and do not alter that object two accesses, "Read" and "Write", are generally used.

Extant systems, however, go a step further and permit accesses to be tailored to the particular object being protected. Some access control mechanisms even permit users to define new types of objects dynamically. For example, in the telephone-service-customer example introduced in the paper discussing the object model, two accesses that altered a telephone-service-customer object were distinguished. "ChangeService" was an access intended for use by the employees responsible for recording cancellation or installation of telephone service. "Charge" was an access intended for use by those employees responsible for customer billing. Both types of employees could alter a telephone-service-customer object, but only in ways appropriate to their responsibilities.

Enforcing access control policies requires knowing who can access what. For this purpose the notion of a right is defined. Performing an access to a particular object requires having the right to perform that access on that object. The term domain will be used to denote the set of rights available to be exercised at an execution site. An access control enforcement mechanism acts as follows. Each time an object is to be accessed, a check is made to determine if the right to perform that access on that object is in the execution domain. If so, the access can be performed; if not, the access, and sometimes the entire execution sequence, is aborted. Note that a domain essentially defines a name space restricted by protection constraints. We speak of those objects named in the rights as being "in" the domain. However, the objects are only available for the purpose of performing permitted accesses on them. It will later turn out to be useful to add to and delete rights from domains; for that purpose a domain is, itself, an object.

To completely define an access control mechanism we need to define three aspects: the protection enforcement check which determines whether a particular access is allowed, how a domain can change, and how execution can be stopped or suspended in one domain and initiated or restarted in another domain.

As an aid to precisely defining an access control mechanism, the information on which it relies can be described as being encoded in a matrix [Lampson71]. A matrix column is defined for each protected object; a row is defined for each domain. Entries in the access matrix are sets of access names. For example, in figure 1 domain D2 has "Read" and "Append" access to File F, and in addition has "Call" access to Procedure P. Domain D1 is responsible for execution in domain D2 and D3 and thus has "Suspend" and "Restart" access to those domains.

Domains	Objects File F	Procedure P	D1	D2	D3
D1		Call		Suspend Restart	Suspend Restart
D2	Read Append	Call			
D3	Write Read Append				

Figure 1: Access Matrix

The first attribute of an access control protection mechanism I will discuss is its <u>Enforcement Rule</u>; it states that no access can be performed on an object except by execution in a domain that includes the right to do so. Interpreted in terms of the access matrix the rule states that domain D can perform access A to object X just in the case the name A appears in the access matrix entry in row D and column X.

The statement that such checks are sufficient to provide access control protection depends on several implicit assumptions which I should state. One is that all objects are uniquely distinguishable, and that a right always names a unique object. The second is the "closed system assumption" that all objects to be protected are under the control of the protection mechanism. They cannot be accessed in any way, unless the protection mechanism determines that such an access is permitted. To simplify further presentations, I will assume dynamic checking, i.e. prior to each and every access the appropriate protection check is made. A third assumption is that name interpretation and enforcement checking are complementary. When domain D requests that an access to a particular object be performed, it uses a name for that object. It is the name interpreter that maps the name to a unique object X; the enforcement check must be made for the same object X. This does not necessarily mean that every object has some system-wide unique name; it does mean that during execution when an object is named, the name interpreter deterministically maps that name to a unique object. Yet a fourth assumption is that the enforcement check is flawless in its design and implementation and in its execution, i.e. failing hardware is not taken into account.

The second attribute of a protection mechanism is its **Rights Movement Rule**. Because a right represents a privilege to perform some action, rights movement must be controlled. Users cannot be permitted to fabricate or pilfer rights. One strategy is to use the protection mechanism itself. To do so, the set of accesses appropriate to each type of object is extended to include some additional accesses for the purposes of rights movement control. For example, in their review paper Graham and Denning [72] propose a right called "Control". If domain D has "Control" access to object X, it is permitted to give any right to manipulate X to any other domain.

Another strategy is to extend each right with tags that indicate how the right-- as opposed to the object it names--can be manipulated. One could define a "Copy" tag that must be present for a right to be copied and a "Transfer" tag that permitted the right to be moved between domains, but not duplicated. The "Transfer" tag permits enforcement of policies in which there are a fixed number of rights to an object which cannot be duplicated, only moved between domains.

An interesting aspect of the rights movement issue that has sparked recent interest is **revocation**: retraction of a right in one domain by action in another domain. A basic tension exists between the amount of autonomy an executing domain should have, and the amount of control a responsible authority should have over an object it controls. For example, once a domain has been given a right and has initiated the performance of some task using that right, one can argue that it should be permitted to continue to completion. On the other hand, there is the classic case of the proprietary program package. If a user who has been given the right to use that package neglects to pays his bills, it seems appropriate that the purveyor of the package be able to retract that user's right to the proprietary package. Redell and Fabry [74] discuss alternative revocation schemes and possible implementations.

The third attribute of a protection mechanism is its **Domain Switching Rule**, i.e. the rule governing suspension of execution in one domain, possibly passage of parameter rights to a second domain, and initiation or restart of execution in that second domain. In the introduction to this paper, I argued that one reason protection is important is that it can be of assistance in the construction and maintenance of software. It is good programming practice for domains to be small, that is, for them to contain only what is needed for performance of a single function. If domains are small, then domain switching is common. In fact, most tasks involve execution of several, probably cooperating, functions in multiple domains.

The concept of a domain is crucial to further development. The term "domain" is commonly used to mean both a set of rights for the accessible objects and an execution site. In some systems domains are dynamically created for the purpose of executing one invocation of a function, then the domain is destroyed. In other systems domains are initially created and then serially reused. In yet other system designs multiple execution sequences concurrently take place in the same domain. The latter is an optimization that will not be discussed because it provides no further functionality and violates good programming practice.

One characteristic of a domain is that it includes some private memory used for execution control. To ensure deterministic, well-behaved programs, the right to alter this memory, which includes at least the program counter and some intermediate storage in the form of registers or a stack, is given to the initiator of execution in the domain, and, subsequently, only to the domain itself. Domain switching for static, i.e. reusable, domains relies on "Enter" rights. To initiate execution in another domain, the currently executing domain exercises its "Enter" right for that other domain. Execution is suspended in the current domain and begins at a specified entry point in the target domain. If it is possible for two domains to concurrently initiate execution in the same target domain, one must wait or fail if the domain is already in use as an execution site.

In the case of dynamically created domains, the protection mechanism relies on procedure objects on which a "Call" access is defined. Part of a procedure is what Linden [76] calls a "template domain". When, as a result of execution in one domain, the "Call" right to a procedure object is exercised, a new domain is created using the domain template of the called procedure. Usually, the domain template includes all those rights which a procedure needs to execute, exclusive of parameters and intermediate storage. Execution is suspended in the calling domain and initiated in the newly called domain at some entry point specified by the procedure object.

An access control mechanism can be defined as a set of operations performing enforcement checks, creation and movement of rights, and domain switching. Presumably, the enforcement check is invoked for each access and that the remaining operations can be invoked at will by users. As usual, each operation can only succeed if the invoking domain contains the appropriate rights. Designing different operations to be part of a protection mechanism means that different sets of security policies can be enforced using that mechanism. Target applications and designer prerogative determine what operations are included. In particular, one must consider the desired grain of protection: how finely divided are the objects that are to be protected? One can protect entire files or segments as units, distinguishing only "Read" and "Write" rights. One may choose to permit users to create new types of objects with a very rich set of accesses tailored to the user's application. Another dimension of the choice of a mechanism is whether a domain is associated with the user, a program, or a procedure invocation. One aspect of this set of protection decisions is cost-effectiveness. A multiplicity of domains and dynamically created objects may be costly. The existence of several contemporary research systems proves that such systems can be built. It remains to be seen that they can be built cost-effectively.

5.1 Implementation of Access Control Protection Mechanisms

Building a reliable, flawless protection mechanism is one case of the general problem of producing reliable, correct software. One construction technique that is being used in several research communities is that of building a security kernel. The strategy is based on the argument that at the core of an operating system should be all, and only, the security relevant portions of the operating system. This small amount of isolated code, called the security kernel, relies on no other portions of the operating system. It should be small enough to be verified, even using the limited techniques available today. A virtual machine monitor, capable of enforcing a policy of isolation, is an example of a security kernel.

An advantage of the security kernel approach is that all system code not relevant to security can be maintained without affecting the integrity of the system's protection mechanism. At MIT the internals of the Multics operating system have been redesigned with the objective of isolating a kernel that is small enough to be audited and certified secure by a set of experts [Schroeder77]. At UCLA a security kernel has been constructed for a PDP-11/45 with the objective of developing a kernel small enough so that a formal proof of correctness can be achieved. This operational kernel supports a general purpose operating system, UNIX [Popek74b,77]. As mentioned earlier, SDC is investigating a redesign of VM/370 to provide a security kernel based on a virtual machine monitor [Gold77].

Viewed in the framework of the object model, such a security kernel must support the basic notions of objecthood, domain, and right, as well as the operations providing the three major activities of the protection mechanism: the protection enforcement check, rights movement, and domain switching. How small this kernel can be and precisely what functions belong in a security kernel are still a matter of research.

As mentioned earlier, our model of protection relies on the closed system assumption. In practice, this assumption cannot be made. When a user wishes to interact with a system, an initial domain is created in which execution on his behalf takes place. In that, or some subsequently called domain, rights to long-lived objects, such as the files in which he has amassed programs and data, will be required. To determine what rights can be included in the users initial domain, the identity of the user must be authenticated. The most often used authentication technique is based on passwords. A user specifies a password which is presumed by the system to be known only by that particular user. For systems equipped only with simple text entry terminals, the password is in the form of a string of symbols. Terminal devices exist that accept entry of identification in the form of a magnetic card. Experimentation proceeds with I/O devices that would detect handwritten signatures.

The system maintains encoded passwords, usually in an encrypted form. The function used for encryption is, ideally, an irreversible function. Even though one might obtain an encrypted encoding of a password, it would be insufficient for determining the user's cleartext password. When the user submits an identifier, the system encrypts it and compares the encrypted value to the encrypted password maintained by the system. If they match, the user's initial domain is augmented with rights to those long-lived objects that are to be accessible to the authenticated user. System security rests on the authentication scheme, whether it is implemented in the security kernel or as a "trusted process".

This notion of isolating security relevant code will not be considered further. Instead, subsequent sections explore two alternative implementations of access control protection mechanisms.

5.2 Authority Lists

The access matrix was used above to structure the encoding of information required for the enforcement checks. Any implementation of an access control protection mechanism must include some means for representing this same information. It would be inefficient to maintain the access matrix as a data structure, both because it is sparse and because at any point in time very few entries are of current interest. One alternative encoding is in the form of an authority list. Intuitively, an authority list implementation encodes with the object itself the information from the access matrix column associated with it. An authority list, then, is a set of pairs, each of the form <domain name, access name>. The protection enforcement check is performed as follows. A domain D is permitted to perform access A to object X if the pair <D,A> is in the authority list associated with X.

The classic application of authority lists is to record protection information in file systems. In the Multics file system, only file type objects are protected. The accesses "Read", "Execute", and "Write" are distinguished. Principal names together with ring numbers are used to identify domains [Graham72].

Notation of who has a right to access an object is maintained with the object itself. The authority list implementation is desirable if objects have "owners" or "controllers", who grant and remove rights to use their object to others. Performing a rights movement operation, such as giving a right to another, involves only the object representation with its associated authority list. Such operations consist of adding or removing pairs from the authority list encoded with the object. Revocation, in particular, is easy to record. To revoke a user's right to an object, the the appropriate pair is deleted from the object's authority list. There is an issue of whether the revocation takes effect as soon as it is recorded in the authority list. Multics is deliberately designed to permit immediate revocation of privilege.

A more general rendering of the notion of authority lists is that an authority list is a set of pairs, each of the form <lock, access name> [Lampson71]. Domains are specified, not by a unique identity, but as a set of keys which can be used to open locks in an authority list. An application of such authority lists is found in compilers for block structured languages. During compilation, object names used in a program are entered in the symbol table, together with an indication of the block depth and lexicographic block number at the point in the program where the object name is declared. The compiler maintains an indication of the dynamic block number and lexicographic block number of the block containing the statement it is currently compiling. The two current block numbers are effectively used as a key to determine whether or not a particular object name for which there exists an entry in the symbol table is accessible to the statement being compiled [Habermann75]. This compiler example is just one example of an application of the access control protection mechanism based on authority lists. Authority list mechanisms are rarely found in the core of an operating system; instead they are useful in subsystems such as a file or data base subsystem.

5.3 Capability Based Implementation

Based on the principle of least privilege, I have argued that domains should be small; consequently, only those few rights in the currently executing domains, i.e. selected rows of the access matrix, need be readily available for use in enforcement checks. This leads to the strategy of encoding protection data with the executing domain, in contrast to storing it in authority lists at the site of the object. A domain can be represented as a set of descriptors or capabilities [Dennis66]. A capability is an encoding of a right; it is a pair that names a unique object, and lists a set of names of accesses applicable to that object. As noted in the paper discussing the object model, a domain expressed as a set of capabilities serves a dual role; it is a basis for both naming and protection of objects. The only objects for which names are needed in a domain are for those objects for which there is a right in the domain. In capability based systems the set of capabilities is structured, in contrast to being a mathematical set, so that terse local names, i.e. indices into the capability structure, can be used to name objects. The protection enforcement check reduces to determining whether the intended access is one whose name appears in the access list portion of the capability used to name the object. For efficiency, this enforcement check can be made in parallel with name interpretation if both are implemented in hardware. Such parallelism cannot be obtained in an authority list system.

To control capability movement the access name list portion of each capability is extended to include some access names which are solely for controlling access to the capability itself. We have already used as examples the "Copy" and "Transfer" accesses which control whether a capability can be duplicated or moved, respectively. Other examples will be illustrated later.

Domain implementations in capability based systems vary markedly. Because domain switching is expected to occur relatively often, the implementation of domains and domain switching is an important aspect of a system. As discussed earlier, there are two philosophies for domain creation and maintenance. One philosophy dictates that domains be created once and repeatedly reused. In the CAL-TSS system [Lampson76], each process was composed of up to eight "sub-processes" (read "domains"). Each sub-process could invoke ("Enter") a subset of the others. The Hydra [Wulf74] and StarOS [Jones77] operating systems exhibit the alternative philosophy of dynamic domain creation. In both of these systems there exists a type of object, that contains at least a domain template as well as the scheduling and state information necessary to initiate execution in a newly created domain. Each of these systems employs a slightly different scheme for encoding the domain data structure. In Hydra [Wulf74] a domain, called a "Local Name Space", is represented as a list of capabilities. When a procedure is called, by exercising the "Call" right to the procedure object, the entirety of the domain template, together with caller specified parameter capabilities, is copied into the Local Name Space. In the StarOS operating system [Jones77] a domain is also maintained as a capability list. One of the capabilities in an executing domain, is for the domain template itself--a separate object, again represented as a list of capabilities--so that the contents of the template need not be copied at the time of invocation.

The Plessey system [England72] employs an interesting variation of dynamic domain creation. The processor is equipped with a set of registers that hold capabilities. An executing program can load and unload them at will. In effect, their contents is the representation of the current domain. When a domain wishes to invoke execution in a second domain, it loads the appropriate registers with parameter capabilities, then exercises an "Enter" capability on an object that is used as the domain template. The Enter operation alters the "Enter" capability of the caller so that the called domain gains the additional right to "Read", and thus exercise, the capabilties from the domain template. The caller only possessed "Enter" rights. Capability registers serve the same purpose as the new domain capability list created at each procedure invocation in Hydra and StarOS. One difference is that the caller can set up parameters in the capability registers; these register values subsequently are part of the called domain. This saves the cost of allocating a domain object during the Enter operation; however, it falls to the caller and the called domain to save capabilities when Entering and Returning. In the other example systems, the operating system provided this save space; in the Plessey system the user apparently must arrange to find it. Because a domain is essentially dynamic, this would appear to require either a capability list private to the domain, or an appropriately supported capability stack. The cost tradeoffs are not at all clear without some experimentation.

Multics provides a textbook example of applying both of the implementation techniques just discussed. Multics protects file objects; the file system maintains an authority list for each file. Multics also uses a capability based naming and protection system to control access to segment objects. A user process has eight statically allocated domains, as specified by the ring mechanism which we do not discuss here. Any specific domain is defined by a sequence of capabilities, which are called "segment descriptors" in the Multics documentation. Protection enforcement on the basis of an individual word access is performed using capabilities, taking advantage of the fact that the enforcement checking can be performed at the domain, without fetching portions of the object itself, for example, its authority list. Basically, Multics has two protection mechanisms and a conversion mechanism so that files can be converted to segments for direct access. Sufficient back pointers are maintained so that if a user revokes the right to a file from a process currently using it, the revocation will take place immediately, because the capabilties for that segment will be "recomputed". Note that validation of any security properties about this system involves analysis of both protection mechanisms including the file/segment conversion mechanism. It is not sufficient to consider the authority list system alone.

5.3.1 Extended Object Types

In most protection systems, only a fixed, few different types of objects can be protected. These are determined by the operating system. One extension, as already noted, is to permit users to define their own types, the so-called "extended types", in such a way that the protection mechanism can provide the same protection service as it does for the types defined by the operating system. This section explores both the notion of extended types and their implementation using capabilities.

First, consider the objects that users wish to create. Except for the most primitive, objects are built up of other objects. The issue of how to express that one object is a component of another arises. It is not unusual for two different objects to share a common component. This precludes representing components inside the representation of the containing object. It is convenient and efficient to encode object components by pointers because of frequent changes of the size and content. Consider the example of a printer queue that contains a sequence of file objects to be printed. One terse representation of a printer queue is as a queue of capabilities for files. If the capabilities are maintained in a list, the front and rear entries will be represented as integers. In the general case, then, an object contains both data and capabilities. The ramifications of this are considerable.

Recording capabilities within arbitrary objects means that alteration of the representation of an object involves the protection mechanism. Capabilities are not merely strings of bits that can be arbitrarily manipulated. The integrity of a capability must be maintained; otherwise, the protection mechanism will be compromised. A tagged architecture has often been proposed [Feustal73] for implementing capabilities so that they can be arbitrarily encoded in the midst of data words. But, in extant capability based systems, capabilities are restricted to capability lists and cannot be intermixed with data. In all cases protection mechanism code must be executed to perform any kind of capability manipulation. Note that this does not necessarily imply inefficiency; in the StarOS and CAP [Needham74] systems, certain capability operations are implemented in microcode to render them as efficient as data operations of similar complexity.

Plessey exhibits one technique for supporting the notion of an extended object, i.e. an object that contains both data and capabilities. It offers the user a minimal, but functional set of building blocks, data segments and capability lists. A capability list is a linear list of capabilities. The printer queue would be represented as a list of capabilities for file objects. Two options are available for maintaining the pointers to the front and the rear of the list of file object capabilities. The first is to define a <u>data capability</u>. A data capability records a bit string, perhaps a word in length, and can be placed in a capability list. Two data capabilities would be sufficient to hold the two integer pointers for the printer queue. The alternative construction of the printer queue object is to reserve the first slot in the capability list representation of the printer queue to hold a capability for a data object. It, in turn, contains the front and rear queue pointers, as well as any other information the printer module maintains, for example, mean time to printing a file. In general, an object requires two segments--both a data and a capability segment--to be represented in a Plessey-like system. Note that if we discount data capabilities, each and every component of an object is a segment and thus incurs the allocation and maintenance overhead of the segment management system.

In Hydra the notion of an object is supported differently. Objects are a mixture of data and code and the separation of the two is ensured by the protection mechanism. It provides operations for manipulating both the data part and the capability part of an object. These two parts are NOT represented as separate segments as in Plessey. Details of their representation are not visible to users. This permits the operating system to maintain information about object maintenance within the object representation. For example, each object contains its own unique 64 bit name for reliability purposes. It also contains reference counts of how many capabilities for the object are outstanding. This is used by the system to know when an object is no longer accessible, i.e. no capabilities exist for it so that the representation can be destroyed. Similarly, reference counts are used to determine when an object's representation can be moved to secondary storage because no capabilities for it are in active use.

Because arbitrary objects can contain capabilities, the question of naming arises again. Objects are related in a directed graph structure in which capabilities serve as the arcs. Therefore, they can be said to have <u>path names</u>. A general path name is of the form i.j.k and is interpreted as follows: i is an index into the domain object. Presumably, i selects a capability for another object that, in turn, is indexed by j resulting in a capability for another object to be indexed by k resulting, finally, in a capability for the object named i.j.k.

Rights movement operations must be designed to permit controlled movement of capabilities and consequent alteration in the graph relation of objects. Hydra provides a rich set of controls [Cohen75]. For example, let the "Delete" right be used to control erasure of a capability--not the object named by that capability. Two domains can share an object Z which, because it contains a capability for X allows them to share the same access to components of X. If the capabilities in X lack "Delete" rights, each domain is ensured that the other cannot destroy its right to the component object.

For a second example of the increased complexity and power of rights movement operations if capabilities can exist in any object, consider a policy of conservation. It is sometimes useful to know that once a capability (say, a parameter capability) is placed in a domain, that it is not moved out into some long-lived object to be made available to other domains or held after the invocation of the operation completes. In Hydra, unless a capability contains the "Environment" right it cannot be moved out of the Local Name Space in which it exists. The Local Name Space is guaranteed to be destroyed when a Return is made to the caller that caused creation of the Local Name Space.

The last ramification of extended types to be discussed involves the content of a domain. As usual, I assume that a domain is entered to perform an operation. The principle of least privilege dictates that a domain should contain only those capabilities required to perform that operations. Certainly, there exist objects which are required for each invocation, for example, code objects and own data. Parameters differ with each invocation. Passing a parameter in the form of a capability transfers a parameter from the calling to the called domain efficiently. Many extant systems do not support the principle of least privilege very well along the parameter dimension; objects destined to be a parameter to a certain set of domains are always accessible from those domains whether the object is involved in a particular invocation or not.

Consider the case of a module that implements a type T. Should the operations for type T have access to all objects of type T whenever the operations are invoked, or should only the parameter objects of type T be accessible during the call? The principle of least privilege and the companion notion of data abstraction [Liskov75] argue for the latter design.

Consider the case that the Called or Entered domain is responsible for implementing an operation for a particular type T. A domain for a type T operation needs to be able to manipulate components of type T objects that are passed to it as parameters. Users of objects of type T should not be able to manipulate the components directly. Two cases are possible: either a domain implementing a type T always has access to the representation of all objects of type T, or it gains access to particular objects of the type only when necessary, e.g. when they are passed as parameters. The first alternative again conflicts with the principle of least privilege. Let us concentrate on the second. An operation called <u>amplification</u> [Jones75a] is used to transform a capability. In this situation it is used to permit the called domain to acquire access to components of an object, thus gaining rights the caller did not have.

Two techniques for achieving amplification have been developed. In the first one, a variation of a capability called an amplification template is defined. An amplification template contains the name of an object type and two rights fields, one recording "necessary rights" and the other encoding "amplified rights". The protection mechanism includes an operation called Amplify, requiring two parameters, a capability C and an amplification template T. The Amplify operation works as follows: if the type of the object named in capability C and the type named in the template T are the same, and if the necessary rights encoded in T are contained in the access name list of C, then a new capability is produced. That capability names the same object as the capability C but the access name list field of the capability is identical to that of the amplified rights field in T.

```
capability C:                          amplification template T:
┌─────┬───────┐                        ┌───────────────┬───────┬──────────┐
│ xxx │ A1,A2 │                        │ printer queue │ A1,A2 │ A2,A3,A4 │
└─────┴───────┘                        └───────────────┴───────┴──────────┘
         └──────────────┐       ┌──────────────┘
                   Amplify operation
                         ↓
                  ┌─────┬──────────┐
                  │ xxx │ A2,A3,A4 │
                  └─────┴──────────┘
```

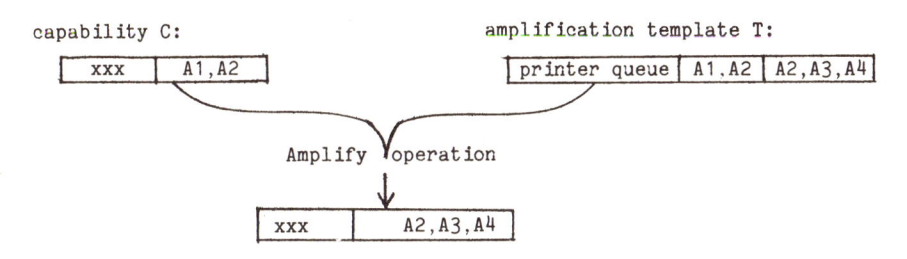

Figure 2. Amplification of a capability for a printer queue object named xxx.

Amplification is graphically shown in figure 2. Assume that capability C contains an internal pointer xxx for an object of type "printer queue" with access rights "A1,A2"; amplification template T specifies type "printer queue", necessary rights "A1,A2", and amplified rights "A2,A3,A4". The Amplify operation determines that object xxx is of type "printer queue" and that the necessary rights in template T do indeed appear in capability C. Therefore it manufactures a new capability for xxx with rights "A2,A3,A4". In Hydra the Amplify operation is automatically invoked for parameter capabilities whenever a procedure Call operation is performed. However, it is also available for direct invocation. Typically in Hydra, a domain implementing a type would use Amplify to obtain the right to exercise, and delete the capabilities in the object and to reference its data part.

The Plessey system [England72] exemplifies a second simpler, albeit less general, technique for amplification. An object, say one created by a type module, can be <u>sealed</u> [Morris74]. Capabilities for the sealed object are distributed among users of that object. Basically, nothing can be done with the capability for the sealed object except to pass it around until it is presented to the appropriate domain as a parameter. The domain in which code implementing the original type of the object has a template which permits it to <u>unseal</u> the object, thus, generating capability for the object so that the components of the object can be manipulated in the domain. The IRIA secure system design uses a very similar technique [Ferrie74].

5.3.2 Status

Several capability based access control systems have been built, for example, CAL-TSS, Hydra, CAP, StarOS, and Plessey. Only the Plessey system is other than a research tool; it is used as a telephone switching computer. To date no major manufacturer has designed and released a hardware/software system employing a general capability mechanism, though some manufacturers have flirted with the idea [Radin76]. Claims have been made that capability based systems are a useful tool for fault detection and containment [Denning76], but these claims are yet to be validated.

The concept of protection enforcement checking is not restricted to operating systems and a dynamic implementation. In 1973 Moore [73] made a proposal to use capabilities with ALGOL-like programs. More recently, the possibility of integrating capability based access control into data abstraction languages, such as Clu and Alphard, has been suggested [Jones76]. A variable can be viewed as a capability: at any instant it names a unique object and specifies a set of rights for the object. Though the object named via a variable can change, the set of permissible accesses cannot. As a result the protection enforcement check can be made at compile-time.

Obviously, one cannot really accomplish <u>all</u> enforcement checking at compile-time. Both separately compiled programs and long-lived objects must be considered. In particular, when an interactive program interrogates the file system for some previously stored object, it is insufficient merely to retrieve the string of bits that represents that object. Both its type and the access rights of the domain which caused the archiving of the object need to be known. Before a variable can be made to name the retrieved object, a type and rights check must be dynamically made. It needs to be made only once; after a variable has been made to name such an object, the compile-time checks are sufficient. Note, however, that the security of programs written in the language relies not only on compiler protection checks, but on the semantics of the object oriented file system.

6. Enforcing Information Control Policies

In the earlier section on security policies, information flow policies were defined to be policies that regulate the transmission of information, however and wherever it is encoded. One such policy is the policy of <u>confinement</u> [Lampson73]. A domain is said to be confined if no information can be transmitted from it, except, perhaps, via parameters given to the domain when it was Entered or Called. The policy is a strict one; even transmission via negative inference or resource usage patterns is prohibited. A number of researchers have proposed information flow techniques for enforcing confinement policies at compile-time [Denning77, Jones75].

The techniques proposed are closely related to those used for flow analysis in compilers. There are cases in which it is possible to use an access control protection mechanism. For example, the domain would be constrained so that it shared access to no objects, other than those parameter objects it was given. The observable execution characteristics of the domain must be constant. If resource usage patterns are visible from another domain, then information could be communicated. Confinement, while difficult, is possible to implement using an access control protection mechanism at great cost. The virtual machine monitor discussed earlier does this by partitioning all resources among the n principals. Each receives exactly his allotted resources each time quantum.

There exists a class of information control policies called <u>value dependent</u> policies that cannot be implemented directly using an access control mechanism. A value dependent policy states that information can or cannot be released, based on the information itself. An example might be the following: Only principals in the personnel department and the president of a company may read the salary of company employees. However, personnel department members cannot read salary figures that exceed 100,000DM. Certainly a protection mechanism which is constrained to deal only in containers of encoded information, i.e. objects, as access control mechanisms are, cannot directly be used to implement a policy that depends on the information encoded within the objects. Fortunately, access control mechanisms are usually a sufficient basis to build up other programs that do implement value dependent policies.

A tax data base was used earlier to illustrate one subclass of information flow policies: statistical access policies. Recall that legislators contemplating tax law changes were permitted to get statistical information based on a subset of tax records for individuals, but were not permitted to obtain information about individuals. The data base system presumably contains a program to derive statistical summaries. Another program would be responsible for determining what statistics could be released to a legislator.

The statistics that can be released without compromising the data base, i.e. by releasing sufficient data to deduce information about an individual, is disappointingly small. Abstract models have been designed to characterize this problem [Dobkin78]. Assume that queries may be made about a data base consisting of n integer elements. Queries can be made about the sum (to pick one operator that will produce a summary result) of any subset of k elements in the data base. Queries are not allowed to overlap, i.e. refer to the same data base elements, by more than r. The user is assumed to already know s elements in the data base. The number of queries required to compromise such a data base is $S(n,k,r,s)$. It turns out that $S(n,k,1,0) \leq 2k - 1$ and $S(n,k,1,1) \leq 2k - 2$, where n is large enough (i.e., $n \geq (k-1)**2 + 2$). For a set of queries of 3 elements with overlap of 1, it requires no more than 6 (5) queries to determine one element exactly, if no (one) element is known a priori.

7. References

Of the following references [Saltzer75], [Popek74a], [Graham72], and [Linden76] are recommended overview articles.

Buzen, J. and U. Gagliardi, The Evolution of Virtual Machine Architecture. AFIPS Conference Proceedings, 42, NCC 1973, 291-300.

Cohen, E. and D. Jefferson, Protection in the Hydra Operating Systems, Proceedings Fifth ACM Symposium on Operating System Principles; ACM Operating Systems Review 9, 5 (November 1975) 141-160.

Denning, D. and P. Denning, Certification of Programs for Secure Information Flow. CACM, 20, 7 (July 1977) 504-512.

Dennis, J. and E. Van Horn, Programming Semantics for Multiprogrammed Computations. CACM 9, 3 (March 1966) 143-155.

Dobkin, D., A. K. Jones, R. Lipton, Secure Data Bases: Protection Against User Inference. Transactions on Data Bases, to be published.

England, D. M., Architectural Features of System 250. Proceedings International Switching Symposium, 1972.

Fabry, R. S., Capability Based Addressing. CACM, 17, 7 (July 1974) 403-412.

Ferrie, J., D. Kaiser, D. Lanciaux, and B. Martin, An Extensible Structure for Protected System Design. Proceedings IRIA International Workshop on Protection in Operating Systems, France, 1974.

Feustel, E. A., On the Advantages of Tagged Architecture IEEE Transactions on Computers, C2,7, 1973, 644-656.

Gold, B., R. Linde, M. Schaefer, and J. Scheid, Final Report: Periods Processing versus KVM/370. System Development Corporation Technical Report, May 1977.

Graham, G. S. and P. J. Denning, Protection--Principles and Practice. AFIPS Conference Proceedings, 40, SJCC 1972, 417-429.

Habermann, A. N., Introduction to Operating System Design. SRA, 1976.

Hoffman, L. J., Modern Methods for Computer Security and Privacy. Prentice Hall, 1977.

Jones, A. K. and W. A. Wulf, Towards the Design of Secure Systems. Software--Practice and Experience, 5 (October-December 1975) 321-336.

Jones, A. K. and R. J. Lipton, The Enforcement of Security Policies for Computation. Carnegie-Mellon University Department of Computer Science Technical Report, May 75.

Jones, A. K. and B. H. Liskov, A Language Extension for Controlling Access to Shared Data. IEEE IEEE Transactions on Software Engineering, SE-2, 4 (December 1976) 277-284.

Jones, A. K., R. J. Chansler, Jr., I. Durham, P. Feiler, and K. Schwans, Software Management of Cm*--A Multiple Microprocessor. AFIPS Conference Proceedings, NCC 1977.

Moore, C. G., Potential Capabilities in ALGOL-like Programs. Cornell Department of Computer Science Technical Report (September 1974).

Lampson, B. W., Protection. Proceedings Fifth Annual Princeton Conference on Information Sciences and Systems (1971) 437-443. Reprinted in ACM Operating Systems Review (January 1974).

Lampson, B. W., A Note on the Confinement Problem. CACM, 16, 10 (October 1973) 613-615.

Lampson, B. W. and H. Sturgis, Reflections on an Operating System Design. CACM 19, 5 (May 76), 251-266.

Linden, T. A., Operating System Structures to Support Security and Reliable Software. ACM Computing Surveys, 8, 4 (December 1976) 409-445.

Liskov, B. and S. Zilles, Specification Techniques for Data Abstractions. Proceedings of the International Conference on Reliable Software, SIGPLAN Notices 12, 3 (1975).

Morris, J. H., Jr., Protection in Programming Languages. CACM, 16, 1 (January 1973) 15-21.

Needham, R. M. and R. D. H. Walker, Protection and Process Management in the CAP Computer, Proceedings IRIA International Workshop on Protection in Operating Systems, France (1974) 155-160.

Popek, G., Protection Structures. <u>Computer</u> (June 1974) 22-33.

Popek, G. and C. Kline, Verifiable Secure Operating Software. <u>AFIPS Conference Proceedings</u> <u>43</u>, NCC (1974).

Popek, G. and D. Farber, A Model for Verification of Security in Operating Systems. <u>CACM</u>, to be published.

Radin, G. and P. Schneider, An Architecture for an Extended Machine with Protected Addressing. IBM Research TR 00.2757, May 1976.

Redell, D. R. and R. S. Fabry, Selective Revocation of Capabilities. IRIA International Workshop on Protection in Operating Systems, France (1974) 197-210.

Saltzer, J. H. and M. Schroeder, The Protection of Information in Computer Systems, <u>Proceedings of the IEEE, 63</u>, 9 (September 1975) 1278-1308.

Saltzer, J. H., Private Communication.

Schroeder, M., Cooperation of Mutually Suspicious Subsystems in a Computer Utility, Doctoral Thesis, MIT Technical Report, 1972.

Schroeder, M, D. Clark, and J. Saltzer, The Multics Kernel Design. Sixth Symposium on Operating System Principles (November 1977).

Wulf, W. A., <u>et al</u>, Hydra: The Kernel of a Multiprocessor Operating System. <u>CACM</u> [17], 6 (June 1974) 337-345.

CHAPTER 3.D.

K. Lagally
Universität Stuttgart
Stuttgart, Germany

Synchronization in a Layered System

SYNCHRONIZATION IN A LAYERED SYSTEM
Klaus Lagally
Institut für Informatik der Universität Stuttgart
Stuttgart, Germany

1. Introduction

In this lecture we study some implementation aspects of the object model in the context of a layered system of cooperating sequential process. A layered system may be viewed as consisting of a linear sequence of layers which, in a step-by-step fashion, transform the hardware interface into the abstract machine on which the user programs may be considered to run. A layer consists of a collection of data, routines and sequential processes which run on an abstract machine implemented by the lower layers. Every layer interface can be represented by a collection of (structured) data objects and the possible operations on them; any further information on the internal structure of the abstract machine defined by the interface is inaccessible to the users of this machine. They may assume that the result of an operation on a date object is consistent irrespective of other users manipulating the same object. We shall describe, and compare on a specific example, several different mechanisms which have been devised to obtain this consistency.

2. General Concepts

2.1 Synchronization

Every object visible at a given interface is associated with a certain extended data type. The type definition gives information about the possible operations on objects of that type, and on their realization. It thus contains among others:

- the description of a data structure which implements objects of the given type by constructing them from more basic objects;
- access operations, which are the only means for the user of the object to manipulate the internal structure.

In a multiprogramming environment, the access operations may be activated by several users simultaneously. This will, at least in general, lead to inconsistencies if no synchronization conditions are observed.

We consider synchronization conditions to be coupled to the date type as a consequence of the internal structure of the object. The effect of synchronization conditions will be that, depending on the state of the object, some access operations will be delayed somewhere during the course of their execution, until an appropriate state of the object is reached by the effect of operations performed by other users.

We thus get a natural subdivision of the access routines into phases which can be considered as the units of synchronization. In general, these phases depend on the chosen internal representation of the data and the access operations, Therefore, it is not always possible to specify the necessary synchronization in terms of the externally accessible operations alone; the user of the object is not aware of, and need not be interested in, the details of the synchronization. It is the implementation's responsibility to maintain consistency by observing suitable constraints.

In order to be more explicit, let us extend our type definition by adding some more components:

- primitive operations on the internal data structure,
- a state description,
- synchronization constraints.

The primitive operations are the building blocks for the access operations. It is important to note that the primitive operations need not necessariliy be mutually exclusive; they can be executed in parallel by different users if no synchronization constraints forbid it. Therefore, we cannot define an "execution history" on our data objects directly as a sequence of executions of primitive operations. If, however, we split the non-exclusive operations into an initiation and a termination phase, we may, without loss of generality, consider these as instantaneous and mutually exclusive to all other operations. We thus can associate to our object a "history" of state transitions which carries all information necessary for correct synchronisation.

The state of the system is determined by the information in which phases of the access operations the individual processes are. State transitions can occur only if a primitive operation is initiated. A state can thus be characterized by the information which primitive operations have been initiated or terminated by the individual processes. Depending on the current state, a transition to another state may be allowed or forbidden. We note that the termination of an operation is always allowed, whereas the initiation may be forbidden. On the other hand, a termination event may lead to a state in which a formerly blocked initiation event becomes enabled; this situation, called "unstable" by Dijkstra [Di71] leads to an immediate state transition.

It may happen that two or more transitions become enabled at the same time. The resulting ambiguity cannot be resolved by synchronization considerations alone; possible additional strategies are e.g.

- priority scheduling: the user with the highest external priority may proceed.
- Fair scheduling: the user is enabled that has been blocked for the longest time (avoidance of "individual starvation").

Every execution of an access operation corresponds to a sequence of initiation/termination events of primitive operations, which is a subsequence of the execution history of the data object. Parallel executions of several access operations correspond to interleaving these subsequences; the synchronization conditions guarantee that no illegal state transitions can occur. The various synchronization tools described in the literature differ mainly in the way in which states and allowable transitions show up.

2.2 Processes and Messages

Up to now, we have made no use of the assumption that we are dealing with a layered system of processes. For the following, we consider the system (including the user programs) to consist of
- a collection of sequential processes executing concurrently with unrelated speed and interacting by a set of standard operations,
- a nucleus, implementing the set of processes in terms of real processors (including peripheral devices) and providing the means for process interaction.

We may distinguish between explicit and implicit process interactions. Implicit interaction occurs if several processes share a common object and have to observe a certain discipline for keeping the object in a consistent state. Explicit interaction occurs if a process has to wait until another process has performed a given task.

It has been noted that explicit synchronization and the passing of information are very closely related so that it is convenient to combine them into a message passing system [BH70, GJL72]. If one process has completed a given task, some result information has been generated, which is deposited by a send-operation into some queue. A process needing the result information will, by an await-operation on the same queue, absorb this information as soon as it becomes available. This mechanism, which is basically nothing else but a producer-consumer pair, was first used in the RC 4000-system [BH70] as the basis for process communication; of the many possible variants we shall describe the BSM message system [GJL72] in some detail.

The passing of information between processes can be considered either as the sending of an "order", calling for some operation to be performed by the called process, or an "answer", notifying a process of the completion of some operation it called for. As we shall see, this distinction, whereas not strictly necessary, is very useful for structuring the system in such a way that it is free from communication deadlocks.

An order is sent by the generic operation

    SEND_ORDER(process, message, key).

The transmitting process will proceed after performing this operation; the result parameter "key" may be used to distinguish between different orders.

We postulate that there will be an answer to every order sent. This answer is received by the operation

    WAIT_ANSWER(buffer, key).

If necessary, the receiving process will be blocked until the answer will be sent by the process that received the corresponding order. The answers for several pending orders can be distinguished by the parameter "key".

A process receives orders by

    WAIT_ORDER(idn, buffer),

where "idn" is an internally generated identification number. If there are no orders present, the process will be put into a wait state until an order becomes available.

Every order received will eventually be acknowledged by

    SEND_ANSWER(idn, answer),

where "idn" identifies the corresponding order. It is the message system's responsibility to identify the sender of this order and to deliver the answer to this process.

Usually, a process will, while working on an order it received, send orders to other processes to have some subtasks performed. If it runs into a wait state, it may wish to proceed with any of a set of pending answers, or even start processing a new order. This can be accomplished by

> WAIT_MESSAGE(msg, idn, buffer, set_of_keys),

which will deliver either an order or an answer out of a set of pending answers and/or orders. It can be used as a "parallel wait" in a process that has issued more than one order and/or accepts orders from other processes. The result parameter "msg" indicates whether an order or an answer was received.

The listed message operations are sufficiently general to include all explicit communications of a process with its environment. Two special cases should be mentioned:

- The sequence SEND_ORDER, WAIT_ANSWER behaves like a subroutine call with value-result-parameters. It can be used to simulate a subroutine which must be protected from its callers.
- The process addressed in SEND_ORDER may in fact execute on a peripheral device; in that case the operation is tranformed by the nucleus into an I/O-channel operation. The I/O-interrupt is converted into an implicit SEND_ANSWER. Thus the peripheral operations can be absorbed into the message system; in this context the WAIT_MESSAGE operation is very useful e.g. when driving several peripheral devices by a single process.

2.3 Process Hierarchy

In the given communications scheme, a process may be blocked for different reasons:

- It may be inside a WAIT_ORDER operation. Then it will be activated if and when some other process, by sending an order, requests some work to be performed by it.
- The process may wait for an answer to an order it has sent to another process. This wait state is potentially dangerous: If the called process may directly or indirectly send orders (not only answers) to the caller then the system may get into a circular wait state.

This possibility of deadlock can be excluded by structuring the system in such a way that the relation "X sends orders to Y" generates a partial ordering of processes. If the answer to any order is computed in a finite number of steps and if every process that is not blocked proceeds with nonzero speed, then it can be shown that the answer to every order will arrive within a finite interval of time, i.e. there is no deadlock.

Obviously, the given partial ordering can in many ways be embedded into a total ordering which can be viewed as a hierarchy of software layers, or abstract machines [Di71]. More generally, with every system process we can associate an abstract machine defined by the collection of operations called by the given process and the objects operated upon. This abstract machine usually is not a sequential automaton; on the contrary, a call on one of its operations generally triggers a parallel activity which must be explicitly terminated by a WAIT_ANSWER operation. The system process itself extends this abstract machine into another one by adding to the existing system functions those it is implementing by the orders it is processing; consequently, some of the old functions are now superseded by the new ones and should only be used by the system process itself, but not by its callers any more. The same considerations apply analogously to the objects and object types visible at the abstract machine interface.

3. Implementation tools

In the following, we give an overview of methods for implementing synchronization constraints. Due to the limited space available, we cannot give a complete survey, but concentrate on a few mechanisms which in our opinion are fundamental and essentially different.

3.1 Semaphores

The oldest, and possibly simplest, synchronization method has been given by Dijkstra [Di68, Di71] and uses semaphores for two completely different purposes:

- One common "mutex" semaphore is used to sequentialize all accesses to the state variables, by collecting all accesses into critical regions guarded by that semaphore.
- To every process, there corresponds a "private" semaphore which is decremented after a critical region which precedes a possibly illegal transition. The decrementing will block the

process if the semaphore has not been incremented inside the
critical region.

If, later, the activity of another process leads to a state in which
the blocked process could proceed, it has to locate the private semaphore of the blocked process and increment it. In case of ambiguity,
the appropriate scheduling discipline has to be observed.

The semaphore solution is obviously sufficiently general for all synchronization problems. However, it suffers from some drawbacks:

- A process has to know about the identity of its potential com-
  petitors in order to activate them again in an unstable situation. This may lead to a sometimes undesirable reduction of
  modularity.
- Semaphore operations must be used with great care. Programs
  that use semaphores are notoriously difficult to verify; programming errors may lead into deadlocks or inconsistent situations which are very difficult to analyze.

These problems may be overcome if the semaphore operations are not co-
ded by a programmer, but generated by a compiler. We therefore now
turn to methods which hide some details of implementation from the
programmer.

3.2 Conditional Critical Regions

A synchronization tool that is, in a certain sense, at the opposite
end of the spectrum from Dijkstra's solution, has been introduced by
Brinch Hansen [BH72a] in the form of "conditional critical regions".
There, the aspects of mutual exclusion and of intermediate blocking
have been taken care of by purely syntactic means:

- The construct
  "region ν do ... end"
  associates to the data object ν an (anonymous) mutex semaphore, which may lock all "region ν" - statements.
- Every access operation of the data object is a "region ν" -
  statement.
- The clause "await B" inside a "region ν" - statement temporarily suspends the execution of the calling process if and so
  long as the condition B on the state variables is false; while
  the process is blocked, the lock associated to ν is open.

When the execution of the process is resumed, B is true and the lock is set.

This synchronization tool allows the programmer to express the synchonization conditions directly; unfortunately, it cannot be implemented in an inexpensive way. The problem is that the conditions "B" have to be evaluated very frequently:

- for avoidance of deadlocks: at least if a process leaves a region or is blocked by an await-clause;
- for minimal blocking: after every change of state variables.

Several mechanisms have been advocated to reduce this overhead: analyzing the dependence of regions [Sch76], predeclaring the conditions [Ke77], restricting the possible forms of the conditions [RV77, Ger77] and/or of the operations on the state variables [RK77]. However, another problem remains, namely that the mutual exclusion of the access operations is sometimes not necessary at all. This leads to unfavourable effects if an access operation makes use of objects in a lower layer and is delayed there; then, the access operation and therefore the given object remains locked unnecessarily, whereas parallel accesses would be logically possible.

Moreover, the case of several possible continuations, which calls for additional scheduling strategies, cannot even be expressed in terms of conditional critical regions; thus, fair scheduling or similar strategies cannot be obtained without the introduction of artificial, explicit interactions, e.g. by permitting waiting conditions to depend on process priorities.

3.3 Monitors

In order to avoid the inefficiency associated with conditional critical regions, Hoare [Ho74] and Brinch Hansen [BH73a] independently introduced the monitor concept. Here, the access operations of a data object are collected in the syntactic context of a type definition and are again locked collectively by a common anonymous lock variable. The mutual interaction, however, has been made explicit by the operations wait and signal (resp. delay / continue):

- The operation "wait(q)" blocks the calling process and puts its process identification on a waiting queue q; the lock on the data object is released.
- The operation "signal(q)" chooses a process from the queue q and activates it; as the lock remains set, the calling process

is suspended until the newly activated process leaves the monitor or is blocked again.

The monitor concept, if used with care, can lead to very efficient implementations; however, it suffers from the same deficiency as conditional critical regions: if monitors are nested, processes may be blocked unnecessarily [JS77, Had77,Lis 77]; the reason is the automatic mutual exclusion on the data object, whereas mutual exclusion on the state variables would suffice [LS77].

Moreover, verification of programs using monitors may be difficult; this is a consequence of the fact that after completion of a wait- or signal-operation, the state may have changed in a rather drastic way. For instance, the process activated by a signal-operation may itself execute a signal-operation which will pass control to still another process, and so on. The situation becomes worse if explicit scheduling disciplines are to be incorporated. Therefore, the utility of monitors for expressing complicated synchronization conditions has remained a controversial issue.

3.4 Path Expressions

A quite different idea has been advocated by Campbell and Habermann [CH74, Ha75]. Their mechanism, called "Path Expressions", is designed to restrict the set of admissible execution histories of primitive operations so that no illegal state transitions are possible.

A path expression has the form
    path S end ,
where S denotes a subsequence of the execution history according to the following syntax:
- S::= S1;S2

    means: the subsequence S1 must be followed by the subsequence S2 and vice-versa.
- S::= S1,S2

    means: either S1 or S2 must follow;
- S::= {S1}

    means: after S1 has been initiated, an arbitrary number of instances of S1 may be initiated. Only after the termination of all of them one may proceed.
- S::= (a-b)^n

    means: at every point in the history, the sequence "a" must have occured at least as often as the sequence "b", and not more than "n"-times more often.

Path expressions may be translated schematically and systematically into a sequence of P- and V-operations that are added as a prolog or epilog onto a given primitive operation so that the postulated synchronization behaviour is fulfilled automatically [CH74, Ha77]. However, if the state depends on the identity and/or the mutual relations of the individual processes, the formulation of the appropriate path expressions is not obvious. Moreover, as the identity of the calling processes does not enter into the description at all, it is not clear how to incorporate explicit scheduling decisions for cases which otherwise would remain ambiguous.

3.5 Object Managers

In the following we describe an implementation that has been used in the experimental operating system BSM [Lag75] and fits well into our model of a layered system of processes. We associate with a type definition a sequential process, called an "object manager", which implements all accesses to the state variables of objects of the given type, and which takes care of the necessary synchronizations [Lag75, JS77]. Every access operation is called by a suitable order to the object manager; as the latter is a sequential process, the state transitions are sequentialized automatically so that the state description is always consistent. On the other hand, the primitive operations on the data itself need not be mutually exclusive; they may be realized by other processes called by the object manager, or by the caller himself after he has obtained the permission from the object manager. An order that cannot be processed completely is put onto an internal queue of the object manager; only after its completion the corresponding answer is sent. The programmer is free to incorporate arbitrary local scheduling strategies for the case that several queued orders simultaneously become enabled to proceed.

The general structure of an object manager is derived from the type definition; its main components are:
- a data structure describing the system state,
- elementary operations performing state transitions,
- waiting queues for blocked transitions,
- a sequential program processing orders and answers.

In order to exploit possible parallelism, the actual data structure and the associated primitive operations are usually not contained in the object manager proper; either they are taken care of by the callers which rely on the object manager only for the purpose of synchronizing, or they rest with some process in a lower layer that is called by the object manager to perform the actual access. The first possibility is analogous to the use of monitors; the second alternative is superior under the aspects of hiding implementation details and protection against misuse. The coding of the object manager is in both cases nearly identical; the main difference is in the signalling of termination events which in the first version arrive as orders, in the second one as answers.

4. Examples

4.1 Readers and Writers

One of the most important synchronization problems is the coordination of several users on a common data object, whose internal structure is not specified any further but that it may be inspected or changed. This is the famous reader-writer-problem that was first published and solved by Courtois, Heymans und Parnas [CHP71]; since then it has been used to test nearly every new synchronization method [e.g. Ag77, BH72, CH74, Ju73, BW74, Ho74, Lam75, Sch76, Ke77]. There are two kinds of users: "writers" modify the object and must thus have exclusive access, whereas "readers" only inspect the object and therefore may share it with other readers. Of the different variants of the problem, we consider the case that writers have priority over readers, which means that if a writer is waiting for access to the object, no new reading operation may begin.

The state may be described by two counters: a reader count rc which counts the processes that are reading at the moment, a writer count wc giving the number of processes either writing or waiting for write access, and a boolean variable $busy$ indicating that a write operation is in progress. In addition we need two waiting lists: rl, the list of waiting readers, and wl for the writers. We assume the existence of procedures put_list, get_list and $empty$ with the following meaning:
- $empty(x)$ tests whether the list x is empty,
- $put\_list(x,y)$ adds the item y to the list x,
- $get\_list(x,y)$ extracts some item from the non-empty list x and assigns it to the variable y.

We must forbid the cases that
- more than one process is writing,

- a process is reading while another is writing.

The first condition already has been taken care of by our choice of state variables; the second may be expressed as

<u>not</u> *busy* ∨ (*rc* = o).

At the end of a write operation or the last one of several concurrent read operations, we get an unstable situation if at least one of the queues *rl* and *wl* is not empty; if both contain elements, we give priority to the waiting writers.

Let us now compare the different formulations of this synchronization problem in terms of the mechanisms introduced in the preceding chapter. In all examples we use PASCAL [Wi71] with some extensions which should be obvious. A reading operation has the form:

<pre>
    procedure read;
    begin   start_read;
            do_read;
            end_read
    end .
</pre>

We are concerned with the procedures *start_read* and *end_read*, which contain the synchronization; the routine *do_read* performs the actual data transfer and is not given here. For convenience, we sometimes use a local procedure *init_read(i)* which activates a given reader process *i*. For writers, analogous considerations apply.

All the given solutions allow writers to lock out readers indefinitely. This is implied by the problem specification and could be overcome by a different scheduling discipline.

4.1.1 Semaphores

a) <u>The general mechanism</u>

We introduce a common semaphore *m* for controlled access to the state variables; in addition, to every process *k* we associate a private semaphore *s[k]* for controlling the blocking of processes. By following the guidelines given in section 3.1, we arrive at the program:

<pre>
    var   rc, wc : integer;
          busy : boolean;
          rl, wl : list of process;
          m : semaphore (1);
          s : array [process] of semaphore (o);
</pre>

```
procedure start_read (i:process);
begin P(m);
      if wc = o then init_read(i)
      else  put_list(rl,i);
      V(m); P(s[i])
      end;

procedure end_read(i:process);
var k:process;
begin P(m); rc -:=1;
      if(rc=o) ∧ not empty(wl) then
      begin get_list(wl,k); init_write(k)
      end;
      V(m)
end ;

procedure start_write(i:process);
begin P(m); wc +:=1;
      if(rc=o) ∧ not busy then init_write(i)
      else put_list(wl,i);
      V(m); P(s[i])
end;

procedure end_write(i:process);
var k: process;
begin P(m); wc -:=1; busy := false;
      if not empty(wl) then
      begin get_list(wl,k); init_write(k)
      end else
      while not empty(rl) do
      begin get_list(rl,k); init_read(k)
      end;
      V(m)
end;

procedure init_read(i:process);
begin rc +:= 1; V(s[i])
end;

procedure init_write(i:process);
begin busy:= true; V(s[i])
end;
```

We notice that a process can only get past the $P(s[i])$-operation in *start_write* if it either has executed *init_write(i)* itself because of the resource being free, or if it has been activated by another process executing *init_write(k)* inside *end_write* or *end_read*. Obviously, only one process at a time can obtain write access, and waiting writers have priority over writing readers. Similarly, readers can only complete *start_read* if there are no active writers. All waiting readers will be activated at the end of a writing phase only if there is no waiting writer. For every blocked process, an identification has been stored on one of the waiting lists; if we specify the criteria by which *get_list* chooses an element from a list, we can implement arbitrary scheduling strategies.

b) <u>The solution of Courtois, Heymans and Parnas</u> [CHP71]

The given solution can very easily be adapted to different scheduling disciplines. However, we must pay for this generality by a considerable overhead which is mainly due to the explicit waiting lists rl and wl. At the cost of flexibility, we can improve on this situation if we make use of the following observations:

- To every set of critical regions there corresponds an implicit waiting list.
- A set of critical regions may be selectively locked so that more than one process of a given class may be in it simultaneously, whereas other processes can have exclusive access.

The selective locking mechanism makes use of the operations [CHP71, CH74]:

<u>procedure</u> PP(m,s : semaphore; c: integer);
<u>begin</u> P(m);
    <u>if</u> c = o <u>then</u> P(s);
    c +:= 1;
    V(m)
<u>end</u>;

<u>procedure</u> VV(m,s : semaphore; c: integer);
<u>begin</u> P(m); c -:= 1;
    <u>if</u> c = o <u>then</u> V(s);
    V(m)
<u>end</u>;

The operation $PP(m,s,c)$ will lock against a $P(s)$-operation and vice versa; however, another $PP(m,s,c)$ with the same parameters will not be locked. $VV(m,s,c)$ is the corresponding unlock operation.

Using this mechanism we arrive at the solution:

```
var   rc,wc : integer;
      m,mr,mw,sr,sw : semaphore (1);

procedure  start_read;
begin P(m); P(sw);
      PP(mr,sr,rc);
      V(sw); V(m)
end;

procedure  end_read;
      VV(mr,sr,rc);

procedure  start_write;
begin PP(mw,sw,wc);
      P(sr)
end;

procedure  end_write;
begin V(sr);
      VV(mw,sw,wc)
end;
```

The *PP*-operation in *start_read* will lock out the *P*-operation in *start_write*, but not the *PP*-operation in other readers; thus, an active reader blocks writers, but not other readers. Conversely, the *P*-operation in *start_write* locks out other *P*- and *PP*-operations; thus, writers have exclusive access.

Priority to writers is obtained in the following way: the $P(sw)-V(sw)$-pair in *start_read* is locked by the first writer executing the *PP*-operation in *start_write*; further writers may pass the *PP*-call. Only when the last writer has executed the corresponding *VV* in *end_write*, readers can again proceed inside of *start_read* to gain access by the *PP*-call. The additional $P(m)-V(m)$-pair in *start_read* has been added to make sure that at most one reader ever waits at sw, whereas any others wait at m [CHP71]. Unfortunately, this is not sufficient to guarantee absolute priority to writers; this is due to the fact that the *PP*- and *VV*-operations are not in the same sense elementary as *P* and *V*, and that the activation order of *V* is undefined. For further details see [Con77].

4.1.2 Conditional critical regions

When using conditional critical regions, we can express the necessary conditions directly:
- no reader may begin reading if a writer is waiting or writing,
- a writer may only write if the object is not being accessed by a reader or writer.

Thus, we get [BH72b], introducing the sharing variable v:

```
var v : shared record rc,wc : integer;
                      busy   : boolean
               end;

procedure start_read;
region v do  await wc = o;
             rc +:= 1
       end;

procedure end_read;
region v do  rc -:= 1
       end;

procedure start_write;
region v do  wc +:= 1;
             await not busy ∧(rc = o);
             busy := true
       end;

procedure end_write;
region v do  wc -:= 1;
             busy:= false
       end;
```

The implementation of the region- and await-statement must make sure that the await-conditions are evaluated sufficiently often so that waiting processes may be activated in time; depending on the sophistication of the compiler this may lead, e.g. to a re-evaluation of the condition "*wc = o*" not only after *end_write*, but also after the await-clause in *start_write* or even after *end_read*. There is no easy way of expressing the knowledge that these latter evaluations are redundant.

The solution correctly delays newly arriving readers if there are writers already waiting; on the other hand, it cannot give writers priority over waiting readers [CHP72, BH73b]. The reason is that there is no way of indicating the evaluation order of the <u>await</u>-conditions.

The variable *busy* can be replaced by putting *do_read* inside a critical region. If we combine the three writer-routines into one, we can omit the variable *busy* altogether:

<u>procedure</u> write;
<u>region</u> v <u>do</u> wc +:= 1;
          <u>await</u> rc = o;
          do_write;
          wc -:= 1
      <u>end</u>;

we cannot apply the same trick to the readers as this would destroy any concurrency.

4.1.3 Monitors

If we explicitly program the blocking and activating of processes and the evaluation of <u>await</u>-conditions, we arrive at Hoare's and Brinch Hansen's monitor concept. If we apply it to our example, we get [Ho74]:

<u>var</u> rc,wc : integer;
    rl,wl : condition;

<u>procedure</u> start_read;
<u>begin</u> <u>if</u> wc ≠ o <u>then</u> rl. wait;
      rc +:= 1; rl. signal
<u>end</u>;

<u>procedure</u> end_read
<u>begin</u> rc -:= 1;
      <u>if</u> rc = o <u>then</u> wl. signal
<u>end</u>;

<u>procedure</u> start_write;
<u>begin</u> wc +:= 1;
      <u>if</u> (rc ≠ o) ∨ (wc o) <u>then</u> wl. wait
<u>end</u>;

<u>procedure</u> end_write;
<u>begin</u> wc -:= 1;
      <u>if</u> wc ≠ o <u>then</u> wl. signal
              <u>else</u> rl. signal
<u>end</u>;

If we compare this version to the explicit semaphore solution, we find that the activation of all waiting readers at the end of *end_write* has been obtained by a trick: a reader that is activated after the operation *rl. wait* inside of *start_read* activates another waiting reader, and so on. We have further assumed that a *signal*-operation on an empty queue has no effect at all.

We can again combine the writer-routines and simplify the wait-condition:

        procedure write;
        begin wc +:= 1;
            if rc ≠ o then wl. wait;
            do_write;
            wc -:= 1;
            if wc ≠ o then wl. signal
                    else rl. signal
        end;

as above, doing the same thing with the reader-routines would give the readers exclusive access. Thus, there can be no monitor for the readers-writers-problem with the only entry-routines *read* and *write*.

4.1.4 Path Expressions

The synchronization conditions for the readers-writers-problem can be expressed by path expressions in a very natural way [CH74]. The fact writers have exclusive access whereas readers may read concurrently may be written as

        path {do_read}, do_write end ,

whereas priority to writers is obtained by

        path   start_read end
and   path   start_read, {start_write; do_write} end ,

which means that readers may execute the operation *start_read* only sequentially and only if no *(start_write; do_write)*-sequence is in progress.

The operations *end_read* and *end_write* are not needed; *start_read* and *start_write* have no other effect but that the execution of the process containing them may be delayed by the synchronization operations the compiler has generated around them when evaluating the path expressions.

A method of directly translating path expressions into semaphore operations has been indicated in [CH74]; the result, for our example problem, is essentially the Courtois-Heymans-Parnas-solution.

4.1.5 Object Managers

a) Explicit Synchronization

All the synchronization mechanism discussed so far have in common that the access operations are called as procedures from the calling processes; thus, if a process is preempted while executing an access operation, the data object may be locked indefinitely. This danger may be avoided by separating the access operations from the callers and collecting them into a sequential process associated to the data object, the "object manager"; an access operation is called by a message operation and proceeds asynchronous to the caller. Only if and when the caller may proceed, the corresponding answer is sent.

The coding of an object manager for the reader-writer-problem can be derived immediately from the given solution using the general semaphore mechanism. In addition to the state variables, we need a local variable *idn* which contains the identification number of the current message, and a variable *buffer* whose value indicates the kind of operation called for. We thus get the following coding for the object manager (let it be called *sync*):

```
process  sync;
var rc, wc : integer;
    busy : boolean;
    rl, wl: list of integer;
    idn: integer;
    buffer: (sr, er, sw, ew);

procedure  start_read;
begin if wc = o then init_read
      else put_list(rl,idn)
end;

procedure  end_read;
begin rc -:= 1; SEND_ANSWER(idn);
      if (rc = o) ∧ not empty(wl) then
      begin get_list(wl,idn); init_write
      end
end;

procedure  start_write;
begin wc +:= 1;
      if (rc = o) ∧ not busy then init_write
```

```
                else put_list(wl,idn)
        end;

        procedure  end_write;
        begin wc -:= 1; busy:= false; SEND_ANSWER(idn);
              if not empty(wl) then
                 begin get_list(wl,idn); init_write
                 end else
                 while not empty(rl) do
                 begin get_list(rl,idn); init_read
                 end
        end;

        procedure  init_read;
        begin rc +:= 1; SEND_ANSWER(idn)
        end;

        procedure  init_write;
        begin busy := true; SEND_ANSWER(idn)
        end;

        begin rc := wc := o;
              busy := false;
              rl := wl := ∅;
              repeat AWAIT_ORDER(buffer,idn);
                     case buffer of
                          sr : start_read;
                          er : end_read;
                          sw : start_write
                          ew : end_write
                     end
              until false
        end;
```

A user now performs a reading operation by the following sequence:
      SEND_ORDER(sync,sr);
      WAIT_ANSWER;
      do_read;
      SEND_ORDER(sync,er);
      WAIT_ANSWER;
a write operation has an analogous structure (we have omitted parameters that are not relevant to our discussion). The orders are received by the AWAIT_ORDER-operation and the case-statement branches to

the appropriate synchronization routines; only after the corresponding answers have been passed, the user process can proceed. Orders that cannot be completed at once are put on the waiting lists rl and wl. They may be later activated again; until then, the user program will wait for the answer and thus be blocked.

b) Implicit Synchronization

The given object manager solution is constructed in analogy to the semaphore solution and is thus equally powerful. Unfortunately, it also shares with the other given solutions a series of drawbacks:
- the users can manipulate the date object in arbitrary, possibly illegal ways,
- the users can bypass the synchronization,
- the users can block each other indefinitely by never releasing the object.

All solutions given up to now depend for correct performance on the cooperative behaviour of the users; the reason is that the access operations *read* and *write* have been split up into synchronization and manipulation routines, and that this structure is visible to the users.

For the sake of system security, it is desirable to have only two kinds of orders; reading and writing. In that case, the actual data transports must be delegated to some other object manager *trans* which is passed a transport description by SEND_ORDER (*trans*, *read/write*, *parameters*) and which acknowledge the completion of the data transport by a suitable answer to its caller.

A reading or writing operation is now processed in the following steps:
- An order from the user, containing the kind of operation and some transport parameters, is received by the manager *sync*.
- As soon as logically possible, *sync* passes the order on to *trans*.
- When the answer from *trans* arrives at *sync*, it is passed on to the user; the state is updated and, if any pending orders have been thereby activated, they are passed on to *trans*.
- The user process can proceed as soon as it has received the answer.

For the sake of simplicity, we shall assume that an answer has the same format as the corresponding order; then the manager *sync* does not need to keep track of the orders it passes to *trans*. We now obtain the new manager *sync* by a slight modification of the old one (we omit the transport parameters):

```
process sync;
var rc,wc : integer;
    busy : boolean;
    rl,wl: list of integer;
    idn : integer;
    msg : (order,answer);
    buffer: record op: (read,write);
                  nr: integer
           end;

procedure init_read;
begin rc +:= 1; SEND_ORDER(trans,(read,idn))
end;

procedure init_write;
begin busy := true; SEND_ORDER(trans,(write,idn))
end;

{other procedures as above}

begin rc := wc := o;  rl := wl := ∅; busy := false
repeat AWAIT_MESSAGE(msg,idn,buffer);
       if msg = order then
           if op = read then start_read
           else start_write
       else begin idn := nr;
                  if op = read then end_read
                  else end_write
            end
until false
end;
```

An access operation now has the simple form

SEND_ORDER(sync,op);
WAIT_ANSWER;

where *op* is *read* or *write* and the value of x is irrelevant. It is now impossible for a reader or writer to tamper with the object, to bypass the synchronization or to block others. Due to the complete isolation by the message system he can only harm himself.

The fact that the actual accesses are provided by *trans* does not imply that they are performed sequentially; *trans* may e.g. be a disk controller driving many disk drives simultaneously.

4.2 The Five Dining Philosophers

The problem of the Five Dining Philosophers, given by Dijkstra [Di71], is instructive because its constraints cannot be easily described in terms of the execution history alone, but must take the individuality of the philosophers into account.

The basic configuration consists of a round table with five seats and five plates; between any two adjacent plates there is a fork. Every philosopher may be in either of two states: "thinking", which in our reduced context is equivalent to doing nothing at all, and "eating" by using the two forks to the right and left of his plate. The problem is now to allocate the forks in such a way that every fork is used by at most one person at a time and that there is no danger of deadlock. Obviously, a request cannot always be granted; we therefore introduce another state "hungry" for the philosophers waiting for some forks to become available.

Dijkstra [Di71] has given a solution using semaphores. We shall not pursue the other possibilities further, but give only the solutions in terms of object managers. Again, the first version obtained by translating the semaphore solution can be improved to a secure mechanism.

We implement the philosophers by sequential processes communicating with an object manager *sync* which takes care of the necessary synchronizations. If we introduce the notation

$x \oplus y = (x+y) \bmod 5, \; x \ominus y = (x-y) \bmod 5$

and otherwise copy Dijkstra's solution, we arrive at the following program:

```
process sync;
var mode: (eat, think);
    idn: integer;
    id: array [0..4] of integer;
    k: 0..4;
    phil: array [0..4] of (thinking, hungry, eating);

procedure init_eat(i);
begin phil[i] := eating; SEND_ANSWER(id[i])
end;
```

```
procedure  stop_eat(i);
begin phil[i] := thinking
end;

procedure  start_eat(i);
begin id[i] := idn;
      if phil[i ⊖ 1] ≠ eating ∧ phil[i ⊕ 1] ≠ eating
      then init_eat(i)
      else phil[i] := hungry
end;

procedure  end_eat(i);
begin stop_eat(i); SEND_ANSWER(idn);
      if phil[i ⊕ 1] = hungry ∧ phil[i ⊕ 2] ≠ eating
      then init_eat(i ⊕ 1) else
      if phil[i ⊖ 1] = hungry ∧ phil[i ⊖ 2] ≠ eating
      then init_eat(i ⊖ 1)
end;

begin for k := 0 to 4 do phil[k] := thinking;
      repeat WAIT_ORDER(idn,(mode,k));
             if mode = eat then start_eat(k)
             else end_eat(k)
      until false
end;
```

The given manager will correctly allocate and deallocate the forks; it always guarantees a correct state of the forks, and will not lead into a deadlock state if the philosophers' behaviour follows the pattern:

```
repeat think;
       SEND_ORDER(sync, eat);
       WAIT_ANSWER;
       eat;
       SEND_ORDER(sync, think);
       WAIT_ANSWER
until false;
```

otherwise, a philosopher may block and harm his neighbours by retaining his forks indefinitely; the same can happen if a philosopher is preempted while in his eating phase. This difficulty is inherent in any explicit synchronization scheme and can only be avoided by hiding the details from the callers, e.g. by delegating the operation *eat* to another manager *trans*. This leads to the following program:

```
process sync;
var msg: (order, answer);
    {idn, id, k, phil: same as above}

procedure init_eat(i);
begin phil[i] := eating; SEND_ORDER(trans(i))
end;
{ other procedures as above}

begin for k := 0 to 4 do phil[k] := thinking;
    repeat WAIT_MESSAGE(msg,idn,k);
        if msg = order then start_eat(k)
        else end_eat(k)
    until false
end;
```

We have again assumed that *trans* will return as result the value of its argument. The program of a philosopher is now:

```
repeat think;
    SEND_ORDER(sync);
    WAIT_ANSWER
until false;
```

as *trans* now does the actual "eating" using the forks allocated by *sync*, a "sleeping" or "mad" philosopher now can only do harm to himself.

5. Conclusion

In the last section, we have presented solutions to the same synchronization problems in several different implementations. If we compare the various mechanisms with regard to their suitability for implementing the object model (in the sense of assisting correct usage of structured data objects) in the context of a layered system of processes (exploiting possible parallelism), we find that none of them is completely free from drawbacks, so that we cannot recommend any of them without reservations. We feel that for choosing a mechanism, other considerations specific to the intended application have to be taken into account. Some of the following observations may be helpful:

- All solutions may be embedded into a class structure [DMN68, BH75], thus making it possible to syntactically associate the access operations with the type declaration, and to check at compile time for correct usage.

- Conditional critical regions, as well as path expressions, contain only local concepts. Therefore, global considerations, such as scheduling behaviour or freedom from deadlocks, cannot be expressed in a natural way.

- Nesting of Monitor calls or of Conditional Critical Regions may lead to unwanted sequentializations.

- The solution of the readers-writers-problem given by Courtois et al. has been tailored specifically to that problem and cannot be easily generalized.

- Of the described mechanisms, only Semaphores, Monitors and Object Managers are sufficiently flexible to express arbitrary scheduling disciplines.

- The "implicit" Object Manager Solution is the only one that does not keep the object locked if a user is preempted while executing an access operation. Thus, users may be scheduled externally without regard to synchronization.

- In the Object Manager Solution, user processes are only loosely coupled to each other and to the Object Manager, and may well have disjoint address spaces. Therefore, this mechanism can easily be adapted for use in a distributed system.

- Semaphores, Monitors and Object Managers have each successfully been used as basic synchronization tools for Complete Operating Systems [Di68, Lag75, BH76].

In our discussion we have always assumed that the number of processes is constant, and that the objects which they access are known from the beginning. The phenomena and considerations that have to be dealt with if we treat transactions, in the sense of sequences of accesses to elements of a Data Base, as the individual actions to be synchronized, are outside the scope of this lecture.

6. References

[Ag77]   Agerwala, T.: Some Extended Semaphore Primitives, Acta Informatica $\underline{8}$, 201-220 (1977)

[BH70]   Brinch Hansen, P.: The Nucleus of a Multiprogramming System. CACM $\underline{13}$, 238-241 (1970)

[BH72a]   Brinch Hansen, P.: Structured Multiprogramming, CACM 15, 574-578 (1972)

[BH72b]   Brinch Hansen, P.: A Comparison of Two Synchronizing Concepts. Acta Informatica 1, 190-199 (1972)

[BH73a]   Brinch Hansen, P.: Operating System Principles, Englewood Cliffs (N.J.): Prentice Hall 1973

[BH73b]   Brinch Hansen, P.: A Reply to Comments on "A omparison of Two Synchronizing Concepts", Acta Informatica 2, 189-190 (1973)

[BH75]   Brinch Hansen, P.: The Programming Language Concurrent Pascal, IEEE Trans. Software Eng. SE-1, 199-207 (1975)

[BH76]   Brinch Hansen, P.: The SOLO Operating System, Software-Practice and Experience 6, 141-205 (1976)

[BW74]   Belpaire, G. and J.P. Wilmotte: "A Semantic Approach to the Theory of Parallel Processes", Proc. ICS 1973, North Holland Publishing Co., Amsterdam 1974, p. 159-164

[CH74]   Campbell, R.H. and A.N. Habermann: The Specification of Process Synchronization by Path Expressions, Lecture Notes in Computer Science 16, 89-102 (1974)

[CHP71]   Courtois, P.J., F. Heymans and D.L. Parnas: Concurrent Control with "Readers" and "Writers", CACM 14, 667-668 (1971)

[CHP72]   Courtois, P.J., F. Heymans and D.L. Parnas: Comments on "A Comparison of Two Synchronizing Concepts" by P.B. Hansen, Acta Informatica 1, 375-376 (1972)

[Con77]   Conradi, R.: Some Comments on "Concurrent Readers and Writers", Acta Informatica 8, 335-340 (1977)

[Di68]   Dijkstra, E.W.: The Structure of the "THE"-Multiprogramming System, CACM 11, 341-346 (1968)

[Di71]   Dijkstra, E.W.: Hierarchical Ordering of Sequential Processes, Acta Informatica 1, 115-138 (1971)

[DMN68]   Dahl, O.J., B. Myhrhaug and K. Nygaard: The Simula 67 Common Base Language, Norwegian Computing Centre, Forskningsveien 1B, Oslo 3

[EGLT76]   Eswaran, K.P., J.N. Gray, R.A. Lorie and I.L. Traiger: The Notions of Consistency and Predicate Locks in a Data Base System, CACM 19, 624-633 (1976)

[Ger77]   Gerber, A.J.: Process Synchronization by Counter Variables, ACM Operating Systems Review 11/4, 6-17 (1977)

[GJL72]   Goos, G., J. Jürgens and K. Lagally: The Operating System BSM viewed as a Community of Parallel Processes, Report 7208, Rechenzentrum TU München, 1972

[Ha75]   Habermann, A.N.: Path Expressions, Carnegie-Mellon University, 1975

[Ha77]   Habermann, A.N.: Personal Communication

[Had77]   Haddon, B.K.: Nested Monitor Calls, ACM Operating Systems Review 11/4, 18-23 (1977)

[Ho74]   Hoare, C.A.R.: Monitors: An Operating System Structuring Concept, CACM 17, 549-557 (2974)

[HR73]   Horning, J.J. and B. Randell: Process Structuring, Comp. Surveys 5, 5-30 (1973)

[JS77]   Jammel, A.J. and H.G. Stiegler: Managers versus Monitors. Proceedings of IFIP Congress 1977. North Holland Publishing Co., Amsterdam 1977, p. 827-830

[Ju73]   Jürgens, J.: Synchronisation paralleler Prozesse anhand von Zuständen, Dissertation, TU München, 1973

[Ke77]   Kessels, J.L.W.: An Alternative to Event Queues for Synchronization in Monitors, CACM 20, 500-503 (1977)

[Lag75]   Lagally, K. (ed.): Das Projekt Betriebssystem BSM, Report 7509, Institut für Informatik, TU München, 1975

[Lam75]   Lamport, L.: The Synchronization of Independent Process, Acta Informatica 7, 15-34 (1975)

[Lis77]   Lister, A.: The Problem of Nested Monitor Calls, ACM Operating Systems Review 11/3, 5-7 (1977)

[LS77]   Lister, A.M. and P.J. Sayer: Hierarchical Monitors, Software-Practice and Experience 7, 613-623 (1977

[RK77]   Reed, D.P. and R.K. Kanodia: Synchronization with Event Counts and Sequencers,
           CACM (to appear); ACM Operating Systems Review 11/5, 91 (1977) (Abstract)

[RV77]   Robert, P. and J.P. Verjus: Toward Autonomous Descriptions of Synchronization Modules, Proceedings of IFIP-Congress 1977, North Holland Publishing Co., Amsterdam 1977, p. 981-986

[Sch76]   Schmid, H.A.: On the Efficient Implementation of Conditional Critical Regions and the Construction of Monitors,
           Acta Informatica 6, 227-249 (1976)

[Wi71]   Wirth, N.: The Programming Language PASCAL,
           Acta Informatica 1, 35-63 (1971).

CHAPTER 3.E.

B. Randell
University of Newcastle upon Tyne
Newcastle upon Tyne, England

Reliable Computing Systems

ABSTRACT

The paper presents an analysis of the various problems involved in achieving very high reliability from complex computing systems, and discusses the relationship between system structuring techniques and techniques of fault tolerance. Topics covered include (i) differing types of reliability requirement, (ii) forms of protective redundancy in hardware and software systems, (iii) methods of structuring the activity of a system, using atomic actions, so as to limit information flow, (iv) error detection techniques, (v) strategies for locating and dealing with faults, and for assessing the damage they have caused, and (vi) forward and backward error recovery techniques, based on the concepts of recovery line, commitment, exception and compensation. A set of appendices provide summary descriptions and analyses of a number of computing systems that have been specifically designed with the aim of achieving very high reliability.

Keywords

fault tolerance, failure, error, fault, system structure, hardware/software reliability.

1 INTRODUCTION

This paper is intended as a set of notes for a course of advanced lectures on computing system reliability. It attempts to provide a general framework, based on concepts of system structuring, for the analysis and comparison of a variety of approaches to the goal of providing continuous and trustworthy service from a computing system, and includes brief descriptions of a number of specific systems that have been designed for highly demanding environments. The paper covers both software and hardware reliability problems, including those arising from design inadequacies, although one very important topic, that of software correctness, is largely ignored, being instead the subject of a companion paper by Popek.

The concept of system reliability is sometimes interpreted rather broadly as a measure of the extent to which a system matches its users' expectations (see for example Naur (NAU77)). The trouble with this view is that these expectations can be mistaken (for example because of inaccurate or inadequate documentation) and can change almost arbitrarily, based perhaps on experience with the system, experience which might turn out to have been quite unrepresentative. In this paper a somewhat narrower interpretation of system reliability is taken, more in line with typical formal, and often quantitative, assessments of hardware reliability. Thus system reliability is related to the success with which a system provides the service specified. By this means the concept of the _reliability_ of a system is separated from that of the _reliance_ placed on a system.

Hopefully of course the reliance placed on a system will be commensurate with its reliability. When this is not the case one or other will have to be adjusted if the system is not to be abandoned. For example, users of a time sharing service that has a tendency to lose the contents of current work spaces are likely to learn to take the precaution of frequently requesting that a copy of their work space be saved, and be satisfied with the quality of the service that they are getting. Notions of reliance therefore can be as much bound up with psychological attitudes as with formal decisions as to the requirement that a system is supposed to satisfy.

In fact the history of the development of computers has seen some fascinating interplay between reliance and reliability. The reliability of early computers was such that relatively little reliance was placed on the validity of their outputs, at least until appropriate checks had been performed, and even less reliance was placed on the continuity of their operation - lengthy and frequent periods of downtime were expected and tolerated. As reliability increased so did reliance, sometimes in fact outdistancing reliability so that additional efforts had to be made to reach previously unattained reliability levels. During this time computing systems were growing in size and functional capacity so that although component reliability was being improved, the very complexity of systems was becoming a possible cause of unreliability, as well as of misunderstandings between users and designers about system specifications.

The subject of system specifications and of how these can be arrived at and documented, validated and updated, is a large and complex topic, well worthy of discussion in its own right. However, given the interpretation of system reliability that we have chosen to make, it is inappropriate to pursue the topic further in the present paper, which takes as its main starting point the set of informal but hopefully rigorous definitions of concepts relating to system reliability that are given in Section 2. These definitions presume the existence of some external specification of the requirements that the system is supposed to meet. Ideally this specification will have previously been agreed and documented; in practice some aspects of it may exist only in the minds of persons authorised to decide on the acceptability of a system's functioning.

As is discussed in Section 3, the growth in the complexity of the functions that computing systems are asked to provide, and the increasing reliance that it is wished to place on them, for example in environments where unreliability can lead to huge financial penalties or even loss of life, has spurred the search for a greater understanding of reliability issues. Aspects of computing systems, such as their software, which were previously virtually ignored in many discussions of reliability problems are now being addressed and causing previous approaches and solutions to be re-evaluated.

The basis for this re-evaluation is provided by recent ideas on system structuring and improved (though still imperfect) understanding of its relationship to reliability, and in particular, to fault tolerance. The likely importance of system structuring was well expressed in the 1973 SRI survey of fault tolerant computing (NEU73) in which it is stated that: "Our assessment of the structured design approach is that it has the potential for providing highly flexible and economical fault tolerance without greatly compromising system cost, system performance and system efficiency. Some qualities of structure are found in the current art, but full realization of this potential requires further development... A serious weakness in the current art is the absence of a design methodology that integrates hardware and software into a systems concept addressing reliability, availability, security, efficiency and functional capability in a unified way. For example, significant benefits can be expected from techniques for structural design and implementation..."

This SRI survey provided a very useful account of the state of the art of hardware fault tolerance, an account which is still of value. Because of the existence of this survey, and much other relevant literature, such as the proceedings of the IEEE Symposia on Fault Tolerant Computing, the present paper does not attempt to describe the present vast array of techniques for hardware fault tolerance in great detail, but rather concentrates on the overall system aspects of reliability. System structuring therefore forms one of the major topics, and is the subject of Section 4. It is this section which provides a basis for describing, in Section 5, different approaches to the attainment of reliable operation, such as masking redundancy, and forward and backward error recovery.

Several sections of the paper are based closely on various earlier papers (LOM77, MEL75, MEL77, RAN75) also emanating from the research project on computing system reliability at the University of Newcastle upon Tyne. It also draws on the writings of a number of other authors, particularly in the appendices, which describe a number of specific approaches to the design of highly reliable computing systems.

2 BASIC CONCEPTS

Our informal, but hopefully precise definitions are based closely on those given in (MEL77). To avoid needless specialisation the terminology is defined in general terms and is not particularly specific to computing systems, leave alone to just hardware or software systems. The terminology we use is intended to correspond broadly to conventional usage, but the definitions of some of the terms differ from previous practice, which typically has paid little attention to design inadequacies as a potential source of unreliability.

2.1 SYSTEMS AND THEIR FAILURES

We define a system as a set of components together with their interrelationships, where the system has been designed to provide a specified service. The components of the system can themselves be systems, and we term their interrelationships the algorithm of the system. There is no requirement that a component provide service to a single system; it may be a component of several distinct systems. The algorithm of the system is however specific to each system individually.

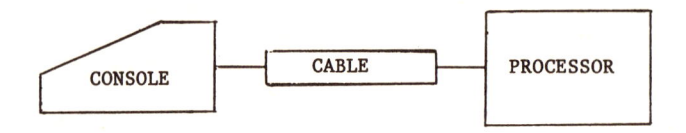

Figure 1 - A Three Component System

Example

Figure 1 is a simple schematic representation of a system consisting of a processor, a console and an interconnecting cable - these three components are interrelated by being plugged together. The interconnecting lines in the diagram represent these interrelationships, rather than any physical component.

The definition of "system", with its insistence that the service provided must be specified (but not necessarily pre-specified), is intended to exclude systems which are "intelligent" in the sense of being capable of determining their own goals and algorithms. At present intelligent systems are not understood sufficiently to permit consideration of their reliability.

The internal state of a system is the aggregation of the external states of all its components. The external state of a system is the result of a conceptual abstraction function applied to its internal state. During a transition from one external state to another external state, the system may pass through a number of internal states for which the abstraction function, and hence the external state, are not defined. The specification defines only the external states of the system, the operations that can be applied to the system, the results of these operations, and the transitions between external states caused by these operations, the internal states being inaccessible from outside the system.

The service provided by a system is regarded as being provided to one or more <u>environments</u>. Within a particular system, the environment of a given component consists of those other components with which it is directly interrelated.

A <u>failure</u> of a system occurs when that system does not perform its service in the manner specified, whether because it is unable to perform the service at all, or because the results and the external state are not in accordance with the specifications. A failure is thus an event. There is however no implication that the event is actually recognised as having occurred. For example, if an environment does not make full use of the specifications of a system (i. e. if what Parnas (PAR71) terms the environment's "assumptions" are a proper subset of the specifications) certain types of failures will have no effect.

2.2 ERRORS AND FAULTS

In contrast to the simple, albeit very broad, definition of "failure" given above, the definitions we now present of "error" and "fault" are not so straightforward. This is because they aim to capture the element of subjective judgement which we believe is a necessary aspect of these concepts, particularly when they relate to problems which could have been caused by design inadequacies in the algorithm of a system.

We term an internal state of a system an <u>erroneous state</u> when that state is such that there exist circumstances (within the specification of the use of the system) in which further processing, by the normal algorithms of the system, will lead to a failure which we do not attribute to a subsequent fault. (The subjective judgement that we wish to associate with the classification of a state as being an erroneous one derives from the use of the phrases "normal algorithms" and "which we do not attribute" in this definition - however further definitions are required before these matters can be discussed properly.)

The term error is used to designate that part of the state which is "incorrect". An error is thus an item of information, and the terms <u>error</u>, <u>error detection</u> and <u>error recovery</u> are used as casual equivalents for erroneous state, erroneous state detection and erroneous state recovery.

A <u>fault</u> is the mechanical or algorithmic cause of an error, while a <u>potential fault</u> is a mechanical or algorithmic construction within a system such that (under some circumstances within the specification of the use of the system) that construction will cause the system to assume an erroneous state. It is evident that the failure of a component of a system is (or rather, may be) a mechanical fault from the point of view of the system as a whole.

Hopefully it will now be clear that the generality of our definitions of failure and fault has the intended effect that the notion of fault encompasses such design inadequacies as a mistaken choice of component, a misunderstood or inadequate specification (of either the component, or the service required from the system) or an incorrect interrelationship amongst components (such as a wrong or missing interconnection in the case of hardware systems, or a program bug in software systems), as well as, say, hardware component failure due to ageing.

Note that the definition of an erroneous state depends on the subdivision of the algorithm of the system into normal algorithms and abnormal algorithms. These abnormal algorithms will typically be the error recovery algorithms. There are many systems in which that subdivision, and hence the designation of states as erroneous, is a matter of judgement.

Example

In a storage system utilising a Hamming Code, one may regard the correction circuits as error recovery mechanisms and a single incorrect bit as an error. Alternatively (particularly with semiconductor storage) the correction circuits may be regarded as normal mechanism, and thus a single incorrect bit would not be regarded as an error, though two incorrect bits would be.

Note also that a demonstration that further processing can lead to a failure of the system indicates the presence of an error, but does not suffice to locate a specific item of information as the error. Consider a system affected by an algorithmic fault. The sequence of internal states adopted by this system will diverge from that of the "correct" system at some point, the algorithmic fault being the cause of this transition into an erroneous state. But there can be no unique correct algorithm. It may be that any one of several changes to the algorithms of the system could have precluded the failure. A subjective judgement as to which of these algorithms is the intended algorithm determines the fault, the items of information in error, and the moment at which the state becomes erroneous. Some such judgements may of course be more useful than others.

The significance of the distinction between faults and errors may be seen by considering the repair of a data base system. Repair of a fault may consist of the replacement of a failing program (or hardware) component by a correctly functioning one. Repair of an error requires that the information in the data base be changed from its currently erroneous state to a state which will permit the correct operation of the system. In most systems, recovery from errors is required, but repair of the faults which cause these errors although very desirable is not necessarily essential for continued operation.

Various formal measures related to a system's <u>reliability</u> can be based on the actual (or predicted) incidence of failures, and their consequences (see, for example, (SHO68)). These measures include Mean Time Between Failures (MTBF), Mean Time To Repair (MTTR) and <u>availability</u> - the fraction of the time that a system meets its specification. Further measures can of course be defined which take into account classifications of the type and seriousness of the failure.

These quantitative measures all concern the success with which the system provides its specified service. The much broader concept of reliability, discussed in section 1, relates to the situation where there is a lack of understanding and/or agreement as to the specification of a system, or where attempts are being made to differentiate between the relative acceptability of the different means by which a system might meet its specifications.

<u>Example</u>

Even where the specification of a storage system lists, without further qualification, both "returns requested word" and "indicates parity error" as acceptable results of a Fetch Operation, no user is likely to be satisfied if all Fetch Operations result in a parity error indication. Clearly what is missing from the specification is some limitation on the relative frequency of parity error indications. The store system would then be regarded, under our definitions, as having failed if this limitation was exceeded, as well as if it, say, returned either the wrong word, or nothing at all to its user.

3   RELIABILITY ISSUES

3.1 REQUIREMENTS

The reliability requirements of different environments can differ enormously. One extreme is the case of air and space-borne computers where only momentary cessation of service can be tolerated, no maintenance or manual repair activity is feasible, and incorrect results are completely unacceptable.

Example

   Depledge and Hartley (DEP77) state that the failure probability of the next generation of computing systems used within civil aircraft flight control systems is likely to be required to be less than 1×10^{-9} per flight of several hours duration. Parsons (PAR77) lists the reliability objective for a computing system for spacecraft as about 0.95, during missions lasting seven years.

Maintenance and manual repair is however usually possible. In some cases the reliability goals can only be met by making it possible for such activity to be carried out while the system is in service. Thus the repair activity is concerning itself with faults, rather than with system failures.

Example

   Very high levels of reliability indeed have been demonstrated in systems, usually of modest complexity, which allow on-line repair activity. Thus for example a number of years ago the STL Dependable Process Computer (DAR70) had achieved a total of 22,000 hours of operation with no unscheduled downtime. During this time 22 errors were detected and the faults that caused them repaired merely by replacing the indicated circuit board, without interfering with the operation of the computer in any way. There was no evidence that any mistakes had been made in any calculations or control actions which the computer performed.

In contrast, in many environments the expense of obtaining very high reliability from a computing system is not worthwhile because so many other failure-prone devices, such as communications lines and mechanical peripherals, are being used or because the cost of failure is comparatively low.

Example

   In computerised telephone systems, relatively infrequent isolated small breakdowns can be tolerated, as long as the overall system remains operational.

Yet another type of reliability requirement is that typical of on-line data base systems, or indeed any systems which are intended to retain extensive amounts of valuable data over lengthy periods of time.

Example

> The reliability objectives of the MULTICS system as described by Saltzer (quoted in the SRI survey (NEU73)) were as follows: "Ideally, the user can rely on the system to have a perfect memory for his files. A secondary availability objective is that the system operates continuously, on a 24-hour basis. Recovery time following a failure is permitted to have a wide variation, but on average on the order of a few minutes. Objectives such as 100% continued operation in the face of any single failure were not attempted."

These examples highlight the fact that reliability is a commodity, whose provision involves costs, either direct, or arising from performance degradation. In theory the design of any non-trivial computing system should involve the designers in careful calculations of trade-offs between reliability, performance, and cost. In practice in complex systems the data and relationships which would be needed for such calculations are quite often unknown, particularly as far as questions of unreliability caused by residual design faults are concerned. Moreover many design efforts concern what can be termed "generic systems", that is systems which are intended for a whole range of different environments, and using a wide variety of different hardware and software configurations. In such circumstances the main thing one can aim for at present is often just incremental improvements to a particular system in a given environment, and reliability and performance predictions based on preliminary statistical data.

3.2 TYPES OF FAULT

Hardware component faults are often classified as __permanent__ or __transient__ (i. e. of limited duration). Such a distinction requires agreement on the maximum time for which a "transient" fault can last for it to be so classified. In general, both types of fault can arise, for example, from statistical uncertainty, degradation of the materials used, or external interference. However as mentioned earlier the generality of our definitions is (as intended) such that the notion of fault also encompasses such design inadequacies as a mistaken choice of component, a misunderstood or obsolete specification (of either the component or the service required from the system) or an incorrect interrelationship amongst components (such as a wrong or missing interconnection).

The distinction between, say, a design inadequacy and a fault due to component ageing might be somewhat arbitrary, since good hardware design practice would involve the provision of appropriate safety margins. This of course is where software differs. The only faults that can be present in a non-physical system such as a software system are algorithmic faults. Algorithmic faults are due to design inadequacies, which will in general arise from unmastered design complexity (and, it must be admitted, incompetence). Naturally some previous fault (of either hardware or software) could cause a particular copy of a software component to be corrupted. This however is not the same as an algorithmic fault in that software component, which would always manifest itself in all correct copies of that component.

Many discussions of computing system reliability assume that algorithmic faults exist only in software. In reality, it is by no means unknown for such faults to be found in the logic circuits of hardware components of modest complexity, even after many years of operational service. Thus the problem of algorithmic faults is not a software problem per se, but rather a problem that becomes a serious one only in complex designs, namely designs where straightforward enumerative design practices are defeated by combinatorics. To date, the relative economics of hardware and software design, production and modification have ensured that as much complexity as possible is left to the software, and the software designer. There is, therefore, little reason to hope that the practices and skills of hardware designers will enable the "problems of software" to be overcome merely by transference to hardware, even though such a move is now made somewhat more feasible by LSI developments.

Hardware designers also classify faults according to their __extent__ , terming faults which only effect single logical values __local__ faults, as opposed to __distributed__ faults, which effect more (perhaps much more) than just a single logic value. This exact distinction is perhaps of less use with respect to software faults. However it does emphasise the fact that, particularly in the case of obscure faults in complex components, many errors may be caused by a given fault before the existence of the fault is revealed by the detection of one of these errors.

The other fault classification used by hardware designers is that of __value__. A fault is said to have a __determinate__ value if the erroneous logic values that it causes remain constant for the duration of the fault. If on the other hand the values vary haphazardly, the fault value is termed __indeterminate__. This classification obviously is applicable to faults originating from, say, physical degradation of components. Its application to software faults is not so obvious and is perhaps inappropriate, since such faults would only cause logic values to change when the software was executed. Certainly, software in which mistakes of processs synchronisation have been made can produce different (and sometimes erroneous) results on different, apparently indentical, occasions. One can either regard this as a transient fault or regard the fault as permanent, but with an indeterminate value.

A quite separate fault category is that causing an erroneous interaction with a system. Such interactions could, for example, include a user providing invalid input data or an operator or maintenance engineer performing invalid operations. These problems can be reduced by an appropriate choice of system specification, and by careful validation and consistency checking within the system. However some interactions, even though valid with respect to the system specification, may later be found to have been wrong. This sort of occurrence, with input data for example, could cause the data in a data base system to drift gradually out of correspondence with the external reality that the data base was intended to model. Such faults can be extremely serious, as well as insidious. (This topic is returned to in Section 4.)

3.3 FAULT INTOLERANCE AND FAULT TOLERANCE

The traditional approach to achieving reliable computing systems has been largely based on what Avizienis has termed <u>fault intolerance</u>. Quoting Avizienis (AVI76): "The procedures which have led to the attainment of reliable systems using this approach are: acquisition of the most reliable components within the given cost and performance constraints; use of thoroughly refined techniques for the interconnection of components and assembly of sub-systems; packaging of the hardware to screen out expected forms of interference; and carrying out of comprehensive testing to eliminate hardware and software design faults. Once the design has been completed, a quantitative prediction of system reliability is made using known or predicted failure rates for the components and interconnections. In a "purely" fault intolerant (i. e. nonredundant) design, the probability of fault-free hardware operation is equated to the probability of correct program execution. Such a design is characterised by the decision to invest all the reliability resources into high-reliability components and refinement of assembly, packaging and testing techniques. Occasional system failures are accepted as a necessary evil, and manual maintenance is provided for their correction."

There are a number of situations in which the fault intolerant approach clearly does not suffice. These include those approaches where the frequency and duration of the periods of time when a system is under repair are unacceptable, or where the system may be inaccessible to manual maintenance and repair activities. An alternative approach to fault intolerance is that of fault tolerance, an approach at present largely confined to hardware systems, which involves the use of protective redundancy. A system can be designed to be <u>fault tolerant</u> by incorporating into it additional components and abnormal algorithms which attempt to ensure that occurrences of erroneous states do not result in later system failures. The degree of fault tolerance (or "coverage") will depend on the success with which erroneous states corresponding to faults are identified and detected, and with which such states are repaired or replaced.

There are many different degrees of fault tolerance which can be attempted. For example, a system designer might wish to reduce the incidence of failures during periods of scheduled operation by designing the system so that it will remain operational even in the presence of, say, a single fault. Alternatively, he might wish to increase the average length of periods of uninterrupted operation by designing the system so that it can tolerate not just the presence of a fault, but also the activity involved in repairing the fault.

Fault tolerant systems differ with respect to their behaviour in the presence of a fault. In some cases the aim is to continue to provide the full performance and functional capabilities of the system. In other cases only degraded performance or reduced functional capabilities are provided until the fault is removed - such systems are sometimes described as having a 'fail-soft' capability.

Example

It is now typical for the computer terminals used in banks to incorporate significant processing and storage facilities. Such terminals enable data input and possibly some limited forms of data validation to continue even when the main computer system is not operational.

Schemes for fault tolerance also differ with regard to the types of fault which are to be tolerated. In particular, many systems which are designed to tolerate faults due to hardware component ageing, electrical interference and the like, make no attempt to cope with algorithmic faults in either the hardware or the software design. This in fact illustrates that fault tolerance and fault intolerance are better regarded as complementary rather than competitive approaches to system reliability. The two different approaches are often used within the same system in an attempt to deal with different types of fault. Indeed both can be used in an attempt to deal with the same type of fault. (In theory one might even use the provision of fault tolerance as an excuse for reducing the amount of effort put into a priori system testing and validation, as has been advocated by Hecht (HEC76). In practice it seems better to use fault tolerance just as a means of augmenting fault intolerance in those situations where this seems worthwhile and practical.)

3.4 DESIGN FAULT TOLERANCE

It is only recently that efforts have been undertaken to extend the fault tolerant approach to cover design faults. The a priori elimination of design faults, assumed in the fault intolerant approach, is the normal (and praiseworthy) aim, so that many writers have equated the notion of reliability with that of correctness, particularly in the case of software. Virtually all research relating to the practice of software development can therefore be claimed to be of direct relevance to software reliability, for example the design of high level languages, formal verification techniques, program design methodologies and tools, debugging aids, etc. However, important as all of these topics are, they can give no guarantee that a complex software design is ever entirely fault-free or that modifications to the design might not introduce new faults. When this is admitted then the only alternative to accepting the (probably unquantifiable) unreliability which results is to seek to improve matters by the use of design fault tolerance.

Most existing approaches to the design of fault tolerant systems make three assumptions: firstly, as mentioned earlier, that the algorithms of the system have been correctly designed; secondly, that all of the possible failure modes of the components are known; and thirdly, that all of the possible interactions between the system and its environment have been foreseen. However, in the face of increasing complexity in systems, the validity of these assumptions must be questioned. This is because the number of possible failure modes of a system increases very rapidly as the system becomes more complex, much more rapidly than the number of correct modes of operation. Equally, the more complex an interface the system has to its environment, the wider the variety of improper interactions that the environment might have with the system. At some stage therefore it must surely become impractical to rely on enumerating all of the possible types of fault which might effect a system, let alone design algorithms to detect or accommodate each possible type of fault individually.

Thus the problem which makes the use of design fault tolerance difficult is essentially that of how to tolerate faults which are unanticipated and unanticipatable, as opposed to previously enumerated and categorised. We would therefore argue that design fault tolerance requires a considerable rethinking of the techniques which have in the past proved suitable for tolerating various kinds of hardware component fault. However, once again quoting Avizienis (AVI76): "The state of the art in design fault tolerance resembles that in operational fault tolerance some ten years ago. The cost and the effectiveness of the design fault tolerance approaches remain to be investigated, and the techniques require much further development and experimentation. The success of operational fault tolerance, however, does strongly indicate that design fault tolerance cannot be safely ignored solely because of the past tradition of fault intolerance in this field."

4 SYSTEM STRUCTURE

Considerations of the reliability problems of complex computing systems, and of means for coping with them, are closely interwoven with various notions that can be collectively termed 'system structuring'. It is almost a truism that structure is our main means of mastering complexity. Yet the topic is an extremely difficult one to discuss with the generality it really demands - this is in part because notions of structure and its perception (or perhaps one should say involuntary imposition) are very much tied up with the whole question of how the human mind recognises, classifies and starts to understand any objects of which it becomes aware. (A valiant attempt to explain these issues has been made by Ross (ROS75).)

In this present account we will take a much more pragmatic view and content ourselves with attempting to discuss those aspects of system structuring that now seem to be comparatively well established as bases for system design practices, and to relate them to issues concerning system reliability. Even so our task is not easy. This is illustrated by the confusion that frequently envelops debates over which of several rival programs has the "best structure", even when the possibility of program design faults and of hardware malfunctions is being ignored. Such debates will often be couched in terms of "aesthetics", when what is really at issue are such quantitative matters as the relative frequency of different types and ranges of data, the likelihood of different requests for program modification, etc. Similarly, even debates about system structure which do concern themselves with matters of reliability and the likelihood of different types of fault usually involve unspoken (and often unrealised) assumptions. In this case the assumptions often concern the possibility, or rather the impossibility, of faults which, so to speak, invalidate the structure. These matters will hopefully be made somewhat clearer by the discussions that follow.

4.1 STATIC STRUCTURE

The definition of system given in Section 2.1 indicates that each system has what might be termed a <u>static structure</u>, which indicates what components it is regarded as being made out of, and how these components are interrelated.

One can of course visualise a given system in terms of many different structures, each implying a different identification of the components of the system.

<u>Example</u>

A programmer visualises a CDC 6600 as having a single sequential main processor and a set of independent peripheral processing units, but the maintenance engineer sees it as consisting of a set of parallel function units, and a single time-shared peripheral processor.

Some static structures will have a more visible reality in the actual system than others - for example, in the case of hardware systems, by corresponding to the interrelated physical components from which the system is constructed. The important characteristic of such "actual" (as opposed to "conceptual") structuring is that the interrelationships between its components are constrained, while the system is operational, ideally to just those that the designer intended to occur. The stronger the constraint, the more the structuring is actual structuring, and the more reasonable it is to base provisions for fault tolerance on that structuring. (The "strength" of a constraint is in fact a measure of the variety of different faults that it will prevent from affecting the planned interrelationship.)

Example

When the various registers and functional units of a central processor are implemented using separate hardware components, the designer can have reasonable confidence that (presuming the absence of electrical or mechanical interference) only those registers and functional units that are meant to communicate with each other do so (along the interconnecting wires that the designer has provided).

The software of a computing system serves to structure that system by expressing how some of the storage locations are to be set up with information which represents programs. These will then control some of the interrelationships amongst hardware components, for example, that the potential communication path between two I/O devices via working store is actually usable.

However, the software can itself be viewed as a system and its structure discussed in terms of the programming language that was used to construct it. Thus in a block-structured language each block can be regarded as a component, which is itself composed out of, and expresses the interrelationships amongst, smaller components such as declarations and statements (including blocks).

The operational software will have "actual" structure matching that of its source language version only to the extent that it consists of components with constrained methods of interacting. Here the constraints are likely to be due to the presence of means of checking attempted interactions, rather than the usually surer constraints "provided" by the absence of means of interaction (such as the interconnecting wires of the last example).

Example

The scope rules in a block-structured language are often enforced by a compiler, which then emits unstructured code. However the compiler could emit code in which the variables of each different block are kept, say, in different segments, and some form of protection mechanism (i. e. disabling mechanism) used to impede access to those variables which are not supposed to be currently accessible. (Such attempted accesses might be a result of hardware addressing faults.)

4.2 DYNAMIC STRUCTURE

Just as the system itself can be regarded as having a static structure, so can its activity be regarded as having a _dynamic structure_. In fact each static structuring of a system implies a dynamic structuring of its activity. The static structure is important for understanding the sorts of faults that might exist in the system and the provisions that have been made for trying to cope with them - the dynamic structure is of equal importance for understanding the effects of these faults and how (or whether) the system tolerates them in order to continue functioning.

The activity of a given system can be visualised in terms of many different structures, depending of which aspects of this activity one wishes to highlight and which to ignore. One basic and now well established concept used for describing some important aspects of the dynamic structure of a system's activity is the "process". Depending on the viewpoint chosen, quite different processes with their interrelationships might be identified as constituting the structure of the system's activity. Again, a dynamic structure will be "actual" rather than merely "conceptual" to the extent to which the interrelationships are constrained to be as the designer intended.

Example

Reasonably "actual" dynamic structure exists in the situation where processes correspond to the application of programs to sets of data, if the programs and data are suitably protected and processes are impeded from interacting other than via, say, an explicit message passing system.

The sequencing, or control flow, aspects of process structuring, namely the creation, existence and deletion of processes, can be shown graphically in some form such as Figure 2. However matters of information flow (intended or unintended) between processes are at least as important as control flow when it comes to considerations of reliability, and in particular the problem of determining the possible damage that a fault has caused. For this reason we need a concept such as that of _atomic action_ (LOM77) as part of our means of expressing the dynamic structure of the activity of a system.

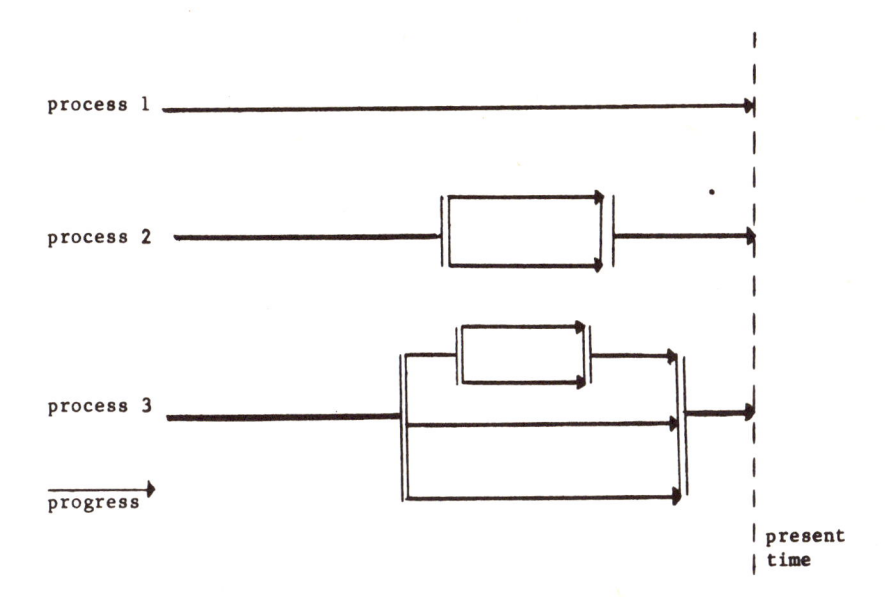

Figure 2 - Control Flow Aspect of Dynamic Structure

4.3 ATOMIC ACTIONS

The activity of the system will be made up of primitive or atomic (i. e. apparently instantaneous) operations which are carried out by the components of which the system is considered to consist. Atomic actions provide a means of generalising such atomic operations. They are in fact a means by which a system designer can specify what process interactions are, if possible, to be prevented in order to maintain system integrity, without having to indicate how this is done. They do this by enabling the designer to indicate the sections of the activity, i. e. the sequences of atomic operations, of a process or a group of processes that are themselves to be executed "atomically". As Lomet (LOM77) has indicated, the important properties of atomic actions can be stated in a number of equivalent ways, such as

1. An action is atomic if the process (processes) performing it is (are) not aware of the existence of any other active processes, and no other process is aware of the activity of the process (processes) during the time the process is (processes are) performing the action.

2. An action is atomic if the process (processes) performing it does (do) not communicate with other processes while the action is being performed.

3. An action is atomic if the process (processes) performing it can detect no state changes except those performed by itself

(themselves) and if it does (they do) not reveal its (their) state changes until the action is complete.

4. Actions are atomic if they can be considered, so far as other processes are concerned, to be indivisible and instantaneous, such that the effects on the system are as if they were interleaved as opposed to concurrent.

The simple version of an atomic action involves just a single process. In the case of software processes, procedures are the means of treating a sequence of primitive operations (typically load, store, add, etc.) as a single action. Lomet therefore suggests that the required programming language feature is the ability to indicate that a particular procedure is to be executed as an atomic action.

Example

Consider a message passing system that maintains a pool of buffers for holding messages, and uses the variable "i" as a buffer frame pointer. The action of inserting an item into the buffer might involve the sequence of operations "i:= i+1" and "buffer(i):= item". It is essential that this sequence of operations is executed as a single atomic action if the buffering scheme is to work properly.

An atomic action could involve several processes, since

1. A process executing a simple atomic action could temporarily create one or more further processes to assist it.

2. Two or more processes could co-operate directly in a shared atomic action, so that their activity is atomic with respect to the remainder of the processes in the system.

These various possibilities are shown in Figure 3, which is based on Figure 2, but where the ovals indicate atomic actions, incomplete ovals representing atomic actions that are still in progress. The lines indicate processes, and should themselves be regarded as consisting of miniscule ovals, placed end to end, corresponding to the primitive operations out of which the processes are constructed.

The figure illustrates that "atomicity" has to be regarded as relative rather than absolute, and that atomic actions can themselves involve atomic actions, as well as the basic atomic operations. It also, by implication, illustrates that atomic actions, by their very nature, cannot overlap, and that any number of processes can be involved as long as the number leaving an atomic action matches the number that entered it. Thus the starting points of atomic actions together with the points at which processes are created are together time-wise nested with respect to the ending points of atomic actions and the points at which processes cease to exist.

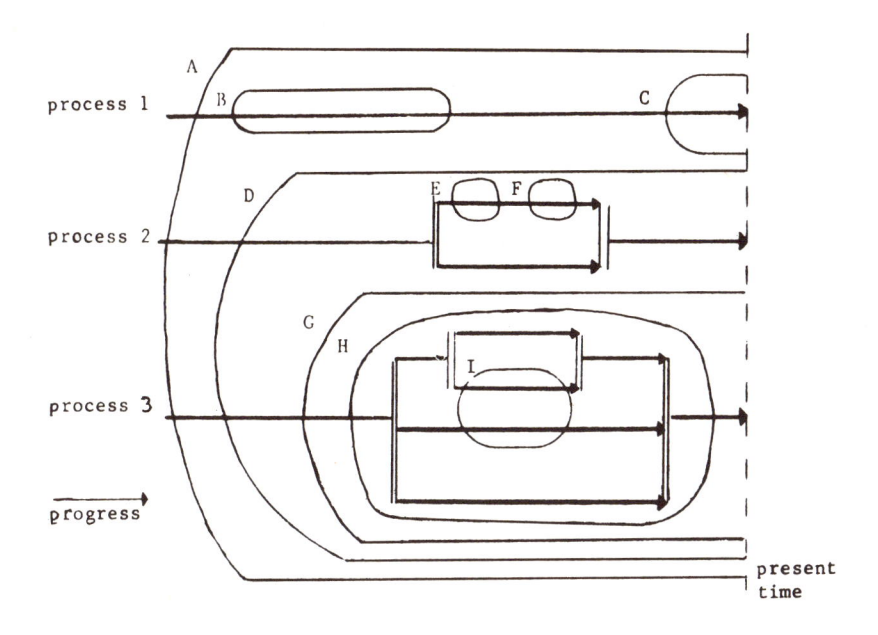

Figure 3 - Processes and their Atomic Actions

We have so far described atomic actions merely as a means for a designer to indicate what system integrity constraints should be met. However, it should be clear that they are of direct relevance to techniques for achieving fault tolerance. This is due to the fact that they provide a means of error detection, and more importantly, a means of delimiting the possible consequences of a fault. Thus it is no coincidence that there are some definite similarities between Figure 3 and those used in (RAN75) to illustrate the concept of a "conversation", and those used in (BJO72) and (DAV72) to illustrate "spheres of control", two concepts which have been introduced in order to provide fault tolerance in systems of interacting processes. The relationships between these various concepts are discussed in Section 5.5.1.

An atomic action is in fact a generalisation of the concept, introduced by data base designers, of a "transaction" (ESW76, GRA75, LOM77). The transaction scheme allows a data base system user to arrange that a sequence of interactions with the data base will be treated as atomic, in order that desired consistency constraints on the data base can be adhered to. A transaction can thus be viewed as an atomic action involving the user and the data base system (or more exactly the process which is the user's activity, and one of the terminal support processes of the system). Atomic actions however need not involve the user - they could for example be used to structure information flows amongst the internal processes of the data base system.

4.4 FORMS OF ATOMIC ACTION

As mentioned earlier, atomic actions provide a way of describing what process interactions are to be prevented, and not how this is to be done. There are indeed a variety of systems whose activity can be described in terms of atomic actions, each involving strategies and mechanisms which might be regarded as conventional in a particular type of computing environment. This point is worth illustrating by a brief survey of these strategies, since atomic actions turn out to be basic to many apparently quite separate approaches to fault tolerance, as Section 5 will make clear.

Atomic actions can of course be provided by having processes implemented by totally independent processors. If the processes are being implemented by multiplexing a single processor, then atomicity could be obtained by executing atomic actions with interrupts disabled, so that an atomic action, once started, would be in sole control of all the resources of the system until it completes. With multiple (non-independent) processors, some centralised scheme of serialising the execution of separate atomic actions would suffice. (Both of these schemes are ones that spring to mind when one thinks of atomic actions as being somewhat similar to monitors (BRI73) and critical regions (HOA74), techniques for directly specifying certain types of synchronisation requirement.)

In many instances however the inherent parallelism of the environment of the system, together with questions of system performance and resource utilisation, precludes such simple strategies. It then becomes necessary to find means of executing atomic actions concurrently. This implies that an individual atomic action does not obtain control of all of the resources of a system, but rather just those that it needs to use, and hopefully just for the time necessary to guarantee atomicity.

Mechanisms for enabling and controlling the parallel activation of separate atomic actions are typically based on the use of "locks" (ESW76, GRA75). Such locks are associated with portions of the set of system resources - for example with individual tables or table entries in a data base system. (The term "granularity of locking" (GRA75) refers to the choice of size of lockable resource.) When the process or processes in an atomic action require exclusive use of a resource the resource must, when available, be locked to prevent (or at least impede) conflicting use by processes outside the atomic action. Locks therefore are, in effect, seized by atomic actions on behalf of the processes they contain, rather than by individual processes themselves.

Systems using locking strategies differ in the extent to which they require that processes, on entry to an atomic action, declare their intentions with respect to resource acquisition and usage. Where some such information is provided it can be used by a scheduler in order to determine constraints on the parallel activation of atomic actions, and so to achieve an "optimum" schedule. But if such information is not given, or is not sufficient, deadlocks are possible, unless appropriate restrictions (e. g. concerning the order in which different resources are acquired and used) are placed on processes (see ESW76) and (GRA75)).

Techniques for coping with, as opposed to avoiding, such deadlocks involve backing up and restarting one or more of the the atomic actions concerned, presuming that the necessary provisions for restart have been made beforehand. The fact that the actions are atomic means that such restarts will have no effect on the outcome of the activity of the system. (These matters are discussed further in Section 5.5.)

As regards the additional mechanisms needed to allow shared atomic actions, the straightforward approach involves synchronising the entries of all the processes involved, and then synchronising all their exits. More sophisticated synchronisation schemes are however possible - these would involve differentiating between operations which involve interactions amongst the processes in an atomic action and operations which only affect resources that are private to an individual process.

4.5 LEVELS OF ABSTRACTION

In choosing to regard a system (or its activity) as made up of certain components and to concentrate on their interrelationships whilst ignoring their inner details, one is deliberately considering just a particular abstraction of the total system. Thus the sorts of structuring that we have discussed so far can be described as structuring within a single level of abstraction, or **horizontal structuring**. When further details of a system (or part of a system) need to be considered, this involves a lower level of abstraction which shows how components and their interrelationships are implemented, in terms of some more detailed components and interrelationships (which will of course in turn just be abstractions of yet more detailed components and interrelationships, and so on).

Various different forms of relationship can exist between the structures that a system is viewed as having at different levels of abstraction. One very common, but limited, form is characterised by the fact that it does not allow for any sharing of subcomponents by separate components. This form often suffices for describing the constructional details of a complicated concrete object, and is frequently the only one considered by hardware designers, and supported by their design aids.

Example

> The computing system consists of three cabinets connected by cables; each cable consists of two connectors and a large number of wires; each cabinet contains power supplies and a number of modules; each module consists of a back plane and a number of populated printed circuit boards, etc.

In choosing to identify a set of levels of abstraction (each of which might relate to the whole system, or just some part of the system) and to define their interrelationships one is once again imposing a structure on a system, but this is a rather different form of structure which we will refer to as <u>vertical structuring</u>. Thus vertical structurings describe how components are constructed, whereas horizontal structurings describe how components interact. The notion of vertical structuring can also be applied to the activity of a system, that is dynamically, as well as statically to the system itself. (The concepts of vertical and horizontal dynamic structure are closely related to the formal concepts of "process abstraction" and "process combination" defined by Horning and Randell (HOR73).)

Less limited types of vertical structuring are possible, in which the relationships between levels are much less straightforward. This is the case when, for example, components, which at their own level of abstraction can be regarded as having separate continuous existences, turn out to owe such existence as they do have to the multiplexing of components from a lower level of abstraction.

Example

> The example given in Section 4.1, of the CDC 6600, shows that it can be visualised as having a two-level structure, the upper level being that seen by programmers as having a single main processor and a set of peripheral processors, the lower level being the very different view seen by the maintenance engineer.

The importance of levels of abstraction is that they allow one to cope with the combinatorial complexity that would otherwise be involved in a system constructed from a very large number of very basic components. The price that is paid is the requirement for well-documented specifications of the external characteristics of each level - such specifications can be thought of as the <u>abstraction interfaces</u> interposed vertically between levels, much as the interrelationships defined between interacting components within a level function as what could be termed <u>communication interfaces</u>. In each case the interface will, if well chosen, allow the designer to ignore (at least to some extent) the workings of those parts of the system which lie on the far side of the interface.

```
4   APL statements
    ─────────────────────────(APL Machine)
3   Instructions
    ─────────────────────────(S/370 Machine)
2   Micro-instructions
    ─────────────────────────(IBM micro-instruction Machine)
1   Hardware logic,
    storage etc.
```

Figure 4 - A Fully Interpretive Multi-Level System

Example

The system shown in Figure 4 has a vertical structure comprising four levels, all but the topmost of which is implemented by an interpreter. Each interpreter is programmed using the set of apparently atomic facilities (objects, operations, etc.) that are provided at one abstraction interface and has the task of providing the more abstract set of (again apparently atomic) facilities that the next higher abstraction interface defines. Because of the fact that each of these abstraction interfaces is fully specified and documented, the designer of the implementation of any one level will normally need little or no knowledge of the design, or perhaps even the existence, of any other levels. (This example involves levels of abstraction which are related by a simple linear ordering. This need not be the case, but this is a matter that we will not pursue further here.)

As with horizontal structuring, so can many different vertical structurings be used to visualise a given system. Equally, some vertical structurings will have a more visible reality in the actual system than others. Once again, the important characteristic of such "actual" (as opposed to "conceptual") structuring is that, while the system is operational, the rules of the abstraction interfaces are, to some degree, constrained or "enforced". The greater the extent of this enforcement, the more the vertical structuring is actual. The role of the enforcement will be to try to prevent faults (or more likely, just certain of the more likely types of fault) from invalidating the abstraction that a level is designed to provide. Were there no possibility of any faults, no enforcement would be needed.

Example

In Dijkstra's THE system (DIJ68), a very influential early example of system design methodology based on using the concept of multiple levels of abstraction, the levels are

almost entirely conceptual. They were used as a means of
factoring the design effort, and of facilitating the
validation of the system design. However no attempt was made
to incorporate mechanisms in the system which would perform
run-time checks on the rules relating to the usage of the
facilities provided at various levels. Thus, for example, if
a memory parity error was detected there was no way of
relating this to a particular level of abstraction, leave
alone of directly incorporating appropriate provisions in each
level for coping with such faults.

However, the more the vertical structuring is actual, the more
reasonable it is to base provisions for fault tolerance on it.

Example

Consider a multi-level interpreter similar to that of Figure
4, but where the microprogram and the program are each held in
a (separate) part of the same store. Naturally, we assume
that the microprogram has been designed to constrain the
program from overwriting the part of the store holding the
microprogram. Then the microprogrammed and programmed
interpreters might well have their own distinct means of
recovering from a reported store parity error. For example a
parity error in a data word at the program level might cause
execution of the program to be restarted, but a parity error
in one of the microprogram instruction words could cause
reloading of the microprogram without affecting (other than
delaying) program execution.

4.6 FAULTS AND STRUCTURING

We have already discussed some examples of how the provision of
"actual" structure in a system makes feasible the provision of
certain types of fault tolerance. Subsequent sections will
develop these points further. However the relationship between
faults and structuring is, as mentioned at the start of our
discussion on System Structuring, really very basic, as well as
subtle. In fact our whole categorisation, given in Section 2.2,
into mechanical faults, algorithmic faults and faults due to
invalid interactions with (i. e. misuse of) a system is based on
system structure. Only after having chosen a particular
perspective on a system, and having identified a vertical and
horizontal structuring, can one say to which of these three
categories a given fault belongs.

Worse than this, the process of identifying a structuring seems
to involve a conscious (or more likely unconscious) assumption
about the sorts of fault that could occur, and should be
considered. Putting this another way, just as it seems
impossible to consider any object as being completely
unstructured, so it seems that we can never, at any one time at
least, avoid limiting the fault possibilities that can be
conceived. Structurings that are useful from the point of view
of considering the reliability of a system (i. e. structurings

which are "actual" structurings) are those which enable designers to think, and to think simply, about those faults which are likely to occur. This is not just a question of considering the relative likelihood of problems with particular pieces of hardware, or from particular types of interface, but in complex systems is also a question of the likelihood of mistakes being made by the designers themselves. Good structuring should reduce the number of such mistakes, but gives no guarantee of their absence.

Here we will leave the topic of system structuring. Hopefully, future discussions will be able to go much further than we have managed towards providing a synthesis of the concepts which we have referred to as horizontal and vertical structuring, and an analysis of the relationship between "actual" structuring and reliability. Such discussions, apart from being much less laboured, will likely make clearer the fact that the idea of "horizontal" versus "vertical" is a local distinction which can be applied uniformly throughout the structure - work which leads in this direction is described in Cohen (COH77). However for our present purposes, namely the classification and comparative description of a variety of existing approaches to the problem of designing reliable systems, the structuring ideas and terms we have introduced and discussed here will (or at any rate will have to) suffice.

5   FAULT TOLERANCE TECHNIQUES

Techniques for attempting to achieve fault tolerance can be classified in various different ways. Here we choose to regard them as comprising, in general, strategies for (i) error detection, (ii) fault treatment, (iii) damage assessment, and (iv) error recovery.

The particular strategies used may differ in different parts of a single system, and at different times during its operation. Indeed it is not always possible to make a positive identification of the components responsible for each of the constituent strategies used in a given fault tolerance technique. The order in which these strategies are carried out can vary, and there can be much interaction between them, but the starting point is always the detection of an error. Once this has occurred, several different approaches to treating the fault that caused the error might be taken, ranging from ignoring its existence, to trying to locate and repair it. Damage assessment might involve exploratory testing, but is frequently based entirely on a priori reasoning, so that no actual assessment algorithm is involved in the operational system. If it is believed that some damage has been done then error recovery will be needed. This can either involve attempting to repair the damage (forward error recovery) or to remove it by abandoning some or all of the results of the recent activity of a system (backward error recovery).

5.1 PROTECTIVE REDUNDANCY

The additional components and algorithms that provide these various strategies in a fault tolerant system constitute what can be termed "protective redundancy". One common classification of such redundancy is into _masking redundancy_, as opposed to _dynamic redundancy_. This distinction is in fact related not so much to the type of strategy used, as to the way in which it is fitted into the structure of the system.

Masking redundancy is redundancy used to mask or hide the effects of faults in a component. Thus, as far as the environment of the component is concerned, the component works perfectly, despite internal faults, at least whilst the masking redundancy is effective. This contrasts with the situation where redundancy is used inside a component so as to provide explicit or implicit indications amongst the outputs of a component as to whether these are erroneous. This internal redundancy would then have to be complemented by external redundancy, in the form of provisions for recovery, in the system that uses the component. Redundancy schemes can also be related to the structure of a system in such a way that they possess attributes of both these classes. Such _hybrid redundancy_ schemes will mask the effects of some types of fault, and provide error indications for some other types.

Masking redundancy is often equated to a form of redundancy which is termed _static redundancy_ because the redundant components that it involves remain in use, and in the same fixed relationship, whether or not any errors are detected. Examples of masking or static redundancy include fault masking via coding, and fixed replication with voting. The canonical example of the latter is Triple Modular Redundancy. This important technique is best described, and related to our discussion of system structuring, in its entirety, rather than as a collection of separate strategies. This is done in the next section, before we attempt more detailed separate discussions of strategies for error detection, fault treatment, etc.

5.1.1 Triple Modular Redundancy

In its standard application, for achieving reliable hardware operation, Triple Modular Redundancy involves the use of three subcomponents (or "modules") of identical design, and majority voting circuits which check the module outputs for exact equality. It is thus designed to mask the failure of any single module, by accepting any output that at least two of the modules agree on. (The TMR structure shown in Figure 5 is assumed to be part of a larger TMR structure, and so has triplicated inputs and outputs.)

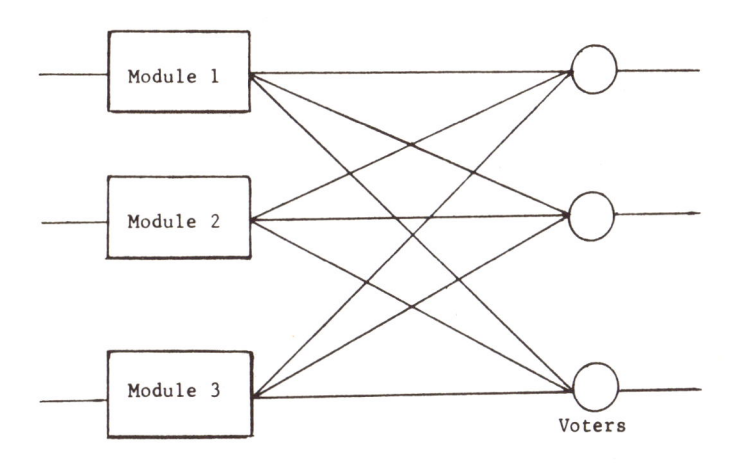

Figure 5 - Triple Modular Redundancy

TMR is feasible at many different levels of a system, and can of course be used in conjunction with other techniques. It would normally be accompanied by some strategy for dealing with the faults whose presence it reveals. This might for example merely involve indicating the identity of the faulty component on a maintenance engineer's panel, so that the component can be manually repaired or replaced. The TMR scheme as described is simply a fault masking technique. It could however be made into a hybrid scheme by, for example, incorporating into its outputs means of indicating when the voting circuits determine that no two outputs agree.

Schemes such as TMR are based on the assumption that failures in the different modules are independent of each other. Thus a design fault which caused all three modules to produce identical but incorrect outputs would not be masked. Equally, it is necessary that the modules do not interact with each other, in other words, that the activity of each is an atomic action. This requirement is difficult to guarantee for modules within a single integrated circuit package, where TMR is therefore inappropriate.

It has been suggested (AVI76) that a TMR-like scheme be used to mask design faults, particularly in software. The hope would be that three modules could be designed, to exactly the same external specification, but sufficiently differently internally (perhaps by different designers) to ensure independence of failures due to design faults. Even if this could be achieved, there is a grave problem of performance degradation caused by the need to synchronise the outputs from the modules, in order that the majority voting can take place. (This can be a non-trivial problem even with hardware modules of identical design.)

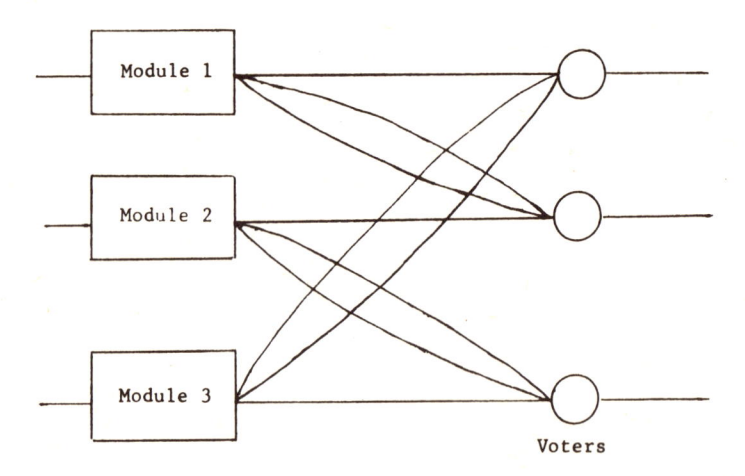

Figure 6 - Would-be Triple Modular Redundancy

Finally there is our point about the way in which each structure that we visualise tends to blind us to certain possible types of fault. With as simple a structuring as one single instance of TMR usage, such as is shown in Figure 5, it is difficult to imagine faults whose existence it might conceal. Figure 6 represents a system with an admittedly highly contrived example of such a fault. The fault is that the voting is not to be carried out on the proper outputs, so that the very essence of the intended TMR structure has been invalidated.

5.2 ERROR DETECTION

The purpose of error detection is to enable system failures to be prevented, by recognizing when they may be about to occur. Ideally, the checks made by error detection mechanisms should be based only on the specification of the service that the system is supposed to provide, and be independent of the system itself. Without such independence there is the possibility of a single fault affecting both the system and the check, and so preventing error detection. If such checks could be designed to cover all of the aspects of the system specifications, and complemented by appropriate means of error recovery, then no single algorithmic or component fault would lead to system failure.

In practice, of course, one has to make do with much less rigorous checking than this. For a start, the system specification may be expressed in terms of information which is external to the system, and in a way which is not amenable to a computational verification. Any checks would therefore have to ignore some aspects of the system specification, because of the necessity of expressing them in algorithmic form which involved only information that was available within the system. Furthermore, the independence of the check and the system being checked cannot be absolute - assessments of the degree of independence will be based on implicit or explicit assumptions about what faults might occur and what faults will not (for example it might be assumed that the software is correct). Even then considerations of cost and effects on performance might further decrease the quality of the check.

<u>Example</u>

  Because of the requirement that checks have to be based on information available in the system, a stock control program cannot guard against being fed valid but incorrect data. It therefore cannot ensure that the actual stock supply situation matches that represented by the information it is holding.

For all of these reasons, therefore, the sorts of checks which can be made in a system will be ones which attempt to enforce some lower standard of behaviour than absolute correctness, a standard usually referred to as "acceptability". All that can be aimed for is the choice of tests for acceptability which provide a very high degree of confidence that any error will be detected.

5.2.1 Types Of Check

Ideally the checks on the functions of a system will be made on its "results" immediately before they leave the system. (This is the principle of minimising "Time of Check to Time of Use" that is described by McPhee (MCP74).) It is often possible, through knowledge of the algorithms of the system, to recognise that certain values of internal data items are erroneous; to do so will save useless processing and enable more speedy recovery. However such checks are an inadequate substitute for checks which are made at the last possible moment and based on the external specifications of the system. Rather, such internal checks, necessarily depending on the internal algorithms of the system, may lack independence from those algorithms.

In many cases the task of establishing the acceptability of the results of a system involves some form of replication, followed by the checking of the consistency of the results obtained. The replications might, for example, involve two or more systems of independent design, two or more copies of the same design, or repeated use of the same system, depending on the sorts of faults that are expected, and on the cost/performance constraints on the system. Such techniques can also be the means by which fault masking is provided, so that separate error recovery is not needed.

A somewhat different kind of check, a reversal check, is sometimes used. This involves processing the results of the system activity in order to determine the corresponding inputs and check them against the actual inputs. Only certain systems lend themselves to this sort of check, namely those where inputs and outputs are in one-to-one or one-to-many relationship.

<u>Example</u>

A reversal check on a system which produces a set of factors of an integer is very convenient, but this is not the case if the system, say, produces a single bit result, indicating whether or not a given integer is a prime number.

Many very effective error detection techniques involve the use of coding as a means of reducing the cost of the check. Techniques such as parity checks, Hamming codes, and cyclic redundancy checks are well established, particularly for detecting certain types of operational error. Checking the acceptability of large and complex masses of data is often infeasible without the use of coding techniques.

<u>Example</u>

Rather than undertake the task of checking that one large set of data is a permutation of another set, it might suffice to confirm that their checksums are correct, and identical.

Any form of error detection based on coding is however at best a limited form of check, whose acceptability must be based on assumptions about the probable characteristics of the errors to be detected. Thus for instance parity checks are regarded as suitable for core stores, but as quite inadequate for telecommunications, because of the different types of fault incurred and hence the different characteristics of the errors.

Error detection mechanisms can of course themselves suffer from faults. Provided that these faults do not cause damage to the system being checked, just two cases need be considered; the mechanism can detect nonexistent errors, or fail to detect actual errors. The detection of an error which does not exist cannot of itself cause the system to fail, though it will use up some of the recovery capability of the system. (If this capability is insufficient a failure will of course ensue.) One can expect that such faults in error detection mechanisms, since they draw attention to themselves, will be quickly identified and remedied. Unfortunately the reverse is true for faults which cause errors to remain undetected.

5.2.2 Interface Checking

Ideal or "complete" checks on the functioning of a system, as described above, would take no account of the design of the system, or of its intended internal structuring. Internal checks are typically based on a combination of suspicion and faith in the structuring of a system. Faith in "actual" structuring is based on the presumed effectiveness of the constraints that are applied to interfaces; faith in "conceptual" structuring on the quality of the thought that went into the design.

Error detection mechanisms within components that serve to check interactions across interfaces (either abstraction or communication) are one means of providing constraints. Checks for division by zero, protection violation, lack of response to a message within a time limit, and power supply irregularities are typical examples of such checks. All these checks of course can be viewed from inside a component as checks on the attempted use made of the component (i.e. system) by its environment. Clearly therefore they can at most guarantee validity of use, as opposed to correctness with respect to environment-level criteria.

The notion that a particular structuring obscures the possibility of certain types of fault has as its counterpart the fact that the choice of an interface makes some sorts of checking of the parts of the system on the far side of the interface impossible or at least impracticable.

Example

It is quite practicable to program a computer to perform a given task in such a way as to incorporate some checking on the correct functioning of the computer (for example of its arithmetic unit or backing store). However it would hardly be feasible to incorporate much or anything in the way of checks on the instruction fetching and decoding, or the store addressing. Indeed, attempts to keep such fault possibilities in mind, while writing, say, an application program, would be most unproductive.

This point leads us to the notion of diagnostic checking - that of periodic attempts to determine whether a component (e. g. the instruction decoder) is presently functioning satisfactorily, interspersed with periods when it is assumed that it is. To be effective the diagnosis must be capable of revealing the existence of likely faults, and the demands made on the component by the diagnostic scheme should approximate to or preferably exceed the demands made during normal use. Such schemes are applicable only in the case of faults that arise through uncontrolled changes to the system (such as component degradation caused by ageing or perhaps inadequately planned modifications), though the diagnosis technique may be invoked in reponse to a failure, in an attempt to locate its underlying cause. The adequacy of diagnostic checking schemes will also depend on the amount of time and resources involved during diagnosis periods, and hence the frequency with which they can be undertaken, as compared to the arrival frequency of faults. The trouble with such schemes is that of the possibly great length of time for which errors might go undetected, whilst damage spreads throughout the system, and beyond.

5.3 FAULT TREATMENT

A detected error is only a symptom of the fault that caused it, and does not necessarily identify that fault. Even where the relationship between the fault and the detected error appears obvious, it will be found that many other possible faults could have caused the same error to be detected. It is often contended that the errors caused by different kinds of faults have fundamentally different natures, that for instance hardware component faults and software design faults are essentially different. We would argue that the differences are superficial. It may be that a pattern sensitive type of fault, which generates an error only for specific patterns of inputs, is more common in software, whilst an abrupt change in behaviour due to a change in internal state is more frequent in hardware. But both types of fault can be present in both hardware and software components (for example a program can damage its data base and be unable to give any further service, and a hardware circuit can be affected by crosstalk).

The task of locating and removing a fault can therefore be a very complex one, whose automation is feasible only in situations which are (or are presumed to be) very simple. An alternative strategy is to ignore the fault and to try to continue to provide a service despite its continued presence, after having dealt in some way with the damage it might have caused. This also involves assumptions, this time about the maximum possible extent of such damage. (In practice it would be unwise not to log the occurrence of an error, and perhaps some information which might aid the later identification of the fault by maintenance personnel. Thus fault repair is not so much avoided, as delayed and left to manual techniques - such techniques can of course be aided considerably by the provision of appropriate tools.)

Continued usage of a component in which there is evidence of the presence of a fault makes sense only when the fault is believed to be one that is effectively a transient fault. For example it is appropriate for faults which arise from sensitivity to a very limited set of specific input patterns, or from occasional time-varying behaviour of sub-components.

Example

> Continued usage could be made of a magnetic tape unit, even though it is occasionally necessary to make repeated attempts at reading a tape before one is successful. If the operating system keeps a record of unsuccessful attempts at reading, this can provide evidence for use during the next period of scheduled maintenance, unless the tape unit deteriorates so rapidly that more urgent remedial action is called for.

If, or more realistically, when, it is decided that some action must be taken to avoid the fault during further operation of the system, or indeed to repair the fault, it must first be located. More exactly, the (assumed) position of the fault must be located to within a component of a size which is acceptable as a unit of replacement (for example a printed circuit board or a sequence of instructions). The search strategy will perforce be influenced by some preconceived ideas about the structure of a system. These will, at least initially, mislead the searcher (whether human or electronic) if a point has been reached where the fault has caused violation of some intended interrelationship between components. This will have occurred, without being detected at the time, because of the absence or inadequacy of constraints on the interrelationship. Where such possibilities have not previously been anticipated, and reflected in at least some existing (preferably documented) viewpoints on the system and its structure, the task of locating the fault can be very difficult indeed, even for a human, since it will in essence involve the generation of a new viewpoint.

Example

> This is what has to be done all the time while debugging a program - it can become a much more difficult task when it concerns residual bugs in a system which has successfully operated for some time, and whose programmers have gained

increased, but misplaced, confidence in the adequacy of their understanding of the system and its structure.

Given that a component has been designated as faulty, and as one whose further use should be avoided, various strategies are possible. Borgerson (BOR73) divides these into replacement and reconfiguration strategies. <u>Replacement strategies</u> are ones in which a previously idle component (a so-called "stand-by spare") is directly substituted for the designated component. <u>Reconfiguration strategies</u> involve arranging for some or all of the responsibilities of the component to be taken over by other components which are already in use by the system. Reconfiguration therefore necessarily involves some degree of performance and/or functional degradation.

Borgerson further classifies such strategies as being either <u>manual</u>, <u>dynamic</u> or <u>spontaneous</u>. In the first category the system takes no part in the strategy, which in the case of hardware may involve manual recabling and the like. In the second category external stimuli cause the system to make use of provisions it contains for reorganising its future activity. Spontaneous replacement and reconfiguration are strategies that are carried out entirely automatically by the system itself, and are sometimes referred to as "self repair"' strategies. The JPL STAR system (see Appendix 3) is one that uses spontaneous replacement to cope with certain types of hardware fault. Spontaneous reconfiguration provides a "fail-soft capability" - Appendix 7 describes the techniques that have been designed for this purpose for the PRIME system.

To date there has been comparatively little work on the design of systems which are specifically intended to tolerate software faults, and on means of spontaneous replacement for this purpose. This is in fact what is provided by the recovery block scheme, (described in Appendix 4), which can be regarded as a technique for using standby spare software components. Here the standby spares are of course of different design to that of the main component. A principle difference between this scheme and that usual with hardware standby sparing is that the spare component replaces the main component only momentarily. This is just in order to cope with the particular set of circumstances (such as the pattern of input data) that has caused a residual design fault to reveal its presence. Thereafter, attempts are made once again to rely on the main component. With hardware standby sparing the spare component, being of the same design, should be as good as the main component was meant to be, and would normally be used as a replacement at least until the main component has been repaired, and more probably until it itself starts to fail.

5.4 DAMAGE ASSESSMENT

Damage assessment can be based entirely on a priori reasoning, or can involve the system itself in activity intended to determine the extent of the damage. Each approach can involve reliance on the system structure to determine what the system might have done, and hence possibly have done wrongly. This approach can be explained, and might have been designed, making explicit use of atomic actions.

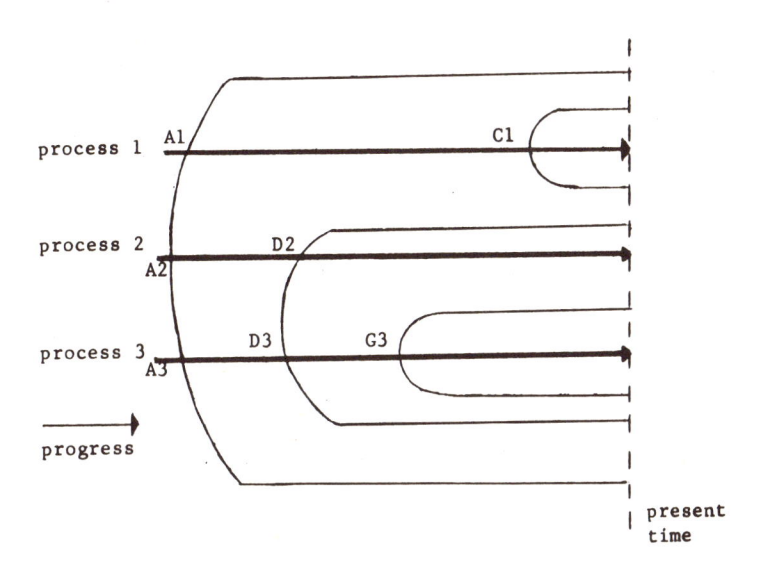

Figure 7 - Extant atomic actions

Figure 7 shows a set of processes and their as yet uncompleted atomic actions. (It is derived from Figure 3 but does not show the complete history of process creation and deletion and of the lifetime of atomic actions. Rather, all completed actions and processes are elided.) The figure therefore indicates, for example, that process 1 has been completely isolated since point C1 in its progress, but that process 2 has perhaps had some interactions with process 3 since they passed points D2 and D3 respectively, but not since process 3 passed point G3.

If process 3 is now detected to be in error, then one possible strategy is to assume initially that what it has done since point G3 is suspect. However if process 2 is the one that is detected to be in error the same strategy would involve an initial assumption that everything it has done since D2 and that process 3 has done since D3 is suspect. These assumptions may of course be too optimistic, in which case greater amounts of recent progress, perhaps on the part of a greater number of processes, will have to be treated with suspicion.

Atomic actions thus provide a simple choice of an a priori delimitation, or rather sequence of delimitations, of amounts of possible damage corresponding to each different error detection point. Such a delimitation can be used to select the area which is inspected for possible damage - a process which is feasible only to the extent that records have been kept of actual information flow and/or meaningful consistency checks can be performed on the system state. Alternatively, and much more simply, one can regard everything within the delimited area as being suspect, so that all must be abandoned. (This is discussed further in Section 5.5.1.) However both these uses assume that the atomic actions are actual, rather than merely hoped for. Thus reliance on atomic actions for damage assessment is reliance on the constraints against unplanned information flow.

In practice damage assessment is often involved closely with efforts at error recovery and at dealing with faults, and is usually a rather uncertain and incomplete affair. Thus effort spent in trying to prevent the spread of damage, by careful definition and monitoring of interfaces between components, is well worthwhile.

5.5 ERROR RECOVERY

Schemes for dealing with the damage that has been assessed as existing when an error is detected are usually classified into backward or forward recovery techniques. Such techniques aim to place the system in a state from which processing can proceed without incurring the failure which has presumably just been averted. _Backward error recovery_ involves first of all backing up one or more of the processes of a system to a previous state which it is hoped is error-free, before attempting to continue further operation of the system or sub-system. (The method of further operation will depend on the fault treatment strategy which is being used.) This technique is thus in sharp contrast to _forward error recovery_, which is based on attempting to make further use of the state which has just been found to be in error. (This distinction is in fact related to the structuring of the system - the system is regarded as having two levels, the lower level consisting of the components that provide the means of backward error recovery. It is only the system state visible at the upper half which is backed up, using information visible only at the lower level. If this classification of the information in the system were not made, one would have to regard all the activity which followed error detection as forward error recovery, by definition.)

5.5.1 Backward Error Recovery

Backward error recovery depends on the provision of _recovery points_, that is a means by which a state of a process can be recorded and later reinstated. Various techniques can be used for obtaining such recovery points. Checkpointing-type mechanisms involve foreknowledge of the resources that the processes could modify whilst they are in the atomic action (e. g. all of working storage). Audit trail techniques involve recording all the modifications that are actually made. Recovery cache-type mechanisms are a compromise which involve recording the original states of just those resources which are modified. Such cache-type mechanisms can be based on saving these original states in a separate set of resources, for reinstatement later if an error is detected (see (AND76) and (VER77)).

Atomic actions are a means of specifying pre-planned limitation of information flow, and hence provide a very useful basis for designing backward error recovery schemes. This is done by arranging that recovery points are saved for a process each time it enters an atomic action and are retained for all processes involved in any given atomic action until all have reached the end of that atomic action. (The straightforward way of ensuring this latter requirement is to arrange that no process is allowed to leave a shared atomic action until all have indicated their readiness to do so - this is the scheduling restriction involved in "conversations" (RAN75).)

Given such a discipline of saving and retaining recovery points, the set of extant atomic actions directly defines the amount of system activity that will be abandoned should an error be detected in any process. (Such an error might be due to a fault in the process, or be due to a deadlock caused by allowing atomic actions to proceed in parallel, as was described in Section 4.4.)

Example

   In Figure 7, if an error is detected in process 1, it could be backed up to recovery point C1. However if an error was detected in process 2, it would have to be backed up to recovery point D2 and process 3 to recovery point D3.

More complex backward error recovery strategies are possible, either instead of, or as supplements to, this atomic action-based strategy. These all involve incorporating strategies into the actual system for determining what information flow has, or might have, occurred. Such strategies therefore can be regarded as ones whose tasks involve both damage assessment and the choice of which recovery points are to be used.

Thus, in contrast to the case of an atomic action-based scheme, the design of such strategies involves the possibly very difficult task of taking into account the effects of any other activity in the system that continues while the strategy is evaluated, and also the possibility of faults occurring during this time. (One can draw a parallel to the distinction between checkpointing and recovery cache mechanisms for saving recovery points - the first of these takes time to complete, but the second can be thought of providing an instantaneous logical checkpoint.) The strategies of course also depend on the accuracy of the records that are used to determine the effects of past activity, just as the atomic action-based scheme depends on the constraints on information flow between processes having been properly enforced.

A major problem with strategies based simply on records of what information flow has, or might have, occurred is that they do not necessarily result in the location of a set of usable recovery points. The problem is illustrated in Figure 8. This shows three processes, each of which has three recovery points in addition to that taken at the point of its entry to the shared atomic action. The dotted lines mark occurrences of information flow between processes.

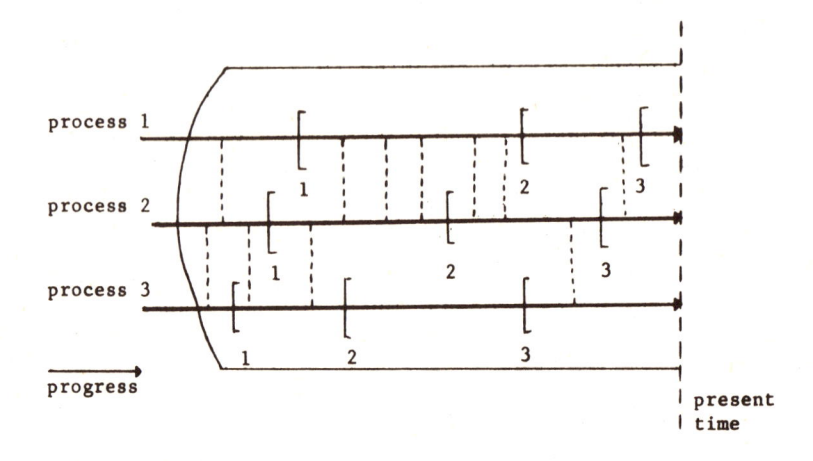

Figure 8 - The Domino Effect

If it should be necessary to back up process 1, this can clearly be done to its third recovery point, without affecting the other processes. If it is process 2 that requires backing up, it will be seen that if this is to its third recovery point, then process 1 will also have to be backed up, and to its second rather than its third recovery point, since its third recovery point postdates interactions between the two processes. However if process 3 has to be backed up, it and the other two processes will have to be backed up right to the start of the atomic action, due to what can be visualised as a sort of "domino effect".

The search for a usable set of recovery points for the process which is in error, and for any other processes which are also affected is in fact a search for a set of consistent recovery points - such a set we will term a recovery line. Each process will at any moment have associated with it a (possibly empty) sequence of recovery lines. A recovery line in fact identifies a set of recovery points, each belonging to a different process, such that

   (a) one of these processes is the process in question,

   (b) no information flow took place between any pair of processes in the set during the interval spanning the saving of their identified recovery points,

   (c) no information flow took place between any process outside the set and any process in the set subsequent to its identified recovery point.

Thus defined, a recovery line identifies a set of process states which might well have all existed at the same moment, and since which all the processes have been isolated from the rest of the system, so that abandoning the activity which postdates these states is a straightforward task. (The concept of recovery line is very similar to that of "sphere of control", introduced by Davies and Bjork (DAV72, BJO72) as a method of representing the system information used for scheduling processes, recording information flow, and preserving recovery points.)

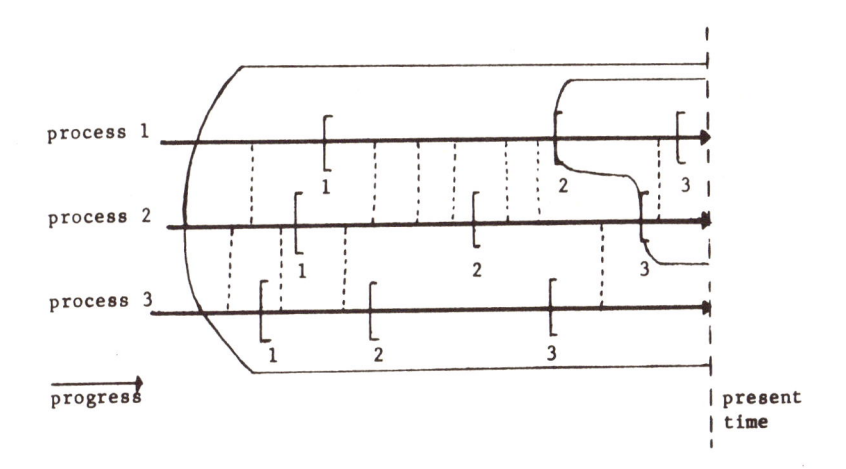

Figure 9 - Recovery Lines

Figure 9 is based on Figure 8, with all the recovery lines drawn in. The line representing the shared atomic action is also a recovery line, since recovery points saved at the start of an atomic action automatically constitute a pre-planned recovery line. Without such pre-planned recovery lines, it may well be the case that, due to the domino effect, one or more processes have no recovery lines at all - such processes must be regarded as being "out of control".

Clearly, therefore, if the scheduling constraints (and hence performance impact) of shared atomic actions can be accepted, they provide a much preferable basis for backward error recovery than what might be termed "information flow analysis" techniques. These scheduling constraints have so far been described in such a way as to imply that shared atomic actions can be used only where there is an explicit requirement for a set of processes to have some private interactions, in furtherance of some common goal. In fact one can imagine the sequencing constraints being imposed on a set of separately designed processes, merely because of a fear of accidental interactions. (An extreme example of this is the act of stopping all the activities of a system so as to take a system-wide checkpoint.) Unfortunately, in some situations resort has to be made instead to the more risky and complicated information flow-based techniques, because of an absence or scarcity of pre-planned recovery lines.

5.5.1.1 Schemes Based on Information Flow Analysis

The essence of such schemes is the search for a recovery line. Recovery lines come into existence through the saving of recovery points. When a recovery line ceases to exist we say that a commitment occurs. A commitment is therefore an impediment to future recovery. (This definition of commitment differs greatly from the various and varied descriptions of commitment given by Davies (DAV72) and by Bjork and Davies (BJO72) but is claimed to capture the essential idea involved.) There are several important varieties of commitment, including what we term "explicit commitment", "interaction commitment" and "accidental commitment".

The deliberate discarding of a recovery point (for example at the end of an atomic action) and hence of any recovery lines of which it was a member constitutes an explicit commitment. Such explicit commitment is therefore the means by which the extent of the resources devoted to error recovery provisions is limited. In some schemes these limitations can be quite severe, so that only a few recovery points ever exist.

Example

File processing systems often have just two recovery points, implemented by the retention of so-called father and grandfather files.

If information is allowed to flow between processes whose latest recovery lines are not identical, and there is no means of "compensating" for this information flow this constitutes an interaction commitment. It means that all recovery lines, for each process, which postdate the latest recovery line which is common to all the processes cease to exist. Such interaction commitments are to be expected for unplanned recovery lines - recovery lines that correspond to uncompleted atomic actions will cease to exist if, for example, the resource locking mechanism fails.

Example

We can re-interpret Figure 7 as a representation of a set of recovery lines for the three processes. Thus process 1 currently has recovery lines (C1) and (A1, A2, A3); process 2 has recovery lines (D2, D3) and (A1, A2, A3) and process 3 has (G3), (D2, D3) and (A1, A2, A3). If there is now an uncompensatable information flow between process 2 and process 3, process 3 will lose its latest recovery line, i. e. (G3).

Compensation (BJO72) is in fact a form of forward error recovery, involving the provision of supplementary corrective information, a technique which is discussed in Section 5.5.2.2. There is however one special case of information flow which does not need compensation, and which does not cause any commitment. This is the case when the recipients are not relying on the accuracy of the information they receive, to the extent that any one of a defined set of possible values will be acceptable, whether or not the sender later regrets having sent it. Bjork and Davies (BJO72) term such information _reference information_, although _insignificant information_ would perhaps be a better term. (A possible example of such information is that obtained by a process which is monitoring the progress of another process.) Barring means of detecting that information is being treated as insignificant, some explicit indication of this intention is needed. Such indications can be used to help determine when back-up is needed, and even as an input to the process scheduler (as described in Section 4.4).

Clearly the task of establishing what recovery lines still exist, rather than have disappeared because of interaction commitments, can be a very difficult one. The rational design of strategies for this task must be based on the assumption that, in the absence of known constraints, information flow will have occurred unless it can be established otherwise (see for example (EDE74)). When such strategies try to take careful account of delays to information flow caused by buffering and the like, and/or account of whether information is actually being treated as insignificant, they can become very complex. However simplicity can always be bought by (hopefully defensible) assumptions about information being insignificant or compensatable.

The third form of commitment poses even worse problems - this is _accidental commitment_, which occurs when something damages the information or the mechanisms that provide one or more (perhaps many more) recovery lines, so making them unusable. The effects of this sort of commitment can be particularly insidious, since its occurrence might be, from the designer's viewpoint, totally unrelated to the activities of many of the processes it may affect. Moreover the commitment may not be noticed at the time that it occurs, so that its effects are only felt later if and when error recovery is needed.

Our approach to understanding, and perhaps even coping rationally with, such problems involves the concept of multi-level error recovery (see Section 5.5.3).

5.5.1.2 Schemes Based on Information Validation

The designs of the backward error recovery strategies described above do not involve any critical assumptions as to which of the processes involved is, or is not, responsible for a particular error. However several important approaches to backward error recovery are based on what are often quite reasonable assumptions about error causes.

For example, some data base systems use audit trails of transactions in order to shield users from the consequences of the system having had to be backed up. Rather than request the user to resubmit the sequence of requests which post-dated the recovery point, the copies of these messages that are held in the audit trail file are reprocessed instead. This technique presupposes that the user's messages were neither themselves the cause of the error nor mistakenly based on erroneous messages from the system itself. (The scheme described by Russell (RUS76) generalises this approach somewhat, so as to deal with networks of interacting processes, rather than a single system interacting with a set of users.)

In effect such techniques assume that the inputs to a process can be presumed valid or can be checked completely. A contrasting scheme would allow a process some means of indicating when its outputs should be regarded as having been certified as correct (with respect to its inputs, and assuming that the process was executed correctly). Then when an error was subsequently detected, such certifications would be regarded as indicating which recovery lines were not worth using because more global error recovery was needed. Whether such global error recovery is actually attempted is another matter.

Example

It might be decided that the risks and consequences of wrongly authorising an automatic cash dispenser to hand out a (limited) sum of money were so small that it would not be worth trying to provide any means of recovery (such as involving a device for photographing the person who extracted the money).

5.5.2 Forward Error Recovery

The relative simplicity of backward error recovery is due to two facts; firstly, that questions of damage assessment and repair are treated quite separately from those of how to continue to provide the specified service; secondly, that the actual damage assessment takes virtually no account of the nature of the fault involved. In forward error recovery these questions are inextricably intermingled, and the technique is to a much greater extent dependent on having identified the fault, or at least all its consequences. Thus generalised mechanisms for backward error recovery are quite feasible (for example, a standard checkpoint/restart mechanism provided by an operating system for use by a variety of application programs). In contrast, forward error recovery schemes have, it seems, to be designed as integral parts of the system they serve. Despite this entanglement with all of the other aspects of a system, forward error recovery techniques can be quite simple and effective. However this simplicity will be based on the assumed simplicity of the faults and the ensuing damage that they are expected to have to cope with. Where such assumptions are justified forward error recovery can be both simple and much more efficient than backward error recovery. (After all, backward error recovery involves undoing everything a system has done since passing its last recovery point, not just the things it did wrongly.) However in many cases the simplicity owes much to the fact that the forward error recovery provisions are not even required to achieve complete error recovery.

<u>Example</u>

In many operating systems, recovery after a crash involves attempting to establish what system resources, and what parts of the data relating to current jobs, seem unharmed. These jobs will then be restarted. On the other hand, jobs which were being executed, or perhaps all jobs that were in main store, when the crash occurred may not be restartable or even recognizable as jobs. Thus although some (perhaps most) users will be unaware of there having been any trouble, others will find that their work has been lost or spoilt, and will themselves have to sort out what should be done about the situation.

The classification of faults that is implied by a choice of a view of the system and its structuring provides us with a means of analysing forward error recovery strategies. Thus they can be provided in a system in order to cope with faults either in the system components, or in systems it is interacting with, or in the design of the algorithm of the system. (It should however be noted that a forward error recovery strategy intended for one of these purposes might, more or less accidentally, on occasion cope with other classes of fault.) Forward error recovery strategies intended for coping with component faults are discussed in section 5.5.2.1, under the heading Exception Handling, and our second category in the following section, under the heading Compensation. It is our opinion that the third case, the deliberate use of forward error recovery to cope with residual design faults in the algorithm of which it is regarded as part, is inappropriate. Should it be wished to provide means of tolerating such faults, backward error recovery seems much more appropriate. Forward error recovery would involve automated diagnosis of design faults, a task whose complexity is such as to be productive of design faults, rather than conducive to the design of reliable systems. Indeed, when the type and location of a design fault can be predicted, it should be removed, rather than tolerated. (This topic is discussed more fully in (MEL77).)

5.5.2.1 Exception Handling

Rational design of an algorithm incorporating strategies for recovering from errors due to faulty components requires prediction of the possible faults, and of how they manifest themselves outside the component. In effect therefore it involves including various possible types of undesirable behaviour amongst the activities that the component is specified as providing. As long as a component does perform one of its specified activities, it will not, by our definitions, have failed. However from the viewpoint of the system there will be a fault when one of the undesired activities takes place, and some (not necessarily easily identified) part of the algorithm of the system will be concerned with coping with it.

Example

> A hardware system can incorporate forward error recovery strategies, based on the use of error correcting techniques and codes, to cope with faulty information storage and transmission components. A given coding scheme will be usable for correcting just a particular, limited, class of errors, (e. g. those involving not more than n successive bits).

It is often desirable to have some means of distinguishing, from each other, and from the main part of an algorithm, those of its parts which have the task of providing forward error recovery for the different kinds of component fault which have been envisaged. Programming language designers have catered for this need by means of language facilities for "Exception handling". The PL/I language provided an early form of such facilities with its "ON Conditions"; more recent proposals include those by Goodenough (GOO75) and Wasserman (WAS76).

Example

> Wasserman's proposals are linked closely with procedure declarations and calls. A procedure can contain statements which will cause particular

exceptions to "hold" (e. g. arithmetic overflow, end of tape, array bound check, etc.). Then each procedure call explicitly, or by default, indicates what is to be done when each possible condition occurs.

Since we regard exception handling as a means of programming forward error recovery, we do not regard it as appropriate for coping with residual bugs in programs. However forward and backward error recovery techniques should be thought of as potentially complementary, rather than competitive, techniques. Thus exception handling can be combined with the recovery block scheme for backward error recovery. An example of such a combination is given in (MEL77). This example shows a program which deals with readily forseeable simple faults, such as invalid input data, by means of exception handling and less likely faults, including those arising from design inadequacies in the exception handlers, by recovery block techniques.

5.5.2.2 Compensation

Compensation, our second form of forward error recovery, fulfills a very different, and indeed much more important need, one which cannot be coped with by backward error recovery. It provides the means for trying to deal with the situation of an error being detected while a system is in communication with an environment which cannot be backed up. As explained in section 5.5.1.2, a <u>compensation</u> is an act by which one system provides supplementary information intended to correct the effects of information that it had previously sent to another system. This requires that both (or more generally, all) the interacting systems are such that, when erroneous information is found to have been sent out or let out by a system, all of the other systems are capable of accepting the corrective information which is then sent out by, or on behalf of, the offending system.

<u>Example</u>

If a stock control data base has been updated because of an input message indicating the issuance of some stocked items, and it is later found that this message was incorrect, it might be possible to compensate for the wrong message by means of another message purporting to record the acquisition of replacement stock items. Such a simple compensation would probably not suffice if, for example, the stock control system had, as a result of the wrong information, recalculated optimum stock levels, or produced purchase orders for the replenishment of the types of stock item involved.

As has already been described, determination of the extent

of information flow, and hence of the requirements for compensation, can be aided by the concept of atomic actions, and by the careful planning of such actions. System algorithms that incorporate compensation strategies can be designed using such structuring techniques as exception handling. However the problem of designing compensation algorithms that will work well, in complex systems, is an immense one, with no obvious general solution - clearly the simple, but unfortunately impracticable solution, is to avoid the need for any compensation by guaranteeing that no incorrect results are ever allowed to leave a system.

Example

>Even recent data base systems which incorporate very sophisticated error recovery strategies can occasionally get the data that they hold into such a state that there is no alternative but to suspend service, and attempt manual correction of the data base, and manual assessment of the damage that thas been done through the provision of wrong information to the organisation using the system (GRA77). The basic requirements for such manual determination of what compensation is necessary are an understanding of the information flow in the environment of the system, and a complete record of all information flow to and from the system (see Bjork (BJO74)). In practice what usually happens is that such manual compensation is neither guaranteed, nor expected, to be complete.

5.5.3 Multi-Level Error Recovery

The advantage of multi-level designs, i. e. designs characterised by the existence of specified (and hopefully well-documented) abstraction interfaces, namely that of enabling each level to be designed independently of the internal designs of other levels, is especially desirable in situations which are complicated by the possibility of faults. Indeed it seems to be the only means we have of mastering problems such as the occurrence of further faults while a previous fault is still being dealt with.

Ideally the algorithm at any level of the system would be designed on the assumption that all of its components, that is the level below, worked perfectly (either faultlessly, or with complete masking of faults). Then error recovery would be needed only for purposes of coping with invalid use of the system and with design faults in the algorithm of the system.

Even when perfection of components is not assumed, it is possible to achieve considerable independence of the design of separate levels, and even of their provisions for error recovery. This in fact is conventional practice in the simple multi-level structures (namely those that relate directly to the physical construction of the system, and involve no sharing of components) that are typical of hardware designs.

Example

The three components, say processors, in a TMR structure might use such internal error recovery strategies as instruction entry and error correcting codes. As long as the faults which cannot be masked by these strategies are independent, and do not destroy the TMR structure, it can mask their effects at the system level.

In more sophisticated forms of multi-level structure, and in systems which have to cope with more than just operational faults in correctly designed hardware components, the situation is more complicated. However in all cases rational design of a system is impossible if it incorporates faulty components which are known to leave themselves in internal states for which no external state (i. e. system level abstraction) is defined.

Therefore one approach, feasible only for faults whose exact consequences can be predicted, is to incorporate the description of the faulty behaviour into the specification of the abstraction interface. The system algorithm then has to be augmented so as to deal with this specified undesirable behaviour, for example by using explicit exception handling facilities, or static redundancy (such as in the above TMR example. Parnas and Wurges (PAR76) give a detailed discussion of one exception handling approach, couched in terms of techniques for programming hierarchies of abstract machines, and based on the use of traps as a means of reporting "undesired events" (i. e. exceptions). An account of how the approach is used in the HYDRA operating system, mainly for coping with hardware faults, is given by Wulf (WUL75).

The technique of augmenting and hence complicating the specification of an abstraction interface by incorporating details of all anticipated (unmasked) faults reduces the practical, if not the theoretical, independence of the designs of the levels it separates. The one alternative means of retaining a large measure of design independence is to require that unmasked faults in the components constituting the lower level cause this lower level to assume a defined state which corresponds to some previous external state. Thus from the system's viewpoint, some sequence of operations end up by having had no effect. In other words, errors detected at one level result in what can be seen from the next level as backward error recovery. Thus, forward progress, as seen at one level, when viewed through an abstraction interface which hides appropriate states and resources can be seen as reverse progress. (An exact analogy is provided by the apparent reverse rotation of the wheels of a stagecoach in a western film). A detailed explanation of a very basic version of such a scheme applicable to levels in a fully interpretive multi-

level system (such as that shown in Figure 5) is described in
(RAN75). More sophisticated versions, which do not require
levels to be fully interpretive, are described in (VER77a,b)
and (BAN77). A detailed general account of multi-level system
design and the problems of recoverability is given in (AND77).

Example

The scheme described in (BAN77) is used to show how
backward error recovery can be provided by an operating
system to independent user processes which are competing
for the resources (e. g. storage space) being managed by
that operating system. Faults in one process do not affect
other processes, and the specification of the operating
system interface remains simple.

When, as in the above example, there is parallel activity on
one or more of the levels of a multi-level system, and perhaps
even different amounts of parallelism perceived at different
levels, the problems of damage assessment and of error
recovery can become very complex. However atomic actions
still provide a very useful means of describing what is going
on, and a basis for the design of largely independent fault
tolerance strategies in the various levels, even though the
atomic actions on different levels cannot be totally
independent of each other.

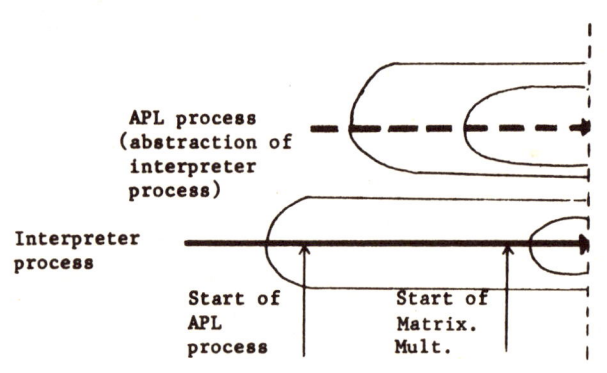

Figure 10 - Atomic Actions in a Two-Level System

The nature of this dependency can be demonstrated using Figure
10, which shows atomic actions in an interpreted process and
in the underlying interpreter process. (The interface between
the levels might, for example, be APL, augmented by some means
of specifying atomic actions.) The atomic actions of the
interpreter either fall within the activity which is seen at
the upper level as comprising a single basic operation, such
as Matrix Multiply, or surround the activity corresponding to
the entirety of an atomic action in the APL process. In other
words, even atomic actions at separate levels of abstraction
of a given process will turn out to have all their entry

points and exits properly nested in time.

The consequences of this dependency are discussed in (RAN75). This shows that many types of interpreter fault can be dealt with either without effecting the APL process, or else by causing the APL process to back up to one of its recovery points. However certain interpreter faults, notably those which prevent it from backing up the APL process, cause it to have to back itself up to a point before the start of interpretation of the APL process.

However all of these strategies for independent design of separate levels of a multi-level system depend absolutely on the vertical structure being "actual", as was discussed in Section 4.5. With respect to error recovery specifically, there would, for example, be little point in having the checkpoints, audit trails, or whatever, that were being kept for different levels, in the same failure-prone storage device. If this were done, and a failure did occur, the level structure would be an impediment to understanding what had happened, rather than an aid to the design of means of tolerating such occurrences.

Multi-level recovery schemes therefore have to be designed with very careful regard for the possibility of an accidental commitment (i. e. destruction of recovery lines) which has as its cause the failure of some system component which is common to the recovery mechanisms used for separate levels. Many possible types of multi-level recovery schemes are possible, with widely varying strategies for achieving a measure of independence between the recovery mechanisms used for the different levels. Perhaps the most common scheme is one which provides two levels of recovery after a system crash, one referred to as enabling a "warm start", the other a more brutal "cold start" (one in which the system retains no information from any of its activity prior to the crash), for use when warm start cannot be achieved. Both levels of recovery are usually incomplete, since even the warm start scheme normally ignores the effects of some interaction commitments, so that some users are left to fend for themselves. This is the case even with the very sophisticated scheme described by Lampson and Sturgis (LAM76). However this scheme, which is based on some quite plausible assumptions about the ways in which storage, communication channels and processors can fail, does guarantee the integrity of the system's distributed shared files, no matter when the crash(es) occur.

6   SUMMARY AND CONCLUSIONS

This paper has attempted to bring out all of the assumptions (justified or not) which are always present in any discussion of the reliability of a complex computing system, and in system designs aimed at providing very high reliability. It has shown how reliability concepts are inextricably intermingled with system structuring concepts, and how a concern for system structuring can help (and hinder) the rational design of fault-tolerant systems.

The aim has been to deal with all possible types of fault, including design inadequacies (both hardware and software) and valid input data which is belatedly identified as incorrect, as well as more obvious faults such as those due to hardware component wear and ageing.

Various basic concepts, such as those of atomic action, level, recovery line, commitment and compensation have been defined and described. As an aid to further explication of these ideas, and to appreciating their manifestations and significance in actual systems, overall descriptions of a number of different approaches to the design of highly reliable systems are given as a set of appendices to this paper. These appendices do not purport to give an up-to-date or complete account of the actual systems described. Rather they are based solely on the particular documents that they reference. The particular selection of systems has been chosen merely to illustrate the wide diversity (but common underlying principles) of current approaches to the design of highly reliable computing systems - it does not purport to be a complete survey of current research and development activity in this area. (No large scale interactive data base systems are included in the selection - this is because data base systems are the subject of a companion paper by Gray.)

The one major moral to be drawn from this paper is the prime importance of the choice and design of interfaces, both communication and abstraction, and of ensuring that they are matched as closely as possible by the "actual" structure of the system. Each interface that is specified allows the system designers to achieve what Dijkstra (DIJ76) terms "a separation of concerns" - this separation may be beneficial, but can be misleading. Particular types of interface are to be preferred (when the cost of providing them can be justified). These are ones which enable all, or at any rate a large proportion of, faults to be masked, and those that enable the existence of complete backward error recovery to be assumed, even in situations involving parallelism. Both types simplify the interface specification, and hence the task of the designer who is trying to provide or make use of the interface. Ideally the design task will be so simplified by appropriate choice of interfaces that it can be carried out faultlessly - if there is reason to doubt this (and there nearly always is), and the needs for high reliability justify attempting to achieve design fault tolerance, we would argue that this should be based on backward error recovery (or possibly replication and voting) rather than forward error recovery.

Forward error recovery can be very effective for predictable faults inside a system - the actual choice of interface will again be important because of the effect it has on the ability of the system to detect errors. (For example results which can have a reversal check applied to them are better in this regard than a single bit result which must either be trusted, or recalculated). However we would suggest that because of the complexity it engenders forward error recovery should be used sparingly, and regarded as an optimisation of backward error recovery, which in any case might still be needed to deal with unanticipated faults. However, forward error recovery, in the form of compensation, may be necessary (as opposed to a mere optimisation) when dealing with environments that cannot be forced to back up, although it is much better to prevent incorrect information flow than to have to compensate for it later.

Ideally all these various design issues would be decided upon, in a particular case, by mainly quantitative methods, based on relative probabilities of faults, the costs and performance characteristics of different strategies and interfaces, etc. Certainly, conventional reliability engineering calculations can and should be used in those parts of the system design task which are sufficiently well understood and codified, such as the construction of simple sub-systems from tried and tested standard hardware components. However it would seem that many of the design tasks involved in achieving high levels of overall reliability from large and complex hardware/software systems will continue for a long time to require large measures of creative skill and experience on the part of the designers.

7   ACKNOWLEDGEMENTS

The ideas presented in this paper, and a number of sizeable portions of the text, owe much to the work of other past and present members of the U.K. Science Research Council-sponsored project, at the University of Newcastle upon Tyne, on the design of highly reliable computing systems. In particular, the preparation of the actual paper has been greatly aided by discussions with Tom Anderson, Ellis Cohen and Santosh Shrivastava. Earlier discussions with Jim Gray, of IBM San Jose, and with members of IFIP Working Group 2.3 on Programming Methodology have also had a strong influence on the paper, as has the pioneering work by Davies and Bjork on spheres of control. Nevertheless the detailed contents and any inadequacies of this attempt at an overall analysis of reliability issues and the role of system structuring in complex computing systems must remain the responsibility of the authors.

8 REFERENCES

(AND76) Anderson, T., R. Kerr. Recovery Blocks in Action: a system supporting high reliability. *Proc. Int. Conf. on Software Engineering* San Francisco (Oct. 1976).

(AND77) Anderson, T., P.A. Lee, S.K. Shrivastava. *A Conceptual Model of Recoverability in Multi-Level Systems.* Technical Report 115, Computing Laboratory, The University, Newcastle upon Tyne (Nov. 1977).

(AVI72a) Avizienis, A. et al. The STAR (Self Testing and Repairing Computer): An Investigation of the Theory and Practice of Fault Tolerant Computer Design. *IEEE Trans. on Computers*, C-20, 11 (Nov. 1971), 1312-1321.

(AVI72b) Avizienis, A., D.A. Rennels. Fault Tolerance Experiments With the JPL-STAR Computer. *IEEE Compcon 72*, (1972), 321-324.

(AVI76) Avizienis, A. Fault-Tolerant Systems. *IEEE Trans. on Computers* C-25, 12 (Dec. 1976), 1304-1312.

(BAN77) Banatre, J.-P., S.K. Shrivastava. *Reliable Resource Allocation Between Unreliable Processes.* Technical Report 99, Computing Laboratory, The University, Newcastle upon Tyne (June 1977).

(BAS72) Baskin, H.B., B.R. Borgerson, R. Roberts. PRIME- A Modular Architecture for Terminal-Orientated Systems. *Proc. AFIPS 1972 SJCC* 40 (1972), 431-437.

(BEL64) *Bell System Technical Journal.* (Sept. 1964).

(BEL77) *Bell System Technical Journal.* (Feb. 1977).

(BJO72) Bjork, L.A., C.T. Davies. *The Semantics of the Preservation and Recovery of Integrity in a Data System.* Report TR 02.540, IBM, San Jose, Calif. (Dec. 1972).

(BJO74) Bjork, L.A. *Generalised Audit Trail (Ledger) Concepts for Data Base Applications.* Report TR 02.641, IBM, San Jose, Calif. (Sept. 1974).

(BOR72) Borgerson, B.R. A Fail-Softly System For Timesharing Use. *Digest of papers FTC-2,* (1972), 89-93.

(BOR73) Borgerson, B.R. Spontaneous Reconfiguration in a Fail-Softly Computer Utility. *Datafair* (1973), 326-331.

(BOR74) Borgerson, B.R., R.F. Freitas. An Analysis of PRIME Using a New Reliability Model. *Digest of papers FTC-4,* (1974), 2.26-2.31.

(BRI73) Brinch Hansen, P. *Operating System Principles.* Prentice-Hall, Englewood Cliffs, N.J. (1973).

(BRI75) Brinch Hansen, P. The Programming Language Concurrent Pascal. *IEEE Trans. On Software Engineering.* SE-1, 2 (June 1975), 199-207.

(CLE74) Clement, C.F., R.D. Toyer. Recovery From Faults in the No. 1A Processor. *FTC-4* (1974), 5.2-5.7.

(COH76) Cohen, E.S. *Strong Dependency: a formalism for describing information transmission in computation systems.* Technical Report, Computer Science Dept, Carnegie-Mellon Univ., Pittsburgh, PA (Aug. 1976).

(COH77) Cohen, E.S. *On Mechanisms for Solving Problems in Computational Systems.* (In preparation.)

(COS72) Cosserat, D.C. A Capability Oriented Multi-processor System for Real-Time Applications. *Int. Conf. On Computer Communications.* Washington, D.C. (Oct. 1972), 287-289.

(DAR70) Darton, K.S. The Dependable Process Computer. *Electrical Review* 186, 6 (Feb. 1970), 207-209.

(DAV72) Davies, C.T. *A Recovery/Integrity Architecture for a Data System.* Report TR 02.528, IBM, San Jose, Calif. (May 1972).

(DEP77) Depledge, P.G., M.G. Hartley. Fault-Tolerant Microcomputer Systems for Aircraft. *Proc. Conf. On Computer Systems and Technology, University of Sussex,* Institute of Electronic and Radio Engineers, London (1977), 205-220.

(DIJ68) Dijkstra E.W. The Structure of the THE Multiprogramming System. *Comm. ACM* 11, 5 (1968), 341-346.

(DIJ76) Dijkstra, E.W. *A Discipline of Programming.* Prentice-Hall, Englewood Cliffs, N.J. (1976).

(EDE74) Edelberg, M. Data Base Contamination and Recovery. *Proc. ACM SIGMOD Workshop on Data Description, Access and Control* (May 1974), 419-430.

(ESW76) Eswaran, K.P., J.N. Gray, R.A. Lorie, I.L. Traiger. The Notions of Consistency and Predicate Locks in a Database System. *Comm. ACM* 19, 11 (Nov. 1976), 624-633.

(FAB73) Fabry, R.S. Dynamic Verification of Operating System Decisions. *Comm. ACM* 16, 11 (1973), 659-668.

(GOO75) Goodenough, J.B. Exception Handling: Issues and a Proposed Notation. *Comm. ACM* 18, 12 (1975), 683-696.

(GRA75) Gray, J.N., R.A. Lorie, G.R. Putzolu, L.L. Traiger. *Granularity of Locks and Degrees of Consistency in a Shared Database.* IBM Research Report RJ1654 (Sept. 1975).

(GRA77) Gray, J.N. (Private Communication).

(HAM72) Hamer-Hodges, K. Fault Resistance and Recovery within System 250. *Int. Conf. On Computer Communications.* Washington (Oct. 1972), 290-296.

(HEA73) Heart, F.E., S.M. Ornstein, W.R. Crowther, W.B. Barker. A new minicomputer/multiprocessor for the ARPA network. *Proc. Of the Nat. Computer Conf.* New York, N.Y. (June 1973), 529-537.

(HEC76) Hecht, H. Fault Tolerant Software for a Fault Tolerant Computer. *Software Systems Engineering.* Online, Uxbridge (1976), 235-348.

(HOA74) Hoare, C.A.R. Monitors: an operating system structuring concept. *Comm. ACM* 17, 10 (Oct. 1974), 549-537.

(HOR74) Horning, J.J., B. Randell. Process Structuring. *Comp. Surveys* 5, 1 (1973), 5-30.

(HOR74) Horning, J.J., H.C. Lauer, P.M. Melliar-Smith, B. Randell. A Program Structure for Error Detection and Recovery. *Proc. Conf. On Operating Systems: Theoretical and Practical Aspects,* IRIA (1974), 177-193. (Reprinted in Lecture Notes in Computer Science, Vol. 16, Springer-Verlag).

(LAM76) Lampson, B., H. Sturgis. *Crash Recovery in a Distributed Data Storage System.* Computer Science Laboratory, Xerox Palo Alto Research Center, Palo Alto, Calif, (1976).

(LIN76) Linden, T.A. Operating System Structures to Support Security and Reliable Software. *Comp. Surveys* 8, 4 (Dec. 1976), 409-445.

(LOM77) Lomet, D.B. Process Structuring, Synchronisation and Recovery using Atomic Actions. *Proc. ACM Conf. On Language Design for Reliable Software.* Sigplan Notices 12, 3 (March 1977), 128-137.

(MCP74) McPhee, W.S. Operating System Integrity in OS/VS2. *IBM System J.* 13, 3 (1974), 230-252.

(MEL75) Melliar-Smith, P.M. *Error Detection and Recovery in Data Base Systems.* (Unpublished, 1975).

(MEL77) Melliar-Smith, P.M., B. Randell. Software Reliability: the role of programmed exception handling. *Proc. ACM Conf. on Language Design for Reliable Software.* Sigplan Notices 12, 3 (March 1977), 95-100.

(NAU77) Naur, P. Software Reliability. *Infotech State of the Art Conference on Reliable Software,* London (1977), 7-13.

(NEU73) Neumann, P.G., J. Goldberg, K.N. Levitt, J.H. Wensley.

<u>A Study of Fault-Tolerant Computing.</u> Stanford Research Institute, Menlo Park, California (July 1973).

(ORN75) Ornstein, S.M., W.R. Crowther, M.F. Kraley, R.D. Bressler, A. Michael, F.E. Heart. Pluribus - a reliable multi-processor. <u>Proc. Of the Nat. Computer Conf.</u> New York, N.Y. (June 1975), 551-559.

(PAR71) Parnas, D.L. Information Distribution Aspects of Design Methodology. <u>Proc. IFIP Congress</u> (1971), TA256-30.

(PAR76) Parnas, D.L., H. Wurges. Response to Undesired Events in Software Systems. <u>Proc. Conf. On Software Engineering.</u> San Francisco, Calif. (1976), 437-446.

(PAR77) Parsons, B.J. Reliability Considerations and Design Aspects of the Hawker Siddeley Space Computer. <u>Proc. Conf. On Computer Systems and Technology, University of Sussex,</u> Inst. Of Electronic and Radio Engineers, London (March 1977), 221-222.

(RAN75) Randell, B. System Structure for Software Fault Tolerance. <u>IEEE Trans. On Software Engineering.</u> SE-1, 2 (June 1975), 220-232.

(REP72) Repton, C.S. Reliability Assurance for System 250, a Reliable Real-Time Control System. <u>Int. Conf. On Computer Communications.</u> Washington (Oct. 1972), 297-305.

(ROH73) Rohr, J.A. Starex Self-Repair Routines: Software Recovery in the JPL-STAR Computer. <u>Digest of papers FTC-3,</u> (1973), 11-16.

(ROS75) Ross, D.T. <u>Plex1: Sameness and the Need for Rigor.</u> Report 9031-1.1, Softech, Inc., Waltham, Mass. (Nov. 1975).

(RUS76) Russell, D.L. <u>State Restoration Amongst Communicating Processes.</u> TR 112, Digital Systems Laboratory, Stanford University, Calif. (June 1976).

(SHO68) Shooman, M.L. <u>Probabilistic Reliability: An Engineering Approach.</u> McGraw-Hill, New York (1968).

(SIM74) Simpson, R.M. A Study in the Design of High Integrity Systems. <u>INFO Software,</u> London (1974).

(STO72) Stoy, J.E., C. Strachey. OS6 - An Experimental Operating System for a Small Computer. <u>Comp. J.</u> 15 (1972), 117-124, 195-201.

(TAY76) Taylor, J.M. Redundancy and Recovery in the HIVE Virtual Machine. <u>Proc. European Conf. on Software System Engineering,</u> London (Sept. 1976), 263-293.

(VER76) Verhofstad, J.S.M. <u>Recovery for Multi-Level Data Structures.</u> Technical Report No. 96. Computing

Laboratory, The University, Newcastle upon Tyne (Dec. 1976).

(VER77) Verhofstad, J.S.M. Recovery and Crash Resistance in a Filing System. Proc. SIGMOD Conference, Toronto (Aug. 1977).

(WAS76) Wasserman, A.I. Procedure-Oriented Exception Handling Medical Information Science, University of California, San Francisco, Calif. (1976).

(WEN72) Wensley, J.H. SIFT - Software implemented fault tolerance. Proc. Nat. Computer Conf., New York (June 1972), 243-253.

(WUL75) Wulf, W.A. Reliable Hardware-Software Architecture. Proc. Int. Conf. On Reliable Software. SigPlan Notices 10, 6 (June 1975), 122-130.

APPENDIX 1: BELL LABORATORIES ESS NO.1A PROCESSOR

The Bell Laboratories Electronic Switching Systems (ESS) represent one of the first major attempts at incorporating extensive fault tolerance in a processor. In this case, the processor is the heart of the electronically controlled switching systems used in the main for telephone exchanges. The first system of this type was in service in 1965.

There are stringent reliability requirements to be met by the ESS systems. For example, those specified for the No.1A ESS (BEL77) require the system to be available for 24 hours a day, and that down time for the total system should not exceed 2 hours over its 40 year life. Moreover, the percentage of calls handled incorrectly should not exceed 0.02%. For the processor itself, the requirement is that its average outage time, that is the time during which established calls are retained but no new calls are established, is not greater than 2 minutes per year.

There are extensive references to the various ESS systems, particularly in the Bell System Technical Journals: for example, the September 1964 issue describes the first system, the No.1 ESS; the October 1969 issue describes No.2 ESS; and a data switching system, No.1 ESS ADF, is described in the December 1970 issue. This appendix will concentrate on the fault tolerant techniques employed in the processor in the No.1A system, a description of which is given in (BEL77) and (CLE74).

A1.1 System Description

The No.1A processor is a self-contained high speed processor developed specifically for the control of Bell ESS systems. Its design is based on the experience gained from the earlier ESS systems. The instruction set of the No.1 processor is a subset of that of the No.1A, thus enabling the well-tested No.1 ESS call processing programs, described in (BEL64), to be used.

The system may simply be regarded as having two levels with hardware components at the bottom level supporting one software level. Figure A1.1, taken from (CLE74), illustrates a static structuring of the hardware components of the No.1A processor. The heart of the system is the Central Control which is fully duplicated (CC0 and CC1). In general, one of the CC modules is designated as the standby, while the active unit controls the system. The timings for the rest of the system originate from a digital clock in the active CC. This provides signals for both the active and standby CCs, which therefore operate synchronously.

The programs to be obeyed by the CCs are stored in the program stores (PS), which are core stores in the No.1A system. The information relating to the processing of telephone calls and the translation (routing) information for the system is stored in the call store (CS) complex (also core stores).

The primary memory in the system can be divided into "protected" and "unprotected" areas. This division is enforced by the active CC, which provides different instructions to write to these different areas, and contains the mapping registers which define the areas. The mapping registers are software controllable via other (special) write instructions. Basically, the protected area contains the parts of the memory that are not duplicated (e. g. the program stores), as well as those areas which vitally affect the operation of the system (e. g. the internal registers of the CC and the disc controllers).

The auxillary unit (AU) system at the bottom of Figure A1.1 consists of the bulk storage devices and their controllers, essentially disc file units (FS) and tape units (TUC). The discs provide a file store for the system, used mainly for holding the backup versions of programs and data, and for holding infrequently used programs. The tape units hold the accounting information that is generated for complete calls, and also hold infrequently used parts of the system database. These auxiliary units operate autonomously, competing with the central control for access to the core memories. The components in the system are interconnected by the three (duplicated) buses indicated in Figure A1.1.

Basically, there are two kinds of interrupt in the No.1A processor; "call processing" interrupts which invoke the "normal" (call processing) algorithms of the software, and "maintenance" interrupts which are discussed below. There are several priority levels in each of the interrupt types. The interrupt structure provides a coarse priority ordering of the tasks to be performed. A finer priority ordering is administered by a control program at each priority level which initiates the tasks at that level as necessary. The call processing programs can be divided into two classes, deferrable and non-deferrable. The deferrable programs are those for whcih the data is already in the system, and the programs are not therefore critically synchronised to real time. The non-deferrable programs are those that must be executed on a strict schedule, otherwise data will be lost. These programs are generally the input/output programs, and are activated by a clock interrupt. For example, one input program which has to be run at regular intervals is the one that detects and receives dial pulses.

The majority of programs in the system are deferrable, and run at what is referred to as the base-level, with all of the interrupts enabled. A main control program at the base-level administers the priority ordering of the tasks to be run at the base level, and multiprograms such tasks together. A further function of the control program is to coordinate the activity of the interrupt level input/output programs and the base-level tasks - for example, it updates the data received from the input programs and distributes it to the task programs for analysis and use. The task programs perform one particular kind of work for a single call at a time. However, it is not clear from (BEL64) whether these tasks operate atomically or not. The communication between interrupt and base-level programs is through shared memory; the input data is assembled into buffers which are inspected by the base-level programs. Similarly, the output data from the base-level is put into buffers, and detected by the interrupt-level output program which unloads the buffer and controls the peripheral equipment. Synchronisation between the interrupt and base-level programs would appear to be achieved via "test and set" type instructions.

A1.2 Reliability Strategies

In order to attempt to reach the reliability requirement of an average of less than 2 minutes outage per year, comprehensive "maintenance" software is provided in the No.1A processor. The various strategies for error detection, fault treatment, damage assessment, and error recovery are closely related. In fact, many of the strategies employed in the No.1A processor have been based closely on the accumulation of experience from the various earlier installed ESS systems as to what sort of faults will occur, and with what exact consequences. Table A1.1, taken from (BEL77), indicates the reliability objectives that have been set for each of the probable causes of outage time in the No.1A system.

	Outage time (minutes/year)
software deficiencies	0.3
hardware reliability	0.4
procedural faults	0.6
abnormal algorithm deficiencies	0.7

Table A1.1 No.1A system outage allocation

Although the 1A system makes use of the well-tested No.1 ESS call processing programs, it can be seen that "software deficiencies" are still expected to result in an outage of 0.3 minutes each year. This time would appear to include outages caused by the integration of new software into the system; facilities for this integration are provided in the No.1A system, but will not be discussed further in this appendix.

The "hardware reliability" category, allocated an average of 0.4 minutes/year, includes faults in the hardware which prevent a working system configuration from being established. Significant effort was placed into the design of the system hardware components in order to make them intrinsically reliable. However, the functions implemented in some units are so critical that the 1A system, in common with the earlier ESS systems, makes significant use of the full duplication of critical units. In general, full duplication is used for the parts of the system whose failure would affect a substantial number of customers, for example the central control, the bus systems and the file stores. (It is stated in (BEL77) that reliability calculations have shown that redundancy greater than full duplicaton is not required.)

Replication of the core memory units is influenced by the ease with which the data contained in the unit can be regenerated. Thus the program stores are supplemented with standby spares, which can be loaded from the file store. The standby spares in the call-store complex are used to provide full duplication for the units containing transient data such as that relating to calls. Figure

A1.1 illustrates the redundancy in the No.1A system.

The third cause of system outage time is that attributed to "procedural faults", which is expected to cause about 0.6 minutes outage per year. In the main, these faults will be caused by the human interface so that particular attention has been paid to the clarity and uniformity of the documentation, and to achieving a reduction in the number of manual operations required.

The largest system outage time in the No.1A system is expected to be caused by "abnormal algorithm deficiencies", i. e. deficiencies in those algorithms in the system that are invoked when an error occurs. As with the earlier systems, the "abnormal algorithms" in the 1A system are mainly implemented at the software level, and the system is dependent on these for its recovery. However, it is recognised that there are a large number of variables involved (the system can be in almost any state when an error is detected), and that system recovery is related to all other maintenance components (for example, recovery can be easily mislead by an incomplete diagnosis). Indeed it is stated in (BEL77) that "there is no guarantee that all impending trouble will be identified and isolated before it can jeopardise system operation".

1) Error Detection

Error detection mechanisms are employed at both the hardware and software levels in the 1A system. The main hardware error detection mechanisms are essentially the same as those employed in earlier ESS systems, namely:-

(a) replication checks
(b) timing checks
(c) coding checks
(d) internal checks i. e. self checking units

Replication checks are the primary mechanism for detecting errors caused by hardware faults in the CC. The CC is fully duplicated; in general two identical modules are fully operational (i. e. static redundancy) with each executing the same instruction atomically, with both units in synchronisation as discussed earlier. Each CC has special (duplicated) circuits which perform consistency (matching) checks between the two CCs. The CCs have access to each other over fast interconnecting buses, which provide for the synchronisation of the CCs as well as providing a route for the data from the CCs for matching. The data that is matched is a function of the operation being performed, and in general these checks guarantee that the data entering and leaving the CCs is identical. The overall action of the CC can therefore be regarded as a shared atomic action which encloses the atomic actions of each processing module. Of course, this type of replication does not detect errors caused by design faults in either the software or hardware. The CC also provides replication checks on the transmissions on the duplicated buses. The duplicated file stores also perform replication checks.

Timing checks are used throughout all of the hardware components in the 1A system. In particular, those on the CC are used to verify that its operations are proceeding in the correct manner. Timing checks are also provided by the CC to the software level (described below). Errors in the clocks used to provide these timing checks are detected by further (hardware) timing checks. (For example, the digital clock in the active CC is checked by an analogue clock.)

Coding redundancy is used to protect all of the words in the system. The error codes used include M-out-of-N codes, parity and cyclic codes, depending on the types of error expected. Thus the interfaces between the components can be checked; for example, the majority of errors caused by faults on the buses or in the memory components can be detected.

Many of the hardware components in the 1A system have been designed to be self-checking. Information concerning the detection of internal faults in a unit is made available to the recovery programs (discussed below) so that extensive software checking may not be required to locate faulty units.

The hardware level also provides error detection mechanisms for use by the software level. These mechanisms are run-time interface and timing checks. The interface checks verify that the addresses used by the programs are within proper limits and that the program does not violate the memory protection described above. Units such as the tape and disc controllers also provide interface checks on the operations they are requested to perform. The timing checks are used to ensure that the program control in the system is not lost because of any software (or hardware) fault.

Essentially, there are two error detection mechanisms at the software level in the No.1A system, namely the audit programs and the diagnostic programs. The audit programs have been designed to detect (and correct) errors arising in the system database, and are run at regular intervals during the normal operation of the system, as well as after hardware failures have been detected. The audit programs provide an independent diagnostic check on the "actual" structure of the database, using the redundancy contained within the database. Replication checks can also be performed, comparing data with its replicated copy. Coding checks are also used by the audit programs, for example to check the non-transient in the program and call stores.

As discussed below, the diagnostic programs play an important role in the treatment of faults in the No.1A system. However, the diagnostics are also used to detect errors in units. Periodically, each unit is removed from service and the diagnostic tests performed to (attempt to) detect latent faults in that unit.

2) <u>Fault Treatment</u>

When an error is detected by the hardware mechanisms described above, the normal call processing operation of the system is interrupted and the fault treatment and recovery programs are invoked. Essentially, there are three priority categories for this interruption:-

(a) immediate interrupt (maintenance interrupt) - if the fault is severe enough to affect the execution of the currently executing program. The priority of the maintenance interrupt is based on the subsystem in which the error was detected.

(b) interrupt deferred until the completion of the currently executing program - if the problem could affect several telephone calls.

(c) interrupt deferred until detected by the routinely executed base-level jobs, if the problem affects only a single call.

The main aim for the fault treatment and recovery programs is to re-establish the call-processing capabilities of the system as quickly as possible. This involves identifying and isolating the faulty hardware unit and (spontaneously) reconfiguring the system to utilise a spare unit. (There are special instructions implemented in the CC to control the call store complex - where no standby spares are available, a unit operating in duplex mode will be preempted to replace a failed unit which was not protected by duplication.

As mentioned above, the main aim for these programs is to restore normal system operation as quickly as possible. Thus an attempt is made to minimise the effects of the non-deferrable maintenance activities. In particular, a technique called "first look" is generally used. With this technique, the fault recognition program examines the information provided by the error detection hardware, which is automatically preserved when a maintenance interrupt occurs, to determine the most likely cause of the problem. The system will then be configured to run without the implicated unit(s), and further diagnostics of those units will be scheduled for deferred processing at the base-level i.e. the diagnostic tests on the faulty unit will be multiprogrammed with the normal operation of the system. For example, if a program store was removed from service, a deferred action would be to run diagnostic checks on that store. (The CC provides special instructions to assist the subsystem fault diagnosis.)

Error records are collected by the fault treatment programs to indicate the units in which errors have been detected and the response of the treatment programs to those errors. If analysis of these records indicates that the system has not been restored to fault-free operation, then at the occurrence of the next error the "first look" strategy is abandoned and a complete check of the implicated units will be performed. If a unit passes all of the diagnostic checks then it is assumed that the fault was transient, and that the unit is now fault-free and can be returned to service, However, anlysis of the error records will result in the isolation of units experiencing a high rate of transient faults.

It can be seen that fault location in the system (and the recovery described below) are program controlled and therefore require (and assume the existence of) a fault free processor. In order to achieve this, "abnormal" algorithms in the hardware level implement a spontaneous reconfiguration mechanism to enable a (hopefully) fault free processor to be configured. The mechanism is invoked by some of the hardware error detection mechanisms described above. For example, program control during recovery actions is monitored by a timer run from the CC clock. This timer is used to detect any loss of program control and to activate the processor reconfiguration. Similarly, it is not valid for both CCs to be active or standby at the same time. Such an occurrence would also invoke the reconfiguration.

There are four steps that can be taken by this mechanism. The first step involves the automatic configuration of a basic processor from the components of the system, consisting of a central control, program store and program store bus. The processor is not capable of full system operation, but only of running fault recognition and spontaneous reconfiguration programs in an attempt to resume normal operation of the system. If this step fails (e. g. detected by timing checks), then it is assumed that the program stores have been corrupted, and the second step involves repeating the first step and reloading the program stores from the discs. If step two fails, then step 3 will configure a basic processor to perform simplified tests, isolating various subsystems until (possibly) fault free operation is restored, and normal operation of the system can be attempted. If this step fails then the last step is to stop the system and wait for manual recovery actions.

The repair of faulty units in the No.1A processor is performed manually. In order to meet the reliability requirements for the hardware (0.4 minutes outage per year) the average repair time for a unit has to be less than 2 hours. Thus a maintenance objective for the No.1A processor was that at least 90% of faults should be isolated to no more than 3 replaceable modules by the (automatic) diagnostic programs, and that such programs should detect at least 95% of the possible faults (as measured using simulation results).

It is clear from (BEL77) that very extensive work has been carried out into the design and development of the diagnostic programs. The diagnosticians and hardware designers work as a team from the start of the design through to the completed system. The hardware and diagnostic designs proceed in parallel, and are used to verify each other. Furthermore, the diagnostic tests are used in many applications, from the initial development of the system (tested using simulation),

to the testing of the various units while a system is being
built and commissioned, and are finally used on-line in the
operational systems. Thus a large amount of experience with
the diagnostic programs is built up.

The design philosophy for the diagnostic program is
essentially that all of the tests on a unit are run, and a
post-processing scheme, the trouble location procedure (TLP),
examines the results of all of the tests to attempt to
determine the problem. Essentially, the TLP performs pattern
matching between a condensed version of the results of the
diagnostic tests and an office resident database (held on
magnetic tape), to produce an ordered list of suspected faulty
modules. The database has been built up (off-line) by circuit
analysis and by the simulation of permanent hardware faults
using a physical or computer model.

3) **Damage Assessment**

The main form of damage assessment in the No.1A system appears
to be based on the a priori reasonings that either a fault
will not result in any damage, or that any damage will
manifest itself as damage to the system database. Damage to
the database will be dynamically assessed by the audit
programs, to invoke various stages of recovery as discussed
below.

Clearly some form of dynamic damage assessment will be
performed by the environment of the No.1A system. For
example, if a call is lost or routed incorrectly, then the
customer will assess the call as "damaged", and (hopefully)
will retry the call. It is not clear from (BEL77) whether the
possiblility of the accounting information being damaged is
considered, or whether this also relies on damage assessment
by the environment.

4) **Error recovery**

The main form of error recovery in the 1A system can be viewed
as forward error recovery at the software level.

Forward error recovery techniques are used to provide recovery
from faults in any of the storage modules in the system whose
contents have been duplicated. If the faulted unit is
replaced, its contents can be recovered from the duplicate:
for example, if a program store fails its contents can be
recovered from the copy of the disc.

Recovery from errors in the systems database is also handled
by forward error recovery, implemented by compensation
algorithms in the audit programs. In general, the algorithms
may read parts of the database as insignificant information,
in that the erroneous information that is detected is removed
(and discarded) from the database, without necessarily being
corrected. This may result, for example, in a (hopefully
small) number of telephone calls being lost, but enabling the

normal operation of the system to be resumed. Clearly the environment of the system will provide the actions required to recover from the system treating some information as insignificant; for example, customers whose call was lost will provide a form of backward error recovery, abandoning the current state of that call and attempting to redial. The amount of information that is treated as insignificant will depend on the damage that is assessed. An "optimistic" approach is adopted for this damage assessment and compensation, i. e. those stages least disruptive to the normal operation of the system will be attempted first. If the damage is assessed as minor then the error recovery will be multiprogrammed with the normal operation of the system. If the damage is more severe (i. e. too extensive to rely on the normal audit to correct the problems), then the call processing is suspended until the appropriate database reinitialisation has been performed.

When an error occurs during the processing of the maintenance programs at the base-level of the system, the currently executing program is terminated (to protect the system against further disruption and to guard against invalid results from the program (BEL77). However, these programs can specify an "abnormal termination algorithm" which is invoked (once) by the "abnormal" algorithms of the software level, if it is assessed that the program caused the error. Thus a program can attempt to provide its own forward error recovery actions. If these fail then that program is terminated, and the normal recovery programs are relied on to resume normal system operation.

A1.3   Reliability Evaluation

It is stated in (BEL77) that, after extensive laboratory testing of the No.1A processor (100,000 processor hours) and greater than 8000 hours in service, the overall performance indicates that the design objectives of the system are being realised. Some early studies were also conducted to evaluate the reliability strategies employed in the system. In one study, 2071 single determinate hardware faults were inserted at random into a normally operating system. Automatic system recovery occurred in 99.8% of these cases, with manual assistance required for only 5 of the faults. Another study which analysed, by simulation, the performance of the diagnostic programs in response to a random selection of 2400 hardware faults indicated that 95% of the faults were detected by the programs. A test of the trouble location procedure was also performed by inserting circuits which were known to be faulty into a system. In only 5 of the 133 simulated repair cases did the TLP fail to include the inserted circuit on its list of suspected modules, and in 94.7% of the lists the faulty component was located within the first five modules.

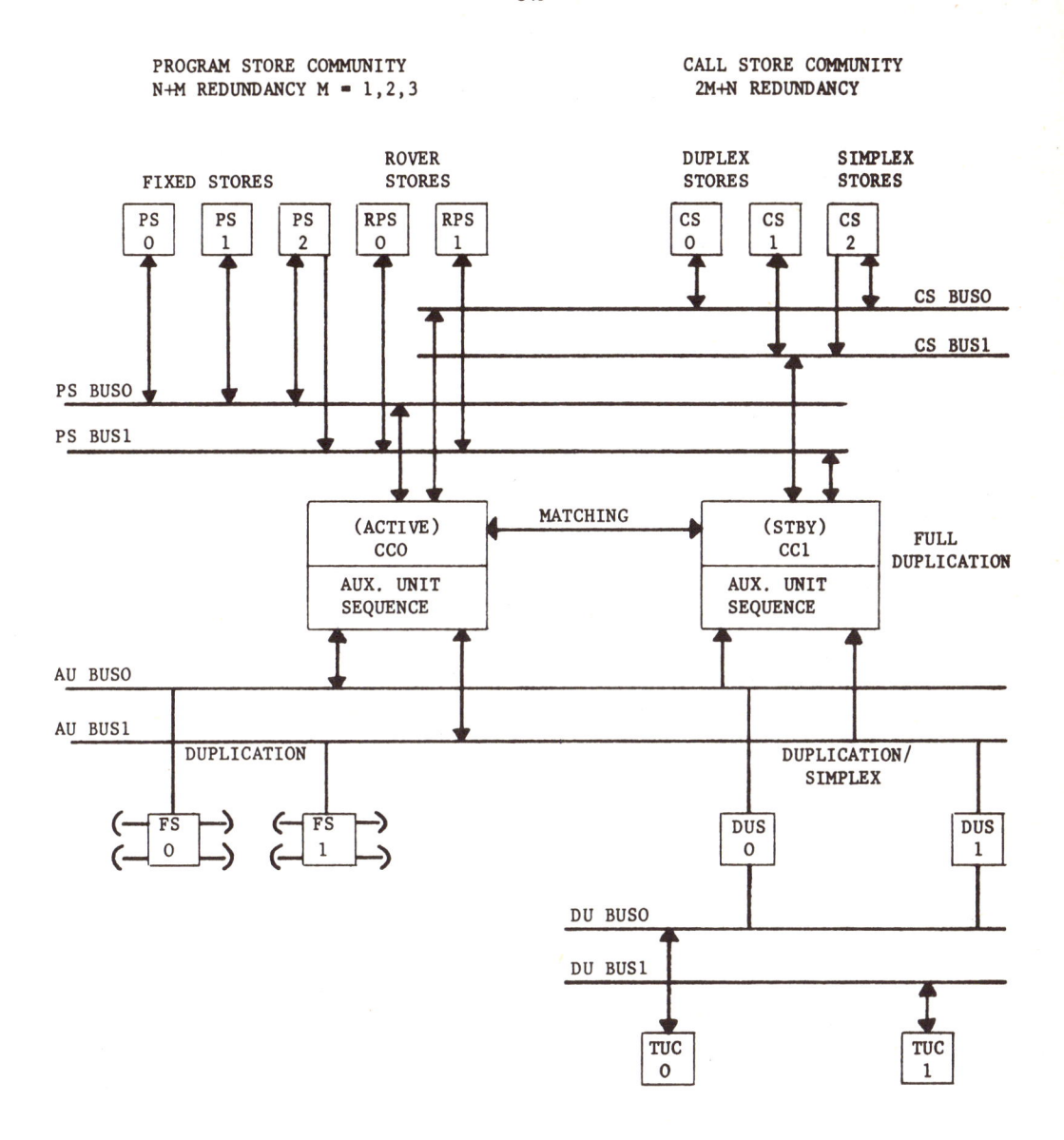

Figure A1.1 - No.1A Processor

APPENDIX 2: HIVE

The HIVE project at the Royal Signal and Radar Establishment (U.K. Ministry of Defence), is concerned with the design and development of a complete software system suitable for implementing large but high integrity dedicated transaction processing systems such as communications switching and database access systems. In particular, one of the basic elements of the HIVE research has been the development and initial implementation of a high integrity virtual machine (i.e. HIVE) which provides useful simplifications, abstractions and hardware independence for the applications programmer, as well as providing features to enable correct transaction processing to be maintained in the presence of faults. (TAY76) presents the main features of the redundancy and recovery in the HIVE virtual machine; this description is based on that report.

A2.1 System Description

The HIVE system can be viewed as a three level system :-

    3   Applications Processes
    2   Kernel Software
    1   Hardware

Level 1 in the system comprises the hardware components, for example discs, core stores, processors and their interconnections. These resources are used by the kernel software at level 2 to implement the HIVE virtual machine interface presented to the applications programmers at level 3. The description presented in (TAY76) concentrates on the virtual machine and does not discuss any of the details of levels 1 and 2.

The HIVE virtual machine provides an arbitrary number of virtual processors (VPs) which can run asynchronously and independently in parallel. The VPs are multiprogrammed together by the level 2 software onto the components provided at level 1.

As mentioned previously, the HIVE system is intended for transaction processing systems. For this purpose, a static structuring of VPs is defined at system build time, in that each VP is dedicated to execute one particular functional program. At run time, the VP executes that program cyclically, for the data of one transaction at a time, during which time it cannot be interrupted by any other transaction or VP. Several VPs can be allocated to perform the same function in parallel but for different transactions.

The HIVE virtual machine is the basic entity to which the other HIVE resources can be allocated. The basic store resources that can be allocated consist of protected objects in the core (core segments) and on secondary storage (file segments or files). The file objects are the permanent objects that comprise the database of the system. A VP can access its protected objects through a capability system, whose function is to provide isolation and protection between VPs. A capability for a store object provides a mapping from the local name that a VP has for that object to the object itself, as well as defining the type of access permitted to that VP. Thus any implementation of a HIVE system must include a suitable set of facilities at level 1 (e.g. base-limit access registers) and at level 2 (e.g. run time checks on capabilities) to ensure that the physical separation between protected objects is enforced.

Input/output facilities for the VPs are provided by a message passing scheme. There are two message interfaces to each VP, the normal interface and the blocking interface. Each interface consists of input and output routes to allow connection to/from other VPs and the hardware devices. (These routes are set up permanently at system build time). A message may contain data parameters, being passed directly to the receiving VP, or capabilities for core or file segments.

The basic execution cycle of a VP consists of processing one message from its normal input interface. Messages that arrive on the normal interface of a VP are queued (by the level 2 software) and do not cause interruption of the execution cycle of the VP. The execution cycle is always terminated by a call of the END (virtual) instruction (see below), which indicates to level 2 that the successful end of the cycle has been reached. This point in the execution of a VP is called the regeneration point. The VP will then become idle until a message arrives on an input route which is specified as a parameter of the END instruction.

The normal output routes of a VP are also buffered; messages that are sent on these routes are buffered (by level 2) until the END instruction is called. At this point these messages are dispatched to their intended destinations. If a VP only made use of its normal message interface, its actions could be regarded as being atomic. However, messages sent on the blocking interface are not buffered, but are sent immediately, and a message is sent back to the requesting VP when the receiving VP has completed the requested action (i.e. when it reaches its regeneration point). The requesting VP can continue processing during this time, and can elect to wait for the reply. Thus the action of a VP may not be atomic.

In the HIVE system a transaction can be regarded as a message being received from the system's environment, and being passed from VP to VP through the system for the various stages of processing. However, while the execution cycle of an individual VP may be atomic, as discussed above, the processing of the transaction is not implemented as a shared atomic action in that information concerning a partly processed transaction can be obtained by (i.e. flow to) VPs processing other transactions. This definition of a transaction is at variance with that defined in Sectin 4.3, and the rest of this discussion will refer to a HIVE transaction as a task.

The data areas required for a task can be regarded as divided into three types: (i) database areas which reside permanently in the system; (ii) task data, i.e. data pertaining to that particular task; and (iii) workspace areas, temporary data areas private to that functional program. The capabilities for the permanent database objects that a particular VP requires access to are defined at system build time (as is the functional program for that VP).

The task data is received via the message passing scheme described above, while the workspace areas can be dynamically created (and deleted) by the VP as required.

The instruction set of a VP can be regarded as consisting of the basic instruction set of the level 1 hardware components (excluding those privileged instructions permitted only to the level 2 software), supplemented by a set of virtual instructions for manipulating the HIVE resources. The kernel software in level 2 is responsible for implementing these virtual instructions, which include the END instruction described above, instructions for the message system and instructions for creating, deleting and accessing the protected objects. In the current implementation of HIVE described in (TAY76), CORAL66 is used as the programming language for the VPs to provide the desired independence from the particular hardware implementation. A second type of language, a system description language SYDEL, has been designed to enable system programmers to specify how these programs are mapped onto the set of HIVE protected objects and VPs, and how the VPs are interconnected to form the complete system. No details were given of this language in (TAY76).

A2.2 Reliability Strategies

As its title suggests, (TAY76) concentrates on the redundancy and recovery features of the HIVE virtual machine. Consequently, the topics of error detection, fault treatment and damage assessment, particularly at levels 1 and 2, are not treated in depth, and this section will therefore concentrate on the facilities provided in HIVE for error recovery.

Essentially, the HIVE system provides a backward error recovery scheme. The most global backward error recovery provided is a "cold start" error recovery; multiple copies of a read-only backstop version of the system are provided. Loading this version into core corresponds to re-establishing the network of application VPs with their permanent capabilities for code and database objects and message routes, with the database objects in their "cold start" states (i.e. with no record of the system's previous activities). This empty network of VPs contains no messages or dynamically created objects.

Backward error recovery for the permanent database objects in HIVE is provided essentially by replication. Each database object is a composite object comprised of at least four versions; two read-only (cold start) and two read-write versions used at run time. These will be distributed across the level 1 secondary storage components to provide tolerance against faults in a particular component. When a VP begins a cycle of execution it is given access (by level 2) to one of the read-write versions of each of the objects that it is permanently associated with, and the objects are locked out to other VPs. If and when that VP reaches its regeneration point, then the other read-write version(s) of that object will be updated, one at a time, by the level 2 software, from the version updated by the VP i.e. explicit commitment of the information takes place. If the regeneration point is not reached, the working version can be reset, from the other versions, to the value it had at the start of that execution cycle ("backdated"). Once updating/backdating is complete, the object can be unlocked for further accesses. The problem of compensation following the committal of erroneous data is not discussed.

Following a major crash (i.e. loss of core or a faulty processor), the initial cold start version of the system is loaded into core, and the code for recovery of the database objects (level 2 code) is entered. (TAY76) does not indicate whether this is an automatic or manual action. This code attempts to access the various versions of the permanent database objects, i.e. those with capabilities built into the cold start version, in order to carry out any necessary backdating/updating of the various versions. Checksums are used to detect partially updated and corrupted versions. When this process is complete, any areas on the discs which have not been accessed are placed on the free list. The basic effect of this recovery is therefore to establish the empty network of VPs, with the database objects in the state prevailing at the most recent regeneration point of the last VP to access it, while the state of all objects created dynamically before the crash (e.g. message data) is lost.

The protection of the task is essentially achieved through a VP checkpointing the data of the task in a permanent (safeguarded) file, which is recovered in the manner described above. This checkpointing will be performed at some stage in the processing of that task, for example when the task enters the HIVE system. Thus, following a crash and the recovery of the database files, the VPs which perform the checkpointing can be executed to re-initialise any of the tasks represented in the checkpoint file. However, as described above, the HIVE system does not implement a task as a shared atomic action, and the recovery points provided for the database objects (i.e. recovery to the most recent regeneration point) and for the tasks (i.e. restart of the task) are not necessarily consistent with each other i.e. a recovery line may not exist. Hence a task which is restarted may already have been processed by some VPs, but not by others, and the state of the database will not be recovered to its state at the time the task was originally started. A task may therefore pass through some stages of processing two (or more) times. According to (TAY76), ensuring that this situation is coped with satisfactorily is an application dependent problem. Essentially this requires that a VP will have to be programmed to provide forward error recovery, in that it will need compensation algorithms to deal with the situation of it being requested to process a particular message for a second (or more) time, without having had its database objects being first backed up to their states when that message was first received. The HIVE system provides a basic facility to enable a VP to detect that such forward error recovery may be required. The VP restarting a task can set a special marker bit in the messages to indicate that this task may have already been processed. This marker bit remains set in all subsequent messages generated in the course of that reprocessing attempt.

A less drastic form of recovery, that of a single VP, is also provided in the HIVE system. (TAY76) suggests that if an individual

VP detects a fault which prevents it from reaching its regeneration point then it can attempt to repeat that cycle. It is claimed that this repetition will not affect the rest of the sysyem because (a) any messages sent over the normal output interface by that VP will have been buffered (b level 2) and not actually sent; and (b) any alterations made to the working versions of any database objects can be reversed (again by the level 2 sofware) by backdating from the other versions. If the action of a VP was atomic, then this would be the case. However, as mentioned earlier, the action may not be atomic because of any messages sent on the blocking interface. The problem of compensating for this information flow if a VP is backed up is not discussed.

APPENDIX 3: THE JPL-STAR COMPUTER

The Jet Propulsion Laboratory Self Testing And Repairing (JPL-STAR) computer was the result of studies, initiated in 1961, into the design of fault tolerant computer systems. The research was sponsored by NASA.

The principal goal stated in (AVI72a) for the design of the STAR was to achieve fault tolerance for a variety of hardware faults, namely transient, permanent, random and catastrophic. In order to achieve this degree of fault tolerance a variety of techniques were used: coding, monitoring, standby spares, replication with voting, component redundancy and program rollback and repetition. No specific provisions were made for possible software faults - rather it would appear that programs that are run on the STAR are assumed to be correct.

The STAR was designed as a general purpose fault tolerant computer, whose main characteristics were chosen to match the requirements of a spacecraft guidance, control and data acquisition system which would be used on long unmanned space missions. Thus the reliability requirements for the STAR were for 100,000 hour survival with a probability of 0.95, and with a maximum time requirement for recovery of 50msecs. It is stated in (AVI72a) that a complete redesign of the STAR was, at that time, being performed to match the exact requirements of a spacecraft computer. An experimental laboratory version of the STAR was constructed and operational in 1969, although it did not implement all of the features of the STAR design. This description will therefore concentrate on the design presented in (AVI72a) rather than on the particular implementation of the STAR. Some of the results from experimentation with the laboratory STAR are presented in (AVI72b), and (ROH73) discusses details of the system software.

A3.1 System Description

The STAR computer may be regarded as a three level system. The bottom (hardware) level of the STAR supports two software levels consisting of a resident executive and the applications programs.

The hardware level of the STAR can be regarded as having a decentralised organisation. A standard configuration of functional subsystems (i.e. components) implements the abstraction interface presented to the higher (software) levels, which essentially has the appearance of a single-cpu system with the required computing capability.

Figure A3.1, taken from (AVI72a), illustrates a static structuring of the bottom level of the STAR computer, consisting of the following functional subsystems:-

(i) control processor (COP) - contains the index registers and contains and maintains the program location counter

(ii) logic processor (LOP) - performs logical operations

(iii) main arithmetic processor (MAP) - performs arithmetic operations

(iv) read only memory (ROM)

(v) read/write memory (RWM)

(vi) input/output processor (IOP)

(vii) interrupt processor (IRP) - handles interrupt requests

(viii) test and repair processor (TARP) - monitors the operation of the computer and implements the recovery.

Communication between the various units is carried out on three buses: the memory-out (M-O) bus; the memory-in (M-I) bus; and the control bus.

The second level in the STAR computer, the resident executive, provides typical operating system features for use by the applications programs in the third level. These features include interrupt control, input/output processing and job scheduling.

The STAR computer operates in two modes; standard mode and recovery mode. In standard mode the stored programs are executed, and the "normal" algorithms of the TARP issue the principal clocking signals and continually monitor the operation of the system. Recovery mode is discussed subsequently.

A3.2 Reliability Strategies

The STAR computer employs a variety of techniques, as already mentioned, to attain the desired hardware controlled self-repair and protection against many types of faults. The TARP implements, in hardware, the majority of these features. The correct operation of the rest of the system is based on the assumption that the TARP is always functioning correctly.

1) Error Detection

> The major error detection mechanisms in the STAR computer are implemented in the hardware (i.e. bottom) level. In particular, the TARP is responsible for monitoring the operation of the computer, and detects errors by two methods:-
>
> (i) testing every word sent over the two data buses; and
>
> (ii) checking status messages from the functional units for predicted responses.
>
> All machine words in the STAR are protected by various error detecting codes. The codes are preserved by arithmetic operations although not by logic operations. (Consequently operation of the logic processor is checked by replication, with two copies operational which indicate when disagreement occurs.) Thus the TARP can detect errors arising from faults

the storage,transmission and processing of words i.e. the TARP checks the abstraction interface between the components at this level.

Each functional unit in the STAR computer generates status messages which are checked in the TARP against the responses that are predicted (independently) by logic internal to the TARP. Thus the TARP can identify, for example, both improperly activated units (unexpected message) and failed units (absence of an expected message).

The types of message that a unit can generate include "disagree with bus" message and "internal fault" message. The "disagree with bus" message is needed for duplex operation of units. The "internal fault" message is produced by monitoring circuits internal to each unit. These circuits utilise redundancy internal to the unit to (attempt to) detect errors in the internal state of that unit.

For example, a reversal check is employed whereby "inverse microprogramming" deduces what the operation/ algorithm should have been from the active gating signals. The deduced result can then be checked against the requested operation/algorithm. The status message generating circuits in each unit are themselves duplicated, enabling some errors in the status messages to be detected by the TARP.

The read/write memory units in the STAR computer have two modes of operation, absolute and relocated. In absolute mode the unit will respond to its own wired in name; in relocated mode the unit responds to an assigned name. The relocated mode can be used by the executive to provide duplicated or triplicated storage for programs and data.

Finally, errors in the TARP itself are detected (and masked) by triple modular redundancy. Three fully powered copies of the TARP are operational at all times with their outputs decoded by a 2-out-of-(n+3) voter. An assumption made, therefore, by the rest of the system is that faults in the TARPs are always masked.

It is not clear from the documentation what error detection mechanisms (if any) are made available to the higher (software) levels in the STAR, apart from the availability of information concerning errors that occurred in the interface with the arithmetic unit (for example, overflow, division by zero).

2) Fault Treatment

Once an error has been detected the TARP exits from standard mode and enters recovery mode (i.e. the "abnormal" algorithms are invoked). In this mode the TARP is responsible for locating and treating the fault. It can be seen from the previous section that the prediction logic of the TARP coupled with the status messages should, in general, enable the TARP to locate the faulty unit causing the error (assuming of course that this prediction logic itself is correct). However, for fault conditions which cannot be resolved by the TARP logic there is a wired-in "cold start" procedure (which is also invoked in the case of temporary power losses).

As the STAR was intended for unmanned space missions, permanent faults are treated by the automatic replacement of the faulty unit. There is no provision for their repair. The standard configuration of functional units is supplemented by one or more unpowered spares of each unit, and the TARP implements a spontaneous replacement strategy. A repeated fault indication in a unit leads to its replacement, implemented by the TARP by power switching. Spare TARP units are also provided; thus if one of the three operational units disagrees with the other two, then the faulty unit can be replaced by a spare.

Fault treatment is also performed by the resident executive in the STAR. Software assistance is required for memory replacement, both for assignment and cancellation of relocation names, and for reloading the replacement memory. Reference is also made in the documentation to a class of diagnostic instructions, which can, amongst other things, exercise the unit status messages and the TARP fault location logic, and also control the power switching to the spare units. The executive apparently implements diagnosis for faulty units, although the interface between this and the TARP is not made clear.

3) Damage Assessment

It would appear that there is no dynamic damage assessment at any level in the STAR computer, as the error recovery described below is always invoked. However, much of the activity of the components in the bottom level could be regarded as consisting of simple atomic actions. Firstly, each functional unit contains its own instruction decoders and sequence generators, as well as storage for the current operation code, operands and results. Apart from overall synchronisation, each unit operates autonomously. It would appear, therefore, that once initiated a functional unit could operate atomically. Hence, if the internal monitoring circuits detected an error, then the damage could be assumed to be localised to that particular unit. The second activity in which atomic actions can be identified is in the operation of the TMR-protected TARPs. Assuming that the activity of each TARP unit is atomic, then any TARP fault should be masked by the voter. Nevertheless, in both of these cases the more global error recovery described below is invoked.

4) Error Recovery

The main form of error recovery in the STAR is implemented by backward error recovery of the software levels. When an error is detected and any replacements have taken place, the TARP issues a reset message which causes all operational units to assume an initial state (presumably the contents of the memories are not reset to an initial state). The program that was running is then forced to rollback, that is to back up to a previous state.

The applications programs are provided with a mechanism for establishing a recovery point. It would appear that it is the responsibility of the programs to establish recovery points as often as is needed for reliable operation (ROH73), and to specify (correctly) the information that needs to be checkpointed. The program also assumes that this operation is performed reliably (and atomically). Moreover, as only one recovery point can be established at one time, an explicit commitment will occur whenever a new recovery point is established. Nothing is said about the problem of compensating for information that has left the system prior to such a rollback - presumably this is the responsibility of the application programmers, as the recovery mechanisms provided would enable the program to perform compensation actions if it so required.

The executive level is responsible for implementing the recovery mechanism provided to the upper level. It uses the rollback point register in the TARP to achieve this. The rollback register can be updated by the executive level, and acts in effect as an interrupt vector, used to restart the executive when a rollback is invoked by the TARP. The rollback of the applications program is then implemented by software in the executive. The executive also uses the rollback register to control non-repeatable events (for instance, input/output operations). The storage of checkpoints for the upper level programs is also the responsibility of the executive, and it provides duplexed storage for this purpose. (ROH73) describes all of these strategies in more detail.

The only other form of error recovery in the STAR is provided by the "cold start" procedure in the TARP, augmented by a "cold start" capability in the resident executive.

A3.3 Reliability Evaluation

According to (AVI72a), early analytical studies using models of dynamically redundant systems had indicated that mean life gains of an order of magnitude or more over a non-redundant system could be expected from dynamically redundant systems, with standby spares replacing failed units. This gain compared favourably with the mean life gain of less than 2 in typical TMR systems. An analysis of a model of the STAR's reliability compared its reliability with that of a simplex computer of equivalent performance and with the Mars Mariner spacecraft computer(MM'69). Some of the results are indicated in Table A3.1, taken from (AVI72a), where the lower bound (k = 1) indicates an equal failure rate of powered and spare units, and the upper bound (k=infinity) indicating a zero failure rate of spare units.

TABLE A3.1

RELIABILITY VERSUS TIME FOR VARIOUS CONFIGURATIONS

Mission Time (h)	MM'69 Computer	Simplex Computer	STAR Computer with S Spares Upper Bound (K=∞) S=3	S=2	Lower Bound (K=∞) S=3	S=2
4368 (≈6 months)	0.928	0.82	0.9999998	0.99997	0.999995	0.99982
43 680 (≈5 years)	0.475	0.14	0.997	0.97	0.966	0.87
87 360 (≈10 years)	0.225	0.019	0.96	0.79	0.71	0.45

It is stated in (AVI72b) that initial experimental tests on the STAR have verified the effectiveness of the error detecting codes used on the STAR words and the coverage provided by the TARP for each functional unit. The tests, involving the introduction of noise bursts on the buses, demonstrated 99.5 - 100% proper recovery. Limited tests on the adequacy of the TARP for error detection, fault diagnosis and recovery demonstrated 90-100% coverage for the various processors and memory modules.

The overhead associated with a STAR computer clearly depends upon the number of spares that are provided. If one spare of each functional unit was provided the extra cost has been estimated at about 150% (i.e. 60% overhead) (NEU72).

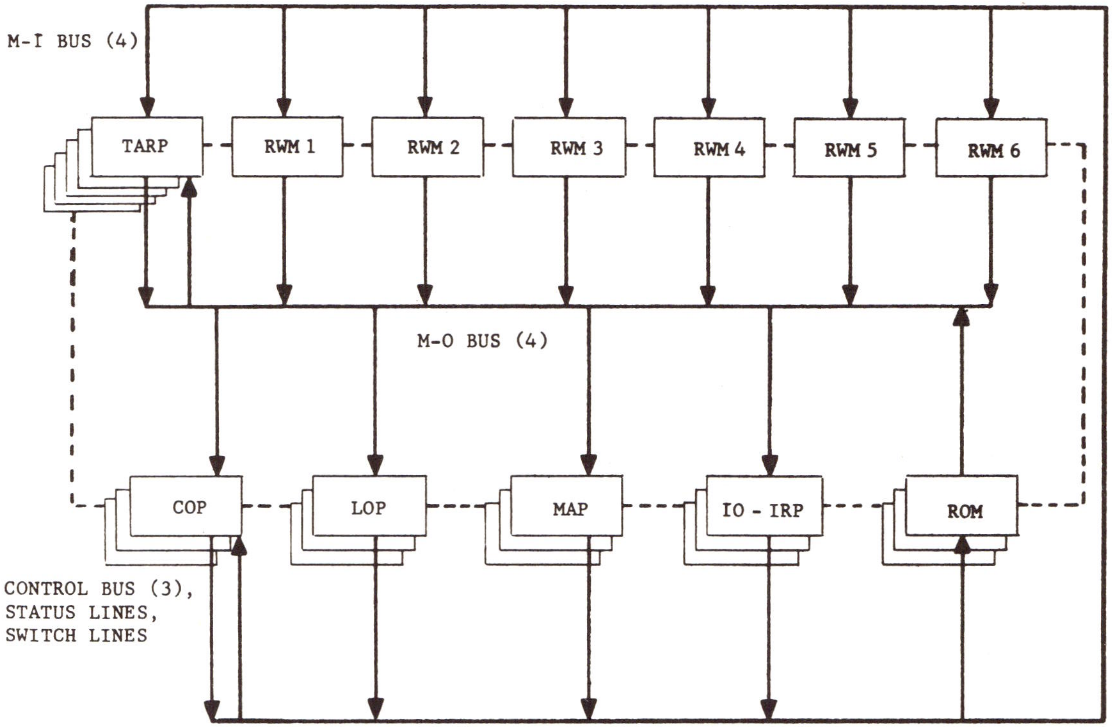

Figure A3.1 - STAR computer organisation

APPENDIX 4: THE NEWCASTLE RELIABILITY PROJECT

The U.K. Science Research Council sponsored research project on the design of highly reliable computing systems was started at the University of Newcastle upon Tyne in 1972. In contrast to the other projects described in these appendices, the principal goal of this project is to investigate techniques for providing fault tolerance for unpredicted faults such as those due to design inadequacies, particularly in complex software systems. This work has led to the development of a number of program structuring techniques and associated mechanisms, several of which have been investigated by means of experimental (software based) implementations.

The initial work concentrated on the problems of fault tolerance in a single sequential process, and is documented in (HOR74). An experimental implementation, the EML system, is summarised in the next section. Extensions of this work to deal with cooperating parallel processes, and systems implemented using multiple levels of interpretation, are discussed in (RAN75). Much more sophisticated fault tolerant multi-level systems are described in (VER77) and (BAN77) which detail, respectively, a filing system implementation, and a scheme for fault tolerance in sets of processes competing for shared resources. A brief description of these two systems, each of which addresses a rather different aspect of the problem of tolerating a wide variety of unanticipated faults, is presented at the end of this appendix.

A4.1 The EML System

As mentioned above, one of the principal goals of the project was to investigate techniques for tolerating faults at the software level in a system. The first experimental implementation in a system supporting fault tolerance for a single sequential process, was the EML system, which is documented in (SIM74) and (AND76).

This system provides facilities for a programmer to specify standby-spare algorithms in a program. The program structure that has been developed for this purpose is called the recovery block structure.

Recovery blocks provide a means for expressing nested atomic actions and for specifying a final programmed check on the acceptability of the results of an atomic action. This check is referred to as the acceptance test. The recovery block structure also enables zero or more alternative algorithms (called "alternates") to act as standby-spares for the atomic action. Figure A4.1 (taken from (AND76) illustrates the form of a simple recovery block example.

<u>ensure</u>

data still valid   "acceptance test"

<u>by</u>

apply fast update   "normal algorithm"

<u>elseby</u>

apply slow but sure update   "standby-spare 1"

<u>elseby</u>

warning ("update not applied") "standby-spare 2"

<u>elseerror</u>

<u>Figure A4.1 A simple recovery block</u>

The functioning of a recovery block is as follows: the first algorithm of the recovery block is executed, followed by the evaluation of the acceptance test. If the acceptance test fails, then the next algorithm in the block is attempted. (This also occurs if an error is detected during the execution of an alternate.) However, before this next algorithm is invoked, the state of the program is automatically reset to its state before the previous alternate was started (i. e. backward error recovery). Thus everything that the program has done since entering the current recovery block is discarded. If the final alternative algorithm (the last standby-spare) does not succeed in reaching and passing the acceptance test, this is treated as an error in the enclosing recovery block (if there is one) which therefore leads to the backward error recovery of the enclosing block.

Because each of the alternates can be designed on the assumption that they start from the same state, their designs can (and preferably should) be independent of each other. The designer of one alternate need have no knowledge of the designs of the other alternates, leave alone any responsibility for coping with any damage that they may have caused. Equally, the designer of a program that contains a recovery block does not necessarily have to concern himself with which of the various alternative algorithms of the recovery block was eventually used. It is therefore argued that the extra size of programs that incorporate recovery blocks as a means of design fault tolerance does not imply any increase in complexity.

The EML system allows the execution of programs in a language which is based on a subset of Pascal, but extended to include recovery blocks. The implementation involves an emulator for the EML language (SIM74), running on one of a pair of linked PDP11/45s. (The second PDP11/45 is used to provide input/output facilities and filestore for these programs - the input/output facilities on the first PDP11/45 are used for injecting faults into, and monitoring the behaviour of emulated programs.)

The system is intended solely as a vehicle for investigating the recovery block approach to the provision of design faults tolerance, and does not contain any specific provisions, nor any replicated hardware components, for dealing with operational faults in the PDP11/45.

A4.2 System Description

The EML system can be thought of as a four level system, although the designs of the bottom two levels, namely the hardware and a small monitor program, are of little relevance to the main aim of the project. Rather, interest is concentrated in the third level, which is the emulator, and the fourth level, the emulated user programs containing recovery blocks.

The emulator interprets what could be described as a "high-level" machine language (EML) which is somewhat akin to that of the Burroughs B6700 computer. Data storage is organised as a stack, and most operations take the top one or two items in the stack as their operands. Information is retained in the EML machine language which indicates the type and range of each variable, and programs are represented as sets of sequences of instructions called "fragments". The fragments reflect the control structure of the original Pascal-like text from which the EML code is compiled.

A4.3 Reliability Strategies

An important role of the third level of the system (the emulator) is to supply an abstraction interface which supports recovery blocks and provides automatic backward error recovery for the user programs (at level 4). The entry to a recovery block establishes a recovery point for the program. However, the programs contain no explicit indication of what needs to be saved in order to provide the recovery point. Rather, the information for the recovery point is automatically saved by the emulator on behalf of the program it is emulating. The recovery point is retained until the successful completion of the recovery block when a deliberate commitment occurs.

1) Error Detection

> The main error detection mechanisms in the EML system are provided at the emulator level (level 3) and at the user program level (level 4).

> The emulator provides all of the (run-time) interface checks on the user program. Such checking detects interface violations such as division by zero, array bound checking, type and range violations, and instruction sequencing errors.

> Error detection at the user level can be programmed in the acceptance test (as well as during the execution of a recovery block by means of assert statements). As described above, the acceptance test, executed at the end of a recovery block,

enables a (programmed) check to be made on the acceptability of the results generated during the execution of that recovery block. This is in accordance with the error detection strategy discussed in Section 5.2.1. That is, the check is (as far as possible) an independent check, made at the last possible moment, before the commitment at the end of the recovery block occurs. The acceptance test takes the form of a boolean expression, but can be based both on the current values of variables, and on the values that the variables had on entry to the current recovery block.

The hardware at the bottom level in the system provides some interface checks on the emulator, and errors such as addressing errors and illegal instructions are detected.

2) Fault Treatment

The form of fault treatment is very simple. Since the intention is to cope with faults whose exact position and form are unanticipated, no attempt is made at fault diagnosis and location, although errors are logged for off-line inspection. Instead, after error recovery (described below) the next alternative algorithm is used as a temporary standby-spare to cope with just the particular set of input data, the normal (first) algorithm will again be used. Thus the aim is to continue to provide service until there is an opportunity for manual fault diagnosis and repair.

3) Damage Assessment

Damage assessment is equally simple, and is based entirely on the a priori reasoning that the damage caused by the user program will be corrected by the error recovery described below. It is also assumed that the emulator program itself will not suffer any damage.

4) Error Recovery

The main error recovery strategy of interest is that provided for the user programs (at level 4). At this level the error recovery is complete backward error recovery of the program, and is implemented by the emulator at level 3 as forward error recovery (and clearly presumes the reliability of the level 3 mechanism for saving recovery points). The backward error recovery is also dependent for its effectiveness on the reasonableness of the overheads involved. The emulator implements the "recovery cache" mechanism (also known as the "recursive cache"), described in (HOR74), in order to implement this backward error recovery. This involves monitoring the activity of a user program, and saving just those components of its state that are modified in a given recovery block, at the time such modification is first attempted. Therefore, only those state components that need to be saved are held in the recovery cache, which in general will consist of a set of "regions", one for each recovery block.

The emulator also utilises forward error recovery, in the form of exception handlers, to deal with errors in its own execution detected by the hardware level of the system. To try to recover from these errors, the emulator (optimistically) assumes that any damage will be confined to the state space of the user programs, and it therefore forces the user program to back up in an attempt (perhaps vain) to repair any damage.

A4.4 Reliability Evaluation

Although no exhaustive evaluation of the EML system has been carried out, various level 4 programs have been written and tested to demonstrate the effectiveness of the recovery block scheme. (AND76) presents a more detailed description of how these programs and the experimiental system coped with both deliberate and accidental faults. One of the features of the emulator is that it allows errors to be injected (at run-time) into the code of the level 4 programs. This facility has been used by the project members and its visitors to corrupt certain sections of a test program in an attempt to prevent the program from producing its correct results. In fact this has rarely been achieved. The few successful attempts, early in the development of the system, were always attributable to design inadequacies, (AND76) reports some cases when successful error recovery was (somewhat fortuitously) achieved.

A4.5 The Recoverable Filing System

This experimental system, which is described in (VER77a), is based on a microprogrammed emulator of O-code running on a Burroughs B1700 computer, and makes use of the OS6 single-user operating system (STO72). This is a system written in BCPL which compiles into O-code. The O-code language and its emulator have been expanded to allow BCPL programs to incorporate recovery blocks, and to provide a recovery cache mechanism for simple variables. However, this system differs from the EML system in that facilities are provided for a programmer to declare new types of variables and provide explicit means of error recovery for them. By doing so, the programmer will effectively be designing a new abstraction interface which provides automatic backward error recovery for the users of that interface. This can be done repeatedly, so as to provide a general form of multi-level system, in which the actual number of levels is not pr-ordained (VER77b).

In most cases a given abstraction interface provides means of resetting only some of the objects to the values that they had at an earlier recovery point. Other objects, so called "unrecoverable objects", will not have this automatic reset facility available. For example, in the particular case of the recoverable filing system, the O-code interface provides recoverable working store words, and unrecoverable backing store blocks. The operating system incorporates error recovery mechanisms in the filing system routines. As a result, users are provided with an abstraction interface in which, should an error be detected, even the information held on the backing store in the filing system will be reset to the state it was in at an earlier user-level recovery point. Full details of this scheme are contained in the referenced papers - other aspects of the recoverable filing system, such as the strategies used for error detection, fault treatment and damage assessment, have much in common with those used in the EML system, so will not be described here.

A4.6   Resource Contention System

In contrast to the two earlier experimental systems, the resource contention system described in (BAN77) attempts to handle some of the problems of fault tolerance among sets of coexisting processes. This system is being implemented on a PDP11/45, the actual implementation being based on that of Concurrent Pascal (BRI75).

The system uses a rather different scheme for providing error recovery in multi-level systems from that used in the recoverable filing system - a detailed analysis of these differences is provided by (AND77). The purpose of the system is to enable a set of otherwise independent concurrent user processes to share a fixed set of common resources. Each type of resource (such as printer, or storage area) is managed by a special kind of monitor termed a "recoverable monitor". User programs are constrained in the way they obtain, make use of, and release resources by programming language features based on the "class" and "inner" concepts in the Simula language.

Each user process can make use of recovery blocks to deal with unanticipated faults. The system enables the user processes to maintain their intended independence, even during error recovery. Thus, despite contention for common resources, there is no risk of the domino effect described in Section 5.5.1, nor any need for the saving and discarding of recovery points to be synchronised, as for example in the conversation scheme discussed in (RAN75).

APPENDIX 5: THE PLESSEY SYSTEM 250 COMPUTER

System 250 (COS72) is a multi-processor system designed by the Plessey Co. Ltd. of the UK for real-time communication applications where highly reliable operation is required. The project, jointly sponsored with the National Research and Development Corporation, started in January 1969 and a prototype was completed by the end of 1971. Currently the system is in quantity production.

The initial application of the system was for stored-program control of a telephone and data switching exchange. A typical requirement for this application is a mean time between system failures of 50 years, where a system failure is defined as a cessation of service lasting over 10 minutes. The system is intended therefore to be resilient against both permanent and transient faults and similarly against software design faults. To achieve this fault tolerance, System 250 uses a variety of techniques including: replication, monitoring, program-rollback, and reconfiguration. A detailed description of the reliability mechanisms is given in (REP72), on which this survey is largely based. One of the diagrams presented here (Figure A5.2) is also taken from this paper, while the other (Figure A5.1) is taken from (COS72).

A5.1 System Description

From the viewpoint of reliability, the Plessey System 250 can be regarded as a four level system. At the lowest level is the hardware and above this at level 2 is the kernel of the recovery system, called "secondary recovery". Level 3 consists of the executive for the system; besides performing basic supervisor, input/output and backing store functions it also contains some "initial recovery" facilities. The final (fourth) level consists of the application programs. Very little information is given on the structure of these applicaton programs in (COS72) and (REP72) thus we will largely ignore them in this survey. In this section we briefly describe the hardware and software (a combined view of levels 2-4) and in the next section the structure of the secondary and initial recovery levels are examined.

Figure A5.1 illustrates a static structuring of the hardware level of System 250, which consists of groups of functionally equivalent processors, stores, buses and input/output devices. Each processor in the system has its own dedicated bus for communicating with the stores or the input/output network. Since processors do not perform dedicated functions in the system, any processor can carry out the tasks of any other processor. Similarly any store can replace any other store.

Two details of the processor hardware are also worth noting, namely the capability and fault interrupt mechanisms (HAM72), because of the influence they have on the reliability aspects of the computer system. The capability mechanism for example, provides a secure store protection facility, thus reducing the possibility of recovery-related programs being over-written in the event of a hardware or software fault. The fault interrupt mechanism provides entry to these recovery programs.

The three levels of software that run on the hardware level are dynamically structured into what (REP72) terms "functional areas". (REP72) implies that functional areas can contain processes but processes cannot contain functional areas. Each functional area besides performing a specific task also contains its own error detection and recovery facilities.

A5.2 Reliability Strategies

The System 250 computer incorporates two separate, but interlinked, reliability strategies. The first of these termed "initial recovery" exists as part of the executive at level 3 and forms a first line of defence. If this level is assessed as having been unable to cope with the situation, responsibility is passed to the "secondary recovery" strategy at level 2. Each of these strategies involves a series of progressively more drastic actions. At the start the action which causes least disruption to the system is used. If this fails to clear the fault, as indicated by further error reports, then increasingly powerful and hence more disruptive recovery actions are used until the fault is presumed cleared, as indicated by the absence of further errors. The initial recovery programs receive simple error indications and provide a number of basic recovery actions. In contrast, secondary recovery software can perform recovery actions that lead, ultimately, to a complete system test and general restart. To give extra reliability secondary recovery software (level 2) is replicated with one complete copy being held in each store module. The mechanisms that implement these two strategies are illustrated by Figure A5.2 and are described below.

1) Error Detection

The error detection mechanisms within System 250 are of three basic types: hardware checking circuits, software checks and test routines. At the hardware level error detection circuits (e.g. capability checks, parity checks, microprogram checks) exist within each processor and, if they detect an error, cause a fault interrupt to be generated automatically. This causes the processor to discontinue execution of the current process and switch to the "fault interrupt" process instead.

Another set of errors are detected by software consistency checks and by time-outs that monitor overall system performance. The final method of detecting errors involves diagnostic test routines (auditors) that are run in background mode and test specific hardware components. As can be seen from Figure A5.2, these software methods of error detection have corresponding modules in both the initial and secondary recovery levels.

2) Fault Treatment

Having detected an error System 250, as shown below, makes an extensive effort to locate and remove the corresponding fault. Information concerning the possible location of faults is built up by the two recovery levels. This information is collected in a variety of ways, often depending on the method of error detection employed. For example if the detection mechanism implicates a particular unit (as indicated at the hardware level by check circuits or test routines) an error count associated with the unit is incremented so as to detect persistently failing devices. In order to test such devices, a process at level 3 called the System Monitor (Figure A5.2) can invoke localised test routines. If a particular hardware unit is identified as containing faults, the system is reconfigured to isolate the unit.

After trying to locate, and failing to remove, a persistent fault, the initial recovery level relinquishes the task to the secondary recovery level (level 2). Level 2 will then make repeated attempts to locate the faulty unit using test sequences that can be extended to cover all units within the control system. As a last resort it will selectively reconfigure the system on a trial basis in an attempt to find a viable system configuration. How quickly this is achieved depends on the nature of the fault; (REP72) states that " a medium sized system can work through all possible combinations of the central control equipment in approximately two minutes".

Processors which have assessed themselves as containing faults (i.e. process a fault interrupt) can automatically remove themselves from the viable configuration in the following way. When a processor detects a fault interrupt it firstly disables all its current capabilities thus preventing further access to the store it was using. It then enters a test program which is arranged as a maze that checks the hardware and "read-only" blocks (programs and data) associated with a processor recovery program. If an error is detected another fault interrupt occurs and the processor attempts the test using programs from the next available storage module. Thus a faulty processor is constrained to cycle repeatedly through the storage system.

3) <u>Damage Assessment</u>

From the System 250 documentation it would appear that damage assessment is integrated with system error recovery at level 2 and 3. For example, if an error is detected by software checks in an application program (level 4), then the initial recovery level seems to assume that any damage is within the functional area or process that detected the error and hence causes the functional area or process to restart. Should this assumption prove incorrect, further repeated errors cause level 2 to perform a general system test.

4) <u>Error Recovery</u>

Three stages of error recovery action which provide progressively more extensive restart facilities are used in System 250. These are referred to as: process restart, area restart and area reload.

Each process in the system has a defined recovery action which can be activated by the initial recovery level if the process detects an error. This is called a process restart and may involve forward error recovery such as regenerating data areas or backward error recovery which may vary from restarting the process to abandoning it.

Each functional area within the system also has a defined recovery action that can be activated by the initial recovery level. This is referred to as an area restart and is used to regenerate read/write data from duplicate files. An area restart can provide complete data regeneration, but often certain processes that were being executed at the time the error was detected are abandoned.

The final stage of recovery is an area reload and can include, at the extreme, reloading the whole system. To achieve an area reload each functional area has a defined recovery line whch will allow processing to be restarted from read-only, sum-checked files. These files are replicated and held on write-protected areas of the backing store. This form of recovery, handled by the secondary recovery level, abandons all current processes and reinitialises the system.

No mention is made in (REP72) of the problems that information-flow between processes and/or functional areas would cause. It is uncertain whether these are in fact atomic actions, or whether such information-flow as does occur is compensated or treated as insignificant.

A5.3 Reliability Evaluation

The designers state that system reliability calculations have been carried out using estimated MTBF's and MTTR's of system hardware modules. These in turn, they say, were calculated from measured failure rates of individual hardware components. The processor self-test program has been tested using a logic level simulation program for the processor, into which a "large number and variety of faults were injected". The reliabiity evaluation is expected to continue for some time, especially in the light of running application programs. No reliability figures are supplied in (COS72) or (REP72).

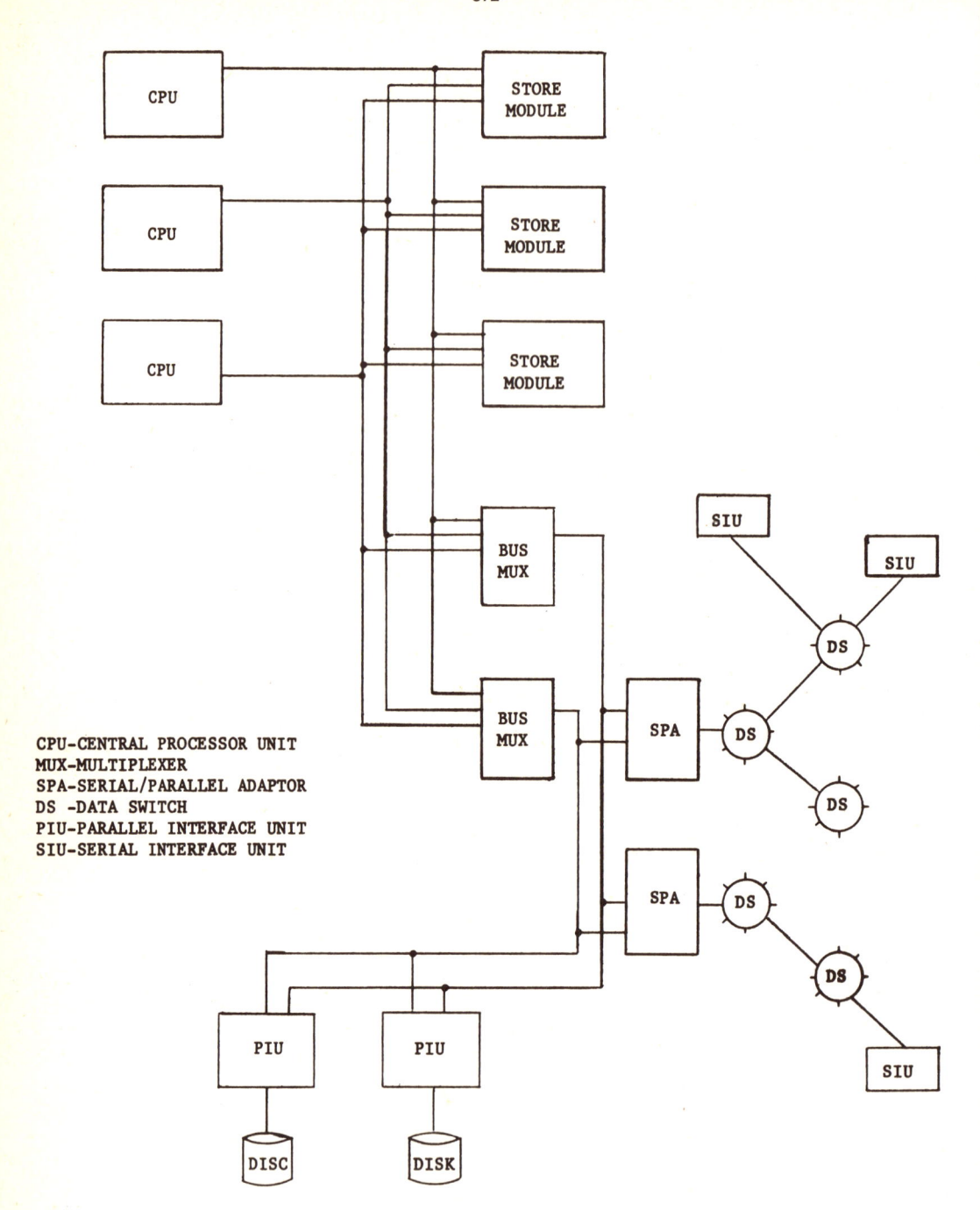

CPU-CENTRAL PROCESSOR UNIT
MUX-MULTIPLEXER
SPA-SERIAL/PARALLEL ADAPTOR
DS -DATA SWITCH
PIU-PARALLEL INTERFACE UNIT
SIU-SERIAL INTERFACE UNIT

<u>Figure A5.1 - System 250 Hardware Configuration</u>

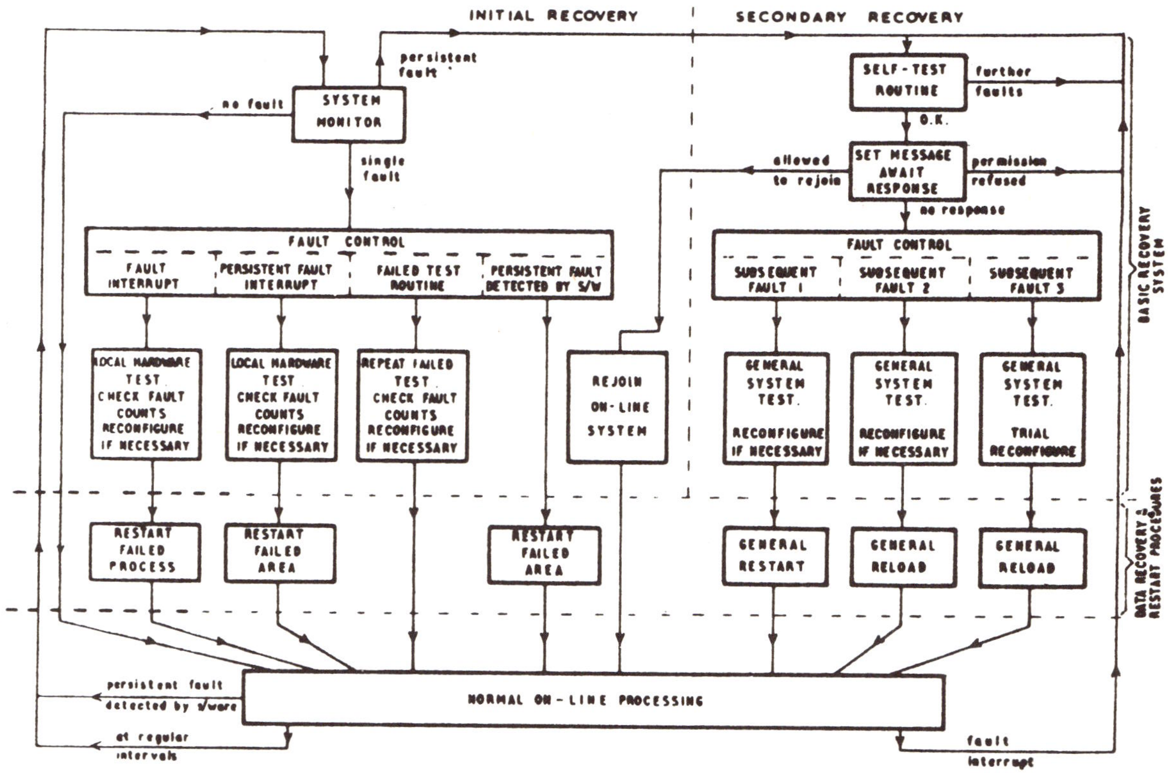

Figure A5.2 - System 250 Reliability Structure

APPENDIX 6: PLURIBUS

Pluribus (HEA73) is a packet-switching communications multi-processor designed as a new form of switching node (IMP) for the ARPA Network. Bolt, Beranek and Newman Inc. started design of the multi-processor system in 1972 and a prototype, 13 processor system was constructed by early 1974.

The machine, besides being capable of a high bandwidth in order to handle the 1.5 megabaud data circuits which are planned for the network, is also intended to be highly reliable (ORN75) operating 24 hours a day, all year round. Pluribus is designed to recover automatically within seconds of detecting an error and to survive not only transient faults but also the failure of any single component. To achieve this fault tolerance Pluribus uses techniques such as: replication, isolation of components (e.g. processors and programs), monitoring, process restart and reconfiguration. The information presented in this survey is primarily based on (ORN75), while Figure A6.1 and A6.2 are taken from (HEA73) and (ORN75) respectively.

A6.1 System Description

When discussing the system structure of Pluribus, particularly with regard to its reliability, we have found it useful to view the system as consisting of four levels and three interfaces.

Levels		Interfaces
4	application program	
	---------------------	IMP
3	second software level	
	---------------------	multi-computer
2	first software level	
	---------------------	hardware architecture
1	hardware	

The bottom level is formed by the hardware (processors, memories, etc.) of Pluribus which supports three software levels. The first and second software levels are concerned with the control and reliability of the system, while the third level consists of the application program that performs the packet-switching role of the IMP.

Figure A6.1 illustrates the hardware level static structure of the Pluribus system. The system is designed round three types of bus (processor, memory, input/output) that are joined together by special bus couplers which allow units on one bus to access those on another. Each bus, together with its own power supply and cooling, is mounted in a separate unit. A processor bus contains two processors each with its own local 4k memory which stores code that is either frequently run or used for recovery purposes. A memory bus contains the segments of a large memory, common to all the processors, while an input/output (I/O) bus houses device controllers as well as central resources such as system clocks. A feature of Pluribus is its treatment of hardware units (processors, memory, buses) as sets of equivalent resources. There is for example, no specialisation of processors for particular system functions and no assignment of priority amongst the processors, such as designating one as master.

The hardware level, in addition to providing conventional processing and storage facilities, contains three components: a "pseudo interrupt device" which facilitates processor scheduling, a "60 Hz interrupt" and a "bus timer". The function of these latter two components relate to the problem of monitoring software activity and assuring its continued progress. The three levels of software seem to be conceptual, based on the assumed correctness of the software design, and to the hardware they appear as a single real-time program. This single program, which includes the application program (i.e. IMP job) as well as the control and reliability programs, is divided into small pieces called <u>strips</u>, each of which handles a particular task. Tasks can initiate other tasks but cannot communicate directly with them while running; communication is handled by leaving messages in common memory.

When a task needs to be performed the name of the appropriate strip is placed on a queue of tasks to be run. Each processor, when it is not running a strip, repeatedly checks this queue for work. When a name appears in the queue the next available processor will remove it and execute the corresponding strip. Since all processors frequently access this queue contention for it is high. For this reason the queue is implemented in hardware by a special pseudo interrupt device (Figue A6.1). By limiting the maximum execution time of a strip to 400 msecs (the time the most urgent task can afford to wait) and priority-ordering the task queue, a number of scheduling and multiprogramming difficulties such as saving and restoring the machine state, have been eliminated.

Above the hardware architecture interface, the first software level views the processors and stores as distinct virtual computers for each of which it creates a context, so that the computer can function reliably. To achieve this reliabilty, two components are used within each computer, called the "code-tester" and the "individual". The code-tester monitors the operation of the computer. It performs such tasks as checking all local memory code and safeguards all control and "lock" mechanisms. With the help of the code-tester, the individual provides an abstraction (multi-computer) interface with the second software level. Each individual finds all memories and processors it considers usable and attempts to form a dialogue with the other individuals so they can work together as reliable virtual computers above the multi-computer interface.

The second software level is concerned with the problem of forming the separate virtual computers provided at the multi-computer interface into a single reliable computer system. This task is performed by three components, called the "consensus", the "IMP-system-reliability" and the "IMP-system". The consensus monitors the interactions of the separate virtual computers and provides a single computer system at the communications interface with the IMP-system-reliability. Specific tasks performed by the consensus include checking all common memory code, finding all usable hardware resources (processors, memories, etc.) from information supplied by the individuals, testing each resource and creating a table of operable ones.

The IMP-system-reliability monitors the operation and, in particular, the data structures of the computer system (the IMP), and helps to assure its reliability. It is assisted in this task by the last component at this level, the IMP-system, which monitors the behaviour of the ARPA Network and will not allow the IMP to cooperate with seemingly irresponsible network behaviour. Above the abstraction (IMP) interface the application program can view the IMP as a reliable, fast sequential computer with a large store.

A6.2 Reliability Strategies

For the purpose of ensuring fault tolerance the hardware and software components of Pluribus are organised into special functional units called <u>reliability subsystems</u>. These reliability subsystems are the components (e.g. code-tester, consensus, etc.) outlined above in the discussion of levels and interfaces. The notion of reliability subsystems seems to assume that all faults are masked above the interface and that the subsystem on the other side of the interface has no responsibility for detecting and coping with errors in the lower subsystem.

A reliability subsystem is some grouping of system resources (hardware, software and/or data structures) whose integrity is verified as a unit by a self-contained test mechanism. Moreover each subsystem contains a reset mechanism which will return it to some specified initial recovery point. (ORN75) describes the entire Pluribus system as being made up of such subsystems, which communicate via data structures, and which appear conceptually to operate asynchronously. Furthermore these subsystems are organised into a "chain" (Figure A6.2) in which each member monitors the behaviour of the next member of the chain, and may externally activate the reset mechanism of that system, if it detects some malfunction.

The monitoring of subsystems is carried out using watchdog timers, which ensure that each subsystem passes through a predefined cycle of activity. This is done by including code in the cycle to restart the timer, so that if the cycle is not executed properly the timer will run out and cause the monitoring subsystem to detect an error. The defined cycle must also contain an execution of a self-test mechanism, so that correct passage through the cycle provides strong evidence of the reliability of the subsystem. Another aspect of the "chain" structure is that subsystems low in the chain attempt to provide and "guarantee" the reliability of some components used by higher subsystems.

1) Error Detection

The error detection strategies used by the reliability

subsystems of Pluribus are mainly based on watchdog timers, supported at the hardware level by the 60 Hz interrupt. These facilities are used within level 2 (the first software level) by the code-tester to monitor the operation of each processor and store. Firstly it sumchecks all low level code (including itself), secondly it ensures that all subsystems are receiving a share of the processors attention and finally it safeguards that "locks" to critical resources do not hang up. Also at level 2 is the individual that performs error detection at the interface with level 3. An individual running from the local store of each processor performs the task of locating all usable resources. This involves addressing every device in the system and every page in memory and listing those which are operable.

At level 3 error detection is handled by the consensus, performing such tasks as sumchecking all common code and maintaining a timer for each processor. The consensus will count down these timers in order to detect uncooperative or dead processors. The IMP-system-reliability also at level 3 detects errors in the IMP-system by monitoring its cycle of behaviour and watching its data structures. Finally at level 3 the IMP-system monitors the behaviour of the other IMPs in the ARPA Network and will not respond to erroneous operations. In return the ARPA Network, through the Network Control Center, monitors the behaviour of the IMP and if it detects a dead IMP trys to restart it remotely.

2) Fault Treatment

Given that an error has been detected in a subsystem of the Pluribus, another subsystem will attempt to locate and remove the fault. For example at the hardware level the bus timer will reset an inactive bus after after 1 sec, which clears any hung device commands. To allow for faults in hardware resources all bus couplers have a program-controllable switch that inhibits transactions via the coupler. The individuals at level 2 use these switches to effectively "amputate" a bus by turning off all couplers from that bus. This mechanism is protected from capricious use by requiring a particular data word (password) to be stored in a control register of the bus coupler before use.

Fault treatment data is built up by each individual (indicating the set of devices considered operable) in regions in common memory. This information is used by the consensus at level 3 to determine the "true" set of usable hardware resources, by a form of replicated voting. The consensus can also run tests on resources to determine the extent of a fault.

3) Damage Assessment

Within Pluribus damage assessment seems to be based entirely on a single strategy - it is assumed that everything that the subsystem has done since starting a task is damaged and hence the task being performed is abandoned. This strategy is adequate in Pluribus, as discussed below, because of the fault tolerant environment in which an IMP operates.

4) Error Recovery

When an error is detected in a reliability subsystem, the monitoring subsystem performs backward error recovery by re-initialising the reliability subsystem. Each processor in the Pluribus system, for example, can reset or reload any other processor by means of password protected paths in the hardware. The notion of reliability subsystems is vulnerable to a simultaneous transient fault (e.g. loss of power) of all processors). However the Network Control Center has access to the above recovery facilities and can therefore restart an IMP if necessary.

A6.3 Reliability Evaluation

The designers of the Pluribus were aided by the fact that the system could be developed under favourable circumstances: (1) the initial application and a prior software implementation in a standard machine were well understood and (2) the application lent itself to fragmentation amongst sets of equivalent resources. Moreover, the environment surrounding a Pluribus system is quite tolerant of faults. Hence if an error is detected in a subsystem the particular task it was performing can be abandoned and the subsystem restarted, since the task will be automatically retried by the ARPA Network. Thus numerous issues concerned with information-flow between the Pluribus and its environment, and such problems as the need for compensation have been avoided.

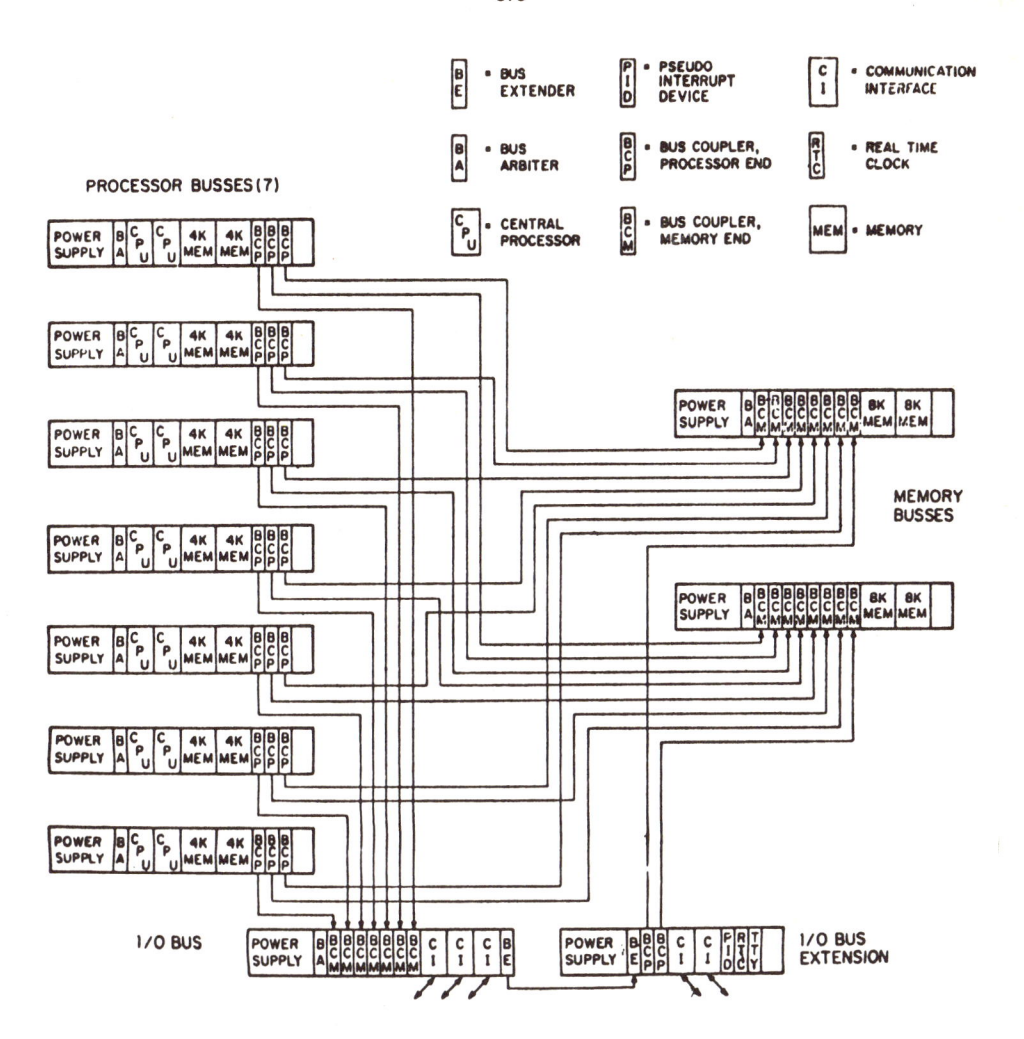

Figure A6.1 - Pluribus Hardware Configuration

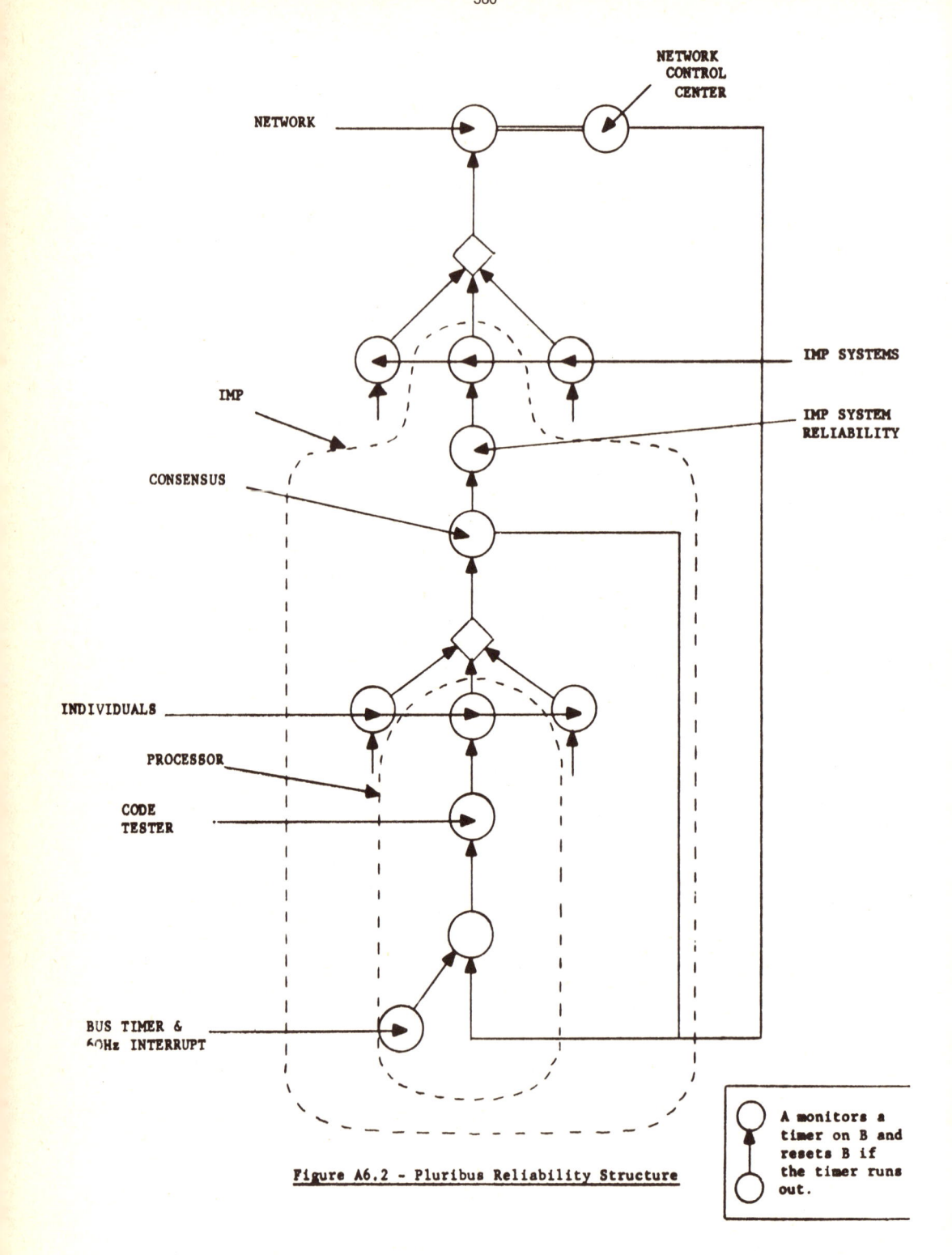

Figure A6.2 - Pluribus Reliability Structure

APPENDIX 7: PRIME

PRIME is a computing system that was being designed and built during 1970 - 1973 at the University of California, Berkeley. The research was sponsored by the Advanced Research Projects Agency. The main description of the PRIME architecture is presented in (BAS72).

The design aim for PRIME was to construct a general purpose multi-access interactive system that would provide a continuous service for the majority of its (terminal) users, despite the occurrence of both hardware and software failures. It is a modular system which has a small set of different functional units (e.g. processors, memory modules, discs) each of which may be replicated many times. These resources are dynamically allocated to the users as required. PRIME was also designed to have a minimum amount of redundant hardware, and thus to be compatible to other systems in terms of cost, computing power and capability, while having signficantly enhanced fault tolerance and availability. The system was aiming to provide continuous availability to the users, with a minimum performance never below 75% of the maximum (NEU72).

A7.1 System Description

The PRIME system can be regarded as a four level system :-
    4   user processes
    3   system software
    2   processing subsystems
    1   hardware modules

At level 1 the PRIME system has a highly modular structure. Figure A7.1 illustrates a static structuring of the components at this level; the main functional units that are replicated include the primary memory modules, secondary storage modules and processing modules. Every processor module is permanently connected to only 64K of primary memory. Each 8K memory block consists of two independent 4K word units and a 4 * 2 switching matrix, with every memory block being connected to at least three processors. The actual mechanism for dynamically allocating and protecting memory is via the Map which is associated with the processing module. The discs in the PRIME system contain special hardware to implement protection for their users. The External Access Network, which is not replicated, basically allows any processor to communicate with any other processor, any disc or any external device. However, at a given time one processor port can be designated as the controlling port and as such has the ability to control such communications. Finally, each terminal in the system is connected to two processors.

Level 2 in the PRIME system consists of processing sub-systems, each comprised of a processor, primary memory and secondary storage. These sub-systems are completely self-contained (and identical), and can function independently. If configured and protected correctly, the sub-systems may be regarded as logically and electrically distinct (BAS72).

The system software controlling the PRIME system can be regarded as being in level 3, and is divided into two parts: the Control

Monitor; and the Extension of the Control Monitor (ECM). The Control Monitor is in general control of the system and its resources. It handles tasks such as scheduling the level 4 user processes on processor sub-systems, resource allocation and communication between processes and communication with the external devices (both via the External Access Network). The Control Monitor also implements the protection between the sub-systems using the mechanisms provided in level 1.

Basically the system operates with one of the processor sub-systems acting as the control processor, running the Control Monitor program. The other processors act as problem processors, dedicated to running the user processes at level 4. The Control Monitor is run continuously, and is never multiprogrammed with user processes.

Each problem processor has some system-wide control functions, and contains the Extension of the Control Monitor (ECM). This is actually part of the Control Monitor, performing local actions on its behalf within each sub-system. These actions include the setting of the Map entries of the memory access and disc control units, and saving, swapping and restoring the state of user processes (as necessary) at the end of their job steps (the problem processors also are not multiprogrammed). Unlike the Control Monitor, the ECM is microprogrammed in the processor. Microcode in each processor is also responsible for controlling the terminals, communicating directly with the Control Monitor; there is no direct relationship between the terminals connected to a processing module and the user processes executing on it.

The user processes in level 4 in the PRIME system consist of a local monitor and the user job. The local monitor is implemented in software and is resident in the problem processor. Each user process may have its own copy of a local monitor. Basically, the local monitor provides file and working-set management for the user process. However, it is only concerned with the user process and does not have any system-wide functions, and it is isolated from the rest of the system. Hence it will not be considered further in this discussion.

Various features have been built into the PRIME system in an attempt to ensure isolation between the processor sub-systems, and to guarantee that no process can gain unauthorised access to the environment of any other processes, even in the presence of software and hardware faults. Memory sharing is not allowed in PRIME; for example, the special hardware in the disc units ensures that a process can access only the disc cylinders that the control processor has allocated to it. Similarly, the control processor is only allowed access to its files and unallocated disc cylinders. Data sharing PRIME is accomplished by having the owner process send the data as a message to the destination process. Interprocess communication takes place via the External Access Network. However, direct communication between problem processors is not allowed and such communication has to take place via the Control Monitor.

A7.2 Reliability Strategies

PRIME is a system that was designed to provide a continuous service to the majority of its users in spite of internal software and hardware failures. The fault tolerance of the system is provided by the replication of the major units in the system, and by the spontaneous reconfiguration mechanism which removes faulty units from the system in order that they can be manually repaired (BOR73). However, there is little significant hardware redundancy in the system; all working units are in use for all of the time and there are no standby spares. When a failure occurs the remaining system is (spontaneously) reconfigured to run without that unit. Thus the PRIME system is a fail-softly system, which provides a graceful degradation in service when a failure occurs (BOR72). Any degradation will remain until the faulty unit has been repaired and returned to the system.

1) Error Detection

   The main error detection mechanisms in the PRIME system reside in level 1 (hardware modules) and in level 3 (system software).

   At level 1, straightforward error detection mechanisms were designed into the logic external to the processors. For example, the primary memory contains a parity bit, and the disc units detect attempted protection violations. Error injection methods are used to periodically confirm the integrity of these detection mechanisms. The processor modules, however, have no internal error detection mechanisms. Instead, each processor has a Control Panel associated with it, which allows software controlled single stepping and monitoring of that processor for the purpose of diagnostic checking.

   The Control Monitor and the Extension of the Control Monitor in level 3 have the responsibility for continually monitoring the system. Error checking and diagnosis of the overall system is performed by the Control Monitor; error, consistency and diagnosis checks local to the processing subsystem are performed by the ECM. The Control Monitor is responsible for diagnostic checking by periodically requesting each problem processor to run a surveillance test on itself and to return a computed result. Such tests are run at the end of a job step. In a similar manner, the problem processors also request the control processor to run a surveillance test on itself.

   Clearly, however, the control processor cannot be permitted to make arbitrary mistakes. The PRIME system attempts to limit the propagation of errors by requiring that an independent interface check is made on every critical function performed by every processor (FAB73). The independent check is performed either by another processor making a consistency check or by a piece of hardware making a validity check. Thus at level 3, the system software has to be designed so that every one of its decisions can be checked independently, for example, functions of the Control Monitor such as resource allocation and file transfers must be double checked. Similarly, as all interprocess communication takes place via the control processor, it can make an independent check on such transmissions.

2) <u>Fault Treatment</u>

When an error is detected a spontaneous reconfiguration scheme is invoked; the first stage of the reconfiguration, implemented by dedicated level 1 components, causes a (hopefully) healthy processor to be established as the control processor (this is described in more detail in (BOR73(). Since all of the processors are identical, any could assume the role of the control processor. Once a control processor has been established, the level 3 Control Monitor is responsible for locating the faulty unit. In the case of a suspected processor (which is prevented from becoming the control processor in the initial reconfiguration), the Control Panel is used by the Control Monitor to step that processor through a set of diagnostic routines. (The documentation does not make it clear what sequence of events enables the other units in the system to be designated as faulty, and what happens if a faulty unit cannot be located). If the faulty unit has been located, the Control Monitor simply removes it from its table of available system resources, after which the unit can be manually powered down for (manual) removal and repair, while the rest of the system continues to run. Thus the PRIME system will fail-softly, i.e. the performance will be (gracefully) degraded as units become faulty.

One unit in PRIME that has not been replicated is the External Access Network. However this unit has been designed as a distributed network so that any internal failure in it manifests itself as a failure of a small part of the network and appears as a failure of a unit that was attached to the node that failed. As the system was designed to run with failures in the units, it should be able to run with arbitrary failures in the network.

3) <u>Damage Assessment</u>

The damage assessment in the PRIME system is apparently based on the a priori assumptions that (a) the double checking scheme described above prevents the propagation of errors; and (b) the level 3 system software and the double checking scheme have all been designed and implemented correctly. In particular, it is assumed that all functions of the Control Monitor (and the ECM) can be independently checked, and as the control processor is assumed to be arbitrarily (but not maliciously) misbehaving at any given time, the double checking scheme can detect both hardware failures that would lead to system wide problems, and software faults that would lead to interprocess interference (BOR73).

Also, the system does not prevent a level 4 process from

corrupting its own data space, either because of a fault in its software or because of a fault in that processor (the processor is only checked out at the end of a job step). It is assumed, therefore, that failures should be confined to a single job step of a single process (BOR73). However, as the system does not insist that the job steps are atomic (intended interprocess intercommunication is allowed), then it would appear that arbritary damage could be done. There do not appear to be any mechanisms in the PRIME system for dynamically assessing such damage.

4) Error Recovery

There does not appear to be any form of explicit error recovery implemented in the PRIME system above level 1. No mechanisms are described for providing error recovery to the level 4 processes, and it appears to be assumed that all other errors, particularly those caused by the level 3 system software, are always detected and masked from higher levels.

A7.3 Reliability Evaluation

There do not appear to be any recent publications concerning the current status of the PRIME system or any empirical evaluations of its reliability. (BOR74) presents an analysis of the PRIME system using a reliability model which allowed the system's reliability to be estimated. This provided evidence that a significant improvement in reliability is obtained in the PRIME system over systems incorporating no fault tolerance, for example the reliability of PRIME after 1000 hours service was estimated as being at least 60% better than that of a system with fault tolerance.

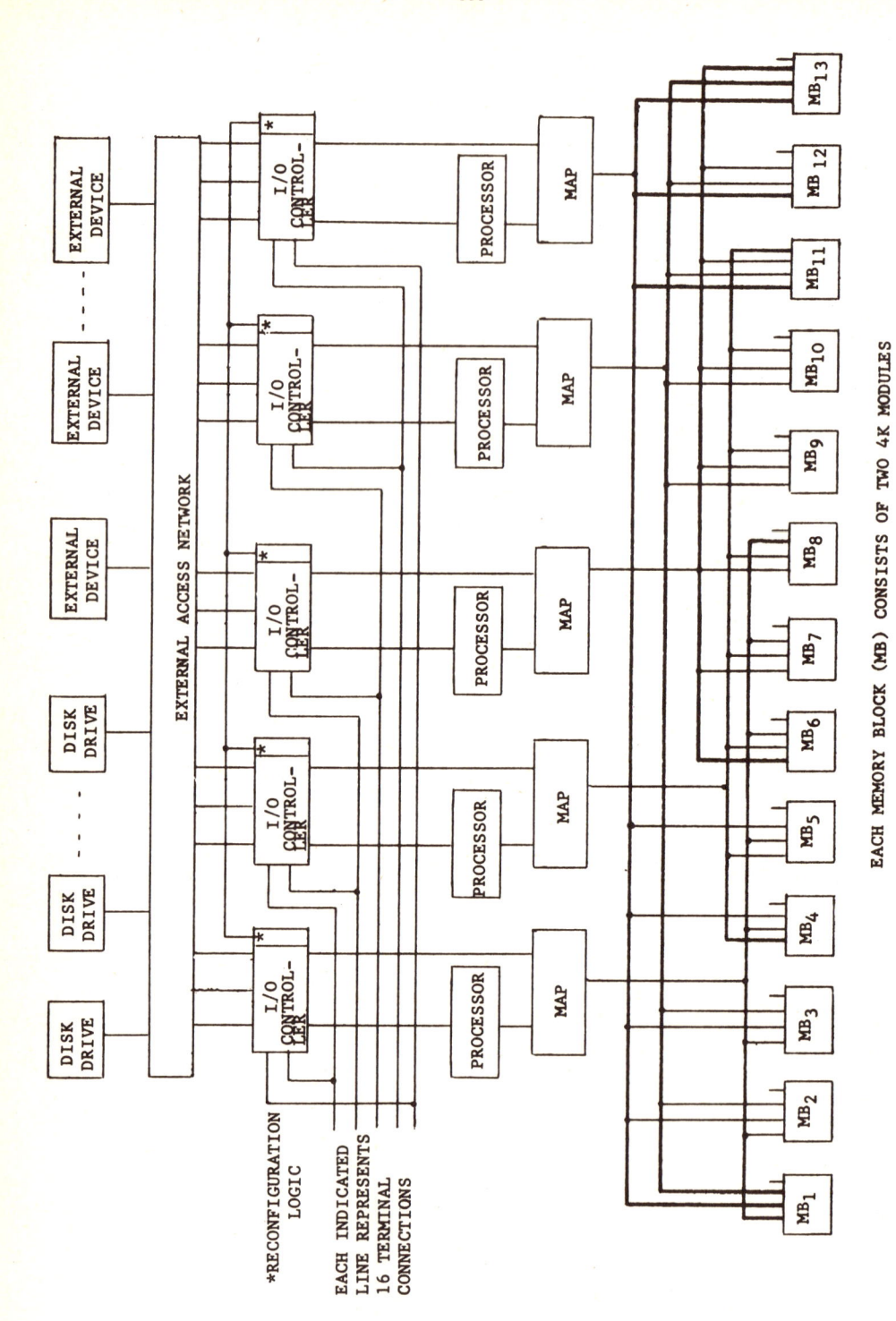

Figure A7.1 - A Block Diagram of the PRIME System

APPENDIX 8: THE SIFT COMPUTER

The Stanford Research Institute SIFT (Software Implemented Fault Tolerance) project (WEN72) was a design study of a fault tolerant digital computer, intended for the control of advanced transport aircraft, performing such tasks as: navigation, stability augmentation, instrument control and blind landing. This application is such that the computer must have approximately 16k words of memory and be capable of performing more than 0.5 MIPS. The project, sponsored by NASA Langley, started in August 1971, an experimental version was completed in 1973 and the final design produced in 1974.

The design was aimed at the task of aircraft control, where the requirement was for a probability of failure of less than 10 during a 10-hour operational period, which translates to a mean time between failures of 10^4 year. The consequences of failure (possible loss of human lives and economic loss) are extremely grave and are claimed to justify the use of extensive redundancy in the computing system, both in terms of extra hardware components (e.g. processors, memories, buses) and processing. As implied by the name, emphasis is placed in SIFT on software techniques for hardware error detection and recovery, with a corresponding de-emphasis on the use of special hardware for these tasks. The details of SIFT presented here (and Figure A8.1) are taken from (WEN72).

A8.1 System Description

The SIFT computer may be regarded as consisting of three levels - a bottom, hardware, level and two software levels comprising the executive and application programs.

The hardware level static structure, illustrated by Figure A8.1, is made up of a number of modules (processor/memory pairs) and the I/O system, interconected by buses. All modules are equivalent and no module is pre-assigned a special role. Individual processors can both read and write to the corresponding memory units, however the intermodule bus organisation (B1,B2,B3) is designed to allow a processor only to read from other memories. The intermodule buses are used as alternative routes rather than as multiple simultaneous transmission paths.

Connected to the buses is the input/output(I/O) system which consists of all the noncomputing units such as transducers, actuators and sensors. Conventional input/output tasks such as formatting or code conversion are handled in the same manner as any other task.

The computations to be executed by SIFT are broken into a number of tasks in such a way that no task requires more computing power than can be supplied by a single processor. (It is clear from (WEN72) that tasks are expected to be atomic actions - presumably storage protection mechanisms are used to attempt to guarantee atomicity.) Each processor is, however, capable of being multiprogrammed over a number of tasks.

Control of the computer resides in level 2 and is carried out by the executive, in which two parts can be identified:-

1) the local executive resident in each processor, which handles all control functions for the processor, e.g. initiating tasks, loading new tasks and reporting errors.

2) the system executive performs all functions that are related to the computer as a whole, e.g. allocation and scheduling of the work load and reconfiguration.

Local and system executive tasks are carried out in the same way as the application program tasks that form level 3, while communication between either executive or user tasks is handled by leaving messages at predefined places in the memories. For example, when the system executive assigns a task to a number of processors, it places a message in its memory for these processors to update their queues of work. When tasks are assigned in this way, the system executive designates the other cooperating processors so that all data required by them may be obtained.

A processor executing a task has the following mode of operation. Data required by a task is assumed to have been generated by each of several processors (including possibly the same one carrying out the task). A check is made to see if the data is available in the corresponding memories. If not the fact is noted in the memory of the processor and the "dispatcher" program entered to determine the next task to be performed. If the data is available, the processor transfers copies from each memory into it's own. A comparison is then carried out on the data and the result of the vote noted in it's memory. If the vote is successful the task is performed and the results, together with a note of the successful completion is placed in memory. The processor then selects the next task to be performed by entering the dispatcher program. (It is unclear (WEN72) how processors keep track of message areas, how this information is passed between tasks or who manages the storage.)

A8.2 Reliability Strategies

The reliability strategy used throughout the software of the SIFT computer is based on hybrid redundancy. Each task to be performed is replicated, being executed by at least three processors and the results generated voted upon by three or more subsequent processors (i.e. TMR - static redundancy) before the results are used. If an error is detected in the voting, backward error recovery is initiated by the system nominating a further set of processors to repeat the task. It would appear that the programs executed by SIFT are assumed to be correct.

One of the stated design aims of the SIFT computer (WEN72) was to use standard hardware components as far as possible. Thus very few reliability features exist at the hardware level apart from the normal mechanisms one would expect to find, such as parity and coding checks. An exception is the intermodule buses that do provide error detection and recovery mechanisms. Logic associated with each bus aims to ensure that only one processor has control of a bus at any time, but also that the length of time is finite, thereby preventing a faulty processor from seizing the bus permanently.

1) Error Detection

The SIFT computer mainly employs software replication and voting, as already mentioned, to achieve fault tolerance. However, the input/output subsystem at the hardware level also assists error detection through replication. Certain input (sensors) can be replicated; each sensor is then individually read and voted on by all modules requiring the input. In the case of outputs it is usually impossible to employ replication, thus a "special voter" is supplied to each output. Efforts are made to ensure that this special voter has the required reliability, presumably by means of such techniques as TMR.

Error detection in the software levels occurs at the start of each new task, when the set of modules nominated to perform the task each vote on the replicated inputs generated by a previous set of modules. A single subroutine within the local executive of each module is used to read and vote on the inputs. This subroutine is the only code outside the system executive that is concerned with detecting and reporting errors.

2) Fault Treatment

Once an error has been detected by the voter a message to that effect is left in the memory for the system executive. The system executive clearly uses these error messages for fault location and treatment, although it is unclear how it performs this analysis. For example to quote (WEN72) "faulty units are not necessarily removed but can either be ignored or assigned to tasks having no overall effect". Likewise no reference is made to what action is taken by the "special" output voters when they detect an error or how the result of the vote is conveyed to the higher software levels.

In the event of faults being detected in one of the executives, the other copies will not use the data computed by it, thereby retaining the (presumed) validity of their results. The error free copies of the executive signal the malfunctioning module to discontinue processing and inform all other modules to ignore the faulty copy. A new copy of the executive is then initiated in another module. Application programs containing faults are handled in a similar way, although it is not apparent how the system treats such faults since bringing in a new copy of the code is clearly inadequate.

3) Damage Assessment

Very little mention is made of damage assessment in the SIFT computer which seems to rely on fault masking to prevent error propagation. The designers claim that error propagation is reduced by the use of read-only memory in the system. However the system executive might also use the error messages generated to determine the extent to which errors might have been propagated.

4) Error Recovery

The main form of error recovery in SIFT is implemented by backward error recovery at the executive level. If three-fold replication is used a single error in the data can be easily detected and a valid set of inputs chosen. Consider next double faults existing simultaneously. Two cases must be distinguished: correlated and uncorrelated errors. Clearly two correlated errors would not be detected by TMR, however two simultaneous but uncorrelated errors should be detected.

Two strategies are suggested by the designers for handling multiple errors in SIFT: the first is to use three-fold replication for all tasks and in the event of any disagreement to avoid using the results until yet further processors have repeated the tasks. Alternatively, one can use five-fold (or greater) replication for all critical tasks. The designers claim that because the processors are not operating in lock-step mode the effects of multiple faults are easier to detect and recover from than in a synchronised system.

With regard to the copies of data generated by the replicated tasks, it is unclear from the documentation (WEN72) how the system decides on when to commit the data. Likewise, no assessment is given in (WEN72) of the effect this replication of processing and data has on the performance of SIFT.

M_1 Memory
P_1 Processor
B_1 Bus

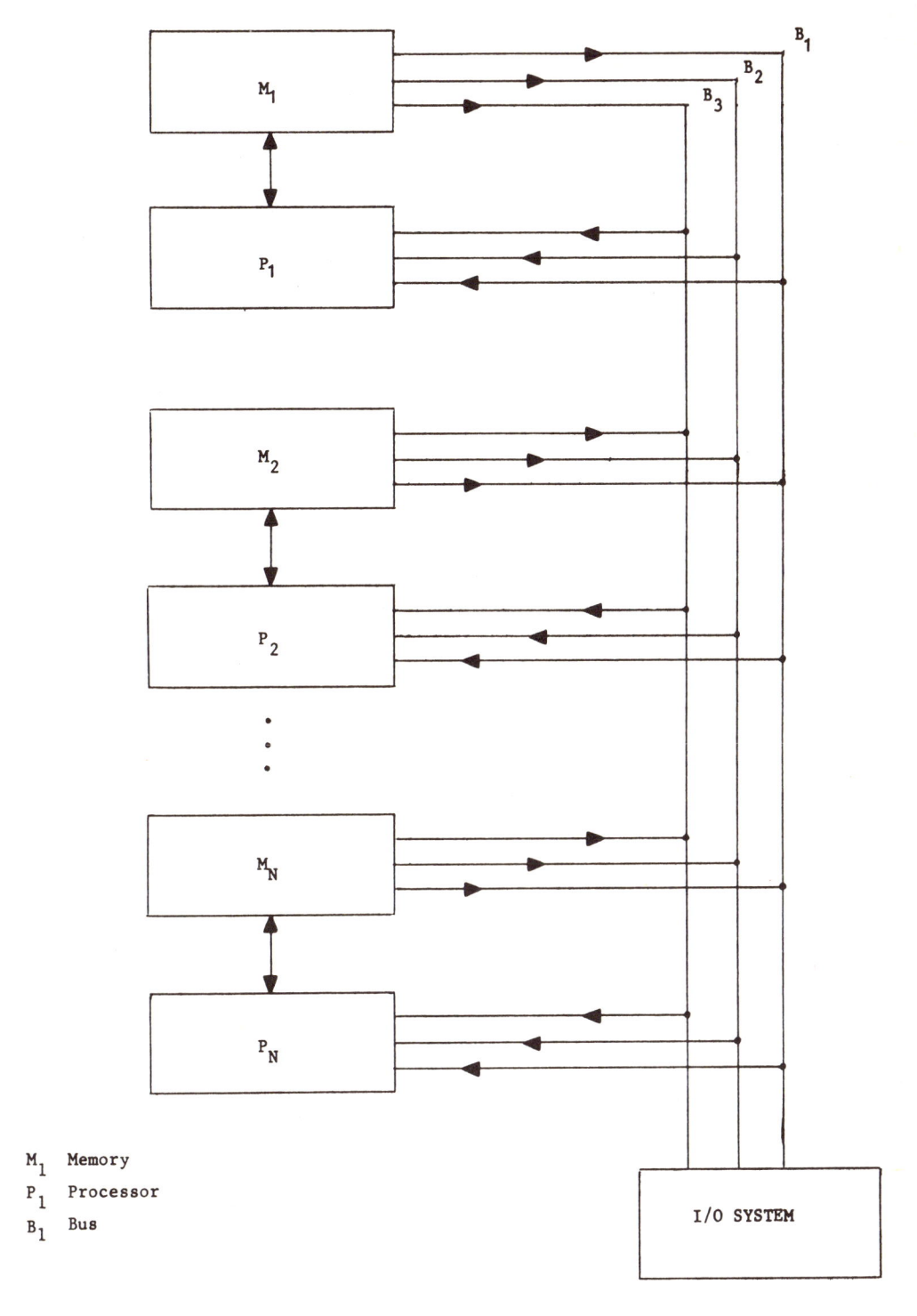

Figure A8.1 - SIFT Hardware Configuration

CHAPTER 3.F.

J. N. Gray
IBM Research Laboratory
San Jose, Ca., USA

Notes on Data Base Operating Systems

Abstract

This paper is a compendium of data base management operating systems folklore. It is an early paper and is still in draft form. It is intended as a set of course notes for a class on data base operating systems. After a brief overview of what a data management system is it focuses on particular issues unique to the transaction management component especially locking and recovery.

Notes on Data Base Operating Systems
Jim Gray
IBM Research Laboratory
San Jose, California. 95193
Summer 1977

ACKNOWLEDGMENTS

This paper plagerizes the work of the large and anonymous army of people working in the field. Because of the state of the field, there are few references to the literature (much of the "literature" is in internal memoranda, private correspondence, program logic manuals and prologues to the source language listings of various systems.)

The section on data management largely reflects the ideas of Don Chamberlin, Ted Codd, Chris Date, Dieter Gawlick, Andy Heller, Frank King, Franco Putzolu, and Bob Taylor. The discussion of views is abstracted from a paper co-authored with Don Chamberlin and Irv Traiger.

The section on data communications stems from conversations with Denny Anderson, Homer Leonard, and Charlie Sanders.

The section on transaction scheduling derives from discussions with Bob Jackson and Thomas Work.

The ideas on distributed transaction management is an amalgam of discussions with Homor Leonard.

Bruce Lindsay motivated the discussion of exception handling.

The presentation of consistency and locking derives from discussions and papers co-authored with Kapali Eswaran, Raymond Lorie, Franco Putzolu and Irving Traiger. Also Ron Obermark (IMS program isolation), and Phil Macri (DMS 1100) and Paul Roever have clarified many locking issues for me.

The presentation of recovery is co-authored with Paul McJones and John Nauman. Dieter Gawlick made many valuable suggestions. It reflects the ideas of Mike Blasgen, Dar Busa, Ron Obermark, Earl Jenner, Tom Price, Franco Putzolu, Butler Lampson, Howard Sturgis and Steve Weick.

All members of the System R group (IBM Research, San Jose) have contributed materially to this paper.

I am indebted to Mike Blasgen, Dieter Gawlick, Jerry Saltzer and especially to John Nauman each of whom made many constructive suggestions about earlier drafts of these notes.

If you feel your ideas or work are inadaquately or incorrectly plagerized, please annotate this manuscript and return it to me.

1. INTRODUCTION

Most large institutions have now heavily invested in a data base system. In general they have automated such clerical tasks as inventory control, order entry, or billing. These systems often support a world-wide network of hundreds of terminals. Their purpose is to reliably store and retrieve large quantities of data. The life of many institutions is critically dependent on such systems, when the system is down the corporation has amnesia.

This puts an enormous burden on the implementors and operators of such systems. The systems must on the one hand be very high performance and on the other hand they must be very reliable.

1.1. A SAMPLE SYSTEM

Perhaps it is best to begin by giving an example of such a system. A large bank may have one thousand teller terminals (several have 20,000 tellers but at present no single system supports such a large network). For each teller, there is a record describing the teller's cash drawer and for each branch there is a record describing the cash position of that branch (bank general ledger). It is likely to have several million demand deposit accounts (say 10,000,000 accounts). Associated with each account is a master record giving the account owner, the account balance and a list of recent deposits and withdrawals applicable to this account. Also there are records describing the account owners. This data base occupies over 10,000,000,000 bytes and must all be on-line at all times.

The data base is manipulated with application dependent transactions which were written for this application when it was installed. There are many transactions defined on this data base to query it and update it. A particular user is allowed to invoke a subset of these transactions. Invoking a transaction consists of typing a message and pushing a button. The teller terminal appends the transaction identity, teller identity and terminal identity to the message and transmits it to the central data manager. The data communication manager receives the message and translates it to some canonical form. It then passes the message to the transaction manager which validates the teller's authorization to invoke the specified transaction and then allocates and dispatches an instance of the transaction. The transaction processes the message, generates a response and terminates. Data communications delivers the message to the teller.

Perhaps the most common transaction is in this environment is the DEBIT_CREDIT transaction which takes in a message from any teller, debits or credits the appropriate account (after running some validity checks), adjusts the teller cash drawer and branch balance, and then sends a response message to the teller. The transaction flow is:

```
DEBIT_CREDIT:
   BEGIN_TRANSACTION;
   GET MESSAGE;
   EXTRACT ACCOUNT_NUMBER , DELTA , TELLER , BRANCH
                           FROM MESSAGE;
   FIND ACCOUNT(ACCOUNT_NUMBER) IN DATA BASE;
   IF NOT_FOUND | ACCOUNT_BALANCE+DELTA <0 THEN
       PUT NEGATIVE RESPONSE;
   ELSE DO;
       ACCOUNT_BALANCE=ACCOUNT_BALANCE+DELTA;
       POST HISTORY RECORD ON ACCOUNT (DELTA);
       CASH_DRAWER(TELLER)=CASH_DRAWER(TELLER)+DELTA;
       BRANCH_BALANCE(BRANCH)=BRANCH_BALANCE(BRANCH)+DELTA;
       PUT MESSAGE ('NEW BALANCE =' ACCOUNT_BALANCE);
       END;
   COMMIT;
```

At peak periods the system runs about thirty transactions per second with a response time of two seconds.

The DEBIT_CREDIT transaction is very "small". There is another class of transactions which behave rather differently. For example, once a month a transaction is run which produces a summary statement for each account. This transaction might be described by:

```
MONTHLY_STATEMENT:
 ANSWER ::= SELECT *
            FROM ACCOUNT , HISTORY
            WHERE ACCOUNT.ACCOUNT_NUMBER=HISTORY.ACCOUNT_NUMBER
            AND   HISTORY_DATE > LAST_REPORT
            GROUPED BY ACCOUNT.ACCOUNT_NUMBER,
            ASCENDING BY ACCOUNT.ACCOUNT_ADDRESS;
```

That is, collect all recent history records for each account and place them clustered with the account record into an answer file. The answers appear sorted by mailing address.

If each account has about fifteen transactions against it per month then this transaction will read 160,000,000 records and write a similar number of records. A naive implementation of this transaction will take 80 days to execute (50 milliseconds per disk seek implies two million seeks per day,) however, the system must run this transaction once a month and it must complete within a few hours.

There is a broad spread of transactions between these two types. Two particularly interesting types of transactions are _conversational_ transactions which carry on a dialogue with the user and _distributed_ transactions which access data or terminals at several nodes of a computer network.

Systems of 10,000 terminals or 100,000,000,000 bytes of on-line data or 150 transactions per second are generally considered to be the limit of present technology (software and hardware).

1.2. RELATIONSHIP TO OPERATING SYSTEM

If one tries to implement such an application on top of a general purpose operating system it quickly becomes clear that many necessary functions are absent from the operating system. Historically, two approaches have been taken to this problem:

- Write an new, simpler and "vastly superior" operating system.
- Extend the basic operating system to have the desired function.

The first approach was very popular in the mid-sixties and is having a renaissance with the advent of minicomputers. The _initial_ cost of a data management system is so low that almost any large customer can justify "rolling his own". The perfomance of such tailored systems is often ten times better than one based on a general purpose system. One must trade this off against the problems of maintaining the system as it grows to meet new needs and applications. Groups which followed this path now find themselves maintaining a rather large operating system which must be modified to support new devices (faster disks, tape archives,...) and new protocols (e.g. networks and displays.) Gradually, these systems have grown to include all the functions of a general purpose operating system. Perhaps the most successful approach to this has been to implement a hypervisor which runs both the data management operating system and some "standard" operating system. The "standard" operating system runs when the data manager is idle. The hypervisor is simply a interrupt handler which dispatches one or another system.

The second approach of extending the basic operating system is plagued with a different set of difficulties. The principal problem is the performance penalty of a general purpose operating system. Very few systems are designed to deal with very large files, or with networks of thousands of nodes. To take a specific example, consider the process structure of a general purpose system: The allocation and deallocation of a process should be _very_ fast (500 instructions for the pair is expensive) because we want to do it 100 times per second. The storage occupied by the process descriptor should also be small (less than 1000 bytes.) Lastly, preemptive scheduling of processes makes no sense since they are not CPU bound (they do a lot of I/O). A typical system uses 16,000 bytes to represent a process and requires 200,000 instructions to allocate and deallocate this structure (systems without protection do it cheaper.) Another problem is that the general purpose systems have been designed for batch and time sharing operation. They have not paid sufficient attention to issues such as continuous operation: keeping the system up for weeks at a time and gracefully degrading in case of some hardware or software error.

1.3. GENERAL STRUCTURE OF DATA MANAGEMENT SYSTEMS

These notes try to discuss issues which are independent of which operating system strategy is adopted. No matter how the system is structured, there are certain problems it must solve. The general structure common to several data management systems is presented. Then two particular problems within the transaction management component are discussed in detail: concurrency control (locking) and system reliability (recovery).

This presentation decomposes the system into four major components:
- Dictionary: the central repository of the description and definition of all persistent system objects.

- Data Communications: manages teleprocessing lines and message traffic.
- Data Base manager: manages the information stored in the system.
- Transaction Management: manages system resources and system services such as locking and recovery.

Each of these components call one another and in turn depend on the basic operating system for services.

1.4. BIBLIOGRAPHY

These notes are rather nitty-gritty, they are aimed at system implementors rather than at users. If this is the wrong level of detail for you (is too detailed) then you may prefer the very readable books:

Martin, *Computer Data-base Organization*, Prentice Hall, 1977. (What every DP vice president should know.)

Martin, *Computer Data-base Organization*, (2nd edition), Prentice Hall, 1976. (What every application programmer should know.)

The following is a brief list of some of the more popular general purpose data management systems which are commercially available:

Airlines Control Program, International Business Machines Corporation.

Customer Information Computer System, International Business Machines Corporation.

Data Management System 1100, Sperry Univac Corporation.

Extended Data Management System, Xerox Corporation.

Information Management System / Virtual Systems, International Business Machines Corporation.

Integrated Database Management System, Cullinane Corporation.

Integrated Data Store/1, Honeywell Information Systems Inc.

Model 204 Data Base Management System, Computer Corporation of America.

System 2000, MRI Systems Corporation.

Total, Cincom Systems Corporation.

Each of these manufacturers will be pleased to provide you with extensive descriptions of their systems.

Several experimental systems are under construction at present. Some of the more interesting are:

Astrahan et. al., "System R: a Relational Approach to Database Management", Astrahan et. al., ACM Transactions on Database Systems, Vol. 1, No. 2, June 1976.

Marill and Stern, "The Datacomputer- A Network Data Utility.", Proc. 1975 National Computer Conference, AFIPS Press, 1975.

Stonebraker et. al., "The Design and Implementation of INGRESS.", ACM Transactions on Database Systems, Vol. 1, No. 3, Sept 1976,

There are very few publicly available case studies of data base usage. The following are interesting but may not be representative:

IBM Systems Journal, Vol. 16, No. 2, June 1977. (describes the facilities and use of IMS and ACP).

"IMS/VS Primer," IBM World Trade Systems Center, Palo Alto California, form number S320-5767-1, January 1977.

"Share Guide IMS User Profile, A Summary of Message Processing Program Activity in Online IMS Systems" IBM Palo Alto-Raleigh Systems Center Bulletin, form number G320-6005, January 1977.

Also there is one "standard" (actually "proposed standard" system):

CODASYL Data Base Task Group Report, April 1971. Available from ACM.

2. DICTIONARY

2.1. WHAT IT IS

The description of the system, the data bases, the transactions, the telecommunications network, and of the users are all collected in the **dictionary**. This repository:

- Defines the attributes of objects such as data bases and terminals.

- Cross-references these objects.

- Records natural language (e.g. German) descriptions of the meaning and use of objects.

When the system arrives, the dictionary contains only a very few definitions of transactions (usually utilities), defines a few distinguished users (operator, data base administrator,...), and defines a few special terminals (master console). The system administrator proceeds to define new terminals, transactions, users, and data bases. (The system administrator function includes data base administration (DBA) and data communications (network) administration (DCA)). Also, the system administrator may modify existing definitions to match the actual system or to reflect changes. This addition and modification process is treated as an editing operation.

For example, one defines a new user by entering the "define" transaction and selecting USER from the menu of definable types. This causes a form to be displayed which has a field for each attribute of a user. The definer fills in this form and submits it to the dictionary. If the form is incorrectly filled out, it is redisplayed and the definer corrects it. Redefinition follows a similar pattern, the current form is displayed, edited and then submitted. (There is also a non-interactive interface to the dictionary for programs rather than people.)

All changes are validated by the dictionary for syntactic and semantic correctness. The ability to establish the correctness of a definition is similar to ability of a compiler to detect the correctness of a program. That is, many semantic errors go undetected. These errors are a significant problem.

Aside from validating and storing definitions, the dictionary provides a query facility which answers questions such as: "Which transactions use record type A of file B?" or, "What are the attributes of terminal 3426?".

The dictionary performs one further service, that of compiling the definitions into a "machine readable" form more directly usable by the other system components. For example, a terminal definition is converted from a variable length character string to a fixed format "descriptor" giving the terminal attributes in non-symbolic form.

The dictionary is a data base along with a set of transactions to manipulate this data base. Some systems integrate the dictionary with the data management system so that the data definition and data manipulation interface are homogeneous. This has the virtue of sharing large bodies of code and and of providing a uniform interface to the user. Ingress and System R are examples of such systems.

Historically, the argument against using the data base for the dictionary has been performance. There is very high read traffic on the dictionary during the normal operation of the system. A user logon requires examining the definitions of the user, his terminal, his category, and of the session that his logon establishes. The invocation of a transaction requires examining his authorization, the transaction, and the transaction descriptor (to build the transaction.) In turn the transaction definition may reference data bases and queues which may in turn reference files, records and fields. The perfomance of these accesses is critical because they appear in the processing of each transaction. These performance constraints combined with the fact that the accesses are predominantly read-only have caused most systems to special-case the dictionary. The dictionary definitions and their compiled descriptors are stored by the data base management component. The dictionary compiled descriptors are stored on a special device and a cache of them is maintained in high-speed storage on an LRU (Least Recently Used) basis. This mechanism generally uses a coarse granularity of locks and because operations are read only it keeps no log. Updates to the descriptors are made periodically while the system is quiesced.

The descriptors in the dictionary are persistent. During operation, many other short-lived descriptors are created for short-lived objects such as cursors, processes, and messages. Many of these descriptors are also kept in the descriptor cache.

The dictionary is the natural extension of the catalog or file system present in operating systems. The dictionary simply attaches more semantics to the objects it stores and more powerful operators on these objects.

Readers familiar with the literature may find a striking similarity between the dictionary and the notion of conceptual schema which is "a model of the enterprise". The dictionary is the conceptual schema without its artificial intelligence aspects. In time the dictionary component will evolve in the direction suggested by papers on conceptual schema.

2.2. BIBLIOGRAPHY

DB/DC Data Dictionary General Information Manual, IBM, form number GH20-9104-1, May 1977.

UCC TEN, Technical Information Manual, University Computing Corporation, 1976.

Lefkovits, Data Dictionary Systems, Q.E.D. Information Sciences Inc., 1977. (A buyer's guide for data dictionaries.)

Nijssen (editor), Modeling in Data Base Management Systems, North Holland, 1976. (All you ever wanted to know about conceptual schema.)

"SEQUEL 2: A Unified Approach to Data Definition, Manipulation, and Control." Chamberlin et. al., IBM Journal of Research and Development, Vol. 20, No. 6, November 1976. (presents a unified data definition, data manipulation facility.)

3. DATA MANAGEMENT

The Data management component stores and retrieves sets of records. It implements the objects: network, set of records, cursor, record, field, and view.

3.1. RECORDS AND FIELDS

A record type is a sequence of field types, and a record instance is a corresponding sequence of field instances. Record types and instances are persistent objects. Record instances are the atomic units of insertion and retrieval. Fields are sub-objects of records and are the atomic units of update. Fields have the attributes of atoms (e.g. FIXED(31) or CHAR(*)) and field instances have atomic values (e.g. "3" or "BUTTERFLY"). Each record instance has a unique name called a record identifier (RID).

A field type constrains the type and values of instances of a field and defines the representation of such instances. The record type specifies what fields occur in instances of that record type.

A typical record might have ten fields and occupy 256 bytes although records often have hundreds of fields (e.g. a record giving statistics on a census tract has over 600 fields), and may be very large (several thousand bytes). A _very_ simple record (nine fields and about eighty characters) might be described by:

```
 DECLARE 1 PHONE_BOOK_RECORD,
          2 PERSON_NAME CHAR(*),
          2 ADDRESS,
            3 STREET_NUMBER CHAR(*),
            3 STREET_NAME CHAR(*),
            3 CITY CHAR(*),
            3 STATE CHAR(*),
            3 ZIP_CODE CHAR(5),
          2 PHONE_NUMBER,
            3 AREA_CODE CHAR(3),
            3 PREFIX CHAR(3),
            3 STATION CHAR(4);
```

The operators on records include INSERT, DELETE, FETCH, and UPDATE. Records can be CONNECTED to and DISCONNECTED from membership in a set (see below). These operators actually apply to cursors which in turn point to records.

The notions of record and field correspond very closely to the notions of record and element in COBOL or structure and field in PL/1. Records are variously called entities, segments, tuples, and rows by different subcultures. Most systems have similar notions of records although they may or may not support variable length fields, optional fields (nulls), or repeated fields.

3.2. SETS

A set is a collection of records. This collection is represented by and implemented as an "access path" that runs through the collection of records. Sets perform the functions of

- relating the records of the set.
- In some instances directing the physical clustering of records in physical storage.

A record instance may occur in many different sets but it may occur at most once in a particular set.

There are three set types of interest:

- Sequential set: the records in the set form a single sequence. The records in the set are ordered either by order of arrival (entry sequenced (ES)), by cursor position at insert (CS), or are ordered (ascending or descending) by some subset of field values (key sequenced (KS)). Sequential sets model indexed-sequential files (ISAM, VSAM).

- Partitioned set: The records in the set form a sequence of disjoint groups of sequential sets. Cursor operators allow one to point at a particular group. Thereafter the sequential set operators are used to navigate within the group. The set is thus major ordered by hash and minor ordered (ES, CS or KS) within a group. Hashed files in which each group forms a hash bucket are modeled by partitioned sets.

- Parent-child set: The records of the set are organized into a two level hierarchy. Each record instance is either a parent or a child (but not both). Each child has a unique parent and no children. Each parent has a (possibly null) list of children. Using parent-child sets one can build networks and hierarchies. Positional operators on parent-child sets include the operators to locate parents, as well as operations to navigate on the sequential set of children of a parent. The CONNECT and DISCONNECT operators explicitly relate a child to a parent. One obtains implicit connect and disconnect by asserting that records inserted in one set should also be connected to another. (Similar rules apply for connect, delete and update.) Parent-child sets can be used to support hierarchical and network data models.

A partitioned set is a degenerate form of a parent-child set (the partitions have no parents), and a sequential set is a degenerate form of a partitioned set (there is only one partition.) In this discussion care has been taken to define the operators so that they also subset. This has the consequence that if the program uses the simplest model it will be able to run on any data and also allows for subset implementations on small computers.

Inserting a record in one set may trigger its connection to several other sets. If set "I" is an index for set "F", then an insert, delete and update of a record in "F" may trigger a corresponding insert, delete, or update in set "I". In order to support this, data manager must know:

- that insertion, update or deletion of a record causes its connection to, movement in, or disconnection from other sets.

- where to insert the new record in the new set:
  - For sequential sets, the ordering must be either key sequenced or entry sequenced.

- For partitioned sets, data manager must know the partitioning rule and know that the partitions are entry sequenced or key sequenced.

- For parent-child sets, the data manager must know that certain record types are parents and that others are children. Further, in the case of children, data manager must be able to deduce the parent of the child.

We will often use the term "file" as a synonym for set.

3.3. CURSORS.

A cursor is "opened" on a specific set and thereafter points exclusively to records in that set. After a cursor is opened it may be moved, copied, or closed. While a cursor is opened it may be used to manipulate the record it addresses.

Records are addressed by cursors. Cursors serve the functions of:

- pointing at a record.

- enumerating all records in a set.

- Translating between the stored record format and the format visible to the cursor user. A simple instance of this might be a cursor which hides some fields of a record. This aspect will be discussed with the notion of view.

A cursor is an ephemeral object which is created from a descriptor when a transaction is initiated or during transaction execution by an explicit OPEN_CURSOR command. Also one may COPY_CURSOR a cursor to make another instance of the cursor with independent positioning. A cursor is opened on a specific set (which thereby defines the enumeration order (next) of the cursor.) A cursor is destroyed by the CLOSE_CURSOR command.

3.3.2. OPERATIONS ON CURSORS

Operators on cursors include:

- FETCH (<cursor> [,<position>]) [HOLD] RETURNS(<record>)
  Which retrieves the record pointed at by the named cursor. The record is moved to the specified target. If the position is specified the cursor is first positioned. If HOLD is specified the record is locked for update (exclusive), otherwise the record is locked in share mode.

- INSERT (<cursor> [,<position>] ,<record>)
  Inserts the specified record into the set specified by cursor. If the set is key sequenced or entry sequenced then the cursor is moved to the correct position before the record is inserted, otherwise the record is inserted at (after) the current position of the cursor in the set. If the record type automatically appears in other sets, it also inserted in them.

- UPDATE (<cursor> ,[<position>] ,<new-record>)
  If position is specified the cursor is first positioned. The new record is then inserted in the set at the cursor position replacing the record pointed at by the cursor. If the set is sequenced by the updated fields, this may cause the record and cursor to move in the set.

- DELETE (<cursor> [,<position>])
  Deletes the record pointed at by the cursor after optionally repositioning the cursor.

- MOVE_CURSOR (<cursor> ,<position>) HOLD
  Repositions the cursor in the set.

3.3.3. CURSOR POSITIONING

A cursor is opened to traverse a particular set. Positioning expressions have the syntax:

```
--+-------------<RID>--------------------+--------------+-;
  +-------------FIRST-------------------+              |
  +-------------N-TH--------------------+  +-CHILD---+-+
  +-------------LAST-------------------+--+---------+
  +--NEXT------+                        +  +-PARENT--+
  +--PREVIOUS--+--<SELECTION EXPRESSION>--+  +-GROUP---+
  +------------+
```

where RID, FIRST, N-th, and LAST specify specific record occurrences while the other options specify the address relative to the current cursor position. It is also possible to set a cursor from another cursor.

The selection expression may be any boolean expression valid for all record types in the set. The selection expression includes the relational operators: =, ¬=, >, <, <=, >=, and for character strings a "matches-prefix" operator sometimes called generic key. If next or previous is specified, the set must be searched sequentially because the current position is relevant. Otherwise, the search can employ hashing or indices to locate the record. The selection expression search may be performed via an index which maps field values into RID's.

Examples of commands are:
  FETCH (CURSOR1,NEXT NAME='SMITH') HOLD RETURNS(POP);
  DELETE (CURSOR1,NEXT NAME='JOE' CHILD);
  INSERT (CURSOR1,,NEWCHILD);

For partitioned sets one may point the cursor at a specific partition by qualifying these operators by adding the modifier GROUP. A cursor on a parent-child (or partitioned) set points to both a parent record and a child record (or group and child within group). Cursors on such sets have two components: the parent or group cursor and the child cursor. Moving the parent cursor, positions the child cursor to the first record in the group or under the parent. For parent-child sets one qualifies the position operator with the modifier NEXT_PARENT in order to locate the first child of the next parent or with the modifier WITHIN_PARENT if the search is to be restricted to children of the current parent or group. Otherwise positional operators operate on children of the current parent.

There are rather obscure issues associated with cursor positioning.

The following is a good set of rules:

- A cursor can have the following positions:
    - Null.
    - Before the first record.
    - At a record.
    - Between two records.
    - After the last record.
- if the cursor points at a null set, then it is null. If the cursor points to a non-null set then it is always non-null.
- Initially the cursor is before the first record unless the OPEN_CURSOR specifies a position.
- An INSERT operation leaves the cursor pointing at the new record.
- A DELETE operation leaves the cursor between the two adjacent records, or at the top if there is no previous record, or at the bottom if there is a previous but no successor record.
- A UPDATE operation leaves the cursor pointing at the updated record.
- If an operation fails the cursor is not altered.

3.4. VARIOUS DATA MODELS

Data models differ in their notion of set.

3.4.1. RELATIONAL DATA MODEL

The relational model restricts itself to homogeneous (only one record type) sequential sets. The virtue of this approach is its simplicity and the ability to define operators that "distribute" over the set, applying uniformly to each record of the set. Since much of data processing involves repetitive operations on large volumes of data, this distributive property provides a concise language to express such algorithms. There is a strong analogy here with APL which uses the simple data structure of array and therefore is able to define powerful operators which work for all arrays. APL programs are very short and much of the control structure of the program is hidden inside of the operators.

To give an example of this, a "relational" program to find all overdue accounts in an invoice file might be:

SELECT ACCOUNT_NUMBER FROM INVOICE WHERE DUE_DATE<TODAY;

This should be compared to a PL/1 program with a loop to get next record, and test for DUE_DATE and END_OF_FILE. The MONTHLY_STATEMENT transaction described in the introduction is another instance of the power and usefulness of relational operators.

On the other hand, if the work to be done does not involve processing many records, then the relational model seems to have little advantage over other models. Consider the DEBIT_CREDIT transaction which (1) reads a message from a terminal, (2) finds an account, (3) updates the account, (4) posts a history record, (5) updates the teller cash drawer, (6) updates the branch balance, and (7) puts a message to the terminal. Such a transaction would benefit little from relational operators (each operation touches only one record.)

One can define aggregate operators that distribute over hierarchies or networks. For example, the MAPLIST function of LISP distributes an arbitrary function over an arbitrary data structure.

3.4.2. HIERARCHICAL DATA MODEL

Hierarchical models use parent-child sets in a stylized way to produce a forest (collection of trees) of records. A typical application might use the three record types: LOCATIONS, ACCOUNTS, and INVOICES and two parent-child sets to construct the following hierarchy: All the accounts at a location are clustered together and all outstanding invoices of an account are clustered with the account. That is a location has its accounts as children and an account has its invoices as children. This may be depicted schematicly by:

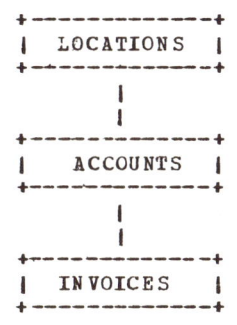

```
+--------------+
|  LOCATIONS   |
+--------------+
       |
       |
+--------------+
|   ACCOUNTS   |
+--------------+
       |
       |
+--------------+
|   INVOICES   |
+--------------+
```

This structure has the advantage that records used together may appear clustered together in physical storage and that information common to all the children can be factored into the parent record. Also, one may quickly find the first record under a parent and deduce when the last has been seen without scanning the rest of the data base.

Finding all invoices for an account received on a certain day involves positioning a cursor on the location, another cursor on the account number under that location, and a third cursor to scan over the invoices:

```
SET CURSOR1 to LOCATION=NAPA;
SET CURSOR2 TO ACCOUNT=FREEMARK_ABBY;
SET CURSOR3 BEFORE FIRST_CHILD(CURSOR2);
DO WHILE (¬END_OF_CHILDREN):
   FETCH (CURSOR3) NEXT CHILD; DO_SOMETHING;
END;
```

Because this is such a common phenomenon, and because in a hierarchy there is only one path to a record, most hierarchical systems abbreviate the cursor setting operation to setting the lowest cursor in the hierarchy by specifying a "fully qualified key" or path from the root to the leaf (the other cursors are set implicitly.) In the above example:

```
      SET CURSOR3 TO LOCATION=NAPA,
                    ACCOUNT=FREEMARK_ABBEY,
                    INVOICE=ANY;
      DO WHILE (¬END_OF_CHILDREN):
         FETCH (CURSOR3) NEXT CHILD; DO_SOMETHING;
      END;
```

Which implicitly sets up cursors one and two.

The implicit record naming of the hierarchical model makes programming much simpler than for a general network. If the data can be structured as a hierarchy in some application then it is desirable to use this model to address it.

3.4.3. NETWORK DATA MODEL

Not all problems conveniently fit a hierarchical model. If nothing else, different users may want to see the same information in a different hierarchy. For example an application might want to see the hierarchy "upside-down" with invoice at the top and location at the bottom. Support for logical hierarchies (views) requires that the data management system support a general network. The _efficient_ implementation of certain relational operators (sort-merge or join) also require parent-child sets requires the full capability of the network data model.

The general statement is that if all relationships are nested one to many mappings then the data can be expressed as a hierarchy. If there are many to many mappings then a network is required. To consider a specific example of the need for networks, imagine that several locations may service the same account and that each location services several accounts. Then the hierarchy introduced in the previous section would require either that locations be subsidiary to accounts and be duplicated or that the accounts record be duplicated in the hierarchy under the two locations. This will give rise to complexities about the account having two balances..... A network model would allow one to construct the structure:

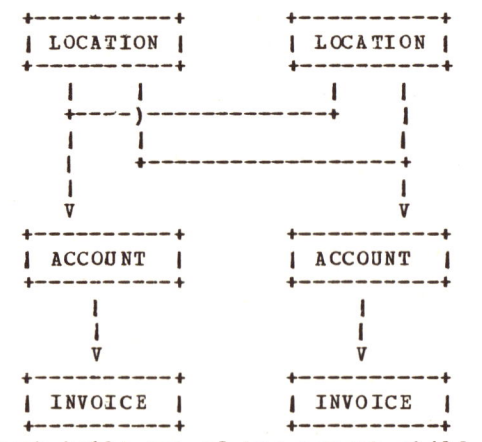

```
          +----------+          +----------+
          | LOCATION |          | LOCATION |
          +----------+          +----------+
             |    |                |    |
             +----)----------------+    |
             |    |                     |
             |    +---------------------+
             |    |                     |
             V                          V
          +----------+          +----------+
          | ACCOUNT  |          | ACCOUNT  |
          +----------+          +----------+
             |                     |
             |                     |
             V                     V
          +----------+          +----------+
          | INVOICE  |          | INVOICE  |
          +----------+          +----------+
```
A network built out of two parent-child sets.

3.4.4 COMPARISON OF DATA MODELS

By using "symbolic" pointers (keys), one may map any network data structure into a relational structure. In that sense all three models are equivalent and the relational model is completely general. However, there are substantial differences in the style and convenience of the different models. Analysis of specific cases usually indicates that associative pointers (keys) cost three page faults to follow (for a multi-megabyte set) whereas following a direct pointer costs only one page fault. This performance difference explains why the equivalence of the three data models is irrelevant. If there is heavy traffic between sets then pointers must be used. (High level languages can hide the use of these pointers.)

It is my bias that one should resort to the more elaborate model only when the simpler model leads to excessive complexity or to poor performance.

3.5. VIEWS

Records, sets, and networks which are actually stored are called __base objects__. Any query evaluates to a virtual set of records which may be displayed on the user's screen, fed to a further query, deleted from an existing set, inserted into an existing set, or copied to form a new base set. More importantly for this discussion, the query definition may be stored as a named __view__. The principal difference between a copy and a view is that updates to the original sets which produced the virtual set will be reflected in a view but will not affect a copy. A view is a dynamic picture of a query, whereas a copy is a static picture.

There is a need for both views and copies. Someone wanting to record the monthly sales volume of each department might run the following transaction at the end of each month (an arbitrary syntax):

```
MONTHLY_VOLUME=
     DEPARTMENT,SUM(VOLUME)
     FROM SALES GROUPED BY DEPARTMENT;
```

The new base set MONTHLY_VOLUME is defined to hold the answer. On the other hand, the current volume can be gotten by the view:

```
DEFINE CURRENT_VOLUME (DEPARTMENT,VOLUME) VIEW AS:
     DEPARTMENT,SUM(VOLUME)
     FROM SALES GROUPED BY DEPARTMENT;
```

Thereafter, any updates to SALES set will be reflected in the CURRENT_VOLUME view. Again, CURRENT_VOLUME may be used in the same ways base sets can be used. For example one can compute the difference between the current and monthly volume.

The semantics of views are quite simple. Views can be supported by a process of substitution in the abstract syntax (parse tree) of the statement. Each time a view is mentioned, it is replaced by its definition.

To summarize, any query evaluates to a virtual set. Naming this virtual set makes it a view. Thereafter, this view can be used as a set. This allows views to be defined as field and record subsets of sets, statistical summaries of sets and more complex combinations of sets.

There are three major reasons for defining views:

- _Data independence_: giving programs a logical view of data, thereby isolating them from data reorganization.

- _Data isolation_: giving the program exactly that subset of the data it needs, thereby minimizing error propagation.

- _Authorization_: hiding sensitive information from a program, its authors and users.

As the data base evolves, records and sets are often "reorganized". Changing the underlying data should not cause all the programs to be recompiled or rewritten so long as the semantics of the data is not changed. Old programs should be able to see the data in the old way. Views are used to achieve this.

Typical reorganization operations include:

- Adding fields to records.

- Splitting records.

- Combining records.

- Adding or dropping access paths.

Simple views of base records may be obtained by:

- Renaming or permuting fields,

- Converting the representation of a field.

Simple variations of base sets may be obtained by:

- Selecting that subset of the records of a set which satisfy some predicate;

- Projecting out some fields or records in the set.

- Combining existing sets together into new virtual sets which can be viewed as a single larger set.

Consider the example of a set of records of the form:

```
-------------------------------------------------------
| NAME | ADDRESS | TELEPHONE_NUMBER | ACCOUNT_NUMBER |
-------------------------------------------------------
```

Some applications might be only interested in the name and telephone number, others might want name and address while others might want name and account number, and of course one application would like to see the whole record. A view can appropriately subset the base set. If the set owner decides to partition the record into two new record sets:

```
PHONE_BOOK                             ACCOUNTS
--------------------------------       --------------------------
| NAME | ADDRESS | PHONE_NUMBER|       | NAME | ACCOUNT_ NUMBER |
--------------------------------       --------------------------
```

Programs which used views will now access base sets (records) and programs which accessed the entire larger set will now access a view (logical set/record). This larger view is defined by:

```
DEFINE VIEW WHOLE_THING:
    NAME,ADDRESS,PHONE_NUMBER,ACCOUNT_NUMBER
    FROM PHONE_BOOK,ACCOUNTS
    WHERE PHONE_BOOK.NAME=ACCOUNTS.NAME;
```

3.5.1 Views and Update

Any view can support read operations; however, since only base sets are actually stored, only base sets can actually be updated. To make an update via a view, it must be possible to propagate the updates down to the underlying base set.

If the view is very simple (e.g., record subset) then this propagation is straight forward. If the view is a one-to-one mapping of records in some base set but some fields of the base are missing from the view, then update and delete present no problem but insert requires that the unspecified ("invisible") fields of the new records in the base set be filled in with the "undefined" value. This may or may not be allowed by the integrity constraints on the base set.

Beyond these very simple rules, propagation of updates from views to base sets becomes complicated, dangerous, and sometimes impossible.

To give an example of the problems, consider the WHOLE_THING view mentioned above. Deletion of a record may be implemented by a deletion from one or both of the constituent sets (PHONE_BOOK and ACCOUNTS). The correct deletion rule is dependent on the semantics of the data. Similar comments apply to insert and update.

My colleagues and I have resigned ourselves to the idea that there is no elegant solution to the view update problem. (Materialization (reading) is not a problem!) Existing systems use either very restrictive view mechanisms (subset only), or they provide incredibly ad hoc view update facilities. We propose that simple views (subsets) be done automatically and that a technique akin to that used for abstract data types be used for complex views: the view definer will specify the semantics of the operators NEXT, FETCH, INSERT, DELETE, and UPDATE.

3.6. STRUCTURE OF DATA MANAGER

Data manager is large enough to be subdivided into several components:

- View component: is responsible for interpreting the request, and calling the other components to do the actual work. The view component implements cursors and uses them to communicate as the internal and external representation of the view.

- Record component: stores logical records on "pages", manages the contents of pages and the problems of variable length and overflow records.

- Index component: implements sequential and associative access to sets. If only associative access is required, hashing should be used. If both sequential and associative access are required then indices implemented as B-trees should be used (see Knuth Vol 3 or IBM's Virtual Sequential Access Method.)

Buffer manager: maps the data "pages" on secondary storage to primary storage buffer pool. If the operating system provided a really fancy page manager (virtual memory) then the buffer manager might not be needed. But, issues such as double buffering of sequential I/O, Write Ahead Log protocol (see recovery section), checkpoint, and locking seem to argue against using the page managers of existing systems. If you are looking for a hard problem, here is one: define an interface to page management which which is useable by data management in lieu of buffer management.

3.7. A SAMPLE DATA BASE DESIGN

The introduction described a very simple data base and a simple transaction which uses it. We discuss how that data base could be structured and how the transaction would access it.

The data base consists of the records

```
ACCOUNT(ACCOUNT_NUMBER,CUSTOMER_NUMBER,ACCOUNT_BALANCE,HISTORY)
CUSTOMER(CUSTOMER_NUMBER,CUSTOMER_NAME,ADDRESS,.....)
HISTORY(TIME,TELLER,CODE,ACCOUNT_NUMBER,CHANGE,PREV_HISTORY)
CASH_DRAWER(TELLER_NUMBER,BALANCE)
BRANCH_BALANCE(BRANCH,BALANCE)
TELLER(TELLER_NUMBER,TELLER_NAME,......)
```

This is a very cryptic description which says that a customer record has fields giving the customer number, customer name, address and other attributes.

The CASH_DRAWER, BRANCH_BALANCE and TELLER files (sets) are rather small (less than 100,000 bytes). The ACCOUNT and CUSTOMER files are large (about 1,000,000,000 bytes). The history file is extremely large. If there are fifteen transactions against each account per month and if each history record is fifty bytes then the history file grows 7,500,000,000 bytes per month. Traffic on BRANCH_BALANCE and CASH_DRAWER is high and is by BRANCH and TELLER_NUMBER respectively. Therefore these two sets are kept in high speed storage and are accessed via a hash on these attributes. That is, these sets are implemented as partitioned sets. Traffic on the ACCOUNT file is high but random. Most accesses are via ACCOUNT_NUMBER but some are via CUSTOMER_NUMBER. Therefore, the file is hashed on ACCOUNT_NUMBER (partitioned set). A sequential set, NAMES, is maintained on these records which gives a sequential and associative access path to the records ascending by customer name. CUSTOMER is treated similarly (having a hash on customer number and an index on customer name.) The TELLER file is organized as a sequential set. The HISTORY file is the most interesting. These records are written once and thereafter are only read. Almost every transaction generates such a record and for legal reasons the file must be maintained forever. This causes it to be kept as an entry sequenced set. New records are inserted at the end of the set. To allow all recent history records for a specific account to be quickly located, a parent child set is defined to link each ACCOUNT record (parent) to its HISTORY records (children). Each ACCOUNT record points to its most recent HISTORY record. Each HISTORY record points to the previous history record for that ACCOUNT.

Given this structure, we can discuss the execution of the CREDIT_DEBIT transaction outlined in the introduction. We will assume that the locking is done at the granularity of a page and that recovery is achieved by keeping a log (see section on transaction management.)

At initiation, the data manager allocates the cursors for the transaction on the ACCOUNTS, HISTORY, BRANCH, and CASH_DRAWER sets. In each instance it gets a lock on the set to insure that the set is available for update (this is an IX mode lock as explained int the locking section 5.7.6.2.) Locking at a finer granularity will be done during transaction execution (see locking section). The first call the data manager sees is a request to find the ACCOUNT record with a given account number. This is done by hashing the account number, thereby computing an anchor for the hash chain. Buffer manager is called to bring that page of the file into fast storage. Buffer manager looks in the buffer pool to see if the page is there. If the page is present, buffer manager returns it immediately. Otherwise, it finds a free buffer page, reads the page into that buffer and returns the buffer. Data manager then locks the page in share mode (so that no one else modifies it). This lock will be held to the end of the transaction. The record component searches the page for a record with that account number. If the record is found, its value is returned to the caller and the cursor is left pointing at the record.

The next request updates account balance of the record addressed by the cursor. This requires converting the share mode lock acquired by the previous call to a lock on the page in exclusive mode, so that no one else sees the new account balance until the transaction successfully completes. Also the record component must write a log record that allows it to undo or redo this update in case of a transaction or system abort (see section on recovery). Further, the transaction must note that the page depends on a certain log record so that buffer manager can observe the write ahead log protocol (see recovery section.) Lastly, the record component does the update to the balance of the record.

Next the transaction fabricates the history record and inserts it in the history file as a child of the fetched account. The record component calls buffer manager to get the last page of the history file (since it is an entry sequence set the record goes on the last page.) Because there is a lot of insert activity on the HISTORY file, the page is likely to be in the buffer pool. So buffer manager returns it, the record component locks it and updates it. Next, the record component updates the parent-child set so that the new history record is a child of the parent account record. All of these updates are recorded in the system log in case of error.

The next call updates the teller cash drawer. This requires locking the appropriate CASH_DRAWER record in exclusive mode (it is located by hash). An undo-redo log record is written and the update is made.

A similar scenario is performed for the BRANCH_BALANCE file.

When the transaction ends, data manager releases all its locks and puts the transaction's pages in the buffer manager's chain of pages eligible for write to disk.

If data manager or any other component detects an error at any point, it issues an ABORT_TRANSACTION command which initiates transaction undo (see recovery section.) This causes data manager to undo all its updates to records on behalf of this user and then to release all its locks and buffer pages.

The recovery and locking aspects of data manager are elaborated in later sections.

I suggest the reader design and evaluate the performance of the

MONTHLY_STATEMENT transaction described in the introduction as well as a transaction which given two dates and an account number will display the history of that account.

3.8. COMPARISON TO FILE ACCESS METHOD

From the example above, it should be clear that data manager is a lot more fancy than the typical file access methods (indexed sequential files).

File systems usually do not support partitioned or parent-child sets. Some support the notion of record, but none support the notions of field, network or view. They generally lock at the granularity of a file rather than at the granularity of a record. File systems generally do recovery by taking periodic image dumps of the entire file. This does not work well for a transaction environment or for very large files.

In general, data manager builds upon the operating system file system so that

- The operating system is responsible for device support.

- The operating system utilities for allocation, import, export and accounting are useable.

- The data is available to programs outside of the data manager.

3.9. BIBLIOGRAPHY.

Chamberlin et. al., "Views, Authorization, and Locking in a Relational Data Base System", 1975 NCC, Spartan Press. 1975. (Explains what views are and the problems associated with them.)

Computing Surveys, Vol. 8 No. 1, March 1976. (A good collection of papers giving current trends and issues related to the data management component of data base systems.)

Date, Introduction to Database Systems, Addison Wesley, 1975. (The seminal book on the data management part of data management systems.)

Date, "An Architecture for High Level Language Database Extensions," Proceedings of 1976 SIGMOD Conference, ACM, 1976. (Unifies the relational, hierarchical and network models.)

Knuth, The Art of Computer Programming: Sorting and Searching, Vol. 3, Addison Wesley, 1975. (Explains all about B-trees among other things.)

McGee, IBM Systems Journal, Vol. 16, No. 2, 1977, pp. 84-168. (A very readable tutorial on IMS, what it does, how it works, and how it is used.)

Senko, "Data Structures and Data Accessing in Data Base Systems, Past, Present, Future," IBM Systems Journal, Vol. 16, No. 3, 1977, pp. 208-257. (A short tutorial on data models.)

4. DATA COMMUNICATIONS

The area of data communications is the least understood aspect of DB/DC systems. It must deal with evolving network managers, evolving intelligent terminals and in general seems to be in a continuing state of chaos. Do not feel too bad if you find this section bewildering.

Data communications is responsible for the flow of messages. Messages may come via telecommunications lines from terminals and from other systems, or messages may be generated by processes running within the system. Messages may be destined for external endpoints, for buffer areas called queues, or for executing processes. Data communications externally provides the functions of:

- Routing messages.
- Buffering messages.
- Message mapping so sender and receiver can each be unaware of the "physical" characteristics of the other.

Internally data communications provides:

- Message transformation which maps "external" messages to and from a format palatable to network manager.
- Device control of terminals.
- Message recovery in the face of transmission errors and system errors.

4.1. MESSAGES, SESSIONS, AND RELATIONSHIP TO NETWORK MANAGER

Messages and endpoints are the fundamental objects of data communications. A __message__ consists of a set of records. Records in turn consist of a set of fields. Messages therefore look very much like data base sequential sets. Messages are defined by message descriptors. Typical unformatted definitions might be: A line from typewriter terminal is a one field, one record message. A screen image for a display is a two field (control and data), one record message. A multi-screen display image is a multi-field multi-record message.

Data communications depends heavily on the network manager provided by the base operating system. ARPANET, DECNET, and SNA (embodied in NCP and VTAM) are examples of such network managers. The network manager provides the notion of __endpoint__ which is the smallest addressable network unit. A work station, a queue, an process, and a card reader are each examples of endpoints.

Network manager transmits rather stylized __transmission records__ (TRs). These are simply byte strings. Network manager makes a best effort to deliver these byte strings to their destination. It is the responsibility of data communications to package messages (records and fields) into transmission records and then reconstruct the message from transmission records when they arrive at the other end.

The following figure summarizes this: application and terminal control programs see messages via sessions. DC in the host and terminal map these messages into transmission records which are carried by the network manager.

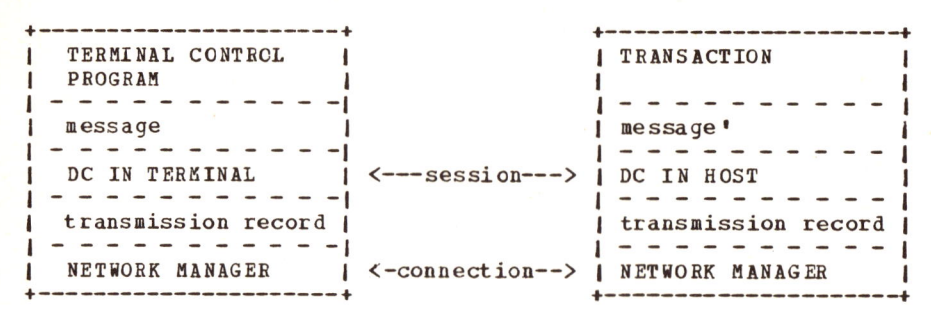

```
+----------------------+                  +----------------------+
|  TERMINAL CONTROL    |                  |  TRANSACTION         |
|  PROGRAM             |                  |                      |
|- - - - - - - - - - - |                  |- - - - - - - - - - - |
|  message             |                  |  message'            |
|- - - - - - - - - - - |                  |- - - - - - - - - - - |
|  DC IN TERMINAL      | <---session--->  |  DC IN HOST          |
|- - - - - - - - - - - |                  |- - - - - - - - - - - |
|  transmission record |                  |  transmission record |
|- - - - - - - - - - - |                  |- - - - - - - - - - - |
|  NETWORK MANAGER     | <-connection-->  |  NETWORK MANAGER     |
+----------------------+                  +----------------------+
```

The three main layers of a session.

There are two ways to send messages: A one shot message can be sent to an endpoint in a canonical form with a very rigid protocol. Logon messages (session initiation) are often of this form. The second way to send messages is via an established _session_ between the two endpoints. When the session is established, certain protocols are agreed to (e.g. messages will be recoverable, session will be half duplex,...) Thereafter, messages sent via the session obey these protocols. Sessions:

- Establish the message formats desired by the sender and receiver.

- Allow sender and receiver to validate one another's identity once rather than revalidating each message.

- Allow a set of messages to be related together (see conversations).

- Establish recovery, routing, and pacing protocols.

The network operating system provides _connection_ between endpoints. A connection should be thought of as a piece of wire which can carry messages blocked (by data communications) into transmission records. Sessions map many to one onto connections. At any instant, a session uses a particular connection. But if the connection fails or if an endpoint fails, the session may be transparently mapped to a new connection. For example, if a terminal breaks, the operator may move the session to a new terminal. Similarly, if a connection breaks, an alternate connection may be established. Connections hide the problems of transmission management (an SNA term):

- Transmission control, blocking and deblocking transmission records (TRs), managing TR sequence numbers and first level retry logic.

- Path control, or routing of TRs through the network.

- Link control, sending TRs over teleprocessing lines.

- Pacing, dividing the bandwidth and buffer pools of the network among connections.

The data communications component and the network manager cooperate in implementing the notion of session.

4.2. SESSION MANAGEMENT

The principal purpose of the session notion is to:

- Give device independence: the session makes transparent whether the endpoint is ASCII, EBCDIC, one-line, multi-line, program or terminal.

- Manages the high level protocols for recovery, related messages and conversations.

Session creation specifies the protocols to be used on the session by each participant. One participant may be an ASCII typewriter and the other participant may be a sophisticated system. In this case the sophisticated system has lots of logic to handle the session protocol and errors on the session. On the other hand if the endpoint is an intelligent terminal and if the other endpoint is willing to accept the terminal's protocol the session management is rather simple. (Note: The above is the way it is supposed to work. In _practice_ sessions with intelligent terminals are very complex and the programs are much more subtle because intelligent terminals can make such complex mistakes. Typically, it is much easier to handle a master-slave session than to handle a symmetric session.)

Network manager simply delivers transmission records to endpoints. So it is the responsibility of data communications to "know" about the device characteristics and to control the device. This means that DC must implement all the code to provide the terminal appearance. There is a version of this code for each device type (display, printer, typewriter,...). This causes the DC component to be very big in terms of thousands (K) Lines Of Code (KLOC).

If the network manager defines a generally useful endpoint model, then the DC manager can use this model for endpoints which fit the model. This is the justification for the TYPE1,TYPE2,... Logical Units (endpoints) of SNA and for the attempts to define a network logical terminal for ARPANET.

Sessions with dedicated terminals and peer nodes of the network are automatically (re)established when the system is (re)started. Of course, the operator of the terminal must re-establish his identity so that security will not be violated. Sessions for switched lines are created dynamically as the terminals connect to the system.

When DC creates the session, it specifies what protocols are to be used to translate message formats so that the session user is not aware of the characteristics of the device at the other end point.

4.3. QUEUES

As mentioned before a session may be:

```
FROM  program        or terminal or queue
TO    program        or terminal or queue
```

Queues allow buffered transmission between endpoints. Queues are associated (by DC) with users, endpoints and transactions. If a user is not logged on or if a process is doing something else, a queue can be used to hold one or more messages thereby freeing the session for further work or for termination. At a later time the program or endpoint may poll the queue and obtain the message.

Queues are actually passive so one needs to associate an algorithm with a queue. Typical algorithms are:

- Allocate N servers for this queue.
- Schedule a transaction when a message arrives in this queue.
- Schedule a transaction when N messages appear in the queue.
- Schedule a transaction at specified intervals.

Further, queues may be declared to be recoverable in which case DC is responsible for reconstructing the queue and it's messages if the system crashes or if the message consumer aborts.

4.4. MESSAGE RECOVERY

A session may be designated as recoverable in which case, all messages traveling on the session are sequence numbered and logged. If the transmission fails (positive acknowledge not received by sender), then the session endpoints resynchronize back to that message sequence number and the lost and subsequent messages are re-presented by the sender endpoint. If one of the endpoints fails, when it is restarted the session will be reestablished and the communication resumed. This requires that the endpoints be "recoverable" although one endpoint of a session may assume recovery responsibility for the other.

If a message ends up in a recoverable queue then:

- If the dequeuer of the message (session or process) aborts, the message will be replaced in the queue.
- If the system crashes, the queue will be reconstructed (using the log or some other recovery mechanism).

If the session or queue is not recoverable, then the message is lost if the transmission, dequeuer or system fail.

It is the responsibility of the data communications component to assure that a recoverable message is "successfully" processed or presented __exactly once__. It does this by requiring that receipt of recoverable messages be acknowledged. A transaction "acknowledges" receipt of a message after it has processed it, at commit time (see recovery section.)

4.5. RESPONSE MODE PROCESSING.

The default protocol for recoverable messages consists of the scenario:

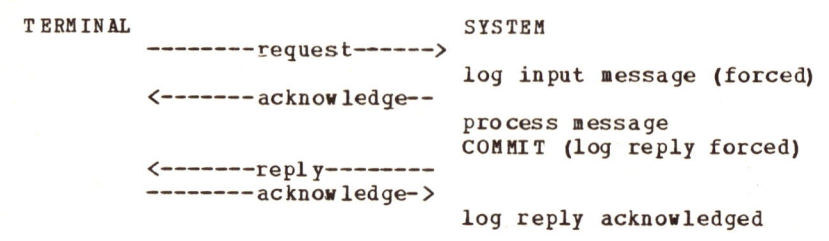

```
    TERMINAL                          SYSTEM
            --------request------>
                                      log input message (forced)
            <-------acknowledge--
                                      process message
                                      COMMIT (log reply forced)
            <-------reply--------
            --------acknowledge->
                                      log reply acknowledged
```

This implies four entries to the network manager (at each endpoint).

Each of these passes requires several thousand instructions (in typical implementations.) If one is willing to sacrifice the recoverability of the input message then the logging and acknowledgment of the input message can be eliminated and the reply sequence used as acknowledgment. This reduces line traffic and interrupt handling by a factor of two. This is the _response_ mode message processing. The output (commit) message is logged. If something goes wrong before commit, it is as though the message was never received. If something goes wrong after commit then the log is used to re-present the message. However, the sender must be able to match responses to requests (he may send five requests and get three responses). The easiest way to do this is to insist that there is at most one message outstanding at a time (i.e. lock the keyboard).

Another scheme is to acknowledge a batch of messages with a single acknowledge. One does this by tagging the acknowledge with the sequence number of the latest message received. If messages are recoverable, then the sender must retain the message until it is acknowledged and so acknowledges should be sent fairly frequently.

4.5. CONVERSATIONS

A conversation is a sequence of messages. Messages are usually grouped for recovery purposes so that all are processed or ignored together. A simple conversation might consist of a clerk filling out a form. Each line the operator enters is checked for syntactic correctness and checked to see that the airline flight is available or that the required number of widgets are in stock. If the form passes the test it is redisplayed by the transaction with the unit price and total price for the line item filled in. At any time the operator can abort the conversation. However, if the system backs up the user (because of deadlock) or if the system crashes then when it restarts it would be nice to _re-present_ the message of the conversation so that the operator's typing is saved. This requires that the group of messages be identified to the data communications component as a conversation so that it can manage this recovery process. (The details of this protocol are an unsolved problem so far as I know.)

4.6. MESSAGE MAPPING

One of the features provided by DC is to insulate each endpoint from the characteristics of the other. There are two levels of mapping to do this: One level maps transmission records into messages. The next level maps the message into a structured message. The first level of mapping is defined by the session, the second level of mapping is defined by the recipient (transaction). The first level of mapping converts all messages into some canonical form (e.g. a byte string of EBCDIC characters.) This transformation may handle such matters as pagination on a screen (if the message will not fit on one screen image). The second level of mapping transforms the message from an uninterpreted string of bytes into a message-record-field structure. When one writes a transaction, one also writes a message mapping description which makes these transformations. For example, an airlines reservation transaction might have a mapping program that first displays a blank ticket. On input, the mapping program extracts the fields entered by the terminal operator and puts them in a set of (multi-field) records. The transaction reads these records (much in the style data base records are read) and then puts out a set of records to be displayed. The mapping program fills in the blank ticket with these records and passes the resulting byte string to session management.

4.7. TOPICS NOT COVERED

A complete discussion of DC should include:

- More detail on network manager (another lecturer will cover that).
- Authorization to terminals (another lecturer will cover that).
- More detail on message mapping.
- The Logon-Signon process.

4.8. BIBLIOGRAPHY.

Kimbelton, Schneider, "Computer Communication Networks: Approaches, Objectives, and Performance Considerations," Computing Surveys, Vol. 7, No. 3, Sept. 1975. (A survey paper on network managers.)

"Customer Information Control System/ Virtual Storage (CICS/VS), System/Application Design Guide." IBM, form number SC33-0068, 1977 (An eminently readable manual on all aspects of data management systems. Explains various session management protocols and explains a rather nice message mapping facility.)

Eade, Homan, Jones, "CICS/VS and its Role in Systems Network Architecture," IBM Systems Journal, Vol. 16, No. 3, 1977. (Tells how CICS joined SNA and what SNA did for it.)

IBM Systems Journal, Vol. 15, No. 1, Jan. 1976. (All about SNA, IBM's network manager architecture.)

5. TRANSACTION MANAGEMENT

The transaction management system is responsible for scheduling system activity, managing physical resources, and managing system shutdown and restart. It includes components which perform scheduling, recovery, logging, and locking.

In general transaction management performs those operating system functions not available from the basic operating system. It does this either by extending the operating system objects (e.g. enhancing processes to have recovery and logging) or by providing entirely new facilities (e.g. independent recovery management.) As these functions become better understood, the duties of transaction management will gradually migrate into the operating system.

Transaction management implements the following objects:

- Transaction descriptor: A transaction descriptor is a prototype for a transaction giving instructions on how to build an instance of the transaction. The descriptor describes how to schedule the transaction, what recovery and locking options to use, what data base views the transaction needs, what program the transaction runs, and how much space and time it requires.

- Process: A process (domain) which is capable of running or is running a transaction. A process is bound to a program and to other resources. A process is a unit of scheduling and resource allocation. Over time a process may execute several transaction instances although at any instant a process is executing on behalf of at most one transaction instance. Conversely, a transaction instance may involve several processes. Multiple concurrent processes executing on behalf of a single transaction instance are called cohorts. Data management system processes are fancier than operating system processes since they understand locking, recovery and logging protocols but we will continue to use the old (familiar name for them).

- Transaction instance: A process or collection of processes (cohorts) executing a transaction. A transaction instance is the unit of locking and recovery.

In what follows, we shall blur these distinctions and generically call each of these objects transactions unless a more precise term is needed.

The life of a transaction instance is fairly simple. A message or request arrives which causes a process to be built from the transaction descriptor. The process issues a BEGIN_TRANSACTION action which establishes a recovery unit. It then issues a series of actions against the system state. Finally it issues the COMMIT_TRANSACTION action which causes the outputs of the transaction to be made public (both updates and output messages.) Alternatively, if the transaction runs into trouble, it may issue the ABORT_TRANSACTION action which cancels all actions performed by this transaction.

The system provides a set of objects and actions on these objects along with a set of primitives which allow groups of actions to be collected into atomic transactions. It guarantees no consistency on the objects beyond the atomicity of the actions. That is, an action will either successfully complete or it will not modify the system state at all.

Further, if two actions are performed on an object then the result will be equivalent to the serial execution of the two actions. (As explained below this is achieved by using locking within system actions.)

The notion of transaction is introduced to provide a similar abstraction above the system interface. Transactions are an all or nothing thing, either they happen completely or all trace of them (except in the log) is erased.

Before a transaction completes, it may be <u>aborted</u> and its updates to recoverable data may be <u>undone</u>. The abort can come either from the transaction itself (suicide: bad input data, operator cancel,...) or from outside (murder: deadlock, timeout, system crash....) However, once a transaction <u>commits</u> (successfully completes), the effects of the transaction cannot be blindly undone. Rather, to undo a committed transaction, one must resort to <u>compensation</u>: running a new transaction which corrects the errors of its predecessor. Compensation is usually highly application dependent and is not provided by the system.

These definitions may be clarified by a few examples. The following is a picture of the three possible destinies of a transaction.

```
     BEGIN              BEGIN              BEGIN
     action             action             action
     action             action             action
       .                  .                action
       .                  .          ABORT=>  .
       .                  .
     action             ABORT
     COMMIT

     A successful       A suicidal         A murdered
     transaction        transaction        transaction
```

A <u>simple</u> transaction takes in a single message does something, and then produces a single message. Simple transactions typically make fifteen data base calls. Almost all transactions are simple at present (see Guide/Share Profile of IMS users). About half of all simple transactions are read-only (make no changes to the data base.) For simple transactions, the notion of process, recovery unit and message coincide.

If a transaction sends and receives several synchronous messages it is called a <u>conversational</u> transaction. A conversational transaction has several messages per process and transaction instances. Conversational transactions are likely to last for a long time (minutes while the operator thinks and types) and hence pose special resource management problems.

The term <u>batch transaction</u> is used to describe a transaction which is "unusually big". In general such transactions are not on-line, rather they are usually started by a system event (timer driven) and run for a long time as a "background" job. Such a transaction usually performs thousands of data management calls before terminating. Often, the process will commit some of its work before the entire operation is complete. This is an instance of multiple (related) recovery units per process.

If a transaction does work at several nodes of a network then it will require a process structure (cohort) to represent its work at each participating node. Such a transaction is called <u>distributed</u>.

The following table summarizes the possibilities and shows the
independence of the notions of process, message and transaction
instance (commit). Cohorts communicate with one another via the
session-message facilities provided by data communications.

	PROCESSES	MESSAGES	COMMITS
SIMPLE	1	1 in 1 out	1
CONVERSATIONAL	1	many in many out	1
BATCH	1	none(?)	many
DISTRIBUTED	many	1 in 1 out	1
		many among cohorts	

We introduce an additional notion of <u>save point</u> in the notion of
transaction. A save point is a fire-wall which allows a transaction to
stop short of total backup. If a transaction gets into trouble (e.g.
deadlock, resource limit) it may be sufficient to back up to such an
intermediate save point rather than undoing all the work of the
transaction. For example a conversational transaction which involves
several user interactions might establish a save point at each user
message thereby minimizing retyping by the user. Save points <u>do not</u>
commit any of the transaction's updates. Each save point is numbered,
the beginning of the transaction is save point 1 and successive save
points are numbered 2, 3, ... The user is allowed to save some data
at each save point and to retrieve this data if he returns to that
point. Backing up to save point 1 resets the transaction instance to

The recovery component provides the actions:

- BEGIN_TRANSACTION: designates the beginning of a transaction.

- SAVE_TRANSACTION: designates a fire-wall within the transaction.
  If an incomplete transaction is backed-up, undo may stop at such a
  point rather than undoing the entire transaction.

- BACKUP_TRANSACTION: undoes the effects of a transaction to a
  earlier save point.

- COMMIT_TRANSACTION: signals successful completion of transaction
  and causes outputs to be committed.

- ABORT_TRANSACTION: causes undo of a transaction.
its initial state.

Using these primitives, application programs can construct groups of
actions which are atomic. It is interesting that this one level of
recovery is adequate to support multiple levels of transactions by
using the notion of save point.

The recovery component supports two actions which deal with system
recovery rather than transaction recovery:

- CHECKPOINT: Coordinates the recording of the system state in the
  log.

- RESTART: Coordinates system restart, reading the checkpoint log record and using the log to either redo committed transactions and undo transactions which were uncommitted at the time of the shutdown or crash.

5.1. TRANSACTION SCHEDULING.

The scheduling problem can be broken into many components: listening for new work, allocating resources for new work, scheduling (maintaining the dispatcher list), and dispatching.

The listener is event driven. It receives messages from data communications and from dispatched processes.

A distinguished field of the message specifies a transaction name. Often, this field has been filled in by data communications which resolved the transaction name to a reference to a transaction descriptor. Sometimes this field is symbolic in which case the listener uses the name in a directory call to get a reference to the transaction descriptor. (The directory may be determined by the message source.) If the name is bad or if the sender is not authorized to invoke the transaction then the message is discarded and and a negative acknowledge is sent to the source of the message.

If the sender is authorized to invoke the named transaction, then the allocator examines the transaction descriptor and the current system state and decides whether to put this message in a work-to-do list or to allocate the transaction right away. Criteria for this are:

- The system may be overloaded ("full".)

- There may be a limit on the number of transactions of this type which can run concurrently.

- There may be a threshold, N, such that N messages of this type must arrive at which point a server is allocated and the messages are batched to this server.

- The transaction may have an affinity to resources which are unavailable.

- The transaction may run at a special time (overnight, off-shift,...)

If the transaction can run immediately, then the allocator either allocates a new process to process the message or gives the message to a primed transaction which is waiting for input.

If a new process is to be created, a process (domain) is allocated and all objects mentioned in the transaction descriptor are allocated as part of the domain. Program management sets up the address space to hold the programs, data management will allocate the cursors of the transaction for the process, data communication allocates the necessary queues, the recovery component allocates a log cursor and writes a begin transaction log record, and so on. The process is then set up with a pointer to the input message.

This allocated process is given to the scheduler which eventually places it on the dispatcher queue. The dispatcher eventually runs the process.

Once the process is dispatched by the transaction scheduler, the operating system scheduler is responsible for scheduling the process against the physical resources of the system.

When the transaction completes, it returns to the scheduler. The scheduler may or may not collapse the process structure depending on whether the transaction is batched or primed. If the transaction has released resources needed by waiting unscheduled transactions, the scheduler will now dispatch these transactions.

Primed transactions are an optimization which dramatically reduce allocation and deallocation overhead. Process allocation can be an expensive operation and so transactions which are executed frequently are often _primed_. A primed transaction has a large part of the domain already built. In particular programs are loaded, cursors are allocated and the program prolog has been executed. The transaction (process) is waiting for input. The scheduler need only pass the message to the transaction (process). Often the system administrator or operator will prime several instances of a transaction. A banking system doing three withdrawals and five deposits per second might have two withdrawal transactions and four deposit transactions primed.

Yet another variant has the process ask for a message after it completes. If a new message has arrived for that transaction type, then the process processes it. If there is no work for the transaction, then the process disappears. This is called _batching messages_ as opposed to priming. It is appropriate if message traffic is "bursty" (not uniformly distributed in time). It avoids keeping a process allocated when there is no work for it to do.

5.2. DISTRIBUTED TRANSACTION MANAGEMENT.

A distributed system is assumed to consist of a collection of autonomous _nodes_ which are tied together with a distributed data communication system in the style of high level ARPANET, DECNET, or SNA protocols. Resources are assumed to be _partitioned_ in the sense that a resource is owned by only one node. The system should be:

- Inhomogeneous (nodes are small, medium, large, ours, theirs,...)

- Unaffected by the loss of messages.

- Unaffected by the loss of nodes (i.e. requests to that node wait for the node to return, other nodes continue working.)

Each node may implement whatever data management and transaction management system it wants to. We only require that it obey the network protocols. So one node might be a minicomputer running a fairly simple data management system and using an old-master new-master recovery protocol. Another node might be running a very sophisticated data management system with many concurrent transactions and fancy recovery.

If one transaction may access resources in many nodes of a network then a part of the transaction must "run" in each node. We already have an

Each node will want to

- Authorize local actions of the process.

- Build an execution environment for the process.

- Track local resources held by the process.

- Establish a recovery mechanism to undo the local updates of that process (see recovery section).

- Observe the two phase commit protocol (in cooperation with its cohorts (see section on recovery)).

entity which represents transaction instances: processes.

Therefore, the structure needed for a process in a distributed system is almost identical to the structure needed by a transaction in a centralized system.

This latter observation is key. That is why I advocate viewing each node as a transaction processor. (This is a minority view.) To install a distributed transaction, one must install prototypes for its cohorts in the various nodes. This allows each node to control access by distributed transactions in the same way it controls access by terminals. If a node wants to give away the keys to its kingdom it can install a universal cohort (transaction) which has access to all data and which performs all requests.

If a transaction wants to initiate a process (cohort) in a new node, some process of the transaction must request that the node construct a cohort and that the cohort go into session with the requesting process (see data communications section for a discussion of sessions). The picture below shows this.

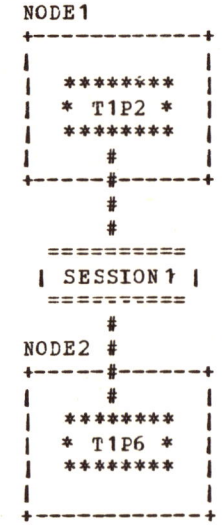

```
                    NODE1
              +------------+
              |            |
              |  *******   |
              |  * T1P2 *  |
              |  *******   |
              |      #     |
              |      #     |
              +-----#------+
                    #
                    #
                ==========
                | SESSION1 |
                ==========
                    #
              NODE2 #
              +-----#------+
              |     #      |
              |  *******   |
              |  * T1P6 *  |
              |  *******   |
              |            |
              |            |
              +------------+
```

Two cohorts of a distributed transaction in session.

A process carries both the transaction name T1 and the process name (in NODE1 the cohort of T1 is process P2 and in NODE2 the cohort of T1 is process P6.)

The two processes can now converse and carry out the work of the transaction. If one process aborts, they should both abort, and if one process commits they should both commit. Thus they need to:

- obey the lock protocol of holding locks to end of transaction (see section on locking).

- observe the two phase commit protocol (see recovery section).

These comments obviously generalize to transactions of more than two chorts.

5.3. THE DATA MANAGEMENT SYSTEM AS A SUBSYSTEM.

It has been the recent experience of general purpose operating systems that the operating system is extended or enhanced by some "application program" like a data management system, or a network management system. Each of these systems often has very clear ideas about resource management and scheduling. It is almost impossible to write such systems unless the basic operating system:

- allows the subsystem to appear to users as an *extension* of the basic operating system.

- allows the subsystem to participate in major system events such as system shutdown/restart, process termination,....

To cope with these problems, operating systems have either made system calls indistinguishable from other calls (e.g. MULTICS) or they have reserved a set of operating systems calls for subsystems (e.g. user SVCs in OS/360.) These two approaches address only the first of the two problems above.

The notion of *sub-system* is introduced to capture the second notion. For example, in IBM's operating system VS release 2.2, notifies each known subsystem at important system events (e.g. startup, memory failure, checkpoint,...) Typically a user might install a Job Entry Subsystem, a Network Subsystem, a Text Processing Subsystem, and perhaps several different Data Management Subsystems on the same operating system. The basic operating system serves as a co-ordinator among these sub-systems.

- It passes calls from users to these subsystems.

- It broadcasts events to all subsystems.

The data manager acts a a subsystem of the host operating system, extending it's basic facilities.

The data management component is in turn comprised of components. The following is a partial list of the components in the bottom half of the data base component of System R:

- Catalog manager: maintains directories of system objects.

- Call analyzer: regulates system entry-exit.

- Record manager: extracts records from pages.
- Index component: maintains indices on the data base.
- Sort component: maintains sorted versions of sets.
- Loader: performs bulk insertion of records into a file.
- Buffer manager: maps data base pages to and from secondary storage.
- Perfomance monitor: Keeps statistics about system performance and state.
- Lock component: maintains the locks (synchronization primitives).
- Recovery manager: implements the notion of transaction COMMIT, ABORT, and handles system restart.
- Log manager: maintains the system log.

Notice that primitive forms of these functions are present in most general purpose operating systems. In the future one may expect to see the operating system subsume most of these data management functions.

5.4. EXCEPTION HANDLING

The protocol for handling synchronous errors (errors which are generated by the process) is another issue defined by transaction management (extending the basic operating systems facilities). In general the data management system wants to abort the transaction if the application program fails. This is generally handled by organizing the exceptions into a hierarchy. If a lower level of the hierarchy fails to handle the error, it is passed to a higher node of the hierarchy. The data manager usually has a few handlers very near the top of the hierarchy (the operating system gets the root of the hierarchy.)

- Either the process or the data management system (or both) may _establish_ an exception handler to field errors.
- When, an exception is _detected_ then the exception is _signaled_.
- Exception handlers are invoked in some fixed order (usually order of establishment) until one successfully corrects the error. This operation is called _percolation_.

PL/1 ON units or the IBM Operating System set-task-abnormal-exit (STAE) are instances of this mechanism. Examples of exception conditions are: arithmetic exception conditions (i.e., overflow), invalid program reference (i.e., to protected storage) wild branches, infinite loops, deadlock, ... and attempting to read beyond end of file.

There may be several exception handlers active for a process at a particular instant. The program's handler is usually given the first try at recovery if the program has established a handler. The handler will, in general, diagnose the failure as one that was expected (overflow), one that was unexpected but can be handled (invalid program reference), or one that is unexpected and cannot be dealt with by the handler (infinite loop). If the failure can be corrected, the handler makes the correction and continues processing the program (perhaps at a different point of execution). If the failure cannot be corrected by this handler, then the exception will percolate to the next exception handler for that process. The system generally aborts any process which percolates to the system recovery routine or does not participate in recovery. This process involves terminating all processing being done on behalf of the process, restoring all nonconsumable resources in use by the process to operating system control (i.e., storage), and removing to the greatest extent possible the effects of the transaction.

5.5. OTHER COMPONENTS WITHIN TRANSACTION MANAGEMENT

We mention in passing that the transaction management component must also support the following notions:

- Timer services: Performing operations at specified times. This involves running transactions at specified times or intervals and providing a timed wait if it is not available from the base operating system.

- Directory management: Management of the directories used by transaction management and other components of the system. This is a high-performance low-function in-core data management system. Given a name and a type (queue, transaction, endpoint,...) it returns a reference to the object of that name and type. (This is where the cache of dictionary descriptors is kept.)

- Authorization Control: Regulates the building and use of transactions.
  These topics will be discussed by other lecturers.

5.6. BIBLIOGRAPHY.

Stonebraker, Neuhold, "A Distributed Data Base Version of INGRESS", Proceedings of Second Berkeley Workshop on Networks and Distributed Data, Lawrence Livermore Laboratory, (1977). (Gives another approach to distributed transaction management.)

"Information Management System / Virtual Storage (IMS/VS) System Manual Vol. 1: Logic.", IBM, form number LY20-8004-2. (Tells all about IMS. The discussion of scheduling presented here is in the tradition of IMS/VS pp 3.36-3.41.)

"OS/VS2 System Logic Library.", IBM, form number SY28-0763, (Documents the subsystem interface of OS/VS pp. 3.159-3.168.)

"OS/VS2 MVS Supervisor Services and Macro Instructions.", IBM, form number GC28-0756, (Explains OS percolation on pages 53-62.)

5.7. LOCK MANAGEMENT.

This section derives from papers co-authored with Irv Traiger and Franco Putzolu.

The system consists of objects which are related in certain ways. These relationships are best thought of as <u>assertions</u> about the objects. Examples of such assertions are:
 'Names is an index for Telephone_numbers.'
 'Count_of_x is the number of employees in department x.'

The system state is said to be <u>consistent</u> if it satisfies all its assertions. In some cases, the data base must become temporarily inconsistent in order to transform it to a new consistent state. For example, adding a new employee involves several atomic actions and the updating of several fields. The data base may be inconsistent until all these updates have been completed.

To cope with these temporary inconsistencies, sequences of atomic actions are grouped to form transactions. Transactions are the units of consistency. They are larger atomic actions on the system state which transform it from one consistent state to a new consistent state. Transactions preserve consistency. If some action of a transaction fails then the entire transaction is 'undone' thereby returning the data base to a consistent state. Thus transactions are also the units of recovery. Hardware failure, system error, deadlock, protection violations and program error are each a source of such failure.

5.7.1. PROS AND CONS OF CONCURRENCY

If transactions are run one at a time then each transaction will see the consistent state left behind by its predecessor. But if several transactions are scheduled concurrently then the inputs of some transaction may be inconsistent even though each transaction in isolation is consistent.

Concurrency is introduced to improve system response and utilization.

- It should not cause programs to malfunction.

- Concurrency control should not consume more resources than it "saves".

If the data base is read-only then no concurrency control is needed. However, if transactions update shared data then their concurrent execution needs to be regulated so that they do not update the same item at the same time.

If all transactions are simple and all data are in primary storage then there is no need for concurrency. However, if any transaction runs for a long time or does I/O then concurrency may be needed to improve responsiveness and utilization of the system. If concurrency is allowed, then long-running transactions will (usually) not delay short ones.

Concurrency must be regulated by some facility which regulates access to shared resources. Data management systems typically use locks for this purpose.

The simplest lock protocol associates a lock with each object. Whenever using the object, the transaction acquires the lock and holds it until the transaction is complete. The lock is a serialization mechanism which insures that only one transaction accesses the object at a time. It has the effect of: notifying others that the object is busy; and of protecting the lock requestor from modifications of others.

This protocol varies from the serially reusable resource protocol common to most operating systems (and recently renamed monitors) in that the lock protocol holds locks to transaction commit. It will be argued below that this is a critical difference.

Responsibility for requesting and releasing locks can either be assumed by the user or be delegated to the system. User controlled locking results in potentially fewer locks due to the user's knowledge of the semantics of the data. On the other hand, user controlled locking requires difficult and potentially unreliable application programming. Hence the approach taken by most data base systems is to use automatic lock protocols which insure protection from inconsistency, while still allowing the user to specify alternative lock protocols as an optimization.

5.7.2. CONCURRENCY PROBLEMS

Locking is intended to eliminate three forms of inconsistency due to concurrency.

- Lost Updates: If transaction T1 updates a record previously updated by transaction T2 then undoing T2 will also undo the update of T1. (i.e. if transaction T1 updates record R from 100 to 101 and then transaction T2 updates A from 101 to 151 then backing up T1 will set A back to the original value of 100 losing the update of T2.) This is called a Write -> Write dependency.

- Dirty Read: If transaction T1 updates a record which is read by T2, then if T1 aborts T2 will have read a record which never existed. (i.e. T1 updates R to 100,000,000, T2 reads this value, T1 then aborts and the record returns to the value 100). This is called a Write -> Read dependency.

- Un-repeatable Read: If transaction T1 reads a record which is then altered and committed by T2 and if T1 re-reads the record then T1 will see two different committed values for the same record. Such a dependency is called a Read -> Write dependency.

If there were no concurrency then none of these anomalous cases would arise.

Note that the order in which reads occur does not affect concurrency. In particular reads commute. That is why we do not care about Read -> Read dependencies.

5.7.3. MODEL OF CONSISTENCY AND LOCK PROTOCOLS

A fairly formal model is required in order to make precise statements about the issues of locking and recovery. Because the problems are so complex one must either accept many simplifying assumptions or accept a less formal approach. A compromise is adopted here. First we will introduce a fairly formal model of transactions, locks and recovery which will allow us to discuss the issues of lock management and recovery management. After this presentation, the implementation issues associated with locking and recovery will be discussed.

5.7.3.1. Several Definitions of Consistency

Several _equivalent_ definitions of consistency are presented. The first definition is an operational and intuitive one useful in describing the system behavior to users. The second definition is a procedural one in terms of lock protocols, it is useful in explaining the system implementation. The third definition is in terms of a trace of the system actions, it is useful in formally stating and proving consistency properties.

5.7.3.1.1. Informal Definition of Consistency

An output (write) of a transaction is _committed_ when the transaction abdicates the right to 'undo' the write thereby making the new value available to all other transactions (i.e. commits). Outputs are said to be _uncommitted_ or _dirty_ if they are not yet committed by the writer. Concurrent execution raises the problem that reading or writing other transactions' dirty data may yield inconsistent data.

Using this notion of dirty data, consistency may be defined as:

Definition 1: Transaction T _sees a consistent state_ if:
 (a) T does not overwrite dirty data of other transactions.
 (b) T does not commit any writes until it completes all its writes (i.e. until the end of transaction (EOT)).
 (c) T does not read dirty data from other transactions.
 (d) Other transactions do not dirty any data read by T before T completes.

Clauses (a) and (b) insure that there are no lost updates.

Clause (c) isolates a transaction from the uncommitted data of other transactions. Without this clause, a transaction might read uncommitted values which are subsequently updated or are undone. If clause (c) is observed, no uncommitted _values_ are read.

Clause (d) insures repeatable reads. For example, without clause (c) a transaction may read two different (committed) values if it reads the same entity twice. This is because a transaction which updates the entity could begin, update and commit in the interval between the two reads. More elaborate kinds of anomalies due to concurrency are possible if one updates an entity after reading it or if more than one entity is involved (see example below).

The rules specified have the properties that:

1. If all transactions observe the consistency protocols then any execution of the system is equivalent to some "serial" execution of the transactions (i.e. it is as though there was no concurrency.)

2. If all transactions observe the consistency protocols, then each transaction sees a consistent state.

3. If all transactions observe the consistency protocols then system backup (undoing all in-progress transactions) loses no updates of completed transactions.

4. If all transactions observe the consistency protocols then transaction backup (undoing any in-progress transaction) produces

a consistent state.

Assertions 1 and 2 are proved in the paper "On the Notions of Consistency and Predicate Locks" CACM Vol. 9, No. 11, Nov. 1976. Proving the second two assertions is a good research problem. It requires extending the model used for the first two assertions and reviewed here to include recovery notions.

5.7.3.1.2. Schedules: Formalize Dirty and Committed Data

The definition of what it means for a transaction to see a consistent state was given in terms of dirty data. In order to make the notion of dirty data explicit it is necessary to consider the execution of a transaction in the context of a set of concurrently executing transactions. To do this we introduce the notion of a schedule for a set of transactions. A schedule can be thought of as a history or audit trail of the actions performed by the set of transactions. Given a schedule the notion of a particular entity being dirtied by a particular transaction is made explicit and hence the notion of seeing a consistent state is formalized. These notions may then be used to connect the various definitions of consistency and show their equivalence.

The system directly supports _objects_ and _actions_. Actions are categorized as _begin_ actions, _end_ actions, _abort_ actions, _share lock_ actions, _exclusive lock_ actions, _unlock_ actions, _read_ actions, and _write_ actions. Commit and abort actions are presumed to unlock any locks held by the transaction but not explicitly unlocked by the transaction. For the purposes of the following definitions, share lock actions and their corresponding unlock actions are additionally considered to be read actions and exclusive lock actions and their corresponding unlock actions are additionally considered to be write actions.

For the purposes of this model, a _transaction_ is any sequence of actions beginning with a begin action and ending with an commit or abort action and not containing other begin, commit or abort actions. Here are two trivial transactions.

```
T1 BEGIN                T2 BEGIN
   SHARE LOCK A            SHARE LOCK B
   EXCLUSIVE LOCK B        READ B
   READ A                  SHARE LOCK A
   WRITE B                 READ A
   COMMIT                  ABORT
```

Any (sequence preserving) merging of the actions of a set of transactions into a single sequence is called a _schedule_ for the set of transactions.

A schedule is a history of the order in which actions were successfully executed (it does not record actions which were undone due to backup (This aspect of the model needs to be generalized to prove assertions 3 and 4 above)). The simplest schedules run all actions of one transaction and then all actions of another transaction,... Such one-transaction-at-a-time schedules are called _serial_ because they have no concurrency among transactions. Clearly, a serial schedule has no concurrency induced inconsistency and no transaction sees dirty data.

Locking constrains the set of allowed schedules. In particular, a schedule is _legal_ only if it does not schedule a lock action on an entity for one transaction when that entity is already locked by some

other transaction in a conflicting mode. The following table shows the
compatibility among the simple lock modes.

```
-----------------------------------------------
|                      |      MODE OF LOCK     |
|     COMPATIBILITY    |-----------------------|
|                      | SHARE    | EXCLUSIVE  |
|----------------------|-----------------------|
| MODE OF  | SHARE     | COMPATIBLE | CONFLICT |
| REQUEST  |-----------------------------------|
|          | EXCLUSIVE | CONFLICT   | CONFLICT |
-----------------------------------------------
```

The following are three example schedules of two transactions. The
first schedule is legal, the second is serial and legal and the third
schedule is not legal since T1 and T2 have conflicting locks on the
object A.

```
T1 BEGIN              T1 BEGIN              T2 BEGIN
T2 BEGIN              T1 SHARE LOCK A       T1 BEGIN
T2 SHARE LOCK B       T1 EXCLUSIVE LOCK B   T1 EXCLUSIVE LOCK A
T2 READ B             T1 READ A             T2 SHARE LOCK B
T1 SHARE LOCK A       T1 WRITE B            T2 READ B
T2 SHARE LOCK A       T1 COMMIT             T2 SHARE LOCK A
T2 READ A             T2 BEGIN              T2 READ A
T2 ABORT              T2 SHARE LOCK B       T2 ABORT
T1 EXCLUSIVE LOCK B   T2 READ B             T1 SHARE LOCK B
T1 READ A             T2 SHARE LOCK A       T1 READ A
T1 WRITE B            T2 READ A             T1 WRITE B
T1 COMMIT             T2 ABORT              T1 COMMIT

legal&¬serial         legal&serial          ¬legal&¬serial
```
The three varieties of schedules (serial&¬legal impossible).

An initial state and a schedule completely define the system's
behavior. At each step of the schedule one can deduce which entity
values have been committed and which are dirty: if locking is used,
updated data is _dirty_ until it is unlocked.

One transaction instance is said to _depend_ on another if the first
takes some of its inputs from the second. The notion of dependency can
be useful in comparing two schedules of the same set of transactions.

Each schedule, S, defines a ternary _dependency relation_ on the set:
TRANSACTIONS X OBJECTS X TRANSACTIONS as follows. Suppose that
transaction T performs action a on entity e at some step in the
schedule and that transaction T' performs action a' on entity e at a
later step in the schedule. Further suppose that T and T' are distinct.
Then:

   (T,e,T') is in DEP(S)
      if a is a write action and a' is a write action
      or a is a write action and a' is a read action
      or a is a read action and a' is a write action

The dependency set of a schedule completely defines the inputs and
outputs each transaction "sees". If two distinct schedules have the
same dependency set then they provide each transaction with the same
inputs and outputs. Hence we say two schedules are _equivalent_ if they
have the same dependency sets. If a schedule is equivalent to a serial
schedule, then that schedule must be consistent since in a serial

schedule there are no inconsistencies due to concurrency. On the other hand, if a schedule is not equivalent to a serial schedule then it is probable (possible) that some transaction sees an inconsistent state. Hence,

Definition 2: A schedule is __consistent__ if it is equivalent to some serial schedule.

The following argument may clarify the inconsistency of schedules not equivalent to serial schedules. Define the relation <<< on the set of transactions by:

T<<<T' if for some entity e (T,e,T') is in DEP(S).

Let <<<* be the transitive closure of <<<, then define:

   BEFORE(T) = {T'| T' <<<* T}
   AFTER(T) = {T'| T <<<* T'}.

The obvious interpretation of this is that the BEFORE(T) set is the set of transactions which contribute inputs to T and each AFTER(T) set is the set of transactions which take their inputs from T

If some transaction is both before T and after T in some schedule then no serial schedule could give such results. In this case, concurrency has introduced inconsistency. On the other hand, if all relevant transactions are either before or after T (but not both) then T will see a consistent state. If all transactions dichotomize others in this way then the relation <<<* will be a partial order and the whole schedule will provide consistency.

The above definitions can be related as follows:

Assertion:
A schedule is consistent
    if and only if (by definition)
the schedule is equivalent to a serial schedule
    if and only if
the relation <<<* is a partial order.

5.7.3.1.3. Lock Protocol Definition of Consistency

Whether an instantiation of a transaction sees a consistent state depends on the actions of other concurrent transactions. All transactions agree to certain lock protocols so that they can all be guaranteed consistency.

Since the lock system allows only legal schedules we want a lock protocol such that: every legal schedule is a consistent schedule.

Consistency can be procedurally defined by the lock protocol which produces it: A transaction locks its inputs to guarantee their consistency and locks its outputs to mark them as dirty (uncommitted).

For this section, locks are dichotomized as __share mode locks__ which allow multiple readers of the same entity and __exclusive mode locks__ which reserve exclusive access to an entity.

The lock protocols refined to these modes is:

Definition 3: Transaction T observes the consistency lock protocol if:
(a) T sets an exclusive lock on any data it dirties.
(b) T sets a share lock on any data it reads.
(c) T holds all locks to EOT.

These lock protocol definitions can be stated more precisely and tersely with the introduction of the following notation. A transaction is well formed if it always locks an entity in exclusive (shared or exclusive) mode before writing (reading) it.

A transaction is two phase if it does not (share or exclusive) lock an entity after unlocking some entity. A two phase transaction has a growing phase during which it acquires locks and a shrinking phase during which it releases locks.

The lock consistency protocol can be redefined as:

Definition 3': Transaction T observes the consistency lock protocol if it is is well formed and two phase.

Definition 3 was too restrictive in the sense that consistency does not require that a transaction hold all locks to the EOT (i.e. the EOT is the shrinking phase). Rather, the constraint that the transaction be two phase is adequate to insure consistency. On the other hand, once a transaction unlocks an updated entity, it has committed that entity and so cannot be undone without cascading backup to any transactions which may have subsequently read the entity. For that reason, the shrinking phase is usually deferred to the end of the transaction; thus, the transaction is always recoverable and all updates are committed together.

5.7.3.2. Relationship Among Definitions

These definitions may be related as follows: if T sees a consistent state in S.

Assertion:

(a) If each transaction observes the consistency lock protocol (Definition 3') then any legal schedule is consistent (Definition 2) (i.e, each transaction sees a consistent state in the sense of Definition 1).
(b) Unless transaction T observes the consistency lock protocol then it is possible to define another transaction T' which does observe the consistency lock protocol such that T and T' have a legal schedule S but T does not see a consistent state in S.

This says that if a transaction observes the consistency lock protocol definition of consistency (Definition 3') then it is assured of the definition of consistency based on committed and dirty data (Definition 1 or 3). Unless a transaction actually sets the locks prescribed by consistency one can construct transaction mixes and schedules which will cause the transaction to see an inconsistent state. However, in particular cases such transaction mixes may never occur due to the structure or use of the system. In these cases an apparently inadequate locking may actually provide consistency. For example, a data base reorganization usually need do no locking since it is run as an off-line utility which is never run concurrently with other transactions.

5.7.4. LOCKING, TRANSACTION BACKUP AND SYSTEM RECOVERY

To repeat, there is no nice formal model of recovery (Lampson and Sturgis have a model in their forth-coming CACM paper on two phase commit processing but the model in the version I saw was rather vague.) Here, we will limp along with a (even more) vague model.

A transaction T is said to be **recoverable** if it can be undone before 'EOT' without undoing other transactions' updates. A transaction T is said to be **repeatable** if it will reproduce the original output if rerun following recovery, assuming that no locks were released in the backup process. Recoverability requires update locks be held to commit point. Repeatability requires that all transactions observe the consistency lock protocol.

The **normal** (i.e. trouble free) operation of a data base system can be described in terms of an initial consistent state S0 and a schedule of transactions mapping the data base into a final consistent state S3 (see Figure). S1 is a checkpoint state, since transactions are in progress, S1 may be inconsistent. A **system crash** leaves the data base in state S2. Since transactions T3 and T5 were in progress at the time of crash, S2 is potentially inconsistent. **System recovery** amounts to bringing the data base to a new consistent state in one of the following ways:

(a) Starting from state S2, **undo** all actions of transactions in-progress at the time of the crash.

(b) Starting from state S1 first undo all actions of transactions in progress at the time of the crash (i.e. actions of T3 before S1) and then **redo** all actions of transactions which completed after S1 and before the crash (i.e. actions of T2 and T4 after S1).

(c) starting at S0 redo all transactions which completed before the crash.

Observe that (a) and (c) are degenerate cases of (b).

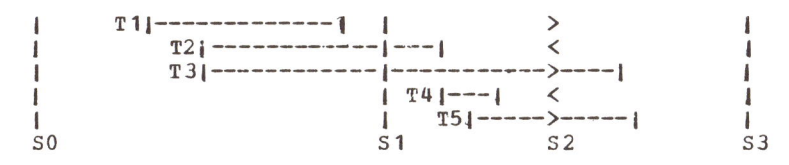

```
|      T1|--------------|  |            >               |
|        T2|-------------|---|         <                |
|          T3|-------------|-----------|----|           |
|                         |  T4|---|  <                 |
|                         |    T5|-----|----->-----|    |
S0                        S1            S2              S3
```

Figure. System states. S0 is initial state, S1 is checkpoint state, S2 is a crash and S3 is the state that results in the absence of a crash.

If some transaction does not hold update locks to commit point then:

- Backing up the transaction may deadlock (because backup must reacquire the locks in order to perform undo.)

- Backing up a transaction may loose updates (because an update may have bee applied to the output of the undone transaction but backup will restore the entity to its original value.)

- Consequentally, backup may <u>cascade</u>: backing up one transaction may require backing up another. (Randell calls this the domino effect.) If for example, T3 writes a record, r, and then T4 further updates r then undoing T3 will cause the update of T4 to r to be lost. This situation can only arise if some transaction does not hold its write locks to commit point. <u>For these reasons, all known data management systems</u> (which support concurrent updators) require that all transactions hold their update locks to commit point.

On the other hand,

- If all the transactions hold all update locks to commit point then system recovery loses no updates of complete transactions. However there may be no schedule which would give the same result because transactions may have <u>read</u> outputs of undone transactions.

- If all the transactions observe the consistency lock protocol then the recovered state is consistent and derives from the schedule obtained from the original system schedule by deleting incomplete transactions. Note that consistency prevents read dependencies on transactions which might be undone by system recovery. The schedule obtained by considering only the actions of completed transactions produces the recovered state.

<u>Transaction crash</u> gives rise to <u>transaction backup</u> which has properties analogous to system recovery.

5.7.5. LOWER DEGREES OF CONSISTENCY

Most systems do not provide consistency as outlined here. Typically they do not hold read locks to EOT so that R->W->R dependencies are not precluded. Very primitive systems sometimes set no read locks at all, rather they only set update locks so as to avoid lost update and deadlock during backout. We have characterized these lock protocols as degree 2 and degree 1 consistency respectively and have studied them extensively (see "Granularity of locks and degrees of consistency in a shared data base", Gray, Lorie, Putzolu, and Traiger, in <u>Modeling in Data Base Systems</u>, North Holland Publishing (1976).) I believe that the lower degrees of consistency are a bad idea but several of my colleagues disagree. The motivation of the lower degrees is performance. If less is locked then less computation and storage is consumed. Further if less is locked, concurrency is increased since fewer conflicts appear. (Note that the granularity lock scheme of the next section is motivated by minimizing the number of explicit locks set.)

5.7.6. LOCK GRANULARITY

An important issue which arises in the design of a system is the choice of <u>lockable units</u>, i.e. the data aggregates which are atomically locked to insure consistency. Examples of lockable units are areas, files, individual records, field values, and intervals of field values.

The choice of lockable units presents a tradeoff between concurrency and overhead, which is related to the size or <u>granularity</u> of the units themselves. On the one hand, concurrency is increased if a fine lockable unit (for example a record or field) is chosen. Such unit is appropriate for a "simple" transaction which accesses few records. On the other hand a fine unit of locking would be costly for a "complex" transaction which accesses a large number of records. Such a transaction would have to set and reset a large number of locks, incurring the computational overhead of many invocations of the lock manager, and the storage overhead of representing many locks. A coarse lockable unit (for example a file) is probably convenient for a transaction which accesses many records. However, such a coarse unit discriminates against transactions which only want to lock one member of the file. From this discussion it follows that it would be desirable to have lockable units of different granularities coexisting in the same system.

The following presents a lock protocol satisfying these requirements and discusses the related implementation issues of scheduling, granting and converting lock requests.

5.7.6.1. Hierarchical Locks

We will first assume that the set of resources to be locked is organized in a hierarchy. Note that this hierarchy is used in the context of a collection of resources and has nothing to do with the data model used in a data base system. The hierarchy of the following figure may be suggestive. We adopt the notation that each level of the hierarchy is given a node type which is a generic name for all the node instances of that type. For example, the data base has nodes of type area as its immediate descendants, each area in turn has nodes of type file as its immediate descendants and each file has nodes of type record as its immediate descendants in the hierarchy. Since it is a hierarchy, each node has a unique parent.

```
            DATA BASE
                |
                |
              AREAS
                |
                |
              FILES
                |
                |
             RECORDS
```

Figure 1. A sample lock hierarchy.

Each node of the hierarchy can be locked. If one requests _exclusive_ access (X) to a particular node, then when the request is granted, the requestor has exclusive access to that node and _implicitly to each of its descendants_. If one requests _shared_ access (S) to a particular node, then when the request is granted, the requestor has shared access to that node _and implicitly to each descendant of that node_. These two access modes lock an _entire subtree_ rooted at the requested node.

Our goal is to find some technique for _implicitly_ locking an entire subtree. In order to lock a subtree rooted at node R in share or exclusive mode it is important to _prevent_ locks on the ancestors of R which might implicitly lock R and its descendants in an incompatible mode. Hence a new access mode, _intention mode_ (I), is introduced. Intention mode is used to "tag" (lock) all ancestors of a node to be locked in share or exclusive mode. These tags signal the fact that locking is being done at a "finer" level and thereby prevents implicit or explicit exclusive or share locks on the ancestors.

The protocol to lock a subtree rooted at node R in exclusive or share mode is to first lock all ancestors of R in intention mode and then to lock node R in exclusive or share mode. For example, using the figure above, to lock a particular file one should obtain intention access to the data base, to the area containing the file and then request exclusive (or share) access to the file itself. This implicitly locks all records of the file in exclusive (or share) mode.

5.7.6.2. Access Modes and Compatibility

We say that two lock requests for the same node by two different transactions are _compatible_ if they can be granted concurrently. The mode of the request determines its compatibility with requests made by other transactions. The three modes X, S and I are incompatible with one another but distinct S requests may be granted together and distinct I requests may be granted together.

The compatibilities among modes derive from their semantics. Share mode allows reading but not modification of the corresponding resource by the requestor and by other transactions. The semantics of exclusive mode is that the grantee may read and modify the resource but no other transaction may read or modify the resource while the exclusive lock is set. The reason for dichotomizing share and exclusive access is that several share requests can be granted concurrently (are compatible) whereas an exclusive request is not compatible with any other request. Intention mode was introduced to be incompatible with share and exclusive mode (to prevent share and exclusive locks). However, intention mode is compatible with itself since two transactions having intention access to a node will explicitly lock descendants of the node in X, S or I mode and thereby will either be compatible with one another or will be scheduled on the basis of their requests at the finer level. For example, two transactions can simultaneously be granted the data base and some area and some file in intention mode. In this case their explicit locks on particular records in the file will resolve any conflicts among them.

The notion of intention mode is refined to **intention share mode** (IS) and **intention exclusive mode** (IX) for two reasons: the intention share mode only requests share or intention share locks at the lower nodes of the tree (i.e. never requests an exclusive lock below the intention share node), hence IS is compatible with S mode. Since read only is a common form of access it will be profitable to distinguish this for greater concurrency. Secondly, if a transaction has an intention share lock on a node it can convert this to a share lock at a later time, but one cannot convert an intention exclusive lock to a share lock on a node. Rather to get the combined rights of share mode and intention exclusive mode one must obtain an X or SIX mode lock. (This issue is discussed in the section on rerequests below).

We recognize one further refinement of modes, namely **share and intention exclusive mode** (SIX). Suppose one transaction wants to read an entire subtree and to update particular nodes of that subtree. Using the modes provided so far it would have the options of: (a) requesting exclusive access to the root of the subtree and doing no further locking or (b) requesting intention exclusive access to the root of the subtree and explicitly locking the lower nodes in intention, share or exclusive mode. Alternative (a) has low concurrency. If only a small fraction of the read nodes are updated then alternative (b) has high locking overhead. The correct access mode would be share access to the subtree thereby allowing the transaction to read all nodes of the subtree without further locking _and_ intention exclusive access to the subtree thereby allowing the transaction to set exclusive locks on those nodes in the subtree which are to be updated and IX or SIX locks on the intervening nodes. Since this is a common case, SIX mode is introduced. It is compatible with IS mode since other transactions requesting IS mode will explicitly lock lower nodes in IS or S mode thereby avoiding any updates (IX or X mode) produced by the SIX mode transaction. However SIX mode is not compatible with IX, S, SIX or X mode requests.

The table below gives the compatibility of the request modes, where null mode (NL) represents the absence of a request.

	NL	IS	IX	S	SIX	X
NL	YES	YES	YES	YES	YES	YES
IS	YES	YES	YES	YES	YES	NO
IX	YES	YES	YES	NO	NO	NO
S	YES	YES	NO	YES	NO	NO
SIX	YES	YES	NO	NO	NO	NO
X	YES	NO	NO	NO	NO	NO

Table 1. Compatibilities among access modes.

To summarize, we recognize six modes of access to a resource:

NL: Gives no access to a node, i.e. represents the absence of a request of a resource.

IS: Gives intention share access to the requested node and allows the requestor to lock descendant nodes in S or IS mode. (It does no implicit locking.)

IX: Gives intention exclusive access to the requested node and allows the requestor to explicitly lock descendants in X, S, SIX, IX or IS mode. (It does no implicit locking.)

S: Gives share access to the requested node and to all descendants of the requested node without setting further locks. (It implicitly sets S locks on all descendants of the requested node.)

SIX: Gives share and intention exclusive access to the requested node. (In particular it implicitly locks all descendants of the node in share mode and allows the requestor to explicitly lock descendant nodes in X, SIX or IX mode.)

X: Gives exclusive access to the requested node and to all descendants of the requested node without setting further locks. (It implicitly sets X locks on all descendants. Locking lower nodes in S or IS mode would give no increased access.)

IS mode is the weakest non-null form of access to a resource. It carries fewer privileges than IX or S modes. IX mode allows IS, IX, S, SIX and X mode locks to be set on descendant nodes while S mode allows read only access to all descendants of the node without further locking. SIX mode carries the privileges of S and of IX mode (hence the name SIX). X mode is the most privileged form of access and allows reading and writing of all descendants of a node without further locking. Hence the modes can be ranked in the partial order of privileges shown the figure below. Note that it is not a total order since IX and S are incomparable.

```
          X
          |
         SIX
          |
     _____|_____
    |           |
    S          IX
    |           |
    |_____|
          |
         IS
          |
         NL
```

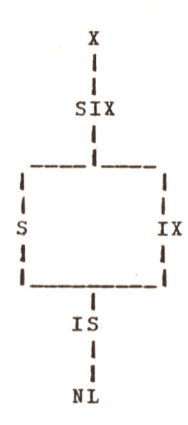

Figure 2. The partial ordering of modes by their privileges.

5.7.6.3. Rules for Requesting Nodes

The implicit locking of nodes will not work if transactions are allowed to leap into the middle of the tree and begin locking nodes at random. The implicit locking implied by the S and X modes depends on all transactions obeying the following protocol:

(a) Before requesting an S or IS lock on a node, all ancestor nodes of the requested node must be held in IX or IS mode by the requestor.

(b) Before requesting an X, SIX or IX lock on a node, all ancestor nodes of the requested node must be held in SIX or IX mode by the requestor.

(c) Locks should be released either at the end of the transaction (in any order) or in leaf to root order. In particular, if locks are not held to end of transaction, one should not hold a lock after releasing its ancestors.

To paraphrase this, locks are requested root to leaf, and released leaf to root. Notice that leaf nodes are never requested in intention mode since they have no descendants. and that once a node is acquired in S or X mode, no further explicit locking is required at lower levels.

5.7.6.4. Several Examples

```
To lock record R for read:
  lock data-base              with mode = IS
  lock area containing R      with mode = IS
  lock file containing R      with mode = IS
  lock record R               with mode = S
```
Don't panic, the transaction probably already has the data base, area and file lock.

```
To lock record R for write-exclusive access:
  lock data-base              with mode = IX
  lock area containing R      with mode = IX
  lock file containing R      with mode = IX
  lock record R               with mode = X
```
Note that if the records of this and the previous example are distinct, each request can be granted simultaneously to different transactions even though both refer to the same file.

To lock a file F for read and write access:
  lock data-base   with mode = IX
  lock area containing F   with mode = IX
  lock file F   with mode = X
Since this reserves exclusive access to the file, if this request uses the same file as the previous two examples it or the other transactions will have to wait. Unlike examples 1, 2 and 4, no additional locking need be done (at the record level).

To lock a file F for complete scan and occasional update:
  lock data-base   with mode = IX
  lock area containing F   with mode = IX
  lock file F   with mode = SIX
Thereafter, particular records in F can be locked for update by locking records in X mode. Notice that (unlike the previous example) this transaction is compatible with the first example. This is the reason for introducing SIX mode.

To quiesce the data base:
  lock data base with mode = X.
Note that this locks everyone else out.

5.7.6.5. Directed Acyclic Graphs of Locks

The notions so far introduced can be generalized to work for directed acyclic graphs (DAG) of resources rather than simply hierarchies of resources. A tree is a simple DAG. The key observation is that to implicitly or explicitly lock a node, one should lock **all** the parents of the node in the DAG and so by induction lock all ancestors of the node. In particular, to lock a subgraph one must implicitly or explicitly lock all ancestors of the subgraph in the appropriate mode (for a tree there is only one parent). To give an example of a non-hierarchical structure, imagine the locks are organized as:

```
            DATA BASE
                |
                |
              AREAS
                |
         _____|_____
         |             |
         |             |
       FILES        INDICES
         |             |
         |_____|
                |
                |
             RECORDS
```

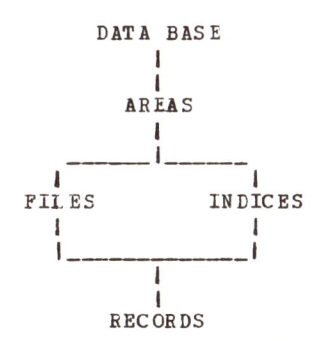

Figure 3. A non-hierarchical lock graph.

We postulate that areas are "physical" notions and that files, indices and records are logical notions. The data base is a collection of areas. Each area is a collection of files and indices. Each file has a corresponding index in the same area. Each record belongs to some file and to its corresponding index. A record is comprised of field values and some field is indexed by the index associated with the file containing the record. The file gives a sequential access path to the records and the index gives an associative access path to the records based on field values. Since individual fields are never locked, they do not appear in the lock graph.

To write a record R in file F with index I:
```
lock data base              with mode = IX
lock area containing F      with mode = IX
lock file F                 with mode = IX
lock index I                with mode = IX
lock record R               with mode = X
```

Note that _all_ paths to record R are locked. Alternatively, one could lock F and I in exclusive mode thereby implicitly locking R in exclusive mode.

To give a more complete explanation we observe that a node can be locked _explicitly_ (by requesting it) or _implicitly_ (by appropriate explicit locks on the ancestors of the node) in one of five modes: IS, IX, S, SIX, X. However, the definition of implicit locks and the protocols for setting explicit locks have to be extended for DAG's as follows:

A node is _implicitly granted in_ S mode to a transaction if _at least one_ of its parents is (implicitly or explicitly) granted to the transaction in S, SIX or X mode. By induction that means that at least one of the node's ancestors must be explicitly granted in S, SIX or X mode to the transaction.

A node is _implicitly granted in X_ mode if _all_ of its parents are (implicitly or explicitly) granted to the transaction in X mode. By induction, this is equivalent to the condition that all nodes in some cut set of the collection of all paths leading from the node to the roots of the graph are explicitly granted to the transaction in X mode and all ancestors of nodes in the cut set are explicitly granted in IX or SIX mode.

By examination of the partial order of modes (see figure above), a node is implicitly granted in IS mode if it is implicitly granted in S mode, and a node is implicitly granted in IS, IX, S and SIX mode if it is implicitly granted in X mode.

5.7.6.6. The Protocol For Requesting Locks On a DAG

(a) Before requesting an S or IS lock on a node, one should request at least one parent (and by induction a path to a root) in IS (or greater) mode. As a consequence none of the ancestors along this path can be granted to another transaction in a mode incompatible with IS.

(b) Before requesting IX, SIX or X mode access to a node, one should request all parents of the node in IX (or greater) mode. As a consequence all ancestors will be held in IX (or greater mode) and cannot be held by other transactions in a mode incompatible with IX (i.e. S, SIX, X).

(c) Locks should be released either at the end of the transaction (in any order) or in leaf to root order. In particular, if locks are not held to the end of transaction, one should not hold a lower lock after releasing its ancestors.

To give an example using the non-hierarchichal lock graph in the figure above, a sequential scan of all records in file F need not use an index so one can get an implicit share lock on each record in the file by:

```
lock data base              with mode = IS
lock area containing F      with mode = IS
```

```
    lock file F                   with mode = S
```

This gives implicit S mode access to all records in F. Conversely, to read a record in a file via the index I for file F, one need not get an implicit or explicit lock on file F:

```
    lock data base                with mode = IS
    lock area containing R        with mode = IS
    lock index I                  with mode = S
```

This again gives implicit S mode access to all records in index I (in file F). In both these cases, <u>only one path was locked for reading</u>.

But to insert, delete or update a record R in file F with index I one must get an implicit or explicit lock on all ancestors of R.

The first example of this section showed how an explicit X lock on a record is obtained. To get an implicit X lock on all records in a file one can simply lock the index <u>and</u> file in X mode, or lock the area in X mode. The latter examples allow bulk load or update of a file without further locking since all records in the file are implicitly granted in X mode.

5.7.6.7. Proof Of Equivalence Of The Lock Protocol

We will now prove that the described lock protocol is equivalent to a conventional one which uses only two modes (S and X), and which explicitly locks atomic resources (the leaves of a tree or sinks of a DAG).

Let $G = (N,A)$ be a finite (directed acyclic) <u>graph</u> where N is the set of nodes and A is the set of arcs. G is assumed to be without circuits (i.e. there is no non-null path leading from a node n to itself). A node p is a <u>parent</u> of a node n and n is a <u>child</u> of p if there is an arc from p to n. A node n is a <u>source</u> (<u>sink</u>) if n has no parents (no children). Let Q be the set of sinks of G. An <u>ancestor</u> of node n is any node (including n) in a path from a source to n. A <u>node-slice</u> of a sink n is a collection of nodes such that each path from a source to n contains at least one node of the slice.

We also introduce the set of lock modes $M = \{NL, IS, IX, S, SIX, X\}$ and the compatibility matrix $C : M \times M \rightarrow \{YES, NO\}$ described in Table 1. Let $c : m \times m \rightarrow \{YES, NO\}$ be the restriction of C to $m = \{NL, S, X\}$.

A <u>lock-graph</u> is a mapping $L : N \rightarrow M$ such that:
(a) if $L(n) \in \{IS, S\}$ then either n is a source or there exists a parent p of n such that $L(p) \in \{IS, IX, S, SIX, X\}$. By induction there exists a path from a source to n such that L takes only values in $\{IS, IX, S, SIX, X\}$ on it. Equivalently L is not equal to NL on the path.
(b) if $L(n) \in \{IX, SIX, X\}$ then either n is a root or for all parents $p_1 \ldots p_k$ of n we have $L(p_i) \in \{IX, SIX, X\}$ ($i=1 \ldots k$). By induction L takes only values in $\{IX, SIX, X\}$ on all the ancestors of n.

The interpretation of a lock-graph is that it gives a map of the explicit locks held by a particular transaction observing the six state lock protocol described above. The notion of projection of a lock-graph is now introduced to model the set of implicit locks on atomic resources acquired by a transaction.

The projection of a lock-graph L is the mapping l: Q->m constructed as follows:
(a) l(n)=X if there exists a node-slice {n1...ns} of n such that L(ni)=X for each node in the slice.
(b) l(n)=S if (a) is not satisfied and there exists an ancestor na of n such that L(na) C {S,SIX,X}.
(c) l(n)=NL if (a) and (b) are not satisfied.

Two lock-graphs L1 and L2 are said to be compatible if C(L1(n),L2(n))=YES for all n ∈ N. Similarly two projections l1 and l2 are compatible if c(l1(n),l2(n))=YES for all n ∈ Q.

Theorem:

If two lock-graphs L1 and L2 are compatible then their projections l1 and l2 are compatible. In other words if the explicit locks set by two transactions do not conflict then also the three-state locks implicitly acquired do not conflict.

Proof: Assume that l1 and l2 are incompatible. We want to prove that L1 and L2 are incompatible. By definition of compatibility there must exist a sink n such that l1(n)=X and l2(n) ∈ {S,X} (or vice versa). By definition of projection there must exist a node-slice {n1...ns} of n such that L1(n1)=...=L1(ns)=X. Also there must exist an ancestor n0 of n such that L2(n0) ∈ {S,SIX,X}. From the definition of lock-graph there is a path P1 from a source to n0 on which L2 does not take the value NL.

If P1 intersects the node-slice at ni then L1 and L2 are incompatible since L1(ni)=X which is incompatible with the non-null value of L2(ni). Hence the theorem is proved.

Alternatively there is a path P2 from n0 to the sink n which intersects the node-slice at ni. From the definition of lock-graph L1 takes a value in {IX,SIX,X} on all ancestors of ni. In particular L1(n0) ∈ {IX,SIX,X}. Since L2(n0) ∈ {S,SIX,X} we have C(L1(n0),L2(n0))=NO. Q.E.D.

5.7.7. LOCK MANAGEMENT PRAGMATICS

Thus far we have discussed when to lock (lock before access and hold locks to commit point) and why to lock (to guarantee consistency and to make recovery possible without cascading transaction backup,) and what to lock (lock at a granularity that balances concurrency against instruction overhead in setting locks.) The remainder of this section will discuss issues associated with how to implement a lock manager.

5.7.7.1. The Lock Manager Interface

This is a simple version of the System R lock manager.

5.7.7.1.1. Lock Actions

Lock manager has two basic calls:

LOCK <lock>,<mode>,<class>,<control>
    Where <lock> is the resource name (in System R for example an eight byte name). <mode> is one of the modes specified above (S | X | SIX | IX | IS). <class> is a notion described below. <control> can be either WAIT in which case the call is synchronous and waits until the request is granted or is cancelled by the

deadlock detector, or <control> can be TEST in which case the
request is canceled if it cannot be granted immediately.

UNLOCK <lock>,<class>
Releases the specified lock in the specified class. If the <lock>
is not specified, all locks held in the specified class are
released.

5.7.7.1.2. Lock Names

The association between lock names and objects is purely a convention.
Lock manager associates no semantics with names. Generally the first
byte is reserved for the subsystem (component) identifier and the
remaining seven bytes name the object.

For example, data manager might use bytes (2...4) for the file name and
bytes (4...7) for the record name in constructing names for record
locks.

Since there are so many locks, one only allocates those with non-null
queue headers. (i.e. free locks occupy no space.) Setting a lock
consists of hashing the lock name into a table. If the header already
exists, the request enqueues on it, otherwise the request allocates the
lock header and places it in the hash table. When the queue of a lock
becomes empty, the header is deallocated (by the unlock operation).

5.7.7.1.3. Lock Classes

Many operations acquire a set of locks. If the operation is
successful, the locks should be retained. If the operation is
unsuccessful or when the operation commits the locks should be
released. In order to avoid double book-keeping the lock manager
allows users to name sets of locks (in the new DBTG proposal these are
called keep lists, in IMS program isolation these are called *Q class
locks).

For each lock held by each process, lock manager keeps a list of
<class,count> pairs. Each lock request for a class increments the
count for that class. Each unlock request decrements the count. When
all counts for all the lock's classes are zero then the lock is not
held by the process.

5.7.7.1.4. Latches

Lock manager needs a serialization mechanism to perform its function
(e.g. inserting elements in a queue or hash chain). It does this by
implementing a lower level primitive called latches. Latches are
semaphores. They provide a cheap serialization mechanism without
providing deadlock detection, class tracking, modes of sharing (beyond
S or X),... They are used by lock manager and by other performance
critical managers (notably buffer manager and log manager).

5.7.7.1.5. Performance of Lock Manager

Lock manager is about 3000 lines of (PL/1 like) source code. It
depends critically on the Compare and Swap logic provided by the
multiprocessor feature of System 370. It comprises three percent of
the code and about ten percent of the instruction execution of a
program in System R (this may vary a great deal.) A lock-unlock pair
currently costs 350 instructions but if these notes are ever finished,
this will be reduced to 120 instructions (this should reduce its slice
of the execution pie.) A latch-unlatch pair require 10 instructions

(they expand in-line). (Initially they required 120 instructions but a careful redesign improved this dramatically.)

5.7.7.2. Scheduling and Granting Requests

Thus far we have described the semantics of the various request modes and have described the protocol which requestors must follow. To complete the discussion we discuss how requests are scheduled and granted.

The set of all requests for a particular resource are kept in a queue sorted by some fair scheduler. By "fair" we mean that no particular transaction will be delayed indefinitely. First-in first-out is the simplest fair scheduler and we adopt such a scheduler for this discussion modulo deadlock preemption decisions.

The group of mutually compatible requests for a resource appearing at the head of the queue is called the <u>granted group</u>. All these requests can be granted concurrently. Assuming that each transaction has at most one request in the queue then the compatibility of two requests by different transactions depends only on the modes of the requests and may be computed using Table 1. Associated with the granted group is a <u>group mode</u> which is the supremum mode of the members of the group which is computed using Figure 2 or Table 3. Table 2 gives a list of the possible types of requests that can coexist in a group and the corresponding mode of the group.

Table 2. Possible request groups and their group mode.
Set brackets indicate that several such requests may be present.

MODES OF REQUESTS	MODE OF GROUP
X	X
{SIX,{IS}}	SIX
{S,{S},{IS}}	S
{IX,{IX},{IS}}	IX
{IS,{IS}}	{IS}

The figure below depicts the queue for a particular resource, showing the requests and their modes. The granted group consists of five requests and has group mode IX. The next request in the queue is for S mode which is incompatible with the group mode IX and hence must wait.

```
*********************************
* GRANTED GROUP: GROUPMODE = IX *
* |IS|--|IX|--|IS|--|IS|--|IS|--*-|S|-|IS|-|X|-|IS|-|IX|
*********************************
```

Figure 5. The queue of requests for a resource.

When a new request for a resource arrives, the scheduler appends it to the end of the queue. There are two cases to consider: either someone is already waiting or all outstanding requests for this resource are granted (i.e. no one is waiting). If waiters exist, then the request can not be granted and the new request must wait. If no one is waiting and the new request is compatible with the granted group mode then the new request can be granted immediately. Otherwise the new request must wait its turn in the queue and in the case of deadlock it may preempt some incompatible requests in the queue. (Alternatively the new request could be canceled. In Figure 5 all the requests decided to wait.)

When a particular request leaves the granted group the group mode of
the group may change. If the mode of the first waiting request in the
queue is compatible with the new mode of the granted group, then the
waiting request is granted. In Figure 5, if the IX request leaves the
group, then the group mode becomes IS which is compatible with S and so
the S may be granted. The new group mode will be S and since this is
compatible with IS mode the IS request following the S request may also
join the granted group. This produces the situation depicted in Figure
6:

```
*******************************************
* GRANTED GROUP GROUPMODE = S        *
* |IS|--|IS|--|IS|--|IS|--|S|--|IS|--*-|X|-|IS|-|IX|
*******************************************
```

Figure 6. The queue after the IX request is released.

The X request of Figure 6 will not be granted until all requests leave
the granted group since it is not compatible with any of them.

5.7.7.3. Conversions

A transaction might re-request the same resource for several reasons:
Perhaps it has forgotten that it already has access to the record;
after all, if it is setting many locks it may be simpler to just always
request access to the record rather than first asking itself "have I
seen this record before". The lock manager has all the information to
answer this question and it seems wasteful to duplicate.
Alternatively, the transaction may know it has access to the record,
but want to increase its access mode (for example from S to X mode if
it is in a read, test, and sometimes update scan of a file). So the
lock manager must be prepared for re-requests by a transaction for a
lock. We call such re-requests <u>conversions</u>.

When a request is found to be a conversion, the old (granted) mode of
the requestor to the resource and the newly requested mode are
compared using Table 3 to compute the <u>new mode</u> which is the supremum of
the old and the requested mode (ref. Figure 2).

Table 3. The new mode given the requested and old mode.

	IS	IX	S	SIX	X
IS	IS	IX	S	SIX	X
IX	IX	IX	SIX	SIX	X
S	S	SIX	S	SIX	X
SIX	SIX	SIX	SIX	SIX	X
X	X	X	X	X	X

So for example, if one has IX mode and requests S mode then the new
mode is SIX.

If the new mode is equal to the old mode (note it is never less than
the old mode) then the request can be granted immediately and the
granted mode is unchanged. If the new mode is compatible with the
group mode of the <u>other</u> members of the granted group (a requestor is
always compatible with himself) then again the request can be granted
immediately. The granted mode is the new mode and the group mode is
recomputed using Table 2. In all other cases, the requested
conversion must wait until the group mode of the other granted requests
is compatible with the new mode. Note that this immediate granting of

conversions over waiting requests is a minor violation of fair scheduling.

If two conversions are waiting, each of which is incompatible with an already granted request of the other transaction, then a deadlock exists and the already granted access of one must be preempted. Otherwise there is a way of scheduling the waiting conversions: namely, grant a conversion when it is compatible with all other granted modes in the granted group. (Since there is no deadlock cycle this is always possible.)

The following example may help to clarify these points. Suppose the queue for a particular resource is:

```
******************************
* GROUPMODE = IS              *
*  |IS|---|IS|----------------------------
******************************
```

Figure 7. A simple queue.

Now suppose the first transaction wants to convert to X mode. It must wait for the second (already granted) request to leave the queue. If it decides to wait then the situation becomes:

```
******************************
* GROUPMODE = IS              *
*  |IS<-X|---|IS|-----------------------------
******************************
```

Figure 8. A conversion to X mode waits.

No new request may enter the granted group since there is now a conversion request waiting. In general, conversions are scheduled before new requests. If the second transaction now converts to IX, SIX, or S mode it may be granted immediately since this does not conflict with the _granted_ (IS) mode of the first transaction. When the second transaction eventually leaves the queue, the first conversion can be made:

```
******************************
* GROUPMODE = X               *
*   |X|-------------------------------------
******************************
```

Figure 9. One transaction leaves and the conversion is granted.

However, if the second transaction tries to convert to exclusive mode one obtains the queue:

```
******************************
*   GROUPMODE = IS            *
*  |IS<-X|---|IS<-X|------------------------
******************************
```

Figure 10. Two conflicting conversions are waiting.

Since X is incompatible with IS (see Table 1), this situation implies that each transaction is waiting for the other to leave the queue (i.e. deadlock) and so one transaction _must_ be preempted. In all other cases (i.e. when no cycle exists) there is a way to schedule the conversions so that no already granted access is violated.

5.7.7.4. Deadlock Detection

One issue the lock manager must deal with is deadlock. Deadlock consists of each member of a set of transactions waiting for some other member of the set to give up a lock. Standard lore has it that one can have timeout or deadlock-prevention or deadlock detection.

Timeout causes waits to be denied after some specified interval. It has the property that as the system becomes more congested, more and more transactions time out (because time runs slower and because more resources are in use so that one waits more). Also timeout puts an upper limit on the duration of a transaction. In general the dynamic properties of timeout make it acceptable for a lightly loaded system but inappropriate for a congested system.

Deadlock prevention is achieved by: requesting all locks at once, or requesting locks in a specified order, or never waiting for a lock, or ... In general deadlock prevention is a bad deal because one rarely knows what locks are needed in advance (consider looking something up in an index,) and consequently, one locks too much in advance.

Although some situations allow a deadlock prevention, general systems tend to require deadlock detection. IMS, for example, started with a deadlock prevention scheme (intent scheduling) but was forced to introduce a deadlock detection scheme to increase concurrency (Program Isolation).

Deadlock detection and resolution is no big deal in a data management system environment. The system already has lots of facilities for transaction backup so that it can deal with other sorts of errors. Deadlock simply becomes another (hopefully infrequent) source of backup. As will be seen, the algorithms for detecting and resolving deadlock are not complicated or time consuming.

The deadlock detection-resolution scenario is:

- Detect a deadlock.

- Pick a victim (a lock to preempt from a process.)

- Back up victim which will release lock.

- Grant a waiter.

- (optionally) Restart victim.

Lock manager is only responsible for deadlock detection and victim selection. Recovery management implements transaction backup and controls restart logic.

5.7.7.4.1. How to Detect Deadlock

There are many heuristic ways of detecting deadlock (e.g. linearly order resources or processes and declare deadlock if ordering is violated by a wait request.)

Here we restrict ourselves to algorithmic solutions.

The detection of deadlock may be cast in graph-theoretic terms. We introduce the notion of the wait-for graph.

- The nodes of the graph are transactions and locks.
- The edges of the graph are <u>directed</u> <u>and</u> <u>are</u> <u>constructed</u> <u>as</u> <u>follows</u>:
  - If lock L is granted to transaction T then draw an edge from L to T.
  - If transaction T is waiting for transaction L then draw an edge from T to L.

At any instant, there is a deadlock if and only if the wait-for graph has a cycle. Hence deadlock detection becomes an issue of building the wait-for graph and searching it for cycles.

Often this 'transaction waits for lock waits for transaction' graph can be reduced to a smaller 'transaction waits for transaction' graph. The larger graph need be maintained only if the identity of the locks in the cycle are relevant. I know of no case where this is required.

5.7.7.4.2. When to Look for Deadlock.

One could opt to look for deadlock:

- Whenever anyone waits.
- Periodically.
- Never.

One could look for deadlock continuously. Releasing a lock or being granted a lock never creates a deadlock. So one should never look for deadlock more frequently than when a wait occurs.

The cost of looking for deadlock every time anyone waits is:

- Continual maintenance of the wait-for graph.
- Almost certain failure since deadlock is (should be) rare (i.e. wasted instructions).

The cost of periodic deadlock detection is:

- Detecting deadlocks late.

By increasing the period one decreases the cost of deadlock and the probability of successfully finding one. For each situation there should be an optimal detection period.

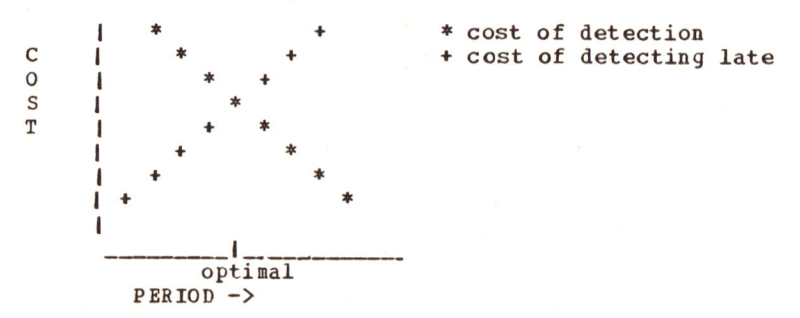

```
        |   *         +         * cost of detection
   C    |    *       +          + cost of detecting late
   O    |     *    +
   S    |      *
   T    |     +  *
        |    +     *
        |   +        *
        |  +           *
        |
        |_____|_____
                optimal
            PERIOD ->
```

Never testing for deadlocks is much like periodic deadlock detection

with a very long period. All systems have a mechanism to detect dead
programs (infinite loops, wait for lost interrupt,...) This is usually
a part of allocation and resource scheduling. It is probably outside
and above deadlock detection.

Similarly, if deadlock is very frequent, the system is thrashing and
the transaction scheduler should stop scheduling new work and perhaps
abort some current work to reduce this thrashing. Otherwise the system
is likely to spend the majority of its time backing up.

5.7.7.4.3. What To Do When Deadlock is Detected.

All transactions in a deadlock are waiting. The only way to get things
going again is to grant some waiter. But this can only be achieved
after a lock is preempted from some holder. Since the victim is
waiting, he will get the 'deadlock' response from lock manager rather
than the 'granted' response.

In breaking the deadlock some set of victims will be preempted. We
want to minimize the amount of work lost by these preemptions.
Therefore, deadlock resolution wants to pick a minimum cost set of
victims to break deadlocks.

Transaction management must associate a cost with each transaction. In
the absence of policy decisions: the cost of a victim is the cost of
undoing his work and then redoing it. The length of the transaction
log is a crude estimate of this cost. At any rate, transaction
management must provide lock management with an estimate of the cost of
each transaction. Lock manager may implement either of the following
two protocols:

- For each cycle, choose the minimum cost victim in that cycle.

- Choose the minimum cost cut-set of the deadlock graph.

The difference between these two options is best visualized by the
picture:

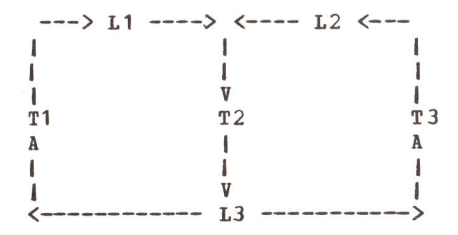

```
        ---> L1 ----> <---- L2 <---
         |            |            |
         |            |            |
         |            V            |
        T1           T2           T3
        A                          A
         |            |            |
         |            V            |
        <----------- L3 ----------->
```

If T1 and T3 have a cost of 2 and T2 has a cost of 3 then a
cycle-at-a-time algorithm will choose T1 and T3 as victims; whereas, a
minimal cut set algorithm will choose T2 as a victim.

The cost of finding a minimal cut set is considerably greater (seems to
be NP complete) than the cycle-at-a-time scheme. If there are N common
cycles the cycle-at-a-time scheme is at most N times worse than the
minimal cut set scheme. So it seems that the cycle-at-a-time scheme is
better.

5.7.7.5. Lock Management In a Distributed System.

To repeat the discussion in the section on distributed transaction management, if a transaction wants to do work at a new node, some process of the transaction must request that the node construct a cohort and that the cohort go into session with the requesting process (see section on data communications for a discussion of sessions.) The picture below shows this.

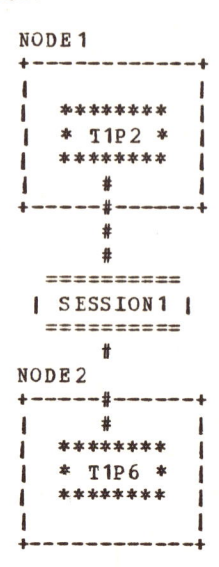

```
               NODE1
            +-----------+
            |           |
            |  *******  |
            |  * T1P2 * |
            |  *******  |
            |     #     |
            +-----#-----+
                  #
                  #
               =========
              | SESSION1 |
               =========
                  #
               NODE2
            +-----#-----+
            |     #     |
            |  *******  |
            |  * T1P6 * |
            |  *******  |
            |           |
            +-----------+
```

A cohort carries both the transaction name T1 and the process name (in NODE1 the cohort of T1 is process P2 and in NODE2 the cohort of T1 is process P6.)

The two processes can now converse and carry out the work of the transaction. If one process aborts, they should both abort, and if one process commits they should both commit.

The lock manager of each node can keep its lock tables in any form it desires. Further, deadlock detectors running in each node may use any technique they like to detect deadlocks among transactions which run exclusively in that node. We call such deadlocks <u>local deadlocks</u>. However, just because there are no cycles in the local wait-for graphs does not mean that there are no cycles. Gluing acyclic local graphs together might produce a graph with cycles. (See the example below.) So, the deadlock detectors of each node will have to agree on a common protocol in order to handle deadlocks involving distributed transactions. We call such deadlocks <u>global deadlocks</u>.

Inspection of the following figure may help to understand the nature of global deadlocks. Note that transaction T1 has two processes P1 and P2 in nodes 1 and 2 respectively. P1 is session-waiting for its cohort P2 to do some work. P2, in the process of doing this work, needed access to FILE2 in NODE2. But FILE2 is locked exclusive by another process (P4 of NODE2) so P2 is in lock wait state. Thus the transaction T1 is waiting for FILE2. Now Transaction T2 is in a similar state, one of its chorts is session waiting for the other which in turn is lock waiting for FILE1. In fact transaction T1 is waiting for FILE2 which is granted to transaction T2 which is waiting for file FILE1 which is granted to transaction T1. A global deadlock if you ever saw one.

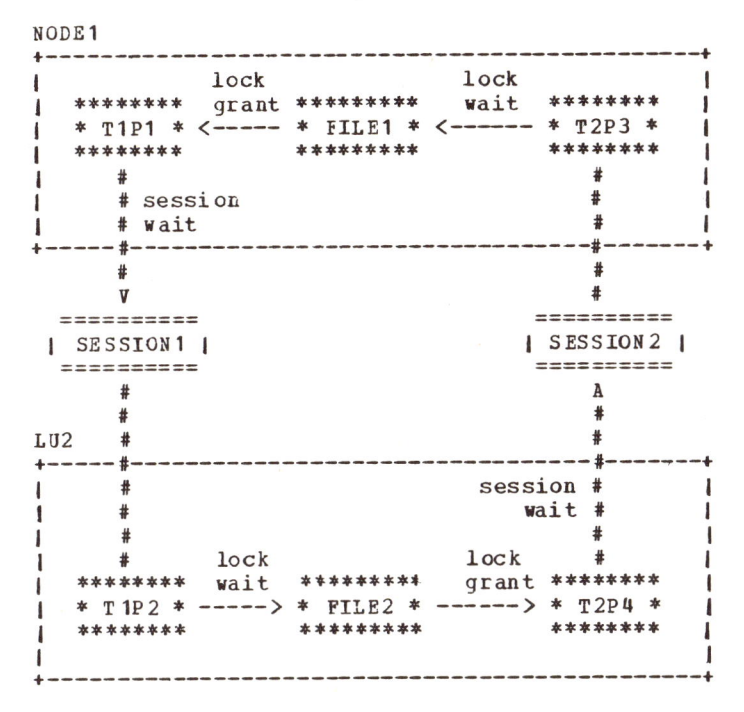

```
         NODE1
    +------------------------------------------------+
    |            lock              lock              |
    |  *******   grant  ********   wait   *******    |
    |  * T1P1 * <-----  * FILE1 * <------ * T2P3 *   |
    |  *******          ********          *******    |
    |     #                                  #       |
    |     # session                          #       |
    |     # wait                             #       |
    +-----#----------------------------------#-------+
          #                                  #
          V                                  #
      =========                          =========
      |SESSION1|                         |SESSION2|
      =========                          =========
          #                                  A
          #                                  #
     LU2  #                                  #
    +-----#----------------------------------#-------+
    |     #                       session #          |
    |     #                       wait    #          |
    |     #                               #          |
    |     #      lock              lock   #          |
    |  *******   wait   ********   grant  *******    |
    |  * T1P2 * ----->  * FILE2 * ------> * T2P4 *   |
    |  *******          ********          *******    |
    |                                                |
    +------------------------------------------------+
```

The notion of wait-for graph must be generalized to handle global deadlock. The nodes of the graph are processes and resources (sessions are resources). The edges of the graph are constructed as follows:

- Draw a directed edge from a process to a resource if

  - the process is in lock wait for the resource,

  - or the process is in session-wait for the resource (session).

- Draw a directed edge from a resource to a process if

  - the resource is lock granted to the process

  - or it is a session of the process and the process is not in session-wait on it.

A local deadlock is a

                lockwait->....->lockwait cycle.

A global deadlock is a

    lockwait->...->sessionwait ->lockwait->...->sessionwait-> cycle

5.7.7.5.1. How to Find Global Deadlocks

The finding of local deadlocks has already been described.

To find global deadlocks, a distinguish task, called the <u>global deadlock detector</u> is started in some distinguished node. This task is in session with all local deadlock detectors and coordinates the activities of the local deadlock detectors. This global deadlock detector can run in any node, but probably should be located to minimize its communication distance to the lock managers.

Each local deadlock detector needs to find all potential global deadlock paths in his node. In the previous section it was shown that a global deadlock cycle has the form:

lockwait->...->sessionwait ->lockwait->...->sessionwait->

So each local deadlock detector periodically enumerates all

session->lockwait->...->sessionwait

paths in his node by working backwards from processes which are in session-wait. (as opposed to console wait, disk wait, processor wait, ...) Starting at such a process it sees if some local process is lock waiting for this process. If so the deadlock detector searches backwards looking for some process which has a session in progress.

When such a path is found the following information is sent to the global deadlock detector:

- Sessions and transactions at endpoints of the path and their local preemption costs.

- The minimum cost transaction in the path and his local pre-emption cost.

(It may make sense to batch this information to the global detector.)

Periodically, the global deadlock detector:

- collects these messages,

- glues all these paths together by matching up sessions

- enumerates cycles and selects victims just as in the local deadlock detector case.

One tricky point is that the cost of a distributed transaction is the sum of the costs of its cohorts. The global deadlock detector approximates this cost by summing the costs of the cohorts of the transaction known to it (not all cohorts of a deadlocked transaction will be in known to the global deadlock detector.)

When a victim is selected, the lock manager of the node the victim is waiting in is informed of the deadlock. The local lock manager in turn informs the victim with a deadlock return.

The use of periodic deadlock detection (as opposed to detection every time anyone waits) is even more important for a distributed system than for a centralized system. The cost of detection is much higher in a distributed system. This will alter the intersection of the cost of detection and cost of detecting late curves.

If the network is really large the deadlock detector can be staged. That is we can look for deadlock among four nodes, then among sixteen nodes, and so on.

If one node crashes, then its partition of the system is unavailable.

In this case, its cohorts in other nodes can wait for it to recover or they can abort. If the down node happens to house the global lock manager then no global deadlocks will be detected until the node recovers. If this is uncool, then the lock managers can nominate a new global lock manager whenever the current one crashes. The new manager can run in any node which can be in session with all other nodes. The new global lock manager collects the local graphs and goes about gluing them together, finding cycles, and picking victims.

5.7.7.6. Relationship to Operating System Lock Manager

Most operating systems provide a lock manager to regulate access to files and other system resources. This lock manager usually supports a limited set of lock names, the modes: share, exclusive and beware, and has some form of deadlock detection. These lock managers are usually not prepared for the demands of a data management system (fast calls, lots of locks, many modes, lock classes,...) The basic lock manager could be extended and refined and in time that is what will happen.

There is a big problem about having two lock managers in the same host. Each may think it has no deadlock but if their graphs are glued together a "global" deadlock exists. This makes it very difficult to build on top of the basic lock manager.

5.7.7.7. The Convoy Phenomenon: Preemptive Scheduling is Bad

Lock manager has strong interactions with the scheduler. Suppose that there are certain high traffic shared system resources. Operating on these resources consists of locking them, altering them and then unlocking them (the buffer pool and log are examples of this.) These operations are designed to be very fast so that the resource is almost always free. In particular the resource is never held during an I/O operation. For example, the buffer manager latch is acquired every 1000 instructions and is held for about 50 instructions.

If the system has no preemptive scheduling then on a uni-processor when a process begins the resource is free and when he completes the resource is free (because he does not hold it when he does I/O or yields the processor.) On a multi-processor, if the resource is busy, the process can sit in a busy wait until the resource is free because the resource is known to be held by others for only a short time.

If the basic system has a preemptive scheduler, and if that scheduler preempts a process holding a critical resource (e.g. the log latch) then terrible things happen: All other processes waiting for the latch are dispatched and because the resource is high traffic each of these processes requests and waits for the resource. Ultimately the holder of the resource is redispatched and he almost immediately grants the latch to the next waiter. But because it is high traffic, the process almost immediately rerequests the latch (i.e. about 1000 instructions later.) Fair scheduling requires that he wait so he goes on the end of the queue waiting for those ahead of him. This queue of waiters is called a _convoy_. It is a stable phenomenon: once a convoy is established it persists for a very long time.

We (System R) have found several solutions to this problem. The obvious solution is to eliminate such resources. That is a good idea and can be achieved to some degree by refining the granularity of the lockable unit (e.g. twenty buffer manager latches rather than just one.) However, if a convoy ever forms on any of these latches it will be stable so that is not a solution. I leave it as an exercise for the reader to find a better solution to the problem.

5.7.8. BIBLIOGRAPHY

Engles, "Currency and Concurrency in the COBOL Data Base Facility", in *Modeling in Data Base Management Systems*. Nijssen editor, North Holland, 1976. (A nice discussion of how locks are used.)

Eswaran et. al. "On the Notions of Consistency and Predicate Locks in a Relational Database System," CACM, Vol. 19, No. 11, November 1976. (Introduces the notion of consistency, ignore the stuff on predicate locks.)

"Granularity of Locks and Degrees of Consistency in a Shared Data Base", in *Modeling in Data Base Management Systems*. Nijssen editor, North Holland, 1976. (This section is a condensation and then elaboration of this paper. Hence Franco Putzolu and Irv Traiger should be considered co-authors of this section.)

5.8. RECOVERY MANAGEMENT

5.8.1. MODEL OF ERRORS

In order to design a recovery system, it is important to have a clear notion of what kinds of errors can be expected and what their probabilities are. The model of errors below is inspired by the presentation by Lampson and Sturgis in "Crash Recovery in a Distributed Data Storage System", which may someday appear in the CACM.

We first postulate that all errors are detectable. That is, if no one complains about a situation, then it is OK.

5.8.1.1. Model of Storage Errors

Storage comes in three flavors with independent failure modes and increasing reliability:

- Volatile storage: paging space and main memory,

- On-Line Non-volatile Storage: disks, usually survive crashes. Is more reliable than volatile storage.

- Off-Line Non-volatile Storage: Tape archive. Even more reliable than disks.

To repeat, we assume that these three kinds of storage have independent failure modes.

The storage is blocked into fixed length units called **pages** which are the unit of allocation and transfer.

Any page transfer can have one of three outcomes:

- Success (target gets new value)

- Partial failure (target is a mess)

- Total failure (target is unchanged)

Any page may spontaneously fail. That is a spec of dust may settle on it or a black hole may pass through it so that it no longer retains it's original information.

One can always detect whether a transfer failed or a page spontaneously failed by reading the target page at a later time. (This can be made more and more certain by adding redundancy to the page.)

Lastly, The probability that N "independent" archive pages fail is negligable. Here we choose N=2. (This can be made more and more certain by choosing larger and larger N.)

5.8.1.2. Mode of Data Communications Errors

Communication traffic is broken into units called messages which travel via sessions.

The transmission of a message has one of three possible outcomes:

- Successfully received.

- Incorrectly received.

- Not received.

The receiver of the message can detect whether he has received a particular message and whether it was correctly received.

For each message transmitted, there is a non-zero probability that it will be successfully received.

It is the job of recovery manager to deal with these storage and transmission errors and correct them. This model of errors is implicit in what follows and will appear again in the examples at the end of the section.

5.8.2. OVERVIEW OF RECOVERY MANAGEMENT.

A transaction is begun explicitly when a process is allocated or when an existing process issues BEGIN_TRANSACTION. When a transaction is initiated, recovery manager is invoked to allocate the recovery structure necessary to recover the transaction. This process places a capability for the COMMIT, SAVE, and BACKUP calls of recovery manager in the transaction's capability list.

Thereafter, all actions by the transaction on recoverable data are recorded in the recovery log using log manager. In general, each action performing an update operation should write an undo-log record and a redo-log record in the transaction's log. The undo log record gives the old value of the object and the redo log record gives the new value (see below).

At a transaction save point, recovery manager records the save point identifier, and enough information so that each component of the system could be backed up to this point.

In the event of a minor error, the transaction may be undone to a save point in which case the application (on its next or pending call) is given feedback indicating that the data base system has amnesia about all recoverable actions since that save point. If the transaction is completely backed-up (aborted), it may or may not be restarted depending on the attributes of the transaction and of its initiating message.

If the transaction completes successfully (commits), then (logically) it is always redone in case of a crash. On the other hand, if it is in-progress at the time of the local or system failure, then the transaction is logically undone (aborted).

Recovery manager must also respond to the following kinds of failures:

- Action failure: a particular call cannot complete due to a foreseen condition. In general the action undoes itself (cleans up its component) and then returns to the caller. Examples of this are bad parameters, resource limits, and data not found.

- Transaction failure: a particular transaction cannot proceed and so is aborted. The transaction may be reinitiated in some cases. Examples of such errors are deadlock, timeout, protection violation, and transaction-local system errors.

- System failure: a serious error is detected below the action interface. The system is stopped and restarted. Errors in critical tables, wild branches by trusted processes, operating system downs and hardware downs are sources of system failure. Most nonvolatile storage is presumed to survive a system failure.

- Media failure: a nonrecoverable error is detected on some usually reliable (nonvolatile) storage device. The recovery of recoverable data from a media failure is the responsibility of the component which implements it. If the device contained recoverable data the manager must reconstruct the data from an archive copy using the log and then place the result on an alternate device. Media failures do not generally force system failure. Parity error, head crash, dust on magnetic media, and lost tapes are typical media failures. Software errors which make the media unreadable are also regarded as media errors as are catastrophes such as fire, flood, insurrection, and operator error.

The system periodically makes copies copies of each recoverable object and keeps these copies in a safe place (archive). In case the object suffers a media error, all transactions with locks outstanding against the object are aborted. A special transaction (a utility) acquires the object in exclusive mode. (This takes the object "off-line".) This transaction merges an accumulation of changes to the object since the object copy was made and a recent archive version of the object to produce the most recent committed version. This accumulation of changes may take two forms: it may be the REDO-log portion of the system log, or it may be a change accumulation log which was constructed from the REDO-log portion of the system log when the system log is compressed. After media recovery, the data is unlocked and made public again.

The process of making an archive copy of an object has many varieties. Certain objects, notably IMS queue space, are recovered from scratch using an infinite redo log. Other objects, notably data bases, get copied to some external media which can be used to restore the object to a consistent state if a failure occurs. (The resource may or may not be off-line while the copy is being made.)

Recovery manager also periodically performs system checkpoint by recording critical parts of the system state in a safe spot in nonvolatile storage (sometimes called the warm start file.)

Recovery manager coordinates the process of system restart system shutdown. In performing system restart, it chooses among:

- Warm start: system shut down in controlled manner. Recovery need only locate last checkpoint record and rebuild control structure.

- Emergency restart: system failed in uncontrolled manner. Non-volatile storage contains recent state consistent with the log. However, some transactions were in progress at time of failure and must be redone or undone to obtain most recent consistent state.

- Cold start: the system is being brought up with amnesia about prior incarnations. The log is not referenced to determine previous state.

5.8.3. RECOVERY PROTOCOLS

All participants in a transaction, including all components understand and obey the following protocols when operating on recoverable objects:

- Consistency lock protocol.
- The DO-UNDO-REDO paradigm for log records.
- Write Ahead Log protocol (WAL).
- Two phase commit protocol.

The consistency lock protocol was discussed in the section on lock management. The remaining protocols are discussed below.

5.8.3.1. Logs and the DO-UNDO-REDO Paradigm.

Perhaps the simplest and easiest to implement recovery technique is based on the old-master new-master dichotomy common to most batch data processing systems: If the run fails, one goes back to the old-master and tries again. Unhappily, this technique does not seem to generalize to concurrent transactions. If several transactions concurrently access an object, then making a new-master object or returning to the old-master may be inappropriate because it commits or backs up _all_ updates to the object by _all_ transactions.

It is desirable to be able to commit or undo updates on a per-transaction basis. Given a action consistent state and a collection of in-progress transactions (i.e. commit not yet executed) one wants to be able to selectively undo a subset of the transactions without affecting the others. Such a facility is called _in-progress transaction backup_.

A second short-coming of versions is that in the event of a media error, one must reconstruct the most recent consistent state. For example, if a page or collection of pages is lost from non-volatile storage then they must be reconstructed from some redundant information. Doubly-recording the versions on independent devices is quite expensive for large objects. However, this is the technique used for some small objects such as the warm start file.

Lastly, writing a new version of a large data base often consumes large amounts of storage and bandwidth.

Having abandoned the notion of versions, we adopt the approach of _updating in place_ and of keeping an incremental _log_ of changes to the system state. (Logs are sometimes called audit trails or journals.)

Each action which modifies a recoverable object writes a log record giving the old and new value of the updated object. Read operations need generate no log records, but update operations must record enough information in the log so that given the record at a later time the operation can be completely undone or redone. These records will be aggregated by transaction and collected in a common system _log_ which resides in nonvolatile storage and will itself be duplexed and have independent failure modes.

In what follows we assume that the log never fails. By duplexing, triplexing,... the log one can make this assumption less false.

Every recoverable operation must have:

* A DO entry which does the action and also records a log record sufficient to undo and to redo the operation.

* An UNDO entry which undoes the action given the log record written by the DO action.

* A REDO entry which redoes the action given the log record written by the DO action.

* Optionally a DISPLAY entry which translates the log into a human-readable format.

To give an example of an action and the log record it must write consider the data base record update operator. This action must record in the log the:
(1) record name
(2) the old record value (used for UNDO)
(3) the new record value. (used for REDO)

The log subsystem augments this with the additional fields:
(4) transaction identifier
(5) action identifier
(6) length of log record
(7) pointer to previous log record of this transaction

```
DECLARE
 1 UPDATE_LOG_RECORD BASED,
   2 LENGTH FIXED(16),    /* length of log record                */
   2 TYPE   FIXED(16),    /* code assigned to update log recs*/
   2 TRANSACTION FIXED(48),/* name of transaction              */
   2 PREV_LOG_REC POINTER(31), /* relative address of prev log*/
                          /* record of this transaction         */
   2 SET    FIXED(32),    /* name of updated set                */
   2 RECORD FIXED(32),    /* name of updated record             */
   2 NFIELDS FIXED(16),   /* number of updated fields           */
   2 CHANGES (NFIELDS),   /* for each changed field:            */
     3 FIELD FIXED(16),   /* name of field                      */
     3 OLD_VALUE,         /* old value of field                 */
       4 F_LENGTH FIXED(16),/* length of old field value        */
       4 F_ATOM CHAR(F_LENGTH),/* value in old field            */
     3 NEW_VALUE LIKE OLD_VALUE, /* new value of field          */
   2 LENGTH_AT_END FIXED(16);/* allows reading log backwards    */
```

The data manager's undo operation restores the record to its old value appropriately updating indices and sets. The redo operation restores the record to its new value. The display operation returns a text string giving a symbolic display of the log record.

The log itself is recorded on a dedicated media(disk, tape,...). Once a log record is recorded, it cannot be updated. However, the log component provides a facility to open read cursors on the log which will traverse the system log or will traverse the log of a particular transaction in either direction.

The UNDO operation must face a rather difficult problem at restart: The undo operation may be performed more than once if restart itself is redone several times (i.e. if the system fails during restart.) Also one may be called upon to undo operations which were never reflected in nonvolatile storage (i.e. log write occurred but object write did not.)

Similar problems exist for REDO. One may have to REDO an already done action if the updated object was recorded in non-volatile storage before the crash or if restart is restarted.

The write ahead log protocol and high water marks solve these problems (see below).

5.8.3.2. Write Ahead Log Protocol

The recovery system postulates that memory comes in two flavors: volatile and nonvolatile storage. Volatile storage does not survive a system restart and nonvolatile storage _usually_ survives a system restart.

Suppose an object is recorded in non-volatile storage _before_ the log records for the object are recorded in the non-volatile log. If the system crashes at such a point, then one cannot undo the update. Similarly, if the new object is one of a set which are committed together and if a media error occurs on the object then a mutually consistent version of the set of objects cannot be constructed from their non-volatile versions. Analysis of these two examples indicate that the log should be written to non-volatile storage _before_ the object is written.

Actions are required to write log records whenever modifying recoverable objects. The log (once recorded in nonvolatile storage) is considered to be very reliable. In general the log is dual recorded on physical media with independent failure modes (e.g. dual tapes or spindles) although single logging is a system option.

The Write Ahead Log protocol (WAL) is:

- Before over-writing a recoverable object to nonvolatile storage with uncommitted updates, a transaction (process) should first force its undo log for relevant updates to nonvolatile log space.

- Before committing an update to a recoverable object, the transaction coordinator (see below) must force the redo and undo log to nonvolatile storage so that it can go either way on the transaction commit. (This is guaranteed by recovery management which will synchronize the commit process with the writing of the phase12 log transition record at the end of phase 1 of commit processing. This point cannot be understood before the section on two phase commit processing is read.)

This protocol needs to be interpreted broadly in the case of messages: One should not send a recoverable message before it is logged (so that the message can be canceled or retransmitted.) In this case, the wires of the network are the "non-volatile storage".

The write ahead log protocol is implemented as follows. Every log record has a unique sequence number. Every recoverable object has a "high water mark" which is the largest log sequence number that applies to it. Whenever an object is updated, its high water mark is set to the log sequence number of the new log record. The object cannot be written to non-volatile storage before the log has been written past the object's high water mark. Log manager provides a synchronous call to force out all log records up to a certain sequence number.

At system restart a transaction may be undone or redone. If an error occurs the restart may be repeated. This means that an operation may be undone or redone more than once. Also, since the log is "ahead of" non-volatile storage the first undo may apply to an already undone (not-yet-done) change. Similarly the first redo may redo an already done change. This requires that the redo and undo operators be repeatable (*idempotent*) in the sense that doing them once produces the same result as doing them several times. Undo or redo may be invoked repeatedly if restart is retried several times or if the failure occurs during phase 2 of commit processing.

Here again, the high water mark is handy. If the high water mark is recorded with the object, and if the movement of the object to nonvolatile storage is atomic (this is true for pages and for messages) then one can read to high water mark to see if undo or redo is necessary. This is a simple way to make the undo and redo operators idempotent.

Message sequence numbers on a session perform the function of high water marks. That is the recipient can discard messages below the last sequence number received.

As a historical note, the need for WAL only became apparent with the widespread use of LSI memories. Prior to that time the log buffers resided in core storage which survived software errors, hardware errors and power failure. This allowed the system to treat the log buffers in core as non-volatile storage. At power shutdown, an exception handler in the data management dumps the log buffers. If this fails a scavenger is run which reads them out of core to storage. In general the contents of LSI storage does not survive power failures. To guard against power failure, memory failure and wild stores by the software, most systems have opted for the WAL protocol.

5.8.3.3. The Two Phase Commit Protocol

5.8.3.3.1. The Generals Paradox.

In order to understand that the two phase commit protocol solves some problem it is useful to analyze the generals paradox.

There are two generals on campaign. They have an objective (a hill) which they want to capture. If they *simultaneously* march on the objective they are assured of success. If only one marches, he will be annihilated.

The generals are encamped only a short distance apart, but due to technical difficulties, they can communicate only via runners. These messengers have a flaw, every time they venture out of camp they stand some chance of getting lost (they are not very smart.)

The problem is to find some protocol which allows the generals to march together even though some messengers get lost.

There is a simple proof that no fixed length protocol exists: Let P be the shortest such protocol. Suppose the last messenger in P gets lost. Then either this messenger is useless or one of the generals doesn't get a needed message. By the minimality of P, the last message is not useless so one of the general doesn't march if the last message is lost. This contradiction proves that no such protocol P exists.

The generals paradox (which as you now see is not a paradox) has strong analogies to problems faced by a data recovery management when doing commit processing. Imagine that one of the generals is a computer in Tokyo and that the other general is a cash dispensing terminal in Fuessen Germany. The goal is to

- open a cash drawer with a million Marks in it (at Fuessen) and
- debit the appropriate account in the non-volatile storage of the Tokyo computer.

If only one thing happens either the Germans or the Japanese will destroy the general that did not "march".

5.8.3.3.2. The Two Phase Commit Protocol

As explained above, there is no solution to the two generals problem. If however, the restriction that the the protocol have some finite fixed maximum length is relaxed then a solution is possible. The protocol about to be described may require arbitrarily many messages. Usually it requires only a few messages, sometimes it requires more and in some cases (a set of measure zero) it requires an infinite number of messages. The protocol works by introducing a commit coordinator. The commit coordinator has a communication path to all participants. Participants are either cohorts (processes) at several nodes or are autonomous components within a process (like DB and DC) or are both. The commit coordinator asks all the participants to go into a state such that, no matter what happens, the participant can either redo or undo the transaction (this means writing the log in a very safe place).

Once the coordinator gets the votes from everyone:

- If anyone aborted, the coordinator broadcasts abort to all participants, records abort in his log and terminates. In this case all participants will abort.

- If all participants voted yes, the coordinator synchronously records a commit record in the log, then broadcasts commit to all participants and when an acknowledge is received from each participant, the cocrdinator terminates.

The key to the success of this approach is that the decision to commit has been centralized in a single place and is not time constrained.

The following diagrams show the possible interactions between a coordinator and a participant. Note that a coordinator may abort a participant which agrees to commit. This may happen because another participant has aborted

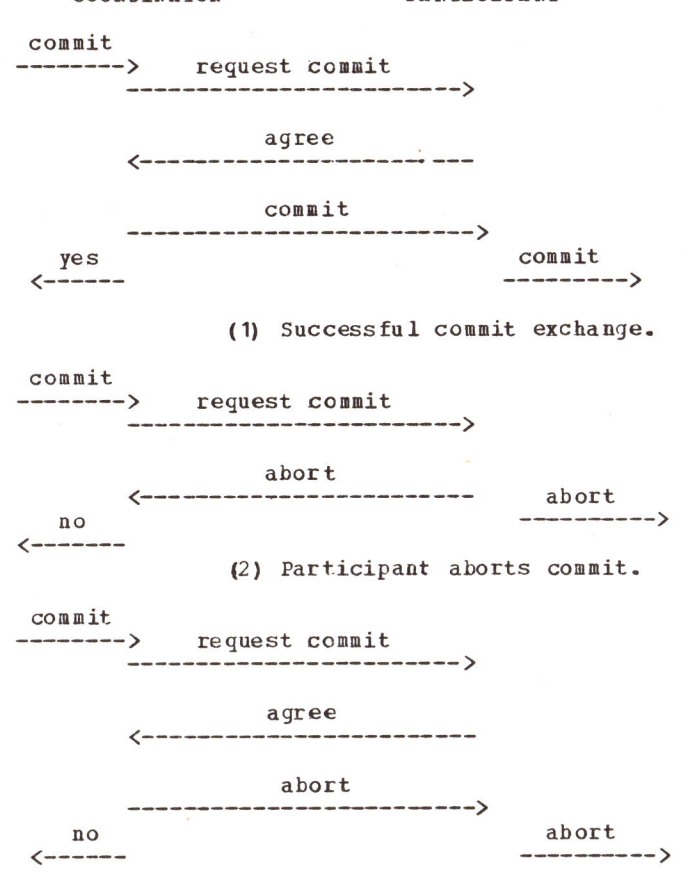

```
           COORDINATOR                    PARTICIPANT
 commit
 -------->    request commit
              ------------------------>

                    agree
              <------------------------

                   commit
              ------------------------>
    yes                                      commit
 <------                                   ---------->

              (1) Successful commit exchange.

 commit
 -------->    request commit
              ------------------------>

                    abort
              <------------------------        abort
                                           ---------->
    no
 <------
              (2) Participant aborts commit.

 commit
 -------->    request commit
              ------------------------>

                    agree
              <------------------------

                    abort
              ------------------------>
    no                                         abort
 <------                                   ---------->

              (3) Coordinator aborts commit.

        Three possible two phase commit scenarios.
```

The logic for the coordinator is best described by a simple program:

```
COORDINATOR: PROCEDURE;
    VOTE='COMMIT';     /* collect votes               */
    DO FOR EACH PARTICIPANT WHILE(VOTE='COMMIT');
        DO;
        SEND HIM REQUEST_COMMIT;
        IF REPLY ¬= 'AGREE' THEN VOTE='ABORT';
        END;
    IF VOTE='COMMIT' THEN
        DO;              /* if all agree then commit*/
        WRITE_LOG(PHASE12_COMMIT) FORCE;
        FOR EACH PARTICIPANT;
            DO UNTIL (+ACK);
            SEND HIM COMMIT;
            WAIT +ACKNOWLEDGE;
            IF TIME LIMIT THEN RETRANSMIT;
            END;
        END;
    ELSE
        DO;              /* if any abort, then abort*/
        FOR EACH PARTICIPANT
            DO UNTIL (+ACK);
            SEND MESSAGE ABORT;
            WAIT +ACKNOWLEDGE;
            IF TIMELIMIT THEN RETRANSMIT;
            END
        END;
    WRITE_LOG(COORDINATOR_COMPLETE);/*common exit*/
    RETURN;
    END COORDINATOR;
```

The protocol for the participant is simpler:

```
PARTICIPANT: PROCEDURE;
    WAIT_FOR REQUEST_COMMIT;       /* phase 1     */
    FORCE UNDO REDO LOG TO NONVOLATILE STORE;
    IF SUCCESS THEN     /* writes AGREE in log */
        REPLY 'AGREE';
    ELSE
        REPLY 'ABORT';
    WAIT_FOR VERDICT;              /* phase 2     */
    IF VERDICT = 'COMMIT' THEN
        DO;
        RELEASE RESOURCES & LOCKS;
        REPLY  +ACKNOWLEDGE;
        END;
    ELSE
        DO;
        UNDO PARTICIPANT;
        REPLY +ACKNOWLEDGE;
        END;
    END PARTICIPANT;
```

There is a last piece of logic that needs to be included: In the event of restart, recovery manager has only the log and the nonvolatile store. If the coordinator crashed before the PHASE12_COMMIT record appeared in the log, then restart will broadcast abort to all participants. If the transaction's PHASE12_COMMIT record appeared and the COORDINATOR_COMPLETE record did not appear then restart will re-broadcast the COMMIT message. If the transaction's COORDINATOR_COMPLETE record appears in the log, then restart will ignore the transaction. Similarly transactions will be aborted if the log has not been forced with AGREE. If the AGREE record appears, then restart asks the coordinator whether the transaction committed or aborted and acts accordingly (redo or undo.)

Examination of this protocol shows that transaction commit has two phases:

- before its PHASE12_COMMIT or AGREE_COMMIT log record has been written and,

- after its PHASE12_COMMIT or AGREE_COMMIT log record has been written.

This is the reason it is called a two phase commit protocol. A fairly lengthy analysis is required to convince oneself that a crash or lost message will not cause one participant to "march" the wrong way.

Let us consider a few cases. If any participant aborts or crashes in his phase 1 then the entire transaction will be aborted (because the coordinator will sense that he is not replying using timeout).

If an participant crashes in his phase 2 then recovery manager as a part of restart of that participant will ask the coordinator whether or not to redo or undo the transaction instance. Since the participant wrote enough information for this in the log during phase 1, recovery manager can go either way on completing this participant. This requires that the undo and redo be idempotent operations. Conversely, if the coordinator crashes before it writes the log record, then restart will broadcast abort to all participants. No participant has committed because the coordinator's PHASE12_COMMIT record is synchronously written before any commit messages are sent to participants. On the other hand if the coordinator's PHASE12_COMMIT record is found in the log at restart, then the recovery manager broadcasts commit to all participants and waits for acknowledge. This redoes the transaction (coordinator).

This rather sloppy argument can be (has been) made more precise. The net effect of the algorithm is that either all the participants commit or that none of them commit (all abort.)

5.8.3.3.3. Nested Two Phase Commit Protocol

Many optimizations of the two phase commit protocol are possible. As described above, commit requires 4N messages if there are N participants. The coordinator invokes each participant once to take the vote and once to broadcast the result. If invocation and return are expensive (e.g. go over thin wires) then a more economical protocol may be desired.

If the participants can be _linearly ordered_ then a simpler and faster commit protocol which has 2N calls and returns is possible. This protocol is called the _nested two phase commit_. The protocol works as follows:

- Each participant is given a sequence number in the commit call order.

- In particular, each participant knows the name of the next participant and the last participant knows that he is the last.

Commit consists of participants successively calling one another (N-1 calls) after performing phase 1 commit. At the end of the calling sequence each participant will have successfully completed phase 1 or some participant will have broken the call chain. So the last participant can perform phase 2 and returns success. Each participant keeps this up so that in the end there are N-1 returns to give a grand total of 2(N-1) calls and returns on a successful commit. There is one last call required to signal the coordinator (last participant) that the commit completed so that restart can ignore redoing this transaction. If some participant does not succeed in phase 1 then he issues abort and transaction undo is started.

The following is the algorithm of each participant:

```
COMMIT: PROCEDURE;
        PERFORM PHASE 1 COMMIT;
        IF FAIL THEN RETURN FAILURE;
        IF I_AM_LAST THEN
           WRITELOG(PHLSE12) FORCE;
         ELSE
           DO;
           CALL COMMIT(I+1);
           IF FAIL THEN
              DO;
              ABORT;
              RETURN FAILURE;
              END;
            END;
        PERFORM PHASE 2 COMMIT;
        IF I_AM_FIRST THEN
           INFORM LAST THAT COMMIT COMPLETED;
        RETURN SUCCESS;
        END;
```

The following gives a picture of a three deep nest:

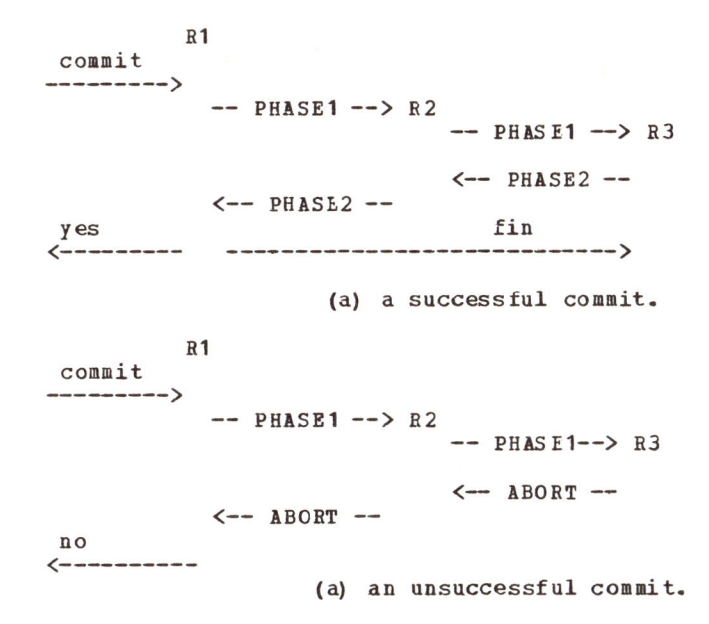

```
              R1
   commit
   --------->
                 -- PHASE1 --> R2
                                  -- PHASE1 --> R3

                                  <-- PHASE2 --
                 <-- PHASE2 --
   yes                              fin
   <---------   ---------------------------->

                  (a)  a successful commit.

              R1
   commit
   --------->
                 -- PHASE1 --> R2
                                  -- PHASE1--> R3

                                  <-- ABORT --
                 <-- ABORT --
   no
   <----------
                  (a) an unsuccessful commit.
```

5.8.3.3.4. Comparison Between General and Nested Protocols

The nested protocol is appropriate for a system in which

- The message send-receive cost is high and broadcast not available.

- The need for concurrency within phase 1 and concurrency within phase 2 is low.

- The participant and cohort structure of the transaction is static or universally known.

Most data management systems have opted for the nested commit protocol for these reasons. On the other hand the general two phase commit protocol is appropriate if:

- Broadcast is the normal mode of interprocess communication (in that case the coordinator sends two messages and each process sends two messages for a total of 2N messages.) Aloha net, Ethernet, ring-nets, and space-satelite nets have this property.

- Parallelism among the cohorts of a transaction is desirable (the nested protocol has only one process active at a time during commit processing.)

5.8.3.4. Summary of Recovery Protocols

The consistency lock protocol isolates the transaction from inconsistencies due to concurrency.

The DO-REDO-UNDO log record protocol allows for recovery of committed and uncommitted actions.

The write ahead log protocol insures that the log is ahead of nonvolatile storage so that undo and redo can always be performed.

The two phase commit protocol coordinates the commitment of autonomous participants (or cohorts) within a transaction.

The following table explains the virtues of the write ahead log and two phase commit protocols. It examines the possible situations after a crash. The relevant issues are whether an update to the object survived (was written to nonvolatile storage), and whether the log record corresponding to the update survived. One will never have to redo an update whose log record is not written because: Only committed transactions are redone, and COMMIT writes out the transaction's log records before the commit completes. So the (no, no, redo) case is precluded by two phase commit. Similarly, write ahead log (WAL) precludes the (no, yes, *) cases because an update is never written before it's log record. The other cases should be obvious.

LOG RECORD WRITTEN	OBJECT WRITTEN	REDO OPERATION	UNDO OPERATION
NO	NO	IMPOSSIBLE BECAUSE OF TWO PHASE COMMIT	NONE
NO	YES	IMPOSSIBLE BECAUSE OF WRITE AHEAD LOG	
YES	NO	REDO	NONE
YES	YES	NONE	UNDO

5.8.4. STRUCTURE OF RECOVERY MANAGER

Recovery management consists of two components.

- Recovery manager which is responsible for the tracking of transactions and the coordination of transaction COMMIT and ABORT, and system CHECKPOINT and RESTART (see below).

- Log manager which is used by recovery manager and other components to record information in the system log for the transaction or system.

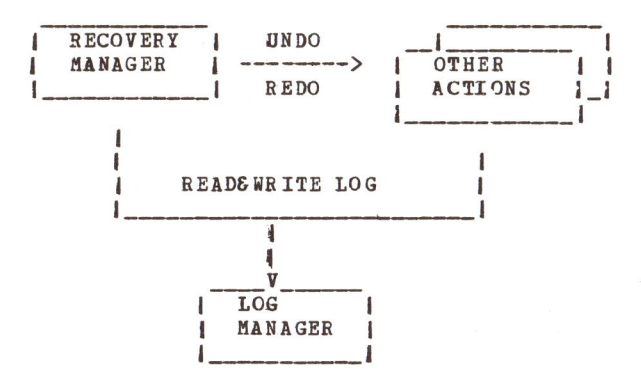

```
 _____       _____
| RECOVERY  |  UNDO    _____
| MANAGER   | -------> | OTHER     | |
|_____|  REDO    | ACTIONS   |_|
                       |_____|
      |
      |
   ___|_____
  |                               |
  |        READ&WRITE LOG         |
  |_____|
              |
              |
            __V__
         | LOG      |
         | MANAGER  |
         |_____|
```

Relationship between Log managers and component actions.

The purpose of the recovery system is two-fold: First, the recovery system allows an in-progress transaction to be "undone" in the event of a "minor" error without affecting other transactions. Examples of such errors are operator cancellation of the transaction, deadlock, timeout, protection or integrity violation, resource limit,....

Second, in the event of a "serious" error, the recovery subsystem minimizes the amount of work that is lost and by restoring all data to its most recent committed state. It does this by periodically recording copies of key portions of the the system state in nonvolatile storage and by continuously maintaining a log of changes to the state, as they occur. In the event of a catastrophe, the most recent transaction consistent version of the state is reconstructed from the current state on nonvolatile storage by using the log to

- undo any transactions which were incomplete at the time of the crash.

- and redoing any transactions which completed in the interval between the checkpoints and the crash.

In the case that on-line nonvolatile storage does not survive, one must start with an archival version of the state and reconstruct the most recent consistent state from it. This process requires:

- Periodically making complete archive copies of objects within the system.

- Running a change accumulation utility against the logs written since the dump. This utility produces a much smaller list of updates which will bring the image dump up to date. Also this list is sorted by physical address so that adding it to the image dump is a sequential operation.

- The change accumulation is merged with the image to reconstruct the most recent consistent state.

Other reasons for keeping a log of the actions of transactions include auditing and performance monitoring since the log is a trace of system activity.

There are three separate recovery mechanisms:
    (a) Incremental log of updates to the state.

(b) Current on-line version of the state.
(c) Archive versions of the state.

5.8.4.1. Transaction Save Logic

When the transaction invokes SAVE, a log record is recorded which describes the current state of the transaction. Each component involved in the transaction is then must record whatever it needs to restore it's recoverable objects to their state at this point. For example, the terminal handler might record the current state of the session so that if the transaction backs up to this point, the terminal can be reset to this point. Similarly, data base manager might record the positions of cursors. The application program may also record log records at a save point.

A save point does not commit any resources or release any locks.

5.8.4.2. Transaction Commit Logic

When the transaction issues COMMIT, recovery manager invokes each component (participant) to perform commit processing. The details of commit processing were discussed under the topics of recovery protocols above. Briefly, commit is a two phase process. During phase 1, each manager writes a log record which allows it to go either way on the transaction (undo or redo). If all resource managers agree to commit, then recovery manager forces the log to secondary storage and enters phase 2 of commit. Phase 2 consists of committing updates: sending messages, writing updates to non volatile storage and releasing locks. In phase 1 any resource manager can unilaterally abort the transaction thereby causing the commit to fail. Once a resource manager agrees to phase 1 commit, that resource manager must be willing to accept either abort or commit from recovery manager.

5.8.4.3. Transaction Backup Logic

The effect of any incomplete transaction can be undone by reading the log of that transaction **backwards** undoing each action in turn. Given the log of a transaction T:

```
UNDO(T):
 DO WHILE (LOG(T) ¬= NULL);
  LOG_RECORD = LAST_RECORD(LOG(T));
  UNDOER = WHO_WROTE(LOG_RECORD);
  CALL UNDOER(LOG_RECORD);
  INVALIDATE(LOG_RECORD);
  END UNDO;
```

Clearly, this process can be stopped half-way, thereby returning the transaction to an intermediate save point. Transaction save points allow the transaction to backtrack in case of some error and yet salvage all successful work.

From this discussion it follows that a transaction's log is a push down stack and that writing a new record pushes it onto the stack while undoing a record pops it off the stack (invalidates it). For efficiency reasons, all transaction logs are merged into one system log which is then mapped into a log file. But the log records of a particular transaction are threaded together and anchored off of the process executing the transaction.

Notice that UNDO requires that while the transaction is active, the log be directly addressable. This is the reason that at least one version of the log should be on some direct access device. A tape based log would not be convenient for in-progress transaction undo.

The undo logic of recovery manager is very simple. It reads a record, looks at the name of the operation that wrote the record and calls the undo entry point of that operation using the record type. Thus recovery manager is table driven and therefore it is fairly easy to add new operations to the system.

Another alternative is to _defer_ updates until phase 2 of commit processing. Once a transaction gets to phase 2 it must complete successfully, thus if all updates are done in phase 2 no undo is ever required (redo logic is required.) IMS data communications and IMS Fast Path use this protocol.

5.8.4.4. System Checkpoint Logic

System checkpoints may be triggered by operator commands, timer facilities, or counters such as the number of bytes of log record since last checkpoint. The general idea is to minimize the distance one must travel in the log in the event of a catastrophe. This must be balanced against the cost of taking frequent checkpoints. Five minutes is a typical checkpoint interval.

Checkpoint algorithms which require a system quiesce should be avoided because they imply that checkpoints will be taken infrequently thereby making restart expensive.

The checkpoint process consists of writing a BEGIN_CHECKPOINT record in the log, then invoking each component of the system so that it can contribute to the checkpoint and then writing an END_CHECKPOINT record in the log. These records bracket the checkpoint records of the other system components. Each component may write one or more log records so that it will be able to restart from the checkpoint. For example, buffer manager will record the names of the buffers in the buffer pool, file manager might record the status of files, network manager may record the network status, and transaction manager will record the names of all transactions active at the checkpoint.

After the checkpoint log records have been written to non-volatile storage, recovery manager records the address of the most recent checkpoint in a warm start file. This allows restart to quickly locate the checkpoint record (rather than sequentially searching the log for it.) Because this is such a critical resource, the restart file is duplexed (two copies are kept) and writes to it are alternated so that one file points to the current and another points to the previous checkpoint log record.

At system restart, the programs are loaded and the transaction manager invokes each component to re-initialize itself. Data communications begins network-restart and the data base manager reacquires the data base from the operating system (opens the files).

Recovery manager is then given control. Recovery manager examines the most recent warm start file written by checkpoint to discover the location of the most recent system checkpoint in the log. Recovery manager then examines the most recent checkpoint record in the log. If there was no work in progress at the system checkpoint and the system checkpoint is the last record in the log then the system is in restarting from a _shutdown_ in a quiesced state. This is a warm start and no transactions need be undone or redone. In this case, recovery

manager writes a restart record in the log and returns to the scheduler
which opens the system for general use.

On the other hand if there was work in progress at the system
checkpoint, or if there are further log records then this is a restart
from a crash (emergency restart).

The following figure will help to explain emergency restart logic:

```
    T1         |---------|       +                                  <
    T2             |------------+------|                             <
    T3                          +           |-------------| <
    T4         |----------------+---------------------------<
    T5                          +                               |---<
                           CHECKPOINT                        SYSTEM
                                                             CRASH
```

Five transaction types with respect to the most recent system
checkpoint and the crash point.

Transactions T1, T2 and T3 have committed and must be redone.
Transactions T4 and T5 have not committed and so must be undone. Let's
call transactions like T1,T2 and T3 <u>winners</u> and lets call transactions
like T4 and T5 <u>losers</u>. Then the restart logic is:

```
RESTART: PROCEDURE;
    DICHOTOMIZE WINNERS AND LOSERS;
    REDO THE WINNERS;
    UNDO THE LOSERS;
    END RESTART;
```

It is important that the REDOs occur before the UNDOs. (Do you see
why?)

As it stands, this implies reading every log record ever written
because redoing the winners requires going back to redo almost all
transactions ever run.

Much of the sophistication of the restart process is dedicated to
minimizing the amount of work that must be done so that restart can be
as quick as possible. (We are describing here one of the more trivial
workable schemes.) In general restart discovers a time T such that
redo log records written prior to time T are not relevant to restart.

To see how to compute the time T we first consider a particular object:
a data base page P. Because this is a restart from a crash, the most
recent version of P may or may not have been recorded on non-volatile
storage. Suppose page P was written out with high water mark LSN(P).
If P contained updates of winners which updated P which logged after
LSN(P), then these updates to P must be redone. Conversely, if it was
written out with a loser's update then these updates must be undone.
(Similarly, message M may or may not have been sent to its destination.
If it was generated by a transaction which is to be undone then the
message should be canceled. If M was generated by a committed
transaction but not sent then it should be retransmitted.) The figure
below illustrates the five possible types of transactions at this
point: T1 began and committed before LSN(P), T2 began before LSN(P) and
ended before the crash, T3 began after LSN(P) and ended before the
crash, T4 began before LSN(P) but no COMMIT record appears in the log,
and T5 began after LSN(P) and apparently never ended. To honor the
commit of T1, T2 and T3 transactions requires that their updates be

added to page P (redone). But T4 and T5 have not committed and so must be undone.

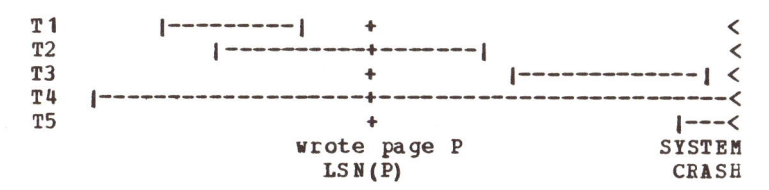

```
T1      |---------|     +                              <
T2            |----------+-------|                     <
T3                       +             |-------------| <
T4      |----------------+---------------------------------<
T5                       +                         |---<
                    wrote page P               SYSTEM
                     LSN(P)                    CRASH
```

Five transactions types with respect to the most recent write of page P and the crash point.

Notice that none of the updates of T5 are reflected in this state so it is already undone. Notice also that all of the updates of T1 are in the state so it need not be redone. So only T2, T3, and T4 remain. T2 and T3 must be redone from HWP(P) forward, the updates of the first half of T2 are already reflected in the page P because it has log sequence number LSN(P). On the other hand, T4 must be undone from LSN(P) backwards. (Here we are skipping over the following anomaly: if after LSN(P), T2 backs up to a point prior to the LSN(P) then some undo work is required for T2. This problem is not difficult, just annoying.)

Therefore the oldest redo log record relevant to P is at or after LSN(P) (The write ahead log protocol is relevant here.) At system checkpoint, data manager records LSNMIN, the log sequence number of the oldest page not yet written (the minimum LSN(P) of all pages, P, not yet written.) Similarly, transaction manager records name of each transaction active at the checkpoint. Restart chooses T as the LSNMIN of the most recent checkpoint.

Restart proceeds as follows: It reads the system checkpoint log record and puts each transaction active at the checkpoint into the loser set. It then scans the log forward to the end. If an COMMIT log record is encountered, that transaction is promoted to the winners set. If a BEGIN_TRANSACTION record is found, the transaction is tentatively added to the loser set. When the end of the log is encountered, the winners and losers have been computed. The next thing is to read the log backwards, undoing the losers, and starting from time T, read the log forward redoing the winners.

This discussion of restart is very simplistic. Many systems have added mechanisms to speed restart by:

- Preventing the writing of uncommitted objects to non-volatile storage (stealing) so that undo is never required.

- Writing committed objects to secondary storage at phase 2 of commit (forcing), so that redo is only rarely required.

- Logging the successful completion of the movement of an object to secondary storage. This minimizes redos.

- Forcing all objects at system checkpoint to minimize "T".

5.8.4.5. Media Failure Logic

In the event of a hard system error (one which causes a loss of non-volatile storage integrity), it must be possible to continue with a minimum of lost work. Redundant copies of an object must be maintained, for example on magnetic tape reels which are stored in a vault. It is important that the archive mechanism have independent failure modes from the regular storage subsystem. Thus using doubly redundant disk storage would protect against a disk head crash, but wouldn't protect against a bug in the disk driver routine or a fire in the machine room.

The archive mechanism periodically writes a checkpoint of the data base contents to magnetic tape, and writes a redo log of all update actions to magnetic tape. Then recovering from a hard failure is accomplished by locating the most recent surviving version on tape, loading it back into the system, and then redoing all updates from that point forward using the surviving log tapes.

While performing a system checkpoint causes relatively few disk writes and takes only a few seconds, copying the entire data base to tape is potentially a lengthy operation. Fortunately there is a (little used) trick: one can take a _fuzzy_ _dump_ of an object by writing it to archive with an idle task. After the dump is taken, the log generated during the fuzzy dump is merged with the fuzzy dump to produce a _sharp_ _dump_. The details of this algorithm are left as an exercise for the reader.

5.8.4.6. Cold Start Logic

Cold start is too horrible to contemplate. Since we assumed that the log never fails, cold start is never required. The system should be cold started once: when its first version is created by the implementors. Thereafter, it should be restarted. In particular moving to new hardware or adding to a new release of the system should not require a cold start. (i.e. all data should survive.) Note that this requires that the format of the log never change, it can only be extended by adding new types of log records.

5.8.5. LOG MANAGEMENT

The log is a large linear byte space. It is very convenient if the log is write-once and then read-only and if space in the log is never re-written. This allows one to identify log records by the relative byte address of the last byte of the record.

A typical (small) transaction writes a 500 bytes of log. One can run about one hundred such transactions per second on current hardware. There are almost 100,000 seconds in a day. So the log can grow at 5 billion bytes per day. (More typically, systems write four log tapes a day at 50 megabytes per tape.) Given these statistics the log addresses should be about 48 bits long (good for 200 years on current hardware.)

Log manager must map this semi-infinite logical file (log) into the rather finite files (32 bit addresses) provided by the basic operating system. As one file is filled, another is allocated and the old one is archived. Log manager provides other resource managers with the operations:

- WRITE_LOG: causes the identified log record to be written to the log. Once a log record is written, it can only be read, it cannot be edited. Write log is the basic command used by all resource managers to record log records. It returns the address of the last byte of the written log record.

- FORCE_LOG: causes the identified log record and all prior log records to be recorded in nonvolatile storage. When it returns, the writes have completed.

- OPEN_LOG: indicates that the issuer wishes to <u>read</u> the log of some transaction or the entire log in sequential order. It creates a read cursor on the log.

- SEARCH_LOG: moves the cursor a designated number of bytes or until a log record satisfying some criterion is located.

- READ_LOG: requests that the log record currently selected by the log cursor be read.

- CHECK_LOG: allows the issuer to test whether a record has been placed in the non-volatile log and optionally to wait until the log record has been written out.

- GET_CURSOR: causes the current value of the write cursor to be returned to the issuer. The RBA returned may be used at a later time to position a read cursor.

- CLOSE_LOG: indicates the issuer is finished reading the log.

The write log operation moves a new log record to the end of the current log buffer. If the buffer fills, another is allocated and the write continues into the new buffer.

When a log buffer fills or when a synchronous log write is issued, a log daemon writes the buffer to nonvolatile storage. Traditionally, logs have been recorded on magnetic tape because it is so inexpensive to store and because the transfer rate is quite high. In the future disk, CCD (nonvolatile?) or magnetic bubbles may be attractive as a staging device for the log. This is especially true because an on-line version of the log is very desirable for transaction undo and for fast restart.

It is important to doubly record the log. If the log is not doubly recorded, then a media error on the log device will produce a cold start of the system. The dual log devices should be on separate paths so that if one device or path fails the system can continue in degraded mode (this is only appropriate for applications requiring high availability.)

The following problem is left as an exercise for the reader: We have decided to log to dedicated dual disk drives. When a drive fills it will be archived to a mass storage device. This archive process makes the disk unavailable to the log manager (because of arm contention.) Describe a scheme which:

- minimizes the number of drives required.

- always has a large disk reserve of free disk space

- always has a large fraction of the recent section of the log on line.

5.8.5.1. Log Archiving and Change Accumulation

When the log is archived, it can be compressed so that it is convenient for media recovery. For disk objects, log records can be sorted by cylinder, then track then sector then time. Probably, all the records in the archived log belong to completed transactions. So one only needs to keep redo records of committed (not aborted) transactions. Further only the most recent redo record (new value) need be recorded. This compressed redo log is called a change accumulation log. Since it is sorted by physical address, media recover becomes a merge of the image dump of the object and its change accumulation tape.

```
FAST_MEDIA_RECOVERY: PROCEDURE(IMAGE,CHANGE_ACCUM);
   DO WHILE (¬End_Of_File IMAGE);
      READ IMAGE PAGE;
      UPDATE WITH REDO RECORDS FROM CHANGE_ACCUM;
      WRITE IMAGE PAGE TO DISK;
      END
   END;
```

This is a purely sequential process (sequential on input files and sequential on disk being recovered) and so is limited only by the transfer rates of the devices.

The construction of the change accumulation file can be done off-line as an idle task.

If media errors are rare and availability of the data is not a critical problem then one may run the change accumulation utilities when needed. This may save building change accumulation files which are never used.

5.8.6. EXAMPLES OF A RECOVERY ROUTINES.

5.8.6.1. How to Get Perfectly Reliable Data Communications

watch this space (a coming attraction)

5.8.6.2. How to Get Perfectly Reliable Data Management

watch this space (a coming attraction)

5.8.7. HISTORICAL NOTE ON RECOVERY MANAGEMENT.

Most of my understanding of the topic of recovery derives from the experience of the IMS developers and from the development of System R. Unfortunately, both these groups have been more interested in writing code and understanding the problems than in writing papers. Hence there is very little public literature which I can cite. Ron Obermark seems to have discovered the notion of write ahead log in 1974. He also implemented the nested two phase commit protocol (almost). This work is known as the IMS-Program Isolation Feature. Earl Jenner and Steve Weick first documented the two phase commit protocol in 1975 although it seems to have its roots in some systems built by Niko Garzado in 1970. Subsequently, the SNA architects, the IMS group and the System R group has explored various implementations of these ideas. Paul Mcjones (now at Xerox) and I were stimulated by Warren Titlemann's history file in INTERLISP to implement the DO-UNDO-REDO paradigm for System R. The above presentation of recovery derives from drafts of various (unpublished) papers co-authored with John Nauman, Paul McJones, and Homer Leonard. The two phase commit protocol was independently discovered by Lampson and Sturgis (see below) and the nested commit protocol was independently discovered by Lewis, Sterns, and Rosenkrantz (see below.)

5.8.8. BIBLIOGRAPHY

Alsberg, "A Principle for Resilient Sharing of Distributed Resources," Second National Conference on Software Engineering, IEEE Cat. No. 76CH1125-4C, 1976, pp. 562-570. (A novel proposal (not covered in these notes) which proposes a protocol whereby multiple hosts can cooperate to provide **very** reliable transaction processing. It is the first believable proposal for system duplexing or triplexing I have yet seen. Merits further study and development.)

Bjork, "Recovery Scenario for a DB/DC System," Proceedings ACM National Conference, 1973, pp. 142-146.

Davies, "Recovery Semantics for a DB/DC System," Proceedings ACM National Conference, 1973, pp. 136-141. (The above two companion papers are the seminal work in the field. Anyone interested in the topic of software recovery should read them both at least three times and then once a year thereafter.)

Lampson, Sturgis, "Crash Recovery in a Distributed System," Xerox Palo Alto Research Center, 1976. To appear CACM. (A very nice paper which suggests the model of errors presented in section 5.8.1 and goes on to propose a three phase commit protocol. This three phase commit protocol is an elaboration of the two phase commit protocol. This is the first (only) public mention of the two phase commit protocol.)

Rosenkrantz, Sterns, Lewis, "System Level Concurrency Control for Data Base Systems," General Electric Research, Proceedings of Second Berkeley Workshop on Distributed Data Management and Data Management, Lawrence Berkeley Laboratory, LBL-6146, 1977, pp. 132-145. also, to appear in Transactions on Data Systems, ACM. (Presents a form of nested commit protocol, allows only one cohort at a time to execute.)

"Information Management System/Virtual Storage (IMS/VS), System Programming Reference Manual, IBM Form No. SH20-9027-2, p. 5-2. (Briefly describes WAL.)

CHAPTER 3.G.

H. Opderbeck
Telenet Communications Corporation
Washington, D.C., USA

Common Carrier Provided Network Interfaces

1. INTRODUCTION

During the last ten years we have seen significant advances in the art of building computer networks. Among the various techniques for implementing large-scale data communication networks, packet switching has proven to be highly successful. From its inception as a research experiment in the ARPANET, packet switching has evolved as the major data communication technique for new public computer networks (TELENET-USA, DATAPAC-Canada, TRANSPAC - France, EURONET). This proves that the major technical problems of building public computer networks have been solved. Therefore the interest has recently shifted from the task of building the network to the task of interfacing the user.

The ARPA experience has already shown that designing and implementing solid and versatile user interfaces is an extremely difficult problem. Even in this private network environment it was very hard to reconcile the conflicting user demands. Without proper standardization this problem is magnified in public networks. Fortunately, recent standardization efforts have been very successful in generating a CCITT standard for connecting data terminal equipment (DTEs), i.e. host computers and terminals, to data circuit-termination equipment (DCEs), i.e. public data communication networks. This standard has become known as X.25 and will be discussed at length in Chapter 5.

Today public networks are only viable if they are able to support the ubiquitous asynchronous terminals in addition to X.25 or packet mode devices. Therefore the designers of X.25 have recently agreed upon an extension of the original X.25 specification. This extension standardizes the handling of asynchronous terminals (called non-packet mode devices) by public networks. This X.25 extension will be discussed in more detail in Chapter 6.

There is no doubt that X.25 will be the most widely used standard for public computer networks in the near future. Today, however, there is a huge number of computers and terminals for which the necessary software and hardware to run X.25 is not yet available. The question arises what can be done to allow these devices immediate access to the available networks. One technique that has proven highly successful is the terminal emulation technique in which the network emulates the operation of a terminal. This network access method will be discussed in Chapter 3.

There is a wide gap of sophistication between the terminal emulation interface (TEI) and X.25. In Chapter 4 we will discuss a third type of interface which overcomes some of the disadvantages of the TEI but is less complex than the X.25 interface. This interface is called the Character Concentration Interface (CCI) since its main property is the multiplexing of several data streams over the same asynchronous channel.

All these interfaces (and many others not mentioned here) have certain characteristics in common. Before we go into the discussion of specific interfaces we will first describe the most important of these common characteristics.

2. Protocol Characteristics

2.1 Connection Establishment and Clearing

A data communication protocol is an agreement on format, meaning and relative timing of information exchanged between two communicating entities. Before any data can be exchanged there needs to be a mechanism by which one end can decide whether or not the other end is operating at all, i.e. able and willing to establish a connection. Similarly, there needs to be a procedure by which one end can indicate that it either wants to establish or break a connection. Simple terminal interfaces use data set signals to convey this information. Depending on the voltage on a particular pin of the interface the terminal indicates that it is either operating or down. For hosts and dial-in devices a more complex sequence of changes in the data set signals is required to establish a connection. More sophisticated protocols require the sending and processing of particular commands to bring up a communication link or to disconnect it.

In the most sophisticated protocols highly structured CALL REQUEST commands can be sent to establish a connection between any two points in a (possibly world-wide) network. To clear such a virtual connection a CLEAR command is used which may carry information about the clearing cause, accounting data, etc.

2.2. Error Control

One of the most important tasks of any data communications protocol is to deal with line errors. Various error detection and correction schemes have been studied and are in use today. They range from simple even or odd parity indication per character to powerful, usually hardware-generated checksums per transmission block. All the more advanced procedures use positive acknowledgement schemes, i.e. the sender waits for an acknowledgement from the receiver. If an acknowledgement is not received within a given time period, the block is retransmitted. Since the acknowledgement may get lost on the line due to a line error, the receiver must be able to distinguish new incoming blocks from retransmissions of previously sent blocks. For this purpose all blocks are provided with a sequence number. Whenever the receiver receives two blocks with the same sequence number he knows that the latter block is a retransmission of the first one and discards it as a duplicate. The receiver will also send an acknowledgement for each duplicate to make sure that the sender eventually learns about the successful transmission.

A well-known technique for acknowledging blocks is to send back to the sender the sequence number n of the next expected block, thereby acknowledging all blocks with sequence numbers n-1 or less. The range of sequence numbers is, of course, limited since they occupy a finite space in each block. If k bits are reserved for the sequence number in the header of a block then they are normally calculated modulo 2**k. In the simplest case k is equal to 1, i.e. each block is labeled as block 0 or block 1. This requires only a single bit in the header for sequence control. This scheme has, however, the disadvantage that block 1 (or 0) can only be sent after block 0 (or 1) has been acknowledged. Therefore the throughput is limited to one message per round-trip time (i.e. the time interval between sending a block and receiving its acknowledgement).

Sequence numbers are also used to detect blocks that reach the receiver out of sequence. In this case two recovery actions are possible. The receiver discards all out-of-sequence blocks and asks the sender to retransmit all blocks from the point on where the first block was missed (reject scheme). The alternative possibility is that the receiver keeps the out-of-sequence blocks and asks the sender only for the retransmission of the missed blocks (selective retransmit scheme).

Figures 1 and 2 demonstrate the use of the reject and the selective retransmit scheme. In both cases message 2 is assumed to get lost on the line. The reject retransmit scheme causes messages 2, 3 and 4 to be retransmitted (Figure 1). The selective retransmit scheme causes only message 2 to be retransmitted (Figure 2).

2.3 Flow Control

To avoid loss of data the average rate at which the receiver is able to accept data must be equal to or greater than the average rate at which the sender is sending it. Alternatively there may be a mechanism by which the receiver can let the sender know that it should stop transmitting or at least slow down. This mechanism is called flow control.

In simple terminal protocols flow control is provided by means of special characters. When the receiver is not willing to accept any more characters, he will transmit a so-called XOFF character. The receipt of this character causes the sender to stop transmitting. To restart the transmission of data the receiver sends the so-called XON character. Since the XOFF and XON characters can be garbled or even generated by line errors this simple scheme can lead to confusion. More sophisticated protocols therefore use checksum protected commands to turn off and restart the flow of data from the sender.

All acknowledgement/retransmission protocols have a built-in natural flow control mechanism. Just by not acknowledging blocks (even though they were received with a good checksum) the receiver can stop the sender. More effective, however, is an extension of the sequence number scheme to cover flow control. In this scheme the receiver returns with the acknowledgment not only the sequence number of the next expected block but also an indication as to how many more blocks the receiver is willing to accept. This indication defines to the sender a window of legal sequence numbers it can use to send data. (Therefore this scheme is called the 'window technique'). Once all sequence numbers in this window are used up, i.e. the window is closed, the sender must stop transmitting and wait for an acknowledgment that may open up the window again. Figure 3 demonstrates the use of sequence number for flow control.

In Figure 1, the sequence number space is represented as a circle. The circle is subdivided into three sectors:

1. Sequence numbers of blocks that have been transmitted but not yet acknowledged (A-B),
2. Sequence numbers that are available for futher transmissions (B-C),
3. Illegal sequence numbers (C-A).

When the sector between B and C becomes empty, the sender has to stop transmitting. Points A and C on the circle are moved by the acknowledgments, point B is moved by the transmissions. The dashed areas represent the sequence number space used up by unacknowledged messages.

This window technique can be simplified by holding the distance between points A and C constant. In this case, it suffices to just send the sequence number for acknowledging blocks. Point C is always moved by the same amount.

2.4 Multiplexing

One of the design goals for data communication protocols is the efficient use of the available line bandwidth, i.e. the protocol should minimize the loss of line capacity due to overhead and/or error control or flow control restrictions. To guarantee the continuous flow of messages over a data communications link, the number of outstanding messages allowed at any time (window A-C) must be larger than the round-trip time divided by the time it takes to transmit one message. If this condition is true the sender will never be blocked by a closed window B-C.

This condition can be relaxed if the protocol supports multiplexing. In this case one can send several data streams over the same physical channel. Each block carries an identifier signifying the data stream it belongs to. Since each data stream is driven by an independent set of sequence numbers, the sender can keep on transmitting even though some of the data streams may be blocked.

The use of independent sequence numbers for each data stream is also important in order to minimize the interference between them. In particular, a protocol must insure that one data stream being blocked does not also block the users of the other data streams.

In most cases where line cost is an important consideration multiplexing becomes necessary to provide the concentration effect that brings down cost. The maximum number of data streams that can be supported in parallel is determined by the size of the data stream identifier field. Since this field itself increases overhead its size needs to be determined judiciously. In practice the theoretical maximum is rarely reached because of bandwidth limitations.

2.5 Synchronization

There are various stages during the exchange of messages at which sender and receiver have to synchronize their activities. The first such synchronization is necessary when the stations become operational, i.e. after the connection has been established. Synchronization may actually be implied in the connection establishment. In many cases it is desirable to also resynchronize the activities without breaking the connection.

The simplest form of synchronization is the bit-synchronization provided by start/stop or asynchronous transmission devices. In this case the receiver resynchronizes after the receipt of every character. In some synchronous protocols a special bit combination (the SYN character) is sent to provide character synchronization. Recently developed full-duplex synchronous protocols specify the sending of continuous flags (01111110) as the idle condition. Any transmission blocks or frames are defined as bit sequences between these flags. This way block synchronization is obtained.

Protocols that use sequence numbers usually provide a mechanism by which these sequence numbers can be reset. This is normally done by means of a sequence number resynchronization command. To make sure that both, sender and receiver, agree on the new value for the sequence numbers a response to the resynchronization command is normally required. Data frames received during the resynchronization are discarded. They can, of course, be retransmitted after synchronization has been reestablished.

2.6 Transparency

Transparency is the ability to send any sequence of bits (in bit oriented protocols) or characters (in character oriented protocols). Asynchronous protocols are in many cases limited to a transparency of less than 8 bits per character because of parity indication and special control characters like XON/XOFF. Synchronous protocols usually provide a mode that allows full transparancy. There are various methods to achieve this. One possibility is to send a character count along with the message to define exactly what characters should be interpreted as data. Another method defines a special character (DLE character) for framing purposes. In case this character is encountered in the data stream it is doubled and can thereby be distinguished from its occurance as a control character. The above mentioned bit-oriented protocols that send 01111110-flags between frames insert a 0-bit after all sequences of 5 continguous 1-bits to insure a flag sequence is not simulated by the data.

3. Terminal Emulation Interface

In the Terminal Emulation Interface (TEI) the network appears to the host as a simple terminal device, i.e. it emulates the operation of a terminal. We will restrict our discussion to the emulation of asynchronous terminals. In this case the host sends and receives serial character streams as it would when connected to an asynchronous terminal with keyboard and printing capabilities.

Because the network emulates terminals for which the host already has support software, the host is provided with a means for quickly and easily accessing the network. As compared to the use of an X.25 interface the use of a TEI introduces certain cost and performance inefficiencies. However, the TEI has proven to be very successful in the context of a new commercial offering. The necessity for a TEI will diminish when the X.25 standard is supported by communications software in most major vendor-supplied host computer systems and terminals.

Standards for connecting terminals over leased or switched communication lines to host computers are well established (e.g. RS 232) and need not be discussed here. Since the TEI processor in the network emulates the operation of a terminal it has to follow the existing conventions. In particular, the connection between host and network is established via an exchange of data set signals. Typically, a host on a TEI would only accept incoming calls but not initiate calls on its own since there is no defined procedure by which it can tell the network what destination port it wants to connect to. An exception to this rule is the so-called autoconnect feature by which a host port is automatically connected to a destination port when it raises its data set signals. The destination is fixed and determined at subscription time.

Connections can be established and broken through the use of data set signals in case the network equipment is directly connected to the host (i.e. no modems in between). The host can either keep DTR (the data-terminal-ready pin on the interface) up all the time in which case he is immediately connected when the network receives a call request for this host. Alternately, the host can keep DTR down and only raise it after the network has raised the ring indicator. Connections can be broken by the host dropping DTR or the network dropping DSR (the data-set-ready pin).

Error control on the TEI is only provided in terms of parity error detection. The network should be capable of supporting odd, even or no parity for characters of 6, 7 or 8 bits.

Flow control, if it is supported by the host at all, is achieved by means of transmitting XON and XOFF characters. The network should be able to provide flow control in both directions, i.e. it should be able to slow down the host as well as accept being slowed down by the host. Also, the actual encoding of the XON/XOFF characters should be selectable by the host at subscription time.

Since there is no multiplexing provided in the TEI, maintaining several TEIs simultaneously requires the use of separate physical access channels. To minimize cost, it is usually more economical to locate at the host site a physical concentrator device which presents the host with these multiple physical connections but which is connected to the network by a single access link. Due to the direct physical connection this arrangement also reduces sharply the error rate observed at the interface.

Bit synchronization over the TEI is obtained via the well-known start/stop bit mechanism. It is also possible to send and receive break signals as is the case with directly connected terminals. The break mechanism can be used to quickly flush data that accumulated in the network (see Chapter 6).

The network must be flexible to support the various requirements for transparency of the data stream. In the fully-transparent mode all characters are passed through the network without being interpreted at all. When flow control characters and/or parity bits are used only a 6-bit or 7-bit transparency is achieved.

In case a concentrator is used to multiplex several TEIs over one high-speed line there are a few performance-related problems that have to be solved. The basic unit of information the network receives from the host is the character. Inside the network the basic unit of information transfer is the packet, each of which may contain between one and M characters. (A typical value of M is 128). Characters are assembled into packets by the TEI concentrator. The 'packaging problem' is to decide at what point during the assembly a packet should be transmitted.

It is clearly inefficient to transmit each character separately in one packet. This not only results in excessive line overhead but may also pose flow control problems. It may also be quite expensive since charging is normally based on the number of packets transmitted. Waiting until the maximum number of M characters is assembled also proves to be impractical in most cases since an entire message may consist of fewer than M characters and no other characters will be output until a response from the terminal has been received and processed. Even where this is not the case, the time to fill an entire packet of M characters over a low speed line may be too long to be tolerated by the user. The TEI concentrator must therefore use criteria for the transmission of packets which are different from the simple 1 or M character accumulations.

One possibility is to trigger the transmission by so-called transmission-forcing characters . This approach is particularly useful when characters are received from terminals. It will be discussed in more detail in Chapter 6. When characters are received from host computers over the TEI, it is not as easy to define the transmission-forcing characters since they are application-dependent and may constantly change during one session at the terminal. For this reason the TEI employs a timer which is reset whenever a character is received by the network and triggers packet transmission whenever it expires. We call this timer an idle timer since it measures idle time on the interface.

For the purpose of decreasing response time in case of a long stream of output characters, a second timer is used which is called an interval timer. The interval timer limits the number of characters transmitted in a single packet to a number smaller than M. It is reset whenever the first character is stored in a packet. When the interval timer expires it also triggers packet transmission.

The correct setting of values for the idle and interval timers is important for the smooth operation of the TEI. The timer values determine how long characters are accumulated into packets before they are sent through the net to the terminal. Therefore they have a direct impact on the response time. Typically, the longer the idle or interval timer values, the longer the response time.

The second important consideration in determining the timer values concerns the average number of packets that are necessary to transmit all characters from the host to the terminal. Since the user is normally charged for the use of the communications facilities on a per packet basis, he wants to keep the packet count as low as possible. Clearly, there are fewer packets sent when the timer values are long. Long timer values, however, conflict with short response times. Therefore, the user has to find a compromise that suits his needs.

4. Character Concentration Interface

The two main disadvantages of the TEI interface are that it does not provide for line error recovery or for character concentration. Let us now discuss a simple host interface which still uses asynchronous lines but defines an acknowledgment/retransmission scheme to recover from line errors and allows the concentration of several character streams over the same physical access channel. We will call this interface a character concentration interface (CCI).

To achieve the concentration effect all characters destined for or received from the same line are sent together in packets. The CCI protocol therefore allows for multiplexing of data streams. Since we are dealing with an asynchronous line, the speed of the line is normally limited to 1800 baud. The number of data streams that can be supported depends, of course, on the traffic statistics. For typical interactive traffic the line should be able to support satisfactorily up to seven 300 baud terminals.

To avoid the monopolization of the line by one data stream, the line bandwidth has to be allocated fairly. Also, the maximum packet size should be small to reduce the interference between the various data streams. Too small a maximum packet size, however, increases the overhead and therefore eliminates any gained advantage. Let us assume that the maximum packet size is seven data characters.

Since characters are sent in packets there needs to be an indication as to what the packet boundaries are. For this purpose a synchronization character is provided which is sent as the first character of each packet. The second character of the packet contains a character count and is therefore used to determine the packet length. This second character is a special control character which also contains the ID of the data stream that the packet belongs to.

Since we want error control on the line, we need to include a checksum character as the last character of the packet. Any simple checksum technique can be used to determine the value of the checksum character. Correctly received packets are acknowledged by special acknowledgement packets.

The use of a retransmission scheme implies that there must be a facility for detecting duplicates. Therefore, each packet needs to carry a sequence number. Since the packets are short the acknowledgement for a successfully transmitted packet is received after a short time. This means that it is sufficient to use only two sequence numbers (0 and 1), i.e. a window size of one. This one-bit sequence number (S-bit) is also carried in the control byte. Figure 4 shows the data packet format of the CCI interface.

Since seven data streams are multiplexed the data stream ID zero can be used to transfer control packets that do not relate to a particular data stream. The acknowledgment packet is such a control packet since it carries the sequence number of the next expected data packet for all seven data streams. To synchronize the sequence numbers at both ends special synchronization commands have to be exchanged. These commands are also sent with a data stream identifier zero and can be distinguished from other commands by means of the character count field. The length of these packets can be deduced from their type.

5. X.25 Interface

5.1 Introduction

The X.25 interface allows a user to establish one or more so-called virtual channels between himself and any other user attached to the same or an interconnected network. All user devices that adhere to the X.25 specification are called data terminal equipment (DTE) operating in packet mode. The network side of the interface is called data circuit-termination equipment (DCE). X.25 therefore defines a protocol for attaching DTEs to DCEs.

The X.25 protocol is based on the concept of a virtual circuit. A virtual circuit is defined as a bi-directional association between a pair of DTEs. Control and data blocks sent and received over a virtual circuit are called packets. Transmission line bandwidth is only assigned to a virtual circuit while there are packets to be transmitted. Thus there is no physical link established between sender and receiver as in traditional communications systems. Rather all virtual circuits share the same physical access path to the network. This sharing of transmission facillities results in lower cost to the user.

There are other properties which distinguish a virtual circuit from the traditional switched or leased lines. A virtual circuit is error-controlled. In contrast to physical circuits it provides a variable delay path between the communicating DTEs. These distinguishing characteristics, however, normally have a negligible impact on the users applications programs. Therefore a conversion to an X.25 interface will typically only involve a change in the communications subsystem of the host system. From the host computers point of view the network may be treated as a hugh, powerful, remote concentrator.

The X.25 specification consists of a hierarchy of three protocol levels which are

1. Physical Interface
2. Link Access Procedure
    and
3. Packet Level Interface

All three levels are defined separately and function independently. Failures on a lower level, however, may affect the operation of the higher levels.

The physical Interface (Level 1) is concerned with the procedure for establishing, maintaining, and disconnecting the physical link between the network and the host. It specifies the use of existing interfaces and therefore does not require any change in the user's interface hardware. Level 1 will not be discussed ant further in this paper.

The Link Access Procedure (Level 2) specifies the communications protocol to be used for data interchange across the link between DTE and DCE. Its function is to provide an error-free link between DTE and DCE.

The Packet Level Interface (Level 3) specifies the packet format and control procedures for the exchange of packets containing control information and user data. In particular, it describes the manner in which virtual circuits are established, used and cleared.

5.2 Link Access Procedure

two sets of procedures for link control have been defined in X.25 called LAP and LAPB. The following discussion will concentrate on the LAP procedure.

The Link Access Procedure (LAP) is defined as a point-to-point symmetric system where both, DTE and DCE, have a send and a receive function which are called primary and secondary functions in X.25. The basic unit of information exchanged between DTE and DCE is called a frame. Frames sent from a primary to a secondary are called commands. Frames sent from a secondary to a primary are called responses. In particular, all information frames (frames carrying user data) are commands, all acknowledgment frames are called responses.

All frames start and end with a flag sequence consisting of one 0 followed by six continuous 1's and one 0. The flags provide the necessary frame synchronization between DTE and DCE. A single flag may be used as both the closing flag for one frame and the opening flag for the next frame.

There are up to four distinct fields inside a frame (see Figure 5):

1. The address field
2. The control field
3. The information field (which may be missing)
   and
4. The frame checking sequence for error detection.

The address field is of minor importance. It distinguishes commands and responses exchanged between the primary in the DCE and the secondary in the DTE from commands and responses exchanged between the primary in the DTE and the secondary in the DCE.

The control field is the most important field since it distinguishes the different types of frames. It will be discussed in more detail below.

The information field is considered data and is not further interpreted by the link access procedure. It is unrestricted with respect to coding or grouping of bits.

Before any data can be exchanged between DTE and DCE a connection must be established ('the line must be brought up'). For this purpose each primary keeps on sending SARM commands (Set Asynchronous Response Mode) until it receives a UA response (Unnumbered Acknowledge) from the secondary station. The link is declared operational only after an SARM/UA command/response pair has been exchanged in both directions. The link can be disconnected by either primary by sending a DISC command (Disconnect) which must be responded to with a UA.

To recover from line errors the link access procedure uses a positive acknowledgment/retransmission procedure. All information frames (or I-frames) are numbered modulo 8. I-frames are acknowledged by means of supervisory frames (or S-frames) which are responses sent from the secondary to the primary station.

All S-frames carry the sequence number n of the next expected I-frame and thereby acknowledge all I-frames with sequence numbers n-1 or less (modulo 8). The REJ response (Reject) also asks the primary station to retransmit all I-frames starting with I-frame number n. An REJ should be sent by the secondary only when the first out-of-sequence I-frame is received. Subsequently received out-of-sequence I-frames should be ignored. Doing otherwise may degrade the throughput severely due to disturbances in the retransmit logic.

If a secondary, due to a transmission error, does not receive a single I-frame or the last I frame in a sequence of I-frames, it will not detect an out-of-sequence condition. Therefore, it will not send an REJ. For this purpose, the primary will retransmit any unacknowledged I-frame after an appropriate time-out period. This also takes care of the case where an acknowledgment frame gets lost due to a line error.

Since I-frames are numbered modulo 8, a primary can send up to seven I-frames without receiving an acknowledgment for the first one. This condition defines the flow control built into the error retransmission scheme. If the secondary station wants to further restrict the flow of I-frames, it may send an RNR S-frame (Receiver-Not-Ready) which tells the primary to stop sending I-frames. To unblock the link again an RR or REJ may be sent. Since this 'unblocking' RR or REJ may get lost due to a transmission error, the primary station should periodically retransmit the next I-frame in sequence to be transmitted even though the link is blocked.

The link access procedure does not provide for multiplexing of multiple data streams. (This is done on the packet level). The primary station can force the reinitialization of sequence numbers any time by sending a SARM command. If the secondary station detects a protocol violation it can initiate a resynchronization by transmitting a CMDR (command reject) response to the primary station.

5.3 Packet Level Interface

The packet level interface provides facilities for establishing and clearing (virtual) connections, for separate flow control on each virtual circuit, for multiplexing of data streams, and facilities for synchronization.

A maximum of 4096 virtual connections can be maintained in parallel through one X.25 interface. Each packet sent across the interface carries a 12-bit identifier indicating what particular virtual circuit it refers to. When a DTE wants to establish a connection it sends a CALL REQUEST control packet to the DCE. The CALL REQUEST packet includes the address of the calling DTE (i.e. the source address), the address of the called DTE (i.e. the destination address), a facility field, and a user data field (see Figure 6). The facility field is optional. It can be used to ask the network to handle the call request differently from what the default values specify. In particular, it allows reverse charging, and variable flow control parameter settings. The user data field that follows the facilities field in the CALL REQUEST packet has a maximum length of 16 bytes. It is passed unchanged to the called DTE. It can be used to convey information to the destination that is relevant for establishing the connection (e.g. a password).

The CALL REQUEST packet is passed through the network to the called DTE and there received as an INCOMING CALL packet. The destination may either accept the incoming call by returning a CALL ACCEPT packet or reject it by returning a CLEAR packet. In case the virtual circuit cannot be established by the network the DCE returns a CLEAR INDICATION packet to the calling DTE. This CLEAR INDICATION packet contains a code indicating the cause for the rejection of the call. Figure 7 shows the sequence of messages exchanged for establishing a connection, transferring data, and the clearing of the connection.

The virtual channel numbers used at both ends of a connection are independent of each other. We mentioned already that the calling DTE selects the virtual channel number it wants to use. The virtual channel number at the called DTE is selected by the network (and included in the INCOMING CALL packet). To minimize the probability of a collision of virtual channel numbers, the DCE normally starts assigning them from 0 on upwards while the DTE will assign them from some upper limit on downwards.

The X.25 interface also defines a permanent virtual circuit which is a permanent association existing between two DTEs. In this case the virtual channel numbers are assigned at subscription time. Therefore no call establishment or clearing of a permanent virtual channel is necessary or even possible.

There is no need for acknowledgment and retransmission of packets since the second level protocol provides an error-free access path to the network (and the network internally insures that no packets get lost, duplicated or sent out-of-sequence). It is, however, important to provide flow control for each virtual connection to guarantee that data is not transmitted at one end of a virtual channel at an average rate that is greater than that at which it can be received at the other end and to avoid interference between virtual channels.

Each data packet consists of a three byte header and a user data field of any number of bits up to some maximum value. The first two bytes of the header are made up by a four-bit format field and the 12-bit virtual channel number. The third byte of the header differentiates the various kinds of packets. Its structure is similar to the structure of the control byte on the second level (which it should not be confused with). In particular, the same sequence scheme is used that is employed by the link access procedure. The sequence numbers, however, have only significance for flow control purposes. The maximum number of data frames that can be sent on a virtual channel without receiving further authorization must never exceed seven. The actual maximum value w is determined at call set-up or subscription time. The transmission of further data packets is authorized by returning receive sequence numbers in data packets travelling in the reverse direction or in RR (Receive Ready) packets. Receiving the receive sequence number n authorizes the sender to send data packets n, n+1,..., n+w-1 (all sequence numbers taken modulo 8). Additional flow control is provided through the use of RNR (Receive-Not-Ready) packets which block a given virtual channel and RR packets which unblock it.

X.25 provides a facility which allows the user to logically group his data into blocks that are larger than the maximum packet size. This facility is called the MORE DATA-bit. If this bit is turned on in the control byte of a full packet the receiver may expect a logical continuation of the data in the next packet. For partially full packets the MORE DATA bit is always assumed to be off. The MORE DATA bit has significance for the network in cases where the maximum packet sizes at both ends of the connection differ. In particular, if the maximum packet size at the receiving end is smaller than that at the sending end, the network will subdivide packets into smaller units and transfer these with the MORE DATA-bit turned on for all but the last unit to convey the logical meaning inherent in the single larger packet delivered by the sender.

To better understand the operation of virtual circuits it can be assumed that there is a process attached to each end of the virtual connection. The information that these processes exchange is carried in data packets. If for some reason a processor stops accepting data there must be a way to nevertheless gain its attention. This is the purpose of the break or interrupt key on most terminals. It provides an out-of-band signal that is interpreted differently from regular data by the host. When communicating through a network this out-of-band signaling capability needs to be retained, i.e. there needs to be a mechanism for sending information across the X.25 interface even though the normal flow of data is blocked by the flow control rules. The X.25 INT (interrupt) command provides this function. It consist of the standard header and a one byte data field. The INT command is not subject to the flow control constraints and is therefore delivered to the destination DTE even in case the virtual link is blocked. To acknowledge the receipt of the INT command the receiver must send an interrupt confirmation command.

The processes that are attached to the virtual circuits will in many cases be terminal handlers. These terminal handling processes will generally reside in equipment operated by the common carriers themselves since the common carriers have a need to not only support X.25 (packet-mode) terminals but also the ubiquitous asynchronous terminals. The question arises as to how a host computer can instruct a terminal handling process to handle the terminals in the specific way that is required for this host system. A more detailed discussion of this problem will be presented in the next chapter. Here, it suffices to say that any control information that is sent from the host to the terminal handling process is distinguished in X.25 from the actual data by a so-called qualifier bit (Q-bit). Thus there are really two levels of data transfer depending on whether or not the Q-bit is set. Both levels share the same flow control and sequencing mechanism. Therefore time and sequence of delivery of the data packets does not depend on the setting of the Q-bit.

The X.25 packet level provides two mechanisms for synchronization: the reset procedure and the restart procedure. The reset procedure is used to reinitialize the virtual circuit and in so doing removes in each direction all data and interrupt packets. The virtual circuit is thereby returned to the state it was in when it was established, i.e. all sequence numbers equal to zero and no packets in transmit. RESET REQUEST and RESET CONFIRMATION control packets are used to reset a virtual circuit.

The restart procedure is used to simultaneously clear all switched virtual circuits and reset all permanent virtual circuits at the DTE/DCE interface. A RESTART control packet would typically be sent by the DTE after a major failure to make sure that the entire interface is properly initialized before service is resumed.

6. Terminal Handling Through Public Networks

6.1 Introduction

Terminal handling is one of the most important issues in data communications. Its design and operation has a direct impact on user satisfaction. Therefore many computer systems have over many years adjusted and fine-tuned their terminal handling procedures to present the user an interface that is easy to use. The specific interface chosen may look quite different for different applications. It is therefore important to recognize that any standard on terminal handling needs to be flexible enough to meet the diverging needs.

The designers of X.25 have recently agreed upon an extension of X.25 to cover the handling of asynchronous terminals (called start/stop mode DTEs in X.25). A proposal for standardization has been submitted to CCITT. In this document the terminal handler is called a PAD (Packet Assembler/Disassembler) since the main function it performs is the assembly and disassembly of packets. Other basic functions of the PAD include establishing and clearing of virtual calls and providing a resetting and interrupt procedure. The PAD communicates with the user via service commands (from the user to the PAD) and service signals (from the PAD to the user). The interaction between the PAD and the remote host computer ('the packet-mode DTE') is done via PAD messages. To provide the necessary flexibility in handling terminals, the operation of the PAD is governed by a set of internal variables known as PAD parameters. The PAD parameters can be set and changed by the user by means of service commands and by the host computer by means of PAD messages (see Figure 8).

6.2. PAD Parameters

There are currently twelve PAD parameters defined. They are identified by decimal reference numbers.

> Reference 1 - Ability to escape from data transfer state.
> If this parameter is set to 0 the user cannot send service commands to the PAD. If it is set to 1 the user can escape from the data transfer state (the state in which he talks to the remote host) by typing the DLE character. If the user wants to send the DLE character to the host, he needs to type two DLE characters on his terminal.

Reference 2 - Echo
: If this parameter is set to 0 no characters will be echoed by the PAD during the data transfer state. While a user is typing in a service command characters are always echoed.

Reference 3 - Selection of data forwarding signal
: This parameter allows to specify whether no character at all, only the carriage return, or all control characters should trigger the transmission of the assembled data when it is typed in.

Reference 4 - Selection of idle timer delay
: This parameter specifies the value of the idle timer (see Chapter 3) in units of 50 msec.

Reference 5 - Ancillary Device Control
: If this parameter is 1 then the PAD will use the XON/XOFF mechanism to control the flow of characters from the terminal to the PAD.

Reference 6 - Suppress PAD Service Signals
: If this parameter is 0 no PAD service signals will be sent to the terminal. This facility is necessary for the operation of cassettes, for example.

Reference 7 - Selection of the procedure on break
: This parameter allows to select one of various actions to be taken when the PAD receives a break from the terminal. Amoung other things it is possible to send a reset on break, to escape from the data transfer state, or to discard output to the terminal until instructed to do otherwise by the host system.

Reference 8 - Discard output
: If this parameter is set to 1 normal data delivery to the terminal is stopped. This parameter is normally used in conjunction with the break procedure.

Reference 9 - Padding after carriage return
: This parameter describes how many padding characters should be transmitted to the terminal after a carriage return or line feed character was sent.

Reference 10- Line folding
: Using this parameter it is possible to specify the maximum number of graphic characters that the PAD may send as a single line to the terminal.

Reference 11- Binary speed
: This parameter describes the binary speed of the terminal. It is a read-only parameter.

Reference 12 - Flow control of the PAD by the terminal
If this parameter is 1 then the terminal is allowed to use the XON/XOFF mechanism to control the flow of characters from the PAD to the terminal.

On initialization a set of preset values of PAD parameters called 'standard profile' is selected. The selection of other profiles via service commands by the user is currently being considered.

6.3 PAD - User Interaction

When the user first connects his terminal to the network he has to send a sequence of characters known as service request to the PAD. The service request allows the PAD to detect the data rate and code used by the terminal. The exact format of the service request has not yet been determined. Typically it consists of 2 or 3 carriage returns. The PAD responds to the service request with a PAD identification service signal (unless messages to the terminal should be suppressed, Reference 6 is 0). The user is now able to type in service commands.

The most important of these commands are:

1. Selection Pad Command Signal
   This command allows the user to specify the address of the host computer he wants to be connected to. The PAD responds with an acknowledgement service signal (carriage return and line feed) and then tries to establish a virtual connection between the terminal and the desired destination. If the connection attempt is successful the PAD sends the 'CON' service signal and the user can now start to talk to the host. If the connect attempt fails the PAD will indicate the reason for the failure and then wait for the next command.
2. Clear Request Pad Command Signal
   If a user wants to clear the virtual call he escapes from the data transfer state and types in the clear request command signal ('LIB'). The PAD responds by transmitting a clear confirmation service signal ('LIB CONF'). The PAD may clear a virtual connection by either disconnecting the line to the terminal or transmitting a clear indication PAD service signal ('LIB' plus a clear cause). Possible causes for clearing a virtual connection are: clearing initiated by the destination host, called number is out of order, local or remote procedure error, etc.

3. PAR? Command Signal
   The user may inquire about the current values of one or several PAD parameters by sending the PAR command signal.
4. SET and SET? Command Signals
   The user may change the values of one or several PAD parameters by sending a SET or SET? command signal. If the SET? command is used the newly set parameter values will be displayed by the PAD.
5. RESET and INT Command Signals
   To force the resetting of the virtual connection or to send an INT packet to the host the user can send the RESET and INT command signal, respectively, to the PAD.

6.4 PAD - HOST Interaction

Each host can influence the handling of the terminals connected to it through the public network by exchanging control information with the PAD. The control information is sent and received in so-called PAD messages. PAD messages are transmitted by the network in sequence with regular user data. They are distinguished from the latter by setting the qualifier bit in the packet header to one (see Section 5.3). The following types of PAD messages are currently defined:

1. SET, READ, and SET-AND-READ PAD messages
   These PAD messages are used by the host to set, read, and set and read the current setting of the PAD parameters. These PAD messages include a list of selected parameters plus, for the SET and SET-AND-READ PAD messages, the desired value for each parameter.
2. Parameter Indication PAD Messages
   The PAD responds with a parameter indication PAD message to a READ or SET-AND-READ PAD message. The parameter indication PAD message contains the list of current parameter values, after any necessary modification, of the PAD parameters to which the message from the host referred.
3. Invitation to Clear PAD Message
   The invitation to clear PAD message is used by the host to request the PAD to clear the virtual connection after transmission to the terminal of all previously transmitted data.
4. Indication of Break PAD Message
   The indication of break PAD message can be used to send a 'break' through the network. It is primarily used in conjunction with the INT feature and the 'discard output' PAD parameter to quickly abort the output of data from the host.

6.5 Network Virtual Terminal

The X.25 PAD functions as described in the preceding sections represent a basic set of facilities that are necessary for terminal handling. There are, however, other concepts that go beyond this basic set and have proven to be very useful. One of these important concepts not yet defined in X.25 is that of a Network Virtual Terminal (NVT).

From the perspective of the host computer system, a network virtual terminal can be viewed as a full-duplex character device having keyboard and display (or printing) capabilities. The NVT has well-defined characteristics concerning code, control characters, etc. The significance lies in the fact that the network is able to map functions of any real terminal it supports into this standard, virtual terminal format and vice versa. In particular, the network does any code conversion, if necessary, and all the device dependent functions (e.g. padding). If the host computer system is able to support the NVT it will therefore automatically be able to exchange information with any real terminal supported by the network (see Figure 9).

Using the NVT mode of operation all the device-dependent functions are performed close to the terminal where they can be done most effectively. They are concentrated in the network where they can be shared by all host systems. Thus the duplication of device-dependent terminal handling functions in all host systems is avoided. Also, augmenting the capabilities of the network terminal handler benefits directly all host systems connected to the network.

References

(1) CCITT Study Group VII Contribution No. 262, December 1975. Submitted by the French PTT and U.K. Post Office.

(2) Hovey, R.B. 'Packet-switched networks agree on standard interface' Data Communications. May/June 1976. 25-39

(3) Kleinrock, L., W.E. Naylor and H. Opderbeck. 'A Study of Line Overhead in the ARPANET'. Communications of the ACM. Vol 19 January 1976, pp. 3-12.

(4) Kleinrock, L. and H. Opderbeck. 'Throughput in the ARPANET-- Protocols and Measurement'. IEEE Transactions on Communications, January 1977, 95-104.

(5) Opderbeck, H. and R.B. Hovey. 'Telenet-- Network Features and Interface Protocols.' Proc. NTG-Conference on Data Networks. Baden-Baden, West Germany, February 1976.

(6) Opderbeck, H. 'The performance of a terminal emulation interface to a packet-switched data network'. Proceedings of the Third International Conference on Computer Communication, Toronto, August 1976, 452-457.

(7) Rybczynski, A., Wessler, B., Despres, R., and Wedlake, J. 'A new communication protocol for accessing data networks - The International packet-mode interface'. National Computer Conference, New York, 1976, 477-482.

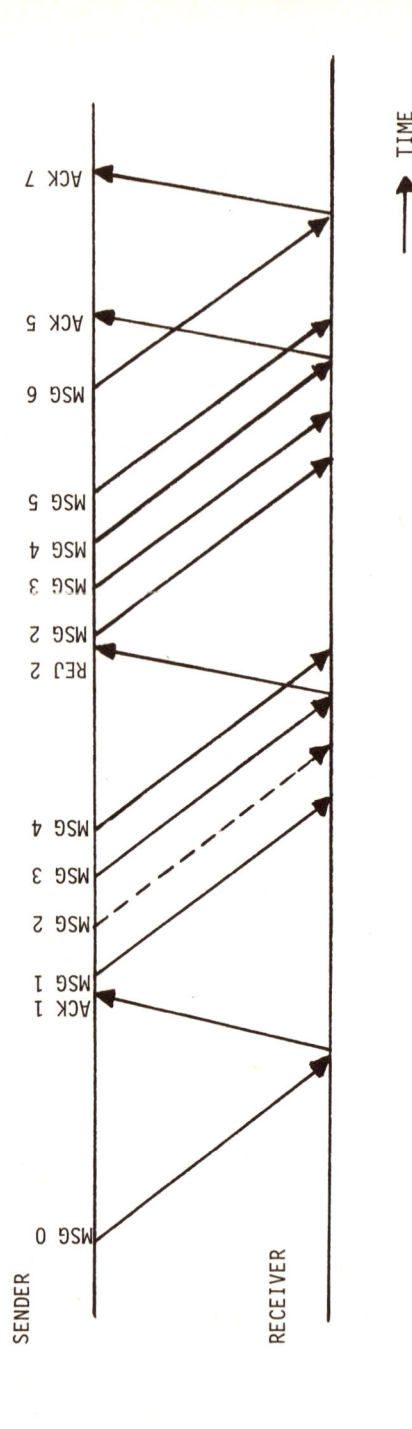

FIGURE 1   "REJECT" RETRANSMIT SCHEME

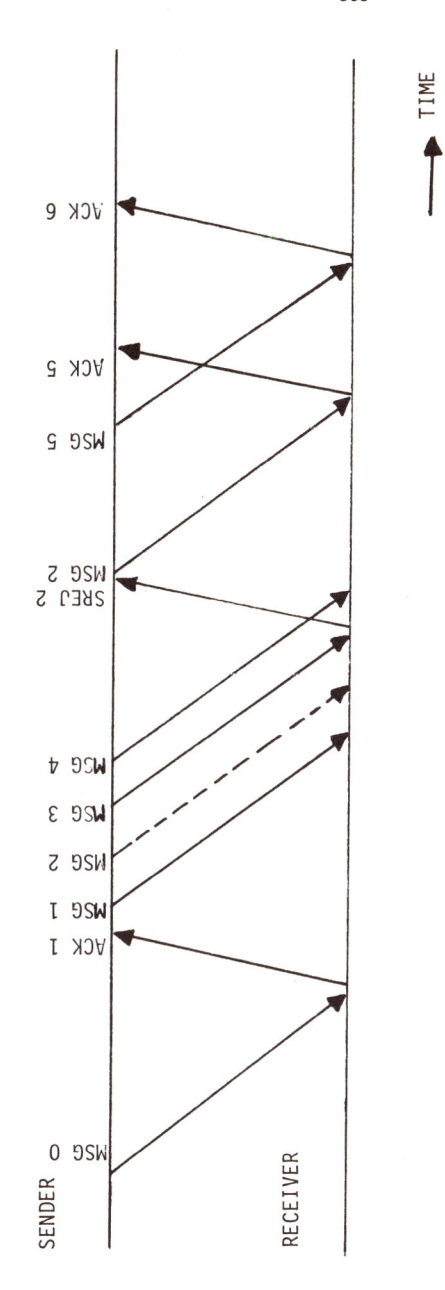

FIGURE 2 "SELECTIVE" RETRANSMIT SCHEME

MSG0 and
MSG1 Sent

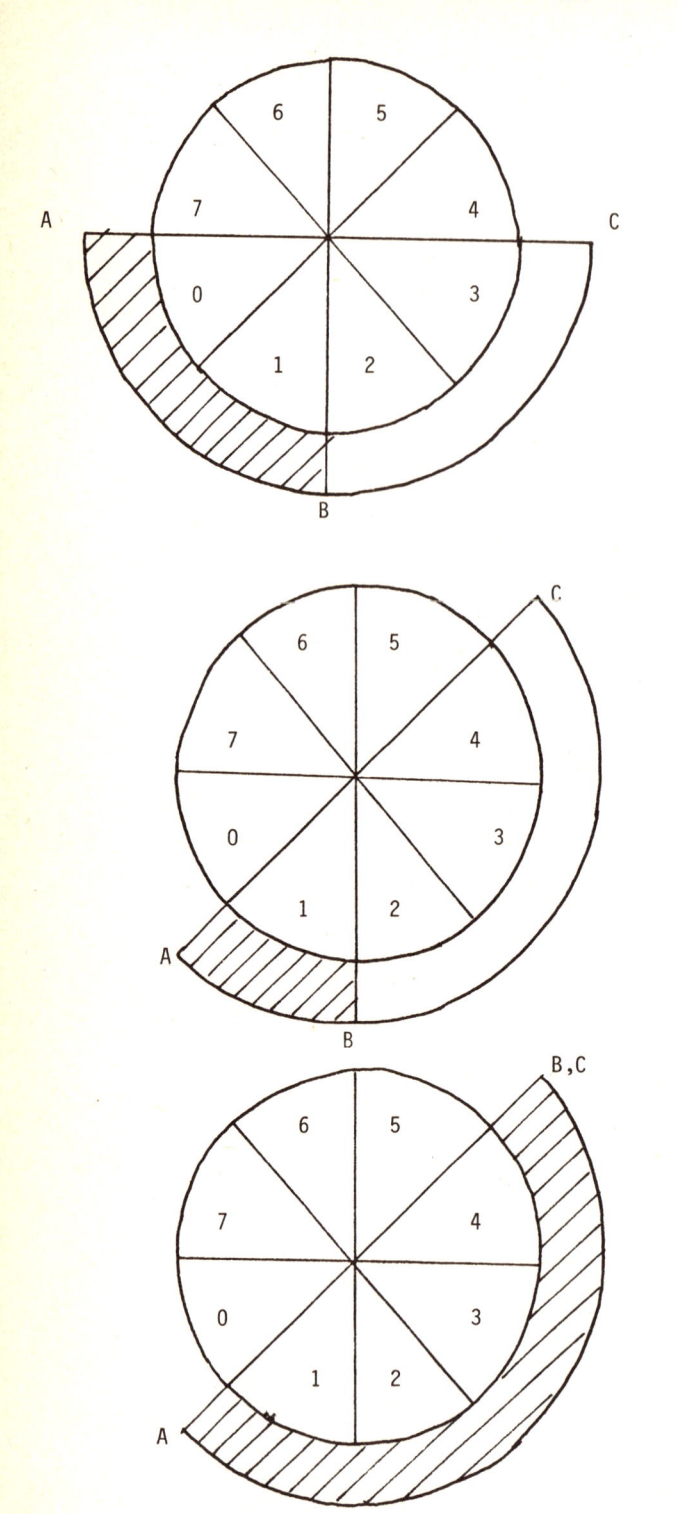

ACK1 received

MSG2, MSG3, and MSG4
Sent

FIGURE 3 Window technique

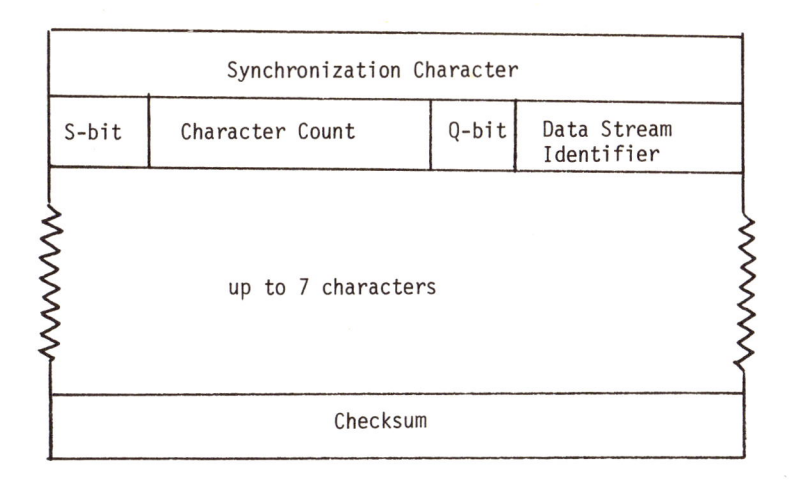

Synchronization Character			
S-bit	Character Count	Q-bit	Data Stream Identifier
up to 7 characters			
Checksum			

FIGURE 4   CCI DATA FRAME STRUCTURE

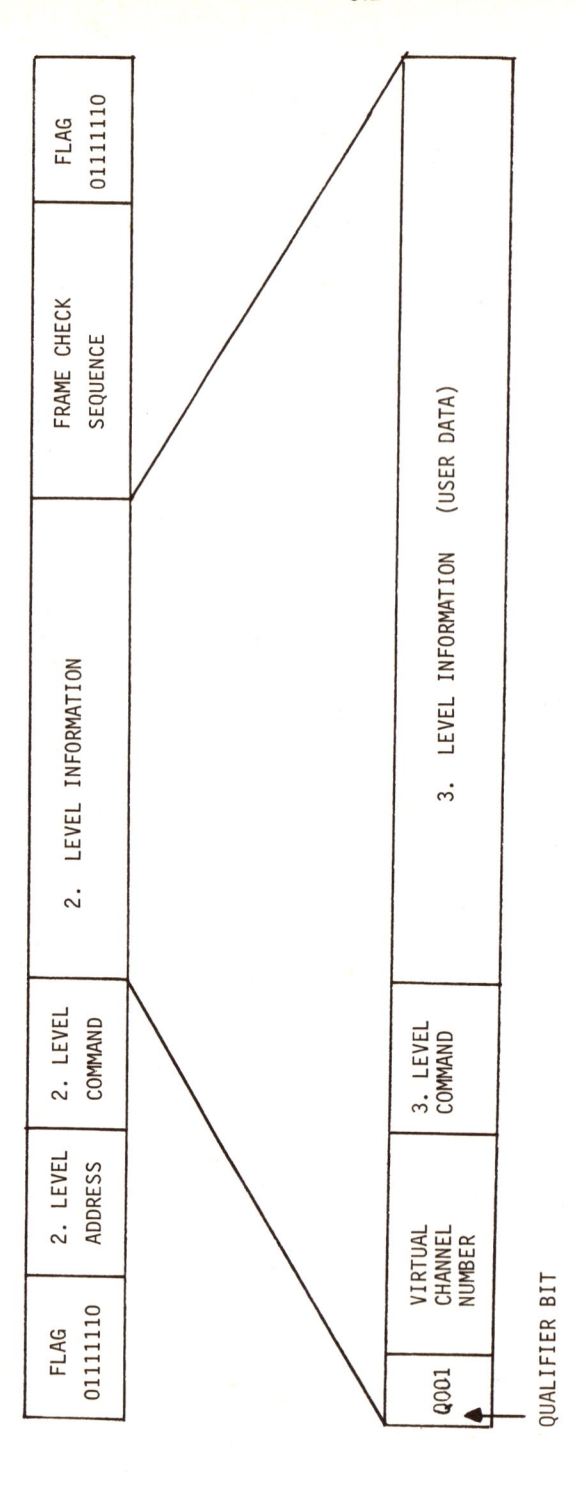

FIGURE 5   X.25 FRAME STRUCTURE

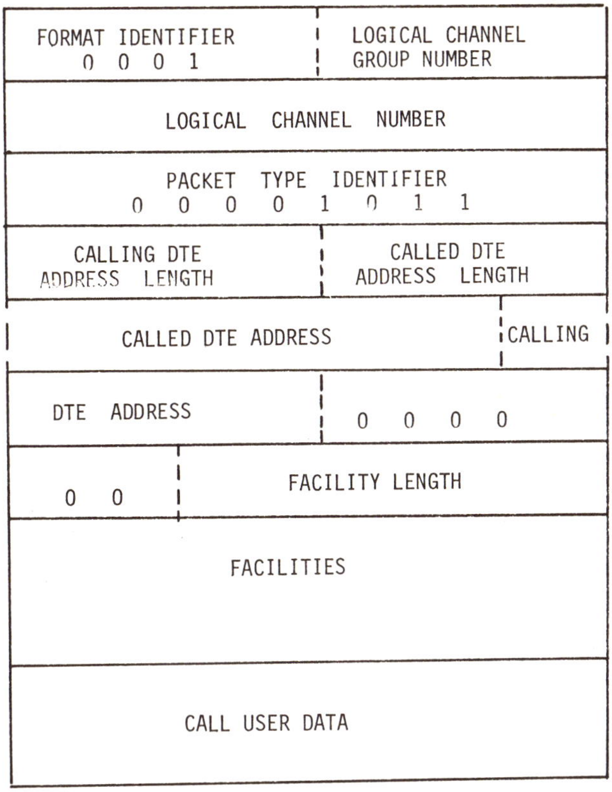

```
+-----------------------------+------------------------+
| FORMAT IDENTIFIER           | LOGICAL CHANNEL        |
|   0  0  0  1                | GROUP NUMBER           |
+-----------------------------+------------------------+
|          LOGICAL  CHANNEL  NUMBER                    |
+------------------------------------------------------+
|            PACKET  TYPE  IDENTIFIER                  |
|          0   0   0   0   1   0   1   1               |
+-----------------------------+------------------------+
|   CALLING DTE               |   CALLED DTE           |
|   ADDRESS  LENGTH           |   ADDRESS  LENGTH      |
+-------------------------------------------+----------+
|          CALLED DTE ADDRESS               | CALLING  |
+-------------------------------------------+----------+
|   DTE  ADDRESS              |   0   0   0   0        |
+---------+-------------------+------------------------+
|  0   0  |        FACILITY LENGTH                     |
+---------+--------------------------------------------+
|                                                      |
|                   FACILITIES                         |
|                                                      |
+------------------------------------------------------+
|                                                      |
|                 CALL USER DATA                       |
|                                                      |
+------------------------------------------------------+
```

FIGURE 6   CALL REQUEST PACKET

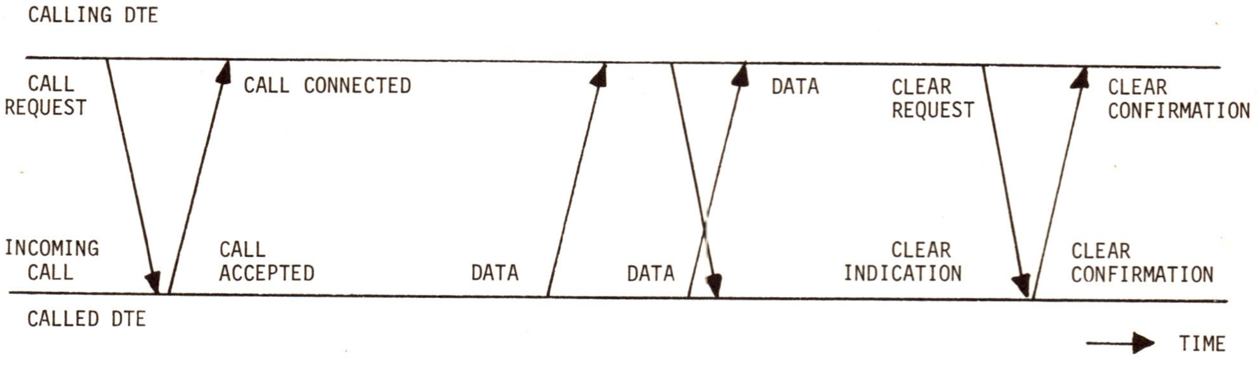

FIGURE 7   CALL ESTABLISHMENT, DATA TRANSFER AND CALL CLEARING

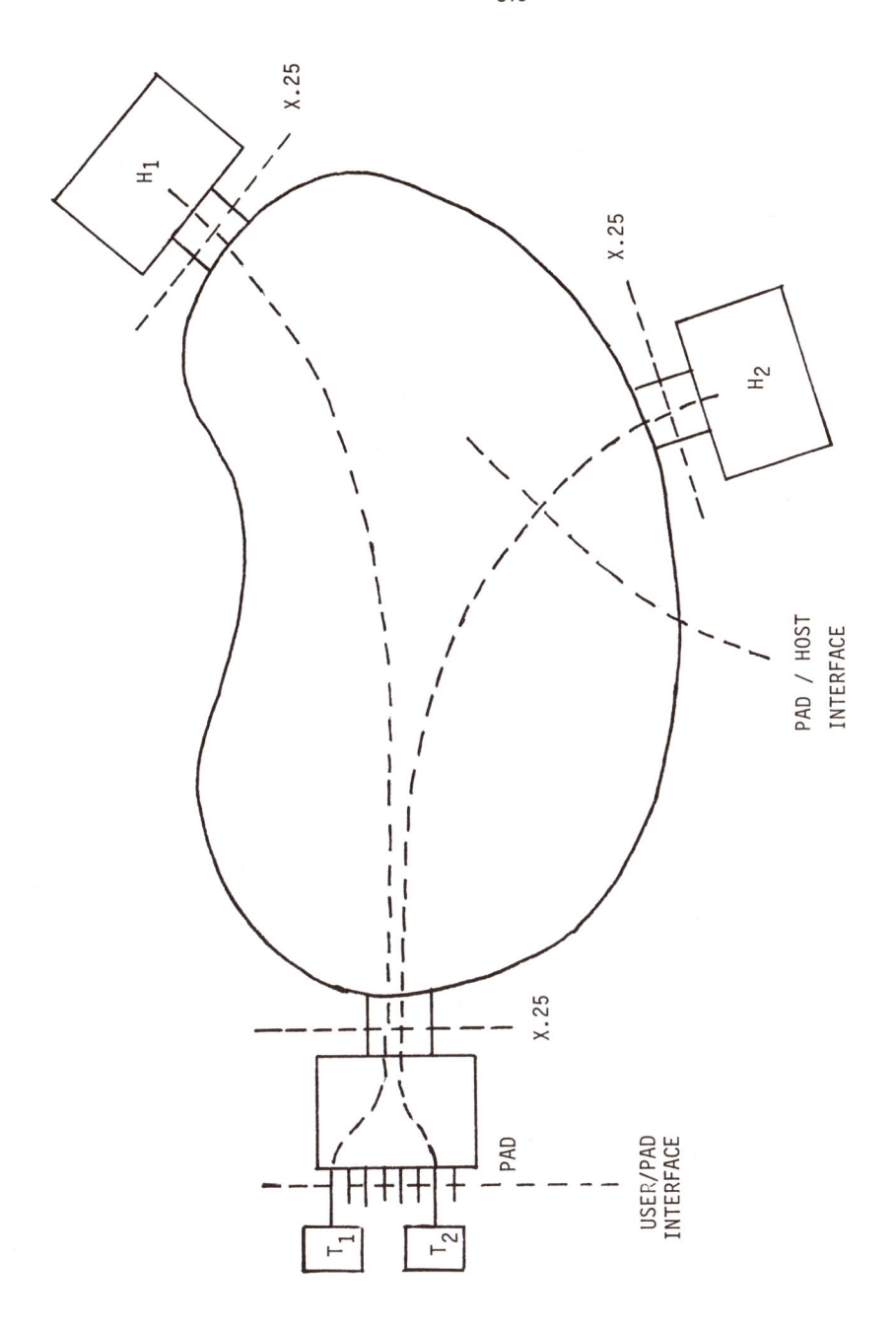

FIGURE 8   USER / PAD AND PAD / HOST INTERFACES

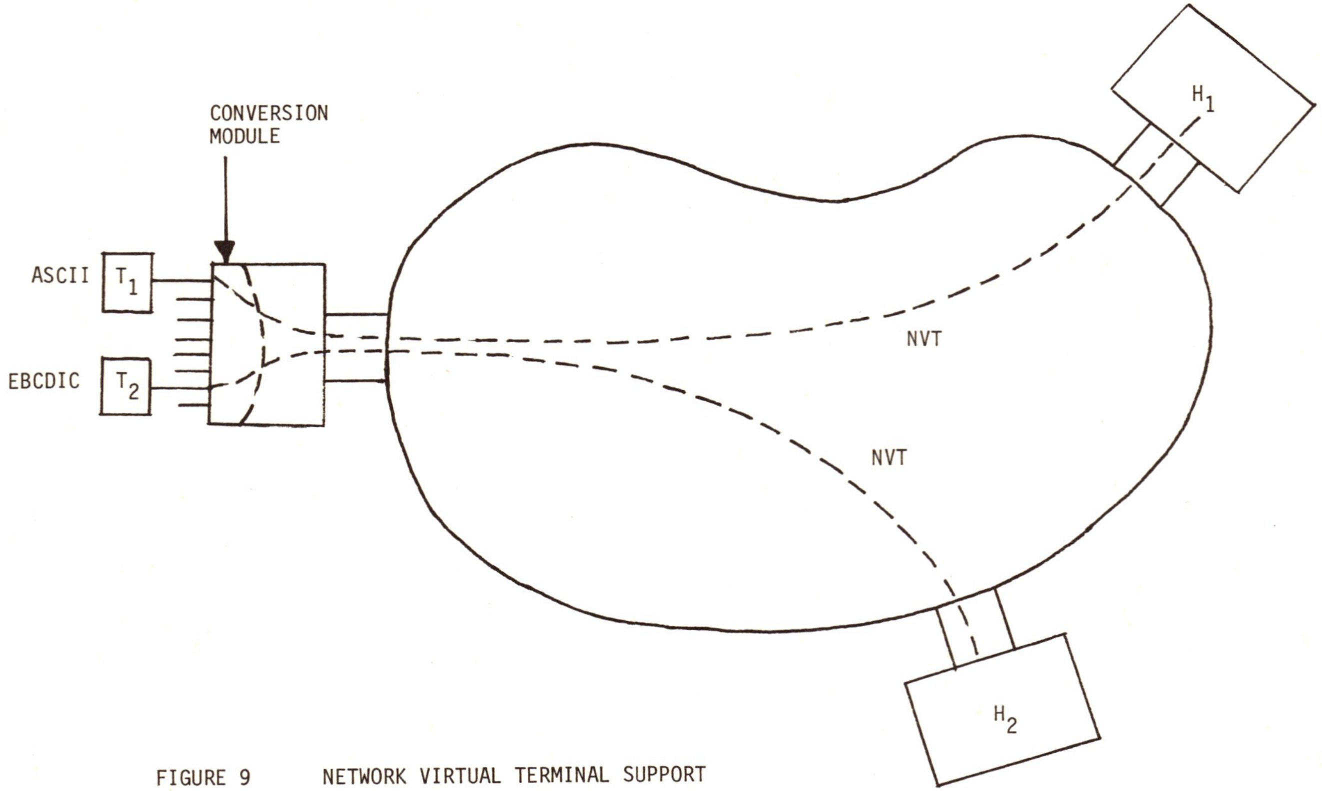

FIGURE 9   NETWORK VIRTUAL TERMINAL SUPPORT

CHAPTER 3.H.

G. J. Popek and C. S. Kline
University of California at Los Angeles
Los Angeles, Ca., USA

Design Issues for Secure Computer Networks

Design Issues for Secure Computer Networks

Gerald J. Popek and Charles S. Kline
University of California at Los Angeles

1. Introduction

It has long been observed that as the cost per unit of equivalent computation in small machines became far less than large centralized ones, and as the technology of interconnecting machines matured, computing would take on a more and more distributed appearance. This change of course is now happening, accelerated by the plunging absolute cost of computation, especially as compared with the more slowly falling cost of communications channels. In many cases users' data manipulation needs can and are likely to be served by a separate machine dedicated to the single user, connected to a network of integrated data bases. Multiprogramming of different users diminishes in importance.

As a result, the nature of the protection and security problem is also beginning to change, from one of considerable, justified concern over the convenience and reliability of the central operating system protection facilities, to the analagous problems in a different form in networks. Given the trends mentioned in the preceding paragraph, one can expect the protection issues in networks to intensify in the future.

The issues of protection in computer networks differ in several fundamental ways from those of centralized operating systems, despite many common characteristics. One of the most important distinctions, with a profound influence on the methods suitable for providing high quality protection, is the fact that the underlying hardware cannot in general be itself assumed secure. In particular, the communications lines that comprise the network are usually not under the physical control of the network user. Hence no assumptions can be made about the safety of the data being sent over the lines. Further, in current packet switched networks, the switches themselves are typically programmed in complex forms of assembly language, and so little can be said with certainty regarding correct delivery of packets.

The only general approach to sending and storing data over media which are not safe is to use some form of encryption. Hence much of the discussion of network security is concerned with integration of encryption methods into the operating systems which are part of the network. Cases where the safety of the entire net can be assured are not discussed here, for issues in that environment are essentially those of distributed operating systems alone.

In networks, as in operating systems, there are several major classes of protection policies that one may wish to enforce. The most straightforward policy, probably satisfactory for most applications, is data security: assuring that no unauthorized modification or direct reference of data takes place. Highly reliable data security in networks today is feasible, and suitable methods will be outlined in the next sections.

A more demanding type of policy is the enforcement of confinement in the network. One of the most often mentioned (and fairly easily solved) confinement problems is traffic analysis: the ability of an observer to determine the various flow patterns of message movement. The conditions under which confinement in general can be feasibly provided in a network are quite limited. Evidence to be presented below indicates that for certain general purpose applications, confinement will be impossible to enforce.

In the following sections, we describe the design problems and alternatives available for the design of secure networks, discuss their utility with respect to data security and confinement, and present an illustrative case study.

1.1 The Environment and its Threats

Because of the inability to make assumptions about the hardware and switches, one typically must expect malicious activity of several sorts.

1. Tapping of lines. While the relevant methods are beyond the scope of this discussion, it should be recognized that it is frequently a simple matter to record the traffic passing through a given commuications line, without detection by the participants in the communication. This problem is present whether the line is private, leased from a common carrier, or part of a broadcast satellite channel.

2. Introduction of spurious traffic. It is often possible to introduce invalid traffic with valid addresses into an operating network, where the injected traffic passes all relevant consistency checks and is delivered as if the traffic were genuine.

3. Retransmission of previously transmitted genuine traffic. Given that it is possible both to record and introduce traffic into a network, it is therefore possible to retransmit a copy of a previously transmitted, genuine message.

4. Breaking lines. It is also possible for the physical connections which comprise the network to be disrupted.

Each of the preceding threats can, in the absense of suitable safeguards, cause considerable damage to an operating network, and make it useless for communication. Tapping of lines leads to loss of privacy of the communicated information. Introduction of false traffic makes reception of any message suspect. Even retransmission of an earlier message can cause considerable difficulty in some circumstances. If that message were part of the sequence by which two nodes communicated their identity to one another, then it may be possible to falsely identify oneself while the valid originator of the message was temporarily out of service.

While all of the previous examples require malicious action, applications of computer networks are becoming increasingly sensitive. Consider the attention that will be directed at such uses as military command and control systems (by which missle firing orders are sent) or commercial electronic funds transfer systems (with billions of U.S. dollars worth of transactions daily). The communicatons network of the Off Track Betting system in New York City has frequently been assaulted in a number of ways.

1.2 Operational Assumptions

This discussion of protection and security in computer networks will be based on several underlying assumptions. The list is as follows.
1. Malicious attacks, including tapping and artificial traffic injection, are expected.
2. There do not exist secure, high bandwidth transmission paths between those sites which wish to communicate in a secure manner.
3. A large number of separately protected logical channels are needed, even though they may be multiplexed on a much smaller number of physical channels.
4. High speed, inexpensive hardware encryption units are available.
5. Reliable, private communication is desired.

It is believed that these assumptions correctly mirror many current environments. In the next sections, we outline relevant properties of encryption. Then the discussion of network security commences in earnest.

2. Relevant Issues in Encryption

Encryption provides a method of storing data in a form which is unintelligible without the "key variable" used in the encryption. Basically, Encryption can be thought of as a mathematical function

$$F: D \times K \rightarrow E$$

where D is the data to be encoded, K is the key variable, and E is the resulting enciphered text. For F to be a useful function, there must exist an F', the inverse of F,

$$F': E \times K \rightarrow D$$

which therefore has the property that the original data can be recovered from the encrypted data if the value of the key variable originally used is known.

However, the use of F and F' is valuable only if it is difficult to recover $d \in D$ from $e \in E$ without knowledge of the corresponding $k \in K$. A great deal of research has been done to develop algorithms which make it virtually impossible to do so, even given the availability of powerful computer tools.

The "strength" of an algorithm is traditionally evaluated using the following assumptions. First, the algorithm is known to all involved. Second, the analyst has available to him a significant quantity of matched encrypted data and corresponding cleartext. He may even have been able to cause messages of his choice to have been encrypted. His task is to deduce, given an additional, unmatched piece of encrypted text, the corresponding cleartext. All of the matched text can be assumed to be encrypted through the use of the same key variable which was used to encrypt the unmatched segment. In particular therefore, the difficulty of deducing the key used in the encoding is directly related to the strength of the algorithm. While cryptanalysis is beyond the scope of this discussion, there are certain properties of such "strong" algorithms worth pointing out.

First, F is invariably designed to mask any statistical properties of the input, or cleartext. The probability of each symbol of the encrypted character set appearing in an encoded message e is equal. Further, the probability of any pairs (digrams) of such characters is also flat. Similarly, it is desirable that the n-gram probability distribution be as flat as possible, for each n. This characteristic is desired even in the face of skewed distributions in the input cleartext, for it is the statistical structure of the input language, as it "shows through" to the encrypted "language" which permits cryptanalysis.

The preceding characteristics, desirable from the protection viewpoint, have other implications. In particular, if any single bit of a cleartext message is altered, then the probability of any particular bit in the corresponding message being altered is approximately 1/2. Conversely, if any single bit in an encrypted message is changed, the probability is approximately 1/2 that any particular bit in the resulting decrypted message has been changed. This property follows because of the necessity for flat n-gram distributions. As a result, encryption algorithms are excellent error detection mechanisms, so long as the recipient has any knowledge of the original cleartext transmission.

In general, it is also true that the strength of an encryption algorithm is directly related to the ratio of the length of the key variable with the length of the transmission being encoded. Perfect ciphers, that completely mask statistical information, require keys of equal lenghs to messages. Fortunately, currently available algorithms are of such high quality that this ratio can be small; i.e. a key can be often reused for subsequent messages.

2.1 Public Key Encryption

Recently, Diffie and Hellman [Diffie 76] proposed a variation of the conventional encryption methods that may in some cases have certain advantages over standard algorithms. In their class of algorithms, there exists

$$F: D \times K \rightarrow E$$

as before to encode the data, and

$$F': E \times K' \rightarrow D$$

to recover the data. The major difference is that the key k' in K' used to decrypt the data is not equal to, and cannot be derived from, the key k in K used to encode the data. Presumably there exists a pair generator $G: I \rightarrow K \times K'$ which based on some input information produces the matched keys with high strength (i.e. resistance to the derivation of k' given k, d in D, and matched e = F(d,k)).

The value of such a public key encryption algorithm lies in some potential simplifications in initial key distribution, since k can be publically known, as well as for "digital signatures". These issues are examined in the section concerning network security. Currently however, strong algorithms of this type are computationally expensive, so that public key methods are not yet practical.

2.2 Algorithms Based on NP Completeness

While conventional cryptanalysis is beyond the scope of this discussion (also much of the superior work is classified), there has been recent work in the development of encryption algorithms using results of complexity theory which may be important, and bears discussion. To begin, it will be useful to summarize the relevant complexity theory results. First, one can often provide an expression for the number of steps required for solution of a particular problem by a particular algorithm, as a function of some measure of the size of the problem at hand. Hence one might be able to demonstrate that a given sorting algorithm requires $O(n^2)$ steps for an n element list. Next, a problem is said to belong to the P (for polynomial) class of problems if there exists a deterministic algorithm whose required number of steps for solution is an expression of polynomial form. Virtually all practically useful algorithms fall into this class.

Another interesting class of problems, called the NP class, includes those problems for which the solution algorithm is non-deterministic, and requires a polynomial number of non-deterministic steps. The usual method to convert a non-deterministic algorithm to a deterministic one yields an algorithm which requires an exponential number of steps if the original required a polynomial number of steps. A problem which requires an exponential number of steps is generally considered "hard", and for sufficient n, quickly becomes computationally intractable, even for the largest computers.

Certainly the P class is contained in the NP class. However, it is not known for certain whether there are problems in the NP class but not in P. A problem p $\in$ NP but p $\notin$ P would therefore not permit a deterministic solution in polynomial time, and would be considered intractable.

A partial result concerns the so called NP Complete class of problems. These are a collection of problems in NP which have been shown to have the following property: If any one of them is shown to have a solution in P, then that general solution method can be used to show that all NP problems are in P. That is, NP = P. However, these issues have been studied for some time now, and it is widely conjectured no such algorithm will be found. This view implies that the NP Complete class is most likely not contained in P, and so composes a collection of intrinsically "hard", computationally intractible problems in general.

The relevance of this complexity theory is simply the following. If encryption algorithms can be developed which have the property that their cryptanalysis under the usual assumptons of available matched clear and encrypted text can be shown equivalent to the earlier "hard" problems, then the algorithm may be a basis for a strong encryption method. This area of research is still quite young, and the only candidate algorithms are computationally expensive. However, a number of researchers believe that the approach will eventually provide a source of strong encryption methods.

2.3 Error Detection

Given the general properties of encryption described in the earlier sections, it is a fairly simple matter to add an error detection (but not correction) protocol to encrypted messages. It is merely necessary that a small part of the message be redundant, in the sense that the receiver knows ahead of time what part of the message should be. In a block with k check bits the probability of an undetected error upon receipt of the block is approximately $1/(2^k)$ for reasonable sized blocks, where the probabilistic assumption mentioned above is valid. Therefore, for example, if three eight bit characters are employed as checks, the probability of an undetected error is less than $1/(10^16)$. In the case of natural language text no special provisions need necessarily be made, since that text already contains considerable redundancy and casual inspection permits detection of errors with very high probability. The check field can also be combined with other information needed in the block for protocol reasons. In fact, most packet switched networks use protocols in which the packet header contains considerable, highly formatted information which can serve the check function. For example, if duplicate transmitted blocks are to be detected by the receiver, which may occur either because of spoofing or through abnormal operation of the network transmission protocols, then it is customary to number each block in order of transmission. If this number contains enough bits and the encryption block size matches the unit of transmission, the sequence number can serve as the check field.

2.4 Block vs Chain Ciphers

Another important characteristic of encryption algorithms which both affects the strength of the algorithm and has implications on computer use is the block or chain nature of the algorithm. A chain cipher, in deciding how to encode the next bits of a message, can use the entire preceding portion of the message, as well as the key and the current bits. A block cipher, on the other hand, encodes each successive block of a message based only on that block and the given key. It is easier to make chain ciphers stronger than block ciphers. One the other hand, chain ciphers are less acceptable for computer use because any error in transmission implies that the rest of the message following the error is lost. If the given message is an entire file, the cost can easily be unacceptably large. Further, if it is desired to be able selectively to update portions of a long encrypted message (or file), then block ciphers permit decryption, update, and reencryption of just the relevant blocks. Therefore block ciphers are preferred. Fortunately, there exist reasonably strong ciphers of this type.

2.5 Applications of Encryption

Four general categories of encryption applications have real utility in computer systems. Each of the four is presented below.

1. Protection of Transmission Lines. The traditional use for encryption has been in communications, where the sender and receiver do not trust the transmission medium, whether it be a hand carried note, or megabytes shipped over high capacity satellite

channels. In computer systems, the use of encryption for protection of transmission becomes crucial in computer networks. This problem is discussed at length in later sections.

2. Removable Media. An obvious application for encyption, related to transmission protection, is the encoding of data on removable media, such as disk packs and tape libraries. In this way, it is not possible for anyone to remove those media and obtain useful information. In fact, so long as the storage of the encryption keys is done in a secure manner, this encryption procedure can block any attempt to substitute foreign media which have been prepared elsewhere to appear like a local disk pack or tape, for checks after decryption will indicate errors in "transmission". This property is important since portions of file systems with file names and protection data specifying access rights may reside on those media.

3. One Way Ciphers. By far the most frequently employed method to identify users to computer systems is to require each user to supply a secret password along with his account when starting a job. Each user has his own password. Clearly, the system must maintain a complete password file for all users. As a result, the password file is critical to the system's security. To increase the safety of this particular file, some systems maintain the passwords in encrypted form. That is, when a new user is added to the system and his password is supplied, it is encrypted by some standard algorithm and stored. Whenever that user wishes to log in, he supplies the password, which is again encrypted and compared with the stored value.

This use for encryption is of interest if the algorithm employed is difficult to invert. That is, given the encrypted text, the cleartext (which must be supplied to the login program) is not easy to obtain. A number of ad hoc proposals for such "non-invertable" transforms have appeared in the professional literature, although without any reasonable justification of their strength.[Evans 74] A superior method of providing a "one way cipher" is to adapt an existing strong standard encryption algorithm. One can break the candidate cleartext password into two parts, one to be treated as key and the other data, and use both as the arguments to the algorithm. In fact, one may even let the entire password be the key, and encrypt a constant, where the constant is the same (and known) for all users!

This last approach can be shown to be effective by the following reasoning. Earlier, the assumptions underlying a strong algorithm were briefly sketched. There it was pointed out that it was to be highly difficult to deduce the key from matched pairs of cleartext and encrypted text. Here, the constant is the cleartext and the stored password is the encrypted text. Since the cleartext password is the key, it should not be practicable to determine it.

However, the additional protection provided by such one way encryption algorithms can be easily lost unless care is taken. For example, suppose it is possible to test candidate cleartext passwords rapidly, either by submitting them to the login facility (perhaps using a microprocessor to generate the test cases) or by executing the login program directly on the system if the encrypted password file is available (as it is in the UNIX operating system). Since virtually all passwords in today's systems are either chosen by users (and therefore are variants of words or names in their native language, or almost pure numerical strings) or by mneumonic nonsense syllable generators, the actual space of inputs to be tested is far smaller than one might suspect for most passwords, and therefore usually can be checked in a practical time. Hence, unless the space of actually used passwords is quite large, or the encrypted passords are not available (which if true would largely obviate the need for one way encryption), the practice of encrypting passwords is of limited value.

4. Authentication. One of the important requirements in computer communications security is to provide a method by which one participant of the comunication can identify itself to the other, and vice versa, in an unspoofable manner. Encryption solves this problem in a quite simple way. Possession of the right key variable is taken as prima facie evidence that the holder is the desired entity, and is therefore able to participate in the message exchanges. The transmitter can be assured that only the holder of the key variable is able to transmit or receive transmissions in an intelligible way. The actual procedures by which keys are distributed in the general case are of course crucial, and will be discussed in subsequent sections. A more general authentication protocol which can detect receipt of previously recorded traffic when the keys have not been changed is also discussed later.

2.6 Limitations of Encryption

While encryption methods can contribute in useful ways to the protection of information in computing systems, there are a number of practical limitations to the class of applications for which it is viable. Several of the issues which limit applicability are discussed below.

1. Processing in Cleartext. Most of the operations that one wishes to perform on data require that the data be supplied in cleartext form, from simple arithmetic operations to the complex procedure of constructing indexes to data bases. Therefore, the internal controls of the operating sytem, and to some extent the applications software, must preserve protection controls while the cleartext data is present. While some have proposed that it might be possible to maintain the encrypted data in main memory, and have it decrypted only upon loading into cpu registers (and subsequently reencrypted before storage into memory), there are serious ques-

tions as to the feasibility of this approach.[Gaines 77] The key management facility required is nontrivial, and the difficulties inherent in providing convenient controlled sharing seem forbidding. Another suggestion sometimes made is that an encoding algorithm be used which is homomorphic with respect to the desired operations. Then the operation could be performed on the encrypted values, and the result can be decrypted as before. Unfortunately, those encoding schemes known with the necessary properties are not strong algorithms.

Therefore, since data must be processed in cleartext, other means are necessary for the protection of data from compromise in the operating system by applications software. Much of the material discussed in other sections on protection is directly applicable.

2. Revocation. Key variables are in many respects similar to simple forms of capabilities. They act as tickets and serve as conclusive evidence that the holder may access the corresponding data. Holders may pass key variables, just as capabilities may be passed. Similarly, selective revocation of access is just as difficult as with simple capability methods. The only practical method is to decrypt the data and reencrypt with a different key. This action invalidates all the old keys, but is obviously not very selective. New keys therefore must be redistributed.

3. Protection against Modification. Encryption by itself provides no protection against inadvertant or intentional modification of the data. However, it can provide the means of _detecting_ that modification. One need merely include as part of the encrypted data a number of check bits. When decryption is performed, if those bits do not match the expected values, then the data is invalid.

Detection of modification, however, is often not enough protection. In large data bases, for example, it is not uncommon for very long periods to pass before any particular data item is referenced. It would be only at this point that a modification would be detected. Therefore, high quality recovery software is necessary to restore the data from old archival records.

4. Key Storage and Management. Every data item that is to be protected independently of other data items requires encryption by its own key. This key must be stored as long as it is desired to be able to access the data. Thus for fine grained protection of long lived data, the key storage and management problem becomes formidable. The collection of keys immediately becomes so large that safe system storage is essential. After all, it is not practical to require a user to supply the key when needed, and it isn't even practical to embed the keys in applications software, since that would mean the applications software would require very high quality protection.

The problem of key storage is also present in the handling of removable media. There however, since an entire volume (tape or disk pack) can be encrypted with the same key (or small set of keys), the size of the problem is reduced. However, if archival media are encrypted, then the keys must be kept for a long period, in a highly reliable way. One approach to this problem would be to store the keys on the unit to which they correspond, perhaps even in several different places to avoid local errors on the medium. The keys would have to be protected, of course; a simple way would be to encrypt them with yet a different "master" key. The protection of this master key is absolutely essential to the system's security.

Furthermore, it is quite valuable for the access control decision to be dependent on the value of the data being protected, or even on the value of other, related data: salary fields are perhaps the most quoted example. In this case, the software involved, be it applications or system procedures, must maintain its own key table storage in order to successfully examine the cleartext form of the data. That storage, as well as the routines which directly access it, require a high quality protection mechanism beyond encryption.

Therefore, since a separate, reliable protection mechanism seems required for the heart of a multiuser system, it is not clear that the use of encryption (which requires the implementation of a second mechanism) is advisable, if the first can be straightforwardly extended to serve both roles. In fact, as this and preceding discussions have suggested, other mechanisms are not necessarily more complicated, but they certainly are more flexible.

Below, methods of network security will be discussed which are robust with respect to the assumptions and limitations outlined above. The methods provide a secure means for large numbers of entities to participate in private, shared or controlled communication in a convenient and low cost manner. That is, we consider the network to be a common carrier, whose task is to provide high quality logical channels.

The discussion, based on conventional encryption methods, is broken into several parts. First the problem of key distribution is presented, and solutions outlined. The use of public key algorithms is discussed separately. Then the issue of how to integrate encryption into a network architecture is examined, in terms of system structure and protocol questions. An illustrative case study is presented, and finally the last section ties together related matters. It is our contention that these questions of key distribution and protocols are the major issues in network security. Other considerations, such as high quality key generation or redundant network topology, are not peculiar to this topic.

3. Key Distribution

For several participants in a network conversation to communicate securely, it is necessary for them to obtain matching keys to encrypt and decrypt the transmitted data. It should be noted that a matched pair of keys forms a logical channel which is independent of all other such logical channels, and as real as any channel created by a network's transmission protocols. Possession of the key admits one to the channel. Without the key, the channel is unavailable. Since the common carrier function of the network is to provide many such channels, the issuing of the keys which create those channels is obviously a central matter.

As there are by assumption no suitable transmission media for the keys other than the physical network, it will be necessary to devise means to distribute keys over the same physical channels by which actual data is transmitted. Of course, the safety of the logical channels over which the keys are to pass is of paramount importance. Unfortunately, the only available method by which any data, including the keys, can be transmitted in a secure manner is through the very encryption whose initialization is at issue. This seeming circularity is actually easily broken through limited prior distribution of a small number of keys by secure means. The usual approach involves designating a host machine on the network to play the role of Key Distribution Center, at least for the desired connection. It is assumed that there have been previously arranged a pair of matched keys between the KDC and each of the potential participants, say A1, A2, ..., Am, in the channel. One of the participants, say Ai, sends a short message to the KDC asking that matched key pairs be distributed to all the A's, including itself. If the KDC's protection policy permits that connection, secure messages over the prearranged channels will be sent to each A, containing the key and other status information. Data can then be sent over the newly established channel. The key distribution channels therefore carry a low quantity of traffic, and thus the keys can be changed relatively infrequently by other means.

This general approach has many variations which have been developed in order to support various desirable properties as distributed protection policy, integrity in face of crashes, and the like. Some of these are discussed below.

1. _Centralized Key Control_. Perhaps the simplest form of the key distribution method employs a single KDC for the entire network. Therefore n prearranged matched key pairs are required for a network with n distinguishable entities. An obvious disadvantage of this unadorned approach is its reliability characteristics. If the node on which the KDC is located crashes, then the establishment of any further secure communication channels is impossible, and if the overall system has been constructed

to prevent any inter-user communication other than in a secure manner, then the entire network stops. This design is in general unacceptable for distributed systems except if the underlying topology is a star and the KDC is located at the center. Note however that this drawback can be fairly easily remedied by the availability of redundant KDCs in case of failure of the main facility. The redundant facility can be located at any site which supports a secure operating system and provides appropriate key generation facilities. Centralized key control can quite easily become a performance bottleneck however.

2. <u>Fully</u> <u>distributed</u> <u>Key</u> <u>Control</u>. Here it is possible for every intelligent node in the network to serve as a KDC for certain connections. If the intended participants A1, A2, ..., Am reside at nodes N1, N2, ..., Nm, then KDCs at each of those nodes can be involved in the protection decision. One node chooses the key, and sends messages to each of the other KDCs. Each KDC can then decide whether the attempted channel is to be permitted, and reply to the originating KDC. At that point the keys would be distributed to the participants. This approach has the obvious advantage that the only nodes which must be properly functioning are those which support the intended participants, necessary anyway. Each of the KDCs must be able to talk to all other KDCs in a secure manner, implying that $n*(n-1)/2$ matched key pairs must have been arranged. Of course, each node needs to store only n-1 of them. For such a method to be successful, it is also necessary for each KDC to talk with the participants at its own node in a secure fashion. This approach permits each host to enforce its own security policy if user software is forced by the local system architecture to use the network only through encrypted channels. This arrangement has obvious appeal in decentralized organizations.

3. <u>Hierarchical</u> <u>Key</u> <u>Control</u>. This method distributes the key control function among "local", "regional", and "global" controllers. A local controller is able to communicate securely with entities in its immediate logical locale; that is, for those nodes with which matched key pairs have been arranged. If all the participants in a channel are within the same region, then the connection procedure is the same as for centralized control. If the participants belong to different regions, then it is necessary for the local controller of the originating participant to send a secure message to its regional controller, using a prearranged channel. The regional controller forwards the message to the appropriate local controller, who can communicate with the desired participant. Any of the three KDCs can select the keys. The details of the protocol can vary at this point, depending on the exact manner in which the matched keys are distributed. This design approach obviously generalizes to multiple levels in the case of very large networks. It is analagous to national telephone exchanges, where the exchanges play a role very similar to the KDCs.

One of the desirable properties of this design is the limit it places on the combinatorics of key control. Each local KDC needs only have prearranged channels for the potential participants in its area. Regional controllers need only be able to communicate securely with local controllers. While the combinatorics of key control may not appear difficult enough to warrant this kind of solution, in certain circumstances the problem may be very serious, as discussed in the section on levels of integration.

The design also has certain characteristics of a property not present in either of the preceding key control architectures: local consequences of local failures. If any component of the distributed key control facility should fail or be subverted, then only users local to the failed component are affected. Since the regional and global controllers are of considerable importance to the architecture, it would be advisable to replicate them, so that the crash of a single node will not segment the network.

All of these key control methods permit easy extension to the interconnection of different networks, with differing encryption disciplines. The usual way to connect different networks, with typically different transmission protocols, is to have a single host called a gateway common to both networks. Inter-network data is sent to the gateway which forwards it toward the final destination. The gateway is responsible for any format conversions as well as the support of both systems' protocols and naming methods. If the networks' transmissions are encrypted in a manner similar to that described here, then the gateway might be responsible for decrypting the message and reencrypting it for retransmission in the next network. This step is necessary if the encryption algorithms differ, or there are significant differences in protocol. If the facilities are compatible, then the gateway can merely serve as a regional key controller for both networks, or even be totally uninvolved.

There are strong similarities among these various methods of key distribution, and differences can be profitably blurred further by designing hybrids to gain some of the advantages of each. Centralized control is a degenerate case of hierarchical control, with little hierarchy. Fully distributed control can be viewed as a variant of hierarchical control. Each host's KDC acts as a local key controller for that host's entities, and communicates with other local key controllers to accomplish a connection. In that case, of course, the communication is direct, without a regional controller required.

3.1 Public Key Based Distribution Algorithms

The class of public key algorithms discussed earlier have been suggested as candidates for key distribution methods that might be simpler than those described in the preceding sections. Recall that k', the key used to obtain the encoded message, cannot be derived from k, the key used for encryption, or from matched encrypted and cleartext. Therefore, each user u, after obtaining a matched key pair <k, k'>, can publicize his k. Another user v, wishing to send a message to u, can employ the publically available k. To reply, u employs v's public key. At first glance this mechanism seems to provide a simplified way to establish secure communication channels. No secure dialog with a key controller to initiate a channel appears necessary.

Unfortunately, as pointed out by Schroeder and Needham[Needham 77], initial connection protocols are not really simplified after all. A Repository for public keys is needed, akin to a key controller. Any user wishing to initiate a connection must first obtain the appropriate public key from the Repository, and it is critical that the Repository issue the correct public key or the message will be decodable by someone other than the intended recipient. This possibility of error was one of the important reasons why encryption is introduced in the first place. Hence an authentication protocol exchange between the requesting node and the Repository is needed just as between the node and a KDC.

One might suspect however that the software required to implement a Repository would be simpler than that for a KDC, and therefore easier to certify its correct operation. If this view were correct, it would still make public key based encryption potentially superior to conventional algorithms, despite the equivalent protocol requirements. It is true that the contents of the Repository need not be protected against unauthorized reference, since the public keys are to be available to all, while the keys used in the authentication protocol between the KDC and the user must be protected against reference. However, the standards of software reliability which need to be imposed on the Repository for the sake of correctness are not substantially different from those required for the development of a secure KDC. Thus public key algorithms may not be of as much value in secure communication over a general network as one might have supposed.

There is one possible exception to the conclusion immediately above. It concerns digital signatures for network mail. The goal in that case is to provide a mechanism by which the recipient of a message can, upon receipt and at some later date, demonstrate that the message was indeed originated by the claimed author. Public key algorithms which are strong when operated symmetrically are more convenient for this purpose than conventional algorithms. Operation is fairly simple. The sender encodes his message by _decrypting_ it with his secret key, and then sends the resulting encoded message to the recipient, who can decode it by _encrypting_ it with the public key of the sender. At any time in the future, the recipient can demonstrate the authenticity to a third party of authorship merely by keeping the encoded version and demonstrating its encryption to cleartext. Schroeder and Needham point out however that this method requires the Repository to keep values of public keys, since the demonstration of authenticity requires a reliable demonstration that the public key being employed is indeed that of the claimed author.

It is more difficult, although not impossible, to obtain digital signatures using conventional encryption algorithms without involving a central Repository in every message. See Rabin [Rabin 77] for one proposal; it is computationally complex, but no more so than current proposed public key algorithms.

4. Levels of Integration

There are many possible choices of endpoints of the encryption channel in a computer network, each with their own tradeoffs. In a packet switched network, one could encrypt each line between two switches separately from all other lines. This is a low level choice, and is often called link encryption. Instead the endpoints of the encryption channels could be chosen at a higher architectural level: at the host machines which are connected to the network. Thus the encryption system would support host-host channels, and a message would be encrypted only once as it was sent through the network rather than being decrypted and reencrypted a number of times, as implied by the low level choice. In fact, one could even choose a higher architectural level. Endpoints could be individual processes within the operating systems of the machines that are attached to the network. If the user were employing an intelligent terminal, then the terminal is a candidate for an endpoint, too. This viewpoint envisions a single encryption channel from the user directly to the program with which he is interacting, even though that program might be running on a site other than the one to which the terminal is connected. This high level choice of endpoints is sometimes called end-end encryption.

The choice of architectural level in which the encryption is to be integrated has many ramifications for the overall architecture. One of the most important is the combinatorics of key control versus the amount of trusted software.

In general, as one considers higher and higher levels in most systems, the number of identifiable and separately protected entities in the system tends to increase, sometimes dramatically. For example, while there are less than a hundred hosts attached to the ARPANET, at a higher level there often are over a thousand processes concurrently operating, each one separately protected and controlled. The number of terminals is of course also high. This numerical increase means that the number of previously arranged secure channels - that is the number of separately distributed matched key pairs - is correspondingly larger. Also, the rate at which keys must be generated and distributed can be dramatically increased.

In return for the additional cost and complexity which results, there can be significant reduction in the amount of software whose correct functioning must be assured for the protection of the communication channel. This issue is very important and must be carefully considered. It arises in the following way. When the lowest level is chosen, the data being communicated exists in the clear form as it is passed from one encrypted link to the next by the switch. Therefore the software in the switch must be trusted not to intermix packets of different channels. If a higher level is selected, from host to host for example, then errors in the switches are of no consequence. However, operating system failures are still serious, since the data exists as cleartext while it is system resident.

In principle then, the highest level integration of encryption is most secure. However, it is still the case that the data must be maintained in clear form in the machine upon which processing is done. Therefore the more classical methods of protection within individual machines are still quite necessary, and the value of very high level end-end encryption may be somewhat lessened. A rather appealing choice of level that integrates effectively with kernel structured operating system architectures is outlined in the case study.

Another small but nontrivial drawback to high level encryption should be pointed out. Once the data is encrypted, it is difficult to perform meaningful operations on it. Many front end systems provide such functions as packing, character erasures, transmission on end of line or control character detect, etc. If the data is encrypted before it reaches the front end, then these functions cannot be performed. That is, any channel processing must be done above the level at which encryption takes place.

5. Encryption Protocols

Network communication protocols concern the discipline imposed on messages sent throughout the network to control virtually all aspects of data traffic, both in amount and direction. It is well recognized that choice of protocol has dramatic impacts on the flexibility and bandwidth provided by the network. Since encryption facilities essentially provide a potentially large set of logical channels, the protocols by which the operation of those channels is managed also can have significant impact.

There are several important questions which any encryption protocol must answer:

1. How is the initial cleartext/ciphertext/cleartext channel from sender to receiver and back established?
2. How are cleartext addresses passed by the sender around the encryption facilities to the network without providing a path by which cleartext data can be inadvertantly or intentionally leaked by the same means?
3. What facilities are provided for error recovery and resynchronization of the protocol?
4. How is flow control done?
5. How are channels closed?
6. How do the encryption protocols interact with the rest of the network protocols?
7. How much software is needed to implement the encryption protocols. Does the security of the network depend on this software?

One wishes a protocol which permits channels to be dynamically opened and closed, allows the traffic flow rate to be controlled (by the receiver presumably), provides reasonable error handling, and all with a minimum of mechanism upon which the security of the network depends. Clearly the more software is involved the more one must be concerned about the safety of the overall network. The performance resulting from use of the protocol must compare favorably with the attainable performance of the network using other suitable protocols without encryption. Lastly, one would prefer a general protocol which could also be added to existing networks, disturbing their existing transmission mechanisms as little as possible. Each of these issues must be settled independent of the level of integration of encryption which is selected, or the method of key distribution.

To illustrate the ways in which these considerations interact, in section six we outline a complete protocol. The case considered employs distributed key distribution and an end to end architecture, all added to an existing network.

5.1 Confinement

Confinement is the problem of guaranteeing that data is not leaked or communicated except through the explicitly controlled paths. Often such communications are possible through subtle, sometimes timing dependent, channels. As an example, two processes, which the security policy desires to prevent from communicating, can attempt to communicate by affecting each other's data throughput. Although such channels are inherently error prone, error detection and correction protocols can be used.

Unfortunately, the confinement problem in computer networks is particularly difficult to handle. This problem results because every general design requires some information to be transmitted in cleartext form. This cleartext information, although limited, can be used for the passage of unauthorized information.

As an example, the communications subnetwork needs the headers which contain network addresses and control information in cleartext form in order to perform its tasks. A malicious user, cooperating with a penetrator, can send data by the ordering of messages among two communication channels. Even though the data of the communications is encrypted, the headers are probably transmitted in cleartext form unless link encryption is also used. In any case, the communications subnetwork requires host addresses in the clear. Thus a penetrator who can capture parts of the subnetwork can receive information. The only solutions to this problem appear to be certification of the secure nature of some parts of the subnetwork and host hardware/software.

Even with such certification, certain confinement problems remain. For example, the protocol implementing software in a given system usually simultaneously manipulates communications for several users. Either this software must be trusted, or data must be encrypted before it reaches this software. Even in this latter case, certain information may be passed between the user and the network software, and thus, potentially, to an unauthorized user. As an example, if a queue is used to hold information waiting to be sent from the user to the network, the user can receive information by noticing the amount drained from this queue by the network software. In almost any reasonable implementation on a system with finite resources, the user will at least be able to sense the time of data removal, if not the amount.

Given the difficulty of confinement enforcement, it is fortunate that most applications do not require it.

5.2 Authentication

Authentication refers to the identification of one member of a communicaton to the other, in a reliable, unforgable way. In early interactive computer systems, the primary issue was to provide a method by which the operating system could determine the identity of the user who was attempting to log in. Typically, the user supplied confidential parameters such as passwords, answers to personal questions, etc. which were already recorded in machine memory for checking at each login attempt. There was rarely any concern over the machine identifying itself to the user.

In networks, however, mutual authentication is of interest: each "end" of the channel may wish to assure itself of the identify of the other end. Quick inspection of the class of methods used in centralized systems show that straightforward extensions of them are unacceptable. Suppose one required that each participant send a secret password to the other. Then the first member that sends the password is exposed. The other member may be an imposter, who has now received the necessary information to pose to other nodes in the network as the first member. Obviously extension to a series of exchanges of secret information will not solve the problem. It only makes necessary a several step posing procedure by the imposter. A different approach is required.

Fortunately, there are a number of straightforward encryption based authentication protocols which provide reliable mutual authentication without exposing either participant. The methods are robust in the face of all the network security threats mentioned earlier. The general principle involves the encryption of a rapidly changing unique value using a prearranged key. Below we outline a simple authentication sequence between nodes A and B. At the end of the sequence, A has reliably identified itself to B. A similar sequence is needed for B to identify itself to A. Typically, one expects to interleave the messages of both authentication sequences.

Assume that A uses a secret key, associated with itself, in the authentication sequence. The reliability of the authentication depends only on the security of that key. Assume that B holds A's matching key (as well as the matching keys for all other hosts to which B might talk).

1. B sends A in cleartext the current time of day as known to B.
2. A encrypts that time of day using its authentication key and sends the resulting ciphertext to B.
3. B decrypts A's authentication message, using A's matched key, and compares it with the time of day which B had sent. If they match, then B is satisfied that A was the originator of the message. If the received time of day is not much older than the current time of day, B is satisfied that the message has not been delayed and retransmitted.

This simple protocol does not expose either A or B if the encryption algorithm is strong, since it should not be possible for a cryptanalyst to be able to deduce the key from the encrypted time of day, even if he knew what the corresponding cleartext time of day was. Further, since the authentication messages change rapidly, it is not possible to record an old message and retransmit it.

Authentication protocols such as these require the prior distribution of secret keys. If data security is the goal, no formal authentication protocol is actually required when all data transmissions are encrypted, since possession of the key serves as prima facie evidence that the participants are the appropriate ones, as well as providing the mechanism empowering the communication. Nevertheless, authentication protocols can give immediate assurance, and protect against the playback of prior recorded traffic.

6. <u>Network Encryption Protocol Case Study</u>:
<u>Process-Process Encryption</u>

Until recently, general purpose protocols for the integration of encryption into network operating systems have not been available. Therefore, we outline here a general protocol for such applications which has been implemented for the ARPANET. For the sake of security, it operates at the relatively high level of process to process communication. In process-process encryption, encoding is performed as data moves from the source process to the system's network software. This approach minimizes the points where data exists in cleartext form, and thus the mechanism which needs to be trusted. Essentially, only a secure operating system kernel is assumed.

The details of the protocol are given for the case of fully distributed key management. Adaptation for the other possibilities is straightforward however.

When a user attempts to send data, a system encrypt function encrypts the data and passes it to the network management software. The network software then attaches headers and sends the data to the subnetwork. Upon reception by the remote network software, the headers and other protocol are removed from the data and the data is passed, via a system decrypt function, to the appropriate user process.

Initial establishment of the communication channel must also be provided in a secure way. When a user process attempts to establish communication, the network software is informed by the system. The network software then communicates with the network software at the remote site. When the two network software packages have arranged for the new communication, the system at each site is informed. At this point in time (actually the order could be reversed), the system software attempts to obtain encryption keys for this communication. This key distribution is accomplished either with local key management software, or via a centralized key distribution center. After the keys have been chosen and distributed (using a previous secure key distribution channel), the user processes are given capabilities to send and receive data through the encrypt and decrypt calls. Thus, the communication channel is established.

In this way, existing network protocols can largely be left undisturbed, and much existing network software is preserved. User processes are blocked, in a reliable way, from communicating with any other user processes anywhere in the network unless the protection policy of both hosts involved in the communication (or the centralized security controller) permit it. Each user's communication is protected from every other user's communication. Perhaps most important, the amount of trusted mechanism required in the system nucleus is quite limited.

6.1 The Encryption Connection Protocol

The details of secure communication establishment, briefly described above, are now presented in more detail. To outline this procedure, we first view the operation from the vantage point of the operating system nucleus, or kernel, and then see how host network protocol software operates making use of the kernel facilities. It is assumed that the reader is familiar with the ideas of operating system security kernels. If not, see the companion paper on the subject in this volume. For brevity, in this discussion, a logical communication channel between two processes will be known as a connection. The host network software will be referred to as the network protocol manager (NPM). In general purpose networks, the role of the NPM is quite sophisticated and requires considerable code to implement the necessary protocols, an important reason not to have security depend on the NPM.

In the discussion below, it will be understood that a pair of matching encryption keys, one held by each of the two hosts involved, defines a secure, simplex channel. A duplex channel between two hosts therefore employs two pairs of keys.[1] Each kernel of each host in normal operational mode has a secure full duplex channel established with each other kernel in the network. How these channels are established concerns the method by which hosts come up, and is discussed later. These kernel-kernel channels are used for exchanging keys that will be used for other channels between the two hosts and for kernel-kernel control messages.[2] The need for these will become apparent as the protocol is outlined. If it is desired, the protocols can be trivially altered to keep the cleartext form of keys only within the encryption units of the hosts. For simplicity of explanation, that requirement is not used here.

A connection will get established in the following way. When hosts come up, their NPMs will establish connections through a procedure analogous to the one we outline here, and described in more detail later. Then, when a user process wishes to connect to a foreign site, the process executes an establish connection call which informs the NPM of the request. The NPM exchanges messages with the foreign NPM using their already existing channel. This exchange will include any host-host protocol for establishing communication in the network. Presumably the NPMs eventually

----
[1] The same key could be used for both directions, but for conceptual clarity here it is not.
[2] In a centralized security controller version, these kernel-kernel secure channels would be replaced by kernel-security controller secure channels.

agree that a connection has been established. At that point the user processes are still unable to communicate, since so far as the kernel is concerned, nothing has been done. The content of NPM exchanges is invisible to the kernel. Rather, at this point, the NPMs must ask the kernel to establish the channel for the processes. This action is performed with kernel function calls. Those calls grant capabilities to the user process so that subsequent requests can be made directly by the process.

In order to explain in more detail, the following four prototype kernel calls are described. The first two are involved in setting up the encryption channel, and presumably would be issued only by the NPM. The second two are the means by which user processes send and receive data over the connection.

GID(foreign-host, connection-id, process-id, state) Give-id. This call (which will typically be made by the NPM) supplies to the kernel an id which the caller would like to be used as the name of a channel to be established. The kernel checks it for uniqueness before accepting it, and also makes relevant protection checks. If state = "init", the kernel chooses an encryption key to be associated with the id (or queries key controller for key). The entry <connection-id, key, process-id, state> is made in the kernel Key Table. Using its secure channel, the kernel sends <connection-id, key, policy-info> to the foreign host. The policy-info can be anything, but in the military case, it should be the security level of the local process identified by process-id. It might also be a network-wide global name of the user associated with the process. If state = "complete", then there should already be an entry in the Key Table (caused by the other host having executed a GID) so a check for match is made before sending out the kernel-kernel message and a key is not included. The NPM process is notified when an id is received from a foreign kernel.

CID(connection-id) Close id. The NPM and appropriate process at the local site are both notified that the call has been issued. The corresponding entry in the Key Table is deleted. Over the secure kernel-kernel channel, a message is sent telling the other kernel to delete its corresponding Key Table entry. This call should be executable only by NPMs or by the process whose Key Table entry indicates that this id is associated with the process, to block potential denial of service problems.

Encrypt(connection-id, data) Encrypt data and buffer for NPM. This call adds integrity information, such as sequence numbers, to the data, encrypts the data using the key corresponding to the supplied id (fails unless the process-id associated with the connection-id matches that of the caller) and places the data in an internal buffer. The NPM is interrupted and informed of the awaiting data.

Decrypt(connection-id, user-buffer) Decrypt data. This call decrypts the data from the system buffer belonging to the connection-id supplied using the appropriate key. The data is moved into the user's buffer. The call fails unless the process-id stored in the Key Table matches the caller and the integrity checks succeed.

An important new kernel table is the Key Table.[1] It contains some number of entries, each of which have the following information:

<foreign-host, connection-id, key, sequence-no, local-process-id>

There is one additional kernel entry point besides the calls listed above, namely the one caused by control messages from the foreign kernel. There are two types of such messages: one corresponding to the foreign GID call and the other corresponding to a foreign CID. The first makes an incomplete entry in the receiving kernel's Key Table, and the second deletes the appropriate entry.

The following sequence of steps illustrate how a connection would be established using the encryption connection protocol. The host processors involved are numbered 1 and 2. Process A is at host 1 and B is at host 2. The two names involved are x and y. Process A, using local name x wishes to connect to B, using local name y.

1. A executes establish connection call which informs NPM@1, saying "conn from x to y@2". This message can be sent locally in the clear. If confinement is important, other methods can be employed to limit the bandwidth between A and the NPM.
2. NPM@1 sends control messages to NPM@2 including whatever Host-Host protocol required.[2]
3. NPM@2 receives an interrupt indicating packet arrival, does I/O call to retrieve it, examines header, determines that it is recipient and processes the message.
4. NPM@2 initiates step 2 at site 2, leading to step 3 being executed at site 1 in response. This exchange continues until NPM@1 and NPM@2 open the connection, having established whatever internal local name mapping they desire.
5. NPM@1 executes GID(connection-id, process-id,"init"), where connection-id is an agreed upon connection id between the two NPMs, and process-id is the local name of the process that requested the connection.
6. In executing the GID, the kernel@1 generates or obtains a key, makes an entry in

----
[1] In some hardware encryption implementations, the keys are kept internal to the hardware unit. In that case, the key entry in the Key Table can merely be an index into the encryption unit's key table.
[2] The host-host protocol messages would normally be sent encrypted using the NPM-NPM key in most implementations.

its Key Table, and sends a message over its secure channel to Kernel@2, who makes corresponding entry in its table and interrupts NPM@2, giving it connection-id.

7. NPM@2 issues corresponding GID(connection-id, process-id', "complete") where connection-id is the same and process-id' is the one local to host 2. This call interrupts process-id', and eventually causes the appropriate entry to be made in the kernel table at host 1. The making of that entry interrupts NPM@1 and process-id@1.

8. Process-id and process-id' can now use the channel by issuing succeeding Encrypt and Decrypt calls.

There are a number of places in the mechanisms just described where failure can occur. If the network software in either of the hosts fails or decides not to open the connection, no kernel calls are involved, and standard protocols operate. (If user notification is permitted, an additional confinement channel is present.) A GID may fail because the id supplied was already in use, a protection policy check was not successful or because the kernel table was full. The caller is notified. He may try again. In the case of failure of a GID, it may be necessary for the kernel to execute most of the actions of CID to avoid race conditions that can result from other methods of indicating failure to the foreign site.

6.2 Discussion

The encryption mechanism just outlined contains no error correction facilities. If messages are lost, or sequence numbers are out of order or duplicated, the kernel merely notifies the user and network software of the error and renders the channel unusable. This action is taken on all channels, including the host-host protocols channels as well as the kernel-kernel channels. For every case but the last, CIDs must be issued and a new channel created via GIDs. In the last case, the procedures for bringing up the network must be used.

This simple minded view is acceptable in part because the expected error rate on most networks is quite low. Otherwise, it would be too expensive to reestablish the channel for each error. However, it should be noted that any higher level protocol errors are still handled by that protocol software, so that most failures can be managed by the NPM without affecting the encryption channel. On highly error prone channels, additional protocol at the encryption level may still be necessary. See Kent [Kent 76] for a discussion of resynchronization of the sequencing supported by the encryption channel.

From the protection viewpoint, one can consider the collection of NPMs across the network as forming a single (distributed) domain. They may exchange information freely among them. No user process can send or receive data directly to or from an NPM, except via narrow bandwidth channels through which control information is sent to the NPM and status and error information is returned. These channels can be limited by adding parameterized calls to the kernel to pass the minimum amount of data to the NPMs, and having the kernel post, as much as possible, status reports directly to the processes involved. The channel bandwidth cannot be zero, however.

6.3 ARPANET Application

To illustrate the viability of the protocol outlined above, extensions have been made to the UCLA secure operating system implementing the encryption protocol for the ARPANET. That effort was instructive with respect to the types of engineering problems one is likely to encounter when retrofitting such facilities into an existing network. An example follows.

In the ARPANET Initial Connection Protocol (ICP), a user process attempts a connection to a special "server socket" (name at the foreign site) for the particular service desired (socket 1 for login, 3 for file transfer, etc.). The protocol is then similar to calling someone and getting a recording to call him at a different number. After establishing this connection, the special server process sends back a socket number for the user to connect to and closes the existing connection. The user process then attempts connections to this new socket. Each of these connections can use the protocol described above to get a secure channel established, and to verify any policy requirements. The current ARPANET ICP protocol just described requires a security policy which allows any user to communicate with the special server processes. These special server processes therefore should be certified to show that they do not allow users to communicate through them in a way that the security policy would not allow. It may be possible to simplify this certification dramatically by making these processes nearly memoryless.

6.4 Efficiency Considerations

In most networks, allocation control for all connections is or should be performed by the centralized network software at the recipient site. Thus, in existing architectures, user processes are usually unaware of the allocation size. In this encryption protocol, the kernels are also unaware, for allocation management is still done by the NPM. However, in cases such as the ARPANET, it is not uncommon for allocations of one or two bytes to be employed. Such small sizes will cause trouble with currently available block ciphers, such as the NBS Data Encryption Standard (D.E.S.), whose block size is 8 bytes or more. Consider the case when a user process wishes to send one byte. An eight byte block will be received by the NPM. However, with small "allocates" (one byte), the NPM must send it one byte at a time. The receiving NPM cannot cause each byte to be decrypted, so they must be buffered until all 8 bytes are received. When all eight are received, a Decrypt call can be executed. It should be clear that when allocates are employed which are small relative to the block size of the cipher being used, there will be considerable extra network traffic generated. For the ARPANET case using the NBS algorithm (8 byte blocks), one byte allocates cause eight times more traffic. One obvious solution is to increase the allocations. Another approach is to use an algorithm which permits byte at a time encryption and decryption. The D.E.S. algorithm, if configured in cipher feedback mode, can be operated in that way, while still avoiding error propagation problems. See [NBS 77] for details.

This problem appears to be the only significant performance implication of the encryption protocol, so long as the actual encryption operation is highly efficient. It is true that additional messages are required to establish a connection, but that is a relatively infrequent event, and so the actual overhead can be neglected.

6.5 System Initialization Procedures

The task of bringing up the network software is composed of two important parts. First, it is necessary to establish keys for the secure kernel-kernel channels and the NPM-NPM channels. Next, the NPM can initialize itself and its communications with other NPMs. Finally, the kernel can initialize its communications with other kernels. This latter problem is essentially one of mutual authentication, of each kernel with the other member of the pair, and appropriate solutions depend upon the expected threats against which protection is desired.

The initialization of the kernel-kernel channel and NPM-NPM channel key table entries will require that the kernel maintain initial keys for this purpose. The kernel can not obtain these keys using the above mechanisms at initialization because they require the prior existence of the NPM-NPM and kernel-kernel channels. Thus, this circularity requires the kernel to maintain at least two key pairs.[1] However, such keys could be kept in read only memory of the encryption unit if desired.

The initialization of the NPM-NPM communications then proceeds as it would if encryption were not present. In the ARPANET example, host-host reset commands would be sent (encrypted with the proper NPM-NPM key). Once this NPM-NPM initialization is complete, the kernel-kernel connections could be established by the NPM. At this

----
[1] In a centralized key controller version, the only keys which would be needed would be those for the key controller NPM-host NPM channel and for the key controller kernel-host kernel channel. In a distributed key management system, keys would be needed for each key manager.

point, the system would be ready for new connection establishment. It should be noted that, if desired, the kernels could then set up new keys for the kernel-kernel and NPM-NPM channels, thus only using the initialization keys for a short time. To avoid overhead at initialization time, and to limit the sizes of kernel Key Tables, NPMs probably should only establish channels with other NPMs when a user wants to connect to that particular foreign site, and perhaps close the NPM-NPM channel after all user channels are closed.

This case study should serve to illustrate many of the issues present in the design of a suitable network encryption facility.

6.6 Symmetry

The case study portrayed a basically symmetric protocol suitable for use by intelligent nodes, a fairly general case. However, in some instances, one of the pair lacks algorithmic capacity, as illustrated by simple hardware terminals or simple microprocessors. Then a strongly asymmetric protocol is required, where the burden falls on the more powerful of the pair.

A form of this problem might also occur if encryption is not handled by the system, but rather by the user processes themselves. Then for certain operations, such as sending mail, the receiving user process might not even be present. (Note that such an approach may not guarantee the encryption of all network traffic.) Schroeder and Needham have sketched protocols that are similar in spirit to those presented here to deal with such cases.

7. Conclusions

This discussion of network security has been intended to illustrate the current state of the art. From it we draw two general conclusions. First, if one's view of security of data in networks is basically a common carrier philosophy, then general principles by which secure, common carrier based, point to point communication can be provided are reasonably well in hand. Of course, in any sophisticated implementation, there will surely be considerable careful engineering to be done. The bulk of this report has been concerned with an explication of those principles.

However, this conclusion rests on one important assumption that is not universally valid. Either there exist secure operating systems to support the individual processes and the required encryption protocol facilities, or each machine operates as a single protection domain. A secure implementation of a Key distribution Center or Repository is necessary in any case. Fortunately, reasonably secure operating systems are well on their way, so that this intrinsic dependency of network security on an appropriate operating system base should not seriously delay common carrier security.

One could however, take a rather different view of the nature of the network security problem: the goal might be to provide a high level extended machine for the user, in which no explicit awareness of the network is required. The underlying facility is trusted to securely move data from site to site as necessary to support whatever data types and operations relevant to the user. The facility operates securely and with integrity in the face of unplanned crashes of any nodes in the network, Synchronization of operations on user meaningful objects (such as Withdrawal on CheckingAccount) is reliably maintained. If one takes such a high level view of the goal of network security, then the simple common carrier solutions merely scratch the surface of the network security problem and a great deal more work remains.

8. Bibliography

Branstedt,D., Security Aspects of Computer Networks, AIAA Computer Networks Conference, April 1973.

Diffie, W. and M. Hellman, New Directions in Cryptography, IEEE Transactions on Information Theory, November 1976, 644-654.

Evans, A. et. al., A User Authentication Scheme Not Requiring Secrecy in the Computer, CACM Vol. 17 No. 8, August 1977, pp437-441.

Gaines, R. S. private communication, September 1977.

Kent, S. Encryption-based Protection Protocols for Interactive User-Computer Communication, Laboratory for Computer Science, MIT, TR 162, 1976.

National Bureau of Standards, Data Encryption Standard, Federal Information Processing Standards Publication 46, January 1977.

Needham, R. and M. Schroeder, Security and Authentication in Large Networks of Computers, Xerox Palo Alto Research Center Technical Report, September 1977.

Rabin, M. "Digital Signatures Using Conventional Encryption Algorithms, Proceedings of the Conference on Fundamentals of Secure Computing, Atlanta Georgia, October 3-5, 1977 Academic Press (to appear).

CHAPTER 4.A.

H. R. Wiehle
Hochschule der Bundeswehr München
München, Germany

On System Specification

A. _Introduction_

A specification of a functional unit or a system of functional units may roughly be characterized as a precise and minimal description of their possible behavior. This description must be complete for the purpose in question. Precision means, in principle, the exclusive application of mathematical formalisms. The principle of _minimality_ (minimality has to be measured relative to the purpose of a specification) requires the suppression of any - with respect to the purpose - unnecessary detail; it does not primarily aim at the number of lines of a specification but at its information contents.

In recent years an increasingly intensive discussion on adequate specification techniques for information processing units (e.g. programs) and especially information storing units (sometimes called "data abstractions" or "abstract data types") has been going on. [Parnas 72], [Liskov 75], [Guttag 76].

Though one goal of these notes is to convey to the reader an idea of what a general and purely mathematical model of an information processing system might look like, in this introduction we shall proceed more or less informally.

In the following the word "system" is always used in the sense of "information processing system". This again should be understood in rather a broad sense, i.e. not necessarily confined to computing machinery. An organization, an organism may be viewed as information processing system, too.

The question might be posed whether system specification should be treated as a topic all by itself, well separated from system design and almost in contrast to system implementation. At least as long as there is no agreement upon the most appropriate techniques and the mathematical tools to be applied, there is indeed a need for specialized investigation. A precise system specification will serve different purposes. First of all, it can be and should be the starting point for any system design if the design process is intended to proceed top-down. Especially in the design of complex systems, precise system specifications are often missing, since it might be too time-consuming, too expensive or simply not known how to produce them.

Another purpose to be fulfilled by a specification of a functional unit is to inform people who intend to use units of this type. A specification is definitely needed if a development contract is to be made.

A demonstration that some system implementation is correct presumes the existence of a precise specification. A rigorous correctness proof can only proceed from a formal system specification.

For a purely "behavioristic" approach it is natural to model the static system structure as a network of functional units, the unidirectional links representing paths for transmission of objects. The interpretation of objects is not restricted; they may represent items of any kind: material or tools. In our example we deal primarily with data objects called message patterns or simply patterns.

Considering most of the examples given in these notes the use of the term "system" will seem to be an exaggeration because of lack of complexity. It is only for the sake of simplicity that we call even the most primitive arrangements of units, e.g. as in Fig. 1, system structures. The examples and the concepts which are defined and discussed will primarily aim at the specification of

- functional units which <u>store data</u>
  (data types, data abstractions)

- systems admitting <u>simultaneity</u> of events.

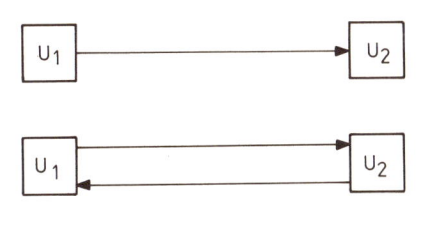

Fig. 1

This statement implicitly determines that the specification of mappings is regarded to be of minor importance, at least for the purpose of these notes. In order to illustrate this point let us assume a system specification where among others the following is stated:
if the functional unit w receives an input message of contents x it will always - independent of what has happened before in the system, especially with the unit w - produce a message of contents y where y=f(x) holds, f designating a certain function applicable to x. Or the relation y ε f(x) could hold where f(x) designates a set. A specification of f would be a part of the system specification but the <u>techniques of specifying f</u> will <u>not</u> be <u>discussed</u> here.

A meta-principle for the invention of system models which we shall accept as a guideline is that a system model should be easily put into correspondence with an appropriate real system. Consequently, we do not start from such concepts as "variable" or "state space" which are not easily to be interpreted by an observer of a real system. We prefer as the only dynamic concept (i.e. having an immediate and strong relationship to time) the transfer of objects between units.

In order to make the following general remarks more conspicuous it seems appropriate to present first a very simple example. One of the most favorite objects of people dealing with specification techniques is the stack[Parnas 72], [Liskov 75].

So the aim is to specify stack-like behavior of a unit ST and to avoid giving any superfluous detail.

The digraph of the communication structure of the system formed by two functional units, a caller C and a stack ST, may be outlined as in Fig. 2.

For the sake of simplicity of the introductory example the stack is assumed to be of unlimited capacity, i.e. it cannot overflow.

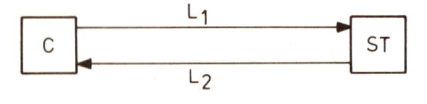

Fig. 2

The specification of the stack ST will be given by defining the possible flow of messages on the channels or links L_1 and L_2. This includes a specification of the unit C (as far as it is a user of ST; other activities of C are not modelled).

In the following a number of restrictions R1, R2, R3 on sets of message transfers (each of these transfers regarded as a primitive event consisting of the link name, the message pattern or contents of the message, and a point of time represented by a real number) is listed. A set of events is called a history of the system C/ST if and only if it fulfills the restrictions R1, R2, R3.

(R1)

(R1.1) Arrangement of events in time: events on L_1 and L_2 occur strictly in alternate order, especially: never simultaneously. The first event of a history belongs to L_1.

(R1.2) If e is an event on L_1 at time t the time t' of the next event on L_2 will be such that

$$t + d1 \le t' \le t + d2$$

holds with the real numbers d1>0, d2>0 being certain universal constants of the system.

Remark: Though forming a sequence of events is necessary, time - regarded as a measurable quantity - will be of no further interest in this example. It is mentioned here since the general framework for specifications (cf. section B.) would be deficient without a measurable time parameter. Arguments in favour of this statement will be discussed later.

(R2) The only possible message patterns (kind of event, contents of message) are

on L_1: - PUSH/string
- POP
- TOP

on L_2: - GO AHEAD
- UNDERFLOW
- UNDEFINED
- string

The word "string" stands for some element of a set of object strings defined somehow. This set does not contain elements which can be confused with one of the other words such as PUSH, POP, GO AHEAD etc. They are regarded as elementary items.

(R3) Let $e_1, e_2, e_3, \ldots, e_r$ be the first r events of a history, the order representing their succession in time.

Let $p_1, p_2, p_3, \ldots, p_r$ be the corresponding sequence of message patterns, i.e. p_i being the pattern of e_i.

(R3.1) If p_i is of type PUSH/string
p_{i+1} must be GO AHEAD

If p_i is a POP
p_{i+1} must be GO AHEAD or UNDERFLOW

If p_i is TOP
p_{i+1} must be of type string or UNDEFINED

(R3.2) If the function SL on pattern sequences ps is defined as
SL(ps) = number of PUSHs in ps

- (number of POPs in ps - number of UNDERFLOWs in ps)

+ 1

and if p_r = POP
then e_{r+1} will have a pattern p_{r+1} = GO AHEAD if and only if
$SL(p_1, p_2, \ldots, p_r) > 0$.

Remark: This restriction (R3.2) assures that for a history h of the system the value of SL can never be negative and can be 0 only if the last event regarded has the pattern POP.

(R3.3) If p_r=TOP then e_{r+1} will have the pattern p_{r+1}=UNDEFINED if and only if $SL(p_1,p_2,\ldots,p_r)=1$.
Otherwise we have $SL(p_1,\ldots,p_r)>1$ (cf. remark at (R3.2)). In this case $p_{r+1}=$ str where str designates an object of type string which can be determined as follows: if $p_1,p_2,\ldots,p_j$, $j<r$, is the longest prefix of $p_1,p_2,\ldots,p_r$, where p_j indicates a push-operation and where $SL(p_1,p_2,\ldots,p_j)=SL(p_1,p_2,\ldots,p_r)$ then p_j=PUSH/str, i.e. contains the string str.

More formally:
$j=\max_i(SL(p_1,p_2,\ldots,p_i)=SL(p_1,p_2,\ldots,p_r))$ for all p_i of type PUSH/string.

This completes the specification of the system Caller/Stack.

Now a series of questions can be raised and discussed with reference to the example.

Question 1. (formality)
Is the specification sufficiently formal? It can be learned from the example that such a specification can be formalized to any conceivable degree though this has not been accomplished here in all details, e.g. the definition of objects named strings could be made much more precise, and so on at various points.

Question 2. (completeness)
Is the given specification complete? Posing this question implies the assumption that there is a (common understanding of the) concept of a stack before a specification has been given. The discussion whether this assumption is justified or not will sooner or later become philosophical. So we shall not go into further details here though one should admit that some arguing may be reasonable whether a proposed specification gives a formalization of a concept not formally described so far.

Remark: As soon as two or more specifications are proposed, the question of their equivalence is a purely mathematical one, and it necessarily poses a well-defined problem.

Our specification of a stack is very likely to be incomplete for someone who intends to make a contract on the delivery of a physical device that behaves like a stack. The buyer of a stack-like unit, among other things, will be interested in its response time characteristics. The two constants d_1, d_2 from restriction R1.2 will probably not suffice. One will have to introduce response time distributions.

Such aspects of system specification as performance, availability and the like are in no way regarded as trivial; they are basically part of the specification business.

They are deliberately and completely ignored in these notes.

Question 3. (comprehensibility)
Is the given specification unnecessarily complex, circumstantial, too large? There is some inherent complexity in a concept which will show up in every specification, but there may still remain considerable differences between several specifications of the same system. Additionally, comprehensibility is rather a subjective measure.

Since it is difficult to argue in general about comprehensibility of certain specification techniques it might be near at hand - especially among programming people - to consider programming languages as a tool of system specification. They might help to make specifications shorter and more comprehensible. For a trained programmer a group of procedures (in conjunction with some global data objects only accessible via these procedures) implementing a stack may be far easier to comprehend than the proposed specification. Some comments will enable him to distinguish between essential features and extraneous details of the programs.

There can be no doubt that a stack-program will be much shorter than the specification given by R1, R2 and R3. The unlimited capacity of the stack may cause some trouble to the programmer.

On the other hand, there is a far-reaching agreement among authors dealing with specification techniques ([Liskov 75], [Guttag 76], [Jones 77]) that programming languages should not be used as a tool for giving specifications. We try to give some reasons for this meta-principle.

First: programs will usually contain extraneous details. The formal characterization of essential and non-essential features of a program will be difficult if at all possible. Thus, programs tend to hurt the principle of minimality.

Second: programs contain variables and assign values to variables. The concept of variable as used in programming languages is not a mathematical concept. The definition of the meaning of assignment-statements is a non-trivial task in the mathematical semantics of programming languages. It is very likely that an explication of the assignment of values to variables essentially comes down to the specification of functional units capable of storing such values. This reveals some kind of vicious circle: specification of systems by means of programs the meaning of which in turn will have to be defined by a system model.

Remark: The basis of this kind of reasoning is the belief that a storage, especially if asynchronously accessible by several users or units, cannot be adequately modelled by a sequence of mappings, a mapping representing the relation between storage locations and their actual contents.

Question 4. (minimality)
Is the proposed specification of stack-like behavior minimal or does it contain extraneous, especially implementation oriented details? Perhaps one could pretend that there are no direct hints to a potential implementor how to design, construct or program a stack. On the other side, from [Liskov 75] one may conclude that the authors would assign to our specification what they call a "representational bias". The criticism would be primarily concentrated on the function SL which might lead an implementor to introduce a ("hidden") state variable that always has as value the actual value of SL (stack-level!).

In [Liskov 75] a set of declarations and axioms, such as

$$pop(push(s,i)) = s$$

which allow to derive formally equations as

$$top(pop(push(push(pop(push(newstack(),cc)),aa),bb))) = aa$$

is regarded to have less or no representational bias.

One may object that the phenomenon of a bracket structure in a string can be described by functions counting the number of opening and closing brackets and by some relationships between the values of these functions. The question is then why the representation by an explicit bracket structure has no representational bias whereas a well known equivalent formalism using "counters" has such a bias.

This arguing against an assumed reproach should stimulate more investigation of the question of minimality and bias of specifications.

Question 5. (generality)
Are the applied techniques of system specification sufficiently general? The purpose of a sufficiently general specification technique is to allow the specification of various kinds of systems at any desirable level of detail. Typical hardware implemented systems and typical programmed systems should be specifiable in the same conceptual framework.

The proposed stack specification is too small a basis for a detailed discussion of the raised question, but some aspects can be mentioned here.

A sufficiently general concept of "system" and of "functional unit" should not enforce a breaking down of the specified unit into many very specialized ("small")

units the behavior of which is very specialized and very different from the usual
behavior of the specified unit. (cf. [Parnas 72], fourth goal, p. 330.) For example,
an a priori classification of functional units in passive ones (storing units, places) and active ones (transforming units, transitions), as it is found in Petri-Nets
and other computational structures, could hurt our criterion of generality. A specification technique has to be judged by its ability to model real world systems in a
natural way, especially without forcing us to introduce unnecessary details, e.g. in
the shape of myriads of microscopic units or items and large quantities of trivial
events.

Moreover, the concept of "system" should be general enough to assure that the class
of systems is closed in the following sense: well-defined combinations of systems
and well-defined abstractions from given systems should not produce systems which
are outside of the class of systems as originally defined. Admittedly this aspect
of generality is quite vague since "combination" and "abstraction" have no precise
meaning yet.

Question 6. (a priori undesirable properties of the specified system?)
Is the proposed specification of a stack consistent? If a system specification is
very complex the question may be justified whether the specification really specifies something. The most basic kind of inconsistency would simply mean that there is
no history (non-empty set of events) fulfilling all the restrictions given in the
specification.

There are weaker kinds of inconsistency, e.g. some type of deadlock: The existence
of finite histories, though not explicitly specified; or, the existence of histories
becoming trivial in some sense ("dead-loop") after a certain number of events.

Another undesirable property may be the following: the difference between the number
of messages received and the number of messages sent by a certain unit U in the system is not bounded in some histories.
It cannot generally be stated that non-decomposability (cf. section D.) is an a priori undesirable property of a specified system.

B. Definitions and Examples

The conceptual framework as given by the following definitions may be outlined as follows: a <u>system</u> consists of a <u>static part</u> and a <u>dynamic part</u>:

- a <u>communication structur</u> represented by a digraph and
- the <u>set of</u> possible (operational) <u>histories</u>.

There is a single primitive concept in the dynamic part, the <u>event</u> which models a (timeless) transmission of an object from one unit to another unit. This includes especially the following: a priori there is <u>no</u> system <u>state</u>. On the one hand it is not obvious that in all cases system states can easily be defined and sometimes it is not obvious that system states are helpful. On the other hand, a system state can be introduced, if necessary, as a set of (past) events or as a set of functions having sets of events as their arguments.

<u>Def. B1</u> (communication structure)

A communication structure CS is a pair $[G,M]$, where

- G is a finite, directed graph, being connected and slingless
- M is some countable set.
  (the elements of M are called message <u>patterns</u> or transmittible items)

<u>Def. B2</u> (event)

An event in a given communication structure $CS=[G,M]$ is a triple $[l,p,t]$.

- l designates a link in G
- p designates an element of M
- t designates a real number, $t \geq 0$

Remark: The event $[l,p,t]$ represents the transfer of item p at time t via the link l.

<u>Def. B3</u> (set of events)

The term "set of events" (or "event set") in a communication structure CS implies that the set ES of events has the following properties:

- ES is a countable set
- there are no two elements $[l_1,p_1,t_1]$ and $[l_2,p_2,t_2]$ of ES such that $l_1=l_2$ and $t_1=t_2$
- if I is a finite closed interval of real numbers and s is defined as the set of all $[l,p,t] \in ES$ with $t \in I$ then s is finite.

Def. B4 (system/histories)
A system S is a pair [CS,DB], where CS is a communication structure and DB is a set of event sets in CS. These sets - the elements of DB - are called the histories of S.

Remark: Definitely nothing is stated about the mathematical tools by which the set of histories of a system should be defined.

Example 1. (System S1)
The digraph of the communication structure is represented by Fig. 3.
The set of patterns is M={s}.
(CL, U, L, s stand for 'clock', 'unit', 'link', 'signal'.)

Fig. 3

If d>0 designates a certain real number, a universal system constant, then a set h is a history of S1 if and only if it is a finite set with elements

$$[L,s,t_i] \quad \text{with } t_i=i*d, \ i=0,1,2,\ldots,r,$$

for some integer r≥0.

This system models a clock sending a signal s every fixed time interval d. It is completely unknown how long the clock will work.

Example 1.1 (System S1.1)
This system has the same communication structure as system S1 but only a single history h, having as elements all tripels [L,s,t], where t=n*d and n is an integer n≥0.
d>0 is a system constant.
S1.1 models a clock which works forever.

Example 2.1 (System S2.1)
S2.1 is a system which is supposed to behave like the Petri-Net in Fig. 4.

The initial marking is relevant. Since a Petri-Net is usually not defined to function in real time (time regarded as a measurable quantity) there is some uncertainty in the specification of a system which "behaves like" a given Petri-Net. It is assumed

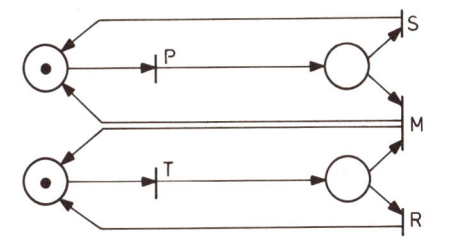

Fig. 4

that the Petri-Net may stop to produce events, but only with a marking identical to the initial marking. The fact that the system will not produce any more events cannot be concluded from its preceding behavior.

The digraph of the communication structure of S2.1 is represented by Fig. 5.

The set M of message patterns has one element, i.e. |M|=1, M={token}.

As a tool for the subsequent definition of the histories of S2.1 we introduce a function D(ES,u,t) in connection with a given communication structure CS. CS is not listed as an argument of D since it is supposed to be fixed in a certain context. The other arguments are

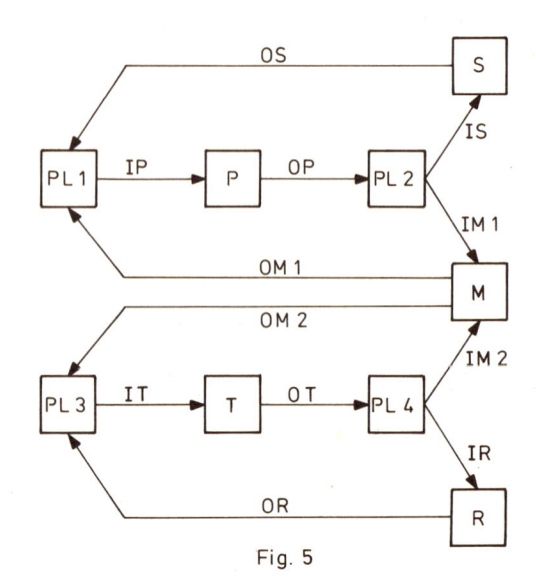

- ES: a finite set of events in CS
- u : a name of a unit (node) in the graph of CS
- t : a real number representing a point of time.

Fig. 5

D(ES,u,t)=$_{Df.}$ number of items received by u in ES until t
- (minus)
number of items sent by u in ES until t

More precisely, first term: number of events [l,p,t'] in ES where l is some link in G (from CS=[G,M]), directed to u, and p ε M, and t'≤t. Second term: correspondingly.

A finite set of events h in the communication structure of S2.1 is a history of S2.1 if and only if

(1) for all t≥0 the following inequalities hold:

0 ≥ D(h,PL1,t) ≥ -1
0 ≥ D(h,PL3,t) ≥ -1

2 ≥ D(h,M,t) ≥ 0   and D(h,M,t) ≠ 1

1 ≥ D(h,u,t) ≥ 0   for u ε {P,S,T,R,PL2,PL4}

(1a) $D(h,u,\bar{t})=0$ for all units, $\bar{t}$ denoting the largest t occurring in some event of h.

(2) every unit has a non-zero delay time in h, i.e. there are no two simultaneous events e_1, e_2 in h such that e_1 is an input event of unit u and e_2 is an output event of the same unit u.

Remark: Specifying the possible flow of events in a system by counting functions and inequalities has a strong similarity to the use of vector addition systems (e.g. [Hack 75]) and some relationship to the use of path expressions (e.g. [Lauer 75]).

Example 2.2 (System S2.2)
The System 2.2 is identical with System 2.1 but the way of defining the histories is quite different. In a first step strings ("skeletons") are defined over an alphabet A where
$$A = \{<, IP, OP, IS, OS, IT, OT, IR, OR, IM1, OM1, IM2, OM2\}$$
i.e. A contains the symbol '<' and the names of the links in the communication structure of S2.2 (identical to the CS of S2.1). Each name is regarded as a single symbol.

In a second step a simple formalism is defined producing histories from a skeleton string: each link symbol will give rise to a single event on that link, a symbol '<' between two link symbols indicating that the resulting events occur one after the other.

We use the notation of production rules for contextfree replacement with certain extensions which will be explained later.

$\langle PSCY \rangle ::= IP<OP<IS<OS \mid \langle EMPTY \rangle$		PS-Cycle
$\langle TRCY \rangle ::= IT<OT<IR<OR \mid \langle EMPTY \rangle$		TR-Cycle
$\langle IPSCY \rangle ::= \langle PSCY \rangle \mid \langle IPSCY \rangle < \langle PSCY \rangle$		iterated PS-Cycle
$\langle ITRCY \rangle ::= \langle TRCY \rangle \mid \langle ITRCY \rangle < \langle TRCY \rangle$		iterated TR-Cycle
$\langle CCPSTR \rangle ::= \{\langle IPSCY \rangle\$< \langle ITRCY \rangle\}$		concurrent composition of iterated cycles

$\langle ESKELETON \rangle ::=$

$\{\langle IPSCY \rangle\}\langle IP<OP\$ \ \langle ITRCY \rangle \ <IT<OT\}<IM1 \ IM2<OM1 \ OM2$

$\langle PSKELETON \rangle ::= \langle ESKELETON \rangle \mid \langle PSKELETON \rangle < \langle ESKELETON \rangle$

⟨SKELETON⟩ ::= ⟨CCPSTR⟩ | ⟨PSKELETON⟩ |

⟨PSKELETON⟩ < ⟨CCPSTR⟩

The three symbols $\{,\$,\}$ are a kind of metasymbols. Once introduced they cannot be replaced by application of normal replacement rules. In so far they behave like terminal symbols. Once x and y consist only of proper terminal symbols the treatment of $\{x\$y\}$ is as follows: the substring $\{x\$y\}$ can be replaced in one step by any "concurrent composition" of the strings x and y, i.e. - spoken informally first - replaced by any string z which can be produced by merging x and y.

The term "concurrent composition" is adopted from [Hack 76]. A string $z=z_1,\ldots,z_r$ is a concurrent composition of strings $x=x_1,\ldots,x_n$ and $y=y_1,\ldots,y_m$ (z_i,x_j,y_k standing for the symbols) if r=n+m and if there is a sequence of n integers $1 \leq l_1 < l_2 < \ldots < l_n \leq r$ with $z_{l_h}=x_h$ for all h=1,...,n and a sequence of integers $1 \leq g_1 < g_2 < \ldots < g_m \leq r$, every l_h being different from all g_f, and $z_{g_f}=y_f$ for all f=1,...,m.

A skeleton-string ss is supposed to contain only proper terminal symbols. ss can be regarded as a representation of a class of histories: the histories compatible with ss. There is a one-to-one mapping between the occurrences of link symbols in ss and the elements of a compatible history h. For two adjacent link symbols l and l' not separated by one or more < symbols the corresponding events [l,token,t], [l',token,t'] occur simultaneously, i.e. t=t'. For two link symbols l,l', separated in ss only by one or more < symbols, l standing left of l', the corresponding events occur one after the other, i.e. t<t'.

A history of S2.2 is defined as a set of events which is related to some skeleton-string in the way described above.

The above rules for generating event sets from skeleton-strings establish a minimum of restrictions. The compatible histories may have to comply with additional restrictions, such as minimum or maximum time distances of subsequent events on certain links, and so on. Nevertheless, for the investigation of many interesting properties of a system a specification will often suffice that defines the communication structure and skeleton-strings only, since these properties do not depend on the mappings of skeleton-strings onto event sets.

A comparison of the two systems S2.1 and S2.2 shows that the same system may be defined in quite different ways. The second definition emphasizes some structural aspects of the histories which are not so obvious from the first definition.

In order to give to the reader the feeling that specifying well-known, sequentially accessed storing units is a matter of routine we add a few short examples. They are deliberately presented in a sketchy manner, with just enough detail to convey the major points of the specification.

For the sake of completeness we start with

Example 3.1 (System 3.1; MS: main store)
This is the ordinary addressable store, maintaining a fixed set of addresses, all of them being always in the same "operational condition".

The digraph of the communication structure is identical with the one of the stack example with MS instead of ST.

For this example and the example 3.2 and 3.3 we assume that all event sets contain events on L_1 and L_2 in alternate order only, the first event occurring always on L_1.

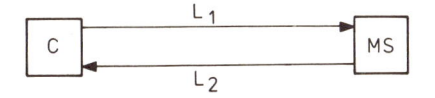

The following message patterns are used between C and MS:

for L_1:   for L_2: (corresponding answers)
- [R,   <address>]   -   <string>
- [W,   <address>, <string>]   -   GO AHEAD

R stands for "read" and W for "write"

An [R,a]-message has to be answered by the string which has been part of the latest preceding write-event with the same address a. If there is no such write-event, some initial value has to be delivered.

Example 3.2 (System S3.2; SS: "set-store")
The storing unit of this system remembers a set of strings. It answers questions whether a string str is in the actual set or not. There are no addresses or the like. One may add and delete stored objects.

The digraph of the communication structure is identical with the one in S3.1 with SS instead of MS. The message patterns are:

for L_1:   for L_2: (corresponding answers)
- [TAKE,   <string>]   -   GOAHEAD or OVERFL
- [DELETE, <string>]   -   GOAHEAD

- [YESORNO, <string>]   - YES or NO

In the following str designates an arbitrary string, but the same string in all cases. The answer to a [YESORNO, str]-message has to be YES if and only if there has been a successful [TAKE, str]-message without a subsequent [DELETE, str]-message. A TAKE-message at time t is successful, i.e. answered by GOAHEAD, if and only if the number of successful and relevent TAKE-messages before time t minus the number of the relevant DELETE-messages before time t is not larger than the CAPACITY (system constant). A successful [TAKE, str]-message is relevant if a [YESORNO, str]-message, replacing it, would have stimulated the answer NO. A [DELETE, str]-message is relevant if a [YESORNO, str]-message, replacing it, would have stimulated the answer YES.

Example 3.3 (System 3.3; TS: tape-like store)
The storing unit to be specified here behaves like a tape-drive with a tape of unlimited length. For simplicity we exclude backspacing.

With the usual digraph, the message patterns are:

for L_1:   for L_2: (corresponding answers):

- [WRITE, <string>]   - GOAHEAD
- READ   - <string> or
                                        - ERROR
- REWIND   - GOAHEAD

For the definition of the histories we introduce the notion of "actual position" to be defined for an event set as argument. The value of the function AP(ES), ES denoting a finite event set is the number of successful READ-messages (i.e. not answered by ERROR or not yet answered at all in ES) plus the number of WRITE-messages, all these events counted from the last REWIND only or from the beginning if there is no REWIND.

For an event e on L_1, e ε ES (ES obeying the rule of alternating events on L_1,L_2) the actual position of e is

$$APE(e,ES) =_{Df.}$$

AP(the subset of ES consisting of all events until e, including e).

An event set H is a history of S3.3 if and only if

- H obeys the rule of alternating events on L_1,L_2, the patterns being used as defined above

- a READ-message r ε H is answered by ERROR if and only if

$$APE(r,H) > APE(\text{latest WRITE-message } w \text{ preceding } r, H)$$

Remark: Obviously, an r cannot be successful unless there is at least one REWIND between w and r.

- if a READ-message r is answered by a string str then str is identical with the string in the latest WRITE-message w, w preceding r and having the same actual position as r, i.e. $APE(r,H) = APE(w,H)$.

C. Sequentializing units

In this section we are discussing a special class of systems comprising a star-shaped communication structure: a central storing unit (CSU) surrounded by a number of callers asynchronously accessing CSU. The term "storing unit" has to be understood in rather a broad sense including a FIFO-storage for readers and writers, reservation systems, and so on.

In some of these systems the CSUs display a behavior under asynchronous accesses which is a very important standard; it can be called "sequentializing" behavior. Roughly spoken, what is meant is that each of the possible results of a set of overlapping accesses $a_1, a_2, \ldots, a_p$ at CSU comes down to a result which could also have been reached by some sequence of (non-overlapping) accesses $a_1', a_2', \ldots, a_p'$, these latter obtainable from $a_1, a_2, \ldots, a_p$ by a rearrangement in time. We are going to make the notions of "access", "overlap" and "sequentialize" somewhat more precise.

Example 1. (System SMMS)

The next example will be the system SMMS (multi-access main store) which is a generalization of the system S3.1 (MS) of section B. The digraph of the communication structure is given by Fig. 7; the patterns associated with the pairs L_{i1}, L_{i2} are identical with those given in S3.1 for the links L_1, L_2.

As a first restriction for the histories we note that the message exchange on L_{i1}, L_{i2} is strictly alternating, starting on L_{i1} for all $i=1,\ldots,r$.

The definition of the set of histories of SMMS will be based to a large extent on the notion of overlapping and non-overlapping accesses.

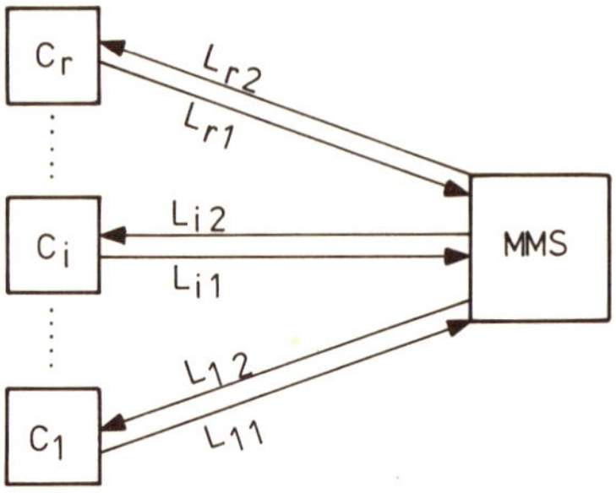

Fig. 7

Def. C1 (accesses to MMS)

If ES is a set of events in the communication structure CS of SMMS then an access in ES is a pair of events $[l_1, p_1, t_1]$ and $[l_2, p_2, t_2]$ such that

- $l_1 = L_{i1}$ and $l_2 = L_{i2}$ for some i from $i=1,\ldots,r$
- $t_1 < t_2$
- there is no other event in ES on l_1, l_2 in $[t_1, t_2 \cdot]$

__Def. C2__ (set of accesses corresponding to an event set)
Let ES be a finite set of events in the communication structure CS of SMMS which conforms to the rule of alternating message exchange on link pairs L_{i1}, L_{i2}, the latest event on a link pair being one on L_{i2}, for all $i=1,\ldots,r$. Then there is a uniquely defined set AS(ES) of accesses where every event $e \in$ ES appears in exactly one $a \in$ AS(ES) and each component from a pair $a \in$ AS(ES) is an element of ES.

A definition of overlapping of two accesses a and b is usually understood to be based on time relations. These time relations can be defined by using a relevant time interval (RTI) of an access.
Some possible definitions of the RTI of an access $a = [[l_1, p_1, t_1], [l_2, p_2, t_2]]$ might be:

- $RTI(a) = [t_1, t_2]$
- $RTI(a) = [t_1+d_1, t_2-d_2]$
  with some suitable constants $d_1 > 0, d_2 > 0$
  (d_1, d_2 may, e.g., depend on p_1 and p_2; it should be assured that RTI(a) is a non-empty interval).
- $RTI(a) = [t_1, t_2+d]$
  this definition is perhaps not reasonable for the MMS but could be useful for later examples in this section.
- $RTI(a) = [(t_1+t_2)/2-d_1, (t_1+t_2)/2+d_2]$
- $RTI(a) = [t_1, t_1+d]$

__Def. C3__ (overlap of accesses to MMS)
Two accesses a and b from a set AS(ES) (cf. Def. C2) overlap if and only if

$$RTI(a) \cap RTI(b) \neq \emptyset .$$

For the following we assume that some definition of an RTI for the accesses has been chosen.

__Def. C4__ (finite histories of the system SMMS)
__1st step__ (non-overlapping histories)
First we define those histories h having an AS(h) which does not contain overlapping accesses, i.e. where the relation < is a linear ordering.
Such a set of events is a history if and only if

(1) there exists a history hms of the system S3.1 (MS; main store) of section B and an order-preserving one-to-one mapping m from AS(h) onto AS(hms) (the accesses in hms defined as in Def. C1), such that the input and output patterns of a and m(a) are identical for all $a \in$ AS(h).

(2) certain time constraints are fulfilled concerning the response time behavior of MMS.

2nd step (inclusion of overlapping histories)
A set ES of events in CS of SMMS (where AS(ES) is assumed to be defined according to Def. C2) is a history of SMMS if and only if

(1) there is an order-preserving one-to-one mapping of AS(ES) onto a set AS(h), where h is a non-overlapping history of SMMS, such that the input and output patterns of a and m(a) are identical for all a ϵ AS(ES).

(2) (same as in the 1st step of the definition.)

Remark: Infinite histories of SMMS may be defined as those infinite event sets in CS which fulfill some obvious compatibility constraints with respect to the finite histories.

We give an example of some overlapping accesses and possible results of read-accesses. All accesses have the same address; the drawing shows their relevant time intervals.

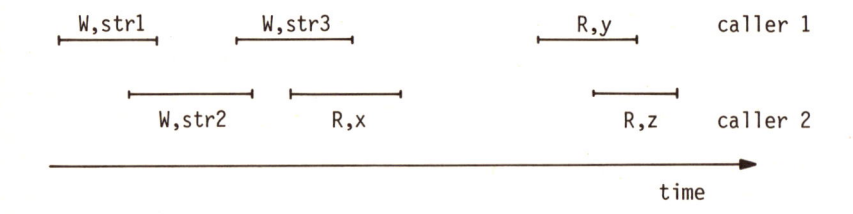

```
    W,str1          W,str3                    R,y         caller 1
      ├──┤           ├──┤                     ├──┤

            ├──┤      ├──┤                        ├──┤
           W,str2    R,x                         R,z        caller 2

    ────────────────────────────────────────────────▶
                                                 time
```

x,y,z denote the strings delivered by MMS.
Applying the definition of histories in SMMS one will find:

- x is str1 or str2 or str3.
- y is equal to str2 or str3.
- z is equal to y.
- additionally: if y is not equal to str3 then both x and y must be equal to str2.

(end of treatment of system SMMS)

We try to outline roughly how a general characterization of the specification technique illustrated by the specification of the system SMMS might look like.

Let U be a unit in a given system S. The concept of a sequentializing unit is not an absolute one, but depends on a notion of access and overlap of accesses.

For the following we need the

Def. C5 (unit-oriented subset of an event set)
With respect to a unit U in a communication structure CS, the unit-oriented subset of an event set ES in CS consists of the events on links which end at U or start at U. This subset of ES is designated by ES/U.

First, what is needed is a definition of accesses which can be given by defining a function AS on certain event sets ES/U where AS(ES/U) is a partition of ES/U. The elements of AS(ES/U) are called accesses in ES/U. The domain T of AS is supposed to include at least all sets H/U where H is a history of system S.

Second, a notion of overlap of accesses has to be introduced. This is done by defining a partial ordering (written '$<_{AS(ES)}$' or simply '<' if no confusion is possible) in each set AS(ES/U), ES ε T. a_1, a_2 ε AS(ES/U) are said to overlap if and only if they are incomparable by <.

Remark: Especially, a definition of a relevant time interval RTI(b) for accesses b establishes a notion of overlap: the partial ordering of the RTIs ($[t_1,t_2] <$ $[t_3,t_4] \leftrightarrow t_2 < t_3$) defines a partial ordering of the corresponding accesses.

Def. C6 (sequentializing unit)
U is called a sequentializing unit in S with respect to a notion of access AS and a partial ordering < of accesses if and only if for each history H of S the event set H/U (cf. Def. C5) can be "sequentialized". H/U can be sequentialized if and only if there is a history $\bar{H}$ of S such that

(C1)   - $\bar{H}$/U is a non-overlapping event set
           (i.e. the ordering < in AS($\bar{H}$/U) is a linear ordering)

(C2)   -   there is a one-to-one mapping m of H/U onto $\bar{H}$/U with the following three properties:

(C2.1) -   m is "access-compatible"
           (i.e. for all e,e' ε H/U: e,e' belong to one access if and only if m(e), m(e') belong to one access)

(C2.2) -   the mapping m_{AS} (defined on accesses by means of m under condition C2.1) from AS(H/U) onto AS($\bar{H}$/U) is order-preserving

(C2.3) -   the patterns of the events e and m(e) are identical for all e ε H/U.

The concept of a "sequentializable" event set, as introduced in Def. C6, may be useful for accomplishing a major step in a system specification of a system S with a starshaped communication structure CS. If the domain T (a set of event sets in CS) of a function AS (defining accesses in the sets g ε T) and the set NOH ⊂ T of the non-overlapping histories of S can easily be characterized, one may define a history of S as an element of T which can be sequentialized (with respect to AS, <, and the set NOH). We do not discuss a definition of systems with a more complex communication structure by means of more than one sequentializing unit.

For the generalization of the concepts of access and overlap of accesses as well as for the mappings of overlapping onto non-overlapping histories cf. [Plickert 77].

Example 2. (System SFIFOS)
As a slightly more interesting and more complicated system than the SMMS we specify a FIFO-storage of unlimited capacity. The FIFO-storage (short: FIFOS) is accessed by a set of delivering units $P_1,...,P_n$ (producers) and by a set of units, $C_1,...,C_m$, asking for stored objects (consumers). The read-accesses of the consumers are destructive.

For the sake of simplicity the sets of producers and of consumers are assumed to have no member in common. We thus have a digraph in the communication structure of the system SFIFOS which can roughly be described as in Fig. 8.

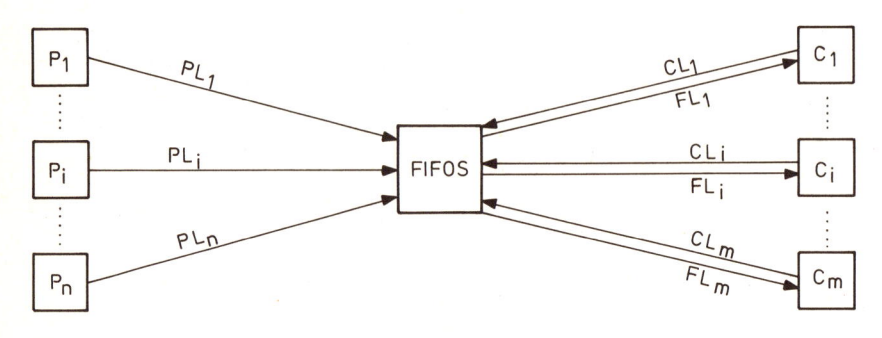

Fig. 8

The fact that there is only a single link connecting a P_i with FIFOS is due to FIFOS' unlimited capacity: a P_i can always deliver an object to FIFOS; an acknowledgement is not needed. A consumer C_j can be successful in requesting some stored object or not, that is to say: the answer can be SORRY or an object (e.g. of type ⟨string⟩). In other words, even for the consumer there is no waiting situation of unknown duration since FIFOS is supposed to answer a request shortly and then to forget about it. Of course, the specification of FIFOS could prescribe a completely different behavior, e.g. to let requesting units wait and to give positive answers only.

<u>1st step</u> of a definition of the histories of SFIFOS

- events on link pairs CL_j, FL_j occur strictly in alternate order. The first event is on link CL_j, for all j=1,...,m. The accesses are defined in analogy to those in system SMMS, Example 1. of this section.
- each event on a link PL_i, i=1,...,n, is regarded to be an access all by itself.
- the relevant time intervals are
  - for accesses on link pairs CL_j, FL_j

    $RTI([\![CL_i, R, t_1]\!], [FL, \langle rp \rangle, t_2]) = [t_1, t_2]$

    where R stands for 'request', $\langle rp \rangle$ for 'response pattern'
  - for an access of a PL_i

    $RTI([PL_i, \langle string \rangle, t_3]) = [t_3, t_3+d]$

    where d>0 is a system constant (of type 'real')
- two accesses of whatever type overlap if and only if their RTIs have a non-empty intersection.

<u>2nd step</u> of a definition of the histories of SFIFOS.

The definition of histories containing no overlapping accesses is given informally since a misinterpretation is almost impossible

- a request at a time t of a C_k will be answered by FIFOS by the delivery of an object string as message pattern if and only if the number of objects delivered to FIFOS (this number being identical with the number of events on the links $PL_1,...,PL_n$) before time t is larger than the number of object strings delivered by FIFOS to the $C_1,...,C_m$ altogether before time t. Otherwise, C_j will receive the answer SORRY.
- the l-th string given by FIFOS to some C_k is identical with the l-th string received by FIFOS from the group of the producers. l is determined by counting through all events in a non-overlapping (!) event set in the order of increasing time.

<u>3rd step</u> of a definition of the histories of SFIFOS.

Starting from those finite event sets ES which obey the rule of alternating message exchange for the consumers we define such an ES to be a history of SFIFOS if and only if it can be sequentialized (cf. Def. C6) on the basis of the 1st and 2nd step.

This version of a producer-consumer relationship via a buffering "device" is rather idealized. E.g., there is no waiting situation modelled for the producers. The system can easily be refined to be more realistic.

Dropping the assumption of FIFOS' unlimited capacity means first a refinement of the communication structure. We introduce links FPL_k, k=1,...,n, from FIFOS to each P_k. Now one has to decide whether a message from FIFOS to P_k means: "the object has been taken over" or "try again later" or even "object not taken over; you will be called on later for delivery". The relevant time interval of a producer-access has to be redefined. For a non-overlapping history it is easy to define when a message pattern on an FPL different from "object taken over" may occur: if and only if the actual stock of objects - delivered to FIFOS and not yet consumed - exceeds FIFOS' capacity.

Even with the refinements the system model is not detailed enough to describe such phenomena as the queueing of consumer requests if a producer intends to deliver a message. Here the interfaces are chosen in such a way that this type of queueing discipline is "internal", is an implementation oriented detail of FIFOS.

Example 3. (System SRES)
A simple reservation system can be obtained from the system SFIFOS by several modifications.

- The message patterns of type $\langle string \rangle$ are replaced by a pair

    [$\langle category \rangle$, $\langle number\ of\ objects \rangle$]

    where categories can be represented by some special kind of string, the number of objects by a positive integer.

- The message pattern of a request (by a consumer) will contain a pair
    [$\langle category \rangle$, n] with an obvious meaning, n>0 being an integer.

- All rules on passing of objects through FIFOS have to be formulated here to be valid for the subsets of histories characterized by some category c taking into account that an access, containing a pattern [c,n] is equivalent (with respect to counting conditions) to n accesses producing or consuming a single object of category c (the c-objects being all identical).

As long as we maintain the distinction between producers and consumers the customers cannot cancel reservations (what is equivalent to delivering objects to RES). A single producer will suffice who delivers objects of category c usually exactly once and in a large bulk. Consumers usually absorb a single c-object or a handful by one request. If k c-objects are requested, RES may deliver k'<k c-objects if there is only a stock of 0<k' c-objects left.

- In order to allow cancellations by customers we simply merge the sets of producers and consumers. The resulting set may be called the set of the partners $P_1,...,P_r$. This, of course, leads to a few additions in the message patterns: the messages going to RES have to be explicitly identified as a delivery or a request. A message exchange in alternate order on all link pairs between RES and one of its partners requires a dummy response by RES to a delivery of objects (we assume that RES has an unlimited capacity).

- Starting from those finite event sets ES which obey the rule of alternating message exchange, we take over accesses and overlap as defined for consumers in SFIFOS, and we define an ES to be a history of SRES if and only if it can be sequentialized (cf. Def. C6) on the basis of the non-overlapping histories of SRES as defined above.

- The specification is incomplete as far as response times, fairness of the treatment of competing customers, availability of the unit RES, and the like are concerned.

We conclude this section by discussing the question whether there are inherently "non-sequentializable" properties.

The inspection of such systems as SMMS, SFIFOS, SRES may lead to the conjecture that most of the asynchronously accessed units (e.g. computer center systems, information systems, reservation systems) are throughout sequentializing units. This conjecture is certainly wrong. We try to give a few examples to demonstrate that inherently non-sequentializable properties (meant are effects that cannot be explained by rearranging overlapping accesses in some appropriate sequence) are far from being artificial.

In the system SRES, we assume two overlapping accesses a_1 and a_2 from two partners P_1 and P_2 respectively, each requesting 3 c-objects, the actual stock being 4 c-objects. There are three reactions of RES possible: to give 1 object to P_1 and 3 objects to P_2, or vice versa, or to give P_1 and P_2 equally 2 c-objects (retaining objects would contradict the overall goal of a reservation system). The equal distribution could never occur if RES were defined to be a sequentializing unit, since a non-overlapped request of 3 objects in combination with a stock of 4 would always receive 3 objects.

A specification of RES could admit a 2/2 distribution in the situation described above though it would perhaps not enforce it. A more elaborate condition than $RTI(a_1) \cap RTI(a_2) \neq \emptyset$ may have to be specified in order to require a levelled distribution. However, admitting a levelled distribution is sufficient to destroy RES' characteristic of being a sequentializing unit.

Another example of a definition of the histories of SRES which cannot be accomplished by reducing all features of overlapping histories to properties of non-overlapping histories deals with a fair treatment of customers. Though we do not refer to absolute response times we could require that RES provides for a fair treatment of partners by obeying the following rule: if there are overlapping request-accesses (no matter what category of objects are requested by the different partners) in the relevant time interval (RTI(A)) of a certain access A of a partner P_i there are embedded at most h RTIs of request-accesses, all coming from a single other partner P_j. h is supposed to be a small positive integer. The restriction has to be maintained for all pairs i,j, 1≤i,j≤r, the partners being $P_1,\ldots,P_r$. (The rule restricts the maximum number of request-accesses embedded in a certain RTI(A) to (r-1)*h.)

Though the message patterns which occur in the events of an arbitrary history may, for specific RES-policies, be explained by reference to the set of non-overlapping histories, the fairness rule obviously cannot be stated by a reference to characteristics of non-overlapping histories.

D. Specification of units and decomposable systems

There are several reasons for investigating whether systems can be composed from separately defined units, e.g. to

- maintain a library of standard units which can be put together in various combinations.
- to define special types of systems by limiting the types of combined units or by restricting the way of combining such units.

Regarding the specification given in Example 2.1 with its inequalities for the message flow through each unit one may conjecture that the system S2.1 is decomposable, though the coordinated behavior of PL2 and PL4 looks somewhat strange under the assumption of completely separate specifications of PL2, PL4 and M. Investigating the decomposability of the system S2.1 means first to introduce a suitable concept of a separate unit specification.

How could a separate specification of unit structure and unit behavior be accomplished so that units can be put together to form a system? As the graph of the communication structure one could use a star-shaped digraph as indicated in Fig. 9 where the unit u in the centre is to be specified. The names of the other units are of no importance. The input links will be referenced by the names il_1, $il_2,\ldots,il_n$, the output links by ol_1, $ol_2,\ldots,ol_m$. The input links could be missing.

The complete communication structure CS_u comprises the two link sets and sets of items (message patterns) $M(il_1),\ldots,M(ol_m)$, each being associated with one of the links.

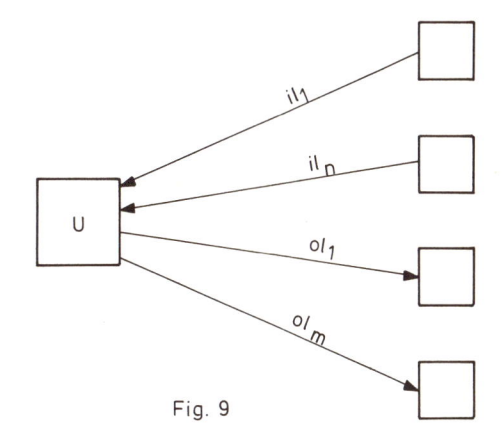

Fig. 9

Under the assumption that "u-consistent" event sets in CS_{u_i} ($1 \leq i \leq r$), which characterize the behavior of the unit u_i, have been defined separately (for units $u_1,\ldots,u_r$) and that the topological aspects of a combination of the star-shaped graphs are left aside (as being relatively easy to handle) the histories of a system composed of units $u_1, u_2,\ldots,u_r$ could be defined as those event sets in the combined communication structure which result in u-consistent event sets in the star-shaped substructure of each unit u (for all units $u_1,\ldots,u_r$).

A unit specification should define the possible <u>reaction</u> of the unit u <u>to any kind</u> of <u>input configuration</u>. A limitation of the possible inputs would restrict the behavior of the adjacent units and contradict the independence of the specifications.

Since the preceding outputs of the unit u may also be significant for its future behavior (if u is non-deterministic these outputs are not entirely implied by their preceding inputs), the basis for determining the next output events has to be a rather general event set.

If we want to specify the dynamic behavior of a unit u by a function $f_u(ES)$ on event sets ES, a value $f_u(ES)$ will have to describe the next possible output events. Because of eventual non-deterministic behavior, in general, there must be a choice among several output events.

Def. D1 (db-function of a unit)
A db-function f_u (dynamic <u>b</u>ehavior) of a unit u with a communication structure CS_u is defined on finite event sets in DS_u, a value of f_u being a finite set of triples

$$[1, M, [minrt, maxrt]]$$

where

- 1 is an output link of u

- $M \subseteq M(1)$

- minrt, maxrt (minimal and maximal response time) are real numbers with $0 \leq minrt \leq maxrt, 0 < maxrt$, maxrt = ∞ being admitted.

Remark: $f_u(ES)$ may be the empty set. This states that u will not produce any output event on the basis of ES.

The meaning of the values of a db-function will be explained below, step by step.

Def. D2 (compatible output event)
An output event [1,p,t] is compatible with a value $f_u(ES)$ of a db-function if and only if there is an element

$$[1', M, [m_1, m_2]] \text{ of } f_u(ES) \text{ such that}$$

$1 = 1'$, $p \in M$, and

$t \in [TMAX(ES) + m_1, TMAX(ES) + m_2]$, if $m_1 > 0$, and

$t \in (TMAX(ES), TMAX(ES) + m_2]$, if $m_1 = 0$

where TMAX(ES) is the largest value occurring as third component in an element of ES ("time maximum"). If ES is empty: TMAX(ES)$=_{Df}$0.

Remark: There is no need of specifying by f_u(ES) a sequence of output events oe_1, oe_2,... This situation is taken care of by a sequence of values: f_u(ES), f_u(ES∪{oe_1}), f_u(ES∪{oe_1,oe_2}), and so on.

On the way of defining a set of events ES to be f_u-consistent (or simply: u-consistent) we introduce the notion of a cut of an event set.

Def. D3 (cut of an event set)
A cut of an event set ES consists of two subsets ES_1 and ES_2 of ES, forming a partition of ES, ES_1 being finite and possibly empty, ES_2 being non-empty and

$$TMAX(ES_1) < TMIN(ES_2)$$

where

$TMAX(ES_1)$ is defined as in Def. D2 and

$TMIN(ES_2)$ is the smallest t occurring as third component in an element of ES_2 ("time minimum").

Before the notion of a db-function is used to define f_u-consistent event sets and the concept of a decomposable system it seems worth while emphasizing some characteristics of the db-functions. It is especially important to recognize that a db-function generally is not identical with an action function (even if this action function is multi-valued, modelling non-deterministic behavior which unconditionally predicts the output behavior of a unit on the basis of a state S (S corresponds to an event set ES). Informally spoken: the value f_u(ES) describes the possible output behavior of u starting from the event set ES as long as u is not disturbed or diverted by an input event. If an input event e (or several simultaneous input events) occurs before the predicted output event, the conditional prediction represented by f_u(ES), is immediately and entirely invalidated. Now f_u(ES∪{e}) is valid. Of course, f_u(ES∪{e}) may contain some or all the elements of f_u(ES), perhaps with times recalculated. For the notion of a divertable unit cf. [Wiehle 73].

Def. D4 (f_u-consistent event set)
A set of events ES in the communication structure CS_u of a unit u is consistent with a db-function f_u of u if and only if for each cut ES_1,ES_2 of ES the subset NE of ES_2 of all events occurring at time $TMIN(ES_2)$ is compatible with $f_u(ES_1)$. NE is compatible with $f_u(ES_1)$ if and only if the following two conditions are fulfilled:
- an output event oe ε NE is compatible with $f_u(ES_1)$(cf. Def. D2)

- if NE does not contain any output event then either $f_u(ES)$ is empty or there must be at least one element $[1,M,[m_1,m_2]]$ of $f_u(ES_1)$ such that

$$TMIN(ES_2) < TMAX(ES_1) + m_2.$$

The intuitive background of definition D4, second condition, may be informally explained as follows: it says that the situation

$$TMIN(ES_2) \geq maxot,$$

maxot=max(TMAX(ES_1)+m_2), the maximum taken from all elements $[1,M,[m_1,m_2]] \in f_u(ES_1)$, is illegal. There is no output event in (TMAX(ES_1), TMIN(ES_2)], i.e. a predicted output event is missing, the admitted time intervals having elapsed.

Remark: The framework proposed so far for separate unit specification is deficient in at least two closely related points:

1. it is not possible to describe which of the possibly simultaneous output events should indeed be enabled to occur simultaneously. If $f_u(ES)$, e.g., contains the two elements $[1_1,a,[m_1,m_2]]$ and $[1_2,b,[m_1,m_2]]$, one may want to be able to specify that never two simultaneous events $[1_1,a,t]$, $[1_2,b,t]$ can occur.

   This deficiency could be removed by extending $f_u(ES)$ by a set of its subsets; a set of simultaneous output events may only occur if there is a corresponding (compatible) subset in the extended $f_u(ES)$.

2. it is not possible to specify by $f_u(ES)$ that, starting from ES, u will have to produce two or more simultaneous output events at some time t, $t \in [t_1,t_2]$, $t_1<t_2$. This deficiency, too, can be removed at the price of additional structure of $f_u(ES)$.

Some examples of values $f_u(ES)$ will demonstrate how the time intervals may be used to define unit behavior.

Example 1. $f_u(ES)$ contains the two elements:

$$[1,a,[m_1,m_2]] \quad \text{and} \quad [1',a',[m_1',m_2']]$$

with simultaneity of the two events being excluded and with the intervals $I=[m_1,m_2]$, $I'=[m_1',m_2']$ overlapping or not. I being before I', $f_u(ES)$ says that, if $e=[1,a,t]$ has not occurred in time, an event $e'=[1',a',t']$ has to be expected.

Example 2. $f_u(ES)$ contains a sequence of elements

$$[1,a,[m_1,m_2]] , [1,a,[m_1+d,m_2+d]] , [1,a,[m_1+2*d,m_2+2*d]] ,...$$

with $[m_1,m_2] \cap [m_1+d, m_2+d] = \emptyset$. This $f_u(ES)$ says that exactly one output event $[1,a,t]$ will occur in one of a sequence of periodical time intervals.

One could model such situations by introducing some artificial output patterns ("dummy output", "empty output") being output at brief intervals (if no other events occur), however, this would violate the principle of keeping the models as close to real systems as possible.

Def. D5 (decomposable system)
A system $S = [CS, DB]$ is decomposable if and only if there is a db-function f_u for each unit u in CS such that the histories of S may be defined as follows: an event set ES in CS is a history of S if and only if, for each unit u in CS, the subset ES_u of ES containing exactly all events on links adjacent to u is consistent with the function f_u (cf. Def. D4).

Remark: The stack-system of section A is obviously decomposable. The separately specified units will simply ignore all inputs that do not conform with the supposed functioning of the partner.

Now the question whether there are non-decomposable systems is near at hand.

Example 3. The system SD3 (two children playing with two balls over a high wall, without shouting at each other), the digraph given by Fig. 10.
M = {ball}, with events occurring always simultaneously on both links at arbitrary points of time $t_1, t_2, \ldots, t_i, t_{i+1}, \ldots$ with $b \geq t_{i+1} - t_i \geq a > 0$, (a,b being system constants) and $b \geq t_1 \geq a$, is not decomposable. Assume A and B have played correctly for a while, having exchanged balls at times $t_1, t_2, \ldots, t_r$.
The set ES (having as elements the 2*r past events) does not contain any more information than what is in the vector $t_1, t_2, \ldots, t_r$. On the basis of this knowledge A cannot exclude any y, $t_r + a \leq y \leq t_r + b$, from being $y = t_{r+1}$, i.e. we have

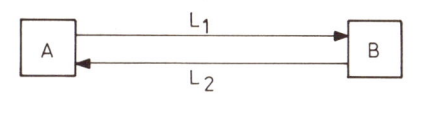

$$f_A(ES) = \bar{f}_A(t_1, t_2, \ldots, t_r) = \{[L_1, \{ball\}, [a,b]]\}$$

Likewise we have

$$f_B(ES) = \{[L_2, \{ball\}, [a,b]]\}.$$

These two values cannot enforce the next two events on the different links to occur simultaneously, more precisely: an event set H, having a cut ES_1, ES_2 with

$$ES_1 = ES \cup \{e_1, e_2\}, \ time(e_1) \ne time(e_2),$$

is consistent up to ES_1 with any pair of functions f_A and f_B.

Remark: The non-decomposability of SD3 depends heavily on the restricted set of message patterns.

Example 4. Since the Example 3 may seem somewhat artificial, we look at system S2.1 of section B., especially at the units PL2, PL4. There we find an analogous phenomenon as in system SD3. Assume an event set of S2.1 with

$$MAXT(ES) = \bar{t} \text{ and } D(ES, PL2, \bar{t}) = D(ES, PL4, \bar{t}) = 1.$$

ES_{PL4} contains no more information than the times of past events on OT,IR,IM2. On the basis of this knowledge $f_{PL4}(ES_{PL4})$ cannot exclude any event on either IM2 or on IR which occurs later than $\bar{t}_4$, where $\bar{t}_4$ is the time of the latest event in ES on the link OT:

$$f_{PL4}(ES_{PL4}) = \{[IM2, \{token\}, [0, \infty]], [IR, \{token\}, [0, \infty]]\}$$

with no simultaneity admitted.

$f_{PL2}(EX_{PL2})$ is defined in analogy to $f_{PL4}(ES_{PL4})$.

The value of $f_M(ES)$ cannot restrict the events occurring on links IM1,IM2. So, these values of db-functions cannot enforce that an event $[IM_1, token, t]$ is accompanied by a simultaneous event $[IM_2, token, t]$.

Since for certain purposes the usefulness of Petri-Nets is unquestioned there are useful system models which are not decomposable. This indicates that a conceptual framework for system models cannot start from unit specifications and proceed via system synthesis since the consequence would be to exclude a priori some useful system models.

E. Some remarks on relations between systems

One of the reasons why we search for adequate and precise system specification is to specify systems at an adequate level of detail, the specification being complete <u>for a certain purpose</u>.

The same real information processing system ("RIHS") can be modelled at different levels of detail and from many different points of view. Each of the model systems $S_1, S_2, \ldots$ of the RIHS is likely to be different from all other model systems. (The term "system" is used here as defined in section B.) The obvious conjecture is that all the systems $S_1, S_2, \ldots$ modelling a single RIHS, must be related to each other in a precise manner, i.e., in principle, these relationships must be describable by mathematical tools and with mathematical precision.

To give an idea of how manifold the relations between systems may be we shall indicate some procedures P_1 to P_5 by which one system S' may be derived from a given system S, thus a relationship between S and S' being established. (It is not claimed that these hints really define the derivation procedures.)

- P1: contraction of subsystems.

    A subset ss of units of S is "contracted" to form a single unit NU in the graph of S'. All links between a unit U outside of ss and a unit of ss become links between U and NU. All the links between units of ss disappear. The histories of S' are derived from the histories of S by simply dropping all events on links inside of ss.

- P2: putting together parallel links.

    The derivation of the histories of S' is obvious if there are no simultaneous events on the parallel links in the histories of S, or, if there are only simultaneous events on these links.

- P3: contraction of sets of events.

    Especially a sequence of events (in S) on a certain link may be mapped - under certain conditions - onto a single event in the histories of S'. Special case: combined contraction of an alternating sequence of events on a link pair between two units, resulting in two events only, one on each link.

- P4: introducing faster units.

    In S a unit u (or several units) is replaced by a faster unit of otherwise identical behavior.

- P5: more complex example/S' with <u>enlarged</u> digraph.

    We roughly outline the relationship between a device-oriented and an employee-oriented reservation system (systems called SRESD and SRESE). We derive SRESD from SRES, section C., by replacing the partners P_i by devices D_j, i=1,...,r, and by adding two types of message patterns: LOGON ⟨identification⟩ and LOGOFF, the meaning and use of these patterns being indicated by the choice of words. Let ⟨identification⟩ be one of the integers 1,2,...,q, q>r by a factor between 2 and 3, or so. The link pairs in SRESD are named DL_{i1}, DL_{i2}, i=1,...,r.

    The digraph of the communication structure CSE of the system SRESE is star-shaped, too, RESP in the centre, each of the employees $E_1,...,E_q$ connected to RESP by a link pair EL_{j1}, EL_{j2}. The message patterns of CSE are identical with those of CSD without the LOGON- and LOGOFF-patterns.

    In SRESD, on a link pair DL_{i1}, DL_{i2} the usual traffic will appear (as defined for such link pairs in SRES) inside a single bracket pair LOGON/j and LOGOFF, each with some trivial response by RESD. The assumption is that there is never an open LOGON for the same j at more than one device.

    If HD is a history of SRESD, completely partitioned into subsets of the structure

    $\{[DL_{i1}, LOGON/j, t_a], rn, a_1, b_1, a_2, b_2, ..., a_w, b_w, [DL_{i1}, LOGOFF, t_e], rf\}$

    (rn,rf designating the trivial responses mentioned above)

    then there is a history HE of SRESE containing exactly all the corresponding event sets $a_1', b_1', a_2', b_2', ..., a_w', b_w'$, where an $a_i'(b_i')$ is derived from $a_1(b_1)$ simply by replacing the link-name $DL_{i1}(DL_{i2})$ by $EL_{j1}(EL_{j2})$.

    (end of P5)

Such a derivation procedure of histories in a communication structure CS_2 from histories in a communication structure CS_1 (CS_1, CS_2 differing considerably) may be called an <u>inductance-rule</u> or a <u>rule of flow-propagation</u>.

What can be learned from the more complex example P5 is that, in deriving systems from systems, the deformation of the digraph of the communication structure may be by far more drastic than in the case of the well-known contraction of subsets of nodes, as outlined in P1. Indeed, the relationship of the digraphs can be very loose, the digraph of the derived system can even be more complex than the one of the original system.

Having gained more experience with precisely established relationships between systems it will become promising to attack the definition of the meaning of such phrases as:

- system S' is isomorphic with system S
- system S is an implementation of system S' (with respect to a certain rule of flow-propagation of S into the communication structure of S')
- system S is a layered system, the layers being the systems $S_1, S_2, \ldots$

Work in this direction will certainly profit from the efforts made by Horning and Randell [Horning 73] in defining such terms as "process image", "abstraction", etc.

References

[Guttag 76]   J.V. Guttag, E. Horowitz, D.R. Musser: The design of data
                   type specifications. Proceedings 2nd International Conference
                   on Software Engineering, IEEE, 414 - 420 (1976)

[Hack 75]   M. Hack: Decision problems for Petri-Nets and vector addition
                   systems. MAC-TM 59, Project MAC, M.I.T., Cambridge, Mass.,
                   1975

[Hack 76]   M. Hack: Petri Net languages. MAC-TR 159, Project MAC, M.I.T.,
                   Cambridge, Mass., 1976

[Horning 73]   J.J. Horning, B. Randell: Process Structuring. Computing Surveys 5, 1, 5 - 30 (1973)

[Jones 77]   C.B. Jones: Program Specifications and Formal Development.
                   Proceedings International Computing Symposium 1977, 537 - 553.
                   North Holland Publishing Company 1977

[Lauer 75]   P.E. Lauer, R.H. Campbell: Formal semantics of a class of high-level primitives for coordinating concurrent processes. Acta
                   Informatica 5, 297 - 332 (1975)

[Liskov 75]   B. Liskov, S. Zilles: Specification techniques for data abstractions. Proceedings of ACM SIGPLAN Conference on Reliable
                   Software. SIGPLAN Notices Vol. 10, 6, 72 - 87 (1975)

[Parnas 72]   D.L. Parnas: A technique for software module specification
                   with examples. Comm. ACM Vol. 15, 5, 330 - 336 (1972)

[Plickert 77]   H. Plickert: Ein Ansatz zur formalisierten Behandlung der Semantik von Speichern mittels eines Maschinenmodells. Doctoral
                   Dissertation, Faculty of Mathematics, Technical University
                   Munich, 1977

[Wiehle 73]   H.R. Wiehle: Looking at software as hardware? Lecture Notes
                   prepared for the International Summer School on Structured
                   Programming and Programmed Structures, Munich 1973

CHAPTER 4.B.

J. H. Saltzer
Massachusetts Institute of Technology
Cambridge, Mass., USA

Research Problems of Decentralized Systems
With Largely Autonomous Nodes

RESEARCH PROBLEMS OF DECENTRALIZED SYSTEMS WITH LARGELY AUTONOMOUS NODES

by

Jerome H. Saltzer

Massachusetts Institute of Technology

A currently popular systems research project is to explore the possibilities and problems for computer system organization that arise from the rapidly falling cost of computing hardware. Interconnecting fleets of mini- or micro-computers and putting intelligence in terminals and concentrators to produce so-called "distributed systems" has recently been a booming development activity. While these efforts range from ingenious to misguided, many seem to miss a most important aspect of the revolution in hardware costs: that more than any other factor, the <u>entry</u> cost of acquiring and operating a free-standing, complete computer system has dropped and continues to drop rapidly. Where a decade ago the capital outlay required to install a computer system ranged from $150,000 up into the millions, today the low end of that range is below $15,000 and dropping.

The consequence of this particular observation for system structure comes from the next level of analysis. In most organizations, decisions to make capital acquisitions tend to be more centralized for larger capital amounts, and less centralized for smaller capital amounts. On this basis we may conjecture that lower entry costs for computer systems will lead naturally to computer acquisition decisions being made at points lower in a management hierarchy. Further, because a lower-level organization usually has a smaller mission, those smaller-priced computers will tend to span a smaller range of applications, and in the limit of the argument will be dedicated to a single application. Finally, the organizational units that acquire these computers will by nature tend to operate somewhat independently and autonomously from one another, each following its own mission. From another viewpoint, administrative autonomy is really the driving force that leads to acquisition of a computer system that spans a smaller application range. According to this view, the large multiuser computer center is really an artifact of high entry cost, and does not represent the "natural" way for an organization to do its computing.

A trouble with this somewhat oversimplified analysis is that these conjectured autonomous, decentralized computer systems will need to communicate with one another. For example: the production department's output will be the inventory control department's input, and computer-generated reports of both departments must be

---

© 1977 by J. H. Saltzer. All rights reserved.

submitted to higher management for computer analysis and exception display. Thus we can anticipate that the autonomous computer systems must be at least loosely coupled into a cooperating confederacy that represents the corporate information system. This scenario describes the corporate computing environment, but a similar scenario can be conjectured for the academic, government, military, or any other computing environment. The conjecture described here has been explored for validity in an undergraduate thesis [d'Oliveira, 1977].

The key consequence of this line of reasoning for computer system structure, then, is a technical problem: to provide coherence in communication among what will inevitably be administratively autonomous nodes of a computer network. Technically, autonomy appears as a force producing incoherence: one must assume that operating schedules, loading policy, level of concern for security, availability, and reliability, update level of hardware and software, and even choice of hardware and software systems will tend to vary from node to node with a minimum of central control. Further, individual nodes may for various reasons occasionally completely disconnect themselves from the confederacy, and operate in isolation for a while before reconnecting. Yet to the extent that agreement and cooperation are beneficial, there will be need for communication of signals, exchange of data, mutual assistance agreements, and a wide variety of other internode interaction. One-at-a-time ad hoc arrangements will probably be inadequate, because of their potential large number and the programming cost in dealing with each node on a different basis.

Coherence can be sought in many forms. At one extreme, one might set a company-wide standard for the electrical levels used to drive point-to-point communication lines that interconnect nodes or that attach any node to a local communication network. At the opposite extreme, one might develop a data management protocol that allows any user of any node to believe that there is a central, unified database management system with no identifiable boundaries. The first extreme might be described as a very low-level protocol, the second extreme as a very high-level protocol, and there seem to be many levels in between, not all strictly ordered.

By now, considerable experience has been gained in devising and using relatively low-level protocols, up to the point that one has an uninterpreted stream of bits flowing from one node of a network to another [Cerf, 1974]. The ARPANET and TELENET are perhaps the best-developed examples of protocols at this level, and local networks such as the ETHERNET [Metcalfe, 1975] provide a similar level of protocol on a smaller scale geographically. In each of those networks, standard protocols allow any two autonomous nodes (of possibly different design) to set up a data stream from one to the other; each node need implement only one protocol, no matter how many other differently designed nodes are attached to the network. However, standardized coherence stops there; generally each pair of communicating nodes must make some (typically ad hoc) arrangement as to the interpretation of the stream of bits: it may represent a stream of data, a set of instructions, a message to one individual, or something else. For several special cases, such as exchange of mail or remotely submitting batch jobs, there have been developed higher-level protocols; there tends to be a distinct ad hoc higher-level protocol invented for each application [Feinler, 1976]. Some workers have explored the problems of protocols that interpret and translate data across machines of different origin [Levine, 1977]. Others have tried to develop a network-wide file system without user-noticeable boundaries [Thomas, 1973; Millstein, 1976].

The image of a loose confederacy of cooperating autonomous nodes requires at a minimum the level of coherence provided by these networks; it is not yet clear how much more is appropriate, only that the opposite extreme in which the physically separate nodes effectively lose their separate identity is excluded by the earlier arguments for autonomy. Between lies a broad range of possibilities that need to be explored.

Coherence and the object model

The first problem is to develop a framework for discussion that allows one to pose much more specific questions. As a way to put some structure on the range of possibilities, it is appropriate to think first in terms of familiar semantic models of computation, and then to inquire how the semantic model of the behavior of a single node might be usefully extended to account for interaction with other, autonomous nodes. To get a concrete starting point that is as developed as possible, let us give initial consideration to the object model [Liskov, 1975; Liskov, 1977; Wulf, 1976]*. Under that view, each node is a self-contained system with storage, a program interpreter that is programmed in a high-level object-oriented language such as CLU or Alphard, and an attachment to a data communication network of the kind previously discussed.

We immediately observe that several interesting problems are posed by the interaction between the object model and the hypothesis of autonomy. There are two basic alternative premises that one can start with in thinking about how to compute with an object that is represented at another node: send instructions about what to do with the object to the place it is stored; or send a copy of the representation of the object to the place that wants to compute with it. (In-between combinations are also possible, but conceptually it is simpler to think about the extreme cases first.) An initial reaction might be to begin by considering the number of bits that must be moved from one node to another to carry out the two alternatives, but that approach misses the most interesting issues: reliability, integrity, responsibility

---

* Two other obvious candidates for starting points are the data flow model [Dennis, 1975; Arvind, 1976] and the actor model [Hewitt, 1977], both of which already contain the notion of communications; since neither is developed quite as far as the object model we leave them for future examination.

for protection of the object, and naming problems. Suppose the object stays in its original home. Semantics for requesting operations, and reporting results and failures are needed. For some kinds of objects, there may be operations that return references to other, related objects. Semantics to properly interpret these references are required. Checking of authorization to request operations is required. Some way must be found for the (autonomous) node to gracefully defer, queue, or refuse requests, if it is overloaded or not in operation at the moment.

Suppose on the other hand, that a copy of the object is moved to the node that wants to do the computation. Privacy, protection of the contents, integrity of the representation, and proper interpretation of names embedded in the object representation all are problems. Yet, making copies of data seems an essential part of achieving autonomy from nodes that contain needed information but aren't always accessible. Considering these two premises as alternatives seems to raise simultaneously so many issues of performance, integrity of the object representation, privacy of its content, what name is used for the object, and responsibility for the object, that the question is probably not posed properly. However, it begins to illustrate the range of considerations that should be thought about. It also suggests the following, more specific, problems that require solutions:

1. To arrange systematically that an object have multiple representations at one point in time but stored at different places. One would expect to achieve reliability and response speed this way [Alsberg, 1976]. An example of non-systematic multiple representation occurs whenever one user of a time-sharing system confronts another with the complaint, "I thought you said you fixed that bug", and receives the response, "I did. You must have gotten an old copy of the program. What you have to do is type..." Semantics are needed to express the notion that for some purposes any of several representations are equally good, but for other purposes they aren't.

2. An object at one node needs to "contain" (for example, use as part of its representation) objects from other nodes. This idea focuses on the semantics of naming remote objects. It is not clear whether the names involved should be relatively high-level (e.g., character-string file names) or low-level (e.g., segment numbers). Ideas involving the interaction among semantics and mechanics of naming in very large address spaces may turn out to have application to the decentralized case [Bishop, 1977].

3. Related to the previous problem are issues of object motion: suppose object A, which contains as a component object B, is either copied or moved from one node to another, either temporarily or permanently. Can object B be left behind or be in yet another node? The answer may depend on the exact combination of copy or new, temporary or permanent. Autonomy is deeply involved here, since one cannot rely on availability of the original node to resolve the name of B. The Distributed Computing System (DCS) at the University of California, Irvine,

provided a first cut trial of this idea by arranging for processes to move from one node to another without having to change their names [Farber, 1972].

4. More generally, semantics are needed for gracefully coping with objects that aren't there when they are requested. (Information stored in autonomous nodes will often fall in this category.) This idea seems closely related to the one of coping with objects that have multiple versions and the most recent version is inaccessible*.

5. Algorithms are needed that allow atomic update of two (or more) objects stored at different nodes, in the face of errors in communication and failures of individual nodes**. There are several forms of atomic update: there may be consistency constraints across two or more different objects (e.g., the sum of all the balances in a bank should always be zero) or there may be a requirement that several copies of an object be kept identical. Process coordination semantics that were adequate for single-node systems do not necessarily stand up under the pressures of robustness and delay of the decentralized system. Reed and Kanodia have developed a promising semantics together with an implementation model in terms of messages [Reed, 1977]. The semantic view that objects are immutable may provide a more hospitable base for extension to interaction among autonomous nodes than the view that objects ultimately are implemented by cells that can contain different values at different times. (The more interesting algorithms for making coordinated changes in the face of errors seem to implement something resembling immutable objects [Lampson, 1976; Thomas, 1976]).

Constraining the range of errors that must be tolerated seems to be a promising way to look at these last two problems. Not all failures are equally likely, and more important, some kinds of failures can perhaps be guarded against by specific remedies, rather than tolerated. For example, a common protocol problem in a network is that some node both crashes and restores service again before anyone notices; outstanding connections through the network sometimes continue without realizing that the node's state has been reset. Careful choice in the semantics of the host-net interface can locally eliminate this kind of failure instead of leaving it as a problem for higher level protocols.

---

* Semantics for dealing systematically with errors and other surprises have not really been devised for monolithic, centralized systems either. However, it appears that in the decentralized case, the problem cannot so easily be avoided by ad hoc tricks or finesse as it was in the past.

** Most published work on making atomic updates to several objects or several sites has concentrated on algorithms that perform well despite communication delay or that can be proven correct [Lamport, 1976 <u>Acta Inf</u>.; Stearns, 1976; Eswaran, 1976; Ellis, 1976; Rothnie, 1977]. Unfortunately, algorithms constructed without consideration of reliability and failure are not easily extended to cope with those additional considerations, so there seems to be no way to build on that work.

The following oversimplified world view, to be taken by each node may offer a systematic way to think about multiply represented objects and atomic operations: there are two kinds of objects, mine and everyone else's. My node acts as a cache memory for objects belonging to others that I use, and everyone else acts as a backing store. These roles are simply reversed for my own objects. (One can quickly invent situations where this view breaks down, causing deadlocks or wrong answers, but the question is whether or not there are real world problems for which this view is adequate.)

Finally, it is apparent that one can get carried away with generalized algorithms that handle all possible cases. An area requiring substantial investigation is real world applications. It may turn out that only a few of these issues arise often enough in practice to require systematic solutions. It may be possible, in many cases, to cope with distant objects quite successfully as special cases to be programmed one at a time. For example, recent measurements on the Multics system suggest that even though that system is designed for maximum ease in sharing data, actual use of the facilities for shared writable objects is mostly quite stylized: the full generality is exploited quite rarely [Montgomery, 1977].

Other problems in the semantics of coherence

Usual models of computation permit only "correct" results, with no provision for tolerating "acceptably close" answers. Sometimes provision is made to report that no result can be returned. In a loose confederacy of autonomous nodes, exactly correct results may be unattainable, but no answer at all is too restricting. For example, one might want a count of the current number of employees, and each department has that number stored in its computer. At the moment the question is asked, one department's computer is down, and its count is inaccessible. But a copy of last month's count for that department is available elsewhere. An "almost right" answer utilizing last month's count for one department may well be close enough for the purpose the question was asked, but we have no semantics available for requesting or returning such answers. A more extreme example would be if the Federal Reserve tried to determine the money supply by interrogating every bank's computer so as to obtain the sum of all checking account balances in the United States. Obtaining an exact result seems unrealistic as well as unnecessary.

A general solution to the problem of providing acceptably close answers seems to require a perspective from Artificial Intelligence, but particular solutions may be programmable if there were available semantics for detecting that one object is an out-of-date version of another, or that a requested but unavailable object has an out-of-date copy. It is not clear at what level these associations should be made.

Semantics are also needed to express constraints or partial contraints of time sequence. (e.g., "reservations are to be made in the order they are requested, except that two reservation requests arriving at different nodes within one minute may be processed out of order.") Lamport has suggested one approach to thinking about this problem [Lamport, March, 1976]. Note that the possibility of unreliable nodes or communications severely complicates this problem.

The semantics of protection of information, just beginning to be understood in the single system case, are a bewildering maze when one considers the decentralized system. The capability model seems to offer little help when the capabilities must be sent from one node to other, potentially hostile ones, since one can't be sure that the capability won't be tampered with. Nevertheless, the capability model may be useful for cases where the nodes are known to be friendly [Donnelley, 1976]. Cryptographic techniques seem to offer some aid in authentication and in protecting control signals in addition to their traditional use in protecting data in transit [Branstad, 1975; Diffie, 1976; Kent, 1976]. Application of information flow models to decentralized systems is a promising idea [Karger, 1977].

The semantics of autonomy are not clear. When can I disconnect my node from the network without disrupting my (or other) operations? How do I refuse to report information that I have in my node in a way that is not disruptive? If my node is overloaded, which requests coming from other nodes can be deferred without causing deadlock? Early work in this area on DCS points the way, but needs to be extended to more cases [Rowe, 1973].

Heterogeneous and Homogeneous Systems

A question that is immediately encountered is whether or not one should assume that the various autonomous nodes of a loosely coupled confederacy of systems are identical either in hardware or in lower level software support. The assumption of autonomy and observations of the way the real world behaves both lead to a strong conclusion that one must be able to interconnect heterogeneous (that is, different) systems. Yet, to be systematic, some level of homogeneity is essential, and in addition the clarity that homogeneity provides in allowing one to see a single research problem at a time is very appealing.

It may be that the proper approach to this issue lies in careful definition of node boundaries. Suppose that we insist that every node present to every other node a common, homogeneous interface, whose definition we hope to specify. That interface may be a native interface, directly implemented by the node, or it may be simulated by interpretation, using the (presumably different) native facilities of the node. This approach allows one to work on the semantics of decentralized systems without the confusion of hetrogeneity, yet it permits at least some non-conforming systems to participate in a confederacy. There is, of course, no guarantee that an arbitrary previously existing computer system will be able to simulate the required interface easily or efficiently.

Conclusion

The various problems suggested here are by no means independent of one another, although each seems to have a flavor of its own. In addition, they probably do not span the complete range of issues that should be explored in establishing an appropriate semantics for expressing computations in a confederacy of loosely coupled, autonomous computer systems. Further, some are recognizable as problems of semantics of centralized systems that were never solved very well. But they do seem to represent a starting point that can to lead to more carefully framed questions and eventually some new conceptual insight.

Acknowledgement

Many of the ideas discussed here were suggested by David D. Clark, David P. Reed, Liba Svobodova, and students in an M.I.T. graduate seminar held during the Spring Semester, 1976-77.

References

Alsberg, P.A., Belford, G.G., Day, J.D., and Grapa, E., "Multi-Copy Resiliency Techniques," University of Illinois Center for Advanced Computation Document #202, May, 1976.

Arvind, et al., "Programming in a viable data flow language," Univ. of Calif. (Irvine) Department of Information and Computer Science, Technical Report 89.

Bishop, P.B., "Computer Systems with a Very Large Address Space and Garbage Collection," Ph.D. thesis, M.I.T. Department of Electrical Engineering and Computer Science, May, 1977, also Laboratory for Computer Science Technical Report TR-178.

Branstad, D.K., "Encryption Protection in Computer Data Communications," *Proc. Fourth Data Communications Symposium*, Quebec, October, 1975, pp. 8.1-8.7.

Cerf, V.G., and Kahn, R.E., "A Protocol for Packet Network Interconnection," *IEEE Trans. on Communications* 22, 5 (May, 1974) pp. 637-648.

d'Oliveira, C., "A Conjecture About Computer Decentralization," B.S. thesis, M.I.T. Department of Electrical Engineering and Computer Science, August, 1977.

Dennis, J.B., "First Version of a Data Flow Procedure Language," M.I.T. Laboratory for Computer Science Technical Memo TM-61, May, 1975.

Diffie, W., and Hellman, M.E., "New Directions in Cryptography," *IEEE Trans. on Info. Theory* 22, 6 (November, 1976) pp. 644-654.

Donnelley, J.E., "A Distributed Capability Computing System (DCCS)," ARPANET Request for Comments #712, Network Information Center, Stanford Research Institute, Menlo Park, California, February, 1976.

Ellis, C.A., "Consistency and Correctness of Duplicate Database Systems," Sixth ACM Symposium on Operating System Principles, November, 1977, pp. 67-84.

Eswaran, K.P., et al., "The Notions of Consistency and Predicate Locks in a Database System," *Comm. of ACM* 19, 11 (November, 1976) pp. 624-633.

Farber, D.J., and Heinrich, F.R., "The Structure of a Distributed Computer System: The Distributed File System," *Proc. First Int. Conf. on Computer Comm.*, 1972, pp. 364-370.

Feinler, E., and Postel, J., ARPANET Protocol Handbook, NIC 7104, Network Information Center, Stanford Research Institute, Menlo Park, California, April, 1976.

Hewitt, C., "Viewing Control Structures as Patterns of Passing Messages," to be published in A.I. Journal.

Karger, P., "Non-Discretionary Access Control for Decentralized Computing Systems," M.S. thesis, M.I.T. Department of Electrical Engineering and Computer Science, May, 1977, also Laboratory for Computer Science Technical Report TR-179.

Kent, S.T., "Encryption-Based Protection Protocols for Interactive User-Computer Communication," S.M. thesis, M.I.T. Department of Electrical Engineering and Computer Science, May, 1976, also Laboratory for Computer Science Technical Report TR-162.

Lamport, L., "Time, Clocks, and the Ordering of Events in a Distributed System," Mass. Computer Associates Technical Report CA-7603-2911, March, 1976.

Lamport, L., "The Synchronization of Independent Processes," Acta Informatica, 7, 1976, pp. 15-34.

Lampson, B., and Sturgis, H., "Crash Recovery in a Distributed Data Storage System," to be published in the Comm. of ACM.

Levine, P.H., "Facilitating Interprocess Communication in a Heterogeneous Network Environment," S.M. thesis, M.I.T. Department of Electrical Engineering and Computer Science, June, 1977.

Liskov, B.H., and Zilles, S., "Specification Techniques for Data Abstraction," IEEE Trans. Software Engineering SE-1, 1, (1975) pp. 7-19.

Liskov, B.H., et al., "Abstraction Mechanisms in CLU," Comm. of ACM 20, 8 (August, 1977), pp. 564-576.

Metcalfe, R.M., and Boggs, D.R., "Ethernet: Distributed Packet Switching for Local Computer Networks," Comm. of ACM 19, 7 (July, 1976) pp. 395-404.

Millstein, R.E., "Second Semi-Annual Report," Massachusetts Computer Associates Report CADD-7608-1611, August, 1976.

Montgomery, W., "Measurements of Sharing in Multics," Sixth ACM Symposium on Operating Systems Principles, November, 1977, pp. 85-90.

Reed, D.P., and Kanodia, R.J., "Synchronization with Eventcounts and Sequencers," to appear in the Comm. of ACM.

Rothnie, J.B., et al., "The Redundant Update Methodology of SDD-1: A System for Distributed Databases," Computer Corporation of America Report CCA-77-02, February, 1977.

Rowe, L.A., Hopwood, M.D., and Farber, D.J., "Software Methods for Achieving Fail-Soft Behavior in the Distributed Computing System," Proc. IEEE Symposium on Computer Software Reliability, 1973, pp. 7-11.

Stearns, R.E., et al., "Concurrency Control for Database Systems," extended abstract, IEEE Symposium on Foundations of Computer Science, CH1133-8 C, October, 1976, pp. 19-32.

Thomas, R.H., "A Resource Sharing Executive for the ARPANET," Proc. AFIPS Nat. Comp. Conf., 1973, pp. 155-163.

Thomas, R.H., "A Solution to the Update Problem for Multiple Copy Data Bases Which Use Distributed Control," Bolt Beranek and Newman Report #3340, July, 1976.

Wulf, W.A., et al., "An Introduction to the Construction and Verification of Alphard Programs," IEEE Trans. on Software Engineering SE-2, 4 (December, 1976) pp. 253-265.